Zarathustra's Dionysian Modernism

PHILOSOPHY   POLITICAL THEORY   AESTHETICS

Judith Butler and Frederick M. Dolan

EDITORS

Stanford University Press
Stanford, California

© 2001 by the Board of Trustees of the
Leland Stanford Junior University

Printed in the United States of America
on acid-free, archival-quality paper.

Library of Congress Cataloging-in-Publication Data

Gooding Williams, Robert.
   Zarathustra's Dionysian modernism /
Robert Gooding-Williams.
        p.   cm. — (Atopia)
   Includes bibliographical references and index.
   ISBN 0-8047-3294-9 (alk. paper) —
ISBN 0-8047-3295-7 (pbk. : alk. paper)
   1. Nietzsche, Friedrich Wilhelm, 1844–1900.
Also sprach Zarathustra.
I. Title.   II. Atopia (Stanford, Calif.)
B3313.A473 G66   2001
193—dc21   00-067942

Original printing 2001

Last figure below indicates year of this printing:
10   09   08   07   06   05   04   03   02   01

Typeset by James P. Brommer in 10.5/13 Garamond

for Sara

Acknowledgments

My blessings are many. Greatest among them are my wife and partner in life, Sara Gooding-Williams, whose love, loyalty, and wisdom have sustained me for over twenty years, and my daughter, Talia Gooding-Williams, whose shining brilliance will never cease to bring me joy.

I also wish to acknowledge the love and support of my father, Ronald Williams, who died of a brain tumor the year I began writing this book; my mother, Arlene Elzadia Williams; my sister, Rhonda Michèle Williams; my paternal grandmother, "Toogie"; and my maternal grandfather, "Papa."

I am also grateful to David Blight, Judy Butler, Ed Casey, Tom Dumm, Janet Gyatso, Tom McCarthy, Lorenzo Simpson, Paul Rockwell, and David Wills for ongoing years of close intellectual and personal friendship.

This book would not have been written—and would not have taken the distinctive shape it has taken—had I not been privileged to be a student at Yale through the 1970s and early 1980s, a time when philosophy and literary criticism still spoke to one another (and were it not for a number of the teachers I had then). I am particularly indebted to Sam Savage, for inspiring in me a love of philosophy and a passion for Nietzsche; to Karsten Harries, for his penetrating insights and his resistance to all-too-tidy readings of Nietzsche that obscure the complexity of his thought; to Seyla Benhabib, for making Hegel come alive; to George Schrader, for his skepticism; to Dewey Faulkner, Jim Winn, Michael Cooke, Peter Demetz, and Ed Casey for introducing me to European literature and literary theory; and to Heinrich von Staden, for his measured judgment, his patience with my fledgling efforts to make sense of *Also sprach Zarathustra*, and his generous spirit.

During the many years that I have thought and written about Nietzsche, I have benefited from the conversation, critical readings, and support of numerous colleagues and friends. I wish especially to mention Linda Alcoff, Bat Ami Bar-On, Robert Bernasconi, Jon Bordo, Bernard Boxill, Stanley Cavell, Cathy Ciepiela,

Dan Conway, Steve Crowell, Larry D'Almeida, Arthur Danto, Adrian Del Caro, Dan Deudney, Richard Drake, Frank Farrell, Jeff Ferguson, Leon Forrest, David Gullette, Margaret Gullette, Amy Gutmann, Rob Hahn, Peter Heller, Kathy Higgins, Amy Kaplan, George Kateb, Larry Langer, Charles L'Homme, Bernd Magnus, Mitch Miller, Royal Naper, Alexander Nehamas, Martha Nussbaum, Ynhui Park, Graham Parkes, Dale Peterson, Peter Pouncey, Diane Raymond, Judith Ryan, Karen Sanchez-Eppler, Starry Schor, Alan Schrift, Ofelia Schutte, Joan Scott, Gary Shapiro, Steve Shaviro, Becky Sinos, Werner Sollors, Doris Sommer, Natasha Stallar, Paul Stern, John Theisen, Kim Townsend, Mary Jane Treacy, Dana Villa, Jonathan Vogel, Larry Vogel, Jeremy Waldron, Georgia Warnke, Tom Wartenberg, Judy Wittenberg, Don White, Iris Young, and Elisabeth Young-Bruehl.

Special thanks are due to Alexander Nehamas, for conversation about some of the key ideas in Chapter 5; to two anonymous reviewers for detailed comments on drafts of the Introduction and Chapter 1; to Tom McCarthy for detailed comments on drafts of the Introduction, Chapter 1, and Chapter 2; to Lorenzo Simpson and Paul Rockwell for detailed comments on a draft of Chapter 2; to Ed Casey, for detailed comments on drafts of Chapters 2 and 4; and to Dan Conway, for the Herculean labor of commenting extensively on the penultimate draft of the book as a whole. Thanks, also, to the Humanities Center at Johns Hopkins University and to the Philosophy Departments at Howard University, the New School for Social Research, Penn State, SUNY Purchase, the University of Richmond, and Vassar College for opportunities to share material contained in this book. Thanks, finally, to Nancy Board and to Kim Gittens for helping me to produce a presentable manuscript.

Portions of this book have appeared in different form in *International Studies in Philosophy*, the *Journal of Nietzsche Studies*, the *Journal of Philosophy*, and the *New German Critique*. Part of Chapter 1 appeared as "Zarathustra's Three Metamorphoses," in *Nietzsche as Postmodernist: Essays Pro and Contra*, edited by Clayton Koelb, and is reprinted here by permission of the State University of New York Press (© 1990 State University of New York; all rights reserved). I am grateful to all for permission to include this material in the present volume.

Let me conclude by expressing my gratitude to the National Endowment for the Humanities, which awarded me the College Teachers Fellowship with which I began to write this book, and to Princeton's University Center for Human Values, which awarded me the Rockefeller Fellowship that enabled me to complete the final chapter.

Contents

Even that Dionysus is a philosopher, and that gods, too, thus do philosophy, seems to me a novelty that is far from innocuous and might arouse suspicion precisely among philosophers.

FRIEDRICH NIETZSCHE, *Beyond Good and Evil*

Explaining the Possibility of Modernism

But the danger of being uncreative—what do you think?
Is it perhaps still only a danger, or is it already a fixed
and settled fact?

THOMAS MANN, *Doctor Faustus*

What is Nietzsche's relationship to modernism? Most contemporary efforts to answer this question arise amidst confusing debates about the defining characteristics of modernity, modernism, and postmodernism. Allusions to Nietzsche in these debates can be puzzling, because the classification criteria for identifying writers as modern or postmodern seem to vary from one discipline to another. Philosophers, social scientists, literary critics, and historians sometimes describe Nietzsche as modern, sometimes as postmodern. Even if they agree as to how he should be classified, they may disagree about the reasons for the classification. Disagreement about reasons obtains, not only between disciplines, but within them. Indeed, there may be little intradisciplinary consensus as to the proper criteria for identifying a given writer as modern or postmodern.

Consider, for example, the case of philosophy. Recent literature suggests that Nietzsche is a postmodern philosopher. But why? On one hand, there are arguments stressing his antirealism and his attack on the myth of the given. Read with reference to these motifs, Nietzsche has been classified as a precursor of various postmodern American philosophers—Goodman, Quine, Sellars, and Rorty, for example.[1] On the other hand, one also finds arguments that Nietzsche is a postmodern philosopher because he proposes that the modern *episteme* is a form of domination. This perspective emphasizes Nietzsche's links to Heidegger, Horkheimer, and Adorno.[2] To be sure, these two views of Nietzsche may not be incompatible. Still, they obviously stress different features of his thought and suggest different criteria for distinguishing the modern from the postmodern.

Disagreement about Nietzsche's relation to modernity is equally evident among intellectual historians and social scientists. For example, Allan Megill distinguishes between a modernist (realist) early Nietzsche and a postmodernist (antirealist) later Nietzsche. He also maintains that the positions Nietzsche articulates in his writings "set the agenda . . . for the whole of modernist and postmodernist art and thought."[3] Richard Wolin is more polemical in his classification, characterizing Nietzsche as an irrationalist who rejected the entire heritage of modernity. In his view, Nietzsche anticipates the contemporary postmodernism of Deleuze and Lyotard. In contrast to Wolin, Marshall Berman celebrates in Nietzsche a classically modernist voice, whose rhythms and range echo Melville, Carlyle, Marx, Whitman, and Ibsen.[4] Finally, both Jürgen Habermas and Daniel Bell tie Nietzsche to aesthetic modernism (Habermas sees Nietzsche as a precursor to surrealism), but also see him as marking a transition from the modern to the postmodern. Yet here again there are important differences. For Bell, postmodernism extends the quest of modernism from art to psychology. Habermas, on the other hand, identifies postmodernism with a thoroughgoing rejection of the emancipatory ideals of the Enlightenment.[5]

What sense can we make of the various ways of categorizing Nietzsche's thought? The multiple and alternative classifications of his work reflect differing conceptions of modernism and its relation to postmodernism. Does "modernism" signify a group of literary or artistic movements, a set of Cartesian or Kantian epistemological commitments, or the progressive traditions of the Enlightenment? Does one place Nietzsche with Melville because of the drama and dynamism in his voice? With Sellars and Quine because he repudiates foundationalism? With the surrealists because he attributes an explosive, irrational power to art? Which aspects of Nietzsche's writings should be stressed? Is one of these aspects more "essential" than the others, and so a surer guide in classifying Nietzsche as a modernist or a postmodernist? Or should contemporary thinkers proclaim that Nietzsche is a modernist in some respects and a postmodernist in others, but that he is also neither?

In keeping with this last proposal, Alexander Nehamas and Robert Pippin have recently argued that Nietzsche's work tends to resist definitive classifications. According to Nehamas, the attempt to fix Nietzsche's ideas as modern or postmodern is "too simple" and pushes him "toward an unequivocal extreme where he does not belong."[6] Similarly, for Pippin, the "tensions" in Nietzsche's thought "undermine the simplicity of any picture of [him] as a pre- or postmodern thinker."[7] In effect, Nehamas and Pippin both suggest that the puzzlement attending contemporary debates about Nietzsche's relation to modernism is as much a function of the complexity of his thought as of the contest between categories. By underlining the ambiguities in Nietzsche's writing, they caution against the temptation to reduce his thought, or phases of his thought (an early Nietzsche, a later Nietzsche), to one or more these categories. Nietzsche, they assert, is infinitely more interesting than the caricatures produced by Nietzsche classifiers.

Let us assume without further ado that Nehamas and Pippin sensibly reject reductionist approaches to Nietzsche, and that trying to determine Nietzsche's significance by characterizing his thought as modernist or postmodernist is a reductionist approach that obscures important features of his thought. Fair appraisals of Berman's and Habermas's readings of Nietzsche bear out this assumption, as would careful evaluations of Bell's, Wolin's and Megill's interpretations.[8] Nietzsche is intellectually interesting, not, finally, because we can find a tidy place for him within our classification schemes, but because he exceeds these schemes and reveals their limitations. Taking Nehamas's and Pippin's remarks to heart, we should be less concerned to discover the right categories for subsuming Nietzsche than we should be to elucidate the polarities in his thinking. Nietzsche's writings tend to put into question all attempts to classify them, because his thinking tends to put itself into question.

Modernism as a Philosophical Problem

How else, then, should we describe Nietzsche's relationship to modernism? One answer to this question, and the one I will explore in this book, is that Nietzsche treats modernism as a philosophical problem. Skeptically eschewing the project of properly classifying Nietzsche as a modernist or postmodernist, I interpret him as a writer who sheds light on issues raised by a concept of modernism that is familiar from the criticism of literature and the arts. It is a concept associated with the idea of an avant-garde. If this concept demands our attention, then Nietzsche does too, not as a writer to be accurately classified, but as a philosopher who thought deeply, subtly, and significantly about a matter that engages us.

In this book, I use a concept of modernism that refers to novelty-engendering interruptions of received practices and traditions. According to this concept, to call a poem, a painting, or a philosophical treatise "modern" is to advert to the advent of the new; it is to assert that there has been a creative break with the past that has produced a work, the essential character of which is unprecedented.[9] Thus understood, the concept of modernism acquires period-specific connotations in the essays of contemporary art critics, precisely where it is used to describe a phase of nineteenth- and twentieth-century art embodying the spirit of Ezra Pound's dictum "Make it new."

According to the critic Rosalind Krauss, modernist aesthetic and critical practices "are functions of [a] . . . discourse of originality."[10] In her view, this discourse represses the concept of the copy in order to fantasize an aesthetic purity that initiates artistic beginnings unstained by the past—so-called "beginnings from ground zero." I turn to Krauss's writing here because it exemplifies a paradox in the conceptualization of postmodernism that illuminates the problem of modernism as Nietzsche saw it. Krauss aims to debunk the discourse of originality and to announce the advent of a new epoch in which the postmodernist "rights of the copy" will receive their due:

> The historical period that the avant-garde shared with modernism is over. That seems an obvious fact. What makes it more than a journalistic one is a conception of the discourse that has brought it to a close. This is a complex of cultural practices, among them a demythologizing criticism and a truly postmodernist art, both of them acting now to void the basic propositions of modernism, to liquidate them by exposing their fictitious condition. It is from this strange new perspective that we look back on the modernist origin.[11]

It is ironic and significant that Krauss, like other critics who adopt her approach, does not displace the discourse of originality. On the contrary, she seems to reinscribe this discourse by identifying *a new perspective that derives from the liquidation of basic propositions*. Krauss trumpets the destruction of the propositional foundations of modernism, because, in effect, it produces a *ground zero* that is no longer contaminated by the influence of the modernist past. Her conception of postmodernism is the fruit of this purified terrain—or so Krauss's modernist rhetoric suggests. In defending postmodernism, in other words, Krauss reproduces the language of modernism. Even as she aims to effect discontinuity, to make a break with the preoccupations of modernism, she reiterates the discourse of originality. Krauss's art-critical interpretation of modernism rebuts her pretensions to postmodernism, for her turn to postmodernism, in the perspective of this interpretation, is, *paradoxically*, a modernist gesture that defeats her claim to have historically surpassed the modernist past.

Krauss's aim is rupture, her achievement repetition. The irony in her effort to displace the discourse of originality is doubly significant. First, it indicates a difficulty involved in *any* self-conscious attempt to make a break with modernism.[12] Second, and more important for my purposes, it signals the persistence in postmodernism of a possibility inherent in modernism: namely, that of failing, despite one's effort, to make an innovative break with a received cultural practice or tradition. As we shall see, it is precisely the possibility of failing in this way that makes modernism a philosophical problem for Nietzsche.

Modernism becomes a problem for Nietzsche because he makes the new, or, more precisely, the creation of new values, a central philosophical concern.[13] Specifically, in *Thus Spoke Zarathustra*, Nietzsche invents Zarathustra, a character who is devoted to the project of creating new values. Zarathustra is a modernist who, articulating his vision of the overman, aspires to create new, non-Christian-Platonic values that will transform European humanity. As distinct from Zarathustra, Nietzsche himself never assumes that this sort of aspiration can be easily fulfilled. Nietzsche knows very well that the enterprise of creating new values *can fail*, and that, as in Rosalind Krauss's case, the attempt to break with the past can result in a repetition of the past. If he shares Zarathustra's modernist ambitions, it is not at the expense of a skepticism that puts their viability into question.

Nietzsche does not merely assent to the proposition that it is possible to create new values; rather, he inquires into how one might go about doing it. How, he wonders, can one satisfy the doubter who holds that the prospect of effecting a radical rupture with one's cultural past can never be fulfilled? Zarathustra's modernism is Nietzsche's literary vehicle for exploring the possibility of value-creation.

Zarathustra *and Nietzsche's Development*

Among recent commentators, Paul de Man is the critic who has most acutely discerned the problem that modernism was for Nietzsche. In his well-known essay "Literary History and Literary Modernity," de Man suggests that Nietzsche's thought, as early on as the second *Untimely Meditation*, "captures the authentic spirit of modernity."[14] In de Man's view, Nietzsche's modernist inclinations involve a desire to forget the past and to reach "a point of origin that marks a new departure."[15] At the same time, de Man also finds in Nietzsche a strong, skeptical sense of the difficulty, if not the impossibility, of satisfying that desire. Specifically, he stresses Nietzsche's insight that the power of the past to enforce its claims on the future constitutes a perpetual threat to the modernist will to innovate: "If history is not to become sheer regression or paralysis," de Man writes, "it depends on modernity for its duration and renewal; but modernity cannot assert itself without being at once swallowed up and reintegrated into a regressive historical process."[16]

De Man is right, I think, to see that for Nietzsche the persistence and repetition of received forms of life is a real threat to the will to innovate. Yet, according to David Hoy, this reading of Nietzsche is misleading. Purporting to side with Nietzsche against de Man, Hoy claims that de Manian doubts about the will to innovate "perpetuate metaphysical assumptions and an ironic cynicism that Nietzsche correctly attempted to undercut."[17] Additionally, Hoy applauds Heidegger for continuing Nietzsche's project: "Heidegger . . . in a very Nietzschean analysis in *Holzwege*, suggests that the world view in which the age sees itself as . . . modern . . . is tied to a self-understanding of man as *subjectum*. The project then becomes one of changing this self-understanding, not just of repeating it."[18] Here, Hoy usefully shows that the central thrust of de Man's reading of Nietzsche has ramifications that go well beyond the discussion of literature. Yet his criticism of de Man, stressing as it does the consequences of de Man's outlook (i.e., that it perpetuates metaphysical assumptions and an ironic cynicism), betrays a question-begging reluctance to take seriously de Man's challenge to Nietzsche and Heidegger. Even if we suppose, with Hoy, that Nietzsche and Heidegger are correct to want to change our self-understanding, it does not follow that change is possible or that repetition can be evaded. Hoy's resolve to resist de Man's views, and thus to avoid the perpetuation of metaphysical assumptions and ironic cynicism, shows neither that de Man is wrong nor that modernist aspirations are viable. Finally, Hoy underplays the ambivalence in Nietzsche's own thinking. De Man's skepticism regarding the possibility of new departures is just the reiteration of a skepticism already present in Nietzsche (see Chapter 2 for a more detailed development of this claim). Indeed, the opposition that Hoy posits, between Nietzsche and de Man, parallels an opposition inherent in Nietzsche's reflection on the nature of modernism. Nietzsche thinks against himself, and in this way investigates the possibility of creating new values.

Even before he wrote the *Untimely Meditations*, Nietzsche addressed the issue of cultural innovation in *The Birth of Tragedy*. Though at the time he had yet to thematize the problem of creating *new values*, Nietzsche's discussion of cultural innovation in his first book can be usefully compared to the approach he takes in later texts such as *Zarathustra*. In *The Birth of Tragedy*, Nietzsche aims to show how it is possible for a scientific, Socratic culture to become a tragic, Dionysian culture. To explain this possibility, he attributes to modern science a self-negating dialectic, arguing that

> science, spurred by its powerful illusion, speeds irresistibly toward its limits where its optimism, concealed in the essence of logic, suffers shipwreck. For the periphery of the circle of science has an infinite number of points . . . noble and gifted men . . . reach . . . inevitably, such boundary points on the periphery from which one gazes into what defies illumination. When they see to their horror how logic coils up at these boundaries and finally bites its own tail— suddenly the new form of insight breaks through, *tragic insight* which, merely to be endured, needs art as a protection and remedy.[19]

In Nietzsche's view, scientific progress undermines and negates the defining assumption of the Socratic spirit: namely, that scientific reason is the measure of the real. When scientific progress reaches the point where the hunger for knowledge turns into despair at the prospect of fully understanding reality, it reveals the possibility, as well as the need, for a new art and a new form of life.[20] Nietzsche believes that science initiates a cultural movement beyond science.[21] He interprets science as a *dynamic*, cultural phenomenon that surpasses itself and effects cultural change.

That Nietzsche has ceased, by the time of *Zarathustra*, to insist on the dynamic character of contemporary culture is clear in his portrait of the last man. To characterize this portrait in terms that are only preliminary,[22] we may say that Nietzsche uses the figure of the last man to *reinterpret* the modern, Socratic, rationalistic culture he describes in *The Birth of Tragedy*. Unlike the early Nietzsche, the later Nietzsche worries that this culture may be prone to inertia. Thus, his image of the last man is the picture of a contented, self-contained form of life that knows nothing of the restless, dialectical contradictions characterizing the modern world in *The Birth of Tragedy*. It is the picture of an "iron cage" from which dynamic change and the possibility of creating new values have been banished. In contrast to this picture, Nietzsche opposes Zarathustra, the personification of a modernist will to cultural change.

In *The Birth of Tragedy*, Nietzsche proposes to explain the possibility of cultural transformation by appealing to a dialectic immanent in contemporary culture. In *Zarathustra*, he refuses such an appeal and asks whether cultural transformation through the creation of new values is possible.[23] Nietzsche aims through his depiction of Zarathustra to describe *one* way that a creation of new values could transpire, notwithstanding the persistence of a rationalistic culture that he associates with the last man. Having grown skeptical of historiographical, dialectical explanation, he turns to literature, to a fictional protagonist, to account for the possibility of cultural innovation. Poetic imagination, as distinct from (putatively) factual narrative, now becomes the medium through which he engages and explores the problem of modernism because he is no longer confident that the promise of radical cultural change is immanent in received historical circumstances.[24]

Zarathustra *and Philosophy*

In an essay written some sixty-five years ago in the idiom of logical positivism, Rudolph Carnap commends *Zarathustra* as an example of metaphysics.[25] To be sure, his praise was not meant to endorse the view proposed in this book that *Zarathustra* should be read as form of philosophical inquiry. According to Carnap, traditional metaphysics lacks theoretical value, yet disguises itself as theory and pretends to be a kind of knowledge. Art, he argues, is the medium of expression proper to metaphysics. In *Zarathustra*, suggests Carnap, metaphysics shows itself for what it really is: namely, a form of art expressing an attitude toward life. He lauds *Zarathustra* for discarding the theoretical pretensions of traditional metaphysics and exposing the artistic essence of all metaphysics. For Carnap, theory is the proper task of empirical science and logical analysis the proper task of philosophy. *Zarathustra*, being a work of art, is neither empirical science nor philosophy, but should be appreciated the way we appreciate the music of Mozart and Beethoven.[26]

Carnap, then, would have been horrified at the suggestion that *Zarathustra*, let alone the writings of Spinoza, Hegel, or Heidegger, should be read as philosophy. He could embrace *Zarathustra* and imply that it is the type of book that Hegel and Heidegger *should have written*, precisely because he assumed that there is a clear and unquestionable distinction between a work of philosophy and a literary fiction. If metaphysics is not philosophy, Carnap thought, then literary fiction, which even metaphysicians will banish from their realm, can make no serious claim on the philosophical mind.

Allan Megill, in his book on Nietzsche, Foucault, Heidegger, and Derrida, develops a contemporary version of Carnap's attempt to close the circle of philosophy. Like Carnap, he focuses attention on *Zarathustra*. Megill, however, writing in a somewhat different intellectual climate than Carnap, suggests that the philosophical claims made in the name of literature, rather than those made in the name of metaphysics, constitute the most important contemporary threat to the integrity of philosophical discourse. The incredulity that logical positivism brought to the works of Hegel and Heidegger, Megill brings to Nietzsche's literary fiction:

> *Zarathustra* simply will not fit a critical or analytical framework. . . . Instead
> of reasons, Nietzsche gives us images; instead of arguments, allegories. . . .
> But Nietzsche fails to make these images part of any coherent argument. . . .
> *Zarathustra* is a work of literature . . . the category of literature seems to be the
> only one within which *Zarathustra* fits at all. . . . The important question here,
> however, is whether *Zarathustra* can also be regarded as a work of philosophy.[27]

What is at stake here? In evaluating *Zarathustra*, Megill seems to presuppose a concept of the *essence* of philosophy. He insinuates that *Zarathustra*, because it fails to satisfy that concept, is not philosophy. Like Carnap, Megill assumes that philosophical writing has well-defined, constitutive conditions—for example, the inclusion of "arguments"—and that some texts, because they do not fulfill those conditions, cannot count as philosophy. Motivated by an interest in drawing a sharp boundary between philosophical and nonphilosophical writing, he would exclude *Zarathustra* from the circle of philosophy for the reason that it lacks characteristics that, in his view, philosophical writing *as such* necessarily possesses.

Perhaps one should respond to the likes of Carnap and Megill by challenging their restrictive notions of the nature of philosophy. Alternatively, one might refuse their assumption that philosophy *has* a "nature" or an "essence." In defending *Zarathustra* against Megill's *specific* complaints, one need not adopt this second alternative, for *Zarathustra* does contain arguments, some of which bear importantly on its central themes (see, for instance, my discussion of Zarathustra's "practical postulate" argument in Chapter 5). In pointing this out, however, I do not begin to do justice to *Zarathustra*'s complex philosophical significance. Moreover, I leave it open to the essentialist to indict *Zarathustra* on *other* grounds —say, because its arguments do not fit neatly into an appropriately "analytical framework." If one is disposed to deny that *Zarathustra* is a work of philosophy, then it will always be possible to justify one's attitude by defining the essence of philosophy in a manner that exludes *Zarathustra*.

Rather than suppose that philosophy has an essence, we might think of it as a specific but fluid intellectual tradition. An important feature of this tradition is that it has not been possible to foretell the nature of significant, forthcoming contributions to it on the basis of received contributions. The tradition we accept as philosophy has had this feature, in part because its boundaries, to the chagrin of the boundary-policing essentialist, have never been and perhaps cannot be strictly defined. If, in some instances, philosophy has overlapped mathematics and psychology, it has also resembled sociology and cultural criticism.[28] Still, philosophy remains a distinct tradition that we can usefully conceptualize as a continuing conversation. The integrity of this conversation derives from the distinctive character of the conversational contributions that have accrued over time. Thus, the unity of philosophy is concrete, historical, and evolving.

More might be said in the way of defending the historicist conception of philosophy I have just sketched. Still, a sketch is sufficient for my present purpose, which is to suggest an alternative to the way that Carnap and Megill would have us construe the question "Is *Zarathustra* philosophy?" We should interpret that question, I am suggesting, not as a query as to whether *Zarathustra* embodies philosophy's essence, but as an invitation to examine *Zarathustra*'s affinities to a received intellectual tradition. The point of such an examination would be to assess the hypothesis that *Zarathustra* has a place within that tradition. Demonstrating that *Zarathustra* is philosophy would amount to showing how it contributes to the conversation of philosophy, without assuming that one can decide in advance, with reference to a well-defined notion of the essence of philosophy, what will count as a contribution to the conversation.

In what follows I further develop the view that *Zarathustra* is philosophy by identifying two ways that, as a literary fiction that poses the problem of creating new values, it contributes to the conversation of philosophy.

Zarathustra *as Philosophical Literature*

Philosophers who deny that literary fictions can be philosophical inquiries may nonetheless admit the existence of "philosophical literature." A standard view of such literature has been succinctly summarized by Lewis White Beck, who notes two ways that philosophy can occur in literature.[29]

First, literary works can *quote* philosophical ideas, that is, they can make "explicit and didactic use of [such] . . . ideas, the author's own, or more often, those he has learned from others."[30] Beck's examples of literature that quotes established philosophical ideas include Lucretius's *De rerum natura* and Pope's *Essay on Man*. In Beck's view, Pope and Lucretius are satisfied to repeat the thoughts of others because they do not bother themselves with the demands of proof.

Second, literary works can *exhibit* philosophical ideas. In other words, they can "embody philosophical stances in situations and character so that the reader can *see* philosophical models instead of having to think about abstract philosophical concepts. Theirs is a logic of images, not concepts."[31] Here, Beck's examples include *The Magic Mountain, Candide, Rameau's Nephew,* and *Huckleberry Finn*. He also mentions Peter Jones's interpretation of *Middlemarch,* according to which Eliot exhibits different philosophies of the imagination in her depiction of different characters.[32] According to Beck, most philosophical literature lies somewhere on the spectrum between "philosophical quotation" and "philosophical exhibition."

Philosophers who challenge Beck's standard view of philosophical literature tend to emphasize literary form at the expense of thematic content. For example, Jean-Paul Sartre and William Gass have encouraged philosophically minded critics to stress not the quotation and exhibition of philosophical ideas in the depiction of character and incident, but rather the expression of these ideas in narrative techniques and other "structural" aspects of a literary work.[33] Though Sartre and Gass were once unusual in advocating the philosophical analysis of literary form, many contemporary critics in the formalist tradition take their position for granted. Among them, Jonathan Culler insists that "a distinction between philosophy and literature is essential to deconstruction's power of intervention . . . the most powerful and apposite readings of literary works may be those that treat them as philosophical gestures by teasing out the implications of their dealings with the philosophical oppositions that support them."[34] If

Culler is right, then deconstructionist literary critics, if not professional philosophers, have steadily begun to satisfy Sartre's and Gass's notions of a genuinely philosophical literary criticism.

Despite the differences between them, there is a deep affinity between Beck's notion of philosophical literature and the position that Sartre, Gass, and Culler advance. Most significantly, the two views assume the availability of a vocabulary *proper* to philosophical discourse. Taken together, they suggest that literary fiction is philosophically significant only if it (1) quotes or (2) exhibits the issues and ideas posed in such a vocabulary, either in (a) content (Beck) or (b) form (Sartre, Gass, and Culler). In general, Sartre, Gass, Culler, and Beck share the belief that the concepts and problems of philosophy are given independently of literary fiction (e.g., in what Beck calls "the source books in the syllabi of professors of philosophy")[35] and that some of this fiction, namely, philosophical literature, displays (quotes or exhibits) these concepts and problems. All that separates Beck from the others is his emphasis on the thematic, as distinct from formal, display of the philosophical issues and ideas that each believes is given in advance.

In Beck's view, the analysis and evaluation of the terms proper to philosophical discourse, as well as the articulation of arguments concerning the appropriate scope of these terms, proceeds through a "logic of concepts." Naturally, none of this logical and conceptual activity requires reference to the literary display of philosophical ideas. Beck suggests that the philosopher's singular concern (qua philosopher) is the philosophical ideas themselves and that these ideas are given antecedently to their literary "appearance" (recall Beck's claim that philosophical literature permits the reader to *see* philosophical models), almost as if they occupied an ethereal Platonic heaven. Likewise, Sartre and Gass tacitly assume that the philosopher can address the themes and problems specific to his discipline (Sartre alludes to metaphysics, Gass, to the principles defining empiricism, skepticism, and stoicism), before analyzing their expression in the techniques and forms of fiction writing. Finally, Culler implies that the deconstructionist critic uses the vocabulary of philosophy to identify and define "philosophical oppositions," before "teasing out" the implications of the way that a particular text handles these oppositions.

For Culler, as well as for Beck, Sartre, and Gass, philosophy as philosophy can dispense with literature. More precisely, each of these writers presupposes that philosophy, together with the vocabulary and the problems that constitute philosophy, is a self-sufficient enterprise, given apart from its manifestations in the forms or contents of literary fictions. Literary fiction, from this point of view, can make philosophical ideas palpable but can contribute nothing to their constitution and development. At best, it provides an interesting distraction for the philosopher as philosopher, who finds his lofty abstractions prettily exhibited in the creations of the imagination.

The conception of philosophical literature that one finds in Beck, Sartre, Gass, and Culler is too narrow. What is missing in this conception is the recognition that literature can contest an established philosophical diction. These authors assume that philosophically significant fiction derives its philosophical importance *exclusively* from already acknowledged philosophical problems. Yet some literary fiction is philosophically significant precisely because it produces new philosophical vocabularies and thus new philosophical problems. Plato's dialogues, for example, were once philosophically significant in this way.[36] Literary fiction that produces new philosophical vocabularies challenges the supposition that some existing vocabulary constitutes the proper mode of philosophical discourse. Such fiction, because it reveals new philosophical problems, may be difficult to grasp from the perspective of traditional philosophical thought. Indeed, such fiction may not be readily accepted as genuinely *philosophical* fiction.

I can summarize my criticism of these authors' analyses of philosophical literature by saying that they neglect literature's capacity for philosophical invention. Literary imagination can function philosophically in much the same way that Kant's productive imagination functions in the pure judgment of taste. In the pure judgment of taste, the productive imagination presents its object but without the benefit of a definite concept. The activity of the imagination, in this judgment, is not dictated in advance by a determinate rule for ordering a manifold. This is not to say that the pure judgment of taste is pure chaos, since the imagination in such a judgment conforms to the form of the understanding in general. Applying Kant's idiom to the authors in question, it can be said that Beck, Sartre, Gass, and Culler ignore the power of the imagination to act independently of given concepts. Philosophical literature, on their account, is the literature of an imagination that re-presents an already constituted array of philosophical ideas. That the productive imagination might achieve a measure of autonomy, that it might act in a nonderivative capacity, and thus produce new concepts and problems, this possibility they do not acknowledge.[37]

The claim that an autonomous productive imagination can be philosophically valuable has some affinity to Richard Rorty's recent defense of narrative philosophy, which he distinguishes from argumentative philosophy. The latter, he asserts, is possible "only if a vocabulary in which to state premises is shared by speaker and audience."[38] Thus, argumentative philosophy presupposes the common recognition that a particular vocabulary is appropriate to philosophical discourse. On the other hand, narrative philosophy challenges the propriety of prevailing philosophical discourse by telling stories "about why we talk as we do and how we might avoid continuing to talk in that way."[39] As examples of narrative philosophy, Rorty cites the works of Nietzsche, Heidegger, and Derrida. He exhorts us not to expect these works "to fill the gaps left vacant by argumentative philosophy."[40] Rather, "the importance of narrative philosophy is that persuasion is as frequently a matter of getting people to drop a vocabulary (and the questions they phrase within it) as of deductive argument."[41]

While Rorty is right to emphasize the critical significance of narration, he underestimates the philosophically productive power of philosophical narratives. In Nietzsche's case in particular, narrative thought is meant not only to free us from old ways of speaking, but also to confront us with new dilemmas, together with new conjectures regarding their resolution. Nietzsche's *Zarathustra* is an example of narrative philosophy in the form of a quasi-novelistic fictional narrative. As a productive act of the imagination, it creates vocabulary, concepts, questions, and concerns that stand at a distance from the mainstream of Western philosophy. The critical notions of the last man, the overman, the higher man, the will to power, and the eternal recurrence are introduced or first developed in *Zarathustra*. Together they constitute a set of anxieties, hopes, questions, and possibilities that I should like to describe as a philosophical world, or form of life. It is only against the background of this world that the unifying theme of *Zarathustra*—namely, the possibility of creating new values—acquires significance. Nietzsche's attempt to explain this possibility is not a response to some widely recognized problem in ethics, epistemology, metaphysics, or even value theory. Rather, the problem of creating new values draws its specific shape and density from the philosophical form of life that *Zarathustra* creates. As narrative philosophy, *Zarathustra* eschews traditional philosophical vocabularies in favor of new modes of philosophical thought.[42]

To be sure, I am not arguing here that *only* fictional narrative can be philosophically inventive. Philosophers as different in outlook as P. F. Strawson and Gilles Deleuze have reminded us that numerous nonfictional works belonging to the canon of philosophy were meant to revise our thinking through the elaboration of new concepts[43]—concepts, for example, like substance (Aristotle) and the *cogito* (Descartes). In some cases, philosophers have noted that the creation of new concepts is connected to the formulation of new problems. Here, a case in point is Kant's suggestion that he was the first philosopher to pose the problem of explaining the possibility of synthetic a priori judgments in part because he was the first clearly to form a concept of the analytic/synthetic distinction.[44] Nietzsche himself exhorts philosophers to "*make* and *create* [concepts],"[45] and, as distinct from most of his precursors, uses a fictional narrative precisely for that purpose. *Zarathustra* shows that fiction, *no less than nonfiction*, can make inventive contributions to the conversation of philosophy.

At this juncture, it seems reasonable to point out that the invention of new concepts *need not* involve a contribution to the conversation of philosophy. Only if the development of new concepts responds to and engages the inherited philosophical tradition—as does, for example, Kant's explication of the analytic/synthetic distinction—does it make sense to speak of some such "contribution." As we shall see in Chapter 2, the vocabulary and concepts Nietzsche invents to explore the problem of creating new values *do* engage the philosophical tradition. Nietzsche suggests that just by posing this problem he questions the validity of a traditional, philosophical interpretation of the origin of value.

Zarathustra *as Philosophical Explanation*

Zarathustra contributes in a second way to the conversation of philosophy by providing a philosophical explanation for the possibility of creating new values. Following Robert Nozick, I take philosophical explanation to be a familiar form of philosophy appropriate to answering questions like: How is it possible for us to have free will, supposing that all actions are causally determined? How is it possible that we know anything, given that it is logically possible that we are dreaming? How can there be stable meanings, granted that all in the world is changing (one of Plato's questions, according to Nozick)? And finally, how is it possible for new values to be created? Philosophical explanations generate explanatory hypotheses that identify putatively sufficient, though not necessary conditions for the phenomena they seek to explain. To "produce . . . [a] . . . possible explanation of *p* is, by seeing one way *p* is given rise to, to see how *p* can be true. 'How is it possible that *p*?' This way: such and such facts are possible and they constitute an explanatory route to *p*."[46] In Nozick's view, a philosophical explanation is a possible account of the possibility of some fact or phenomenon. To produce such an explanation is to chart a possible path of jointly sufficient conditions to the possibility one aspires to explain. Philosophical explanations are speculative, hypothetical conjectures that tell us what could be, what some conceivable account of this or that possibility looks like.

Philosophical explanations tend to be motivated by the identification of *apparent excluders*. In other words, the questions prompting these explanations typically have the following form: "How is one thing possible, *given (or supposing) certain other things?*"[47] By "other things," Nozick means a set of statements, R1 . . . Rn, *that appear to exclude* p's *holding true*, where *p* is the possibility to be explained (in the examples cited above, these "other things," or apparent excluders, are "that all actions are causally determined," "that it is logically possible that we are dreaming," and "that all in the world is changing"). The point of a philosophical explanation is to show that some facts or principles, if they were to obtain, would give rise to p, either despite the truth of $R_1 \ldots Rn$ (e.g., that such-and-such facts and principles would give rise to free will, despite the truth of the claim that all actions are causally determined) or where one need not accept as true one or all of $R_1 \ldots Rn$. In both cases, the explanatory aim is to show how p is possible, notwithstanding some reasons for denying that p is possible.[48]

The concept of an apparent excluder can help us to see how *Zarathustra* works as a philosophical explanation. As I have argued, Nietzsche thinks against himself in his reflection on the nature of modernism. Though he sympathizes with the modernist intentions Zarathustra personifies, he also doubts the possibility of fulfilling those intentions. The tension in Nietzsche's thought, between sympathetic and doubtful attitudes toward the modernist desire to create new values, structures the plot of *Zarathustra* as a whole. That tension appears in the book as a conflict between Zarathustra's will to innovate and the many skeptical voices that, in the course of Zarathustra's career, speak against his will. Throughout *Zarathustra*, these voices function as apparent excluders.

Let me be more precise: in the course of striving to move himself and others to become creators of new values, Zarathustra encounters a variety of figures (e.g. the saint, the jester, the soothsayer, and the spirit of gravity), all of whom suggest in one way or another that a creation of new values is not possible. In each instance, this suggestion threatens to dissuade Zarathustra from his effort to become a cultural innovator and, accordingly, threatens to shipwreck his project altogether. Zarathustra can become a creator of new values only if he persists in his commitment to becoming such a creator. The figures who speak against his project function as apparent excluders, because the consequence of their skepticism is, typically, to undermine his commitment. Here, then, skepticism produces an effect that is another reason for skepticism. For Nietzsche, part of showing how it is possible to create new values is showing how it is possible for someone and, in particular, for Zarathustra, to maintain his commitment to becoming a creator of new values despite the truth of the claim that assertions of skepticism tend repeatedly to undermine and could even obliterate that commitment.

In resisting the aforementioned assertions of skepticism, Zarathustra characteristically adopts a posture of defiance, the distinctive content of which will be a central theme of this book. By repeatedly embracing that posture, he repeatedly reaffirms his commitment to becoming a cultural innovator. Zarathustra's enactments of a posture of defiance estrange him from his capacity to be affected by passional chaos, a capacity that (as we shall see in Chapter 4) he must acknowledge if he is to create new values. More exactly, his defiant behavior requires that he disown that capacity and deny that he possesses it. Paradoxically, then, Zarathustra's strategy for maintaining his commitment to creating new values impedes his fulfillment of that commitment. Put another way, his manner of resisting the skeptical voices that beset him appears in its own right to *exclude* the possibility of him becoming a creator of new values. Thus, showing how it is possible to create new values involves showing how Zarathustra could do that, given the truth of the assertion that he has become self-estranged.

Supposing that Zarathustra were to free himself of his self-estrangement, there is no guarantee that he would then become a new-values creator: for this, an experience of passional, Dionysian chaos is essential.[49] Roughly the second half of *Zarathustra* concerns Zarathustra's recognition that, even if he acknowledges a *capacity* to be affected by passional chaos, the onslaught of the social conditions he associates with the last man will have eliminated from his and his disciples' bodies the passions that otherwise might chaotically have seized them. At this stage in Zarathustra's development, accounting for the possibility of creating new values involves showing how Zarathustra could become a new-values creator given that that option seems to have been ruled out by the destruction of the passions required for such creation.

Zarathustra contributes to the conversation of philosophy, first, by inventing vocabulary and concepts for posing a new problem that engages the philosophical tradition, and second, by exemplifying a familiar style of philosophical speculation—what Nozick calls "philosophical explanation"—in addressing that problem.[50] For Nietzsche, explaining the possibility of creating new values amounts to demonstrating how Zarathustra could come to be a creator of new values despite the skepticism, the self-estrangement, and the passion-eradicating social conditions that haunt his will to innovate. By telling Zarathustra's story, Nietzsche charts one path—that is, one trajectory of putatively sufficient conditions—for becoming a new-values creator. In effect, he dramatizes a sequence of events—among them Zarathustra's acts of defiance and his acknowledgment of his ability to be affected by passional chaos—which, in tandem, would suffice to foster a creation of new values.[51] Nowhere does Nietzsche proclaim that these events or events like them are likely to occur in the world outside his fiction. Neither is he confident that there exist individuals in that world able to emulate Zarathustra.

Reading Zarathustra

Thus far I have been discussing the concepts—modernism, narrative philosophy, and philosophical explanation—that frame my reading of *Zarathustra* in the chapters that follow. In the remainder of this introduction, I outline the specifics of that reading.

As I have suggested, the plot of *Zarathustra* is shaped by the reiteration of a conflict between Zarathustra's will to innovate and one or another of the incredulous voices (and apparent excluders) that oppose his will. Chapter 1 of the present book develops this suggestion by arguing that the action of Nietzsche's narrative is generally structured by an opposition between (1) Zarathustra's intentions to become a creator of new values and to inspire others to do the same, and (2) the doubts of skeptical figures who claim (or imply) that Zarathustra's future harbors no creations of new values, but only the repetition in human life of received, Christian-Platonic values. In subsequent chapters, I describe these skeptical personae as *representations of repetition*. The aforementioned opposition I describe as *an antithesis of intention and repetition*.

Chapter 1 explains this antithesis by comparing *Zarathustra* to Hegel's *Phenomenology of Spirit* and by interpreting Nietzsche's narrative with reference to Edward Said's and Peter Brooks's literary criticism of the novel. Said's and Brooks's works help to contextualize my reading of *Zarathustra*, because they show how antitheses quite similar to the antithesis of intention and repetition function as principles of plot formation in other works of nineteenth-century fiction. In addition, they help to frame my response to Tracy Strong's provocative (but undeveloped) idea that "*Zarathustra* is, among other things, a counter to Hegel's *Phenomenology*."[52] Following Strong, I contrast *Zarathustra* to the *Phenomenology*, stressing in each case the connection between plot structure and philosophical outlook. *Zarathustra*, I submit, can be read as a modernist "rewriting" of the *Phenomenology*.

The final sections of Chapter 1 complicate my account of the plot of *Zarathustra*. In particular, I focus on Zarathustra's speech on the three metamorphoses (the first speech of Part 1 of *Zarathustra*). There, Zarathustra depicts a triptych of forms of action describing his typical responses to representations of repetition and his picture of what it is to be a creator of new values. When Zarathustra falls victim to representations of repetition, he becomes a weight-bearing camel. When he resists and defies these representations, he becomes a heroic, Promethean lion. When, finally, the creation of new values is imminent, he becomes a yea-saying child. The speech on the three metamorphoses is Nietzsche's sketch of the way *Zarathustra* works as a philosophical explanation: in adopting the defiant posture of the lion, Zarathustra reaffirms his commitment to becoming a new-values creator, despite the harsh incredulity of "this" or "that" representation of repetition; in becoming a child (which he becomes only at the end of the book), he becomes a new-values creator, notwithstanding the fact that he has become self-estranged and notwithstanding the persistence among men of passion-eradicating social conditions.

Chapter 1 establishes the basis for my interpretation of the prologue[53] and four parts of *Zarathustra* in Chapters 2–6. In Chapter 2, where I concentrate on the prologue I investigate the irony framing Zarathustra's initial effort to create new values, as well as the setbacks prompting him to recognize that creating new values may not be possible. Zarathustra aims to alert his auditors to the possibility of experiencing the Dionysian chaos involved in such creation. In my discussion of the prologue, I analyze the frustrations Zarathustra suffers in attempting to realize his aim, interpreting his actions in terms of the three metamorphoses of the spirit and the antithesis of intention and repetition. In this context, I also revisit Paul de Man's reading of Nietzsche, acknowledging, however, that de Man is right to identify in Nietzsche's thought a skepticism regarding the modernist will to innovate. De Man errs, I argue, in proposing that this skepticism represents a stable, final phase in the development of Nietzsche's thought.

Chapter 3 turns to Part 1 of *Zarathustra* and reconstructs in detail Zarathustra's theory of value creation. Central to that theory is the thesis that the body is a field of passions and, as such, the primary bearer of human culture. The chapter begins by expanding the analysis (sketched in this introduction) of *The Birth of Tragedy*'s approach to the problem of cultural innovation. More specifically, I argue that Nietzsche's early vision of a tragic, Wagnerian culture is predicated on the view that the German nation is the proper vehicle for realizing a Dionysian cultural transformation of the modern world. Nietzsche's early concept of the German nation is riddled with self-contradiction. By the time he writes *Zarathustra*, he has rejected this concept and has harshly repudiated the *Volksgeist* nationalism he had earlier embraced. For the later Nietzsche, the *healthy human body*, as distinct from the *German body politic*, is the conduit through which Dionysus-sponsored cultural innovation, now understood as new-values creation, can transform the modern world. Zarathustra's theory of new-values creation is his attempt to show how the healthy human body can function as a conduit to such creation.

The prologue and Part 1 of *Zarathustra* highlight Zarathustra's search for companions. As philosophical explanation, they emphasize his subjection, as a camel, to representations of repetition, and his repeated enactment of the posture of the lion in resisting these representations. In his search for companions in Part 1, Zarathustra speaks in the voice of a lion and addresses himself to individuals who can be or who have become lions. He also outlines an ethics that is appropriate to living as a lion. Nowhere in the prologue or Part 1, however, does he entertain the possibility that to become a heroic, Promethean lion is to become self-estranged.

Only in Part 2 does this possibility receive Zarathustra's attention, when he experiences the self-estrangement of the lion as a form of suffering. Chapter 4 of the present book proposes a reading of Part 2 that connects Zarathustra's self-estrangement and suffering to his will to truth. Zarathustra sees, ultimately, that he must relinquish his will to truth, as well as the heroic sense of the sublime it engenders, if he is to cease to be self-estranged and become a creator of new values. Zarathustra can become a creator of new values, despite the fact that he has become self-estranged, because he learns to renounce the heroic, leonine sensibility that has caused his self-estrangement. As we shall see, Nietzsche also relates Zarathustra's self-estrangement to the Cartesian tendency to view human beings as noncorporeal subjects. In effect, he suggests that adherence to a Cartesian self-understanding precludes the possibility of creating new values.

Eternal recurrence is the central theme of the final two chapters of this book, where I argue that the thought of recurrence proceeds through three phases of development in *Zarathustra*, each of which corresponds to one of the three metamorphoses of the spirit. In charting the evolution of this thought, I trace a sequence of events marking the final path on the route of Nietzsche's explanation of the possibility of creating new values. In becoming a camel and a lion one final time, and a child for the first time, Zarathustra brings to a conclusion a narrative that shows how, despite persistent representations of repetition, the recurrence of the trauma of self-estrangement, and the pervasive destruction of human passions in the age of the last man, it is still possible to become a creator of new values.

Chapter 5 focuses on the final third of Part 2 (sections 14–22) and on Part 3. Near the end of Part 2, the soothsayer's speech alerts Zarathustra to the imminent elimination of bodily passions from human life. Zarathustra's interpretation of that speech causes him to believe that he has fallen victim to the endless perpetuation of Christian-Platonic values in the person of the last man—the first stage in the development of the thought of recurrence. In Part 3, Zarathustra struggles to defy this belief, conjecturing that he can do so without becoming self-estranged. Ultimately, however, he fails in his effort to reconcile heroic, leonine defiance with an acknowledgment of his capacity to be affected by passional chaos. At the end of Part 3, Zarathustra envisions his soul as an eternal "now" that encompasses the whole of time. This vision marks the second stage in the development of the thought of recurrence.

Chapter 6 tells the tale of Zarathustra's adventures in the fourth and final part of *Zarathustra*. Through most of Part 4, Zarathustra anticipates the appearance of the "children" and "right men" in whose company he hopes to become a creator of new values. While awaiting these men, he soon discovers a group of the "wrong men," the so-called "higher men," whose nausea and despair he palliates by means of a drunken, theatrical parody of his performance of the second (leonine) phase of the thought of recurrence in Part 3. In the aftermath of that parody, with the advent of the "right men" seemingly at hand, Zarathustra takes leave of the higher men and becomes a child-creator. As Part 4 draws to a close, he enacts the third and final phase of the thought of recurrence, which involves the belief that the passions and the possibility of experiencing passional chaos have been returned to European modernity, thereby enabling him and his children to become creators of new values.

Zarathustra ends, of course, without the appearance of Zarathustra's children (they are said to be "near") and without a creation of new values. The book's conclusion shows Zarathustra believing that a creation of new values is imminent, yet hardly insists that his modernist optimism is well founded. And why should it? Having explained how new values *could be* created, *Zarathustra* ultimately leaves unresolved the question of whether what could be *will be* in the future. I return to this question in Chapter 6, in anticipation of my discussion of *Zarathustra*'s relationship to *Beyond Good and Evil.*

CHAPTER ONE

Philosophizing with a Stammer

Look here! That is the very difference! Our reality doesn't change: it can't change! It can't be other than what it is, because it is already fixed for ever. It's terrible.

LUIGI PIRANDELLO, *Six Characters in Search of an Author*

History, Stephen said, is a nightmare from which I am trying to awake.

JAMES JOYCE, *Ulysses*

Zarathustra is a fiction that confuses its readers by offering them multiple but disparate clues about what genre it belongs to. At first glance, it seems to be a mock-religious or perhaps religious book that repeatedly parodies biblical sayings and consistently imitates the syntax of Luther's Bible. Yet a closer examination of the text shows that its uses of allusion and parody extend far beyond the Old and New Testaments. At decisive moments in the development of the plot, *Zarathustra* emulates, mimics, or satirizes the works of Plato, Goethe, Byron, Schopenhauer, Wagner, and others. These secular allusions often have as much bearing on our understanding of *Zarathustra* as its references to the Bible. There is, furthermore, an atmosphere of make-believe about *Zarathustra*, in which biblical and secular allusions alike are embedded. Like Carl Spitteler's *Prometheus and Epimetheus*, a work that probably inspired important features of the plot and the style of *Zarathustra*, Nietzsche's fiction unfolds against the backdrop of a mythical mountain landscape in which animals speak and characters like "Life" and "Wisdom" are personified. The "oriental" lineage of its protagonist enhances the mythical strangeness of *Zarathustra* and lends the book a typically *fin de siècle* exoticism that Nietzsche elsewhere suggests is a symptom of Wagnerian decadence. The affinity to Wagner can be pressed further by noting that *Zarathustra*, if performed, would incorporate poetry, song, and dance, and to that extent would resemble a *Gesamtkunstwerk*. The more we read *Zarathustra*, the more difficult it is to classify. Nietzsche's masterpiece is oriental myth, Wagnerian opera, spirited evangelism, and secular culture critique, yet never seems reducible to any one of these categories.[1]

The problem of classifying *Zarathustra* is further complicated by the claim that this book is a work of philosophy. How can a narrative fiction that seems to be so many things, yet nothing in particular—how can such a fiction be a philosophical explanation? More generally, how can a text that appears to participate in such a motley assortment of genres exhibit an articulate structure that renders it intelligible as a form of speculative inquiry? In a recent discussion of *Zarathustra*, Hans-Georg Gadamer gives what seems to me to be the proper answer to these questions. In his view, the philosophically decisive feature of *Zarathustra* is "the drama that happens in the telling of this book."[2] Gadamer holds further that "when we behold this work as a dramatic action, including all Zarathustra's speeches . . . we free ourselves from that serial form which gives to this collection of speeches . . . the tone of a sermon that simply goes on."[3] If Gadamer is correct, then the action of *Zarathustra* surpasses in philosophical importance the biblically cadenced didacticism that imbues it with religious overtones. To extend Gadamer's point, I would add that the action of *Zarathustra* also surpasses in philosophical importance its parodies, mythical qualities, and affinities to Wagner's *Gesamtkunstwerke*. This is not to deny, by any means, that these other aspects of Nietzsche's fiction are philosophically significant, but only to insist that they derive their philosophical value from their connection to the book's plot.[4] The plot of *Zarathustra*, the *patterning of its action*, organizes it as a unified whole.[5]

Zarathustra provides a variety of clues as to the general form of the tale it tells.[6] Of particular interest, in this respect, are Zarathustra's self-descriptions. In this chapter, I propose to read two of these self-descriptions as descriptions of *Zarathustra* itself, that is, as metaphors for the book's plot structure. In Part 3 of *Zarathustra*, in the section entitled "On Old and New Tablets," Zarathustra asserts that like poets he stammers (*stammelt*) and that he is ashamed that he must still be a poet (as he puts it, *ich schäme mich, dass ich noch Dichter sein muss*). Later, in the same section, he claims that he is a prelude (*Vorspiel*) to better players (*Spieler*).[7] Bearing these remarks in mind, I shall show that the plot of *Zarathustra* is constructed both as a stammer and as a prelude. I will additionally maintain, perhaps paradoxically, that *Zarathustra* is articulate as a prelude because its action has the form of a stammer. *Zarathustra* is an articulate stammer and, as such, a prelude to the play it anticipates. Finally, I shall argue that Zarathustra's speech on the three metamorphoses specifies modes of action by which Zarathustra submits to, defies, and triumphs over *Zarathustra*'s stammering.

Zarathustra's *Stammering*

Stammering is characterized by an opposition between a speaker's intentions and her involuntary repetition of words she has already spoken.[8] Stammers suggest that, despite a speaker's intentions, her future is destined to repeat her past. The plot of *Zarathustra* resembles a stammer, because it is structured by an analogous opposition. In fine, it is structured by a conflict between Zarathustra's intentions and the various characters who claim that, despite his intentions, humanity's future is destined to repeat its past. *Zarathustra*'s "textual" stammering evinces a clash between Zarathustra's intentions and personae whose words and actions portend the defeat of his intentions. But just what are Zarathustra's intentions and who are the personae that oppose them?

Speaking in preliminary terms that anticipate a detailed reading of "Zarathustra's Prologue" (see Chapter 2), we may say that Zarathustra is defined essentially by two intentions. One is his *poetic intention* to speak poetically and thereby to inspire others to become creators of new values. The second is his *personal intention* to become a value-creator in his own right and hence someone who need not settle for the lesser, poet's vocation of inspiring others to become value-creators. If Zarathustra is ashamed that he *must still be a poet*, it is in part because he has thus far failed to fulfill and must keep trying to fulfill his poetic intention, but also because he has thus far failed to fulfill and must keep trying to fulfill his personal intention. Zarathustra's failures seem necessary to him, one suspects, because he has overheard the soothsayer's prophecy near the end of Part 2. As we shall see (in Chapter 5), the central claim of this prophecy is that the destruction of the passions presupposed by all new-values creation is imminent. If the soothsayer speaks the truth, then Christian-Platonic values will persist in humanity's future and Zarathustra's two (personal and poetic) intentions will never be fulfilled. Conjuring up the stammerer's specter of a future that relentlessly repeats the past, the soothsayer implies that Zarathustra's attempts to realize these intentions will forever be futile.

The appearance of the soothsayer marks the most important but not the first time that Zarathustra's personal and poetic intentions meet with the antithetical personae I call "representations of repetition." In "Zarathustra's Prologue," for example, Zarathustra encounters a saint, townspeople, and a jester, all of whose words and/or actions raise doubts as to the possibility of overcoming man through the creation of new values. In each case, the implication of these doubts is that the pervasive, repetitive perpetuation of Christian-Platonic values in human life is inescapable. Later, in Part 2 (before the appearance of the soothsayer), Zarathustra hears caricatures of his teachings that make a related point, arguing that Zarathustra himself, notwithstanding his efforts to the contrary, re-iterates and promotes Christian-Platonic values. In Part 4, finally, Zarathustra discovers "higher men" who appear symbolically to confirm the soothsayer's view that the future must repeat the past.

In the chapters that follow I say more about each of these representations of repetition. Here, I simply mention them in order to begin to substantiate my suggestion that the action of *Zarathustra* is patterned like a stammer. *Zarathustra's* plot is punctuated by stammers that harass Zarathustra. The plot first stammers when Zarathustra meets the saint in the forest. It stammers again in the prologue, Part 2, Part 4, and in various other places. The plot of *Zarathustra* stammers precisely when one or another representation of repetition suggests to Zarathustra that the project of creating new values is futile. Nietzsche explains how new-values creation is possible by showing how Zarathustra, notwithstanding this stammering, can succeed in realizing his personal and poetic intentions.[9]

In general, then, the action of *Zarathustra* exhibits a pattern of conflict between Zarathustra's intentions and the figures that resist those intentions by (explicitly or implicitly) representing the future as repeating the values of the past and as involving no creation of new values. This pattern, or structure, which I describe as an antithesis of intention and repetition, is central to Nietzsche's thinking: it betokens both his sympathy with, and skepticism about, Zarathustra's modernism. I have to insist, therefore, that J. P. Stern is wrong to suggest that Nietzsche dogmatically downplays the claims of custom and the past in favor what is outstanding, unique, and novel. On the contrary, by dramatizing Zarathustra's confrontations with nay-saying representations of repetition, Nietzsche expresses his own skeptical sense that the (Christian-Platonic) past may be a nightmare from which Zarathustra will never awake. Though Stern is right to doubt that it is possible to create new values that would be discontinuous with old ones, he is mistaken to suggest that Nietzsche shows no interest in the "logic of conversion." Not only is Nietzsche interested in this "logic," he devotes *Zarathustra* to it. In other words, Nietzsche uses *Zarathustra* to produce a coherent, intelligible explanation of the possibility of transforming human beings into new-values creators. The antithesis of intention and repetition frames this philosophical explanation and structures Nietzsche's attempt to see how modernist intentions can prevail against representations of repetitions.[10]

At this juncture, a careful, nuanced analysis of *Zarathustra's* relationship to other works of literature would distract us from the central concerns of this chapter. Still, we may begin to appreciate *Zarathustra's* distinctiveness, as well as its affinities to other narrative fictions, by briefly considering it in the perspective of Edward Said's and Peter Brooks's recent, plot-centered theories of the novel.[11] As we shall see, these theories attribute to the novel structural oppositions similar to the antithesis of intention and repetition that is evident in *Zarathustra*.

Examining a literary tradition that stretches from Cervantes to Conrad, Said describes a structural opposition between authority and molestation. "Authority" is his term for the power of an individual to sustain and render effective an intention to begin something new (a "beginning intention"). According to Said, the pursuit of novelty is a central theme of the classical novel and is often evident in the aspiration of a protagonist—for example, Dickens's Pip and Eliot's Dorothea Brooke—to create a new and alternate life for herself. Typically, the protagonist's effort to realize her aspiration is stymied—"molested" is Said's term—by inhibiting and destructive powers that enforce the claims of reality and insist that her envisioned "new life" necessarily is a fiction. Summarizing his theory, Said finds in the classical novel both "a desire to create or author an alternate life and to show (by molestation) this alternative to be at bottom an illusion with reference to "life."[12]

Said's description of the classical novel is strikingly similar to Peter Brooks's treatment of nineteenth-century narrative fictions. Brooks interprets novelistic plots and plotting as forms of deviance and abnormality. Accordingly, where Said sees molestations of authority, he discerns a conflict between the desire to plot (that is, to deviate from a state of normality) and novelistic elements that subvert and "cure" that desire. Brooks also claims that novels represent plots as errors in the evaluation of what realistically is possible, an assertion that recalls Said's judgment that such texts demonstrate the illusory character of the alternate lives they depict: "the nineteenth-century novel in general . . . regularly conceives plot as a condition of deviance and abnormality. . . . Deviance is the very condition for life to be 'narratable': the state of normality is devoid of interest, energy, and the possibility of narration. In between a beginning prior to plot and an end beyond plot, the middle—the plotted text—has been in a state of *error*: wandering and misinterpretation."[13]

As described by Said and Brooks, novels often oppose modernism, arguing against the viability *in fact* of the desire for novelty and plot that they contrast to "true life" and normality. Were *Zarathustra* like a novel in this respect, it would depict as ultimately futile Zarathustra's intentions to become a creator of new values and to inspire others to do the same. To use Said's language, it would tell the tale of the decisive thwarting of Zarathustra's intentions by representations of repetition that molested his authority to create new values. Needless to say, Nietzsche never grants that Zarathustra's intentions are futile. Indeed, part of his purpose in *Zarathustra* is to justify those intentions by explaining the possibility of their realization. *Zarathustra* is philosophically at odds with Said's and Brooks's "antimodernist" novels, for it is ambivalent in its appraisal of Zarathustra's modernism. In the end it envisions the fulfillment, not the thwarting, of Zarathustra's intentions, yet still allows that the "new life" it seems to grant Zarathustra (a life of creating new values) may be a fantasy born of unjustifiable optimism.

The action of *Zarathustra, because* it envisions the fulfillment of Zarathustra's intentions, can be read as an anticipatory prelude to the creation of new values. It can also be read as a prelude to the advent of Zarathustra's "better players." The creation of new values and the advent of better players are inextricably related. As a prelude to both, the action of *Zarathustra* expresses a revisionary conception of philosophy. In the next section of this chapter I explicate this conception, first, by relating the advent of better players to Nietzsche's idea of a "philosophy of the future," and second, by comparing *Zarathustra* to Hegel's *Phenomenology*. The plot structure of *Zarathustra* is closely related to the idea of a philosophy of the future that breaks with philosophical tradition. Nowhere does this become clearer than in contrasting *Zarathustra* to the *Phenomenology*. Compared to the *Phenomenology*, *Zarathustra* looks like a "rewriting" of the earlier book that embodies a modernist sensibility. If Hegelian phenomenology receives its materialist transformation in Marx, it receives its modernist transformation in Nietzsche.

Zarathustra and Hegel's Phenomenology

The subtitle of *Beyond Good and Evil* is *Prelude to a Philosophy of the Future*. Thus, to read *Zarathustra* as I do, with reference to the idea of a philosophy of the future, is to raise the question of the relationship between *Zarathustra* and *Beyond Good and Evil*.

Commentators have long puzzled over the connection between these books because Nietzsche completed *Beyond Good and Evil* soon after writing the fourth and last part of *Zarathustra*. Some have proposed that *Zarathustra* is the philosophy of the future to which the later book is a prelude. Still others have insisted that *Beyond Good and Evil* is supposed to clarify the ideas that Nietzsche develops "poetically" in *Zarathustra*. To these views, I wish to add a third: namely, that *Beyond Good and Evil* articulates a point of view corresponding to the portrait of Zarathustra in the closing section of Part 4 ("The Sign"). This is not to deny that *Beyond Good and Evil* helps to illuminate *Zarathustra*, though I reject emphatically the claim that *Zarathustra* itself is Nietzsche's philosophy of the future. *Beyond Good and Evil* and *Zarathustra* are *perspectivally continuous*, because *Beyond Good and Evil* elucidates and elaborates a perspective that Zarathustra personifies at the end of Part 4.

For Nietzsche, the phrase "philosophy of the future" signifies a conception of philosophy that defines philosophy as an activity of value-creation. *Zarathustra* and *Beyond Good and Evil* are preludes to Nietzsche's philosophy of the future, for they envision the advent of "philosophers of the future," or "new philosophers," whose distinctive task is to create new values. In other words, both works look forward to the arrival of avant-garde philosophers who, like avant-garde artists, embody a modernist aspiration to innovate. The individuals belonging to this avant-garde are, I want to suggest, Zarathustra's children and better players: philosopher-creators who can play well the game of creating new values. The action of *Zarathustra* is a prelude to better players, because, in explaining the possibility of creating new values, it anticipates the appearance of these individuals. *Beyond Good and Evil* can be said to begin where *Zarathustra* ends because it presents itself as having been written from the perspective of Zarathustra's expectation, as Part 4 comes to an end, that his better players' appearance is imminent.

In Chapter 6, in an addendum to my reading of the fourth part of *Zarathustra*, I develop at greater length my interpretation of *Zarathustra's* relationship to *Beyond Good and Evil.* Here, I presuppose the validity of that interpretation in order to outline a framework for comparing *Zarathustra* to the *Phenomenology*. Like *Zarathustra*, the *Phenomenology* is a prelude to philosophy; more precisely, it is a propaedeutic to the scientific philosophy that begins with *Science of Logic*. Hegel's conception of this philosophy—his conception, that is, of what I shall call "philosophy proper"—is in many respects deeply traditional. As we shall see, some of the differences that separate Hegel's philosophy from Nietzsche's conception of a philosophy of the future reflect a more general opposition between Nietzsche's thinking and certain traditional philosophical commitments.

In what follows, I argue that the most salient differences between Hegel's philosophy and Nietzsche's philosophy of the future—namely, the differences between their contrasting relationships to time—express themselves in the "formal," or nonthematic, characteristics that distinguish *Zarathustra* from the *Phenomenology*. The plot of *Zarathustra* is structured as if to show the kind of text the *Phenomenology* would be—or how it would differ from the text that it is— were it written as a preface not to logic, but to Nietzsche's modernist philosophy of the future. *Zarathustra* can be interpreted as a re-creation of the *Phenomenology* that expresses a modernist rejection of traditional philosophy.[14]

Here, of course, it may be objected that Nietzsche nowhere suggests that

Zarathustra should be read in connection to the *Phenomenology*. Still, a comparison of these two texts can provide valuable insights into the relationship between literary "form" and philosophical "content" in *Zarathustra*. A precedent for the sort of contrastive and philosophically informed reading I intend here is Louis Mackey's interpretation of Kierkegaard's *Either/Or* as a parody of Goethe's *Wilhelm Meister*. Whether Kierkegaard *meant* to parody Goethe or not, Mackey's comparison of these two *Bildungsromane* remains a useful and important account of the ways that Kierkegaard's existentialist theory of the self is implicated in his choice of a literary form.[15]

The *Phenomenology* follows spirit (*Geist*), the protagonist of Hegel's narrative, through a series of manifold metamorphoses that terminates in absolute knowledge. Absolute knowledge obtains just when spirit transcends all the divisions that have beset it, thus becoming transparent to itself and for-itself what it is in-itself. The *Phenomenology* describes the dynamic by which spirit negates, preserves, and surpasses its succeeding determinations, and discovers finally that each of these determinations is a necessary expression of its essence. This dynamic, the perpetual *Aufhebung* of self-consciousness, is also a process of recollection (*Erinnerung*) through which spirit remembers and reveals the truth of being. This truth, Hegel claims, is absolute knowledge. For Hegel, the *Phenomenology* is a prelude to *philosophy proper*, because philosophy, strictly or *properly* conceived [that is, philosophy conceived as science (*Wissenschaft*)] takes the revealed truth of being as its point of departure.[16]

For Hegel, absolute knowledge is the "spiritual site" of properly philosophical thought and the real subject matter of *Science of Logic*. This site lies beyond the ambit of the ordinary, nonphilosophical consciousness that is immersed in the facticity of time and history. The *Phenomenology* resembles a *Bildungsroman* because it describes the educational process by which ordinary consciousness annuls the historical and temporal conditions of its existence.[17] When spirit becomes for-itself what it is in-itself, it overcomes its temporal manifestations, recollects that its truth is timeless, and brings ordinary consciousness to the extra-ordinary site of philosophical thought. Hegel is a traditional philosopher, an heir to Plato, inasmuch as he makes the transcendence of temporal existence a precondition of philosophical knowledge. Thus, he can write that *Science of Logic* reveals God "as he is in his eternal essence before the creation of nature and a finite mind."[18] In Hegel's view, the transcendence that belongs to philosophical insight is the transcendence that belongs to eternity with respect to time. The *Phenomenology*, like Socrates in the *Symposium*, asserts that a finite, temporal being, by way of a *Bildungsprozess*, can surpass time and bear witness to philosophical truth.[19]

Nietzsche's philosophy of the future is distinguished from Hegel's philosophy proper, as well as from traditional philosophy in general, by the relationship it bears to time. The spiritual site proper to Nietzsche's philosophy of the future is not a timeless truth available to absolute knowledge but an avant-garde consciousness that the future can differ radically from the present and the past. Rather than transcend time and possess a knowledge of eternal being, this consciousness surpasses the past toward the future in order to create new values. Nietzsche's notion of a philosophy of the future is founded on his rejection of European philosophy's traditional belief in the existence of timeless truth and being. *Zarathustra* presupposes that timeless truth and being *do not* exist and inaugurates Nietzsche's attempt to conceptualize a philosophy of the future on the basis of this presupposition. Nietzsche's modernist reconception of philosophy ascribes to new philosophers an extra-ordinary "knowledge," not of what is and has been, but of possibilities that have yet to be fulfilled. His new philosopher seeks rupture and discontinuity, not with time, but within it.

Let me now consider the ways that Nietzsche's revisionary conception of philosophy finds expression in some of the nonthematic characteristics distinguishing *Zarathustra* from the *Phenomenology*. *Zarathustra* is intelligible as a prelude to Nietzsche's philosophy of the future because it is structured by an antithesis of intention and repetition. By showing how representations of repetition can be endured, defied, and ultimately refuted, Nietzsche explains the possibility of creating new values. By depicting the strategies Zarathustra uses to cope with these repesentations, he shows how it is possible to become a new philosopher. Nietzsche anticipates the advent of new philosophers by demonstrating that Zarathustra can fend off the representations of repetition that burden him and fulfill his modernist intentions.

In contrast to the intentions that sustain the action of *Zarathustra*, the purpose that animates the action of the *Phenomenology* aims toward and not away from a repetition of the past. More precisely, the *Aufhebung* of self-consciousness is a movement by which spirit recollectively *returns* to itself in order to know rather than transcend what it is and has been. This movement is intelligible as a prelude to philosophy proper—that is, as a preface to the philosopher's explication of the truth of being—because it is a movement by which that truth is disclosed to the philosopher as a complete and integrated object of thought. Because Nietzsche conceptualizes his philosophy of the future as a movement that transcends the past toward the future, he structures his prelude to philosophy as a stammering struggle that culminates in a refutation of, and final triumph over, representations of repetition. Hegel, on the other hand, because he conceives philosophy proper as the contemplation of spirit's essential truth, structures his prelude to philosophy as a movement that restores spirit to a full recognition of its timeless essence.

Zarathustra and the *Phenomenology* structure action differently. What is more, they narrate it differently. The narrative difference, like the structural one, is a function of the contrasting relationships of Nietzsche's philosophy of the future and Hegel's philosophy proper to time.

In his introduction to the *Phenomenology*, Hegel describes the book as "the Science of the *experience of consciousness*."[20] By characterizing the *Phenomenology* as science, he implies that the phenomenological narration of spirit's development presupposes absolute knowledge. Absolute knowledge, Hegel believes, is not possible absent the completion of this development. Thus, as a description of the experience of consciousness, Hegelian phenomenology is a recollective representation of a journey that has already come to an end. Phenomenology is the recollection of a movement of recollection through which spirit attains absolute knowledge and thus the capacity for phenomenological narration.[21] Because phenomenology expresses the standpoint of absolute knowledge, it discloses the timeless necessity of the development it describes. Spirit is blind to this necessity prior to possessing absolute knowledge.

In contrast to the *Phenomenology*, *Zarathustra* never proposes that it has been narrated from a standpoint that has annulled time. Moreover, in various places, Nietzsche suggests that *Zarathustra* expresses a temporally (historically) situated projection of a future possibility: namely, that of creating new values.[22] Whereas the *Phenomenology* represents as ineluctable a movement that has already occurred, *Zarathustra* articulates a speculative (hypothetical) account of a possibility that has yet to be realized. Put simply, Hegel's narrative is retrospective and identifies a necessary course of development while Nietzsche's is prospective and identifies a possible route to a possible future. Nietzsche can write a prelude to a philosophy of the future absent a knowledge of eternal truth, because that prelude is a conjecture as to how the possibility he envisions could be realized. His goal is not to show that an achieved philosophical perspective is the timelessly necessary result of past experience.

Both the *Phenomenology* and *Zarathustra* are preludes to philosophy. Considered as such, the differences between them are primarily attributable to Nietzsche's modernist rejection of traditional philosophy. In other words, the structural and narrative differences that separate the *Phenomenology* and *Zarathustra* (the differences between the *Aufhebung* of spirit and the antithesis of intention and repetition; between retrospective narration and prospective narration; between a narrative that demonstrates necessity and one that hypothesizes possibility; and between narration in the perspective of absolute knowledge and narration as situated conjecture) derive from a more fundamental opposition between a traditional philosophy that seeks ontological truth and a philosophy of the future involving the creation of new values. *Zarathustra* may be construed as a modernist "rewriting" of the *Phenomenology* because it reconceives the notion of a prelude to philosophy on the assumption that philosophy can be the modernist enterprise of a visionary avant-garde that surpasses past and present toward the creation of the new. Embodying the structure of a stammering prelude and narratively projecting the possibility of new-values creation, *Zarathustra* implicates a clear break with philosophical tradition.[23]

In aligning philosophy with the modernist creation of new values, Nietzsche rethinks the relationship of philosophy to time. In Chapter 2, I explore the implications of this "rethinking" by evaluating Nietzsche's rejection of some Christian-Platonic assumptions about the nature and genesis of value. To be specific, I argue that his rejection of these assumptions is closely related to his interest in formulating a new philosophical vocabulary (an interest that I began to explain in the Introduction). For the remainder of this chapter, I postpone further consideration of such issues in order to show how *Zarathustra* can be both a stammering prelude to a philosophy of the future *and* an example of philosophical explanation.

The Three Metamorphoses and Philosophical Explanation

Zarathustra's speech on the three metamorphoses has inspired readings of the most diverse sort, from the traditional biographical gloss to an alchemical analysis of Zarathustra's language.[24] For my purposes, this speech is significant because it bears on the plot structure of *Zarathustra*. If Nietzsche's fictional narrative has the form of a stammer, then, to extend the metaphor, "On the Three Metamorphoses" describes modes of action through which Zarathustra copes with *Zarathustra*'s stammering.[25]

In order to clarify the relationship between "On the Three Metamorphoses" and the plot of *Zarathustra*, we may recall that the figure of the child, with which this speech ends, is the figure the old saint applies to Zarathustra in the second section of the prologue. In asserting that "Zarathustra has become a child" the saint suggests that Nietzsche's protagonist, when he descends from his cave for the first time, embodies the child's capacity for new beginnings. In the eyes of the saint, Zarathustra personifies the sort of value-creating activity that Nietzsche associates with the new philosophers. I would argue, however, that when the saint first sees Zarathustra, Zarathustra intends to become, but has still not become, a child and a value-creator.

The saint's assertion notwithstanding, Zarathustra has yet to fulfill his personal intention when he initially descends from his mountain. The story narrated in *Zarathustra* is, in part, the story of how Zarathustra comes to fulfill this intention by becoming the new beginner that he believes he is destined to become. That there is a story here to be told at all presupposes that the realization of Zarathustra's personal intention has been deferred, or, in other words, that he has *not immediately* become a child. Ideal-typical modes of action, marked and delineated by the speech on the three metamorphoses, structure Zarathustra's attempt to become the value-creator he aspires to be when he meets the old saint. In contrast to the metamorphoses of the spirit that express the *necessity* of the movement through which Hegelian self-consciousness achieves absolute knowledge, the metamorphoses of Zarathustra's spirit characterize his *contingently chosen* modes of response to the varying circumstances.

Nietzsche's protagonist normally enacts the first metamorphosis of the spirit, symbolized by the figure of a camel, upon encountering representations of repetition that discourage his desire to create new values and to inspire others to do the same. He performs the second metamorphosis, symbolized by the figure of a lion, by placing himself in defiant opposition to these representations of repetition. Zarathustra effects the third metamorphosis, signified by the figure of a child, when he forsakes the defiant posture of the lion and becomes a value-creator. The saint's claim that Zarathustra has become a child, though false, suggests that he has already become a camel and a lion when *Zarathustra* begins. As the plot of the book unfolds, we find Zarathustra becoming a camel and a lion on several other occasions until, finally, at the end of the book, he enacts the role of child and value-creator.[26]

Zarathustra becomes a camel when he submits to the belief espoused by representations of repetition that the creation of new values is impossible; that is, when he assents to this belief and, accordingly, is tempted to resign his commitment to cultural innovation through value-creation. Representations of repetition tend to evoke in Zarathustra a spirit of resignation that undermines his value-creating enterprise. Were this spirit to persuade Zarathustra to renounce his will to innovate, Zarathustra could not become a creator of new values. The reason for this is simple: embodying a will to become a creator of new values is a necessary if not sufficient condition of becoming one. In his portrait of the child-spirit, which I examine later in this chapter, Zarathustra suggests as much, and in Part 1 (as I will show in Chapter 3) he develops this point further.

In the Introduction I claimed that representations of repetition function as apparent excluders because they subvert Zarathustra's commitment to becoming a new-values creator. For Nietzsche, then, part of explaining the possibility of creating new values is to show how Zarathustra persists in his commitment to be-coming a new-values creator notwithstanding the skepticism that threatens that commitment. The central figure in Nietzsche's depiction of Zarathustra's persist-ence is the lion, who in defying incredulous representations of repetition denies that the human future must be governed by the perpetuation of Christian-Platonic values. When Zarathustra becomes a camel, he submits to the outlook of the personae who personify the stammers that punctuate the plot of *Zarathus-tra*. In becoming a lion, however, he repudiates this outlook, insists that he *can* become a new-values creator, and, if he has fallen prey to the camel's temptation to resign his commitment to becoming a new-values creator, banishes that temp-tation and persists in his commitment.

As we shall see, the speech on the three metamorphoses affords a less detailed account of the metamorphosis from lion to child than of the two other meta-morphoses it describes. This is a detail worth some reflection, since the third metamorphosis, no less than the first and the second, marks an important junc-ture in *Zarathustra*'s explanation of the possibility of creating new values. We can make sense of the difference if we consider the place of "On the Three Metamorphoses" in Zarathustra's development. When Zarathustra delivers this speech, he has already had the experience of becoming a camel and a lion in the prologue (for examples, see my discussion of the prologue in Chapter 2), but he has not had the experience of becoming a child. Presumably, it is this want of experience that explains the sketchy character of his description of the child, as well as his failure to say how the lion becomes a child. As is evident from Zara-thustra's description of the three metamorphoses, he knows at the beginning of Part 1 *that* the lion-spirit cannot create new values, yet he appears not to know *why* the lion-spirit cannot create new values. Throughout Part 1, moreover, he seems to be naively oblivious to the issue posed by this "why." It is only in Part 2 that Zarathustra recognizes that the lion-spirit is self-estranged and that the self-estrangement of the lion-spirit apparently excludes the possibility that a lion-spirit will create new values. Part of explaining how such creation is possible is to explain how—notwithstanding his self-estrangement—an individual who has become a lion-spirit can become a child.

As will become evident in Chapter 4, showing how Zarathustra can become a child involves showing how he can rid himself of his leonine self-estrangement. However, as I noted in the Introduction, freedom from leonine self-estrangement is a necessary but not a sufficient condition of the third metamorphosis. In the person of the soothsayer, Zarathustra comes face to face with this fact. In effect, he sees that the soothsayer's prophecy envisions social conditions that, even for someone who has renounced the self-estranging spirit of the lion, appear to exclude the possibility of new-values creation. In Parts 3 and 4, Nietzsche completes his explanation of the possibility of creating new values: first, by exploring Zarathustra's lion-spirited reaction to the plot-stammering the soothsayer personifies; and second, by showing how Zarathustra can become a child-creator notwithstanding the occurrence of the social conditions the soothsayer prophesies. By becoming a child-creator, Zarathustra once and for all refutes and triumphs over the skeptical voices and plot-stammerings that have relentlessly molested him.

The Camel

I will now consider the three metamorphoses individually. Each metamorphosis defines an ideal type, a generally conceived mode of action that on various occasions Zarathustra's particular actions more or less approximate as he copes with representations of repetition. By considering these ideal types in some detail, we can more fully appreciate the roles they play in Nietzsche's philosophical explanation of the possibility of creating new values.

I begin with the figure of the camel. Christian-Platonic asceticism defines the cast of mind that Nietzsche identifies with this figure. To use the language Nietzsche employs in *On the Genealogy of Morals*, the camel embodies an attitude according to which nothingness, or the ascetic ideal, is the purpose of human existence. For Nietzsche, the ascetic ideal expresses a "hatred of the human, and even more of the animal, and more still of the material, this horror of the senses, of reason itself, this fear of happiness and beauty, this longing to get away from all appearance, change, becoming, death, wishing, from longing itself—all this means—let us dare to grasp it—*a will to nothingness*."[27] Zarathustra describes the camel's life as a desert (*Wüste*) because the camel denies and represses everything vital in human existence, transforming it eventually into something barren and lifeless. The asceticism of the camel is tied inextricably to certain values, an adherence to which promotes the will to nothingness. In "On the Three Metamorphoses," Zarathustra characterizes these values in terms of the "thou shalt" (*du sollst*) morality of the Old Testament. Here, as elsewhere, he insists that Christian-Platonic values, which the camel reveres, burden the camel in the manner of a heavy (*schwer*) weight that is difficult to bear. In Zarathustra's view, the camel is an image of life turned against itself, of a will that stands in awe of values that threaten to crush the will and destroy it.[28]

Nietzsche offers at least two reasons for his belief that Christian-Platonic values express a will to negate life. First, he maintains that these values, in virtue of their *content*, slander the passions, sensuality, beauty, and so on. They identify as wrong or sinful aspects of human life that seem essential to embodied being in time. Second, and perhaps more important, Christian-Platonic values express an unconditional morality, and "confronted with morality (especially Christian, or unconditional, morality), life *must* continually and inevitably be in the wrong, because life *is* something essentially amoral—and eventually, crushed by the weight of contempt and the eternal no, life *must* then be felt to be unworthy of desire and altogether worthless."[29] When Nietzsche alludes to unconditional morality, he refers to values that present themselves as having a justification that is not dependent on considerations concerning the preferences and situations that distinguish and divide human beings. Such values are unconditional because they claim to be binding on all individuals regardless of the interests and circumstances that separate them. Unconditional morality is hostile to life, Nietzsche believes, because it expresses a desire to eliminate conflict among alternative schemes of interests and values—a form of conflict that Nietzsche thinks is *essential* to life—in favor of the universal rule of one and only one value scheme. Christian-Platonic values express this desire by purporting to be the only values that human beings should ever observe.[30]

It is with reference to the unconditional morality of the camel that Zarathustra introduces the second metamorphosis of the spirit:

> In the loneliest desert, however, the second metamorphosis occurs: here the spirit becomes a lion who would conquer his freedom and be master in his own desert.
>
> Here he seeks out his last master: he wants to fight him and his last god; for ultimate victory he wants to fight with the great dragon.
>
> Who is the great dragon whom the spirit will no longer call lord and god? "Thou shalt" is the name of the great dragon. But the spirit of the lion says, "I will." "Thou shalt" lies in his way, sparkling like gold, an animal covered with scales; and on every scale a golden "thou shalt."
>
> Values, thousands of years old, shine on these scales; and thus speaks the mightiest of all dragons: "All value of all things shines on me. All value has long been created, and I am all created value. Verily there shall be no more 'I will.'" Thus speaks the dragon.[31]

Zarathustra's portrait of the second metamorophosis is rich in allusive significance. Depicting the lion-spirit in the image of a god-defying Prometheus, he describes the God of Christianity's unconditional morality using a biblical metaphor for Satan—"the great dragon"—which also, if Erich Heller is right, refers to Siegfried's clash with the dragon Fafner in Wagner's *The Ring of the Nibelung*.[32] As we shall see later in this book, some of these allusions afford insight into Zarathustra's interpretation of his situation in Parts 2, 3, and 4. Here, however, in analyzing Zarathustra's speech, I focus on the explicit content of his characterization of the lion-spirit's conflict with the Christian God.

The Lion

Let me turn, then, to what Zarathustra actually says about the lion and the great dragon. What defines the lion, in essence, is his defiance of the dragon's unconditional, Christian morality. Zarathustra identifies the dragon with this morality ("thou shalt," besides being emblazoned on each of the dragon's scales, is also his name), and thus suggests that the lion-spirit's last god (*letzter Gott*) is indeed the Christian God. The great dragon is a figure for the absolute power and authority that the camel invests in the values that govern his existence: "All value of all things shines on me . . . and I am all created value," speaks the great dragon. The lion's defiance of the great dragon and his repudiation of the asceticism of the camel are actions having a complex significance. I elucidate the meaning of these actions by highlighting three distinct but related themes: supersession, priority, and freedom.

The theme of supersession appears for the first time in Zarathustra's claim that the lion "would . . . be master [*Herr*] in his own desert" where "he seeks out his last master [*letzten Herrn*]." These words imply that the lion means to be master just where the dragon has been master. The lion wants to supplant the dragon as the lord of a desert in which the dragon has previously prevailed. From the lion's perspective the dragon is a usurper, the master of a domain—the lion's *own* desert—in which the lion alone is entitled to hold sway. The desert, once again, is Zarathustra's figure for the impoverishing impact of ascetic self-denial on human existence. Life is a desert for the lion because he is heir to the asceticism of the camel. To be more precise, the life the lion has inherited has *become* a desert because the ascetic ideal has dominated that life. Although the lion rejects the ascetic ideal, the life he claims for himself is its creation. To perform the second metamorphosis is not to endorse the impact of the will to nothingness on human life, but it is to subject that life, without qualification, to a new master: namely, the lion's will. The lion's will seeks neither no masters nor many masters, but aims to be by itself the only master. In essence, the lion's will is a will to rule human existence with an unrestricted power and authority. The lion seeks out his *last* master, that is, his last master other than himself, in order to destroy a last restriction on his will. This will, or, as Zarathustra puts it, the lion's "I will," now claims for itself the same exclusive and absolute power and authority to command human existence that the camel worships in the great dragon and his "thou shalt" morality.

What motivates Nietzsche to construe the defiant spirit of the lion as a will to supersede the great dragon? In other words, what considerations move him to view the lion's nay-saying to Christian asceticism as a desire to *supplant* the Christian God? One plausible and instructive answer to this question is that Nietzsche conceptualizes the conflict between the lion's will and the Christian God in Reformation terms. According to Martin Luther, it is in the nature of man's "natural will" not only to want to be a god but also to want to be the one and only god in the place of the one and only God who actually exists. From this monotheistic perspective, which allows the possible existence of none but one God, the will to be a god cannot be a will to be just one god among many. Rather this will must be a will to annihilate the one God in order to possess in his place his power and authority. In Luther's view, the will to annihilate God can be undone only by an act of grace.[33]

Nietzsche's lion, I want to suggest, is modeled on Luther's conception of a natural will that has been unaffected by an act of grace. The lion, like this natural will, refuses to share the divinity he seeks. He simply will not countenance a polytheistic world in which many gods (or masters) effectively limit each other's power and authority. No less than the Christian God himself, the lion and the natural will that has not been touched by grace are monotheistic in their theological commitments. Each admits the existence of only one God and master, which God and master *each* strives to be. If the lion is to be the absolute power and authority he wants to be, then the great dragon must be slain. Like Luther's natural will, the lion's "I will" must will God's (the dragon's) annihilation. In fact, the lion's "I will" and the dragon's "thou shalt" cannot but exclude each other. Each can prevail only if the other fails to triumph. That even the dragon knows this is only too clear from his insistence, "Verily, there shall be no more 'I will.'"

The act of supersession is in essence an act of negation. It is, in other words, the sort of act that Nietzsche identifies elsewhere as reactive. As is typical of reactive agents, Zarathustra's lion defines himself in and through the denial of his difference from a force that dominates him. By willing to supersede the Christian God, he wills to obliterate his own difference from the power and authority that this God represents.[34] In this way, the lion denies that God's power and authority transcend him, or, what is the same, asserts that there is nothing to distinguish this power and authority from the "I" (his "I") that wills. But this is just another way of saying (or implying) that the lion's will wills God's annihilation or that the "I will" excludes the "thou shalt." For from the perspective of the lion's will, modeled as it is on Luther's natural will, to identify oneself with God's power and authority (to take God's place) is at once to have annihilated God, along with all of his unconditional moral commands.

The theme of priority, meanwhile, is related to the idea that the lion's will is a will to supersede the Christian God. I will approach this theme by carefully considering the only words that Zarathustra attributes to the great dragon: "All value of all things shines on me. All value has long been created, and I am all created value. Verily there shall be no more 'I will.'" Part of what the dragon asserts here is that the morality he represents is unconditional. He implies that the values constituting this morality are all, and thus are the only values that apply to human existence. In effect, the dragon proclaims the unqualified and universal validity of a single scheme of values. But this is not the end of what he insinuates. In addition to depicting Christian values as unconditional, the dragon invests them with historicity. Speaking retrospectively, he avers that the "thou shalt" morality is a created morality that has been handed down from the past as an inescapable facticity. Speaking prospectively, he avers that all values have long been created (*Aller Werth ward schon geschaffen*), or, in other words, that all values that ever could have been created have already been created. He holds that there will be no more creation of values—no more "I will"—which is to say that the future will afford nothing in the way of new values. From the dragon's point of view, or from that of Christianity as Nietzsche understands it, Christian values are and must be the only values, now and forever. Besides demanding an unqualified and universal obedience to its values, Christianity insists that there are not and simply cannot be any others.

This background helps explain my claim that Zarathustra enacts the first metamorphosis of the spirit when he encounters representations of repetition that discourage his desire to create and inspire the creation of new values. As we have seen, the figure of the camel signifies an absolute submission to the Christian view of human existence. In part, this submission involves acceptance of the proposition that the future will yield no new values, a proposition that follows from the great dragon's belief that already-existing Christian values are and must be the only values. For the camel, the future offers no escape from the values that burden human life and thus no release from the facticity that is part of the legacy of the Christian God.[35] From the camel's point of view, the future must repeat the past because human beings must persist in living their lives in accordance with Christian values. As we shall see, Zarathustra undergoes the first metamorphosis on occasions that move him to see things as a camel sees them. He becomes a camel only when he confronts representations of repetition that reiterate the claim that the future will be or has to be a repetition of the Christian past.

To be a camel is to internalize the outlook of the great dragon; it is to suppose that the "thou shalts" dictated by God exhaust all possibilities of value-creation. The camel assumes, in effect, that God's will has expressed itself *prior* to every other will and thus preempted for itself the creation of all possible values. It is no wonder, then, that Zarathustra is tempted to resign his commitment to becoming a creator of new values when he becomes a camel. The great dragon proclaims that there shall be no more "I will," for his divine "I will," which is the source of his divine "thou shalt," has left nothing for any will to accomplish in the manner of value-creation. Although the camel accepts this dogma, the lion does not. On the contrary, says Zarathustra, the lion assumes "the right to new values."[36] How does the lion come to this conclusion? By denying the priority of the divine will. This denial is implicit in the lion's will to have for himself the power and authority that the camel cedes to God. As we have seen, it is in the nature of the lion to will God's annihilation; to will, that is, that God not exist in order that the lion may possess God's power and authority. To will that God not exist is, for the lion, to will that there not exist a will that has exhausted all possibilities of value-creation *prior* to the lion's assertion of his will. When the lion claims for himself God's power and authority, when he puts himself in God's place, he preempts for himself all possibilities of value-creation. This is not to say that the lion actually creates values—indeed, Zarathustra explicitly denies this—but only that the lion, in attributing to himself God's power and authority, denies that there can be any creation of value that is not entirely due to the power and the authority of his will. Whereas the great dragon purports to represent the accomplished creation of all possible values, the lion asserts that there will be no value-creation that does not (rightfully) have its origin exclusively in his will. In the perspective of the lion, leonine willing is both a necessary and a sufficient condition for the creation of new values.

The theme of freedom is implicit in the lion's reactions to representations of repetition. The lion defies representations of repetition by denying that Christian values necessarily will govern the future. His act of denial is at once an assertion of independence and an anticipation of the creation of new values: "To create new values—that even the lion cannot do; but the creation of freedom for oneself for new creation—that is within the power of the lion."[37] As a figure intermediate between the camel and the child, the lion personifies a freedom *from* Christian values and a freedom *for* the creation of new ones.[38] Declaring that the Christian God is a nonexistent fiction (saying "no" to duty, he wills the annihilation of the "thou shalt" he has loved "as most sacred" by finding "illusion and caprice even in the most sacred"),[39] he withdraws his allegiance from values that, as a camel, he believed to express a preemption of his will. By the same declaration he asserts that the values of the future need not be those of the Christian past, thereby affirming his liberty to create new values.[40] In becoming a lion Zarathustra can persist in his commitment to becoming a new-values creator, because as a lion he believes that he can create new values—though in fact, qua lion, he *cannot*.

The Child

Nietzsche's characterization of the third metamorphosis may have been inspired by Goethe's *Novelle*.[41] Whatever its origin, his interpretation of the movement from lion to child has special significance. Zarathustra initiates this movement at the beginning of *Zarathustra* (in Said's language, he endeavors to enact his personal, "beginning intention" to effect the third metamorphosis) but succeeds in finally becoming a child only at the book's end.

Zarathustra describes this final transformation as follows: "The child is innocence and forgetting, a new beginning, a game, a self-propelled wheel, a first movement, a sacred 'Yes.' For the game of creation, my brothers, a sacred 'Yes' is needed: the spirit now wills his own will, and he who had been lost to the world now conquers his own world."[42] Zarathustra's portrait of the child occupies about a quarter of the space allotted to his individual depictions of the camel and the lion, and seems vague and insubstantial.[43] This should come as no surprise. To repeat an earlier point, Zarathustra, when he delivers "On the Three Metamorphoses," has not yet had the experience of becoming a child. To some extent, then, the portrait he draws is conjectural. It should also be remembered that a central purpose of *Zarathustra* is to fill out this portrait by explaining how becoming a child—or a "better player" or a "new philosopher"—is possible. So while the description of the child in "On the Three Metamorphoses" is thin, much of what we find in the rest of the book compensates for it. In this chapter, then, I limit myself to a preliminary discussion of this figure. In particular, I focus on two of its features: innocence and forgetting.

Because the image of the child is so burdened with romantic connotations, it is not easy to do justice to the particular significance Nietzsche attributes to it. The problem is rendered even more complex by Nietzsche's ongoing obsession with romanticism. This obsession involves Nietzsche's repeated but often unsuccessful attempts to distance himself from romantic writers, as well as occasional palinodes expressing the self-critical insight that sometimes these attempts have faired poorly.[44] One is not surprised, then, to discover an overriding disposition among Nietzsche commentators to interpret the figure of the child in essentially romantic terms. Among recent critics, Erich Heller's attempt to assimilate Nietzsche's conception of this figure to the categories of romanticism is especially explicit. In Heller's view, Nietzsche's child is the symbol of a paradise regained (or attained). He is a figure for a naiveté, innocence, and unity with nature that signify a dissolution of self-consciousness. In all of these respects, claims Heller, Nietzsche's child symbolizes a vision of "pure and unselfconscious being" that Nietzsche shares with Rousseau, Schiller, Kleist, Wordsworth, and Hegel.[45] Like Heller, J. P. Stern finds in Nietzsche's child a metaphor for Wordsworthian innocence. Similarly, Karl Löwith, and again, recently, Joan Stambaugh and Roger Hollinrake, suggest that this figure betokens an immediate oneness with being.[46]

Löwith, Stambaugh, and Hollinrake all base their views on the assumption that Nietzsche identifies the child with the motto "I am." This assumption finds some support in one of Nietzsche's posthumously published notes: "Higher than 'thou shalt' ranks 'I will' (the heroes); higher than 'I will' ranks 'I am' (the gods of the Greeks)."[47] The affinity of this remark to what Zarathustra says in his first speech is obvious. It is less obvious, however, that "I am" should be identified with the figure of the child that emerges in "On the Three Metamorphoses." Although the phrases "thou shalt" and "I will" do appear in Zarathustra's accounts of the lion and the camel, respectively, the expression "I am" nowhere occurs in his discussion of the child. Indeed, the only "I am" in "On the Three Metamorphoses" is the "I am" attributed to the great dragon who says that "I am all created value." The essence of the third metamorphosis is not a transition from willing to being (that is, from "I *will*" to "I *am*"), but a shift in self-understanding that involves a disappearance of the idea of a substantial subject (a so-called "doer behind the deed") to whom various acts of willing can be ascribed. The child, far from saying "*I* am" or "*I* will," does not say "I" at all. Rather he "wills his own will," thereby appearing to acknowledge no substantial subject but only the act of willing itself.

To be sure, none of this shows that the motto "I am" is irrelevant to the attempt to make sense of the figure of the child. Still, I do want to insist on a reading of "On the Three Metamorphoses" that precludes the soundness of both Hollinrake's suggestion that the child is simply being and Stambaugh's romantic claim that the child is "wholly immersed in its being."[48] If the figure of the child signifies "being", then the being it signifies has a complexity characterizing a form of willing that bears a *reflexive* relation to itself: the will of the child wills itself.[49] The child cannot be simply being, or wholly immersed in being, or, as Heller suggests, pure unselfconscious being, if only because the child exists *for-itself* as will. It is in willing to will that the child commits himself to becoming a creator of new values, having repudiated the leonine interpretation of self-commitment and willing as stemming from a substantial subject.

By stressing the complexity of the child, I do not mean to imply that he represents an "organized innocence" that encompasses divided self-consciousness within a mediated or "higher" unity. Because the child acknowledges no substantial subject, it would be implausible to suppose that he is a figure for the substantial "super-subject" that idealism and romanticism sometimes envision as surmounting all divisions and differences.[50] I emphasize that Nietzsche's child exists for-itself only to justify the contention that the innocence of the child cannot be the innocence of unmediated being. This contention is true, not only because the child's will wills itself, but also because the child's willing is a new beginning, an example of *intentional activity* that transcends what is ("being," as Heller understands it) toward what is yet to be. Above all else, the child is defined by his fulfillment of his intention to become a creator of new values.

Zarathustra identifies neither the camel nor the lion as innocent. We may infer, then, that the camel and the lion have an affinity that distinguishes them from the child. As we have seen, the lion, no less than the camel, believes that all created values have their origin in a cause that is the first and only cause of all created values. And despite his nay-saying to those values that seem to derive from the Christian God's power and authority, the lion still embraces *one* Christian value: namely, the value of possessing the sole and unrestricted power and authority to create values. The lion's will, like Luther's natural will, because it wants to supersede God never questions the good of *being God*.[51] In fact, the lion's act of accrediting divine power and authority to himself is precisely the act by which he seems to redeem (make good or valuable) the impoverished existence he inherits from the camel. But what is it to be God? What is the nature of the *being* that the lion claims for himself when he attributes to himself God's power and authority?

Answers to these questions can be found in the language that frames the lion's struggle against the great dragon. This language interprets willing as a deed done by a doer; that is, as an action performed by an ego substance that underlies but does not depend for its being on its actions, thoughts, and desires. The doer-deed dichotomy and the fiction of a substantial subject are implicated in the lion's "I will," in the dragon's "thou shalt," and even in the "I am" that the dragon applies to himself.[52] When the lion supersedes the great dragon he purports to put his ego substance, his "I," in the place of the "I" of his nemesis. In the lion's view, to supplant God is to envision one's own ego substance as the only possible origin of created value. To *be* God, from this perspective, as well as from the perspective of the Christian camel, is to be the ego substance or substantial subject in whom all created values originate and inhere.

As I noted above, the child rejects the view that willing is the activity of a substantial subject. An important passage in *Twilight of the Idols* suggests that this refusal of substantialist thinking extends to the child's vision of the world as a whole. The same passage explains Zarathustra's claim that "the child is innocence":

> There is nothing besides the whole. That nobody is held responsible any longer, that the mode of being may not be traced back to a *causa prima*, that the world does not form a unity either as a sensorium or as "spirit"—that alone is the great liberation; with this alone is the innocence of becoming restored. The concept of "God" was until now the greatest objection to existence. We deny God, we deny responsibility in God: only thereby do redeem the world.[53]

With this statement, Nietzsche questions the principle that there is always a reason that things are thus and not otherwise (the principle of sufficient reason). He criticizes as well a particular application of this principle according to which God, his sensorium, or his spirit is the sufficient reason for the world's mode of being. According to Nietzsche, one experiences becoming innocently only by relinquishing the opinion that the unity of the world ("the whole") is the product of a *causa prima*. More generally, he implies that innocence entails abandoning the view that the character of the world derives ultimately from a deed done by a first doer or ego substance. On this account, the innocence of the child has nothing to do with the experience of an immediate oneness with being. Rather it expresses the assumption that there is no God or godlike substance that is the origin and ground of all else. In "On the Three Metamorphoses," this same assumption seems evident in the child's obliviousness to the prospect of becoming the first and singular cause of all created value. As distinct from the camel, the lion, and the great dragon, the child pays no heed to concerns prompted by the metaphysics of monotheism because he believes that this metaphysics is false.

Zarathustra's claim that "the child is . . . forgetting" is intrinsically related to his understanding of the child's innocence. The child forgets not himself but a theologically informed self-interpretation. Unlike the camel and the lion, for example, he does not define himself with reference to the belief that it is good to be the one and only God. The child's forgetting may seem, then, to sustain and reinforce the lion's nay-saying antipathy to Christianity by extending that antipathy to the very value of being God. Yet Zarathustra never describes the child as a defiant naysayer. Rather he attributes to him a sacred "yes" that contrasts with the sacred "no" of the lion. In other words, Zarathustra does not believe that the child is a reactive spirit who constitutes his identity through acts of resistance to already established values. Whereas the lion says "no" to the dragon's "thou shalt," the child says nothing of the sort to the view that it is good to be God. Forgetting, unlike nay-saying, is not an act that negates or contradicts previously posited theses. To contradict a thesis is to oppose that thesis to an antithesis. To forget a thesis, on the other hand, is to render conscious opposition to it impossible. The yea-saying child reacts neither to the dragon's "thou shalt" nor to the claim that it is good to be God because he has consigned both assertions to oblivion. The power of forgetting is not the power of reaction, but the power to abandon and distance oneself from those claims that otherwise engender reaction.[54]

My treatment of the child's innocence and forgetting leaves some critical questions unanswered. How, for example, is the child's abandonment of the view that willing stems from a substantial subject (an ego substance) related to the creation of new values? Does the abandonment of that view facilitate such creation? Does it result from such creation? To what, furthermore, is the child's yea-saying responsive, if not to the dragon's "thou shalts," or to the good of being the one and only God? As we have seen, the portrait of the child given in "On the Three Metamorphoses" is just too limited to provide clear answers to these questions. This is not to say, however, that there are no answers available. As the plot of *Zarathustra* unfolds, Nietzsche elaborates his conception of the child. The depiction of Zarathustra in "Zarathustra's Prologue," the discussion of creation in Part 1, and Zarathustra's response to the soothsayer in Part 3 all illuminate this conception, though most illuminating is the ending of *Zarathustra*, Part 4. The importance of this ending cannot be overestimated, because it is here that Zarathustra becomes a child and, as he fulfills his personal intention, anticipates the advent of companions through whom he can fulfill his poetic intention.

I will conclude my analysis of the three metamorphoses by emphasizing again that these figures define ideal types. I stress this point, because in the pages that follow we will see that Zarathustra's actions, when they *approximate* some one of these types (here, I refer primarily to the camel and the lion types, since Zarathustra becomes a child only at the end of *Zarathustra*), do not display each and every one of its features. For example, the evidence for interpreting a given action as camel-like, or as leonine, though clear, is not always so detailed as to converge with the full-fledged portraits of the camel and the lion presented in "On the Three Metamorphoses." The convergence is greatest when Zarathustra becomes a camel in first *forming* the thought of eternal recurrence (Part 2) and then a lion in *trans-forming* it the first time (Part 3).

CHAPTER TWO

Incipit *Zarathustra*: A Reading of "Zarathustra's Prologue"

> Near and
>
> Hard to grasp is
>
> The God.

FRIEDRICH HÖLDERLIN, "Patmos"

In his recent book on the concept of modernism, Astradur Eysteinsson interprets the aesthetic practices of modernist literature as attempts to "*interrupt . . . modernity.*" Drawing on the insights of Habermas, Kristeva, and various other critics, he argues that these practices promote "a *liberation from the repressive forces of rationality.*"[1] Eysteinsson's theory of modernism is persuasive, though not conclusive. Still, it pertains directly to this study because it captures so well the spirit of Zarathustra's will to innovate. Descending from his cave for the first time, Zarathustra aims to interrupt the modern, rationalistic culture that he associates with the last man and that the early Nietzsche describes as "Socratic." Expecting immediately to fulfill his personal and poetic intentions, he aspires to hinder and even to thwart the reproduction of this culture by becoming a new-values creator who inspires other human beings to follow his example.

"Zarathustra's Prologue" recounts Zarathustra's initial struggle to interrupt European modernity. In this chapter I chart the course of that struggle, interpreting the plot of the prologue in terms of the three metamorphoses of the spirit and in light of Nietzsche's belief that modernity is characterized by nihilism. Zarathustra engages the threat of nihilism (unwittingly, at first) by exhorting his contemporaries to become new-values creators. Unable to move his auditors as he pleases, he explains his perlocutionary failure in historical terms. In investigating the significance of Zarathustra's perlocutionary failure, I sketch and defend an account of Nietzsche's skepticism about Zarathustra's modernism. Unlike Paul de Man, I deny that this skepticism defines a stable, final phase in the evolution of Nietzsche's thought.

After explaining his inability to move his auditors, Zarathustra sees that his efforts to interrupt modernity and to vanquish the threat of nihilism may be tragically futile. Recognizing that the fulfillment of his personal and poetic intentions will not be immediate, he no longer takes for granted the success of his enterprise. Still, "Zarathustra's Prologue" ends on an optimistic note, with Zarathustra reaffirming his commitment to becoming a creator of new values by performing the second metamorphosis of the spirit.

Nihilism and the Will to Truth

In *Twilight*, Nietzsche concludes his famous story of how the true world became a fable with a reference to the beginning of *Zarathustra*: "Noon; moment of the briefest shadow; end of the longest error; high point of humanity; INCIPIT ZARATHUSTRA."[2] The story's last phrase, "INCIPIT ZARATHUSTRA" (Zarathustra begins), situates *Zarathustra* with respect to a brief history of the concept of truth that refers penultimately to the demise of the "true world." In essence, Nietzsche is claiming that *Zarathustra* is a coda to European humanity's recognition that its belief in a "true world" has been in error. Envisioning historical time as discontinuous, Nietzsche writes a fiction that assumes the end of the old as it beckons the advent of the new. As he depicts it, *Zarathustra* occupies the *interregnum* between past and future.

Nietzsche explains European humanity's rejection of its belief in the "true world" in a paragraph preceding the expression "INCIPIT ZARATHUSTRA": "The 'true world'—an idea which is no longer good for [*nütz*] anything, not even obligating—an idea which has become useless [*unnütz*] and superfluous—*consequently*, a refuted idea: let us abolish it."[3] Here, Nietzsche seems to be claiming that considerations of utility can be blamed for the destruction of Europe's belief in the "true world." His representation of these considerations, because it questions the *value* of the idea of a "true world," echoes his rather extensive discussion of truth in *Genealogy*. In that book, Nietzsche ties the concept of truth to what he subsequently calls the "true world": "The truthful man [*der Wahrhaftige*], in the audacious and ultimate sense presupposed by the faith in science, *thereby affirms another world* than that of life, nature, and history. . . . It is still a *metaphysical faith* that underlies our faith in science."[4] As distinct from the treatment of truth in *Twilight*, the treatment of this theme in *Genealogy* charts the sequence of events through which the value of truth is put into question. In short, Nietzsche argues that Europe's will to truth (especially in the practice of natural science) subverts its belief in God, thereby prompting it to reject the view that truth has the highest value because it is divine: "From the moment faith in the God of the ascetic ideal is denied, a *new problem arises*: that of the *value* of truth."[5]

Nietzsche's discussion of truth and divinity in *Genealogy* complements the story he subsequently tells of how the "true world" became a fable. It also involves a historical analysis that is different from the analysis proposed in *Twilight*, where Nietzsche highlights the *theoretical* consequences that ensue from the critique of the value of truth. One of these consequences is a thoroughgoing denial of the existence of the "true world." A second and equally important consequence is a rejection of the traditional and Christian-Platonic way of characterizing the sensible or "untrue" world. "The true world—we have abolished. What world has remained? The apparent one perhaps? But no! *With the true world we have also abolished the apparent one.*"[6] In *Genealogy*, Nietzsche focuses on the practical, or, broadly speaking, *ethical* results of critical inquiry into the value of truth.[7] To be precise, he stresses the relevance of such inquiry to human beings' efforts to answer the question "How should I live my life?" From the perspective of *Genealogy*, "INCIPIT ZARATHUSTRA" is not simply a challenge to the truth/appearance distinction, but a proposal to revalue human existence in light of that challenge. The argument of *Genealogy* brings out the full significance of what Nietzsche, in *Twilight*, notes only in passing: namely, that the beginning of *Zarathustra* marks a "high point of humanity," what Heidegger calls a "peak of decision" concerning the destiny of man.[8]

In *Genealogy*, Nietzsche claims that Europe's commitment to truth, its will to truth, is the essence (*Kern*) of the ascetic ideal. Arguing that to will truth is to will nothingness, he tacitly ties the will to truth to the figure of the camel in "On the Three Metamorphoses." The will to truth and nothingness acquires supreme power over European humanity through the ideology and actions of the ascetic priest. The priest's great achievement, says Nietzsche, is his interpretation of human suffering from the perspective of guilt. This interpretation is significant, for by positing nothingness as the goal of willing it rescues (*rettet*) suffering life from the inclination to renounce willing. The priest's rescue operation, though it fulfills the same function that Nietzsche assigns Apollonian and Dionysian art in *The Birth of Tragedy*, is especially harsh and repressive because it asserts that the purpose of human willing is the unconditional annihilation of what is sensuous and time-bound in human existence. But, says Nietzsche, "man would rather will *nothingness* than *not* will."[9]

The argument of *Genealogy*, no less than that of *The Birth of Tragedy*, assumes that a disposition to abdicate willing haunts the human experience of suffering.[10] In Nietzsche's view, the ascetic ideal has functioned historically to prevent human beings from acting on that disposition. But when the will to truth turns against itself; when, in other words, the will to truth questions the desirability of truth—and, therefore, the desirability of willing the truth—then the value of truth becomes a problem and the specter of resignation reasserts itself.

For Nietzsche, this "self-overcoming" of the will to truth is a "self-overcoming" of the will to nothingness that undermines the belief that nothingness is the proper end of human existence. Left bereft, and without a clear understanding of how they should live their lives, suffering human beings who have sought comfort and meaning in one version or another of the will to nothingness now find themselves seized and driven again by the compulsion to renounce willing.

Nietzsche published *Genealogy* in 1887. A number of his notebook entries from that same year suggest that one of the central themes of this book is the history of European nihilism.[11] Consider, for example, the passage that asks "What does nihilism mean?" Nietzsche's answer is "*That the highest values devaluate themselves.* The aim is lacking; 'why?' finds no answer."[12] Nietzsche implies here that nihilism is the historically specific experience of *meaninglessness* ("'why?' finds no answer") produced by a critique of the highest values—truth included—in the name of the highest values.[13] Thus understood, nihilism is precisely the experience Nietzsche portends when, in the concluding sections of *Genealogy*, he describes the "self-overcoming" of the will to truth.

In another notebook entry, also belonging to the period of *Genealogy*, Nietzsche connects nihilism to a particular moment in Europe's history. To be specific, he suggests that nihilism is an artifact of a historical interval between the demise of "the world of being" (*Twilight*'s "true world") and the revaluation of "becoming and the apparent world."[14] Read with reference to the later "INCIPIT ZARATHUSTRA," Nietzsche's notebook entry suggests that *Zarathustra* belongs essentially to the experience of European nihilism. In other words, it suggests that *Zarathustra* is a response to the *horror vacui* that Nietzsche sees seizing the human animal as it confronts the void (*Lücke*) of meaninglessness produced by the self-inflicted destruction of the will to truth and nothingness.[15]

By assigning human life a new purpose—that being to overcome "man" through the creation of new values—*Zarathustra*'s protagonist attempts to fill this void, or, as he suggests in the prologue, to build a bridge (*Brücke*) across the abyss (*Abgrund*) of nihilism. Nietzsche himself, because he never takes for granted the viability of this bridge-building enterprise, structures *Zarathustra* as an antithesis of intention and repetition that argues for, no less than against, the ineluctability of nihilism.

In *Zarathustra*, Nietzsche elaborates a post-Christian-Platonic theory of the sensible or "untrue" world in order to make intelligible the possibility of creating new values. Thus, he proposes to characterize the nature of this world, but without relying on any version of the received Christian-Platonic distinction between truth (or being) and appearance. More generally, as I argued in the Introduction to this book, Nietzsche attempts the articulation of a new philosophical vocabulary that breaks completely with traditional and, to his mind, Christian-Platonic philosophizing about the nature of what is.[16] The demand for such a vocabulary derives in part, he believes, from the diminishing theoretical viability of Christian-Platonic thinking in the face of the self-destruction of the will to truth. Perhaps more important, however, is Nietzsche's suggestion that, from a Christian-Platonic point of view, his inquiry into the possibility of creating new values will seem absurd. Christianity, as Nietzsche conceives it—for example, in his portrait of the Christian God (the great dragon) in "On the Three Metamorphoses"—asserts that all the values that could ever be created *have been* created by God. The Platonist's view is no more appealing, because it identifies value per se with eternal form (the good conceived as the form of forms) and asserts that all the particular forms (or values) that could ever be have *never not been* (from the Platonist's perspective, temporal manifestations of value indicate the imitative participation [*methexis*] of transient appearances in eternal values). Neither the Christian nor the Platonist believes that *new values* can be created from within the world of time and appearances. Thus, neither will find much sense in Nietzsche's effort to explain how human bodies that inhabit that world could become new-values creators. Just in entertaining the possibility that time-bound human bodies could give birth to new values, Nietzsche questions the validity of traditional, Christian-Platonic philosophical assumptions about the origin of value and suggests the need for a new vocabulary and concepts to challenge those assumptions.[17]

By employing a new philosophical vocabulary, Nietzsche provides for the characterization of new-values creators, the individuals whom he also names "new philosophers" and "better players." In other words, he uses his new vocabulary to produce a new conceptual framework for describing the new philosopher's philosophical enterprise. Here, Nietzsche's project recalls Plato's efforts (e.g., in the *Republic*) to characterize the philosopher's vocation in terms belonging to a general theory of human nature. Still, Nietzsche breaks with Plato by identifying the creator of new values and not the knower of eternal forms as the philosopher.[18] For Plato, the philosopher knows the origin of value (the form of the good) by cognitively transcending time. For Nietzsche, we shall see, the creator of new values knows the origin of value by being an embodied being in time. Nietzsche calls creators of new values "new philosophers" because he shares Plato's belief that knowing the origin of value distinguishes the philosopher from other human beings. Yet Nietzsche rejects Plato's view that the origin of value transcends time. Contra Plato, he relates the philosopher's knowledge of value-origins to the temporality of value-creation.[19]

Presupposing the self-destruction of the will to truth and the advent of nihilism, the expression "INCIPIT ZARATHUSTRA" points to Nietzsche's use of a new philosophical vocabulary to conceptualize a new purpose for human life; to his attempt to rethink in an original way the relationship between value and time; and to his related rejection of the Platonic distinction between the creator (the artist) and the philosopher. As we shall see, "Zarathustra's Prologue," the story with which *Zarathustra* does in fact begin, forcefully engages and develops each of these themes.

Incipit Tragoedia, Incipit Parodia

That *Zarathustra* offers an alternative to Christianity and Platonism could be nowhere clearer than in the opening section of the prologue. According to the first sentence of this section, Zarathustra "was thirty years old when he left his home and the lake of his home and went into the mountains."[20] Here Nietzsche's narrative suggests that Zarathustra is similar to Jesus by recalling the reader to the New Testament Gospels—for example, to Luke's (4:1–2)—according to which Jesus was thirty years old when the holy spirit led him into the wilderness to be tempted by the devil ("und ward vom Geist in die Wüste geführet; Und ward vierzig Tage lang von dem Teufel versucht," in Luther's translation of the Bible).[21] In the next sentence, and in what follows, Zarathustra's relationship to Jesus begins to seem more ambiguous, the two men significantly different. Whereas Jesus resides in the wilderness for forty days and nights, Zarathustra remains alone for ten years. And unlike Jesus, who fasts, grows hungry, and suffers the temptation of the devil, Zarathustra delights in his spirit, in his solitude, and, "like a bee that has gathered too much honey," in the sun's overflow.[22] In comparison to Zarathustra's stay on his mountain, Jesus's stay in the wilderness was brief and apparently wanting in joy and fulfillment.

In Part 1 of Nietzsche's text, Zarathustra distinguishes himself from Jesus explicitly: "Would that he had remained in the wilderness [*in der Wüste geblieben*] and far from the good and the just! Perhaps he would have learned to live and to love the earth—and laughter too. Believe me my brothers! He died too early; he himself would have recanted his teaching had he reached my age. Noble enough was he to recant. But he was not yet mature. Immature is the love of the youth, and immature his hatred of man and the earth. His mind and the wings of his spirit are still tied down and heavy [*schwer*]."[23] Zarathustra differs from Jesus, he argues, because he (Zarathustra) lived longer in solitude than Jesus and could thereby overcome the ascetic hatred of the earth that Jesus never overcame. In this context, Zarathustra's use of the terms *Wüste* and *schwer* is significant because it explicitly recalls his depiction of the camel in "On the Three Metamorphoses" (where Kaufmann translates *Wüste* not as "wilderness" but as "desert") and suggests that Zarathustra, before *he* matured, was himself a Christlike camel, dominated by the will to truth and nothingness. Burdened, like the weight-bearing spirit of the ascetic, Zarathustra carried (*trug*) his ashes (a standard figure for the penitent disposition informing Christian asceticism) to the mountains, where, in the company of his animals, he seems to have achieved a lion's freedom from the dour heaviness of Christian values. As *Zarathustra* commences, Zarathustra initiates and anticipates a third metamorphosis (*Verwandlung*), when, we are told, "a change came over his heart" (*aber verwandelte sich sein Herz*).[24] In other words, he inaugurates (in his heart) a transformation of spirit that he successfully completes only at the end of Part 4.

The opening passages of *Zarathustra* are no less anti-Platonic than they are anti-Christian. Of particular significance in this respect are Zarathustra's agonistic allusions to Plato's *Republic*, especially to the Myth of the Cave.[25] Consider, for example, that Plato's sun hovers above the cave and its dwellers whereas Zarathustra's sun *comes up* to the cave in which he resides (*Zehn Jahre kamst du hier herauf zu meiner Höhle*).[26] Given the allegorical significance that the sun and cave images possess in Plato's myth—the sun representing the world of the forms, the cave the world of time and appearances—Zarathustra's emphasis on the sun's *temporal* trajectory (we are told, in fact, not only that the sun comes up to the cave in the morning, but also, later, that it sets: *Ich muss, gleich dir, untergehen*)[27] challenges the Platonist view that the source of all value (for Plato, the world of the forms) transcends the world of time and appearances. Zarathustra's claim that the sun depends for its well-being on those who live in the cave ("what would your happiness be had you not those for whom you shine?") further suggests that, contra Plato, the originating source of time-bound manifestations of value, whatever it may be, relies in some important and essential way on the reality of time and appearances.[28]

Nietzsche modeled the opening section of "Zarathustra's Prologue" on the nearly identical concluding aphorism of the first edition of *The Gay Science*, which begins with the expression *Incipit tragoedia*. In the preface to the second edition of *The Gay Science*, Nietzsche recalls this expression and its suggestion that *Zarathustra* is a tragedy: "'*Incipit tragoedia*' we read at the end of this awesomely aweless book. Beware! Something downright wicked and mischievous is announced here: *incipit parodia*, no doubt."[29] That *Zarathustra* does indeed express something of the spirit of a playful and malicious parody is certainly borne out by what I have said so far about the book's beginning passages. Nietzsche parodies Plato's *Republic* and the Bible by imitating and investing with new significance their imagery (the sun and the cave) and action (a sojourn into solitude at the age of thirty). His artful repetition and revision of these "precursor texts" is ironic, and to that extent mischief-making, because it argues implicitly against the metaphysical perspectives (Christian asceticism and Plato's understanding of the relationship between time and value) that he believes these texts articulate.[30] What, however, of Nietzsche's suggestion that *Zarathustra* is properly read as a tragedy? Is Nietzsche's concept of tragedy *already* implicated in the first section of "Zarathustra's Prologue"? And if so, how does Nietzsche weave a connection there between parody and tragedy? How, in other words, does he deploy parody at the beginning of *Zarathustra* (*incipit parodia*) in order to construct *Zarathustra*, from the beginning, as a tragedy (*incipit tragoedia*)? I shall answer these questions by considering further the ways that the opening section of *Zarathustra* parodies Christianity and Platonism. In particular, I will show that the use of parody at the beginning of *Zarathustra* generates an aporia concerning *Zarathustra*'s readers' ability to know the significance of Zarathustra's descent. I shall argue, ultimately, that this aporia exposes the plot structure of *Zarathustra* (which is defined, I have argued, by an antithesis of intention and repetition), and that it represents this structure in a manner corresponding to the concept of tragedy that Nietzsche develops in *The Birth of Tragedy*.

As we have seen, the sun imagery that dominates the opening section of *Zarathustra* alludes directly to Plato's *Republic*. Yet equally important are its allusions to the *Timaeus* and, more generally, to the Neoplatonic philosophical tradition that grows out of the *Timaeus*.[31]

In the *Timaeus*, the eponymous speaker explains the genesis of the world of becoming and appearances, claiming that the Demiurge, being good and devoid of envy, "desired that everything should be so far as possible like himself."[32] According to Timaeus, the Demiurge's goodness inspired the Demiurge's creative activity, the telos of which was to expand the scope of his goodness as widely as possible. Plato's Neoplatonic successors, Plotinus among them, develop Timaeus's view of cosmological creation using the concept of *emanation*. They hold that the One, the timeless, self-sufficient first good and origin of value, overflows its plenitude, emanating first the Forms and then a subordinate deity, the Universal Mind. The Universal Mind, like Plato's Demiurge, creates in its turn the sensible world of nature (animals and plants), modeling its creations on the Forms. For Plotinus, sensible reality derives its being and value from the superabundant, expansive fecundity of the One, which expresses itself through the creative activity of the Universal Mind.[33]

Macrobius, in a fifth-century commentary on one of Cicero's writings, vividly summarizes the Platonic and Neoplatonic idea of a creative activity that is the envyless and superabundant outpouring of some supersensible good or goodness:

> Since, from the Supreme God Mind arises, and from Mind Soul, and since this in turn creates all subsequent things and fills them all with life, and since this single radiance illumines all and is reflected in each, as a single face might be reflected in many mirrors placed in a series; . . . the attentive observer will discover a connection of parts, from the Supreme God down to the last dregs of things, mutually linked together and without a break. And this is Homer's golden chain, which God, he says, bade hang down from heaven to earth.[34]

I quote this passage in full, because two of the metaphors it employs, the golden chain and the series of reflecting mirrors, figure for centuries to come in the transmission of Neoplatonic thought and, significantly, have clear reverberations in the first section of *Zarathustra*. "Bless the cup that wants to overflow [*überfliessen*]," says Zarathustra to the sun, "that the water may flow from it golden [*golden*] and carry everywhere the reflection [*Abglanz*] of your delight."[35] The Neoplatonism resonating in this reference to water that conveys everywhere the sun's golden reflection echoes as well in Zarathustra's depiction of the sun as a superabundant, overflowing source of delight (*Wonne*) and in his earlier claim, reminiscent of Plotinus's fifth *Ennead* no less than of the *Timaeus*, that the sun knows nothing of envy (*Neid*).[36] Finally, Zarathustra's expressed desire to carry the sun's reflected delight to the netherworld recalls the Neoplatonic figure of a Demiurge-like subordinate deity who mediates and facilitates the descending overflow of the One.

To be sure, none of this is meant to imply that Nietzsche intends to represent Zarathustra as a Neoplatonist. Rather my point is that here, as in his allusions to Plato's *Republic*, Zarathustra repeats and revises a received group of images and metaphors so as to invest them with new significance. By emphatically temporalizing the sun, and by insisting that the sun depends on cave dwellers for its happiness, Zarathustra suggests that temporal manifestations of value have an origin that is bound essentially to time. By depicting the sun in the image of the timeless Neoplatonic One, he further suggests that the creation of value, while temporal in character, derives from a superabundant, expansive fecundity that characterizes the origin of all value. Readers of Nietzsche's other books will see in this second suggestion a clue to the *identity* of the time-bound origin of value that Zarathustra invokes by parodying the image of the sun. Nietzsche's name for this origin, a name that never appears in *Zarathustra*, is "Dionysus," the "god" whose epiphany he describes time and again in his mature writings with metaphors of fullness, overfullness, and overflowing fecundity. Zarathustra's use of similar metaphors in his first speech intimates that the sun is a figure for Dionysus and that his own Demiurge-like task is to mediate the manifestation of Dionysus to the world of men. Zarathustra's knowledge of Dionysus he calls his "wisdom" (*Weisheit*). His claim to possess such knowledge, and thus to be full of Dionysian inspiration, marks him as a would-be new philosopher and child whose departure from his cave promises a creation of new values stemming from the temporal source of all values.[37]

The interpretation of Zarathustra's sun as a figure for Dionysus is perhaps startling, for the image of the sun is the Apollonian image par excellence. Yet this clash between figure and content cannot come as a complete shock, because Nietzsche, even as he is writing *The Birth of Tragedy*, suggests that Apollonian imagery is a viable vehicle for symbolizing Dionysus. He argues, in fact, that the ancient Greeks, because Apollonian representations were clear to them and Dionysian reality obscure, appropriately used the former to explain the latter. He claims too that modern Europeans understand the Dionysian world but, opposite from the ancients, require Dionysus to explain the world of Apollonian appearance (a requirement that Nietzsche himself exploits in *The Birth of Tragedy*).[38] In letting Apollo symbolize Dionysus in *Zarathustra*, Nietzsche suggests that he no longer holds to this view of modern Europeans. His change in perspective is understandable, for when he wrote *Zarathustra* he had ceased to believe *The Birth of Tragedy*'s thesis that there is a dialectic in contemporary culture rendering the advent of Dionysus historically imminent. For the later Nietzsche, an appeal to Dionysus is an appeal to possibilities of cultural interruption and rupture that are not and may never be immediately available. To his mind, no less than to the minds of the ancient Greeks, Dionysus has become an obscure and perhaps fictional god who might best be approached indirectly and circumspectly through the image-language of Apollo. Nietzsche's use of the Apollonian sun to invoke Dionysus,[39] though perhaps the most wickedly mischievous aspect of his portrait of Zarathustra's descent, may betray his sense that for his fellow contemporary Europeans Dionysus, like the god Hölderlin invokes in the first stanza of "Patmos," will be difficult to grasp and comprehend.[40]

Thus far, my interpretation of Zarathustra's descent may raise more questions than it answers. What, after all, does the figure of Dionysus signify? And what is meant by the suggestion that Dionysus is the *origin* of all values? To be sure, my reference to Dionysian inspiration involves an interpretation of the yea-saying responsiveness of the child (and new philosopher) that Zarathustra aspires to be when he leaves his cave. But how is this responsiveness connected to the possibility of new-values creation? In subsequent sections of this chapter, I begin to provide answers to these questions. In what immediately follows, however, I set aside these questions in order to conclude my interpretation of Zarathustra's first speech and descent in the opening section of "Zarathustra's Prologue."

I have claimed that the use of parody in the opening section of the prologue generates an aporia that exposes the plot structure of *Zarathustra* as a whole. In order to show that this is so, I will examine closely the final three lines of this opening section.

Zarathustra completes his first speech, saying, "Behold, this cup wants to become empty [*leer*] again, and Zarathustra wants to become man again." The narrative assertion that follows these remarks, "Thus began Zarathustra's going-under [*Untergang*]," concludes the opening section of the prologue.[41] Read with reference to Nietzsche's parody of Neoplatonism, these lines suggest that Zarathustra has begun his descent, or going-under, as a cuplike carrier of Dionysian overfullness who will bring Dionysus to men and inspire them to create new values by emptying himself of his overfullness. According to this reading, Zarathustra descends to men, not to shore up some human deficiency, but because he needs men to receive his overflow.[42] This reading suggests that Zarathustra will soon discover that men as he finds them are altogether capable of receiving his overflow.

This interpretation of Zarathustra's descent is persuasive, and perfectly consistent with what Zarathustra and the narrative actually say. However, the language of the final three lines is no less suggestive of a second and very different reading of Zarathustra's descent, which, while antithetical to the first interpretation, is just as compelling. The epistemic aporia that haunts the opening section of "Zarathustra's Prologue" derives from the difficulty of deciding between these two equally plausible interpretations.

The key to the second interpretation, again, is the use of parody. Once more the object of Nietzsche's parody is a biblical text: not, this time, the Gospel of Luke, but St. Paul's epistle to the Philippians (2:6–11). In particular, I have in mind the six-stanza hymn that Paul uses to describe the incarnation, death, and resurrection of Christ. The first three stanzas are especially important to the purposes of my argument:

His nature is from the first, divine,
And yet he did not see in the rank of Godhead,
A prize to be coveted;

He dispossessed himself,
And took the nature of a slave
Fashioned in the likeness of men,
And presenting himself in human form;

And then he lowered his own dignity,
Accepted an obedience which brought him to death,
Death on a cross.[43]

In the above translation the word "dispossessed" translates the third-person singular aorist of the Greek "*kenóō*," which means "to empty out."[44] According to Paul, Christ in the act of incarnation empties himself of his divinity in order to become man "in all the circumstances of his servitude."[45] To become man, Paul believed, is fully to embrace man's condition and therefore to embrace death, the ultimate consequence of original sin.[46]

The topic of the second half of Paul's hymn is the resurrection of Christ. The fact of the resurrection is, of course, central to the story Paul aims to tell, as without that fact his story would end where the third stanza ends: namely, with the apparent triumph of death over divinity and the tacit suggestion that humanity and divinity mutually and necessarily exclude each other. For Paul, Christ's resurrection is a divine victory over death and the renewal of human nature through the power of the holy spirit.[47]

In the three lines that conclude the first section of "Zarathustra's Prologue," Zarathustra alludes to Paul's hymnal interpretation of Christ's incarnation and death. He tells us first that he wants to *become empty again* (*wieder leer werden*), and then that he wants to *become man again* (*wieder Mensch werden*). Read as a parody of Paul's letter to the Philippians, these remarks suggest that Zarathustra aims to purge himself of his Dionysian divinity in order to take on a human identity. The statement following these remarks, "Thus began Zarathustra's going-under," suggests a further repetition and revision of Paul's text, because *Untergang*, which Kaufmann translates as "going-under" or "to go-under," can be translated equally well as "ruin" or "destruction." Zarathustra's going-under resembles the death-dealing incarnation of Paul's Christ: it is a descent to a ruinous fate that inevitably awaits him once he embraces the human condition.

Nietzsche's parody of Paul has profoundly pessimistic implications. When Zarathustra leaves his cave, he wants to become man. In his view, "man" is Christian-Platonic man (a point that becomes clear as the plot of the prologue develops): that is, man as he has been formed by the Christian-Platonic interpretation of human existence. In order to "become man," Zarathustra empties himself of his Dionysian divinity and embraces the human condition as Platonism and Christianity have constituted it. Thus constituted, the human condition promises to cause the ruin (*Untergang*) of Zarathustra's creative enterprise (a direct consequence of his embracing the human condition), that is, to destroy his already depleted effort to bring Dionysus to man. As prefigured in the opening section of the prologue, which evokes no image of a resurrected Zarathustra, the anticipated destruction of this effort seems irrevocable. Nietzsche's parody of Paul intimates the irreversible triumph of Christian-Platonic man over Zarathustra-Dionysus, as well as the irreversible defeat of Zarathustra-Dionysus's attempt to effect a creation of new values.

Read as a parody of Paul, the opening section of *Zarathustra* suggests that man is at once the *object* of Zarathustra's poetic intention—Zarathustra aspires to shower and imbue man with Dionysian inspiration—and the *obstacle* that keeps Zarathustra from fulfilling that intention. Christian-Platonic man, as this parody envisions him, incarnates the permanent death of Zarathustra's modernist enterprise and is in essence inadequate to receiving Zarathustra's overflow. Indeed, his relentless and recurring presence (Zarathustra suggests that man is insistently there, ever to be encountered *again* [*wieder*]) seems to entail the repulsion of that overflow. Because Nietzsche's parody of Paul restricts itself to the first half of Paul's hymn, it implies that Christian-Platonic man and Dionysian divinity mutually and necessarily exclude one another (man prevails to the exclusion of Dionysus in the world below; Dionysus appears, but only with Zarathustra, atop Zarathustra's mountain). Were this implication true, Dionysus could not enter into the human world to which Zarathustra descends and Zarathustra could not inspire others to become creators of new values. Moreover, Zarathustra, in becoming man again, could not become a new-values creator in his own right and thus fulfill his personal intention.

We know, of course, that this implication need not be true, since it presupposes an interpretation of Zarathustra's descent that is open to question because it is but one of two equally viable though mutually contradictory interpretations of Zarathustra's descent. Read as a parody of Neoplatonism, Zarathustra's descent suggests that men, as Zarathustra finds them, are equal to the possibility of receiving his Dionysian overflow; read as a parody of Paul, it suggests that they are not equal to that possibility. Read as a parody of Neoplatonism, Zarathustra's descent portends the inspirational manifestation of Dionysus in men's lives; read as a parody of Paul, it augurs the death of Dionysus wherever men subsist. And finally, read as a parody of Neoplatonism, Zarathustra's descent promises the fulfillment of his poetic and personal intentions to overcome Christian-Platonic man through the creation of new values; read as a parody of Paul, it represents the repetition and persistence of old, Christian-Platonic values through the recurrence (perhaps the eternal recurrence) and perpetuation of Christian-Platonic man. The meaning of Zarathustra's descent is genuinely ambiguous, for as readers of the opening section of "Zarathustra's Prologue" we cannot know which interpretation is correct.

The aporia we face at the start of *Zarathustra*, produced by two incompatible and reciprocally antagonistic readings of Zarathustra's descent, is not simply a case of a text underdetermining its interpretations.[48] Our hermeneutical dilemma is more complicated than that because it exposes and highlights the plot structure of *Zarathustra* as a whole. As my third formulation of this aporia suggests, the conflict between interpretations of Zarathustra's descent opposes Zarathustra's poetic and personal intentions to a representation of the repetition of Christian-Platonic values. Thus, this conflict prefigures the antithesis of intention and repetition that throughout *Zarathustra* structures Zarathustra's encounters with figures who skeptically question the viability of his Dionysian modernism.

As we have seen, Zarathustra's speech itself helps to generate the aporia affecting our reading of his descent. Zarathustra speaks of the sun's overflow, of its lack of envy, and of water carrying the reflection of the sun's delight to the world below, thus alluding to the Neoplatonic notions of emanation and the great chain of being. He also speaks of "becoming empty" and of "becoming man," thus recalling the first half of Paul's hymn. He does not mention, however, at least explicitly, his impending death and destruction. To be sure, Zarathustra does use the word *untergehen* (the verbal root of "*Untergang*") before he speaks of "becoming empty" and of "becoming man," but only to compare his going-under to the light-bearing descent and setting of the sun for which the common German expression is *Sonnenuntergang*: "I must descend to the depths as you do . . . when you go behind the sea and still bring light to the underworld, you overrich star. Like you [*gleich dir*] I must *go-under* [*untergehen*]—go down, as is said by man to whom I want to descend [*zu denen ich hinab will*]." Here, Zarathustra explicitly and narrowly intends the word *untergehen* to signify his sunlike descent to man, not his destruction. That this descent may entail his destruction is, we have seen, suggested by the statement that concludes the opening section of the prologue. The use of the noun *Untergang* there, unlike Zarathustra's use of the verb *untergehen*, works not to eliminate semantic ambiguity, but ironically to suggest that what Zarathustra understands simply as his descent may as well result in his ruin and demise. The upshot of this irony is a certain asymmetry between Zarathustra's view of his descent and *Zarathustra's* readers' view of it. Reading the opening section's concluding statement, just after we learn that Zarathustra wishes to "become empty" and to "become man," we have been primed to sense in the narrative use of *Untergang* reverberations of the deathly forebodings already evident in Zarathustra's allusions to the second stanza of Paul's hymn. Zarathustra, however, because he does not see the connotations of these allusions, remains blind to the equivocal character of his situation. What I mean to suggest here is that Nietzsche's fictional protagonist, despite his verbal "Paulinism," retains a naively optimistic and one-sided view of his descent. Because he speaks of "becoming empty" and of "becoming man" only *after* he restricts the meaning of *untergehen*, and only *after* he portrays himself as a Dionysian demiurge, Zarathustra invites the impression that his references to Paul's hymn are unintentional and meant simply to elaborate a sanguine vision of his descent.

Although Zarathustra echoes Paul, he seems not to know what he is saying. Anticipating later encounters with representations of repetition, the pessimism in his speech is nonetheless inadvertent. From Zarathustra's perspective, his descent unequivocally marks the inspirational entry of Dionysus into the world of men. Nietzsche, however, by casting that perspective in an ironic light, entertains a skeptical appraisal of Zarathustra's modernist pretensions.[49]

We are now in a position to see how Nietzsche's parodies of Neoplatonism and of Paul's letter to the Philippians work in tandem in the opening section of "Zarathustra's Prologue" to construct *Zarathustra* as a tragedy. Our point of departure will be a brief, selective review of the theory of tragedy that Nietzsche expounds in *The Birth of Tragedy*.

According to Nietzsche, Dionysian or tragic art forces us

> to recognize that all that comes into being must be ready for a sorrowful destruction [*Untergange*]; we are forced to look into the terrors of the individual existence—yet we are not to become rigid with fear: a metaphysical comfort tears us momentarily from the bustle of the changing figures. We are really for a brief moment primordial being itself. . . . In spite of fear and pity, we are the happy living beings, not as individuals, but as the *one* living being, with whose creative joy we are united.[50]

With these remarks, which begin section 17 of *The Birth of Tragedy*, Nietzsche continues the discussion of tragic heroes and metaphysical comfort begun in sections 7, 10, and 16, and briefly explains his understanding of the tragic plot (*mythos* in Aristotle's sense, not Nietzsche's).[51] In Nietzsche's view, the tragic hero is a mask of Dionysus. Following Aristotle, he also asserts that the tragic hero is prey both to error (*hamartia* for Aristotle and *Irrthum* for Nietzsche) and reversal (*metabole*). But where Aristotle distinguishes recognition, peripety, and pathos as three modes of reversal, Nietzsche restricts himself to discussing the reversal effected by the tragic hero's destruction (as he puts it in section 17) and annihilation (*Vernichtung*).[52] Like Aristotle, Nietzsche holds that this reversal arouses feelings of pity and fear in the spectator. Like Schopenhauer, he suggests that it encourages feelings of resignation (section 7). Nietzsche breaks with Aristotle and Schopenhauer, however, by insisting that tragedies, after exciting the emotions of pity, fear, and resignation, evoke in their audiences a sense of metaphysical comfort (*Trost*) that saves (*rettet*) these men and women from the temptation to resign life.[53]

How is Zarathustra related to Nietzsche's notion of a tragic hero? By parodying Neoplatonism, Nietzsche depicts Zarathustra as an individualized, demiurgic expression of Dionysian inspiration. In effect, he suggests that Zarathustra is a mask of Dionysus. Nietzsche adds to his portrait of Zarathustra as a tragic hero by parodying Paul and thereby anticipating Zarathustra's destruction. Nietzsche's parody of Paul also demonstrates Zarathustra's susceptibility to error, or, more precisely, to a blindness that lets Zarathustra mistake ambiguous circumstances for clearly defined ones. The ironic perspective that this blindness grants *Zarathustra*'s readers marks Zarathustra as the type of tragically ironic hero that, according to Northrop Frye, lacks a knowledge that the readers of his story possess.[54] As we have seen, this lack of knowledge finds poignant expression in Zarathustra's failure to recognize the full semantic range of *untergehen*, a word that reverberates and continues to haunt him in the narrative use of *Untergang*. Here, as in *Antigone*, tragic irony deploys the vehicle of linguistic equivocacy to show us a tragic hero who, in the words of Jean-Pierre Vernant, "finds himself literally 'taken at his word,' a word which turns itself against him in bringing him the bitter experience of the meaning which he insisted on not recognizing."[55]

When Zarathustra first descends from his mountain he has yet to anticipate, let alone to experience, a ruinous "reversal" of his will to innovate. In other words, he has yet to have the sort of experience that typically excites pity, fear, and resignation in a tragedy. Nietzsche engages the themes of resignation and fear in section 6 of the prologue, and returns to these themes in the main body of *Zarathustra*, where he also engages the theme of pity. In Part 3, finally, Nietzsche describes the conclusion of Zarathustra's tragedy. Having rejected the earlier notion of metaphysical comfort—arguing, in essence, that it is irredeemably romantic—he develops a concept of tragic-heroic comfort to displace it, a concept, as we shall see in Chapter 5, that is closely related to the second phase of the thought of eternal recurrence.

Zarathustra and the Saint

In the second section of "Zarathustra's Prologue," the old saint reproduces the pessimistic, Pauline interpretation of Zarathustra's descent. My discussion of Zarathustra's conversation with the saint focuses on the words that pass between the two men just after the saint says to Zarathustra that "Zarathustra has become a child."

> Zarathustra is an awakened one; what do you now want among the sleepers? You lived in your solitude as in the sea, and the sea carried [*trug*] you. Alas, would you now climb ashore? Alas, would you again drag [*schleppen*] your own body? Zarathustra answered: "I love man." "Why," asked the saint, "did I go into the forest and the desert [*Einöde*]? Was it not because I loved man all-too-much? Now I love God; man I love not. Man is for me too imperfect a thing [*unvollkommene Sache*]. Love of man would destroy [*umbringen*] me." Zarathustra answered: "Did I speak of love? I bring [*bringe*] men a gift." "Give them nothing!" said the saint. "Rather take part of their load and help them to bear it [*trage es mit ihnen*]—that will be best for them, if only it does you good! And if you want to give them something, give them no more than alms, and let them beg for that!"
>
> "No," answered Zarathustra. "I give no alms. For that I am not poor enough."[56]

Read from the perspective of "On the Three Metamorphoses," the saint's words seem initially to suggest that, though Zarathustra aspires to become a child, his renunciation of solitude will require that he revert to being a camel. Zarathustra's approach to human community will demand that he exchange the sensation of effortless becoming ("and the sea carried you") for the camel-like sufferance of a heavy burden ("would you again drag your own body?"). It is no surprise that the saint instructs Zarathustra to help men bear their load. In the saint's view, the recalcitrant facticity of men's circumstances will defeat Zarathustra's modernist intentions and transform Zarathustra's life into a grave and cumbersome burden.[57]

Obsessed with human imperfection, the saint sees a fundamental, ineradicable deficiency in human facticity, a deficiency that he believes frustrated his former desire that human beings be better than they are. The saint suggests, in fact, that man's deficiency is such an unyielding and weighty force that it can destroy (*umbringen*) the aspirations of individuals like Zarathustra and perhaps the saint himself (when he loved man "all-too-much"), who work lovingly to transform man. Like Nietzsche's parody of Paul's hymn, the saint intimates that Zarathustra's encounter with man will be the ruin of Zarathustra's hopes. From the saint's point of view, which denies the possibility of changing man, human existence can only be the deficient reality that it is. That is why the saint remains in the forest, far away from the human beings he once dangerously wanted to perfect.

After Zarathustra proclaims to the saint that he loves man, he hears the saint argue that man is not worthy of love, repudiates his earlier proclamation, and announces that he is bringing men a gift. Zarathustra's self-correction is significant, because it shifts attention away from men to the gift that Zarathustra wishes to bring them. Man now matters, not for his own sake, but for the sake of what Zarathustra's gift can do to him. By correcting himself, Zarathustra deflects without refuting the saint's suggestion that human facticity will destroy Zarathustra's will to innovate. Rather than disprove the saint's vilifying portrait of man, Zarathustra renounces any interest in what man actually is (an interest that the saint infers from the statement "I love man") in order to proclaim an interest in the effect his gift could have on man. I do not mean to imply here that Zarathustra accepts as true the view that man is *inessentially* imperfect (as distinct from the saint's view that man is *essentially* imperfect), or that he regards his gift as a means to perfecting man. If Zarathustra believed that human beings are lacking in some respect, then his response to the saint's suggestion that he offer men alms would not be what it is. Zarathustra, by insisting that he is not poor enough for the charity of almsgiving, reminds us that his descent was not motivated by the belief that human beings are in some way deficient, but by a superabundant and self-transcending fecundity that needed and sought human beings to receive its overflow. Man is important to Zarathustra, not for what he is (be he imperfect or perfect), but for what he can become through the reception of Zarathustra's Dionysian gift.[58]

Zarathustra's conversation with the saint dramatizes for the first time in *Zarathustra* the antithesis of intention and repetition. In the figure of the saint, Zarathustra's poetic and personal intentions discover a figure who rejects the belief that man can be overcome. Arguing that human existence can only be the deficient reality that it is, the old hermit implies that man will never escape his Christian-Platonic heritage by creating new values. In appraising Zarathustra's modernism, the saint reiterates a pessimism that is already evident in Nietzsche's parody of Paul's hymn. As we have seen, he expresses this pessimism in his suggestion that Zarathustra cannot become man again without becoming a camel again. Zarathustra responds to that suggestion, in the manner of a lion, by defying the saint and by reaffirming his commitment to becoming a new-values creator. Zarathustra defies the saint by repudiating the latter's obsession with human deficiency. He reaffirms his commitment to becoming a new-values creator by envisioning himself as a gift giver whose Dionysian gift will stimulate others to consort with him in his effort to overcome man.

When Zarathustra meets the old saint, he views man as essentially a *possibility*. In other words, he sees man as a being that is fundamentally defined by its capacity to become another kind of being. Oblivious to the thought that human facticity could offer even a little resistance to his will, Zarathustra believes that he can transform man as he (Zarathustra) wishes. One of his reasons for holding this belief is his assumption that God is dead: that is, his assumption that belief in God has ceased to be intellectually defensible in the modern world (as we have seen, Nietzsche explains this assumption with reference to the history of the will to truth).[59]

"God is dead" is the last phrase Zarathustra pronounces in section 2 of the prologue. As astute readers of *Zarathustra* have observed, *"I teach you the overman"* is the first sentence he utters in section 3. Passing promptly from one italicized expression to the next, Zarathustra seems to believe that if God is dead then man can be overcome. Because Zarathustra also assumes that God in fact is dead, he can logically infer, by *modus ponens* ("method of affirming"), that man can be overcome. Man is available, Zarathustra supposes, to be transformed at will. The saint is oblivious to the possibility of overcoming man, Zarathustra suggests, because his worship of God blinds him to other purposes—including the Dionsyian purpose that is Zarathustra's gift: "'With singing, crying, laughing, and humming I praise the god who is my god. But what do you bring us as a gift?' When Zarathustra had heard these words, he bade the saint farewell and said: 'What could I have to give you? But let me go quickly lest I take something from you.'"[60]

Zarathustra's understanding of the saint's obliviousness is inaccurate. According to the saint himself, his turn to God succeeded his disenchantment with man. Thus, he became skeptical of the possibility of transforming man *before* he devoted himself to his religion. Apparently transposing earlier and later events, Zarathustra mistakes the saint's disenchanting practical knowledge of human facticity—derived, presumably, from the holy hermit's efforts to perfect man—for a form of blindness stemming from his belief in God. The saint is oblivious to the possibility of overcoming man not because he blindly worships God, but because he knows man all too well.

Zarathustra interprets the saint's continuing belief in God as an effect of the saint's ignorance ("Could it be possible? The old saint in the forest has not yet heard anything of this, that *God is dead*!" he says).[61] However, it *can* be interpreted otherwise. Suppose, for example, that though his knowledge of human facticity impels him to believe that man cannot be overcome, the saint agrees with Zarathustra that if God is dead then man can be overcome. Granting this supposition, we can conjecture that the saint believes in God, not because he is ignorant, but because he validly infers that belief in God has not ceased to be intellectually defensible; that is, because he validly infers that God is not dead. Proceeding from the premises (1) that if God is dead then man can be overcome and (2) that man cannot be overcome, the saint logically concludes, by *modus tollens* ("method of denying"), that God is not dead. Having reason to believe that belief in God has remained intellectually defensible, he is moved to maintain his belief in God.

When Zarathustra and the saint leave each other, Nietzsche's narrative states that "they separated, the old one and the man, laughing as two boys laugh."[62] This remark is significant, for it implies that Zarathustra and the saint, regardless of the differences between them, share a perspective that is youthful and naive. Given my interpretation of the saint's belief in God, we can conjecture that the substance of this perspective is the proposition that if God is dead then man can be overcome. Or, to put it differently, that the death of God is a sufficient condition for the possibility of overcoming man. Taking this proposition as his first premise, Zarathustra assumes as his second premise that God is dead and concludes (again, by *modus ponens*) that man can be overcome. Taking the same proposition as his first premise, the saint assumes as his second premise that man cannot be overcome and concludes (again, by *modus tollens*) that God is not dead.

Zarathustra begins his descent believing that his conclusion is true and that the saint's is false. As the action of the prologue unfolds, however, he has experiences that recall the saint's profound disenchantment with man; that strongly support the saint's second premise; and that suggest that Zarathustra's own conclusion is false. As a result of these experiences, Zarathustra begins to notice man's recalcitrance to change and to suspect that, although God is dead, overcoming man is not possible. In sum, he begins to doubt the proposition that he and the saint seemed naively to endorse.

Zarathustra loses his naiveté gradually. The attenuation of his credulity is evident in sections 3–5, when he fails to fulfill his poetic intention and then attempts to explain his failure. It is also evident in section 6, when he witnesses a dramatic rendition of the thought that all striving to overcome man is futile. In confronting this thought, Zarathustra recognizes that human life could persist as a pointless affair, despite his fervent struggle to provide it a new point in the aftermath of the death of God. Zarathustra is transformed by the nihilistic prospect of human life "enduring in vain," because it forces him to face the possibility that his descent is fated to catastrophe.

Zarathustra's Speeches on the Overman

In section 3, Zarathustra identifies the overman as the purpose of human existence: "*I teach you the overman.* Man is something that shall be overcome. What have you done to overcome him?"[63] The rhetoric of evolution he uses to describe the overman, with its reference to the movement from worm to ape to man to overman, clearly depicts the overman as a sensible and worldly being (a contrast to the supersensible and otherworldly God of Christian asceticism) distinct from man. Keeping in mind that by "man" Zarathustra means Christian-Platonic man, we may take him to be saying that the overman is a kind of human being that, though it has yet to be, may be in the future.[64]

The evolution from man to overman that Zarathustra envisions is not an effect of natural selection; rather, Zarathustra conceptualizes this transition as a process of self-transformation. He argues that in the Christian-Platonic past the soul disdained the body and the ascetic ethic of the soul ruled human existence. He further suggests that the Christian and Platonic values that have defined that ethic—happiness, reason, virtue, justice, goodness, and pity—have been the means by which the soul cruelly subjected the body to its hatred of earthly, sensible reality. For Zarathustra, values constitute human selves as selves of a particular type, and Christian-Platonic values constitute human selves as selves of the type "man." The sort of self-transformation that is essential to overcoming man requires that these values be viewed with a great contempt ("as poverty and filth and wretched contentment") that will prompt not only their destruction, but the destruction of this contempt itself (since contempt depends for its existence on the existence of the very values it denounces).[65] To the extent that Zarathustra declines to identify the overman with the creation of particular non-Christian-Platonic values, his concept of the overman remains empty.[66] Zarathustra insists, however, that any esteeming or value-creating that gives rise to the overman must appreciate the sensuous, physical being of the body. Whereas the ascetic ideal demands the destruction of the passions of the "earth"—Zarathustra's metaphor for the kinds of desire that commonly claim human bodies—the creation of the overman requires the inspiration of passional chaos. In creating the overman, one prizes the passions of the body in order to embody the "meaning of the earth [*der Sinn der Erde*]."[67]

Zarathustra's second speech to the townspeople uses their language to articulate his vision of the overman. The townspeople interpret Zarathustra's first speech as describing the tightrope walker whose performance is about to begin. Zarathustra responds to this interpretation by transforming the figure of the tightrope walker into a metaphor for the possibility of overcoming man. Thus, his second speech is an attempt further to elaborate in terms accessible to his audience the argument he initially espoused. "Man," says Zarathustra, "is a rope tied between beast and overman—a rope over an abyss [*Abgrund*]. A dangerous [*gefährliches*] across, a dangerous on-the-way, a dangerous looking-back, a dangerous shuddering and stopping. What is great in man is that he is a bridge [*Brücke*] and not an end: what can be loved in man is that he is a *going-over* [*Übergang*] and a *going-under* [*Untergang*]."[68] With these words, Zarathustra twice characterizes the human condition ambiguously. He suggests first that man resembles a stable and secure tightrope ("a rope over an abyss") no less than a worried and imperiled tightrope walker ("a dangerous looking-back, a dangerous shuddering and stopping"). He also suggests that man is a bridge (or going-over) to the overman, as well as a bridge-forsaking feat of self-destruction (or going-under). As we shall see, both of these ambiguities are significant, as both pertain to Zarathustra's understanding of man's capacity to transform himself.[69]

The first ambiguity suggests that the tightropelike security of human existence is essentially affected by the hazardous possibility of losing that security. The apparent point here is that man is not reducible to the Christian-Platonic interpretation of his existence and that he must risk the abandonment of the Christian-Platonic values that have fixed his identity if he is to overcome himself. The figure of the abyss (*Abgrund*) amplifies this point, by alluding to the experience of a groundless disorientation that the demise of a stable identity and reliable values must inevitably entail. The second ambiguity complicates the significance of the first by relating the disorienting and ruinous destruction (*Untergang*) of Christian-Platonic man to the transformative transition (*Übergang*) from man to overman. Zarathustra's attempt to clarify this ambiguity, as his second speech unfolds, is only partially successful.

Zarathustra's second speech is for the most part a sequence of assertions, each having the form "I love . . ." In some of these assertions, Zarathustra distinguishes the individuals who will go-under and sacrifice themselves from the individuals who will "cross-over" and become overmen. In effect, he glosses the equivocal suggestion that man is at once a going-over and a going-under by implying that *some* men will be the self-sacrificial means enabling *other* men to become overmen (Zarathustra says, for example, that he loves those "who sacrifice themselves for the earth, that the earth may some day become the overman's"). There can be no doubt that Zarathustra admires the forerunners of the overman who will go-under but not go-over. Still, his distinction between forerunners and eventual overmen has limited hermeneutical value, because it does not explain the second ambiguity as it applies to someone whose going-under will lead to his own going-over. When Zarathustra speaks of those "who do not know how to live, except by going-under, for they are those who cross over;" or when he purports to love him whose "virtue is the will to go under" and who "strides over the bridge as spirit;" he very clearly suggests that the second ambiguity pertains not only to the distinction between forerunners and overmen, but equally to the self-transformation of particular individuals. Thus, in order completely to clarify this ambiguity, Zarathustra needs to show how going-over and going-under can be phases of the same movement; or, in other words, how the movement by which someone repudiates what he is and has been can become the movement by which he makes himself into a new type of human being.[70]

Though Zarathustra never accounts fully for the second ambiguity, he provides two clues that help to clarify its significance. The first of these is his repeated use of *zu Grunde gehen* ("to perish") in the second half of his second speech. To be sure, his use of this phrase is semantically of a piece with the use of *Untergang* ("going-under"), since both terms connote death and destruction. Taken literally, however, *zu Grunde gehen* suggests a descent to the ground (*Grund*) of human existence.[71] Zarathustra's use of *zu Grunde gehen* intimates that the groundless abyss (*Abgrund*) that man must embrace in abandoning the security of traditional, Christian-Platonic values is, in its own way, a foundation that can support and sustain a radical transformation of human existence. Going-under and going-over converge, Zarathustra's language suggests, because the abyss in which man goes under can be a ground, or a bridge, across which he goes over.

A second clue is implicit in the allusiveness of Zarathustra's language. Significantly, the opening lines of Zarathustra's second speech, with their talk of a dangerous movement across a bridge that spans an abyss, echo the first stanza of Hölderlin's "Patmos." Even a cursory perusal of the poem's first few sentences suggests that Hölderlin's language is the language Zarathustra uses to characterize the way to the overman:

> Nah ist
> Und schwer zu fassen der Gott.
> Wo aber Gefahr ist, wächst
> Das Rettende auch.
> Im Finstern wohnen
> Die Adler und furchtlos gehn
> Die Söhne der Alpen über den Abgrund weg
> Auf leichtgebaueten Brücken.

> Near and
> Hard to grasp is
>   The God.
> But where danger is,
>   Deliverance also grows.
> The eagles
>   Dwell in obscurity
> And across chasms fearless go
>   The sons of the Alps, on bridges
> Lightly built.[72]

By repeating the language of "Patmos," Zarathustra tacitly links the danger and abyssal terror of going-under to the epiphany and saving inspiration of a god. In effect, he postulates a connection and a continuity between the destruction of the self (as it is and has been) and the renewal of the self, between going-under and going-over. Going-under and going-over can be the same movement, Zarathustra suggests, if to go-under is to embrace a divine and sustaining inspiration that, in keeping with the implications of the first clue, bridges the way between man and overman.

I have previously maintained that "Dionysus" is Nietzsche's name for the god whose arrival among men is essential to the creation of the overman. The central idea implicit in Zarathustra's use of Hölderlin's metaphors—that this god is at once an abyss and a ground—can be developed further by relating it to the proposition that the creation of the overman requires the inspiration of bodily, passional chaos. Dionysus *is* this chaos, I want to suggest, but not simply this chaos.[73] In Part 1, Zarathustra analyzes the relationship between the body's passions and the creation of new values, but he has already alluded to that relationship in mentioning the human abyss that is also a bridge to the overman. For Zarathustra, Dionysian passional chaos is the abyssal dissolution of established values and the founding possibility of new values.[74]

Let us now consider Zarathustra's struggle to find language adequate to his persuasive purpose. Zarathustra wants his second speech to correct the belief that his first speech referred to the tightrope walker. One of the townspeople, who seems to speak for the others, expresses this belief: "Now [*nun*] we have heard [*hörten*] enough about the tightrope walker; now let us see [*sehen*] him too!"[75] Notwithstanding his later effort to adapt the figure of the tightrope to his vision of the overman, Zarathustra remains frustrated, ultimately, by the townspeople's failure to comprehend his message: "'There they stand,' he said to his heart; 'there they laugh. They do not understand me; I am not the mouth for these ears. Must one smash their ears before they learn to hear [*hören*] with their eyes? Must one clatter like kettledrums and preachers of repentance? Or do they believe only the stammerer.'"[76] Though full of exasperation, these last remarks illuminate the townspeople's reaction to Zarathustra's first speech. As they interpret it, this speech describes someone (the tightrope walker) who is present "now" (*nun*), not simply to be heard about, but immediately to be seen ("now let us see him too"). As Zarathustra himself interprets it, especially when he speaks of "hearing eyes," it has a very different significance.

Hearing eyes, I presume, would not hear and listen as ears hear and listen. Why smash a person's ears, if the only point is to produce eyes that do what ears do anyway? In order to appreciate the genuinely paradoxical nature of Zarathustra's talk of "hearing eyes," we must interpret it as saying that there could be eyes that, functioning as eyes function, still do what ears do. According to this interpretation, "hearing eyes" would be eyes that hear *by* seeing, eyes that somehow see what ears hear. Zarathustra imagines eyes that see sounds (one can think analogously, here, of "seeing ears," that is, of ears that hear colors and shapes). Such eyes, as distinct from ordinary eyes, would be eyes that could see what is ordinarily not present to be seen. The reference to "hearing eyes" suggests that Zarathustra meant neither his first nor his second speech to describe someone present to be seen, but that he intended each speech to bring into view a possibility that, like sounds, lay beyond what is visibly present. By speaking catachrestically, he retrospectively interprets his speeches as attempts to turn the townspeople's sights from the present that is man toward the future that is the overman.

By figuring his vision of the overman as a sighting of sounds, Zarathustra conflates an apprehension of Apollonian form (visible appearances) with an attunement to Dionysian sonority (audible music).[77] As in his opening apostrophe to the sun, he invokes Apollo to conjure Dionysus. The overman is a future possibility grounded in passional, Dionysian chaos. Using the catachresis of "hearing eyes," Zarathustra develops this idea, proposing to awaken his auditors' sight to the prospect of suffering such chaos. By summoning the townspeople to envision in their passions the potential soundings of a chaos that is not present to be seen, Zarathustra hopes to stimulate the creation of new values.

The difference between Zarathustra's and the townspeople's interpretations of Zarathustra's first speech is the difference between (1) viewing that speech as an attempt to perform a perlocutionary act (as an attempt to produce an effect *by* saying something) and (2) viewing it as an effort to constate a fact (as an effort to state, or to report, a fact).[78] In the judgment of the townspeople, Zarathustra endeavored in his first speech to describe the tightrope walker by relating certain facts about him. Thus, they construe that speech to have been an attempt to re-present verbally something factually present and at hand. Considered in the perspective of Zarathustra's subsequent allusion to "hearing eyes," the townspeople's interpretation of Zarathustra's speech mistakes language that was meant to persuade his auditors to envision a future possibility (e.g., "Behold [*Seht*], I teach you the overman") for language that was intended to characterize an existing state of affairs. Zarathustra responds to this error by struggling to restore the perlocutionary efficacy of his language; that is, by metaphorically using the figure of the tightrope walker to redirect his listeners sights toward the future. Thus, he resists the townspeople's belief that his speech is a form of repetition (again, verbal re-presentation) and reaffirms the power of his speech to reveal a possibility that transcends what is here and now. When Zarathustra bemoans the fact that the townspeople do not hear with their eyes, he is implying that, despite his perlocutionary efforts, they remain myopically bound to the facticity of the present.

Zarathustra's encounter with the townspeople pits his passion for the future against their obsession with the present, dramatizing the antithesis of intention and repetition. Zarathustra's poetic intention is to induce in his auditors a vision inspiring them to become new-values creators. As we have seen, his belief that his speech can fulfill that intention contradicts the townspeople's view that his words pertain only to the here and now. Insisting that Zarathustra's language can only repeat or re-present what is present, the townspeople are camel-like representatives of repetition who fail to see how the future can differ from the past and thus to see the point of speech meant to reveal new possibilities. Lion-like, Zarathustra responds to the townspeople by resisting their attempt to implicate him in re-presentational talk about the tightrope walker. Saying "no" to their belief that he is constrained to use language to describe existing facts, he asserts his freedom to create new values by imagining a future unlike the present and the past. Although Zarathustra does not now become a child, he reaffirms his commitment to becoming one, and to inspiring others to become children, not, as before, by depicting himself as a gift giver, but by using the figure of the tightrope walker to persuade others to join him in envisioning the possibility of overcoming man.

Man, as the saint in the forest foresaw, proves impervious to Zarathustra's exhortations. By adducing the figure of the stammerer ("Or do they believe only the stammerer"), which figuratively captures the power of representations of repetition to undermine his creative intentions, Zarathustra ties man's imperviousness to the antithetical structure of *Zarathustra* as a whole. Having labored in vain to speak persuasively, and thus to produce the perlocutionary effects he purposed to produce, Zarathustra is left, if not speechless, then momentarily stymied by his failure to do with his speech what he wanted to do. This failure is significant, for it shows that the success of Zarathustra's effort to bring Dionysus to men will turn in part on the potency of his language.[79]

As we shall see, Zarathustra's speech on the last man explains in historical terms his failure to awaken his auditors to the possibility of overcoming man. Zarathustra's explanation is, broadly speaking, *historical*, because it attributes his failure to the fact that his auditors *have become* persons of a certain sort (persons who closely resemble the last man). The speech on the last man concerns the asceticism of modern social practices. Zarathustra falters, it implies, because human life has become a repressed and diminished affair under the sway of these practices. In Part 2, Zarathustra qualifies this explanation by allowing that he himself is partly to blame for his inability to reach his auditors (see Chapter 4). Here, his account is again historical, for it attributes his perlocutionary failure to the fact that he has *become* a person of a certain sort (a person who is self-alienated).

Perlocutionary failure need not be explained historically. An alternative account, suggested by Paul de Man, is that failure of this sort is due to the constitutive limits of human knowledge. By endorsing an epistemological explanation of perlocutionary failure, de Man implies that historical explanations are beside the point. More exactly, he suggests that ineluctable ignorance spells the miscarriage of speech acts intended to move others, regardless of what human beings have become and regardless of the changes that would alter what they have become. De Man's analysis of perlocution merits attention for two reasons. The first is that it purports to draw on insights derived from Nietzsche's own writings. The second and, for my purposes, the more important, is that it forms the basis of de Man's view of Nietzsche's skepticism about modernism. Nietzsche's thought is marked by an ambivalent tension between his sympathetic sense that Dionysian, modernist aspirations can be fulfilled and his doubt that they are viable; or, again, between his belief that new-values creation is possible and his skeptical worry that it is not. De Man's treatment of Nietzsche resolves this tension in favor of Nietzsche's skepticism. He suggests that Nietzsche's thought comes to rest in a tensionless, final phase of development in which Nietzsche no longer questions the authority of his skepticism.

In the next section of this chapter, I dispute de Man's view of Nietzsche. Digressing from my interpretation of "Zarathustra's Prologue," I reconstruct the central argument of de Man's essay "Rhetoric of Persuasion,"[80] emphasizing its implications for the explanation of perlocutionary failure. Subsequently, I submit that this argument exemplifies the antipathy to Dionysus and to Dionysian modernism that generally characterizes de Man's thought. I conclude my analysis of de Man's treatment of Nietzsche by sketching and then criticizing what I infer to be his reading of *Zarathustra*—a reading that attributes a decided authority to a skeptical, ironical interpretation of Zarathustra's descent.

An Excursus: Nietzsche and de Man

Paul de Man's "Rhetoric of Persuasion" is a reading of two passages belonging to Nietzsche's posthumous notes. One of these passages (*The Will to Power*, no. 516) concerns constative speech. In it, Nietzsche skeptically suggests that the belief that speech states facts may be due to the deceptive workings of rhetorical operations escaping conscious control.[81] (Here, Nietzsche's remarks recall Descartes's skeptical suggestion that belief in the existence of an external world is due to the deceptive machinations of an evil genius.) He implies that this belief could be the effect of linguistic acts that, though they appear to report facts, serve only to postulate or posit (*setzen*) the existence of facts.[82]

In a second posthumous passage (*Will to Power*, no. 477), Nietzsche issues a second skeptical conjecture, namely, that in asserting that there exist subjects who think we rely on the fiction of the "the deed" as well as that of "the doer."[83] Taken in tandem, the two passages analyzed by de Man prompt the following line of argument:

> The first passage (section 516) . . . showed that constative language is in fact performative, but the second passage (section 477) asserts that the possibility for language to perform is just as fictional as the possibility for language to assert. Since the analysis has been carried out on passages representative of Nietzsche's deconstructive procedure at its most advanced stage, it would follow that, in Nietzsche, the critique of metaphysics can be described as the deconstruction of the illusion that the language of truth (*episteme*) could be replaced by a language of persuasion (*doxa*). . . . the target which one long since assumed to have been eliminated has merely been displaced. The *episteme* has hardly been restored intact to its former glory, but it has not been definitively eliminated either. The difference between performative and constative language (which Nietzsche anticipates) is undecidable. The deconstruction leading from one model to the other is irreversible but it always remains suspended, regardless of how often it is repeated.[84]

It is important to note that de Man's primary paradigm of performative speech is not the illocutionary act that has consequential effects due to social convention, but the persuasive, perlocutionary act that has consequential effects *not* due to social convention, (hence the title, "Rhetoric of Persuasion").[85] In de Man's view, Nietzsche's "first passage" proposes that the (false) belief that speech reports facts is a rhetoric induced, perlocutionary speech effect. As he interprets it, this passage gives us reason to doubt that apparently constative speech is truly constative. Nietzsche's "second passage" complicates matters by giving us reason to doubt that speech "acts" or "performs" in any way whatsoever. Together, the two passages suggest that one can never *know* that apparently constative speech is constative or that apparently performative speech is performing. Thus, one cannot know that apparently constative speech is constative *and not performative*, or that apparently performative speech is performative *and not constative*. In other words, one cannot tell one of these forms of speech from the other. In de Man's jargon, the difference between constative and performative speech is epistemically "undecidable."

De Man's argument bears significantly on the interpretation of Zarathustra's perlocutionary enterprise. De Man himself suggests as much when in "Rhetoric of Persuasion" he refers to Nietzsche's protagonist. Describing Zarathustra as "that irrepressible orator," he conjectures that Nietzsche earned the right to create a character who exploits the perlocutionary power of rhetoric by "the . . . labor of deconstruction that makes up the bulk of his [Nietzsche's] more analytical writings."[86] Were this conjecture true, de Man suggests, it would "allow for the reassuring conviction that it is legitimate to do just about anything with words, as long as we know that a rigorous mind, fully aware of the misleading power of tropes, pulls the strings."[87] But if "it turns out that this same mind does not even know whether it is doing or not doing something, then there are considerable grounds for suspicion that it does not know *what* it is doing."[88]

De Man's belief that no one knows *whether* her speech is doing or not doing something rests on the premise that the difference between performative and constative speech is undecidable. His "grounds" for suspecting that no one knows *what* her speech is doing appear to presuppose that "doing something" is the perlocutionary act of producing an effect *by saying something*: if one does not know *whether* she is producing or not producing any effect at all by saying something, then it is doubtful that one could know *what* sort of effect she is producing by saying words of "this" or "that" sort. More exactly, it is doubtful that one could possess the instrumental knowledge—for instance, that speech acts of a certain sort, due to their power to mislead, produce effects of a certain sort—that de Man invokes as the standard of "legitimate" persuasive speech. In de Man's view, one can "pull the strings" of persuasive speech, and thereby produce the perlocutionary effects one aims to produce, *only if* one possesses such knowledge—or so his use of the figure of a "fully aware" and "rigorous" mind seems to intimate. Absent such knowledge, one will fail in one's manipulative, "string pulling" efforts to fulfill one's perlocutionary intentions.[89] Because de Man doubts that the instrumental knowledge (of speech acts and effects) pertinent here can belong to any mind, he suggests that perlocutionary failure of the kind Zarathustra exemplifies is the ineluctable result of an ineluctable human ignorance.

De Man derives the assertion that persons with perlocutionary intentions do not know what they are doing from the premise, $P2$, that they do not know that (or whether) they are doing anything. He derives this premise from the prior assumption, $P1$, that the difference between constative and performative language is undecidable. In de Man's view, $P1$ expresses Nietzsche's "final insight . . . that . . . 'rhetoric' is precisely the gap [between rhetoric as trope and rhetoric as persuasion] that becomes apparent in the pedagogical and philosophical history of the term."[90] Putting the same point somewhat differently, he writes that "the aporia between performative and constative language is *merely a version* of the aporia between trope and persuasion" (emphasis mine).[91] For de Man, $P1$ states a general claim concerning the nature of rhetoric. By presenting that claim as Nietzsche's concluding or "final" insight, he implies that Nietzsche's thinking, in the last phase of its development, acknowledged a truth that de Man himself adduces in one of its versions as the first, foundational premise of his own argument.

De Man's argument in "Rhetoric of Persuasion" begins, he believes, where Nietzsche's thinking ends. Proceeding from a version of the view that rhetoric is aporetical, de Man suggests that, due to the inevasible limits of human knowledge, attempts to move auditors by means of persuasive speech should never be expected to succeed. De Man's argument bears on the concerns of this chapter because it purports to locate in Nietzsche's writings the basis for an ahistorical explanation of the kind of perlocutionary failure that is depicted in "Zarathustra's Prologue." If such failure is the inevitable function of an ignorance to which human beings are constitutively and thus always subject, then, despite Zarathustra's hopes to the contrary, it is not an historical effect (not an effect of what human beings have become) or susceptible to historical transcendence (not suitable to being remedied by altering what human beings have become).

For various reasons, de Man's argument is not conclusive. As at least one critic has noticed, it depends on a questionable interpretation of Nietzsche's views regarding the relationship between language and action.[92] Moreover, it rests on the doubtful presupposition that the performative-constative distinction, though epistemically undecidable in any given instance, is otherwise tenable (a presupposition that both Austin and Searle reject).[93] It is also worrisome that de Man's argument assumes an unanalyzed and perhaps too stringent a notion of knowledge (*episteme*). Still, the argument merits attention, for regardless of whether it is sound or unsound, it paints a plausible and even tempting *picture* of Nietzsche's mature thought and of his skepticism vis-à-vis Dionysian modernism—a picture that we ought to reject.

Through much of his career, de Man persisted in attacking the "aesthetic ideology" characteristic of high romanticism. In particular, he repeatedly criticized the belief that language (especially poetic language) can dissolve the rift that separates words and things; mind and nature; human intentions and historical circumstance.[94] De Man's suggestion that all must fail in their efforts to use speech to move others is of a piece with his more general view that the realities of nature and history are destined to frustrate the linguistically mediated demands of the human will.[95]

Applied to *Zarathustra*, de Man's critique of aesthetic ideology implies that Zarathustra would be foolish to believe that he could interrupt modernity and turn the course of history by persuading men to "hear with their eyes." From the perspective of this critique, and from the standpoint of Nietzsche's "final" insight and "most advanced" deconstructive procedure[96] as de Man construes it, the Pauline reading of Zarathustra's descent, in casting an ironic light on the optimism with which Zarathustra descends to man, correctly suggests that Zarathustra's perlocutionary failure is inevitable: from a Pauline point of view, "man" and Dionysus necessarily exclude one another. Taking de Man's view, we should have to say that that reading articulates the implications of Nietzsche's most sophisticated thinking. In general, de Man endorses the ironic and deconstructive elements in Nietzsche's writing that contradict Zarathustra's Dionysianism. And despite his suggestion elsewhere that one should hesitate to interpret the "history" of Nietzsche's work as a movement from blindness to insight, his talk of "final" and "advanced" developments invites just such an interpretation.[97] For de Man, the conclusion and culmination of Nietzsche's intellectual evolution is his repudiation of Dionysus.

To be sure, de Man's impulse to oppose the ironic, deconstructivist Nietzsche to Nietzsche the philosopher of Dionysus pertains not only to his reading of *Zarathustra*, but also to his interpretation of *Genealogy* and *The Birth of Tragedy*—books that, notwithstanding the differences between them, could readily be called "Dionysian."[98] In "Rhetoric of Persuasion," de Man refers explicitly to the first of these books and, specifically, to a passage in which Nietzsche, in the course of discussing the Dionysus-related concepts of doing, effecting, and becoming (Dionysus-related because they apply to the flux and instability that essentially characterize the action of Dionysian "going-under"), writes that "the deed is everything." In opposition to this remark, de Man privileges the post-humously published claim that "the deed as well as the doer are fictions," argu-ing that

> one cannot expect the same strategy with regard to valorization in a book like
> the *Genealogy* explicitly designated as a pamphlet and destined to condemn
> and convince, as in the more speculative treatises that Nietzsche's later book (or
> books) were . . . destined to be. On a specific question (such as the ontological
> authority of acts) the speculative statements should be given at least equal
> consideration next to the emphatic, persuasive ones.[99]

Reminiscent of Heidegger's reading of Nietzsche, de Man suggests here, how-ever reservedly, that Nietzsche's deepest insights can be found in notes that an-ticipate the speculative magnum opus he was planning near the end of his philosophical career. In the development of Nietzsche's thought, de Man sug-gests, Nietzsche the deconstructivist epistemologist ultimately supersedes Nietz-sche the pamphleteer, orator (like Zarathustra), and philosopher of Dionysus.[100]

In "Literary History and Literary Modernity," de Man prefigures the critique of "the deed" evident in "Rhetoric of Persuasion."[101] Like the later essay, this piece foregrounds elements of Nietzsche's thinking that contradict the spirit of Zarathustra's modernism.[102] Still, neither essay is as explicit as "Genesis and Ge-nealogy" in identifying the anti-Dionysian motifs implicit in Nietzsche's pub-lished works. In "Genesis and Genealogy," de Man argues that *The Birth of Tragedy*, notwithstanding its pathos and exaltation, ironically disputes and "de-constructs" the Dionysian authority that it otherwise invokes.[103] Here again, then, he locates an anti-Dionysian element in Nietzsche's writing, but without revealing the motivation that underlies his strategy of reading. What is it that moves de Man not only to read Nietzsche against Nietzsche, but even to suggest that the endpoint of Nietzsche's thinking is an ironic spurning of his prior at-tachments to Dionysus? And why, extending the same line of questioning, does he ever so reticently invite us to condemn precisely those among Nietzsche's books that, he says, were themselves designed to condemn?

An answer to these questions is available, I think, in de Man's "Wordsworth and Hölderlin," which, though it neither mentions nor seems explicitly to be about Nietzsche's Dionysus, invokes him rhetorically. This essay appeared before the articles on Nietzsche I have mentioned, first in German (1966) and later in English translation (1984).[104] Of particular interest is the language de Man uses to discuss some passages in *The Prelude* in which Wordsworth considers the dan-ger posed by radical revolutionaries to the cloister of the Grande Chartreuse. The setting is a 1790 journey through France, during which Wordsworth and his companion meet a group of delegates to the *états généraux*. After this meeting, the two travelers head toward the Simplon Pass, which they mistakenly bypass.

According to de Man, Wordsworth's treatment of the Chartreuse-Simplon sequence links the political passion of revolutionaries to the experience of erroneously bypassing one's goal:

> When the travelers unsuspectingly set to climbing a mountain that already lies beyond their goal, or when the insurgents head towards destroying the cloister of the Grande Chartreuse with the same naive enthusiasm, there is no doubt that they are driven by the same, almost divine wish and stand under the influence of the poetic faculty. This gives them the power to direct themselves decisively toward the future. But it is just as certain that in this same instant, this faculty is conscious of neither its power nor its limits [*Grenzen*], and that it errs through excess [*Masslosigkeit*].[105]

When de Man speaks here of "limits" and of error brought about by "excess," he recalls and anticipates similar passages (in the same essay) in which he speaks of the insurgents' "lack of measure" (*Masslosigkeit*), their "intoxication with the act" (*der Trunkenheit der Tat*), their "loss of self in the intoxication of the instant" (*des Selbstverlustes in der Trunkenheit des Augenblicks*), and their "Titanism" (*der Titanismus*), the last of which he relates to "an excess issuing from a fullness which causes us to transgress our own limits" (*eines Übermasses, das aus einer Fülle hervorgeht, die uns die eigenen Grenzen überschreiten lässt*).[106] For my purposes, each of these passages is significant, because they echo the rhetoric and conceptual framework of *The Birth of Tragedy* in characterizing the revolutionary and poetic wills (wills that are in essence the same, in de Man's view) for which "the movement of our [human] wishes . . . correspond[s] to that of the age."[107] Indeed, we need only remember that Nietzsche explicitly contrasts Apollonian measure (*Maass*) and respect for limits (*Grenzen*) to Dionysian excess (*Uebermaass*) and intoxication (*Rausch*) to see that de Man, though he never refers to Dionysus in this essay, relies on Nietzsche's portrait of this god to describe "a . . . hubris of the will" that aspires to dictate the course of human events. (Although Nietzsche uses *Rausch* and not *Trunkenheit*, he clearly aims to associate the former term with the *drink-inspired* drunkenness that the latter term connotes. Consider, for example, his claim that Dionysian intoxication can result from the influence of a "narcotic draught" [*des narkotischen Getränkes*].) In suggesting that this hubris bespeaks a titanic feeling of fullness, de Man also echoes Nietzsche's description of Dionysian creativity as "titanic" (*titanische*) and as proceeding from the "distress of fullness" (*der Noth der Fülle*).[108]

In "Wordsworth and Hölderlin," de Man's Nietzschean rhetoric suggests that

he interprets Dionysus as a figure for the human will's striving to find fulfillment in history ("the movement . . . of the age"). This striving, he thinks, since
it always involves an attempt to exceed human limitations, cannot but fail: error, in de Man's view, is inevitable. The finite subject can never bridge the rift
separating her will from the facticity of historical circumstance. Her romantic
dream of a perfect correspondence between what she intends and what history
becomes must remain forever out of reach. De Man repudiates Dionysus, because, as the language of "Wordsworth and Hölderlin" so strongly intimates, he
identifies Dionysus with the blind will to do what cannot be done.

De Man's antipathy to Dionysus pertains to both Nietzsche's early and late
writings, for despite Nietzsche's rejection of Schopenhauer's dualism, and despite his rejection of the belief that Dionysian renewal will issue from a dialectic evident in contemporary culture, he persistently invokes Dionysus as a figure
for his attempt to conceptualize and explain the possibility of a humanly (if not
altogether autonomously) willed interruption of European modernity. For de
Man, the attempt to explain this possibility is an absurd and futile enterprise.
Thus, from his perspective, it makes perfect sense to privilege the deconstructive and ironic elements of Nietzsche's thought in contradistinction to the Dionysian elements. Indeed, if one starts from the assumption that Dionysus signifies error, then, like de Man, one will reasonably infer that the deconstruction
of Dionysian thinking marks a genuine "advance" in the direction of those speculative and "final insights" that compel us to condemn as mere "pamphlets" the
writings that embody the philosophy of Dionysus.

We are now in a position to begin to see just where Nietzsche's point of view
differs from de Man's and why we should reject de Man's suggestion that his argument begins where Nietzsche's thinking ends. In this context, I shall find it
useful to develop my earlier conjecture that, viewed from de Man's perspective,
the implications of Nietzsche's most sophisticated and "advanced" thinking are
evident in the ironic reading of Zarathustra's descent prompted by Nietzsche's
parody of St. Paul. Central to my argument is de Man's undeveloped suggestion
that *Zarathustra* should be read as an ironic allegory.[109] In what follows, I pursue this suggestion by showing that an interpretation of *Zarathustra* as an ironic
allegory accords with an ironic appraisal of Zarathustra's descent and, in fact,
with the more general claim that the plot structure of *Zarathustra* is defined by
an antithesis of intention and repetition. I also argue that the description of
Zarathustra as an ironic allegory implies that *Zarathustra* expresses an ironic repudiation of Zarathustra's Dionysianism corresponding to what de Man believes is the "final" stage in the development of Nietzsche's thought.

In examining the concept of an ironic allegory, we should bear in mind that de Man decries metaphor for pretending to eliminate the rift separating mind and language from nature and historical circumstance but that he privileges allegory, irony, and metonymy for compelling us to acknowledge that rift. Keeping these valorizing commitments in mind, we can reinterpret the irony at work in the opening section of *Zarathustra* with reference to the distinction between metaphor and metonymy. We can also see why the narrative of *Zarathustra*, if we assume that it is structured by an antithesis of intention and repetition, can be said to sustain the metonymically-based irony of the opening section through the extended elaboration of an ironic allegory.

Following de Man, let us say that a metaphor is "an exchange or substitution of properties" based on resemblance that relies on "resemblance as a way to disguise differences," and that a metonymy is a change of name based on "contingent association."[110] The metaphor "Juliet is the sun" attributes properties characteristic of the sun to Juliet, thereby exchanging those properties for the properties that otherwise belong to Juliet. The metonymy "I have read all of Shakespeare" gives the works of Shakespeare the name of someone I associate with them: to wit, their author. The opening section of *Zarathustra*, due to the way it parodies Neoplatonism, can be seen to represent Zarathustra's descent as resembling metaphor; that is, as representing that descent as effecting a metaphorical "exchange of properties." This same section's parodying of Paul's hymn can be seen to represent Zarathustra's descent as resembling a name that metonymically migrates from one object to another; that is, as representing that descent as Zarathustra's migration from one object to another.

By parodying Neoplatonism, Nietzsche represents Zarathustra as a Dionysian demiurge who aspires to bear the properties of Dionysus to man ("Zarathustra wants to become man again") in order to exchange those properties for the (Christian-Platonic) properties that man otherwise possesses. Resemblance, we know, is the motivating basis for this property exchange, since Zarathustra's clearly stated goal is to re-create man in the image of Dionysus ("Bless the cup that wants to overflow . . . and carry everywhere the reflection [*Abglanz*] of your delight"). Read as a parody of Neoplatonism, Zarathustra's descent is the *vehicle* of an extended metaphor-like action that conveys to the *tenor*, man, the properties of Dionysus.[111]

By parodying Paul, Nietzsche portrays Zarathustra as a Dionysian divinity, but suggests too that Zarathustra divests himself of his divinity when he descends to man. Considered from a Pauline perspective, Zarathustra detaches himself from Dionysus and attaches himself to man (Zarathustra becomes man again). Migrating from one object (Dionysus) to a second object (man) that he associates with the first, he conveys to the second object *none* of the properties of the first. In this perspective, Zarathustra does not behave as the vehicle of a metaphor-like action that re-creates man in the image of Dionysus. Rather he behaves as a name that migrates from one object to another without representing the second object as resembling the first (when I say "I have read all of Shakespeare," I detach the name "Shakespeare" from its literal referent, attach it to the works of Shakespeare, but do not represent those works as resembling Shakespeare). By parodying Paul, Nietzsche depicts Zarathustra's descent as a metonymy-like renaming of man that does nothing to heal the rift between Dionysus and man. Man, Nietzsche's parody suggests, will persist at being man.[112]

If we read Zarathustra's descent as a parody of Neoplatonism, then we read it as a metaphor. If we read it as a parody of Paul, then we read it as a metonymy. The precise meaning of Zarathustra's descent is hermeneutically ambiguous. Reinterpreting the irony of Zarathustra's first speech, we may now say that irony is a function of Zarathustra's blindness to the possibility of viewing his descent as having not the character of a metaphor but that of a metonymy.

De Man conceptualizes irony as a synchronic structure that "knows neither memory nor prefigurative duration."[113] This notion captures the irony in Zarathustra's opening speech, which invites the optimistic interpretation that Zarathustra favors, even as at the same time it invites the pessimistic interpretation to which he is blind (Nietzsche simultaneously parodies Neoplatonism and Paul's hymn when he has Zarathustra say, "Behold, this cup wants to become empty again, and Zarathustra wants to become man again"). The narrative statement that concludes the prologue's first section, "Thus began Zarathustra's going-under (*Also begann Zarathustras Untergang*)," reinforces the irony in Zarathustra's speech and marks a transition in the text from irony to allegory.

According to de Man, allegory achieves through diachronic narration what irony achieves synchronically: "allegory appears as a successive mode capable of engendering duration as the illusion of a continuity that it knows to be illusionary. Yet the two modes (allegory and irony), for all their profound distinctions in mood and structure, are the two faces of the same fundamental experience of time."[114] The "experience of time" to which de Man alludes is, essentially, the experience of the divide, or rift, separating mind and language from nature and historical facticity. Allegory distinguishes itself from irony by figuring the demystification (the critical debunking) of efforts to eradicate this divide, not as concurrent with these efforts, but as subsequent to them. Allegory represents "de-mystification as a temporal sequence . . . in which the conditions of error and of wisdom have become successive."[115]

Proceeding from de Man's concept of allegory, we may interpret the assertion

"Thus began Zarathustra's going-under" as allegorical. The use of "began" (*begann*) is critical here, for it temporalizes the demise (*Untergang*) and demystification of Zarathustra's tacit suggestion that his descent can be likened to a linguistic action (a metaphor) that eradicates the divide separating a word (a metaphoric vehicle) bearing the attributes of Dionysus from a historically evolved humanity (Christian-Platonic man). In other words, the use of "began" suggests that the demystification of Zarathustra's self-understanding, though it has "thus" (*Also*) begun, will be truly accomplished only in the future.[116] Following de Man, we can call this narrative designation of a beginning "allegorical" because it signals the postponement of the demystification of Zarathustra's self-understanding.

Zarathustra is not simply an allegory, de Man suggests, but an ironic allegory. De Man defines ironic allegory as a form of narrative that narrates sequentially the reiteration of one and the same trope: namely, irony. An ironic allegory is an allegory *of* irony, he believes, for it is an allegory that takes the reiteration of irony as its principal theme and subject matter.[117] De Man's understanding of ironic allegory may at first seem wanting, because it fails explicitly to explain how any allegory, let alone an allegory *of* irony, can be ironic in its own right. The difficulty disappears, however, if we attribute to de Man the view that every allegory of irony is ironically allegorical. We may plausibly attribute this view to him, for it is invited by the assumption that an allegory of irony is, *by definition*, a narrative marked by the reiteration of irony. This assumption suggests that the event of demystification that every allegory of irony, qua allegory, postpones has, ironically, always already been effected through one or another use of irony. It suggests, in other words, that all allegories of irony are, as allegories, ironic.[118]

In the first section of *Zarathustra*, the allegorical prefiguration of Zarathustra's demystification, precisely because it marks a transition from irony to allegory, is ironic. As we have seen, the narrative conclusion of this section ("Thus began Zarathustra's going-under") postpones the demystification of Zarathustra's self-understanding, but only *after* Zarathustra's self-understanding has been parodically and ironically demystified (by Nietzsche's parody of Paul). *Zarathustra* can be read as an ironic allegory because the irony that marks its opening section has always already effected the demystification its allegory defers. This allegory, in its turn, can be read as an allegory of irony, for one of its principal themes is the reiteration of irony.

Zarathustra narrates this reiteration, precisely to the extent that it is structured by an antithesis of intention and repetition. As we have seen, the plot of the book's narrative repeatedly confronts Zarathustra's personal and poetic intentions with representations of repetition (e.g., the saint and the townspeople) that *echo* the demystifying irony created by Nietzsche's parody of Paul. *Zara-*

thustra is an allegory of irony, because its narrative, in reiteratively confronting Zarathustra with representations of repetition, recapitulates as a feature of its plot the opening section's ironic juxtaposition of metonymic and metaphoric interpretations of Zarathustra's descent (e.g., where Zarathustra views himself as the metaphoric vehicle of a [Dionysian] gift, the saint, expressing his sense of man's recalcitrant facticity, sees him as a metonymic migrant from a buoyant [Dionysian] sea to a human shore that, far from resembling that sea, offers Zarathustra nothing but resistance; and where Zarathustra presumes that his first speech will communicate a transformative vision of Dionysian possibility, the townspeople interpret his words as a metonymic renaming of the tightrope walker). Read as an ironic allegory of irony, *Zarathustra*'s initial, recurrent, and final teaching is an ironically and metonymically expressed skepticism regarding the prospect of ever fulfilling Zarathustra's poetic, metaphoric, intention. In fine, to read *Zarathustra* as de Man reads it is to claim a decided authority for an ironic interpretation of Zarathustra's descent.[119]

We have seen that de Man, in "Rhetoric of Persuasion," rejects his conjecture that Nietzsche's "considerable labor of deconstruction" justified his creation of that "irrepressible orator," Zarathustra. While this labor "*seems to end* in a reassertion of the active performative function of language," Nietzsche's "*final* insight" into the nature of rhetoric, by entailing that even a rigorous mind will not know what it is doing by deploying putatively persuasive speech, undermines the legitimacy of such speech once and for all.[120] Put succinctly, de Man maintains that Nietzsche's thinking concludes with a deconstructionist point about rhetoric, not, as he initially suggests, with the rehabilitation of persuasion.[121] De Man holds that because Nietzsche recognized that philosophical thought cannot transcend the perspective of deconstruction he remained skeptical, ultimately, of the pretensions of persuasive speech. De Man also implies that in *Zarathustra*, no less than in Nietzsche's most sophisticated and "advanced" deconstructive writings, Nietzsche skeptically disowns the rhetorically compelling Dionysianism he ascribes to Zarathustra.[122]

De Man's proposed reading of *Zarathustra* misrepresents Nietzsche's philosophical thinking. To the extent that *Zarathustra*'s structure is defined by an antithesis of intention and repetition, it possesses features characteristic of an ironic allegory. Still, *Zarathustra* is *not* an ironic allegory. Rather, as I argue throughout this book, it is best understood as an instance of a speculative (conjectural) Dionysian thinking that proceeds by way of a ruthless and ironic skepticism regarding its ambition to explain and render intelligible the modernist possibility of creating new values. Since, for Nietzsche, explaining this possibility is tantamount to explaining how human beings can go-under to Dionysus and overcome themselves, *Zarathustra* can be described as Nietzsche's attempt to account for the possibility of a specifically Dionysian modernism.

As we have seen, Nietzsche questions the viability of Zarathustra's Dionysianism through the persistent (reiterated) use of irony, for he never *assumes* that the rift separating Dionysus and man can be dissolved. But refusing this assumption is not equivalent to claiming a decided authority for an ironic reading of Zarathustra's descent. Although Nietzsche is always skeptical of Zarathustra's Dionysian pretensions, he never ceases to question his skepticism and to think speculatively beyond it. As a philosopher of Dionysus, he challenges the authority of his irony and skepticism no less than, as an ironist and a skeptic, he challenges the authority of his own Dionysian thinking. The essence of Nietzsche's rigor is his relentless, if often stressful practice of thinking against himself.[123]

Pace de Man, I have been arguing that Nietzsche's philosophical thought, far from coming to rest in a skeptical and ironical repudiation of Dionysus, remains always and insistently loyal to the task of Dionysian speculation. In *Zarathustra*, Nietzsche sets about this task by attempting to develop a vocabulary in light of which he can explain the possibility of creating new values. Explaining this possibility, we have seen, involves showing how values can originate within the world of time and appearances. Since neither the Platonist nor the Christian believes that new values can be created from within that world, Nietzsche is compelled to reinterpet it in terms of a post-Christian-Platonic philosophical vocabulary and conceptual apparatus. As I have previously argued, the notions of the overman, the last man, the higher man, the earth, the body, the passions, the will to power, the eternal recurrence, and so forth belong to this conceptual apparatus. Together, they provide a philosophical framework for Nietzsche's project. In elaborating these notions Nietzsche advances the enterprise of speculative, Dionysian thinking, for to account for the possibility of new-values creation is to account for the possibility of Dionysian self-overcoming. Nietzsche persists in this enterprise after he completes *Zarathustra*, even in the period that de Man associates with his "final insight."[124]

Though I have been insisting that, throughout *Zarathustra*, Nietzsche pits Dionysian speculation against his own irony and skepticism, I am not claiming that he wants dogmatically to insist on the efficacy of persuasive speech. De Man can easily refute the conjecture that Nietzsche's "considerable labor of deconstruction" justifies the creation of Zarathustra, because this conjecture is a straw man. De Man knows, moreover, that Nietzsche himself never embraces this conjecture. But this is not, as de Man suggests, because he endorses a "final insight" leading him to abandon the possibility of rehabilitating persuasion;

rather it is because Nietzsche views the rehabilitation of persuasion as part of a speculative project that acknowledges the implications of his own skeptical (deconstructivist) insights without treating them as conclusive. Nietzsche acknowledges these implications at the start of *Zarathustra* by depicting Zarathustra's descent as a metonymy-like action that will fail, inevitably, to persuade men to envision Dionysus. Still, as *Zarathustra* unfolds, Nietzsche persists in looking beyond this depiction (and beyond the repesentations of repetition that echo it) to the possible fulfillment of his protagonist's poetic and personal intentions. Thinking against his own skepticism, he hopes to show how Zarathustra could come eventually to move other individuals to "hear" and to "see" the possibility of going-under to Dionysian chaos.

Zarathustra's Speech on the Last Man

I divide my discussion of Zarathustra's speech on the last man into three parts. First, I investigate the self-understanding of the last man. Second, I interpret Zarathustra's speech on the last man as Zarathustra's genealogical explanation of his own perlocutionary failure. As I have already suggested, this explanation merits comparison with de Man's ahistorical and epistemological approach to the problem of perlocutionary failure. Finally, I consider the figure of the last man in the perspective of Nietzsche's understanding of nihilism.

The last man claims to know "everything that has ever happened" and (in the case of his most acute representatives) to have liberated himself completely from the delusions of the past.[125] As Zarathustra characterizes him, he purports to possess an error-free and perfect knowledge of all that is and has been. This knowledge, he believes, distinguishes him from his predecessors. Reminiscent of the Hegelians whom Nietzsche derides in the second of his *Untimely Meditations*, the last man believes that all of human history has become "transparent and comprehensible" in his person. Thus, he ascribes to himself a dispassionate and objective understanding of human affairs and possibilities. Like the Socratic, theoretic man of *The Birth of Tragedy*, he takes rationally grounded knowledge to be the measure of the real; like Hegelian man, he attributes his possession of that knowledge to historical progress.[126]

The knowledge of the last man is first and foremost instrumental knowledge. His claim "Wir haben das Glück erfunden," which Kaufmann translates as "We have invented happiness," could just as easily have been translated "We have discovered happiness."[127] By putting the semantically ambiguous *erfunden* into the mouth of the last man, Nietzsche implies that what the last man discovers (*erfindet*) and knows is what he invents (*erfindet*). He implies, in fact, that the last man's knowledge is primarily a knowledge of the techniques and practices he has invented to make himself happy (e.g., avoiding regions where it is hard to live, avoiding conflict with others, using a bit of poison to produce agreeable dreams, etc.). Nietzsche develops this point by inviting us to regard the last man as a utilitarian who knows what means he requires to realize his dream of happiness.[128] The last man, we have seen, puts the invention of these means in the past ("We *have invented* happiness") and thus suggests that his dream of happiness, no less than his dream of perfect knowledge, has in his own person found historical fulfillment. Wanting nothing in his world to be different than it is ("Everybody wants the same, everybody is the same: whoever feels different goes voluntarily into a madhouse"), the last man views the happiness he has invented as the *summum bonum* of human existence. Dwelling blissfully in the here and now of complacent satisfaction, he is the absolute antithesis of a Faustian spirit.[129]

Twice in his speech on the last man, Zarathustra ties the last man's happiness to his blinking; twice, in fact, Zarathustra utters the following sentence: "'We have invented happiness,' say the last men, and they blink." Zarathustra's references to the last man's blinking are altogether in keeping with his ongoing preoccupation with the theme of "seeing" (recall his recurrent use of *Seht* and his reference to "hearing eyes"). The implication of these references is, presumably, that the last man is a figuratively "blind" man who repeatedly "closes his eyes" to a dimension of human possibility that Zarathustra would have men see. By using an involuntary physical phenomenon to figure the last man's blindness, Zarathustra likens it to forms of behavior whose meanings the persons engaged in those behaviors need not recognize.[130] Resembling an hysterical symptom, the last man's blinking appears in tandem with an expressed self-understanding (expressed, for example, in the last man's claim to have "invented happiness") that offers no insight into the significance of his blinking. If we would find meaning in the last man's blinking and blindness, then we must look beyond his self-understanding to discover that meaning, just as the psychoanalyst must look beyond the self-understanding of his or her patient to discover the significance of some involuntary, neurotic tic.

Genealogy is Nietzsche's method of "looking beyond" an individual's (or a culture's) self-understanding in order to trace the genesis of that individuals' beliefs, practices, and blindnesses. Thus, it is a mode of historical inquiry that can *expand* one's self-understanding. Genealogy emphasizes the contingent character of the shapes and forms that human life typically assumes. By highlighting the origins of these shapes and forms, the genealogist shows them to be dispensable and unnecessary features of the world we inhabit. By unmasking the contingency that the dogmatist (the person who denies that things could be otherwise) disguises, she illuminates possibilities of change and transformation.[131]

The speech on the last man hints at a genealogical explanation of the last man's blindness and of Zarathustra's perlocutionary failure. Because this explanation is genealogical, it suggests that such blindness and failure can be historically remedied by altering what human beings have historically but contingently become. In the former case, Zarathustra elucidates the meaning of the last man's blindness by identifying the origins of his blindness. In the latter case, he suggests an alternative to de Man's dogmatist view that perlocutionary failure stems from a disenabling ignorance to which human knowers are constitutively subject.

An exploration of the historical significance of the speech on the last man can begin by noting that *letzte Mensch*, which I translate as "last man," can also be translated as "ultimate man"[132]—a phrase that suggests that the man in question personifies human nature in its most extreme and developed form. It suggests, in other words, that the last man achieves in his person the utmost expression of man's "essence." For Nietzsche, as distinct from the Hegelians he describes in the *Untimely Meditations*, this "essence" is not a developing self-consciousness that progressively works its way to the "end of history." Rather it is embodied in the values of an ascetic ethic that has been produced by the Christian-Platonic interpretation of human existence. Nietzsche's last and ultimate man is the man who most fully realizes these values. He is, in short, the heyday and the utopia of a historically specific ethic of asceticism.

Zarathustra represents the last man's blindness and happiness as effects of asceticism. The last man's avoidance of hardship ("one has left the regions where it was hard to live") and conflict ("a fool whoever still stumbles over stones or human beings"); his use of drugs to ensure a quiet sleep ("A little poison now and then: that makes for agreeable dreams"); his resistance to exertion, including the stresses of entertainment ("one is careful lest the entertainment be too harrowing"); and his careful effort to eliminate indigestion ("One still quarrels, but one is soon reconciled—else it might spoil the digestion") collectively suggest a form of life ruled through and through by repression.[133] At each and every turn, the last man works to control, to contain, and, as Zarathustra suggests, to domesticate life.[134] His great distinction, of course, is that his effort succeeds. Christian asceticism finds its utopia in the last man because he has produced worldly means by which to satisfy the will to nothingness: his happiness, his heaven on earth, is a secular fulfillment of the priest's desire to destroy the body's passions.[135] Because the last man has obliterated his passions, he is blind to the possibility of experiencing passional chaos. Not knowing that he is blind, he attaches no significance to his blindness. Zarathustra, however, because he looks beyond the horizon of the last man's knowledge and self-understanding, sees his blindness as symptomatic of a repressive asceticism.

By explaining the last man's blindness as a product of asceticism, Zarathustra in effect explains his own perlocutionary failure. To be sure, Zarathustra tells his auditors that they can still experience the chaos that creation demands: "one must still have chaos in oneself to be able to give birth to a dancing star. I say unto you: you still have chaos in yourselves."[136] Yet, as the townspeople's expressed sense of affinity to the last man suggests ("Give us this last man. . . . Turn us into these last men"), he may be wrong. No less than the last man, the townspeople appear to have lost sight of the possibility of going-under to passional, Dionysian chaos. In view of their responses to Zarathustra's first and second speeches to them, it is evident that their blindness to this possibility is intractable. The townspeople, if they are not last men, seem to be immediate forebears of last men and indistinguishable from them. In other words, they themselves seem to be the products of an ascetic life that has banished from its midst the possibility of experiencing Dionysian chaos.[137] It would appear, then, that Zarathustra's inability to stir his auditors is an effect of repressive asceticism. Even if they wanted to, the townspeople could not be persuaded to "see" and to "hear" within their bodies the possibility of going-under to passional chaos, because their bodies' passions have been extirpated. Considered in the perspective of his speech on the last man, Zarathustra's perlocutionary failure to move his last-man-like auditors is a consequence of the impact that the forces of modern asceticism have had on them.

Zarathustra's interpretation of the last man's blindness and, implicitly, of the townspeople's explains his perlocutionary failure as an effect of the modern, secular history of the ascetic ideal. Because Zarathustra provides a historical, genealogical account of his failure, he can also look beyond it to the possibility of his perlocutionary success. In Zarathustra's view, it is conceivable that the possibility of experiencing passional chaos has not been banished from all human lives (perhaps not all humans have begun to resemble the last men), and, if it has, that it could be returned to some human lives in the future. (Zarathustra does not seriously entertain the thought that this possibility could be banished from all human lives until he hears the soothsayer speak in Part 2.) Even if, due to the historically contingent practices of asceticism, all human lives have been rendered passionless, one can still imagine that a resurgence of the passions will again alter these lives in the future. (Perhaps Nietzsche imagines this when, in *Genealogy*, he envisions Zarathustra as the man who could redeem the world from "the curse that the hitherto reigning ideal has placed on it.")[138] In contrast to de Man, who sees perlocutionary failure as inevitable, Zarathustra suggests that he would fulfill his poetic, perlocutionary intentions were his auditors either persons whose passions had not been obliterated or persons whose passions had been obliterated but in whom, subsequently, the passions were reborn. By putting a historical explanation of perlocutionary failure into Zarathustra's mouth, Nietzsche challenges and thinks against the skepticism that both he and de Man bring to the appraisal of Zarathustra's Dionysian modernism.

Zarathustra's depiction of the last man crystallizes a vision of European modernity that dominates Nietzsche's later philosophy. According to Nietzsche, the most characteristic political ideologies of European modernity—liberalism, socialism, communism, feminism, and so on—are all ideologies of the last man. Despite the differences between them, Nietzsche sees each of these ideologies as but one more secular attempt to rationalize an ascetic way of life that is the contemporary legacy of Christianity. Some commentators have held that Nietzsche's depiction of the last man is meant first and foremost to be a critique of communism.[139] To be sure, there is some justification for this claim. Still, the simple identification of the last man and communist man misrepresents the *scope* of Nietzsche's reaction to modern politics.[140] The concept of the last man is a *limit-concept* of the ascetic tendencies that Nietzsche believes feminists, liberals, socialists, and communists equally perpetuate.[141] By repudiating *all* forms of modern politics, Nietzsche highlights his worry that secular asceticism, through the agency of multiple and often conflicting ideologies, will destroy the Dionysian preconditions of self-transformation.[142]

By claiming that the concept of the last man is a "limit-concept," I mean to suggest again that the last man is a figure for the secular fulfillment of the priest's will to nothingness. Where the last man prevails, the will to nothingness has reached its ultimate limit. Because the last man has extirpated his body's passions, he cannot see the possibilities of self-overcoming that Zarathustra, hoping to heal the rift between Dionysus and man, would persuade him to see. With the ability to experience passional chaos gone from his life, he finds contentment in the nothingness that has displaced his passions and harbors no wish to become something other than he is. Complacent to the end, the last man is oblivious to the advent of nihilism. Bearing witness to the death of God and to the self-destruction of the ascetic ideal, he remains indifferent to both events. Having *realized* the old goal (nothingness), he pursues it no longer, and so is not disturbed by the fact that his forebears' commitment to it has destroyed its viability. Neither, however, does he pursue a new goal. Wholly satisfied and without suffering, the last man has no desire to achieve something he has not achieved or to make himself into something he is not. He does not aspire to direct his will to a new goal, for one aspires to do that, Nietzsche insists, only if one suffers.[143] Because the last man does not suffer and want for a goal, it matters not to him that his will lacks a goal. Unheedful of the advent of nihilism, he knows nothing of the encroaching worry that an "aim is lacking."[144]

Because the last man is oblivious to the advent of nihilism, he can be distinguished from the "higher man" who appears in *Zarathustra*, Part 4. Cousin to the last man, the higher man is also a product of the ascetic tendencies that have driven from the modern world the possibility of experiencing passional chaos. Thus deprived of the Dionysian preconditions of self-transformation, the higher man is no more able to overcome himself than the last man. Still, he differs from the last man because he *suffers* from the ascetic impoverishment of life that the last man calls "happiness." The higher man's suffering prompts him to seek a new meaning for human existence in the face of the advent of nihilism. Precisely because he suffers, he cannot bear the experience of meaninglessness. Neither, however, can he effectively pursue the goal that Zarathustra avows, for this would require that he possess the ability to overcome himself. Now Zarathustra, we know, when he delivers his speech on the last man, assumes that not all men have become last or higher men. In other words, he assumes that the possibility of experiencing Dionysian chaos has yet to be banished from *all* men's lives ("I say unto you: you still have chaos in yourselves") and therefore that some of his contemporaries can still be brought to "see" and to "hear" the possibility of going-under and overcoming themselves. These contemporaries will suffer, Zarathustra supposes, though less from the impoverishment of life than from an excess of passional, Dionysian energies. As *sufferers*, they will want to interpret their lives in light of some goal. As *Dionysian* sufferers, they will be able to achieve the goal that Zarathustra would have them pursue.[145]

Zarathustra's assumption that he can awaken some of his contemporaries to the possibility of going-under is implicit in his belief that, by descending to man, he can heal the rift separating Dionysus from man. Nietzsche's parody of Paul, the saint's forebodings, and the townspeople's interpretation of Zarathustra's speech all question this assumption—albeit not with the same force and explicitness with which the drama enacted in section 6 of the prologue challenges it. The central message of this drama is that there are not now and will not be men in existence who are something other than last or higher men. Supposing that this message were true, then neither now nor in the future would there exist persons who could suffer the Dionysian chaos essential to self-overcoming— persons, that is, whom Zarathustra could persuade to "hear with their eyes." The "play" performed in section 6 brings the action of the prologue to a climax by depicting Zarathustra's persuasive, perlocutionary enterprise as doomed to fail. Shattering what remains of his naiveté, this drama forces Zarathustra to acknowledge that catastrophe may be a consequence of his descent. More to the point, it forces him to acknowledge that though God and the ascetic ideal are dead, overcoming man may never be possible.

The Tragedy of the Tightrope Walker and Beyond

The most notable and bizarre event of section 6, which makes "every mouth dumb and every eye rigid," is the jester's leap over the tightrope walker.[146] In order to construe this event and its consequences as I have proposed—that is, as a challenge to Zarathustra's understanding of his descent—it is necessary to interpret the tightrope walker and the jester as characters of essentially allegorical significance.[147] Zarathustra "sets the stage" for so interpreting these figures by deploying the image of the tightrope walker to represent the possibility of overcoming man in his second speech to the townspeople. The jester's remarks to Zarathustra later in the prologue and Zarathustra's speech "On the Flies of the Market Place" also support an allegorical reading of the jester and his bizarre action.

When the jester confronts Zarathustra he speaks in the name of "the good and the just"[148]—terms that, for Zarathustra, refer primarily to the last man.[149] Zarathustra makes this reference explicit in his speech "On Old and New Tablets," as does Nietzsche, in a passage alluding to that speech, when he comments that "Zarathustra calls the good now, 'the last men,' now the 'beginning of the end.'"[150] Considered in tandem, Zarathustra's speech and Nietzsche's comments suggest that Nietzsche intends to present the jester as a figure for the last man by having him speak in the name of the good and the just.

In "On the Flies of the Market Place" Zarathustra characterizes jesters as actors.[151] Moreover, his description there, of jesters and actors as "great men" whose "great noise" and "faith" (in themselves) excites and "overthrows" their flatterers, is nearly identical to Nietzsche's descriptions elsewhere of Wagner (whose art Nietzsche sees as the art of the actor) and, more broadly, of the higher men, among whose number Nietzsche counts Wagner.[152] The remarkable similarity of these descriptions suggests that the jester is a figure for the higher men in general and for Wagner in particular. Since the jester is also a figure for the last man, his allegorical significance is triply overdetermined.

Having established the basis for an allegorical reading of the drama of section 6, I should also like to argue that Nietzsche's depiction of that drama represents it as a tragedy. The play Zarathustra observes in section 6, precisely because it is a tragedy, challenges his optimistic interpretation of his descent. In what follows, I identify the features of the play that mark it as a tragedy, and then show how tragedy and allegory collaborate in this *mise en scène* to cast doubt on the viability of Zarathustra's modernist struggle to defeat the specter of nihilism.

Nietzsche shapes the drama of section 6 in accordance with his notion of the tragic reversal caused by the emotionally affecting annihilation (*Vernichtung*) of a tragic hero. First, he prompts us to see the tightrope walker as a tragic hero by picturing him in the image of Sophocles' Oedipus: "Forward lamefoot," the jester says to the tightrope walker. Second, he dramatizes a reversal resulting from the annihilation (the death) of the tightrope walker. Third and finally, Nietzsche ties the tightrope walker's demise to the arousal of fear and resignation, tragic emotions that he believes tragedies excite through the destruction of tragic heroes but overpower through the creation of metaphysical comfort.

Regarding the evocation of fear, the narrative description of the jester's leap—"the dreadful thing [*das Erschreckliche*] . . . which made every mouth dumb and every eye rigid [*starr*]"—recalls Nietzsche's earlier insight that the fear (*Schrecken*) caused by the annihilation of tragic heroes can petrify (*erstarren*) the spectator.[153] In section 6, apparently, Nietzsche applies this insight in his representation of the tightrope walker's demise as the fear-arousing and eye-petrifying annihilation of a tragic protagonist. As for the evocation of resignation, the tightrope walker's response to the jester's leap is critical. The tightrope walker falls, we know, because he cannot bear to see his rival win. Prompted by the sight of the victorious jester, he abdicates his will to reach the end of his rope with a self-denying gesture of renunciation: "This man . . . seeing his rival win, lost his head and the rope, tossed away his pole, and plunged into the depth."[154] By quitting his performance, the tightrope walker confronts his spectators with the temptation to renounce willing, thus threatening to call up in them feelings of resignation similar to his own.

We can further explain the tightrope walker's death if we allegorically interpret the tightrope walker as a figure for the possibility of overcoming man and the jester as a figure for the last and the higher men. When the tightrope walker sees (*seht*) his rival, the jester, win, he sees *man* win: what he sees before him, in other words, is *not* the possibility of overcoming man, but a personification of man in the modes of the last man and the higher man. Hoping that he has left the last man and the higher man (and, indeed, all forms of Christian-Platonic man) behind him in the past, the tightrope walker continues to find both sorts of men beside him in the present (personified by the jester when he is "but one step behind" the tightrope walker) and ahead of him in the future (personified by the jester after he has leaped ahead of the tightrope walker). More exactly, he finds that the last man and the higher man exhaust man's present and future fate. As neither the last nor the higher man can overcome himself, he discovers, in effect, that overcoming man is not possible in the present and will not be possible in the future.

Like Sophocles' Oedipus, the tightrope walker confronts in his future the destiny he sought to escape: for Oedipus, the destiny to kill his father and marry his mother; for the tightrope walker, the persistence of man. The jester's leap implies that man will persist forever and exclusively in the modes of the last man and the higher man. It suggests, therefore, that man will never overcome himself. The tightrope walker quits his performance because the jester's leap is a representation of repetition that signals both the endless recurrence of man and the eternal exile of Dionysus from man's world. As a tragic hero and "mask" of Dionysus, he is doomed to "go-under" (*Untergang*)[155] and to die a permanent death if the future harbors no men but last and higher men.

Let us now consider the tightrope walker's tragedy, treating the jester as a figure for Wagner. By leaping over the tightrope walker and displacing him, the jester recalls the discussion of "stage-stealing" in *The Birth of Tragedy*. In particular, he recalls the claim that Euripedes' aesthetic Socratism usurped the place of Dionysus in the Greek theater.[156] In Nietzsche's first book, Wagner appears as a savior who restores Dionysus to the stage from which Euripedes banished him. In section 6, he appears as a jester who thwarts the Dionysian tightrope walker. For the later Nietzsche, Wagner's art is a symptom, not of Dionysian renewal, but of the destruction of Dionysus by the will to nothingness.[157] Where the will to nothingness prevails, Nietzsche suggests, jesters like Wagner dominate the stage of public life. Rather than offer an alternative to the temptation to quit a life from which the possibility of experiencing Dionysian chaos seems forever to have been banished, they tend to foster and perpetuate the spirit of resignation. Since the "comfort" their entertainment provides is at best a brief blunting of that temptation, they are wanting as sources of Dionysian renewal. If, however, their art is the only art possible, as they claim it is, then such renewal is impossible anyway, and a Dionysian tragedy such as the tightrope walker's cannot but end on a note of Schopenhauerian pessimism.

In "Zarathustra's Prologue," Schopenhauer's theory of tragedy frames Nietzsche's engagement with the theme of nihilism. This is the central implication of Zarathustra's claim that "human existence is uncanny and still without meaning: a jester can become man's fatality [*Verhangnis*]."[158] For Schopenhauer, the tightrope walker's tragedy would properly conclude, *just as it does*, with the resignation and resignation-inspiring death of the tightrope walker. According to this finale, human existence cannot realize the meaning that Zarathustra wishes it to realize because overcoming man is not and will never be possible. With its Schopenhauerian ending, the clear message of the tightrope walker's tragedy is that, though God and the ascetic ideal are dead, Zarathustra must fail in his endeavor to assign a feasible purpose to lives that will persist, for as long as they last, "in vain." In the perspective of this ending, human existence is fated to an endless nihilism.

The tightrope walker's tragedy implicates Zarathustra because the destruction of the tightrope walker, read allegorically, is the destruction that the "Pauline" and metonymic interpretation of Zarathustra's descent predicts will befall Zarathustra. Like the *Untergang* that this interpretation anticipates, the *Untergang* of the tightrope walker indicates an irreversible annihilation of Dionysian hopes—not the self-overcoming that is the topic of Zarathustra's second speech. Upon witnessing the demise of the tightrope walker, Zarathustra lets go the blind optimism with which he first interpreted his descent, as well as the naive belief he shared with the saint. Acknowledging now the catastrophic potential of his endeavor, he recognizes, in effect, that his *Untergang* could be an adventure in nihilism that affords no bridge to his or anyone else's *Übergang*.

Perhaps the best indication of this recognition is Zarathustra's conversation with the tightrope walker. Just before he dies, the tightrope walker demonstrates his attachment to the Christian-Platonic view of human existence ("I have long known that the devil would trip me. Now he will drag me to hell"), a view that Zarathustra might be tempted to revive, given the jester's message that overcoming man is impossible. Zarathustra, however, remains steadfast in his belief that God and the Christian-Platonic interpretation of human existence are dead ("Your soul will be dead even before your body: fear nothing further"). Confronted with that belief, the tightrope walker responds that he loses "nothing" in losing his life and that he is "not much more than a beast." In effect, he points indirectly to the nihilism that would result if—with God dead—*the meaning that Zarathustra has assigned human existence seemed unrealizable.*

Zarathustra declines to contradict the tightrope walker's suggestion that his life is meaningless (that he loses nothing in losing his life). We have seen, in fact, that he explicitly endorses this suggestion in the next section ("Human existence is . . . still without meaning"). Zarathustra insists, however, that the tightrope walker can be distinguished from a beast, not because he has a soul, and thus an "otherworldly" vocation (which is what the tightrope walker appears to believe), but because he has made danger his vocation. The danger is the danger of meaninglessness: it is, again, the danger of a "going-under" and "perishing" ("Now you perish [*gehst du . . . zu Grunde*] of your vocation," says Zarathustra), that encounters the empty abyss of nihilism rather than the saving abyss of Dionysian chaos. In Zarathustra's view, the tightrope walker's complaint that his life is not unlike the meaningless life of a beast shows ironically that, unlike any beast, he can suffer the experience of meaninglessness. Reading the tightrope walker's *Untergang* as an allegory of a danger immanent in his own *Untergang*—to which danger he was originally blind—Zarathustra recognizes that his descent, regardless of his intentions, may do naught but leave humanity suffering the experience of meaninglessness.[159]

Still, Zarathustra resists the thought that he cannot defeat the catastrophe of nihilism, insisting that he "will *teach* men the meaning of their existence—the overman" (emphasis mine).[160] Persisting in his belief that the meaning and purpose he teaches can be realized, he purports to have seen his way beyond the Schopenhauerian ending of the tightrope walker's tragedy. As night falls, however, Zarathustra remains haunted by the tightrope walker's demise. Indeed, the depiction of Zarathustra in the next section of the prologue suggests that he has embraced the view that overcoming man is impossible, despite his earlier reassertion of his teaching.

Section 8 of the prologue figuratively represents Zarathustra as a camel. By hoisting the dead tightrope walker on his back, Zarathustra symbolically assumes as his "camel's burden" the death of the possibility of overcoming man. Having assumed that burden, he subsequently encounters individuals who interpret his fate with reference to the tragedy of the tightrope walker.

For example, the jester and the gravediggers warn that the tightrope walker's death prefigures Zarathustra's. ("Tomorrow I will leap over you, one living over one dead," says the jester. "If only the devil were not a better thief than Zarathustra: he will steal them both, he will gobble up both," say the gravediggers.)[161] Rather than repeat this warning, the hermit hints that it has come true. Declining to discriminate between the live man and the dead one, he feeds them both, thus suggesting that Zarathustra, though apparently living, might as well be dead.

Because the tragedy of the tightrope walker signifies the death of the possibility of overcoming man, the remarks of the hermit, read figuratively, suggest that Zarathustra attests to that death and embraces it as his own in enacting the role of the camel.[162] As befits that role, by the close of section 8, Zarathustra can imagine no route to the possibility of overcoming man: in the double entendre of Nietzsche's narrative, "he did not see a path [*Weg*] anywhere."[163]

The advent of dawn, or morning, recalls Zarathustra's attempt, just a morning earlier, to bring Dionysus to man and to become a child. For Zarathustra, morning is the time proper to Dionysian self-overcoming. It is significant, then, that Zarathustra sees nothing of the dawn and morning mentioned at the start of section 9 ("For a long time Zarathustra slept, and not only dawn [*Morgen-röthe*] passed over [*gieng über*] his face but the morning [*Vormittag*] too").[164] By letting Zarathustra sleep through the morning, Nietzsche continues to depict him as a camel who sees no route to the possibility of overcoming man. Were Zarathustra to remain asleep, he would be resigning once and for all his attempt to see his way beyond the Schopenhauerian ending of the tightrope walker's tragedy; thus, he would be abdicating his commitment to becoming a new-values creator. We know, of course, that Zarathustra does not remain asleep. We know too that, when he awakens, he sees a new truth and a new way to his goal: "Then he rose quickly . . . for he saw a new truth. . . . Living companions I need, who follow me because they want to follow themselves—wherever I want."[165] I do not mean to suggest here that Zarathustra has suddenly become a new-values creator. Rather, with his awakening, he again enacts the second metamorphosis of the spirit.

Noon is the time proper to the second metamorphosis. It is the time when Zarathustra parts from and bids farewell to the burden he bore as a camel:

> And you, my first companion, farewell! I buried you well in your hollow tree. . . . But I part from you; the time is up. Between dawn and dawn a new truth has come to me. No shepherd shall I be, nor gravedigger. Never again shall I speak to the people: for the last time have I spoken to the dead.
>
> I shall join the creators, the harvesters, the celebrants: I shall show them the rainbow and the steps to the overman. To the hermits, I shall sing my song, to the lonesome and the twosome. . . .
>
> To my goal I will go—on my own way; over those who hesitate and lag behind I shall leap. Thus let my going be their going-under.
>
> This is what Zarathustra had told his heart when the sun stood high at noon.[166]

In his speech on the three metamorphoses, Zarathustra characterizes the lion as creating a freedom for new creation. As I argued in Chapter 1, the lion creates this freedom by asserting his independence from the outlook of the camel and the great dragon, for whom all future willing is in thrall to past value creations. In section 9, Zarathustra enacts the lion's assertion of independence by parting from the tightrope walker and proposing that, in addition to shepherds and herds, there also exist creators.

For Zarathustra, the creator is the harvester (*der Ernter*), the person in whom there still resides the possibility of experiencing a Dionysian chaos from which that person can harvest the fruit of new values: "Companions, the creator seeks, and fellow harvesters; for everything about him is ripe for the harvest."[167] Proclaiming that creators still exist, Zarathustra repudiates the message of the jester's leap: namely, that the shepherdlike higher man and the herdlike last man exhaust the present and future destiny of human existence. Turning to the future, he bids farewell to the role of the camel who sees no route to the possibility of overcoming man. When Zarathustra addresses himself at noon, he implies that he can persuade *some* of his fellow men to "see" within themselves the possibility of self-overcoming. Speaking in the voice of the lion, he reaffirms his commitment to becoming a new-values creator in the company of creator-companions.

All this said, we must be careful to remember that noon is not morning. At noon, Zarathustra again occupies the perspective he occupied before beginning his morning-time descent (the descent described in section 1 of the prologue) but after carrying his ashes to his cave and performing the second metamorphosis of the spirit. (As we shall see, it is significant that this perspective corresponds to the presence of Zarathustra's animals, to whom Zarathustra refers in section 1 of the prologue and at noon). When Zarathustra begins his descent, he mistakenly believes that the time is ripe to complete the third metamorphosis of the spirit. In other words, he falsely supposes that this literal morning is, figuratively speaking, the "new morning" of Dionysian self-overcoming.[168] More circumspect than Zarathustra, Nietzsche suggests in *Twilight* that the literal morning is, figuratively speaking, "noon" (noon, it will be remembered, is the moment Nietzsche marks with the words "INCIPIT ZARATHUSTRA"), the time that *Zarathustra* associates with the second metamorphosis.[169] As distinct from Zarathustra himself, Nietzsche doubts that Zarathustra's transformation from lion to child is imminent when Zarathustra begins his descent. As we have seen, he initially expresses this doubt by representing Zarathustra's first speech as an inadvertent parody of Paul's letter to the Philippians.

Having again enacted the second metamorphosis in section 9 of the prologue, Zarathustra has yet to become a child or to meet anyone who has become a child. He has, however, seen his way beyond a Schopenhauerian ending to the tightrope walker's tragedy. Confronted with the jester's representation of repetition and with the spirit of resignation fostered by the jester's destruction of the tightrope walker (which spirit initially transforms Zarathustra into a camel), Zarathustra renews, in a noontime act of leonine self-assertion, his hope for the Dionysian renewal of human existence.[170] Fending off the spirit of resignation, he defiantly envisions a future that is different from the Christian-Platonic past.

I conclude this section with a discussion of Zarathustra's animals; in particular, the appearance of Zarathustra's animals in the tenth and final section of the prologue. Here, Nietzsche uses the figures of the serpent and the eagle to begin to conceptualize a distinctly leonine modality of Dionysian experience.[171]

In section 1 of the prologue, Zarathustra's parody of Neoplatonism represents the sun as Dionysus and Zarathustra as a Dionysian demiurge. Viewed from the perspective of this parody, and in light of a Hermetic symbolism that resonates with Neoplatonic metaphysics, the *coiled* serpent Zarathustra sees in section 10 (this serpent, we are told, "kept herself wound around [*geringelt*]" the neck of Zarathustra's eagle)[172] signifies a reversal of his descent. In the Hermetic tradition, with which Nietzsche seems to have been familiar, the image of a coiled serpent, or ouroboros, indicates a "departure from" and "return to" the original source of all things.[173] Thus it connotes the very movements Plotinus attributes to emanation (the procession of beings from the One) and epistrophe (the return of beings to the One).[174] Read with reference to Zarathustra's parody of Neoplatonism, the appearance of an ouroboros in section 10 betokens a "departure from" and "return to" Dionysus. The prologue begins with Zarathustra departing from Dionysus in a demiurgic effort to mediate the manifestation of Dionysus to man. It ends with an epistrophe through which Zarathustra seems to unite himself with the god he sees as the origin of all values. Sighting his serpent at noon, Zarathustra appears no longer as a demiurge, but, like the sun in section 1, as the superabundant Dionysus himself.

After Zarathustra sees his animals, whom he identifies as his pride (*Stolz*) and his prudence (*Klugheit*), Nietzsche's narrative describes them as follows: "An eagle soared through the sky in wide circles, and on him there hung a serpent, not like a prey but like a friend: for she kept herself [*sie hielt sich*] wound around his neck."[175] This description first creates and then undermines the expectation that the serpent is the eagle's quarry. It further suggests that the serpent, by keeping herself coiled about the eagle's neck (thus imitating the motion of the eagle's flight), lets us see that she has become his friend. In sum, Nietzsche's portrait of Zarathustra's serpent suggests that the serpent's promise of prudence (for what else could *this* serpent possibly promise) has prompted Zarathustra's eagle to see as an *ally* an animal that normally is the plunder of his hunt.

Within a Christian interpretive framework, the suggestion that human pride (here, again, Zarathustra's eagle) could find an ally in a serpent that should be its victim recalls the Old Testament story of the Fall. In that story, a serpent tempts Eve's pride and wins her as an ally by persuading her that eating from the tree of knowledge will make her prudent (*klug*).[176] By alluding to this biblical tale, Nietzsche suggests that Zarathustra reenacts the Judeo-Christian fall in allowing his pride to be tempted by the promise of prudence. Nietzsche uses the figure of the ouroboros, not only to signify Zarathustra's reunion with Dionysus, but also to note the tendency of human pride to antagonize the Christian God.

To elucidate the connection between the Neoplatonic and Christian connotations of Zarathustra's ouroboros, let us consider a Christian interpretation of human pride that, arguably, Nietzsche derives from Luther's treatment of the story of the Fall. A significant feature of Luther's version is his account of *what* the serpent says to Eve in order to persuade her that eating of the tree of knowledge will make her prudent. Where, for example, the King James Bible has the serpent remark that "your eyes shall be opened, and ye shall be as gods, knowing good and evil," Luther has him say, "so werden eure Augen aufgethan, und werdet sein wie Gott, und wissen, was gut und böse ist."[177] It is evident here that Luther has the serpent speak of *God* (*Gott*) where the King James translation has him speak of *gods*. The use of the singular *Gott* should not be surprising, for, as I emphasized in Chapter 1, Luther believes that the human will to be God is a monotheistic will to supplant the one and only God. Luther's Eve is persuaded to eat the forbidden fruit, not by the promise that she will become as *a* god, but by the promise that she will become as *God*. The prudence that tempts her and that her pride desires is a singular prudence that she could possess only by becoming God in God's place.

As it appears in section 10, Zarathustra's pride also desires a singular and divine prudence, for it is a lion's pride (viz., a pride that attaches to the leonine posture Zarathustra personifies when, in section 10, his eagle appears) that seems to have been modeled on Luther's conception of the human will to be God. By willing to be God, the leonine Zarathustra, like Eve, pridefully wills to supplant God. By willing to supplant God, he envisions himself as the one and only possible creator of values. From a biblical, Christian point of view, no less than from a Neoplatonic and Hermetic perspective, the prologue's figure of an eagle-borne ouroboros marks Zarathustra as *the* being in whom all values originate. Looking to the sky to praise his animals, he appears not only as Dionysus, but as a "fallen," irreverent lion who would usurp the place of the Christian God by becoming that being.

By portraying Zarathustra as Dionysus himself, and not as a demiurge who mediates the manifestation of Dionysus to men, the concluding sections of the prologue illuminate a distinctive mode of Dionysian experience. Reminiscent of Plato's Good and Plotinus's One, Zarathustra-Dionysus at noon appears as a self-contained source of value, albeit as a source that has still to show itself for what it is. As distinct from the Good and the One, however, Zarathustra-Dionysus has his home *within time*. Through the figure of Zarathustra at noon, Nietzsche conceptualizes Dionysus as an intratemporal origin of value, but without conflating that origin with the experience of going-under to passional chaos. Nietzsche distinguishes between (1) the Dionysian creator, child, and new philosopher who purports to *know* Dionysus by going-under and creating new values, and

(2) the Dionysian "hero," or lion, who creates no new values but nonetheless purports *to be* Dionysus and thus *to be* the unique and unprecedented origin of all values. Zarathustra, imagining that he is such a hero, denies that any values have been created prior to his assertion of his will. At noon, then, he rejects the claim of the great dragon and the jester that no values can be created that have not been created.

Conclusion

In "Zarathustra's Prologue," Zarathustra's attempt to interrupt modernity proceeds by way of a journey that returns him to the leonine perspective he occupied before beginning his morning-time descent. Only at the end of the journey is it suggested that this perspective involves a mode of Dionysian experience; or, more exactly, that to enact the second metamorphosis is in some sense to identity oneself as Dionysus. Time and again in the prologue, Zarathustra encounters representations of repetition—the saint, the townspeople, and the jester, for example—who antagonize his will to innovate. Functioning as apparent excluders, these skeptical voices tend to subvert his commitment to fulfilling his personal and poetic intentions. Now for Nietzsche, we have seen, a part of explaining the possibility of creating new values is to illustrate the leonine acts by which Zarathustra, despite the skepticism he encounters, reaffirms and persists in his commitment to fulfilling those intentions. By intimating that Zarathustra's performing such acts means that he envisions himself as Dionysus, Nietzsche complicates our understanding of their significance.

In the next chapter, I interpret Zarathustra's speeches in Part 1 in light of the leonine posture he adopts at the end of the prologue, and with specific reference to the theory of the body he advances to explain the process of going-under and creating new values. In Chapter 4, however, I return to the question, left unresolved here, about the relationship between knowing Dionysus and being Dionysus; or, to be precise, between the child who suffers Dionysian chaos in order to create new values and the lion who feels that he is the Dionysian origin of all values. Indeed, through a close reading of *Zarathustra*, Part 2, I argue that the leonine experience of Dionysus is a mode of *Dionysian self-alienation* through which the person who purports to be Dionysus estranges him- or herself from the possibility of having the child's knowledge and experience of Dionysus. Because Dionysian self-alienation apparently excludes the possibility of creating new values, explaining how new-values creation is possible involves showing how Zarathustra, notwithstanding the fact that he has become self-estranged, can become a new-values creator.

All that said, it will be evident that my analysis of Dionysian self-alienation remains incomplete: for it does not say *why* the figure of Dionysus should play any role at all in Nietzsche's conceptualization of the heroic/leonine posture that Zarathustra adopts in reaction to representations of repetition. In Chapter 5, I address this issue in connection to my discussion of the development of the thought of eternal recurrence in *Zarathustra*, Part 3.

CHAPTER THREE

Dionysus, the German Nation, and the Body

It may be assumed that the healthy spirit of the Reformation
was saved by Luther's glorious *chorale*, for it swayed heart
and mind.

    RICHARD WAGNER, *Beethoven*

If a person learns to sing . . . all the notes that are within his
natural compass are easy to him, while those beyond the
compass are at first extremely difficult. But, to be a vocalist,
he must have them all at command. Just so with the poet—
he deserves not the name while he only speaks out his few
subjective feelings; but as soon as he can appropriate to
himself, and express, the world, he is a poet. Then he is
inexhaustible, and can be always new.

    JOHANN WOLFGANG VON GOETHE,
    Conversations with Eckermann

Power ceases in the instant of repose; it resides in the moment
of transition from a past to a new state, in the shooting of the
gulf, in the darting to an aim. This one fact the world hates;
that the soul *becomes*; for that forever degrades the past, turns
all riches to poverty, all reputation to a shame, confounds the
saint with the rogue, shoves Jesus and Judas equally aside.

    RALPH WALDO EMERSON, *Self-Reliance*

In the Introduction to this book I claimed that when Nietzsche wrote *Zarathustra* he had grown skeptical of *The Birth of Tragedy*'s claim that the promise of
radical cultural change is immanent in received historical circumstance. I also
suggested that Nietzsche's skepticism in this respect is evident in his use of an explicitly fictional narrative to account for the possibility of modernism. In *Zara-*

thustra, I argued, Nietzsche lets fiction do the explanatory work done by historiography in *The Birth of Tragedy*.

In this chapter I return to *The Birth of Tragedy* in order further to explore Nietzsche's change in explanatory strategies. In his first book, Nietzsche envisions the German nation, or folk, as the proper vehicle for realizing a Dionysian interruption of modernity. In short, he identifies the German body politic as the conduit through which Dionysus can reclaim modern, European culture. Yet Nietzsche's notion of a Dionysian, German nation suffers from self-contradiction. By exploring the conceptual sources of this contradiction, I show that *The Birth of Tragedy* impugns the modernism it otherwise endorses; or, to put the point a bit differently, that it dramatizes a Schopenhauerian view of history that prefigures the "stammering" representations of repetition that stand athwart Zarathustra's modernism.[1]

By stressing Nietzsche's early nationalism, I hope to throw into relief a central motif of *Zarathustra*: namely, its interpretation of the physical body as a potential medium of Dionysian energies. In philosophically explaining the possibility of creating new values, Nietzsche presupposes a general view of the nature of cultural innovation in the mode of new-values creation. Critical to this view is the thesis that new-values creation has its roots in the passional, Dionysian experience of "going-under" (see Chapter 2). In the speculative vision of *Zarathustra*, the body that goes under is the conduit through which Dionysus can enter the modern world. Turning from historiography to fiction to explain the possibility of cultural innovation, Nietzsche seeks the advent of Dionysus not in the German nation, but in the healthy human body. As we shall see, his turn to the body both frees the idea of a Dionysian modernism from the contradictions that initially haunted it and expresses a conviction that the German nation has been corrupted by the forces of modernity.

In the opening section of this chapter, I examine in detail the Dionysian nationalism of *The Birth of Tragedy*. In the following section, I reconstruct the theory of Dionysian value-creation that Zarathustra sketches in Part 1 of *Zarathustra*. Finally, in the third section, I interpret Zarathustra's speeches in Part 1 with reference both to his theory of value-creation and the leonine posture he adopts at the end of the prologue. In Part 1, Zarathustra aspires to speak as a lion to other lions who can become value-creators.

Dionysus and the German Nation

In *The Birth of Tragedy*, Nietzsche explains the transition from a Socratic to a Dionysian and new form of cultural life as the necessary consequence of a dialectic immanent in Socratic culture. A "sublime metaphysical illusion accompanies science as an instinct and leads science again and again to its limits at which it must [*muss*] turn into *art—which is really the aim of this mechanism.*"[2] The art Nietzsche envisions here, that of Wagner's music, he interprets as generically Dionysian and specifically German. For the early Nietzsche, Wagner's music embodies the artistic self-reformation of a self-estranged German spirit. Expressing the Dionysian "root" and essence of the German spirit, it effects that spirit's "return to itself," bringing its manifest spiritual "form" into harmony with its essence.[3]

According to Nietzsche, Wagner's musical re-formation of the German spirit is the culmination of a cultural movement that Luther began with his re-formation of German religion. Nietzsche suggests that Luther's initiative had an essentially Dionysian and musical character that prefigured the development of German music from Bach to Beethoven to Wagner: it is from a primordial Dionysian abyss that "the German Reformation came forth; and in its chorales the future tune of German music sounded for the first time . . . —as the first Dionysian luring call breaking forth from dense thickets at the approach of spring."[4]

By representing Wagner's music as the cultural fulfillment of the German Reformation, Nietzsche identifies it as the apex of a distinctively Germanic reaction to the Alexandrian-Romanic culture he associates with the figure of Socrates. Effecting a "return to itself of the German spirit," Wagner's music marks the final phase of the purification (*Läuterung*) of that spirit.[5] Purification, in this context, entails the "elimination of everything Romanic" (*der Ausscheidung des Romanischen*) from the German spirit, including the Socratic and secularizing tendencies that estranged it from its "sacred," Dionysian essence, leaving it rootless, exhausted, and prey to a "homeless roving" that seeks nourishment from "foreign tables." In the modern world, the "abstract education; abstract morality; [and] abstract law" essential to Alexandrian-Romanic culture have subjected a Dionysian and distinguishably German sensibility to a logic-driven, Socratic cast of mind that privileges no attachments to German (or any) national culture (e.g., "native myth"). Thus, German spiritual renewal requires that German culture purge itself of its "forcibly implanted" Alexandrian-Romanic elements. To be sure, Nietzsche allows that Prussia's victory over "Romanic" France in the Franco-Prussian War may have abetted the self-purgation of the German spirit. Still, he urges genuine advocates of German cultural purity to continue to draw their primary inspiration from Luther and from Germany's great artists and poets.[6]

In the wake of war, Nietzsche exhorts German cultural purists to the project of German spiritual renewal. Advocating a specifically *cultural* nationalism, he exalts the cultural potential of the German nation (*Volk*), not Bismarck's found-

ing of a new *Reich* ("let him never believe that he could fight similar fights without the gods of his house, or his mythical home, without 'bringing back' all
German things! And if the German should hesitantly look around for a leader
who might bring him back again into his long lost home . . . let him merely listen to the ecstatically luring call of the Dionysian bird that hovers above him
and wants to point the way for him").[7] The German spirit's return to itself,
which Nietzsche equates with the fulfillment of German cultural potential, portends, in his view, the cultural self-determination of the German people, striving "boldly and freely before the eyes of all nations [*Völkern*] without being attached to the lead strings of a Romanic civilization."[8] Like Herder before him,
Nietzsche uses the chauvinistic language of German nationalism to promote the
pursuit of German cultural autonomy.[9] His high praise of German culture entails an aggressive antipathy to foreign cultures, precisely to the extent that he
sees them as colonizing forces that have stifled the cultural self-expression and
self-reformation of the German spirit.[10]

Other commentators have noted the nationalism evident in the concluding
chapters of *The Birth of Tragedy*. Less frequently noted, however, is the *supra-
national* thrust of that nationalism. Following Etienne Balibar, I conceptualize
supranationalism as a form of nationalism that represents the nation as embodying some *transnational* reality, force, or identity (e.g., Aryan racial identity). *The
Birth of Tragedy* is a supranationalistic text, for it represents the German nation
as the epitome of a transnational, Dionysian reality.[11] This reality is the Dionysian thing-in-itself and subsists independently of the Apollonian appearances to
which the "history of nations" belongs. It is transnational because it exceeds in
its being the boundaries of individual nations.

For Nietzsche (in *The Birth of Tragedy*), Dionysian reality embodies a dissolution of distinct identities in which dissolution there is no place for the boundaries and differences characterizing the Apollonian world of appearances. Thus,
there is no place for the boundaries and differences distinguishing one nation
from another.[12] By characterizing the German national spirit as intrinsically
Dionysian, Nietzsche implies that an essential feature of that spirit is a property
(the property of partaking in Dionysian reality), the expression of which would
inherently entail the dissolution of the differences constituting the distinctness
of the German nation. That Nietzsche does not acknowledge this implication,
but, on the contrary, represents the self-expression of an essentially Dionysian,
German spirit as entailing the cultural self-determination of a persistently distinct and purely German national entity, is evidence, I shall argue, of the conceptual difficulties informing his attempt to portray Dionysus as a specifically
cultural presence.[13]

We can better assess Nietzsche's notion of a Dionysian nation by contrasting it to his representation of Dionysus as the metaphysical ground of appearances. Regarding the former, Nietzsche's language is one of *exclusion* and *collection*, a rhetoric that celebrates the elimination of foreign (Alexandrian-Romanic) elements from the German spirit, while unifying under the rubric of that spirit the likes of Luther, Bach, and Beethoven, along with Kant, Schopenhauer, and Wagner. In fine, it represents the German nation by constructing a spiritual pedigree in the form of a cultural canon. In articulating the contents of that canon, Nietzsche aggregates some texts and compositions (those of Luther, Bach, Beethoven, etc.) under the notion of the "spiritually German," yet excludes from that notion all texts and compositions having a non-Germanic origin. Nietzsche amasses numerous cultural elements under a single concept, but denies that there exist cultural affinities between precisely those elements and the foreign ones he bars from his picture of a spiritually pure German culture.[14]

Regarding his representation of Dionysus as the metaphysical ground of appearances, Nietzsche's language is one of *nonexclusion*. The Dionysian in-itself is the one and only "truly existent" being; there is, therefore, nothing that it excludes from its being. Moreover, the Dionysian in-itself is metaphysically *simple*: it does not consist of a collection of components and therefore cannot be distinguished from other entities (of which, strictly speaking, there are none) by identifying its constituent elements. (For Nietzsche, the metaphysical analog to the mythical "dis-memberment" [*Zerstückelung*] of Dionysus is not the division of the thing-in-itself into composite parts, but the manifestation of an *unreal* [*Wahrhaft-Nichtseiende*] world of Apollonian appearances.)[15] Because the Dionysian ground of appearances neither excludes nor includes *any* elements, it excludes no foreign elements, includes no native ones, and so cannot be accurately understood as a nation different from other nations. In describing the German national spirit as a distinct yet essentially Dionysian entity, Nietzsche characterizes it in contradictory terms. Conceptualized as an exclusive collection, whose essence is nonexclusive and simple, the notion of a spiritually pure Dionysian nation is internally inconsistent.

As we shall see, Nietzsche's notion of a tragic, Dionysian chorus is similarly inconsistent. This should come as no surprise, for much of what Nietzsche says about the German national spirit recalls his earlier descriptions of the Greek chorus. Consider, for example, the opening pages of *The Birth of Tragedy*, which describe the chorus as imitating the reveling (*schwärmende*) throng of Dionysian votaries and as consisting of individuals who are Dionysian revelers (*Schwärmer*).[16] Echoing this description, Nietzsche subsequently represents the musical tradition issuing from Luther's chorales as a "solemnly exuberant procession of Dio-

nysian revelers [*Schwärmer*] . . . to whom we are indebted for German music—
and to whom we shall be indebted for *the rebirth of German myth.*"[17] Here, by
resounding his earlier characterization of the tragic chorus, Nietzsche portrays
Luther and his successors (Bach, Beethoven, and Wagner) as a modern group of
Dionysian singers. In effect, he characterizes a musically reborn German national spirit as a chorus of Dionysian votaries singing its songs to a Europe still
dominated by the ethos of Socratic rationality. Whereas Nietzsche saw the ancient chorus as the origin of ancient tragedy, he envisions the modern chorus of
German composer-revelers as the origin of a modern rebirth of tragedy and
tragic myth.

Like the German spirit, the Greek chorus appears in Nietzsche's text as an *exclusive collection.* The chorus is, first of all, a *collection* of individuals who aggre-
gate themselves under the unifying rubric of a ritual devotion to Dionysus. This
collection is an *exclusive* one, not only because it includes some individuals and
not others, but, likewise, because it constitutes a community (*Gemeinde*) that dissociates itself from the civic functions and status obligations shaping the life of
the larger society: "the dithyrambic chorus is a chorus of transformed characters
whose civic [*bürgerliche*] past and social status have been totally forgotten: they
have become timeless servants of their god who live outside the sphere of society."[18] As a *collection,* the satyr chorus is the template for Nietzsche's representation of the German nation as a cohort of chorale inspired Dionysian composers-
revelers. As an *exclusive* collection, it prefigures his depiction of the nation
expressing itself through the elimination of "foreign elements." Just as the Greek
chorus could be what it was only by maintaining its distance from the preoccupations of civic and political life, the German nation can flourish as the chorus
of modern Europe only by freeing itself from an Alexandrian-Romanic culture
whose predominantly civic preoccupations squelch the manifestation of Dionysian energies.[19]

The concept of a Dionysian chorus, like that of a Dionysian nation, is self-
contradictory. Representing the chorus and the nation as exclusive collections,
Nietzsche depicts them as distinct Apollonian phenomena. In short, he uses the
language of exclusion and collection to *individuate* these phenomena, thereby
distinguishing them from *other* domains of social life (e.g., politics and the
world of Alexandrian-Romanic civilization). Nietzsche views the chorus and the
purified nation as *distinct* social spheres that (1) exist apart from other social milieu and (2) harbor the revelers and revelous activities marking them as Dionysian. Society as a whole he seems to see as a complex arrangement of mutually
delimiting social spheres and practices.[20] Regarding the chorus in particular,
Nietzsche notes that its practices and performances are surrounded by a "world

of culture."²¹ Unlike the institutions making up that world, the chorus incarnates a "Dionysian reality" (*dionysischen Wirklichkeit*) that destroys the boundaries (*Schranken*) separating different social spheres.²² Similarly, but unlike the institutions of Alexandrian-Romanic civilization, the purified German nation also embodies a "Dionysian reality." By depicting the chorus and the nation as distinct dwelling places of Dionysian epiphanies, Nietzsche represents both as exemplifying the self-contradictory notion of a distinct Apollonian phenomenon that embodies the nullification of all distinctions.

That Nietzsche embraced this contradiction seems evident from his account of what he calls "the most important moment" in the history of the cult of Dionysus.²³ This moment involved a reconciliation of Dionysus and Apollo: to borrow Peter Sloterdijk's phrase, it constituted an "Apollonian compromise" that made it possible to distinguish the Dionysian *culture* of the Greeks from the Dionysian *barbarism* of non-Greek peoples.²⁴ According to Nietzsche, Dionysian barbarism "centered in excessive [*überschwänglichen*] sexual licentiousness, whose waves [*Wellen*] overwhelmed all family life and its venerable traditions; the most savage natural instincts were unleashed, including even that horrible mixture of sensuality and cruelty which has always seemed to me to be the real 'witches brew.'"²⁵ Here, the image of a superabundant sexuality overflowing the norms of social taboo suggests that the Dionysian barbarian desired *literally* to efface "the rigid, hostile barriers that necessity, caprice, or 'impudent convention' have fixed between man and man."²⁶ What the Dionysian barbarian wanted, ultimately, was to be "fused" sexually with each and every one of his family members and neighbors in order to return the Apollonian order of nature to a simple Dionysian oneness. The Dionysian Greek, on the other hand, repudiated the literalism of the barbarian and strove *figuratively* to express Dionysian excess.²⁷ Rejecting the barbarian's effort to restore nature to its "primordial unity," he believed that the Dionysian "essence of nature is . . . to be expressed *symbolically*" through "the entire symbolism of the body . . . the whole pantomime of dancing, forcing every member into rhythmic movement."²⁸

With the advent of the figurative, symbolic performance of Dionysian excess, "the destruction of the *principium individuationis* for the first time becomes an artistic phenomenon."²⁹ Because the artistic and specifically *cultural* rendition of this destruction (as opposed to the barbaric attempt literally to realize it) is generally compatible with the persistence of communally shared traditions and conventions, the Dionysianism of the Greek poses little threat to social stability. As Nietzsche puts it, the "horrible 'witches brew' of sensuality and cruelty becomes ineffective."³⁰ The artistic representation of Dionysian excess is a ritual phenomenon that, confined to a distinct festival or theatrical "space," leaves standing the surrounding fabric of social relations. The ritual transmutation of Dionysian excess involves an *Apollonian* compromise, for it recasts that excess as a bounded and distinct Apollonian phenomenon: "the Delphic god, by a seasonably effected reconciliation, now contented himself with taking the destructive weapons from the hands of his antagonist."[31]

To summarize: Dionysus, to the extent that he is a *cultural* modality no longer in the grips of a savage barbarism, has always already been compromised by Apollonian boundaries and distinctions. Thus, Nietzsche implies that the concept of an *authentically* Dionysian culture—the concept, that is, of a culture that *literally* incarnates and communicates a distinction-nullifying Dionysian excess—contradicts itself. He also lets us see that the contradictions evident in his notions of *particular* Dionysian cultures and institutions—for example, in his notions of the Hellenic chorus and a purified German nation—exemplify this more general self-contradiction.[32] In fine, Nietzsche's discussion of Dionysian Greeks and barbarians suggests that self-contradiction is the logical "price" he is willing to pay in order to imagine the possibility of a culture that, notwithstanding its supposed Dionysian "roots" and "reality," must remain, qua culture, a socially safe Apollonian *surrogate* for such roots and reality.

Social stability is compatible with the symbolic, if not the literal expression of Dionysian excess. Symbolic revelry, precisely because it substitutes figurative for literal performance, produces a self-contained sphere of aesthetic activity that ultimately becomes the tragic theater. Symbolic revelry nullifies the socially destabilizing consequences of Dionysian excess by replacing that excess with its figurative representations. Hardly a revolutionary force, the bounded figuration of Dionysian boundlessness, be it in the Greek tragic chorus or in the Luther-inspired German national chorus, no more effects or embodies a *veridical* dissolution of the *principium individuationis* than do the characteristic cultural expressions of Hellenic (Homeric) and Alexandrian (Socratic) cultures. All three of these cultures—that of beautiful forms, of the opera, and of the chorus—belong, metaphysically speaking, to the appearances side of the divide between appearances and the will-in-itself. None of them, therefore, not even the culture of the chorus, can claim *qua culture* to incarnate and communicate that distinction-obliterating and boundless excess which is the Dionysian ground of appearances. Nietzsche himself seems to make a similar point in the paragraph that begins section 18 of *The Birth of Tragedy*:

> It is an eternal phenomenon: the insatiable will always finds a way to detain its creatures in life and compel them to live on, by means of an illusion spread over things. One is chained by the Socratic love of knowledge and the delusion

of being able thereby to heal the eternal wound of existence; another is ensnared by art's seductive veil of beauty fluttering before his eyes; *still another by the metaphysical comfort that beneath the whirl of phenomena life flows on indestructibly* [emphasis mine]—to say nothing of the more vulgar and almost more powerful illusions which the will always has at hand. These three stages of illusion are actually designed only for the more nobly formed natures, who actually feel profoundly the weight and burden of existence, and must be deluded by exquisite stimulants into forgetfulness of their displeasure. *All that we call culture is made up of these stimulants* [emphasis mine]; and according to the proportion of the ingredients, we have either a dominantly *Socratic* or *artistic* or *tragic* culture; or if historical exemplifications [*Exemplificationen*] are permitted, there is an Alexandrian or a Hellenic or Buddhistic culture.[33]

Nietzsche's claim here, that every culture is a mode of illusion that hides the true nature of things, suggests that culture in general is but a form of false appearance that communicates nothing of the will-in-itself's boundless excess. This assertion troubles many commentators, for it seems to contradict the suggestion in various places in *The Birth of Tragedy* that tragic cultures, at least, far from dissimulating the true, Dionysian nature of things, embody an undistorted expression of the will's "true, undissembled [*unverstellten*] voice."[34] Consider, in this connection, the following remarks:

Dionysian art, too, wishes to convince us of the eternal joy of existence: *only we are to seek this joy not in phenomena, but behind them.* We are to recognize that all that comes into being must be ready for a sorrowful end; we are forced to look into the terrors of the individual existence—yet we are not to become rigid with fear: *a metaphysical comfort tears us momentarily from the bustle of the changing figures.*

We are really for a brief moment primordial being itself, feeling its raging desire for existence . . . the struggle, the pain, the destruction of phenomena, now appear necessary to us, in view of the excess of countless forms of existence which force and push one another into life, in view of the exuberant fertility of the universal will.[35] (emphasis mine)

Nietzsche suggests here that Dionysian art, the centerpiece and essence of tragic culture, is the source of a metaphysical comfort that affords human beings an unmediated knowledge of the will-in-itself. On this view, tragic cultures communicate an authentic and literal experience of Dionysian ecstasy and boundlessness. But recall section 18, where Nietzsche implies that tragic cultures cover over and conceal the true nature of the will, providing human beings with an experience not of Dionysian ecstasy, but of an illusion that dissimulates Dionysian ecstasy. From the point of view of section 18, the notion of a tragic culture whose metaphysical comforts involve a direct experience of "primordial being itself" is self-contradictory. From this perspective, forming such a notion is conceptualizing the possibility of a *culture* that is *authentically Dionysian*, and thus the possibility of a *dissimulation* of Dionysian reality that is *not a dissimulation*.[36]

Like Nietzsche's remarks regarding Dionysian Greeks and barbarians, section 18 supports my analysis of his notions of a Dionysian chorus and a Dionysian nation, for it suggests that internal inconsistency is implicit *whenever* one represents a distinct culture or cultural form as expressing being- or the will-in-itself as it is in-itself. The fundamental source of this inconsistency, particulars aside, is the conflict between Nietzsche's metaphysical dualism—that is, his appropriation of Kant's and Schopenhauer's distinction between things-in-themselves and appearances—and his belief that tragic cultures nullify that distinction by affording human beings an unmediated experience of reality as it is in-itself. To put the point bluntly, the depiction of the Greek chorus and the German chorus/nation as Apollonian instantiations of a distinction-obliterating Dionysian boundlessness, like the representation of tragic cultures in general as mediating "primordial being," violates the dualist assumption that there can be no incarnation or revelation of being-in-itself, as it is in-itself, in the world of Apollonian appearances.

It may be objected here that in investigating inconsistencies in *The Birth of Tragedy* I have ignored the most obvious culprit: namely, Schopenhauer's theory of music. Schopenhauer asserted that music is an "unmediated image of the will" (*unmittelbares Abbild des Willens*).[37] If, following Paul de Man, this proposition is viewed as a "logical absurdity," then the contradictions I have identified can be traced to it. Inconsistency infects the representations of the Greek chorus and the German nation, one might argue, because Nietzsche believed that these phenomena, precisely to the extent that they had a *musical* character, could dissolve the opposition between the thing-in-itself and appearances. Because Nietzsche appears uncritically to quote Schopenhauer's assertion that music is a mode of unmediated representation, one could suppose that he had foolishly endorsed it, unaware that it is logically absurd.

There are two decisive objections to this view, both of which Henry Staten identifies in his very careful critique of de Man's reading of *The Birth of Tragedy*.[38] First, de Man mistakenly holds that Schopenhauer, in referring to an "unmediated image of the will," is asserting that there can be representations that render *immediately present* what they represent: that is, re-presentations that present their objects absent the mediation of re-presentation. Were this what Schopenhauer were claiming, then, indeed, his theory of music would involve the absurdity of logical contradiction. But de Man gets Schopenhauer wrong, for when the latter insists that "music is 'immediately' the image of the will . . . he does not at all mean the absurdity that de Man ascribes to him; by 'immediate image' he means . . . that music is, unlike the other arts, not a *representation at two removes*, not a representation of the Platonic or species ideas, but a representation of the original which the Platonic ideas also copy."[39]

Second, and perhaps more important, Nietzsche breaks with Schopenhauer by developing a causal and nonrepresentationalist notion of music's relationship to the Dionysian will. More exactly, he proposes that music can cause an unmediated knowledge and experience of the will's ecstasy and boundlessness. For Nietzsche, music communicates the Dionysian immediacy embodied in the chorus, but, in Staten's words, "not as representation: it is a matter of the communication of force . . . (of) 'forces merely felt, and not condensed into images.'"[40]

The following passage, drawn from section 7 of *The Birth of Tragedy*, very clearly highlights Nietzsche's causal conception of the relationship between choral music and the experience of the will as it is in-itself. It also suggests that the contradictions informing the concepts of the Dionysian chorus and the Dionysian nation have not to do with the idea of unmediated representation, but, as I have been arguing, with Nietzsche's attempt to conceptualize the possibility of an Apollonian instantiation of Dionysian reality:

> The Greek man of culture felt himself nullified in the presence of the satyric chorus, and this is the most immediate effect [*die nächste Wirkung*] of the Dionysian tragedy, that the state and society and, quite generally, the cleavages [*Klüfte*] between man and man give way [*weichen*] to an overwhelming feeling of unity [*Einheitsgefühle*] leading back to the very heart of nature [*welches an das Herz der Natur zurückführt*].
>
> The metaphysical comfort—with which I am suggesting even now, every true tragedy leaves us—that life is at the bottom of things [*im Grunde der Dinge*], despite all changes of appearances [*Erscheinungen*], indestructibly powerful and pleasurable—this comfort appears in incarnate clarity in the chorus of satyrs [*erschient in leibhafter Deutlichkeit als Satyrchor*], a chorus of natural beings who live ineradicably, as it were [*gleichsam*], behind all civilization and remain eternally the same, despite the changes of generations and of the history of nations [*Völkergeschichte*].[41]

According to these remarks, the metaphysical comfort felt by tragic audiences is not the content of an "unmediated (musical) representation" but an *effect (Wirkung)* caused by the singing of the satyr chorus. The chorus personifies the comforting experience of Dionysian oneness, even as it communicates the immediacy of that experience by means of the sheer feeling its song and presence generate. For Nietzsche, the chorus is an *incarnate appearance of metaphysical comfort* (because the chorus of satyrs *appears* [*erscheint*], it belongs to the world of *appearances* [*Erscheinungen*]), a distinct Apollonian phenomenon that embodies a Dionysian dissolution of the Apollonian "cleavages" separating phenomena.

Nietzsche's reference in section 7 to "the history of nations" links his effort philosophically to explain the possibility of modernism to some of the contradictions I have been discussing. As we have seen, Nietzsche believes that Germany's self-reformation will free it from the oppressive forces of Alexandrian-Romanic culture. By re-forming itself, the German nation will enact a process of historical development that has for its end the Dionysian self-expression of the German spirit. According to the closing pages of *The Birth of Tragedy* (sections 19–25), the German nation will participate in the "history of nations," incorporating into that history the full-fledged incarnation of a Dionysian reality that, in the perspective of section 7, exists separately from the apparent world of nations, civilizations, and changing generations. Once again, then, Nietzsche's thought founders on the contradiction between his metaphysical dualism and his belief that "tragic" cultures or cultural phenomena—the Dionysian German nation, for instance—can nullify the divide between Dionysian reality and Apollonian appearance. Section 7 is significant, because it tacitly ties this contradiction to Nietzsche's contention that the German nation is the conduit through which Dionysus can reclaim modern, European culture.

Section 7 is significant also for a second reason: namely, that it throws into relief the conflict between *The Birth of Tragedy*'s Hegelian and Schopenhauerian sensibilities. On one hand, Nietzsche's first book is written in the spirit of Hegel's philosophy of history, obvious differences notwithstanding. Thus, the suggestion that the history of the self-purifying German spirit will culminate in the Dionysian re-formation of the German nation echoes the argument, expressed in *Reason in History*, that "the goal [of history] is that it bring a spiritual world to existence which is adequate to its own (sc., the world's) concept, that it realize and perfect its truth, that religion and the state be so produced by it that it becomes adequate to its concept."[42] Like Hegel, Nietzsche represents historical change as a teleological movement geared to the full realization or incarnation of the essence of a historically developing spirit (for Hegel, the rational essence of the world-spirit; for Nietzsche, the Dionysian essence of the modern, German spirit) in some concrete community or nation. (Hegel, like Nietzsche, uses the term *Volk*, though he restricts himself, in his philosophy of history, to discussing *Völker* who form states.)[43] And like Hegel, Nietzsche believes that some but not all historically emergent communities adequately embody that essence, and that they mark an advance over those that do not. Hegel's example of such a community is the modern state; Nietzsche's is the purified German nation.

On the other hand, the Schopenhauerian impulses evident in *The Birth of Tragedy*—in section 7, for example—contradict Nietzsche's quasi-Hegelian historical argument and, specifically, the proposition that the Dionysian essence of the German spirit can meet with adequate historical realization. Schopenhauer, we know, criticized Hegel's philosophy of history:

> For we are of opinion that anyone who imagines that the inner nature of the world can be *historically* comprehended, however finely glossed over it may be, is still infinitely far from a philosophical comprehension of the world. But this is the case as soon as a *becoming*, or a *having-become*, or a *will-become* enters into his view of the inner nature of the world; whenever an earlier or later has the least significance; and consequently whenever points of beginning and of ending in the world, together with a path between the two are sought and found, and the philosophizing individual even recognizes his own position on this path. . . . For all such historical philosophy, whatever airs it may assume, regards *time*, just as though Kant had never existed, as a determination of things in-themselves, and therefore stops at what Kant calls the phenomenon in opposition to the thing-in-itself, and what Plato calls the becoming never the being in opposition to the being never the becoming, or finally what is called by the Indians the web of Maya.
>
> Finally, as regards the attempt specially introduced by the Hegelian pseudophilosophy . . . the attempt, namely, to comprehend the history of the world as a planned whole, or, as they call it "to construct it organically," a crude and shallow *realism* is actually at the root of this. Such realism regards the *phenomenon* as the *being-in-itself* of the world and imagines that it is a question of this phenomenon and of its forms and events.
>
> The Hegelians, who regard the philosophy of history as even the main purpose of all philosophy, should be referred to Plato, who untiringly repeats that the object of philosophy is the unchangeable and ever permanent, not that which now is thus and then otherwise. All who set up such constructions of the course of the world, or, as they call it, of history, have not grasped the principal truth of all philosophy, that that which is is at all times the same, that all becoming and arising are only apparent, that the Ideas alone are permanent, that time is ideal.[44]

For Schopenhauer, historical becoming belongs to the illusion-world of mere appearance and reveals nothing of the being of things-in-themselves (the being of the inner nature of the world). Because he denies that the being of things-in-themselves can appear, he rejects the view that some mode of appearance, for the reason that it had rendered the being of things-in-themselves fully manifest, could have greater significance than an earlier or later occurring mode of appearance. In Schopenhauer's view, all appearances remain equally and infinitely estranged from the being of things-in-themselves, from which it follows that no historical change from one mode of appearance to another can put human beings more closely in touch than they have been in the past with what truly is. Thus, Schopenhauer dismisses the Hegelian contention that history can engender forms of phenomena (e.g., the modern state) that adequately embody and reveal the world's being and essence (for Hegel, the being and essence of the world-spirit). For similar reasons, he would have dismissed Nietzsche's claim that some particular historical phenomenon—the purified and re-formed German nation—could reduce to nought the divide between appearances and things-in-themselves by embodying and expressing a (its) Dionysian essence that Nietzsche identifies with things-in-themselves.

It is perhaps clear now that Nietzsche echoes Schopenhauer when, in section 7 of *The Birth of Tragedy*, he opposes Dionysian being to the history of nations, and when, in section 18, he characterizes phases of history as examples (*Exemplificationen*) of modes of illusion that hide the true nature of things. For Schopenhauer, history progresses neither from illusion to truth, nor from a state-of-affairs that fails adequately to incarnate being-in-itself to one "great and glorious" that does.[45] Thus, he rejects the belief "that time may produce something actually [*wirklich*] new and significant; that through it or in it something positively real [*schlechthin Reales*] may attain to existence [*Daseyn*]." Schopenhauer insists that history "is . . . the long, heavy, and confused dream of mankind."[46] As voiced in *The Birth of Tragedy*, Schopenhauer's anti-Hegelian sensibility insists that the transition from a Socratic and Alexandrian-Romanic culture to a Dionysian and tragic-Germanic one is a transition from one illusory mode of appearance to another, not a momentous cultural advance or musical re-formation that can truly be said to reveal a Dionysian essence.

The Schopenhauerian perspective that speaks in *The Birth of Tragedy* holds that the book's historical explanation of the possibility of radical cultural transformation rests on a false assumption: namely, that the rift between Dionysus and man can be dissolved. According to this view, human life, inasmuch as it is life amidst the world of appearances, can know nothing of the comforting reality of "primordial being." By reasserting Schopenhauer's view of history, Nietzsche prefigures the many voices and actions that speak in "Zarathustra's Prologue" against Zarathustra's effort to bring Dionysus to man. Like the parody of Paul, the forest-saint's portrait of man, the townspeople's interpretation of Zarathustra's speech, and the jester's fatal leap over the tightrope walker, his reiteration of this view suggests that human life is fated to remain uninspired by Dionysus. Schopenhauer's voice, as Nietzsche resounds it in his first book, is the prototype for the stammering representations of repetition that oppose Zara-thustra's modernism. Perhaps, too, one hears an echo of this voice in Paul de Man's critique of the world-transforming pretentions of the Dionysian will.

After he has completed *Zarathustra*, Nietzsche explicitly recants *The Birth of Tragedy*'s Schopenhauerian and Hegelian tendencies, along with the book's cel-ebratory but contadictory vision of a Dionysian German national spirit. Thus, in the 1886 "Attempt at a Self-Criticism," he writes:

> that in those days I still lacked the courage (or immodesty?) to permit myself
> in every way an individual *language of my own* [emphasis mine] . . . and that
> instead I tried laboriously to express by means of Schopenhauerian and
> Kantian formulas strange and new valuations which were basically at odds
> with Kant's and Schopenhauer's spirit and taste. . . . How differently Dionysus
> spoke to me! How far removed I was from all this resignationism—But there
> is something far worse in this book, something I now regret still more than
> that I obscured and spoiled Dionysian premonitions with Schopenhauerian
> formulations: namely, that I *spoiled* the grandiose *Greek problem*, as it had
> arisen before my eyes, by introducing the most modern problems! That I
> appended hopes where there was no ground for hope, where everything
> pointed all too plainly to an end! That on the basis of the latest German music
> I began to rave about the "German spirit" as if that were in the process even
> then of discovering and finding itself again—at a time when the German spirit,
> which not long before had still had the will to dominate Europe and the
> strength to lead Europe, was just making its testament and *abdicating* forever,
> making its transition, under the pompous pretense of founding a Reich, to a
> leveling mediocrity, democracy, and "modern ideas."[47]

In the posthumously published *Ecce Homo*, Nietzsche adds to these self-criticisms, suggesting now that Hegel, not Schopenhauer, is the thinker whose legacy he felt most strongly in writing *The Birth of Tragedy*:

> It smells offensively Hegelian, and the cadaverous perfume of Schopenhauer
> sticks only to a few formulas.
>   An "idea"—the antithesis of the Dionysian and the Apollonian—translated
> into the realm of metaphysics; history itself as the development of this "idea."[48]

Considered in tandem, Nietzsche's post-*Zarathustra* readings of *The Birth of Tragedy* point to at least four ways in which, in his later works, he attempts to free his Dionysianism of contradiction. First, he rejects "Schopenhauerian and Kantian formulas," including, presumably, the divide between the thing-in-itself and appearances. Second, he reconceptualizes the identity of Dionysus, something he must do if, in light of his rejection of Schopenhauer's and Kant's dualism, he no longer views this deity as the ground of Apollonian appearances. Third, he repudiates his earlier belief that the spirit of the German nation is the medium through which Dionysus will enter into and transform modern European culture. Finally, he rejects the Hegelian proposition that history is the teleological development of an "idea" or spiritual essence.

Notwithstanding his disillusion with Hegelian teleology, Nietzsche continues to philosophize about the conditions of radical and significant cultural change, and thus to resist the antagonism to such philosophizing that links Schopenhauer to de Man. Still, Nietzsche unequivocally follows Schopenhauer in criticizing the Hegelian attempt to construct history "organically." Subsequent to Foucault's engagement with Nietzsche's philosophy, it has become commonplace to observe that Nietzschean genealogy, with its rejection of teleology and its emphasis on contingency, entails a critique of the Hegelian view that history is the self-realization of the world-spirit. As we have seen, moreover, *Zarathustra* can be read as a modernist "rewriting" of the *Phenomenology*, which, rather than describing a necessary course of teleological development, identifies a merely possible route to a possible future. For the later Nietzsche, as distinct from the early Nietzsche and Hegel, historical genealogy (as in *Genealogy*) and future-oriented fictional narrative (as in *Zarathustra*) preserve the modernist hope for a future that is not a repetition of the past, yet without depicting historical change as the inevitable outgrowth of some past process of historical development.

As the "Attempt at a Self-Criticism" demonstrates, the later Nietzsche shows nothing but contempt for his earlier belief that the German nation could serve as the agent of a historical change leading to the Dionysian transformation of European humanity. This contempt is especially evident in Nietzsche's suggestion that, under Bismarck, the German spirit has fallen victim to the modernity of the last man ("leveling mediocrity, democracy, and 'modern ideas'"), and thus come to embody a repression and a negation of the possibility of Dionysian renewal. In *Zarathustra*, disillusionment with the German body politic leads Nietzsche to envision the healthy physical body as the agent of a Dionysian interruption of the last man's modernity. In order to keep attuned to the possibility of going-under, the healthy body must keep its distance from the "cold monster" Bismarck's *Reich* has become.[49] In *Zarathustra*, physical health represents the only real hope that Dionysus can reclaim modern Europe.

For the later Nietzsche, then, the healthy body is a Dionysian body, but not because it has an essence that partakes in the being of things-in-themselves. Having rejected the thing-in-itself/appearances dichotomy and, more generally, all versions of the distinction between a true world and an apparent one, the later Nietzsche develops a "language of . . . [his] . . . own" (what I described in the Introduction to this book as a new philosophical vocabulary) for conceptualizing the possibility of a genuinely Dionysian modernism. The concept of a Dionysian body—that is, of a body that can go-under to passional chaos and subsequently overcome itself—is the centerpiece of this putatively post-Christian-Platonic philosophical project. In the speculative imagination of the later Nietzsche, the Dionysian body incarnates the reconciliation of Dionysus and man, thereby fostering the creation of new values.

With respect to the problem of explaining the possibility of modernism, Nietzsche's methodological shift from historiography to fiction corresponds to a thematic shift from the German nation to the healthy body. In *The Birth of Tragedy*, Nietzsche's historical, dialectical explanation of the possibility of cultural interruption rests on an interpretation of the German nation as a self-purging Dionysian spirit. Analogously, in *Zarathustra*, his fictional explanation of the possibility of cultural interruption rests on an interpretation of the healthy body as (potentially) a value-creating Dionysian body. In the next section of this chapter, I analyze Nietzsche's interpretation of the healthy body, drawing largely on Parts 1 and 2 of *Zarathustra*.

Dionysus and the Body

In *Zarathustra*, Part 1, Zarathustra describes the self, which he identifies with the body, as a site of conflicting passions (*Leidenschaften*). This description of the self is not unique to *Zarathustra*, and is of a piece with Nietzsche's depictions elsewhere (e.g., in *Beyond Good and Evil*) of the self, the body, and/or the soul ("something about the body," in Zarathustra's view) as sites of multiple and opposing instincts, desires, affects, or passions. According to Nietzsche, "the evidence of the body reveals a tremendous multiplicity."[50] Through Zarathustra, Nietzsche conceptualizes values as *esteemed passions* and as features of the self and body. He conceptualizes *new* values as the effects of bodily transformation and self-overcoming.

Zarathustra defines men's values as the "good and evil" they give themselves.[51] But in at least two places in Part 1, he appears to identify this "good and evil" and implicitly men's values with their virtues. Consider, for example, the speech "On the Thousand and One Goals":

Good and evil have always been created by lovers and creators. The fire of love glows in the names of all the virtues [*Tugenden*].
Zarathustra saw many lands and many peoples. No greater power did

Zarathustra find on earth than the works of the lovers: "good" and "evil" are their names.[52]

Zarathustra here draws no distinction between values in general—the "good and evil" that a person or a people gives him-, her-, or itself—and virtues—in his view, the characteristics of individual selves that individuals and/or groups value.[53] The inadvertent shifts in his speech, from talk of good and evil to talk of virtues, and then again to talk of good and evil, suggests at the very least that he identifies the values of persons and peoples first and foremost with their virtues. This suggestion is born out earlier in the same speech, when, in identifying the values promoted by various peoples, Zarathustra describes different peoples' conceptions of virtue: that is, their different conceptions of the characteristics that individual selves have to possess in order to be worthy of the praise of other members of their communities. Zarathustra's examples include the Greeks, who praised the human being who excelled all others; the Persians, who celebrated the individual who spoke the truth and handled the bow and arrow well; the Jews, who honored the person who honored his or her father and mother; and the Germans, who revered the individual who practiced loyalty for its own sake.

"On the Gift-Giving Virtue" is the second place in Part 1 in which Zarathustra seems to characterize all values as virtues.

> Upward goes our way, from genus to overgenus. But we shudder at the degenerate sense which says "Everything for me." Upward flies our sense [*Sinn*], thus it is a parable [*Gleichniss*] of our body, a parable of elevation [*Erhöhung Gleichniss*]. Such parables of elevation [*Solcher Erhöhungen Gleichnisse*] are the names of the virtues [*Tugenden*].
>
> Thus the body goes through history, becoming and fighting. And the spirit—what is that to the body? the herald of all its fights and victories, companion and echo.
>
> All names of good and evil are parables: they do not define, they merely hint. A fool is he who wants knowledge of them.
>
> Watch for every hour, my brothers, in which your spirit wants to speak in parables: there lies the origin [*Ursprung*] of your virtue. There your body is elevated [*Erhöht*] and resurrected [*auferstanden*].[54]

Virtues, Zarathustra says, are bodily states of elevation that virtue-naming parables designate. The history of bodies, he claims, is the history of these states, which states spirits "herald" and "echo," presumably by speaking in parables. (Zarathustra lends support to this presumption when, a few lines later, he anticipates that the spirits of his "brothers" will speak in parables referring to bodily states of elevation that signal the origin in each of them of a new "gift-giving" virtue ["your virtue"].) Read in light of these remarks, Zarathustra's subsequent insistence that "all names of good and evil are parables" suggests that all such names, and thus all the names of all values (keeping in mind that Zarathustra defines men's values as the "good and evil" they give themselves), are parables precisely of the sort he has been discussing: that is, virtue-naming parables that record the history of the body. Zarathustra reinforces this suggestion in the very next paragraph, where the parables to which he alludes appear again to be parables pertaining to bodily elevations.

The thesis I have been advancing, that Zarathustra regards values in general as virtues, is consistent with Zarathustra's speech, in section 3 of the prologue, on overcoming man, as well as with his speech in Part 2 on self-overcoming. In the first of these speeches, Zarathustra argues that to overcome man is to liberate him from Christian-Platonic values and to transform him (see my discussion in Chapter 2). Similarly, in the speech on self-overcoming, he equates the process by which selves overcome themselves with the destruction of old values and the creation of new ones. Both speeches seem to identify value-change with self-change and suggest that to change values is to remake the self by fixing anew the value of the self's already valued characteristics. To revalue these characteristics is, in Zarathustra's view, to produce a new self with new virtues and thus new bodily states of elevation.[55]

Before exploring further the connection between producing new bodily states of elevation and revaluing the self's characteristics, I will consider an important objection to the claim that Zarathustra views values in general as virtues. Such a claim is implausible, this objection holds, for, as Nietzsche notes elsewhere, humans value things other than the characteristics of human selves (e.g., the practices in which they participate). That humans value such things is of course true. But this fact speaks less strongly against my understanding of Zarathustra's "theory of value" than one might suppose. After all, Nietzsche believes that the nature of the values one ascribes to anything that is not a characteristic of the self is a function of the type of self (and body) one is.[56] And because he also believes that the type of self one is is a function of the values one assigns to characteristics of the self (see below my discussion of the body's passions), he reasonably concludes that the creation of new values must always begin with the self and with the self's transformation (Zarathustra says: "Change of values—that is a change of creators").[57] It is plausible, then, that for the sake of explaining the possibility of creating new values Nietzsche has concentrated his attention on the virtues—even to the point of creating a protagonist who conflates the distinction between virtues and values in general—in order to underline the idea that the transformative revaluation of the self's characteristics is fundamental to *all* value creation.

Zarathustra's clearest statement of the nature of virtue occurs in a section of Part 1 entitled "On Enjoying and Suffering the Passions": "Once you suffered passions and called them evil. But now you have only your virtues left: they grew out of your passions. You planted [*legtest*] your highest goal in the heart of these passions: then they became your virtues and passions you enjoyed."[58] In interpreting this passage, I first consider the relation between having a goal and transforming a passion into a virtue. I then turn to the matter of Zarathustra's reference to a specifically *highest* goal. Finally, I return to Zarathustra's discussion of the gift-giving virtue.

Lester Hunt has recently and usefully analyzed the relation between having a goal and transforming a passion into a virtue as a three-term relation.[59] According-ing to Hunt's analysis, the creation of virtue occurs where a particular *agency* (i.e., means or instrumentality) assigns a particular *function* to a particular *passion*. Translated into Zarathustra's language, this amounts to asserting that one's passions become virtues when one (exerting some agency) uses them (thus ren-dering them functional) to nourish the realization of one's highest goal. For Zarathustra, the self/body is a site of multiple passions and affects—enmity, reverence, the desire for sex, the drive to revenge, and so on—that present them-selves as uncreated, raw material for the creation of virtues.

Hunt's explication of his view of the creation of new virtues refers to Nietz-sche's discussion of the will to power in section 12 of the second essay of *Genealogy*. There, Nietzsche characterizes the will to power as an agency whose interpretive activity consists in imposing a purpose or function on some an-tecedently given procedure (e.g., the procedure of punishment) or other subject matter. In what follows, I show that Zarathustra articulates an understanding of valuing as esteeming that involves a similar conception of the will to power and that helps further to illuminate the assertion that the virtues grow out of the passions.[60]

Only man placed values in things to preserve himself—he alone created a meaning for things, a human meaning.

Therefore, he calls himself "man," which means: the esteemer.

To esteem [*Schätzen*] is to create: hear this you creators. . . . Through esteeming alone is there value. . . .

There is much that life esteems more highly than life itself; but out of the esteeming itself speaks the will to power.[61]

Taken together, these passages suggest a plausible though preliminary interpretation of Zarathustra's understanding of the relationship between passions and virtues. One's virtues are simply the passions one esteems. To create a virtue is to transform a passion into a value—to constitute it as "good"—by esteeming it. To esteem a passion, finally, is to subject that passion to one's will to power.

For Zarathustra, the will to power is the will to be master (*Herr*).[62] He suggests, moreover, that the will to be master is a dimension of bodily existence and that it is present in *all* living bodies. "Where I found the living, there I found will to power; and even in the will of those who serve I found the will to be master."[63] For Zarathustra, then, the act of esteeming a passion is, more fundamentally, an act of mastering a passion. From his point of view, there is no difference between esteeming a passion and mastering it.

To master a passion is to make it into a virtue: this, I propose, is the meaning of Zarathustra's claim that to create a virtue is to plant one's "highest goal" in the heart of a passion. Thus, to master a passion is to render it functional visà-vis the realization of some goal or purpose. Because Zarathustra also holds that to master a passion is to esteem it, he is tactily committed to the proposition that causing a passion to serve some purpose is equivalent to prizing it for serving that purpose. Zarathustra draws no distinction between constituting a passion as "good" (esteeming it and transforming it into a virtue) and rendering it effective in some purposive or functional capacity. To constitute a passion as "good" is, in his view, to use it, to adapt it to and literally make it "good for" the realization of some function. By representing the will to power as a purpose-imbuing will to be master, Zarathustra prefigures Nietzsche's general claim in *Genealogy* that "all events in the organic world are a subduing, a *becoming master* [*Herrwerden*], and all subduing and becoming master involves a fresh interpretation, an adaptation [*Zurechtmachen*] through which any previous 'meaning' and 'purpose' are necessarily obscured or obliterated."[64]

I will now turn now to Zarathustra's suggestion that human beings create virtues when they use their passions to realize their specifically *highest* goals and purposes. I will focus first on the relationship between Zarathustra's view of value-creation and the historic reign of the ascetic ideal as man's highest goal. I then discuss the connection between this same view of value-creation and Zarathustra's exhortation to make the overcoming of man man's highest goal.

For Zarathustra, to overcome man is to overcome Christian-Platonic man. As we have seen, Christian-Platonic man is constituted in his identity by his subjection to the ascetic ideal—the ultimate end or "highest goal" of his existence—and by his embodiment of Christian-Platonic values. Interpreting the body of Christian-Platonic man in light of the view of values (virtues) and value-creation that Zarathustra articulates in Part 1, it follows that that body is one in which the will to power uses the body's passions to realize the ascetic ideal. Furthermore, because nothingness is the ascetic ideal, it also follows that the body of Christian-Platonic man incarnates a will to power that uses the passions to annihilate the passions. Nietzsche describes a will to power of this sort in the third essay of *Genealogy*:

> An ascetic life is a self-contradiction; here rules a *ressentiment* without equal, that of an insatiable instinct and power-will [*Machtwillens*] that wants to become master [*Herr*] not over something in life, but over life itself, over its most profound, powerful, and basic conditions; here an attempt is made to employ force to block up the wells of force. . . . All this is in the highest degree paradoxical: we stand before a discord that *wants* to be discordant, that *enjoys* itself in this suffering and even grows more self-confident and triumphant the more its own presupposition, its physiological capacity for life, *decreases*.[65]

A will to power (or power-will) that wills nothingness aims to eradicate "life itself" and not simply to destroy a part of life, or "something in life." It wants to master life by imposing on life and *all* of life's passions the purpose of being annihilated. From the perspective of such a will, the function of each and every passion is the destruction of that passion. To make a passion serve that function is to esteem it, for in destroying a passion one uses it to realize the ascetic ideal, prizing that passion for its instrumental efficacy. A passion becomes a Christian-Platonic virtue to the extent that, in succumbing to annihilation, it becomes effective as a means to satisfying the will to nothingness.[66]

Christian-Platonic man esteems the passions in proportion to the measure in which they yield to destruction. In his view, a man achieves perfect virtue only by eradicating his passions. Nietzsche puts the point well when he writes that "the [Christian] moralist's madness . . . demands, instead of the restraining of the passions, their extirpation. Its conclusion is always: only the castrated man is a good man."[67] Nietzsche puts the point again when he relates Christianity's "anti-natural morality" to the condemnation of both the lowest and highest desires of life and when he proclaims that the corruption of men (the loss of their instincts) is greatest where they "have so far aspired most deliberately to 'virtue' and 'godliness.'"[68]

In the wake of the self-destruction of the ascetic ideal, Zarathustra urges Christian-Platonic man to make overcoming man his *highest goal*. In order to realize that goal, a given individual would need to effect in his person a revaluation of at least some of his body's passions—a process that would effect the overcoming of man (in a particular instance), precisely to the extent that it resulted in the creation of a self of a sort other than that of Christian-Platonic man. Of course, any number of revaluations, resulting in the creation of any number of different sorts of non-Christian-Platonic selves, would achieve this goal. What they would all share in common is the use of at least some of the body's passions, not to effect these passions' annihilation, but to form selves in which these passions thrived.

For man to be overcome, passions that the will to nothingness sought to extirpate must flourish. To be precise, a (Christian-Platonic) man overcomes himself if, and only if, he uses some of his passions, and thus some of the passions the will to nothingness aimed to destroy (for the will to nothingness aimed to destroy *all* passions), to create a self/body that takes delight in and draws inspiration from the passions it incorporates. Nietzsche suggests in many places that to create such a self would be to form one's passions into a coherent and ordered whole, and thus to make oneself into a joyful work of art.[69] His explication of this notion of self-creation is especially clear in *The Gay Science*:

> *One thing is needful.*—"To give style" [*Stil geben*] to one's character—a great
> and rare art! It is practiced by those who survey all the strengths and weakness
> of their nature and then fit them into an artistic plan until every one of them
> appears as art and reason and even weaknesses delight [*entzückt*] the eye. . . .
> In the end, when the work is finished, it becomes evident how the constraint
> of a single taste governed and formed everything large and small. . . . It will
> be the strong and domineering natures that enjoy their finest gaiety [*ihre
> feinste Freude geniessen*] in such constraint and perfection under a law of
> their own.[70]

To use one's passions to create a being beyond man (an "overman") is to "stylize" and hence to revalue those passions; it is, in other words, to unify them and, by unifying them, to render them effective (functional) as sources of that self-enjoyment and delight that come from subjecting oneself to "the constraint of a single taste." As the act of creating a being beyond man can yield indefinitely many sorts of selves, there is no unique recipe for achieving the unity of self that produces this self-enjoyment and delight.[71]

In his speech on the gift-giving virtue, Zarathustra seems not to distinguish the joy and delight of self-creation (creating new virtues) from the experience of bodily states of "elevation."[72] As we have seen, he also seems to claim that all virtues are states of elevation. Yet there are passages in Zarathustra's speech in which his references to states of elevation pertain neither to virtue in general, nor to every virtue, but specifically to those *new* virtues and values that make "holy" the instincts that were subject to repression under the reign of the ascetic ideal.[73] These virtues and values have a special relation to the virtue Zarathustra calls "the gift-giving virtue." Moreover, they can be distinguished from Christian-Platonic virtues, which are also states of elevation.

Even before his speech on the gift-giving virtue, wherein he describes Christian-Platonic virtues as virtues that have "flown away" from the earth, Zarathustra suggests that these virtues are states of elevation:[74]

> It was the sick and the decaying who despised body and earth and invented the heavenly realm and the redemptive drops of blood: but they took even these sweet and gloomy poisons from body and earth. . . . Ungrateful, these people deemed themselves transported [*entrückt*] from their bodies and this earth. But to whom did they owe the convulsions and raptures of their transport [*Entrückung*]? To their bodies and this earth.[75]

Here Zarathustra proposes that even the will to nothingness elevates the body, though not by elevating the body's passions. Rather, by destroying the passions, the will to nothingness elevates the body beyond the passions, making it feel that it has been transported beyond itself. Christian-Platonic virtues are states of elevation—in a sense, privative states of passionlessness—that obtain when the passions become virtues by succumbing to annihilation. In at least one place, Nietzsche describes the feeling of trans-portation that accompanies these states as an excruciating pain that relieves sick bodies of their weariness and depression.[76]

The *new* virtues and values Zarathustra envisions are states not only of the body's "elevation" (*Erhöhung*), but also of its "resurrection" (*Auferstehung*).[77] Echoing the Bible's description of the resurrection of Christ, Zarathustra imagines the creation of a body that would be, not passionless, but brimming with passion, a body in which repressed and dying passions were "brought back to life." The resurrected body to which Zarathustra alludes would be elevated, not because it was raised beyond its passions, but because it raised up its passions beyond the clutches of death.

As we saw in Chapter 2, the transmutation of passions into new values—figured in "On the Gift-Giving Virtue" as the "resurrection" of the body, but also in the prologue as the "harvesting" of new values—requires the existence of Dionysian bodies that go-under and overcome themselves. The resurrected body is a Dionysian body, for it is the body of someone who goes-under to passional, Dionysian chaos, in this case in order to reclaim his previously repressed passions and make them sources of self-enjoyment. The gift-giving virtue contributes to the creation of resurrected bodies, because it is the virtue of reclaiming or *in-corporating* previously repressed and dying passions: that is, of rendering these passions functional as thriving features of the body and self. The gift-giving virtue is the virtue of finding a place within one's body for passions that one hitherto willed to exterminate.

In order to resurrect one's body, one must go-under to a passional chaos that the last man cannot experience. More exactly, one must surrender one's ascetic will to annihilate one's passions (that is, to master them and render them functional *by* annihilating them) and *then* go-under to passional chaos. Going-under, then, is a necessary condition of the resurrection of the body. But it is not a sufficient condition. Going-under, by itself, does not result in the reclamation and integration of previously repressed passions. Additionally, the resurrection of the body requires that one wills to acknowledge and embrace as aspects of oneself—again, to incorporate into one's self—desires and passions that one previously wished to destroy.

Zarathustra identifies the gift-giving virtue as the *highest virtue.*[78] This identification implicitly relates the gift-giving virtue to esteeming, since, in an earlier speech, Zarathustra describes "esteeming" as "of all esteemed things the most estimable treasure."[79] By claiming that esteeming is what he esteems most, Zarathustra represents esteeming as a virtue and as the highest virtue.

Now all esteeming, we have seen, is will to power. To esteem esteeming, then, is to esteem the will to power and to make it into a virtue. A particular individual could make her will to power into a virtue, only by assigning it some function. That individual would acquire the *gift-giving virtue* only if she assigned to her will to power the function of transforming her self and body by incorporating some previously repressed passions. To acquire the gift-giving virtue, in other words, she would have to make her will to power effective as a means of self-resurrection.[80]

> Verily, a new good and evil is she. . . . Power is she, this new virtue, a ruling thought is she. . . . Remain faithful to the earth . . . with the power of your virtue. Let your gift-giving love and your knowledge serve the meaning of the earth. . . . Do not let them fly away from earthly things and beat with their wings against eternal walls. Alas, there has always been so much virtue that has flown away. Lead back to the earth the virtue that flew away, as I do—back to the body, back to life, that it may give the earth a meaning, a human meaning.
>
> In a hundred ways, thus far, have spirit as well as virtue flown away and made mistakes. Alas, all this delusion and all these mistakes still dwell in our body: they have there become body and will.

In a hundred ways, thus far, spirit as well as virtue has tried and erred. Indeed, an experiment was man. Alas much ignorance and error have become body within us. . . .

With knowledge the body purifies itself; making experiments with knowledge, it elevates itself; in the lover of knowledge all instincts become holy; in the elevated, the soul becomes gay.[81]

The gift-giving virtue is power; it is power the will to power exercises in creating new values ("a new good and evil is she . . ."). The will to power exercises this power by effecting a "ruling mastery" over previously repressed passions and instincts, thereby rendering them effective as sources of self-enjoyment (*Selbst-Lust*).[82] Functioning in the role of the gift-giving virtue, the will to power serves the purpose of re-valuing the passions and creating a new sort of self. Thus, it serves the purpose of creating a being beyond man, which purpose is "the meaning of the earth." The knowledge that abets this purpose is that "seeing" and "hearing" of the possibility of going-under and overcoming oneself to which Zarathustra exhorts his auditors. It is a knowledge that envisions a future different from the past and that I have attributed to new philosophers and to the child of "On the Three Metamorphoses." To draw inspiration from that knowledge, and thus to own rather than disown the uncreated passions that are its subject matter, would be to "experiment" with the self by going-under and fashioning a new self. A refashioning of the self would "purify" the body of the repression that the practice of asceticism has perpetuated, for it would resurrect the passions as features of a newly integrated body. Virtue that had "flown away" from the earth, by becoming indistinguishable from the privation of earthly and bodily passions, would be "led back" to the earth and flourish there as states of elevation in which instinct and desire claimed and moved human existence.

As we have seen, to esteem esteeming is to esteem the will to power and to make it into a virtue. And because all esteeming is will to power, it follows that the will to power becomes a virtue when it esteems itself and assigns itself some function. The *gift-giving virtue* appears just when the will to power assigns itself the function of incorporating some previously repressed passions, aiming thereby to render them effective as sources of self-enjoyment and delight. Though a new virtue and value in its own right, the gift-giving virtue also constitutes *other* new virtues and values *as* virtues and values (as esteemed passions). I noted above (parenthetically) that Zarathustra's allusion to the elevation and resurrection of the body ("watch for every hour . . . in which your spirit wants to speak in parables: there lies the origin [*Ursprung*] of your virtue. There your body is elevated and resurrected") pertains to the origin in the body of the gift-giving virtue, which he calls "your virtue." But this allusion also pertains to the origin of virtue other than the gift-giving virtue, because the appearance of the gift-giving virtue entails the resurrection of previously repressed passions and thus the revaluing, or "re-virtuing," of those passions. In other words, the esteeming of esteeming always involves the esteeming of features of the self other than esteeming.

The relation between the gift-giving virtue and other new virtues can best be characterized as that between first-order and second-order passions. By the former I mean those passions and desires that most immediately claim the body, inclining it and sometimes moving it to act or not to act in one way or another. The passions I cited earlier, including enmity, reverence, and the desire for sex, are good examples of the passions or desires that Nietzsche would count as "first-order." By second-order passions I mean one's desires to have or not have, or to render effective or ineffective in some capacity, some first-order desire or desires. Second-order passions express one's capacity for self-evaluation, one's ability to want to be or not to be the sort of person one is.[83]

For Nietzsche, all second-order desire is will to power. When the will to power seeks virtue in nothingness, it wills that a given body's first-order passions be destroyed. When the will to power seeks virtue in resurrection, it wills that a given body's previously repressed first-order passions function effectively as sources of self-enjoyment. Relative to these previously repressed first-order passions, the will to power (of a given individual), in exemplifying the gift-giving virtue, functions as a second-order passion.[84] The will to power functions as a second-order passion only if it *makes itself* function in this way (by esteeming its own esteeming). Thus, the will to power (of a given individual), in exemplifying the gift-giving virtue, behaves as a higher-order passion relative to its own second-order activity of resurrecting first-order passions. Pursuing the purpose of overcoming man, the will to power causes itself to revalue the passions and thus to transform the character of human existence.

The will to power that causes itself to revalue the passions is the will to power of the child: it is the self-reflexive will to power of a spirit that, as we saw in Chapter 1, "wills its own will." Now, the child-spirit, I have argued, embodies an intention to create new values. The child-spirit realizes this intention, I can now add, just to the extent that he wills his will to power to revalue his passions. In revaluing his passions, the child-spirit affirmatively responds to the experience of going-under to passional chaos—which experience, we have seen, is a necessary but not sufficient condition for the resurrection of the body. The essence of this affirmation, the child-spirit's "yes" to the game of creation, is the transformation of passional chaos into a newly integrated body.

Zarathustra ends his explicit discussion of the gift-giving virtue with the following remarks:

Physician help yourself: thus you help your patient too. Let this be his best help that he may behold with his eyes the man who heals himself.

There are a thousand paths that have never yet been trodden—a thousand healths and hidden isles of life.

Even now, man and man's earth are unexhausted [*Unerschöpft*] and undiscovered.

Wake and listen, you that are lonely! From the future come winds with secret wing beats; and good tidings are proclaimed to delicate ears. You that are lonely today, you that are withdrawing, you shall one day be the people: out of you, who have chosen yourselves, there shall grow a chosen people—and out of them the overman. Verily, the earth shall yet become a site of recovery. And even now a new fragrance surrounds it, bringing salvation—and a new hope.[85]

With these words, Zarathustra relates his account of the gift-giving virtue to themes he introduces early in Part 1. In particular, he suggests that health is incompatible with the exhaustion of man's earth—or, more exactly, that the availability of "a thousand healths" implies that "man and man's earth are unexhausted"—thereby recalling his previously expressed interpretation of bodily health and sickness. Zarathustra initially states this interpretation in "On the Afterworldly" and "On the Despisers of the Body," the speeches of Part 1 that immediately follow "On the Teachers of Virtue." In "On the Teachers of Virtue," Zarathustra depicts Christian-Platonic teachers of virtue whose commitment to the ascetic ideal has moved them to equate virtue with the suppression of life and life's passions (Zarathustra describes as "opiate [*mohnblumige*] virtues" the virtues such teachers praise; as we have seen, these virtues ultimately stem from wills to power that will nothingness).[86] In "On the Afterworldly" and "On the Despisers of the Body," he fills out this depiction, describing the ascetic teaching of virtue as a product of sick bodies whose sickness is a symptom of exhaustion.[87]

In "On the Afterworldly," Zarathustra claims that the creation of "afterworlds" is due to "suffering and incapacity [*Unvermögen*]"; to a "poor ignorant weariness that does not want to want anymore"; and to "the sick and dying who despised body and earth." In "On the Despisers of the Body," he explains his idea of incapacity, arguing that incapacity breeds contempt for the earth: "Your self . . . wants to die and turns away from life. It is no longer capable [*Nicht mehr vermag*] of what it would do above all else: to create beyond itself. . . . But now it is too late for . . . this. . . . For you are no longer able [*nicht mehr vermögt*] to create beyond yourselves. And that is why you are angry with life and the earth." Despisers of the earth cannot re-create themselves, for they have *ex-*

hausted their capacities to do so. They "despair" of their weary, suffering, sick bodies, and invent "the heavenly realm," because they cannot find within their bodies the living impulses and inspiration they need to make something different of themselves.[88]

Uninspired bodies unable to create beyond themselves have fallen ill. In "On the Afterworldly," Zarathustra implies that these bodies no longer voice "the meaning of the earth."[89] Still, he later asserts that *man and man's earth have yet to be exhausted.* In "On the Gift-Giving Virtue," in other words, Zarathustra expresses his "new hope" that not *all* human bodies have become so wanting in inspiration and so ill that they cannot be awakened ("Wake and listen," Zarathustra says in "On the Gift-Giving Virtue") to the possibility of self-overcoming. Zarathustra's hope is an expectation he first articulates near the end of "Zarathustra's Prologue." It is, in essence, his wishful belief that the reign of asceticism in the age of the last man has not thoroughly annihilated the passional preconditions of self-overcoming. From the perspective of "On the Afterworldly" and "On the Despisers of the Body," Zarathustra's hope appears to express a faith— a Dionysian faith—that the sickness and exhaustion leading some individuals to become afterworldly ascetics have not become pandemic through these individuals' teaching. (Prefiguring the priest of *Genealogy*, the "afterworldly" and the "despisers of the body" seem to be teachers of asceticism whose teaching has spread the very sickness and exhaustion that engendered *their* asceticism.)[90] Echoing his judgment of the teachings of ascetic teachers of virtue—"if life had no sense [*Sinn*] and I had to choose nonsense [*Unsinn*], then I too should consider this the most sensible nonsense [*Unsinn*]"—Zarathustra admits that ascetic doctrines have held sway over human bodies for a long time, thereby propagating a sickness he wishes to see healed: "mistakes still dwell in our body . . . they have there become body and will . . . over the whole of humanity there has ruled so far only nonsense—no sense [*Unsinn, der Ohne-Sinn*]. . . . Physician, help yourself."[91] Still, Zarathustra believes that these doctrines, notwithstanding their repressive, sickness-causing effects, have not exhausted human health, that they have left at least *some* individuals healthy enough to find within their "perpendicular" (*rechtwinklige*) bodies living passions that can inspire them to create beyond themselves.[92]

Here, it should be noted that Nietzsche's interest in the theme of bodily exhaustion was typical of the late nineteenth century. Indeed, he shared with many of his contemporaries—scientists, physicians, and novelists among them —the belief that modern civilization was fast succumbing to the forces of physical fatigue. Neither was Nietzsche alone in tying physical exhaustion to cultural decay, or in envisioning the possibility of bodies liberated from fatigue.[93] He seems to have distinguished himself, however, by proposing that freedom from fatigue is the privilege of the healthy, Dionysian body. Moreover, Nietzsche's concept of a healthy body seems to reflect less the speculations of his contemporaries than the influence of Goethe on his thinking. Particularly interesting in this connection is Goethe's treatment of the theme of exhaustion in the *Conversations with Eckermann*, a book that Nietzsche described as "the best German book there is."[94] For Goethe, poets can remain new and inexhaustible (*unerschöpflich*) only by means of a "healthy effort . . . directed from the inward to the outward world." The healthy poet, he thought, speaks not "his few subjective feelings," but makes the world his own and expresses it (*sobald er die Welt sich anzueignen und aussprechen weiss, ist er ein Poet*).[95] Goethe's sense that one could resist the exhaustion of one's creative capacity, by opening one's self to forces that subjective poets have disowned, prefigures Nietzsche's representation of Dionysian bodies as reclaiming and incorporating previously repressed and dying passions. For Nietzsche, Dionysian self-overcoming is less a matter of expressing the self's feelings and passions than of opening the self to and embracing passions that it previously willed to obliterate. It is this Goethean opening of the self that Nietzsche celebrates when he says that Goethe "took as much as possible upon himself, over himself, into himself" and that he could "afford the whole range and wealth of being natural."[96] Nietzsche interprets Goethe's belief that the world would always answer to his openness, that he would never deplete the inspiring riches it provided him, as the "highest of all possible faiths," a faith that Nietzsche baptizes with the name "Dionysus."[97] Like Zarathustra, Nietzsche's Goethe affirmed a Dionysian faith in the persistence in human experience of the natural, uncreated passions that fuel creation.

In conceptualizing the healthy and perhaps Goethean body as the conduit of a Dionysian interruption of modern, European culture, Nietzsche assumes that that culture is founded on the will to power's esteeming and functional ordering of bodily passions. For the later Nietzsche, the distinctive character of a given culture derives from the perpetuation over time of one and the same functional ordering of the passions by the embodied wills to power (second-order desires) active in that culture. In other words, the distinctive character of a culture reflects a distinctive style of embodiment (Eric Blondel is right, then, to view Nietzschean genealogy as a "stylistics of the will to power and the body").[98] Furthermore, when Zarathustra, or Nietzsche, criticizes a given culture, he highlights the possibility of revaluing the passions to which the wills to power active in that culture have assigned a particular purpose or set of purposes and thereby produced a distinctive style of embodiment. By recalling men to the earth, or to the possibility of going-under to passional, Dionysian chaos, Zarathustra would persuade his auditors to see that they *can* restyle their bodies and remake European culture by compelling their passions to fulfill a purpose (effectiveness as a source of self-enjoyment) other than the purpose (destruction) that they have hitherto served.

It would be a mistake, then, to take Zarathustra's references to the body, the earth, or, as he sometimes puts it, life, as invoking a nature/culture dualism that displaces but somehow echoes the thing-in-itself/appearances dualism that shapes the argument of *The Birth of Tragedy*.[99] In claiming that "man and man's earth are unexhausted," Zarathustra does not mean to imply that self-overcoming entails the interruption of a particular culture, or form of life, by a precultural Dionysian reality that subsists apart from all forms of life. Rather, his point is that some of the desires that modernity's ascetic culture has wanted to annihilate have yet to be annihilated; they persist *within that culture* as impulses that, though they have been assigned the purpose of being destroyed, can be revalued. Zarathustra's appeal to "man and man's earth" is an exhortation to persons who share a form of life (the ascetic culture of modernity) to "wake and listen" to the impulses that animate that form of life and that those persons could will to function in new ways. For Zarathustra, to listen to the body and the earth is to attune oneself to passions within one's self and culture that one could use to interrupt the reproduction of a culturally normative and dominant style of embodiment.[100] Resistance to culture is cultural, though it must also be said that "culture," for Zarathustra, like "soul," is a word for something *about* the body.[101]

Zarathustra's Search for Companions

Near the end of the prologue, after he departs from the tightrope walker and performs the second metamorphosis of the spirit, Zarathustra seeks companions who could join him in the project of creating new values. As we have seen, individuals of this sort would have to have bodies that still harbored the possibility of going-under; unlike the townspeople Zarathustra addresses in the prologue, they would be able to experience passional chaos in spite of their exposure to the practices of modern asceticism. Zarathustra finds hope in the belief that such individuals exist, for he has explained his perlocutionary failure in *historical* terms, suggesting not that his failure was due to the constitutive limits of human knowledge (as would de Man), but to the fact that passion-eroding modern asceticism had extirpated the passions of the townspeople he addressed.

In Part 1, Zarathustra's search for companions takes the form of a series of speeches that repeatedly draws on the rhetoric and the conceptual framework developed in "On the Three Metamorphoses." Whereas the camel-lion-child scheme implicitly shaped Zarathustra's actions in the prologue, it explicitly frames his speaking and thinking in Part 1. In Part 1, moreover, *Zarathustra's* thematic focus shifts from Zarathustra's gradually dawning recognition that overcoming man may not be possible to his attempt to articulate what he calls at one point "the way of the creator." In adumbrating this "way," Zarathustra relies on the figures of the camel, the lion, and the child to describe the psychological pitfalls, the tempting distractions, and the helpful allies that the individual who would perform and sustain in his own person the metamorphosis from camel to lion is likely to encounter. Zarathustra also sketches a form of life, an ethics of sorts, that is compatible with being a lion who may one day become a child.[102]

Having enacted the second metamorphosis of the spirit, just prior to the ending of the prologue, Zarathustra's speech in Part 1 is a lion's speech meant for potential and actual lions. Zarathustra's search for companions who can go-under is also a search for fellow lions, for, in becoming a lion-spirit, one maintains one's commitment to becoming a creator of new values—one's encounters with representations of repetition notwithstanding—absent which commitment going-under and becoming a creator of new values is not possible. It is paradoxical, therefore, that in becoming a lion-spirit, and thus maintaining one's commitment to becoming a creator of new values, one alienates oneself from one's ability to go-under and defeats the possibility of fulfilling that commitment. Zarathustra acknowledges the paradox the lion-spirit embodies and learns *why* that spirit cannot create new values only in Part 2. In Part 1, he evinces no knowledge of these matters.

As I argued in Chapter 1, a lion-spirit believes that newly created values would derive from his will and his will alone. Thus, a lion-spirit cannot acknowledge that other lion-spirits could become new-values creators. It is ironic, then, that Zarathustra in Part 1 seeks fellow lions who can become new-values creators. Apparently unmindful of his leonine belief that new values must stem exclusively from his will, he speaks and acts precisely as if this belief were false. Again, it is only in Part 2 that Zarathustra begins to evince self-knowledge, and to admit that, *qua lion*, and despite his claims to the contrary, he has not been able to discern in other lion-wills the power and the authority to create new values.

"On the Pale Criminal" is the first speech in Part 1 in which Zarathustra evaluates a lion-spirited individual. Greg Whitlock is right, I think, to see the person Zarathustra discusses here as a "lion . . . in crisis," someone who, though he is disposed to transgress the "thou shalt" morality to which the camel submits, reverts almost immediately to the ethos of Zarathustra's "beast of burden."[103] A paradigmatic product of the Christian-Platonic interpretation of man, the pale criminal is the victim (1) of a Christian-Platonic "reason" (*Vernunft*) that wants to restrict the power of bodily desire to control human action, and (2) of a Christian-Platonic morality that is obsessed with the idea of sin.

The pale criminal's soul interprets his body's suffering and coveting as "murderous lust and greed for the bliss of the knife." This soul, moreover, having ascribed to the pale criminal's body a desire for the bliss of the knife, seems to want that body (1) to desire that bliss and (2) to commit a crime, acting from and satisfying its desire for bliss.[104] In effect, the pale criminal has a second-order desire to have a desire for blood (the bliss of the knife) and to have that desire become effective as a motive.[105]

Now, from the perspective of the pale criminal's "poor reason," the desire to be motivated by a desire for blood is madness and a cause for shame. Speaking in a utilitarian voice reminiscent of the last man, this reason asks, "What matters blood," thereby suggesting that no good is to be gained from actions motivated only by a desire for blood. The poor reason also proclaims that actions motivated by a desire to steal are reasonable and hence shameless. Here, being reasonable seems to amount to little more than being intelligible as the expression of an instrumental rationality bent on finding the best means appropriate to the realization of some material gain (here, the acquisition of a good through theft). The pale criminal's reason aims to tame the pale criminal by persuading him (1) to repudiate his second-order disposition to be motivated, *no matter what the consequences*, by his body's urgings—for instance, by his desire for blood—and (2) to want to be motivated *only* by those bodily urgings the satisfaction of which will also produce some material gain. "'What matters blood?' it asked; 'don't you want at least to commit a robbery *with it* [*dabei*]'" (emphasis mine).

Keeping in mind that Zarathustra later interprets second-order desire as will to power, one could say that the primary aim of the pale criminal's poor and Christian-Platonic reason is to enlist the pale criminal's will to power in repressive practices that promote the ascetic ideal. The central message of this poor reason is that bodily desires should be renounced if their satisfaction is not compatible with the demands of an instrumental rationality geared toward material acquisition. Letting his sick body get the best of him, the pale criminal finds that he is hungry for blood and, lionlike, disposed to transgress the "thou shalt" morality of the camel. Still, he remains prey to the camel's asceticism, even in enacting his transgression, because he heeds his poor reason and robs when he murders. The pale criminal is a "lion in crisis," for in becoming a thief he submits to an ethos of renunciation that will be enforced by a repressive will to power. After he performs his murderous deed, the pale criminal's crisis becomes a complete relapse:

An image made this man pale. He was equal to his deed when he did it; but he could not bear its image after it was done. Now he always saw himself as the *doer of one deed.* Madness I call this: *the exception now became the essence* for him. A chalk streak stops a hen. . . .

And now the lead of his guilt lies upon him, and again his poor reason is so stiff, so paralyzed, so heavy. If only he could shake his head, then his burden would roll off: but who could shake this head?[106]

Having committed his crime, the pale criminal sees himself as, and only as, a criminal, the guilty agent of a wrongful deed. In effect, he subjects himself to what Nietzsche describes elsewhere, in words that echo Zarathustra's character-ization of the pale criminal, as "the *'idée fixe'* of sin, the hypnotizing of the hen by the chalk line 'sin.'"[107] In his own eyes, the pale criminal is naught but a sin-ner; his exception (*Ausnahme*) becomes his essence (*Wesen*), because he regards his singular flouting of Christian morality as defining, once and for all, the na-ture of his being. Confronting the image of his deed, the pale criminal repudi-ates forever the thought that he could be anything other than a sinner.

In judging himself to be a sinner, the pale criminal interprets his deed in the perspective of Christian morality.[108] In conceptualizing his sinfulness as his en-tire essence, he denies the possibility of being anyone other than the person he is in that perspective. Zarathustra appropriately describes the pale criminal in terms recalling the camel spirit (e.g., as bearing a heavy [*schwer*] burden), because the pale criminal, once he has performed his deed, cannot envision the possibility of a future in which he would be judged by values other than those of Christian morality. His vision paralyzed by his guilt, the pale criminal is pathologically prey to what Zarathustra calls "madness after the deed": he sees Christian moral val-ues as the only possible values, as the only values in light of which his actions could be judged, and as justifying a judgment of his actions that reveals the quid-dity of his being. In the pale criminal's view, his "sinfulness" is *not* an interpreta-tion of a fact, but a metaphysically necessary feature of his identity.[109]

The four speeches that follow the speech on the pale criminal—"On Reading and Writing," "On the Tree on the Mountainside," "On the Preachers of Death," and "On War and Warriors"—constitute Zarathustra's attempt to clearly charac-terize the spirit of the lion and to address himself to persons who, though they as-pire to be lions, have yet to complete the second metamorphosis of the spirit. Un-like the pale criminal, the auditors who concern Zarathustra in these speeches are not individuals in whom some version of Christian-Platonic reason or morality has been so thoroughly ingrained that their efforts to perform the second meta-morphosis are doomed from the start. Rather they are individuals whose attempts to say "I will" need to be encouraged and nourished, potential companions who could one day achieve the leonine independence from Christianity and Platonism that Zarathustra believes he himself personifies.

In "On Reading and Writing," Zarathustra alludes to his speech on the pale criminal and professes a taste for aphorisms written in blood. Thus expressing his literary appetite for sanguineous adages, he underlines the affinity of his own transgressive spirit to the pale criminal's desire to be moved by the desire for blood. Zarathustra also resembles the pale criminal in expressing a taste for bodies, though not for the bliss of the knife. Zarathustra's taste is instead for "tall and lofty" physiques, for the upright, perpendicular forms that "On the After-worldly" attributes to healthy bodies. In Zarathustra's view, aphorisms written in blood—aphorisms that, like his speeches, bespeak and encourage the transgressive spirit of the lion—nourish healthy bodies.

Zarathustra's leonine antipathy to the camel-spirit is evident throughout "On Reading and Writing." For example, he takes issue with the belief that life is a gloomy and ponderous enterprise ("I no longer feel as you do: this cloud which I see beneath me, this blackness and gravity [*Schwere*] at which I laugh—this is your thundercloud"); with the sentiment that life is too "hard to bear" (*schwer zu tragen*); and with the solemn sensibility of "the spirit of gravity" (*der Geist der Schwere*), the "devil" through whom "all things fall."[110] In general, Zarathustra rejects the camel-spirit's belief that life is a difficult and weighty burden. In alluding to the spirit of gravity—whom he later blames for the camel-spirit's submission to Christian values[111]—Zarathustra also recalls the jester of the prologue, a literal spirit of gravity and the devil (when he leaps over the tightrope walker, the jester's cry is described as "devilish")[112] through whom the tightrope walker falls. In Part 3, the spirit of gravity returns to haunt Zarathustra and, again reminiscent of the jester, propounds the belief endorsed by the camel and the great dragon that striving to create new values is futile.

By repeatedly adopting the grammatical form of the first-person singular in "On Reading and Writing" (I count nineteen instances in this speech, as compared to five in the one immediately preceding it), Zarathustra persistently echoes the self-assertive "I" of the lion's "I will." Likewise, in this speech, he elaborates his earlier suggestion that the lion is combative (in "On the Three Metamorphoses," Zarathustra asserted that the lion-spirit wanted to struggle [*ringen*] for victory [*Sieg*] against the great dragon), implying that the courage and character of the warrior is critical to maintaining an "elevated" freedom from the spirit of gravity ("Brave, unconcerned, mocking, violent—thus wisdom wants us: she is a woman and always loves only a warrior").[113] Having repudiated the camel's outlook on life, Zarathustra concludes "On Reading and

Writing" with a description of his leonine experience of rising high above the ominous spirit who would thwart his modernist ambitions: "Come, let us kill the spirit of gravity! I have learned to walk: ever since, I let myself run. I have learned to fly: ever since, I do not want to be pushed before moving along. Now I am light, now I fly, now I see myself beneath myself, now a god dances through me."[114]

In "On the Tree on the Mountainside," Zarathustra meets a lad who hopes to personify the spirit of the lion but who has trouble bearing the independence ("I no longer trust myself since I aspire to the height") and the loneliness ("nobody trusts me . . . Nobody speaks to me") required to say no to established values. The young man's claims to aspire "to the height" and to hate "the flier" suggest that he has taken to heart and even learned by heart Zarathustra's speech in "On Reading and Writing." (Zarathustra encouraged this response to his speech in remarking that "whoever writes in blood and aphorisms does not want to be read but to be learned by heart.") Wishing to emulate Zarathustra, the lad strives for the elevated freedom from the spirit of gravity that Zarathustra claims for himself. He is frustrated, however, not only by the difficulty of his task, but by his envy of one better than himself: "Behold," he says to Zarathustra, "what am I, now that you have appeared among us? It is the *envy* of you that has destroyed me." Answering his envious admirer, Zarathustra feels compelled to tell him that he is not yet free: "To me," says Zarathustra, "you are still a prisoner who is plotting his freedom."

The youth on the mountainside "wants to create something new and a new virtue." Still, he merely anticipates his freedom and remains captive to old virtues and values, presumably for want of the confidence that he can act independently and say "I will." The danger facing Zarathustra's admirer is not that he will devote himself to preserving old virtues (like "the good"), but that his envy and self-doubt will make him "an impudent one [*Frecher*], a mocker [*Höhnender*], [and] a destroyer [*Vernichter*]," one who repudiates his "highest hope" and slanders "all high hopes." Having faltered in his efforts to personify the autonomy and self-trust of the lion, the young man, notwithstanding his attachment to traditional values, will still deride them even as he derides *all* aims that merit esteem. Taking revenge on the entire human enterprise for his personal failure, he is destined to become a spirit of negation who denies that there are any ends justifying serious and heroic commitment: "Once they thought of becoming heroes: now they are voluptuaries. The hero is for them an offence and a fright."[115]

It is the almost Schopenhauerian pessimism threatening the youth on the mountainside that explains Zarathustra's next speech. Supposing that this youth did come to see in the voluptuary's life his only escape from the feeling that human ends have no value, he would be ripe for the central teaching of pessimism, the doctrine of renunciation (*Abkehr*). In "On the Preachers of Death," Zarathustra warns against that doctrine in its many versions, hoping to discredit it in the eyes of individuals who, like the youth on the mountainside, might be drawn to it.[116] It seems clear, however, that the attack on pessimism advanced in this speech, while it could succeed in prompting resistance to feelings of resignation, offers nothing to replace them. Indeed, Zarathustra says nothing that begins to make good his final words to his tormented companion: "Hold holy your highest hope!" Is there any point to such a command, one wonders, if it is addressed to an individual whose envy and self-distrust have defeated his aspiration? And won't Zarathustra's words seem useless, if one's struggle to say "I will" has left one unable to acknowledge the worth of anything?

Seemingly sensitive to these questions, Zarathustra more persuasively engages the issues they pose in "On War and Warriors." Here, he addresses individuals like the youth on the mountainside, men who aspire to the autonomy of the lion ("Your enemy you shall seek, your war you shall wage—for your own thoughts," Zarathustra says to his warriors) but who remain frustrated in their aspiration by the envy and hatred in their hearts.[117] Still, it seems, these men, with proper guidance and training, could one day become the lion-spirits they long to become (a fact about them that, again, distinguishes them from the pale criminal).

There is, of course, a very obvious objection to this reading of "On War and Warriors." Although Zarathustra's rhetorical emphasis on courage and war directly recalls his representation of the lion-spirit in "On Reading and Writing"; and although his talk of struggle ("Let your work be a struggle [*Kampf*]"), of enemies ("You should have eyes that always seek an enemy [*Feinde*]"), and of victory ("Let your peace be a victory [*Sieg*]") reproduces some of the key ideas he uses to describe the lion-spirit in "On the Three Metamorphoses," his claim that "to a good warrior, 'thou shalt' sounds more agreeable than 'I will'" suggests that his speech about war and warriors is directed *not* to potential lions but to individuals destined ultimately to be camels.[118] I would suggest, however, that this claim be read ironically, for the command, or "thou shalt," that Zarathustra would have his warriors obey as their "highest hope" is that "man is something that shall be overcome."[119] Presumably, and paradoxically, obeying *this* "thou shalt" (in the manner outlined in "On the Three Metamorphoses") would involve a leonine repudiation of *all* "thou shalts," Zarathustra's included, and, subsequently, a performance of the third metamorphosis of the spirit. In other words, Zarathustra's command involves a deontic paradox analogous to the paradox of the liar: his "brothers in war" can obey his command (i.e., they can overcome themselves in the manner he advocates) only if, by enacting the lion-spirit's nay-saying to all "thou shalts," they disobey his command and subsequently become child-creators. Zarathustra's "thou shalt," though seemingly intended to transform his auditors into reverent camels of a sort, is designed in fact to promote their efforts to become lions and eventually children.

Zarathustra commands the likes of the youth on the mountainside to overcome man, but he does not urge them to assert their independence or to see in Zarathustra the measure of their achievements. Insisting that they obey *his* "thou shalt," Zarathustra never explicitly asks these men to test their capacities to say "I will." Depicting himself as a leader to be obeyed, he declines as well to pose as a potential equal whose independence they might envy and wish to emulate. Zarathustra calls his warriors to overcome man, thereby exhorting them, implicitly, to become lions and thereafter children. By representing his exhortation as a command, however, he permits them the temporary *illusion* that self-overcoming is possible for someone who has not entirely renounced the camel's attachment to values imposed by others, values embodied in the camel's revered "thou shalts." Under the auspices of Zarathustra's "thou shalt," his warriors will take issue with imposed values, cultivate a confidence in their capacities for independence, but remain free of the debilitating envy and lack of self-trust that too often result from denying the authority of all "thou shalts." These warriors will renounce the authority even of Zarathustra's "thou shalt"—in effect, they will throw away the "ladder" they have used to "climb" to the height of the lion's "I will"—when they complete the second metamorphosis of the spirit. Only then will they have won the battle to claim for themselves the freedom and right to create their own thoughts and values.

In the aftermath of "On War and Warriors," in Part 1, Zarathustra devotes his attention to persons who have enacted the second though not the third of the three metamorphoses of the spirit.[120] In the three speeches that immediately follow "On War and Warriors"—"On the New Idol," "On the Flies of the Marketplace," and "On Chastity"—he attends to claims and voices that compete with his own voice for the hearing of the lion-spirited individual. In these speeches, Zarathustra worries that rival claims and voices will distract the lion-spirit from his proper calling, which is to go-under and become a child-creator of new values.

In "On the New Idol," for example, Zarathustra suggests that the modern state, with its many enticements, may all too easily win the devotion of his auditors:

> It is not only the long-eared and short sighted who *sink to their knees* . . . it
> detects you too you *vanquishers* [*Besieger*] of the old god. You have grown weary

with fighting and now your weariness still serves the new idol. . . . It will give you everything if you will adore it, this new idol: thus it buys the splendor of your virtues and the look of your proud eyes. It would use you as bait for the all-too-many."[121] (emphases mine)

Although he has conquered the old god, the lion-spirit has grown weary from his struggle. With little difficulty, it seems, he could fall victim to a new idol that threatens to transform him again into a kneeling camel, one who worships a "cold monster" rather than a "great dragon." If he is to resist these persuasions, Zarathustra suggests, the lion-spirit must choose a life that is free of the preoccupations and the rituals of modern state politics:

Foul smells their idol, the cold monster: foul they smell to me altogether, these idolators.

My brothers, do you want to suffocate in the fumes of their snouts and appetites? Rather break the windows and leap to freedom.

Escape from the bad smell! Escape from the idolatry of the superfluous!

Escape from the bad smell! Escape from the steam of these human sacrifices!

The earth is free even now for great souls. There are still many empty seats for the lonesome and the twosome, fanned by the fragrance of silent seas.

A free life is still free for great souls. Verily, whoever possesses little is possessed that much less: praised be a little poverty.

Only where the state ends, there begins the human being who is not superfluous: there begins the song of necessity, the unique and inimitable tune.

Where the state *ends*, look there my brothers! Do you not see it, the rainbow and the bridges of the overman.[122]

Reminiscent of Socrates, who urged Alcibiades to abandon Athenian politics for his own good, Zarathustra exhorts the lion-spirit to forsake the politics of the modern state for his own good.[123] Yet while Socrates directed Alcibiades' attention *away* from the body, Zarathustra affirms the bodily vocation of self-overcoming by invoking the figure of the overman. Using the same language he used in the prologue to describe the leonine companions he sought, Zarathustra again attributes this vocation to "the lonesome [*Einsame*] and the twosome [*Zweisame*]."[124] And anticipating "On the Gift-Giving Virtue," where he speaks of the fragrance (*Geruch*) of an earth on which lonely and resurrected bodies could flourish, he alludes to a fragrance that is fanning the empty, "stateless" places where the lonesome and the twosome could dwell.[125] In general, "On the New Idol" argues that the lion-spirit must renounce the politics of the modern state if he is to attend to the bodily possibility of going-under and revaluing his passions. The argument does *not* assert that the project of self-overcoming is essentially apolitical, but only that affiliation with the state obscures the power of healthy bodies to effect radical and politically significant cultural transformation.

"On the Flies of the Marketplace" focuses on public opinion, which also distracts the lion-spirit from his vocation. Typically, the public's pundits (journalists, critics, commentators, etc.) exhort the lion-spirit to decide immediately and unequivocally what he thinks about a given issue (a quick, unambiguous decision is essential, if the lion-spirit is to be seen to have made legitimate contributions to "public debate"). Thus, they demand that he forgo the slow (*langsam*), searching engagement with experience (*Erleben*) through which decisions about value are made.[126] Not surprisingly, Zarathustra urges the lion-spirit to distance himself both from the public's pundits and the flies ("the people") that attend them. Echoing his earlier appeals to the lonesome and the twosome, he recommends a life of "solitude" (*Einsamkeit*). Only by deafening themselves to the "masters of the hour" and their epigone can the men Zarathustra addresses learn to listen for the Dionysian "good tidings" that he ascribes to healthy bodies and an "unexhausted earth": "Flee, my friend, into solitude! I see you dazed by the noise of the great men and stung all over by the stings of the little men. Woods [*Wald*] and crags know how to keep a dignified silence with you. Be like the tree that you love with its wide branches: silently listening [*aufhorchend*] it hangs over the sea."[127]

As if to recall precisely these words, Zarathustra begins "On Chastity" by invoking the appeal of the forest: "I love the woods [*Wald*]. It is bad to live in cities: there too many are in heat [*Brünstigen*]."[128] For Zarathustra, a solitary life in the forest can be a source of relief, not only from the "noise of . . . great men," but likewise from the impulse to lose oneself to sexual desire. He worries, it seems, that sexual desire, if felt as intensely as urban life may make one feel it, can transform the lion-spirit into a hedonist who has lost sight of his proper vocation: "And behold these men . . . they know of nothing better on earth than to lie with a woman. Mud [*Schlamm*] is at the bottom of their souls."[129]

Zarathustra's worry explains in part his advice that chastity should be avoided by those who find it difficult. In such cases, abstention renders sexual desire ever more insistent: "They abstain, but the bitch, sensuality, leers enviously out of everything they do. . . . Those for whom chastity is difficult [*schwer*] should be counseled against it, lest it be their road to hell—the mud [*Schlamm*] and heat [*Brunst*] of their souls."[130] The use of *schwer* here suggests that chastity can become a vexing burden that transforms the spirit of the lion into that of a camel. Arguing that the weight of this burden can pull the soul down into a hellish, muddy, sexual "heat," Zarathustra implies that the chaste sensualist, no less than the hedonist, is mired in an obsession with sexual desire that renders him, in the manner of all camels, oblivious to the possibility of creating new values. In the instance of a given lion-spirited individual, Zarathustra can endorse either chastity *or* nonabstention, just to the extent that the option chosen does not foster a preoccupation with sexual desire that obscures the possibility of going-under and becoming an overman.[131]

Having taken an adversarial stance toward the state, the pundits of public opinion, and a potentially preoccupying sexual desire, Zarathustra finally identifies a clear ally to his cause in the speech that follows "On Chastity." Friendship, he suggests in "On the Friend," is an intimacy of adversaries: "You should be closest [*nächsten*] to [your friend] with your heart when you resist him." The intimacy of friendship exists not for its own sake, but for friends to challenge one another to assert themselves as independent individuals. Ultimately, friends should support each other in cultivating the solitude ("Are you pure air and solitude and bread and medicine for your friend?") that Zarathustra ties to the quiet listening to oneself that is the path to self-overcoming ("The friend," he says, should be "an anticipation of the overman").[132] A friend's purpose, then, is not to guarantee that an otherwise solitary and lion-spirited individual will never be alone; rather, a friend should be a voice that helps that individual to combat the sort of preoccupying introspection that can, in the manner of the spirit of gravity, undermine one's belief that one can become a creator of new values. In essence, the friend is the lion-spirit who spurs other lion-spirits (his friends) to preserve their spiritual "height" and their commitment to becoming new-values creators despite the depressing, downward pull of a self-undermining self-interrogation: "I and me are always too deep in conversation: how could one stand that if there were no friend? For the hermit, the friend is always the third person: the third is the cork that prevents the conversation of the two from sinking into the depths [*Tiefe*]. Alas, there are too many depths [*Tiefen*] for all hermits; therefore they long so for a friend and his height [*Höhe*]."[133]

By representing friendship as a form of intimacy that has self-overcoming in solitude as its end, Zarathustra exposes his teaching to two misinterpretations. The first is that he believes that self-overcoming is a private affair void of public significance. In this view, the advent of the overman will be without political consequence, for it will not affect the character of any of the actions, practices, or institutions in which human beings jointly participate. The second misinterpretation is that the intimacy Zarathustra endorses is a form of neighborliness. In the speeches that follow "On the Friend"—"On the Thousand and One Goals" and "On Love of the Neighbor"—Zarathustra discredits both misinterpretations. He thus refines his account of friendship and clarifies his understanding of the forces tending to distract the lion-spirit from his proper vocation.

In "On the Thousand and One Goals," Zarathustra suggests that self-overcoming is not an end in itself but a means to the end of transforming humanity into a *people*. In advancing this position, he recalls his earlier speech on the new idol, where he proclaimed the "death of peoples" and attacked the modern state for pretending to be a people. According to Zarathustra, a people is united by common customs, a common faith, and a singular sense of good and evil. Every people, he says, "speaks its tongue of good and evil. . . . It has invented its own language of customs and rights."[134] In contrast, the modern state, in the absence of people-unifying faiths and customs, lies "in all the tongues of good and evil."[135] For Zarathustra, the death of peoples and the appearance of the modern state stem from the rise of the "clever ego . . . that desires its own profit in the profit of the many."[136] The modern state rules modern egos, he holds, not only by lying, but by coercion and the manipulation of desire.[137] As we have seen, Zarathustra exhorts the modern, lion-spirited ego to dwell apart from the rituals of state power in order to attend to the possibility of overcoming himself. In entertaining this possibility, such an ego could well imagine himself the founder and ruler of a new people:

> Change of values—that is a change of creators.
>
> First peoples were creators; and only in later times, individuals. Verily, the individual himself is still the most recent creation.
>
> Once peoples hung a tablet of good over themselves. Love which would rule [*herrschen*] and love which would obey have together created such tablets.
>
> Zarathustra saw many lands and many peoples. No greater power did Zarathustra find on earth than the works of the lovers: "good" and "evil" are their names.
>
> Verily a monstor is the power of praising and censuring. Tell me, who will conquer [*bezwingt*] it, O brothers? Tell me, who will throw a yoke [*Fessel*] over the thousand necks of this beast?
>
> A thousand goals have there been so far, for there have been a thousand peoples. Only the yoke for the thousand necks is still lacking [*fehlt*]: the one goal is lacking. Humanity still has no goal.
>
> But tell me my brothers, if humanity still [*noch*] lacks a goal—is humanity itself not still lacking too?[138]

Zarathustra's assertion that humanity *still* lacks a goal poignantly recalls a thought he expressed in the immediate aftermath of the tightrope walker's tragedy: "Human existence is uncanny and still [*immer noch*] without meaning; a jester can become man's fatality."[139] Before the tightrope walker dies, Zarathustra assigns to man the meaning and goal of overcoming man through the creation of new values. After the tightrope walker dies, he claims that human existence is *still* without a meaning, for he begins to suspect that overcoming man will prove impossible and that his descent to man will do naught but leave humanity suffering the catastrophe of nihilism.[140] In "On the Thousand and One Goals," Zarathustra reiterates this suspicion, complicating it, however, with political considerations.[141] If none of his auditors can be persuaded to pursue the end of overcoming man, then, Zarathustra worries, they will suffer the nihilistic experience of meaninglessness, which is to suffer the lack in lacking a goal. Moreover—and this is the political point—none of them will assume responsibility for transforming humanity into a people, for one could assume that responsibility only if one had overcome oneself and become a creator of new values.

In the wake of the demise of peoples, the creator's responsibility for transforming humanity into a people *must fall to individuals* ("First people were creators; and only in later times, individuals"). This responsibility is a *political* responsibility, Zarathustra implies, for it will implicate the individuals who undertake it in the project of ruling others and thus in shaping the practices in which human beings jointly participate. Subjecting the whole of humanity to the rulership that peoples once exercised over themselves, the lovers-creators Zarathustra envisions will use the values they create to yoke the remains of previous peoples into a common way of life based on a unifying vision of good and evil.

The politics Zarathustra imagines in "On a Thousand and One Goals" is what Nietzsche later calls "great politics," the global politics predicted in *Beyond Good and Evil*: "a new caste that [will] rule Europe," a "time [when] petty politics [will be] over: the very next century will bring the fight for the dominion of the earth—the *compulsion* to great politics [*grossen Politik*]."[142] In Chapter 1, I suggested that *Zarathustra* resembles *Beyond Good and Evil* in prefiguring the advent of a new caste of new-values-creating philosophers; in Chapter 6, I explore further the connections between these two texts. Here, however, I restrict myself to noting that the notion of a new-values creation does not require that a new-values creator undertake to be the founder and ruler of a new people. Zarathustra envisions his lion-spirited addressees as potential value-creators *and* as potential rulers, but nothing in his *concept* of new-values creation rules out the possibility of a new new-values creator who declined to dedicate himself to the aims of "great politics." New-values creation cannot be without *some* political consequences, for it entails a disruption of culturally dominant styles of embodiment. But these consequences could flow from a "micropolitics" that has renounced the planetary imperialism of "great politics" and seeks within the interstices of modern life, and beyond the rituals of state power, possibilities of bodily and cultural transformation.[143]

In this chapter, I have argued that the nationalism of *The Birth of Tragedy* is founded on a supranationalist and essentialist concept of the German nation and people. (In his translation of *The Birth of Tragedy*, Kaufmann uses "nation" to translate *Volk*; in his translation of *Zarathustra*, he renders it "people.") Because the early Nietzsche believes that the German nation and people embody a transnational Dionysian essence, he can embrace a patriotic politics the telos of which is the expression of that essence by way of a cultural re-formation of the German spirit.[144] Zarathustra, meanwhile, no less that the early Nietzsche, thinks politically in terms of the concept of a people (*Volk*). Yet nothing could be further removed from Nietzsche's early, *expressivist* understanding of German cultural politics than Zarathustra's vision of a people that is created by creators of new values. For Zarathustra, creating a people is not a matter of fostering the expression of an already *given* spiritual or cultural identity; rather it entails the fabrication of some such identity by means of a revaluation of the body's passions.[145] The creation of a people is Dionysian, not because it reveals the Dionysian essence of a group's spirit, but because it involves an experience of going-under that reveals no such essence. Zarathustra's "great politics" aims not to unearth an otherwise concealed cultural or human nature, but to replace one form of spiritual existence (as constituted by Christian-Platonic values) with a radically different one. A nonimperialistic micropolitics would be less ambitious, though no less free of expressivist assumptions.

Zarathustra's speech "On Love of the Neighbor" makes explicit the conflict between radical spiritual change and neighborliness. The central theme of this speech is the difference between love of the neighbor and love of the friend: "Let the future and the farthest be for you the cause of your today: in your friend you shall love the overman as your cause. My brothers, love of the neighbor [*Nächstenliebe*] I do not recommend to you: I recommend to you love of the farthest."[146] In criticizing "love of the neighbor," which is love of the closest, Zarathustra recalls his earlier claim that "You should be closest [*nächsten*] to [your friend] with your heart when you resist him." For Zarathustra, closeness to another is not an intrinsic good. It is valuable, he suggests, only if it prompts a person to love the farthest and thus to overcome himself. In the case of the friend, closeness to another may be effective in this way. In the case of the neighbor, it can be a hindrance: "One man goes to his neighbor because he seeks himself; another because he would lose himself. Your bad love of yourselves turns your solitude into a prison."[147] Whoever he is, the neighbor is the person in whose company one flees the solitude required for self-overcoming and radical spiritual change. Even a friend becomes a neighbor, if he fosters the avoidance of solitude.

"On the Thousand and One Goals" and "On Love of the Neighbor" conclude a sequence of speeches conveying Zarathustra's most urgent advice to potential and actual lions. In his next speech, "On the Way of the Creator," Zarathustra recapitulates this advice, reciting numerous themes and images. Among these are the idea of freedom ("You call yourself free? . . . Free *from* what? As if that mattered to Zarathustra! But your eyes should tell me brightly: free *for* what"); the figure of "height" ("Alas there is so much lusting for the heights!"); the emotions of envy and hatred ("You pass over and beyond them: but the higher you ascend, the smaller you appear to the eye of envy. But most of all they hate those who fly"); the inclinations to murder and self-judgment ("Can you be your own judge and avenger of your law? . . . But are you capable of this—to be a murderer?"); and, most important, the value of solitude ("Lonely one [*Einsamer*], you are going the way of the lover").

By reiterating the central ideas of his previous speeches to potential and actual lions, "On the Way of the Creator" summarizes the substance of Zarathustra's attempt in Part 1 to describe the experience of the individual who wishes to become a lion and/or to maintain the posture of the lion on his way to becoming a child. With its psychological pitfalls, tempting distractions, and helpful allies, this is the experience of the person who would defy (or aspire to defy) representations of repetition in order to reaffirm and persist in his commitment to becoming a child, or new-values creator. To be sure, "On the Way of the Creator" alludes specifically to the child-spirit ("Are you a new strength and a new right? A first movement? A self-propelled wheel?"), but says less to define that spirit than to point the way to the possibility of personifying it.[148] That way, we have seen, is a path to a quiet solitude that is essential to self-overcoming: "Is it your wish, my brother, to go into solitude [*Vereinsamung*]? Is it your wish to seek the way to yourself? Then linger a moment, and listen to me."[149]

By highlighting the pitfalls and distractions that haunt the way of the creator, Zarathustra complicates *Zarathustra*'s philosophical explanation of the possibility of creating new values. As we have seen, part of explaining this possibility is showing how Zarathustra, despite the representations of repetition that threaten his commitment to becoming a new-values creator, reaffirms and persists in that commitment by enacting the second metamorphosis of the spirit. Having shown that, however, one can demand a more detailed explanation by treating the *explanans* as an *explanandum*, asking how is it possible to enact the second metamorphosis of the spirit; or, if someone has enacted it, how it is possible for that person to keep attuned to his proper calling. Part 1 addresses these questions by suggesting (1) that though the possibility of becoming a lion-spirit appears to be excluded by the human-all-too-human tendencies to envy and self-doubt, these psychological pitfalls can be avoided ("On War and Warriors"); and (2) that though the possibility of remaining attuned to one's proper calling appears to be excluded for the lion-spirit who is tempted by the modern state, public opinion, and insistent sexual desire, such a spirit, despite these distractions, can remain attuned to his proper calling by cultivating lonesomeness (in places "fanned by the fragrance of silent seas"), solitude, and the company of friends ("On the New Idol," "On the Flies of the Marketplace," "On Chastity," and "On the Friend").

"On the Way of the Creator" ends with Zarathustra bidding a tearful farewell to his companion, exhorting him to the solitary task of self-overcoming: "With my tears [*Thränen*] go into your loneliness [*Vereinsamung*], my brother. I love him who wants to create over and beyond himself and thus perishes [*zu Grunde geht*]."[150] Elegaic in his sentiment, Zarathustra seems to lament in advance the loss of his "brother." Grieving is appropriate, he suggests, because self-overcoming entails the death (perishing) of the self as it presently is. Zarathustra's tears express the pain with which he foresees that his companion, having fulfilled the vocation Zarathustra has assigned him, will in a significant sense cease to be.[151] If Zarathustra is not inconsolable, notwithstanding his anticipation of his companion's demise, it is because he envisions that demise as a bridge to an end (the creation of a being beyond man) that is genuinely worthy of his love.

In proclaiming to "love him who wants to create over and beyond himself and thus perishes," Zarathustra echoes the language and central preoccupations of his speech in section 4 of the prologue. The farewell scene that accompanies his proclamation suggests that he has come full circle: after conveying his message to the townspeople, who could not see what he would have them see, Zarathustra seems finally to have found an individual who has absorbed his teaching and stands ready to enact it. There is, in other words, something conclusive about "On the Way of the Creator," a sense in which this speech, with its mournful yet hopeful final episode, provides a kind of closure to Zarathustra's search for proper companions: here, at last, he *seems* to have found one. Given the dramatic force of this episode, succeeding, as it does, the recapitulation of themes that is otherwise the substance of "On the Way of the Creator," I am inclined to read the five speeches that follow it, and that bring Part 1 to an end, as an extended coda to a signal pedagogical achievement. This is not to say that these speeches should be ignored, but only that they concern "unfinished business," like the musical codas that follow the recapitulation of musical themes in certain sonatas.[152]

The unfinished business of four of these speeches—"On Little Old and Young Women," "On the Adder's Bite," "On Child and Marriage," and "On Free Death"—is the lion-spirited individual who, unlike the companion appearing in "On the Way of the Creator," has not yet embarked upon the solitary path of perishing and self-overcoming. Speaking in these speeches of war and warriors, of the happiness of saying "I will," of letting "your victory [*Sieg*] and . . . freedom [*Freiheit*] long for a child," and of the importance of dying one's death victoriously (*seigreich*), Zarathustra addresses the lion-spirited individual who has *deferred* the task of becoming a child. What he offers this individual is, in effect, an ethics: a brief account of how he can live as a lion in a world he shares with *other* human beings, not many of whom have completed the second metamorphosis of the spirit. Zarathustra's disciples now *need* an ethics, because they have put off for the time being the self-isolation they require to create over and beyond themselves.[153] Zarathustra satisfies his disciples' need by prescribing a set of norms and attitudes appropriate to their involvement with women (here, as elsewhere, everything suggests that Zarathustra's disciples are men), child-rearing, marriage, people who injure the lion-spirit, people the lion-spirit injures, and death. Zarathustra believes, apparently, that this ethics is compatible with the possibility of effecting eventually in one's own person the third metamorphosis of the spirit.[154]

In "On the Gift-Giving Virtue," the last of the speeches that conclude Part 1, Zarathustra returns to the problematic presented by the companion he addresses in "On the Way of the Creator." Here, the "unfinished business" he engages is that of clarifying the nature of the body's experience of self-overcoming. As I have already shown in this chapter, Zarathustra characterizes this experience as a delight produced by the resurrection of repressed passions and instincts. Thus, by means of his speech on the gift-giving virtue, Zarathustra completes the business of showing how the way of the creator is the way of the living body.

In the wake of his paean to the gift-giving virtue, which is the single virtue necessarily possessed by all who resurrect previously repressed passions (for resurrecting such passions is possible only if the will to power assigns itself the second-order function of resurrecting previously repressed passions), Zarathustra prepares to take leave of the companions who have yet to take leave of him: "Now I go alone [*allein*], my disciples. You too go now, alone."[155] Speaking as a genuine friend should speak, he urges the men who still attend him to go the way of the one whose departure brought him tears: the solitary way of the creator. Knowing that his disciples will get lost along this way, Zarathustra predicts that he will return to them and later be with them a "third time" in order to celebrate the advent of the overman.[156]

Zarathustra does not foresee that, with his return to his disciples (Part 2), he will learn that in performing the second metamorphosis of the spirit he has alienated himself from his ability to go-under. Neither does he foresee that, through his encounter with a soothsayer, he will lose his Dionysian, Goethean faith in the persistence in human experience of the uncreated passions required to create new values. In the next chapter, I explore the Dionysian self-estrangement, or self-alienation of the lion-spirit. I also show that the dramatization of Dionysian self-estrangement advances the philosophical explanation of the possibility of creating new values. In Chapter 5, I consider Zarathustra's loss of Dionysian faith. Via the figure of the soothsayer, Nietzsche yet again expresses the skeptical thought that the modernist aspirations Zarathustra represents are not viable. As we shall see, he suggests that the modern human body is no better equipped than the modern German nation to foster a Dionysian interruption of modernity.

CHAPTER FOUR

Cartesian Subjects, Promethean Heroes, and the Sublime

I disdain'd to mingle with
A herd, though to be a leader—and of wolves.
The lion is alone, and so am I.

GEORGE GORDON, LORD BYRON, *Manfred*

And isn't it by forgetting the first waters that you achieve
immersion in your abysses and the giddy flight of one who
wings far away, perched at such heights that no sap rises there
and no thread secures his way.

LUCE IRIGARAY, *Marine Lover of Friedrich Nietzsche*

As Zarathustra searches for companions in Part 1, he does not once mention that his limitations as a lion may hinder his effort to become a child. In other words, he never explicitly entertains the possibility that his identity as a lion, constituted as it is through a defiant nay-saying to representations of repetition, is inherently defined by a form of self-understanding that precludes new-values creation. Exhorting his auditors to "see" and "hear" that they can go-under, Zarathustra seems oblivious to the fact that one is strictly speaking incapable of such seeing and hearing while one remains a lion-spirit. As Zarathustra suggests in his earlier speech on the three metamorphoses, a lion-spirited individual can realize his freedom for new creation only if he ceases to be lion-spirited. In Part 2, the first thirteen sections of which I discuss in the present chapter, Zarathustra takes this suggestion to heart and attempts to say *why* the lion-spirited individual is unable to create new values.

In his speech on the three metamorphoses, Zarathustra also suggests that each lion-spirited individual believes in himself as the sole potential creator of new values. It is odd, therefore, that Zarathustra spoke in Part 1 as a lion to other lions, implying that there were lion-spirited individuals other than he who could become new-values creators. In "The Night Song" in Part 2, Zarathustra makes explicit the ironic nature of these earlier harangues by admitting, in effect, that his leonine belief that he alone can create new values has affected his view of other lion-spirits.

A paradox haunts the figure of the lion, for the lion-spirited individual, in reaffirming his commitment to becoming a new-values creator, nullifies his ability to go-under and defeats the possibility of fulfilling that commitment. This paradox bears on Zarathustra's personal intention to go-under and overcome himself, inasmuch as Zarathustra, in striving to realize his personal intention, speaks and acts as a lion. It also bears on Zarathustra's poetic intention to inspire and "touch the souls" of others. In "The Night Song," in fact, it will seem that Zarathustra has failed to realize his poetic intention, not or not only because his auditors have become men like the last men, but because he speaks in the spirit of the sort of man—a lion—who can neither "see" nor "hear" the possibility of self-overcoming that he has wished his auditors to see and hear. It is a case of the blind leading the blind.

Zarathustra's interpretation of the lion's inability to create new values illuminates and helps to connect two of the central theses of the present book: that *Zarathustra* is Nietzsche's philosophical explanation of the possibility of creating new values, and that the depiction of Zarathustra in "Zarathustra's Prologue" points to a distinction between two modalities of Dionysian experience: that of the Dionysian, Promethean, leonine hero and that of the Dionysian child-creator. A creator's Dionysian experience is the passional chaos of the body, an indispensable moment in the process of creating new values. The hero, on the other hand, experiences Dionysus as the superabundant source of all values.

As philosophical explanation, *Zarathustra* shows (in "Zarathustra's Prologue") how Zarathustra's enactment of the second metamorphosis of the spirit defies representations of representation that threaten his commitment to becoming a new-values creator. It also shows (in Part 1) how Zarathustra, or perhaps a disciple, could become a lion-spirit and how a lion-spirit could remain attuned to his proper calling regardless of his exposure to various psychological pitfalls and worldly temptations. As we will see in the present chapter, Part 2 further develops *Zarathustra*'s explanation of the possibility of value-creation by asking how Zarathustra (or, again, a disciple) could become a new-values creator, even though he has become a self-estranged lion (a fact that apparently excludes the possibility of him becoming a new-values creator). Part 2 answers this question by dramatizing Zarathustra's genealogical interpretation of the creational impotence of the lion-spirit. Suggesting that the lion's inability to create new values is rooted in a heroic yet self-estranging act of will that engenders an experience of the sublime—a mode of aesthetic experience that Part 2 also ties to the modern, Cartesian concept of the thinking subject—Zarathustra holds that he (or another lion-spirit) could become a new-values creator, even though he has become a self-estranged lion, were he to discard the heroic will sustaining his self-estrangement.

Chapter 2's distinction between two modes of Dionyian experience is linked to the project of philosophical explanation, for showing how a self-estranged lion can become a new-values creator is tantamount to showing how a Dionysian hero could become a Dionysian child. Essential to that transformation, I shall argue, is exchanging the Promethean experience of Dionysus for the experience of Dionysus as passional chaos, and forsaking the transcendence of the sublime for the graciousness of the beautiful.

Zarathustra concludes his inquiry into the creational impotence of the lion-spirit with "On Those Who Are Sublime," by the end of which he has fully developed a distinctive interpretation of human being-in-time, drawing on the new and putatively post-Christian-Platonic vocabulary he elaborated in the prologue, Part 1, and Part 2. Having introduced the language of the last man, the earth, the healthy body, and the will to power, and having complicated his understanding of the second and third metamorphoses of the spirit, Zarathustra will now face the greatest challenge imaginable to his personal and poetic intentions, one that grants him the basic terms of his reinterpretation of human being-in-time. Taking the form of a soothsayer's prophecy, this challenge inspires a formation of the thought of eternal recurrence that I take up in Chapter 5 and that I term the camel's thought of recurrence.

Zarathustra's Will to Truth

In the first section of Part 2 ("The Child with the Mirror"), Zarathustra reports a dream suggesting that his disciples have denied him, just as he predicted they would at the end of Part 1:

> Why was I so frightened [*erschrak*] in my dream that I awoke? Did not a child step up to me, carrying a mirror [*das einen Spiegel trug*]? "O Zarathustra," the child said to me, "look at yourself in the mirror." But when I looked into the mirror I cried out, and my heart was shaken: for it was not myself I saw, but a devil's [*Teufels*] grimace and scornful laughter. Verily, all-too-well do I understand the sign and admonition of my dream: my *teaching* is in danger; weeds pose as wheat. My enemies have grown powerful and have distorted my teaching till those nearest to me must be ashamed of the gifts I gave them; I have lost my friends; the hour has come to seek my lost ones.[1]

In the midst of a dream, Zarathustra's devil, the spirit of gravity, appears to him in a mirror. The meaning of the dream, as Zarathustra reads it, is that Zarathustra's disciples have mistaken him for his devil. As I noted in Chapter 3, the spirit of gravity holds that striving to create new, non-Christian-Platonic values is futile: thus, he believes that overcoming man is not possible.[2] To mistake Zarathustra for his devil is to imply that the teaching of the overman, despite its claim to envision a future different from the past, is but a disguised reiteration of Christian-Platonic teachings that Zarathustra believes cannot be eclipsed. Zarathustra's disciples have denied him, he believes, because they now see in his teaching a shameful allegiance to the very Christian-Platonic values they thought he repudiated.[3]

Seeing his image transformed into a representation of repetition—a figure for the belief that Christian-Platonic man cannot be overcome and for the view that the recurrence of Christian-Platonic man and his values will pervade the future—Zarathustra leaps up "like a seer and a singer who is moved by the spirit," after which he asks, "Have I not changed [verwandelt]?"[4] Only momentarily is Zarathustra frightened by the thought that the future must repeat the past; only momentarily does he remain lying on his bed, as if, with his heart shaken, he would submit, camel-like, to a distortion of his teaching that his disciples, figured by his dream-child, have come to know already as a burden (the dream-child carries this burden in the form of the mirror that contains Zarathustra's distorted image). When Zarathustra leaps up, he puts behind him his moment of hesitation. The spiritual transformation (Verwandlung) he experiences is that of the second metamorphosis of the spirit. Zarathustra, in short, is moved by the defiant, self-assertive spirit of the lion.

Zarathustra explicitly suggests that he is animated by the spirit of the lion when he describes his "wild wisdom" (wilden Weisheit) as his "lioness."[5] Departing from his cave, he appears as the agent of a leonine wisdom, as one propelled by the spirit that says "I will." Journeying to the "blessed isles," Zarathustra imagines his disciples living lives reminiscent of the heroes who occupied the blessed isles of Greek mythology, lives separate from other men and that justify the hope that man can be overcome.[6] Zarathustra's aim on these isles will be to retrieve the truth of his teaching, to free his image from the disfiguring caricature that his enemies have created in the eyes of his disciples. While the speeches of Part 1 emphasized the earth, the healthy body, and the idea of the overman, Zarathustra's "new speech" stresses his desire to distinguish his teaching from the teachings with which it has been conflated.[7]

When Zarathustra arrives upon the blessed isles, he begins immediately to mark off his teaching from Christian-Platonic teachings. The focus of his speech is the difference between the Christian conjecture that God exists and his con-jecture that the overman will exist in the future. Zarathustra's treatment of the difference between these conjectures falls into two parts, in the first of which he addresses his disciples as lovers of knowledge (*Erkennenden*) and presents them with an epistemological critique of the God-conjecture:

> God is a conjecture: but I desire that your conjectures should not reach beyond your creative will. Could you *create* a god? Then do not speak to me of any gods. But you could well create the overman. Perhaps not you yourselves, my brothers. But into fathers and forefathers of the overman you could re-create yourselves: and let this be your best creation.
>
> God is a conjecture; but I desire that your conjectures should be limited by what is thinkable [*Denkbarkeit*]. Could you *think* a god? But this is what the will to truth should mean to you: that everything be changed into what is thinkable [*Denkbares*] for man, visible [*Sichtbares*] for man, feelable [*Fühlbares*] by man. You should think through your own senses [*Sinne*] to their consequences.
>
> And what you have called world, that shall be created at first by you [*soll erst von euch geschaffen*]: your reason, your image, your will, your love shall thus be realized. And verily for your own bliss, you lovers of knowledge [*Erkennenden*].
>
> And how would you bear life without this hope, you lovers of knowledge. You could not have been born either into the incomprehensible [*Unbegriefliche*] or into the irrational [*Unvernünftige*].[8]

As distinct from the overman-conjecture, the God-conjecture postulates the exis-tence of something that Zarathustra's disciples could not create. Arguing that his disciples should limit their conjectures to what they *can* create, Zarathustra also suggests that they should refrain from supposing that the God-conjecture is true.

Zarathustra does not stop here. Prefiguring the logical positivists, he also sug-gests that the God-conjecture is not, strictly speaking, a *thinkable* conjecture (the positivists would speak, not of thinkable conjectures, but of meaningful statements). Thinkable conjectures pertain to what human beings can see or feel, or, more generally, to what they can know by way of their senses. Accord-ing to Zarathustra's will to truth, a conjecture is true of reality only if it is think-able and thinkable only if it postulates the existence of what can be known in sense-experience. What *can* be known in sense-experience, and what rightly can be said to be real, or to exist (what rightly can be "called world"), is and is lim-ited to what knowing subjects *create* in sense-experience (e.g., by their reason, imagination, will, and love). Nothing exists that cannot be known in sense-experience, and to think otherwise would be to suppose that human beings had been born into the "irrational" or the "incomprehensible." The God-conjecture is neither thinkable nor true, for it postulates the existence of something that human beings could not create and hence something that they could not know in sense-experience.

Reminiscent of Descartes, though giving a greater due to sense-experience than Descartes ever could, Zarathustra's epistemology reduces reality to what can be known by human beings.[9] In effect, his modern sounding "critique of knowledge" represents "man" as an all-knowing subject and "the world" as a wholly knowable object—an object having no reality beyond what the knowing subject can know of it through the exercise of her or his senses.

Compare Zarathustra's critique of knowledge to his earlier characterization of knowledge in "On the Gift-Giving Virtue." In that speech, Zarathustra described a knowledge that involved "seeing" and "hearing" the possibility of self-overcoming, a knowledge on the basis of which, he claimed, the self could experimentally "purify" itself. Notice, moreover, that this "gift-giving" knowledge concerned *uncreated* passions and instincts, whereas the knowledge described on the blessed isles refers exclusively to entities produced by knowing subjects. Resembling Kant perhaps more than Descartes, but likewise recalling a more radical, post-Kantian idealism that denies that our knowledge of objects relates to "given" intuitions, Zarathustra's "new speech" restricts knowledge to entities that the knowing subject him- or herself has actively created, or generated. More generally, he outlines an anthropocentric epistemology typical of early modern European philosophy. Embracing a decidedly post-Cartesian and quasi-idealist will to truth, Zarathustra rejects those wills to truth that, having failed to subject knowledge to rigorous critique, permit themselves conjectures (e.g., that God exists) exceeding the limits of human experience.[10]

In the second part of "Upon the Blessed Isles," Zarathustra speaks not from the head (not as an epistemologist) but explicitly from the "heart."[11] His shift to a more personal tone is telling, for it hints that his epistemological critique of the God-conjecture has not exposed the deepest, experiential roots of his opposition to it. In the remainder of this chapter, I explore the implications of Zarathustra's epistemology, highlighting its connection to the Promethean posture of the lion-spirit. In Chapter 6, I revisit his explicitly "heartfelt" remarks, because they illuminate his response to the soothsayer's prophecy. In that context, I look more closely at the second half of "Upon the Blessed Isles."

In "On the Pitying," "On Priests," and "On the Virtuous," the three speeches that follow "Upon the Blessed Isles," Zarathustra resumes his effort to dissociate his teachings from Christian-Platonic doctrines. "On the Pitying" begins with

Zarathustra reporting a remark that his enemies probably meant for him to hear: "My friends, a gibe was related to your friend: 'Look at Zarathustra! Does he not walk among us as if we were animals?'"[12] Had Zarathustra reacted defensively to this taunt, as no doubt his enemies hoped he would, then he would have insisted that his feelings for his fellow human beings were compassionate, not disdainful. Refusing to respond in this manner, Zarathustra fails to confirm his enemies' suspicion that he, like his Christian predecessors, is a teacher of pity (*Mitleiden*). Though he sometimes experiences pity ("If I must pity, at least I do not want it known; and if I do pity, it is preferably from a distance"), Zarathustra's teaching stresses shame. Bidding himself not to shame others, he has feelings of shame for the sake of the shame of those who suffer.[13] Implicit in Zarathustra's feelings of shame is his sense of responsibility for others, a sense that is likewise evident when he remarks that "all great love is even above all its pity."[14] Pity, as in the case of the pity for man that the "devil" claims killed God, can inspire a desire to renounce life.[15] Zarathustra's "great love" remains "above" its pity in order to assume responsibility for re-creating the lives that the pitying would renounce.

In "On Priests," Zarathustra confronts the Christian teachers of pity.[16] Acknowledging his connection to these "evil enemies" (Zarathustra claims that his blood "is related to theirs" and that he suffers and has suffered with them), Zarathustra emphasizes nonetheless his repudiation of their life-denying and repulsive teachings, central to which is their notion of a "Redeemer." Noting that the priests "wrote signs of blood on the way they walked," Zarathustra affirms that "blood is the worst witness of truth."[17] With this remark, he also suggests that his earlier claim to "love only what a man has written with his blood" should not be *misread* as aligning him with the ethos of Christian asceticism.[18]

When Zarathustra says of the priests that "nothing is more vengeful than their humility," he introduces an idea that he repeatedly advances in Part 2 to *diagnose* the teachings with which his teaching has been confused.[19] Each of these teachings, it seems, expresses something of the spirit of revenge. This is true not only of the teachings of the Christian priests (including, e.g., their teaching on pity), but, as Zarathustra argues in "On the Virtuous," of all the many teachings of virtue in which virtue is a matter of "revenge, punishment, reward, [and] retribution."[20] Zarathustra's justification of virtue proclaims neither that virtue should be rewarded nor that its absence should punished and avenged ("punishment," Zarathustra later says, is what revenge calls itself). Rather it argues that one should love one's virtue and want to act virtuously because one sees one's self in one's virtue ("You love virtue as a mother her child," Zarathustra proclaims).[21] Eschewing the utilitarian logic of reward and retribution, Zarathustra holds that virtuous action stems from a self-love that is a love of the virtues (the esteemed passions) that constitute the self.[22] Acting virtuously, he believes, is matter of maintaining one's integrity.[23]

Having disabused his disciples of their misinterpretation of his teaching on virtue, Zarathustra turns his attention in his next two speeches to the modern practice and theory of equality.[24] In "On the Rabble," Zarathustra demonstrates his distaste for the practices of modern Europe's egalitarian public culture. In "On the Tarantulas," meanwhile, he returns to the theme of revenge and insists that his teaching should not be confused with the revenge-driven theories of justice that rationalize modern Europe's egalitarian public culture.

The rhetoric of Zarathustra's speech on the rabble (e.g., his talk of the rabble's "snouts" [*Mäuler*], of their power to poison life, and of the stench they cause) recalls "On the New Idol" and "On the Flies of the Marketplace," two of the speeches he delivered in Part I.[25] In those speeches, Zarathustra portrayed the public culture of modern European society—a culture dominated by the rituals of state politics and the discourse of public opinion—as a force that could divert the potential lions among his disciples from their proper vocation. In "On the Rabble," he elaborates his critique of this culture, highlighting the popular politics of the "power-rabble" (mass movements that higgle and haggle for power with those who rule), the popular press of the "writing-rabble" (journalists and other pundits of public opinion), and the popular hedonism of the "pleasure-rabble" (the pursuit of "low" and sexually titillating forms of entertainment).[26] In "On the Flies of the Marketplace," Zarathustra emphasized the egalitarian outlook animating the public culture of the rabble (viz., the rabble's profound dislike for the human being who seems to stand out and apart from others) and urged his disciples to "escape" and "flee" the rabble. Here, however, he declines to repeat his earlier exhortation, choosing instead to describe his own escape and flight:

> The bite on which I gagged the most is not the knowledge that life itself requires hostility and death and torture-crosses—but once I asked, and I was almost choked by the question: What? does life require even the rabble? Are poisoned wells required, and stinking fires and soiled dreams and maggots in the bread of life?
>
> Not my hatred but my nausea gnawed hungrily at my life. . . . And I turned my back on those who rule when I saw what they now call ruling: higgling and haggling for power—with the rabble. I have lived with closed ears among people with foreign tongues: would that the tongue of their higgling and their haggling for power might remain foreign to me. And holding my nose, I walked disgruntled through all of yesterday and today. . . .
>
> Like a cripple who has become deaf and blind and dumb: thus have I lived

for many years lest I live with the power-, writing- and pleasure-rabble. Laboriously and cautiously my spirit climbed steps; alms of pleasure were its refreshment; and life crept along for the blind as if on a cane.

What was it that happened to me? How did I redeem myself from my nausea? Who rejuvenated my sight? How did I fly to the height where no more rabble sits by the well [*am Brunnen sitzt*]? Was it my nausea itself which created wings for me and water-divining powers? Verily I had to fly to the highest spheres that I might find the fount of pleasure [*den Born der Lust*] again.

Oh, I found it, my brothers! Here, in the highest spheres, the fount of pleasure wells up for me [*quillt mir der Born der Lust*]! And here is a life of which the rabble does not drink.

Gone is the hesitant bloom of spring! Gone the malice of my snowflakes in June. Summer I have become entirely, and summer noon! A summer in the highest spheres with cold wells [*kalten Quellen*] and blissful silence: oh come, my friends, that the silence may become still more blissful.[27]

Zarathustra's description of his experience of flight and transcendence identifies both negative and positive modalities of feeling. On the negative side, Zarathustra's belief that the rabble is essential to life ("What? does life require even the rabble?") made him nauseous. Believing that he was powerless to enjoy a life set free of the rabble, he closed his eyes and ears to life, and even refused to speak of it. In effect, he learned to accept a spiritually withdrawn and desensitized life (a "crippled" life) in order to live as if he were not living amidst "the power-, writing- and pleasure-rabble" (just as one blind and deaf might live as if she were not living amidst many of the things she neither sees nor hears). On the positive side, Zarathustra's redemption from his nausea came when he suddenly found a life divorced from the life of the rabble, a life over which the rabble exercised no dominion. Free and immune from the influence of the rabble, he could now lay claim to a life he once thought it vain to imagine: "For this is *our* height and our home: we live here too high and steep for all the unclean and their thirst."[28]

In depicting his flight to a height above the rabble, Zarathustra seems to be recounting his lion-spirit's experience of transcending the spirit of gravity, a feeling he first describes in "On Reading and Writing." (Significantly, Zarathustra rebukes the rabble, even in this earlier speech: "Once the spirit was God, then he became man, and now he even becomes rabble.")[29] In "On the Rabble," Zarathustra relates this feeling to the leonine belief that the creation of new values is possible, claiming that he built his nest "on the tree, Future" and thereby intimating that by escaping and transcending the rabble he has preserved his hope for a future that overcomes the values of the past. But what is the nature of the elevated height and life that enable this hope? The speech on the rabble, while showing that Zarathustra knows no empathy for them, and while prefiguring his criticism of theoreticians who rationalize the rabbles' egalitarian public culture, says little to address this question. Suggesting that the fount of pleasure he has found is a well among "cold wells," and declaring a wish to live "like strong winds" (*wie starke Winde*) over the rabble, Zarathustra only begins in this speech to define the character of his life-divorced-from-life.[30]

In "On the Tarantulas," Zarathustra interprets modern doctrines equating justice and equality as expressions of the spirit of revenge. Conceptualizing revenge as "repressed envy" and "aggrieved conceit," he will only later (in "On Redemption") arrive at a notion of this phenomenon that highlights its connection to human finitude. Here, however, Zarathustra focuses on modern theorists of justice—the tarantulas—who want to avenge themselves against all whose equals they are not. In particular, he attempts to distinguish his views from the views of those who preach *his* "doctrine of life," yet only because their enemies, the powerful, preach death. Speaking against the tarantulas, Zarathustra argues that his ascent to a life-divorced-from-life let him see that life itself refutes the modern theorist of justice. It let him see, he suggests, that ascending to heights and establishing hierarchies is essential to life, an insight that sharply differentiates his outlook from that of the egalitarians with whom he has been confused: "Life wants to build itself up into the *heights* with pillars and steps; it wants to look into vast distances and out toward stirring beauty: therefore it requires *height*. And because it requires *height*, it requires steps and contradiction among the steps and the climbers. Life wants to climb and to overcome itself climbing"(emphases mine).[31]

Zarathustra reveals the nature of his transcendent height and life in his speech on the famous wise men. According to Zarathustra, famous wise men lack the commitment to truth that characterizes his own lion-spirit. Though they pretend to will the truth, their first priority is to profit the people, to be camel-like "beasts of burden" that pull the people's cart: "You have served the people and the superstition of the people, all you famous wise men—and *not* the truth." The spirit of the lion knows no such priority, Zarathustra insists, and sacrifices comfort for the sake of the truth: "Hungry, violent, lonely, godless: thus the lion-will wants it. Free from the happiness of slaves, redeemed from gods and adorations, fearless and fear-inspiring, great and lonely: such is the will of the truthful." In the lion-willed individual, as Zarathustra describes him, spirit is "the life that cuts into life" and a form of life that "with its own agony . . . increases its knowledge." More exactly, the lion's will is an expression of life that subjects life itself to the will to truth: like a surgeon, this will "cuts into life" in order to make what is remote and inaccessible in life available to the scrutiny of the knowing subject.[32] Driven by the will to truth, the spirit of the lion makes life into an object of knowledge, yet takes delight in the experience, foreign to the famous wise men, of being genuinely wise and knowing:

> You are lukewarm to me, but all profound knowledge [*tiefe Erkenntniss*] flows cold [*kalt*]. Ice cold [*Eiskalt*] are the inmost wells [*innersten Brunnen*] of the spirit: refreshing for hot hands and men of action. You stand there honorable and stiff with straight backs, you famous wise men: no strong wind [*starker Wind*] and will drives you.
>
> Have you ever seen a sail go over a sea, rounded and taunt and trembling with the violence of the wind? Like the sail, trembling with the violence of the spirit, my wisdom [*Weisheit*] goes over the sea—my wild wisdom.[33]

With his allusions here to ice-cold wells and a strong wind, Zarathustra clearly echoes his speech on the rabble; he also insinuates that the leonine cold well and strong wind wherein he took refuge from the rabble are a well and wind of knowledge and wisdom. Animated by the spirit of the lion, Zarathustra has raised himself to a height transcending the rabble and discovered a life of knowledge that is a "fount of pleasure" from which the rabble never drinks. The nature of this transcendent height and life is his subjective experience of a will to truth that relentlessly subjects life to the objectifying pursuit of knowledge. Zarathustra's will to truth is the strong wind and will that drives him, as well as the spirited substance of his "wild wisdom." A form of the life that "cuts into life," it is the essence of his identity as a knowing subject and the essence of the lion-spiritedness that propels him from the beginning of Part 2 to the end of his speech on famous wise men.

Prior to "The Night Song," Zarathustra's primary aim in Part 2 is to produce a truthful account of his teachings. Attacking caricatures of his beliefs that conflate them with Christian-Platonic doctrines, he highlights the differences between his views and the revenge-driven views of the priests, the virtuous, and the tarantulas. Notwithstanding the verdicts of his enemies, Zarathustra implies that he is not an agent of the spirit of gravity and that his disciples need not be ashamed of him. Promoting his will to truth to show that he is not a representation of repetition, he preserves his leonine belief that he can create new values.

Yet Zarathustra's will to truth is ambiguous, for it also casts doubt on this belief. Expressing a quasi-idealist epistemology, Zarathustra's will to truth reduces reality to what the human subject can know and limits human knowledge to what the human subject has created. From the perspective of his will to truth, there exist no entities that have not been created by human subjects. Indeed, from that perspective, talk of "listening" to the body, and of "seeing" within it the possibility of going-under to "given" passions that have not been created— talk Zarathustra has relied on to exhort men to become new-values creators—is talk of nothing at all. Taking refuge from the rabble in the transcendent height and life of the knowing subject's will to truth, Zarathustra tacitly refuses to admit the reality (the existence) of uncreated passions that claim human bodies. In effect, he disclaims the possibility of suffering a chaos of such passions, which he must suffer to create new values. Although he has explicitly endorsed this possibility (e.g., in the prologue) his will to truth forbids him to acknowledge it. It estranges him from his ability to go-under.

I argued in Chapter 3 that Zarathustra, in Part 1, avows a Dionysian, Goethean faith that the energies required to create new values persist in human experience despite the ravages of modern asceticism. For Zarathustra, these energies constitute the natural furniture of human facticity, the uncreated passions that commonly affect human bodies and that he names "the earth" in the prologue. In embracing the posture and, implicitly, the epistemology of the lion, Zarathustra, even in Part 1, has inadvertently denied the existence of the earth and unwittingly betrayed his faith that uncreated passions continue to claim human existence. This is the message of the middle sections of Part 2. In "The Night Song," Zarathustra expresses the suffering caused by his act of betrayal.

Crisis and Cure

The first of the three songs that follow "On the Famous Wise Men," "The Night Song" begins to show why a self-estranged, lion-spirited individual, if he is to become a new-values creator, must exchange one form of Dionysian experience for another. As we shall see, moreover, Zarathustra's interpretation of the lion-spirit's creational impotence, because it has self-referential ramifications, helps him to cope with his own self-estrangement. Indeed, in developing this interpretation—in "The Night Song," The Dancing Song," "The Tomb Song," "On Self-Overcoming," and "On Those Who Are Sublime"—Zarathustra subjects himself to a sort of therapeutic self-analysis that suggests a cure for his self-estrangement.

> Night has come; now all fountains [*Brunnen*] speak more loudly. And my soul too is a fountain.
>
> Night has come; only now all the songs of lovers awaken. And my soul too is the song of a lover.
>
> Something unstilled [*Ungestilltes*], unstillable [*Unstillbares*], is within me; it wants to be voiced. A craving for love [*Eine Begierde nach Liebe*] is within me; it speaks the language of love.

Light am I; ah, that I were night! But this is my loneliness that I am girt with light. Ah, that I were dark and nocturnal! How I would suck at the breasts of light! And even you would I bless, you little sparkling stars and glowworms up there, and be overjoyed with your gifts of light.

But I live [*lebe*] in my own light; I drink [*trinke*] back into myself the flames that break out of me; I do not know the happiness of those who receive [*des Nehmenden*].[34]

Depicting his soul as a fountain (*Brunnen*) and well (*Brunnen*) of light, Zarathustra suggests here that his rabble-transcending life of knowledge, a life he once experienced as a "fountain of pleasure," has suddenly become a well of anguish.[35] What is the source of this anguish? At first blush, the answer is that Zarathustra suffers because he cannot experience the love of another. He imagines his love as a light source that, because it emits light, cannot know what it is to feel the light he imagines the love of another to be. Thus, his "ah, that I were night" seems in essence to express his longing to exchange his role as a lover for that of one beloved. Consider, however, that Nietzsche's comment on "The Night Song" in *Ecce Homo* describes it as Zarathustra's "immortal lament at being condemned by the overabundance of light and power, by his sun-nature, *not to love*."[36] For Nietzsche, Zarathustra's craving *for* love involves a craving *to* love and thus a craving to play the role of a lover he has been condemned not to play. His explanation of Zarathustra's anguish complicates the account I originally suggested, as it implies that Zarathustra's desire to be beloved is, at bottom, a desire to love as one beloved loves when he or she *responsively returns* the love of his or her lover. Zarathustra is condemned *not to love* as one beloved loves, precisely because he has been barred from the beloved's experience of being touched and moved by the love of another.

Yet the roots of Zarathustra's anguish run deeper than his estrangement from the love of others; ultimately they derive from a kind of self-estrangement. Zarathustra is a stranger to the love of others because he has become a stranger to himself.

Many suns revolve in the void: to all that is dark they speak with their light—to me they are silent. Oh, this is the enmity of the light against what shines: merciless it moves in its orbit. Unjust in its heart against all that shines, cold [*kalt*] against suns—thus moves every sun.

The suns fly like a storm in their orbits, that is their motion. They follow their inexorable [*unerbittlichen*] will: that is their coldness [*Kälte*].

Oh, it is only you, you dark ones, you nocturnal ones, who create [*schafft*] warmth out of that which shines. It is only you who drink [*trinkt*] milk and refreshment out of the udders of light.

> Alas, ice is all around me [*Eis ist um mich*], my hand is burned by the icy [*an Eisigem*]. Alas, thirst is within me that languishes after your thirst.[37]

Having begun his night song by implying that his fount of pleasure has become a well of anguish, Zarathustra approaches his song's conclusion by tacitly depicting his well of anguish as a *cold* well. What makes it cold, Zarathustra proposes—and here he advances a diagnosis that nowhere accompanies his talk of cold wells in "On the Rabble" and "On the Famous Wise Men"—is his *inexorable will*. Fountainlike suns are cold against one another, for they offer one another no warmth. They offer one another no warmth because not one of them possesses the darkness necessary to create warmth. To possess such darkness, one of Zarathustra's suns or fountains would have to relinquish its light. In other words, a will that "spoke" with its light would have to cease to be inexorable in its self-assertion. Zarathustra, for example, would have to *surrender* the leonine will and light that sustains his wild wisdom and that cuts into life for the sake of knowledge. Only then could he be touched and warmed by the light of another sun, as one beloved is touched and warmed by the love of a lover. Only then, in fact, could Zarathustra be touched and warmed *by his own light*. For even as he drinks "back into himself" the flames that have broken out of him, he remains surrounded by ice. Zarathustra, it seems, *is unable even to warm himself*. He has become estranged from himself, because he has become a stranger to his ability to be affected, touched, or moved by anything at all, including himself.[38] Having lost that ability, it is inevitable that he should be barred from sensing the love of others and hence that he should be a stranger to the feel of that love.

As we saw in Chapter 1, the leonine individual believes that new values must originate in his will and in his will alone. Thus, he implicitly denies that there can exist new-values creators other than himself. It is ironic, then, that Zarathustra in Part 1 spoke a lion's speech meant for potential and actual lions. Notwithstanding his exhortations to his disciples (see Chapter 3), the leonine Zarathustra had to have believed that newly created values would stem exclusively from his will. Zarathustra attests to the irony of his earlier attempts to cultivate fellow lions in "The Night Song," where he laments his inability to sense and feel the love of other suns and so figuratively admits that he cannot discern in other inexorable lion-wills the power and the authority to create new values.

If we consider "The Night Song" from the perspective of the Kantian epistemology that Zarathustra sometimes echoes, we can begin to appreciate the nature of Zarathustra's self-estrangement. "Our knowledge," says Kant, "springs from two fundamental sources of the mind": "sensibility," or "the *receptivity* of [the] mind, its power of receiving representations in so far as it is in any wise affected"; and "understanding," or "the mind's power of producing representations from itself, the *spontaneity* of knowledge." Only through the union of these two powers is knowledge possible, according to Kant. Neither of them is privileged with respect to the other: "Without sensibility no object would be given to us, without understanding no object would be thought. Thoughts without content are empty, intuitions without concepts are blind."[39]

Human knowledge, Kant claims, is always a knowledge of something "given," and thus of intuitions that *affect* the mind independently of the mind's spontaneous activity. Sensibility is essential to knowledge, he insists, because it is the mind's capacity to be affected by mind-independent intuitions.[40] Applying Kant's language to "The Night Song," we may say that Zarathustra's self-estrangement is a form of *in-sensibility* and that Zarathustra is in-sensible because he has disowned his *power of receptivity*. Oblivious to this power, Zarathustra can be affected neither by his own activity (e.g., he is like a sun that cannot warm itself) nor by anything that is given independently of that activity (e.g., he is like a sun that cannot be affected by the light of other suns). Singing his night song, he personifies a *pure spontaneity* that knows no "given" element in anything it experiences. Zarathustra's idealism comes as no surprise, for his will to truth reduces reality to what can be known and limits knowledge to what the knowing (human) subject creates. Reminiscent, perhaps, of Fichte, who radicalizes Kant's idealism by denying the existence of "given" intuitions, he views the sensible objects of knowledge (what he calls "world" and Fichte "not-self") as effects that the knower who knows those objects has generated.[41] By disowning his power of receptivity, Zarathustra obscures the reality of what in his experience most resists being construed as such an effect—namely, his body and his body's passions.

An important implication of "The Night Song" is that the lion-spirit is defined by a will to truth that precludes the creation of new values. So long as he is a lion-spirit, Zarathustra cannot create new values, for he will have disowned his power of receptivity. In embracing the lion-spirit's will to truth, Zarathustra dissociates himself from his own ability to be affected and moved *by anything*. Thus, he dissociates himself from his ability to be affected and moved by his body's "given," uncreated passions. Inasmuch as his will to truth denies that such passions exist, Zarathustra disclaims and estranges himself from his power to go-under to them.

To the extent that the will to truth of the lion is *inexorable*, it will no more relinquish its light that it might reclaim the power to be gripped by passional chaos than it will relinquish that light in order to be illuminated by other suns. Thus, it will persist in cold estrangement from both the body's ability to go-under and from the light of other suns. By discarding his will to truth and ceasing to be a lion, Zarathustra can look beyond his quasi-idealist view of reality and acknowledge his capacity to be moved by Dionysus. Only then, in fact, can he have the experience of going-under, which is a necessary if not sufficient condition of the possibility of creating new values.

Although he has disowned his power to go-under to Dionysian chaos, Zarathustra in "The Night Song" has not ceased to be Dionysian figure. Nietzsche in fact links Zarathustra to Dionysus when he comments in *Ecce Homo* on the anguish Zarathustra suffers in "The Night Song": "Nothing like this has ever been written, felt, or *suffered*: thus suffers a god, a Dionysus."[42] Taken in tandem, Nietzsche's remark and my reading of "The Night Song" suggest that the singer of the song is Dionysus but that he knows no capacity to be moved by Dionysus. How is such a paradox possible? How is it possible, in other words, for Zarathustra to personify Dionysus, and thus to suffer as Dionysus suffers, yet to personify him in a way that disowns the power to go-under to Dionysian chaos? To pose these questions is, in effect, to pose again a question I posed at the end of Chapter 2: What is the relationship between the Dionysian lion and the Dionysian child, or, again, between the Dionysian hero and the creator of new values? In the concluding section of the prologue, Nietzsche uses Neoplatonic imagery to suggest that Zarathustra has enacted an epistrophic recuperation of Dionysian superfecundity; Zarathustra appears there, I argued, as a source of values that has yet to reveal itself as a source. In "The Night Song," Nietzsche again represents Zarathustra in Neoplatonic terms, and again as an ultimate source and origin. To be precise, he uses Plotinus's standard figures for the emanation of the One—the overflowing fountain and the radiant sun—to depict Zarathustra's will to truth.[43] In both cases Zarathustra is a Dionysian lion, yet in neither case is he touched by the chaos that claims the child who creates new values. What can we make of this?

Nietzsche himself offers helpful clues about this question. Section 10 of *The Birth of Tragedy* recalls two distinct states of Dionysus in Greek myth, each of which prefigures the representation of Dionysus in *Zarathustra*:

> Dionysus appears in a variety of forms, in the mask [*Maske*] of a fighting [tragic] hero, and entangled [*verstrickt*], as it were, in the net of the individual will [*Einzelwillens*]. . . . In truth, however, the hero is the suffering Dionysus of the mysteries, the god experiencing in himself the agonies of individuation, of whom wonderful myths tell that as a boy he was torn to pieces by the Titans and now is worshipped in this state [*Zustande*] as Zagreus. Thus it is intimated that this dismemberment [*Zerstückelung*], the properly Dionysian *suffering*, is like a transformation into air, water, earth, and fire, that we are therefore to

regard the state of individuation as the origin and primal cause of all suffering, as something objectionable in-itself. . . . In this existence as a dismembered god, Dionysus possesses the dual nature of a cruel, barbarized demon and a mild, gentle, ruler. But the hope of the epopts looked toward the rebirth of Dionysus, which we must now dimly conceive as the end of individuation. It was for this coming [*kommenden*] . . . Dionysus that the epopts' roaring hymns of joy resounded. And it is this hope alone that casts a gleam of joy upon the features of a world torn asunder and shattered into individuals; this is symbolized in the myth of Demeter, sunk in eternal sorrow, who *rejoices* once again for the first time when told that she may *once more* give birth to Dionysus.[44]

Considered in the perspective of these remarks, Zarathustra's night song can be heard as the lament of a suffering Dionysus-Zagreus.[45] It is the song of Dionysus in a state of *individuated* existence, which is likewise the state in which Dionysus appears as a tragic hero. The tragic hero suffers, Nietzsche suggests, precisely *because* he is an individuated representation or Apollonian "mask" of Dionysus. As applied to Zarathustra, whose appearance as a tragic hero and mask of Dionysus I explored in Chapter 2, this suggestion implies that de-individuation is the way beyond the anguish of "The Night Song." Here, however, we must be careful. De-individuation, in the context of *The Birth of Tragedy*, entails the restoration of the world to a oneness that Nietzsche associates with the "thing-in-itself." Because the later Nietzsche rejects the thing-in-itself/appearances distinction, it is obvious that de-individuation could not have this significance in *Zarathustra*. But that is not to imply that this concept has no application in *Zarathustra*. On the contrary, it is clearly implicated in Zarathustra's conception of going-under, a movement whereby the body lets go of an established and distinct (Christian-Platonic) self in order to embrace passional chaos. For Zarathustra-Zagreus, then, de-individuation would entail an experience of passional chaos, and passional chaos would be the identity of the "coming" Dionysus. De-individuation would be the way beyond Zarathustra's anguish, because Zarathustra's anguish reflects his estrangement from his ability to go-under.[46]

Zarathustra is Zagreus when he appears as a Promethean and leonine hero who defiantly asserts his will against representations of repetition. As Zagreus, for example, he departs from the dead tightrope walker in section 9 of the prologue. And as Zagreus, he opposes his will to truth to his enemies' distortions of his doctrines. More generally, Zarathustra-Zagreus is the Zarathustra in whom the self-assertion of the will functions as an Apollonian *mask* that estranges him from his ability to experience passional chaos. (Nietzsche's remarks in section 10 of *The Birth of Tragedy* suggest that the hero's will *masks* Dionysus *by entangling him*.) In Part 2, prior to "The Night Song," Zarathustra-Zagreus's self-assertive will to truth is the heroic and epistemological mask that causes his self-estrangement. Were Zarathustra-Zagreus to discard his will to truth, and acknowledge his power to go-under, he would reclaim the ability to experience a chaos of uncreated passions that is the "coming" Dionysus. In effect, he would be forsaking one mode of Dionysian experience for another.

In *Zarathustra*, Nietzsche preserves the distinction between Dionysus-Zagreus and Dionysus the coming god.[47] It is this distinction, indeed, that explains how Zarathustra in "The Night Song" can personify Dionysus, and thus *be* the god Nietzsche claims he is, even as he disowns his power to be affected by Dionysian chaos. Zarathustra personifies Zagreus, yet has no experience of the coming god's chaos. As Zagreus, in fact, he is barred from this experience, to which he would have access only by discarding his heroic will and reclaiming his power to go-under—only, that is, by ceasing to be Zagreus. Zarathustra can personify Dionysus-Zagreus, even as he disowns his power to be affected by the coming god's epiphany as passional chaos, for maintaining a will that disowns this power is *essential* to being Dionysus in the mode of Zagreus.[48]

Though Zarathustra-Zagreus can envision his will as the unique source of all values, as in sections 9 and 10 of the prologue, he cannot suffer the chaos one has to suffer to be able to create new values. Indeed, he could become a creator of new values only if he exchanged his Promethean, leonine experience of Dionysus (as Zagreus) for the creator-child's experience of Dionysus (as the coming god). Zarathustra's descent at the beginning of *Zarathustra* seems to be an attempt to reclaim his power to go-under and so to effect this exchange. Zarathustra goes-under, we observed, in order to become man again; in order, that is, to dissolve the rift between Dionysus and man. In leaving his mountain cave, he intends to spend his leonine superfecundity (atop his mountain, it may be recalled, Zarathustra had already enacted the second metamorphosis of the spirit) by rendering it accessible to man as passional chaos. In effect, then, he abandons his Zagrean and Promethean experience of Dionysus—as the overrich source of all possible values—in order to embrace and stimulate the human ability to experience Dionysus as the coming god. In this way, he attempts to become a creator of new values and to exhort others to become creators of new values.

Zarathustra's descent courts tragedy, "Zarathustra's Prologue" suggests, because the possibility of experiencing Dionysian chaos may have disappeared from the world to which Zarathustra descends. Appearing to be a self-spending Promethean hero when he begins his descent, Zarathustra soon shows himself to be a self-emptying tragic hero who is blind to the possibility that his descent will leave standing the rift between Dionysus and man. When Zarathustra finally faces this possibility (in the wake of the tragedy of the tightrope walker), he takes the view that the problem then confronting him is that of finding companions in whom the possibility of suffering Dionysian chaos has not been exhausted.

Prior to "The Night Song," the *only* problem Zarathustra acknowledges is that of finding the "right men." In Part 2, this problem is complicated by the fact that Zarathustra's disciples, among whom he hopes to find the companions he seeks, have fallen victim to caricatures of his teachings. Driven by the "strong wind" of his will to truth, Zarathustra leaves his cave to attack these distortions. Yet, as we have seen, Zarathustra's assertion of his will to truth is a mixed blessing that brings to light his self-estrangement. At the beginning of the prologue, Zarathustra aimed to abandon his Zagrean experience of Dionysus and, like the sun, go-under ("Like you, I must *go-under* [*untergehen*]"), bringing Dionysus, the coming god, to man. At the beginning of Part 2 he neglects to speak of going-under, although he does express a desire to "go down" to his friends and enemies. The rift between Dionysus and man persists in Part 2—"They receive from me, but do I touch their souls?" Zarathustra asks in "The Night Song"— but it seems unlikely that Zarathustra, so long as he embraces the posture of the lion, will be the one to heal that rift.[49] Supposing that Zarathustra's leonine will to truth and Zagrean experience of Dionysus preclude *his* "seeing" and "hearing" the possibility of going-under, it strains credulity to believe that he could inspire his disciples to such seeing and hearing. Even if there existed persons who still embodied the possibility of going-under, it is doubtful that they could be moved by a leonine Zarathustra. In "The Night Song," Zarathustra responds to his feeling of pedagogical impotence by plotting *revenge* against his disciples. This response is ironic, of course, for he has been led to it by his devotion to a will to truth that insistently distinguished his views from the revenge-driven doctrines with which they had been confused.[50]

In "Zarathustra's Prologue," Zarathustra suggests that his perlocutionary and pedagogical failure to realize his poetic intention was due to the fact that his auditors had become men like the last men (see my discussion in Chapter 2). In Part 2, we learn that this failure has also been due to Zarathustra's limitations as a lion-spirit—again, the case seems to be one of the blind leading the blind. This second account of Zarathustra's perlocutionary failure, like the one Zarathustra presents in the prologue, is *historical* (and, therefore, at odds with the de Manian explanation I explored in Chapter 2). Both accounts explain the perlocutionary failure by highlighting the sort of persons people have *become*: the prologue highlights the sort of persons the townspeople have become, and Part 2 highlights the sort of person Zarathustra has become. In "The Night Song," Zarathustra laments the suffering he has induced simply by becoming a lion-spirit.

In "The Dancing Song," Zarathustra begins to grapple with the crisis to which his leonine will to truth has led him. His first attempt to "resolve" this crisis is quite significant, for it involves a radical inversion of his image of himself. Having come upon a group of girls who cease to dance when they see him, Zarathustra characterizes the "devil" as the spirit of gravity and then describes himself:

> Indeed, I am a forest and a night of dark trees [*eine Nacht dunkler Bäume*]: but he who is not afraid of my darkness [*Dunkel*] will also find rose slopes under my cypresses. And he will also find the little god whom girls like the best: beside the well [*Brunnen*] he lies, still, with his eyes shut. Verily, in bright daylight [*am hellen Tage*] he fell asleep, the sluggard! Did he chase after butterflies too much? Do not be angry with me, you beautiful dancers, if I chastise the little god a bit. He may cry and weep—but he is laughable even when he weeps. And with tears in his eyes he shall ask you for a dance, and I myself will sing a song for his dance: a dancing and mocking song on the spirit of gravity, my supreme and most powerful devil, of whom they say he is "master of the world."
>
> And this is the song that Zarathustra sang while Cupid and the girls danced together.[51]

Zarathustra's inversion of his self-image is dramatic: the character who in "The Night Song" intoned "Light am I; ah, that I were night" now identifies himself with night and darkness. Considered in the perspective of the longing expressed in "The Night Song," Zarathustra's allusion to his darkness may be read as his acknowledgment, finally, of his power of receptivity. This reading is confirmed by Zarathustra's claim that, within the darkness, Cupid, the god of love, fell asleep "beside the well . . . in bright daylight." Here, Zarathustra admits that, as he enjoyed his transcendent "well" and life of knowledge, he permitted his "dark" ability to love responsively—to love as one beloved loves—to lie dormant, and so was able to identify himself exclusively with the bright daylight of the will to truth that seemed to imprison him in "The Night Song." By now identifying himself with his nightlike power of receptivity, and by awakening his Cupid's ability to receive and respond to the claims of another, Zarathustra seems to have suspended his will to truth, and to have solicited an experience of life that is not predicated on this will's reduction of reality to what knowing subjects have created and know. Zarathustra's metaphor for his reclaimed openness to life is Cupid's dance, a dance with girls who, when they first recognized Zarathustra, stopped dancing, as if they had sensed his allegiance to a will to truth that renders him a stranger to the dancing body's power to be moved by the uncreated passions that claim it.

While Cupid and the girls dance together, Zarathustra sings "a dancing and mocking song [*Ein Tanz- und Spottlied*] on the spirit of gravity."[52] But almost immediately, his intention to mock the spirit of gravity is made to appear ironic: "Into your eyes I looked recently, O life! And into the unfathomable [*Unergründliche*] I then seemed to be sinking [*sinken*]. But you pulled me out with a golden fishing rod, and you laughed mockingly [*spöttisch*] when I called you unfathomable."[53] Although he aims to mock the spirit of gravity, Zarathustra falls prey to that spirit, and so finds himself "sinking," like a heavy weight, as his life laughs and ridicules him. By suspending his will to truth, which is the essence of his "wild" wisdom, Zarathustra relinquishes his primary means for showing that he is not a representation of repetition and for maintaining his leonine repudiation of the spirit of gravity's belief that creating new values is not possible. Without his will to truth, Zarathustra reclaims his power of receptivity, yet leaves himself vulnerable to this belief through which "all things fall."[54] No longer envisioning his life from the perspective of his will to truth, Zarathustra now believes that his life's meaning is unknowable—that it is "unfathomable"—and that it offers him no firm and intelligible basis for speaking against the spirit that scorns his highest hope.

The remainder of "The Dancing Song" expresses the dilemma Zarathustra now faces. Portrayed as an erotic triangle, with Zarathustra torn between his loyalties to life and wisdom (his "wild" wisdom), the dilemma, in essence, is this: if Zarathustra keeps faith with his wisdom and will to truth, then he must disown his power to be moved by life in ways to which his wisdom and will to truth must remain oblivious; if, however, he suspends his will to truth, in order to enrich his experience of life, he sacrifices his primary means for resisting the spirit of gravity. Life offers a solution to Zarathustra's dilemma (a solution that is figured by her golden fishing rod) when she depicts herself as "changeable and wild, and a woman in every way."[55] Although Zarathustra later accepts and sees the point of life's self-depiction (in "The Tomb Song" and "On Self-Overcoming"), he initially responds to her remarks with disbelief ("I never believe her . . . when she speaks ill of herself"). He then alludes to his wisdom's jealous anger at his praise for life, and notes that, though he loves "only life," he remains well disposed toward wisdom "because she reminds [him] . . . of life." When, finally, Zarathustra describes his wisdom to life, in language similar to the language life used to describe herself, life suggests that Zarathustra has unwittingly described her. Confused about the nature of life and her relation to wisdom, Zarathustra has not resolved his dilemma by the end of "The Dancing Song." A retreat to the "sunlit" perspective of "The Night Song" would be a dead end. Yet the "sunset" perspective of "The Dancing Song" ("The sun has set long ago," Zarathustra tells us) offers nothing better. The questions Zarathustra asks at the end of "The

Dancing Song"—"What? Are you still alive, Zarathustra? Why? What for? By what? Whither? Where? How? Is it not folly still to be alive?"—show that he has still to find a way *both* to reclaim his power of receptivity and to refute the spirit of gravity's belief that the aim of creating new values and overcoming man is a "Why?" and a "What for?" whose pursuit is futile.[56]

Zarathustra wonders if living is folly, for without his will to truth he has lost faith in the possibility of overcoming man. In "The Tomb Song," Zarathustra begins to combat his loss of faith by reflecting on the losses he suffered in the past. Carrying an evergreen wreath to the "isle of tombs," he mourns the passing of his youth's "visions and apparitions"; singing in a profoundly personal voice, he blames his "enemies" for killing his visions, and then for stealing his nights and selling them into sleepless agony.[57] In general, Zarathustra portrays his life as pervaded by loss, and so corroborates life's description of herself in "The Dancing Song" as "changeable." In Zarathustra's life, change and the loss it brings seem inevitable. Still, Zarathustra finds sustenance in the wake of loss from his silent and unchanging will. His will, he implies, resurrects and justifies the lost visions that otherwise seem irretrievable: "You [my will] are still alive and your old self. . . . You have still broken out of every tomb. What in my youth was unredeemed lives on in you; and as life and youth you sit there, full of hope, on yellow ruins of tombs."[58] As long as Zarathustra has a will that lives, and that can renew and confirm his lost visions—and, we may assume, his lost faith—he need not despair at life's changes, nor worry that living is folly. To redeem his hope and faith that man can be overcome, Zarathustra requires a will that can reassert and validate that hope and faith. Such a will, however, is not his will to truth.

The concluding sentences of "The Tomb Song" allude indirectly to Zarathustra's solution to the dilemma he faces in "The Dancing Song." As I hope now to show, Zarathustra states this solution explicitly in the speech that follows "The Tomb Song" ("On Self-Overcoming") in the form of a critique of the will to truth:

"Will to truth," you who are wisest call that which impels you and fills you with lust?

A will to the thinkability [*Denkbarkeit*] of all beings; this *I* call your will. You want to *make* all being thinkable [*denkbar*], for you doubt with well-founded suspicion that it is already thinkable [*denkbar*]. But it shall yield and bend for you. Thus your will wants it. It shall become smooth [*glatt*] and serve the spirit as its mirror and reflection [*und dem Geiste unterthan, als sein Spiegel und Widerbild*]. That is your whole will, you who are wisest: a will to power—when you speak of good and evil too, and of valuations. You still want to create the world before which you can kneel: that is your ultimate hope and intoxication.[59]

Although Zarathustra addresses himself here to the "wisest," his discussion of the will to truth of the wisest clearly echoes the epistemological position *he* advanced in "Upon the Blessed Isles." Recall, for example, his conception of the will to truth: "But this is what the will to truth should mean to you: that everything should be changed into what is thinkable [*denkbares*] for man."[60] In "Upon the Blessed Isles," Zarathustra held that a conjecture is true of reality only if it is thinkable. When he suggests, then, that the wisest envision reality as the mirror image of the knowing spirit's thinkable representations, he implicates himself as one of the wisest. If "On Self-Overcoming" is Zarathustra's critique of the will to truth of the wisest, it is also a self-critique. And if Zarathustra can now distinguish himself from the truth seekers he criticizes, it is because the insight he acquired in "The Dancing Song," and then refined in "The Tomb Song," has led him away from the epistemology he still embraced in "The Night Song."

For Zarathustra, the will to truth is but one expression of the will to power. It is in the nature of the will to power, moreover, to undermine the will to truth. The wills to truth of the wisest, Zarathustra argues, create and represent as true the many worlds of value within which peoples live and act. The primary threat to these worlds, their ever present "danger and . . . end," he claims, is the will to power itself.[61] In order to explain further to the wisest the conflict between the will to power per se and the will to power as will to truth, Zarathustra proffers an interpretation of life that he bases on a "secret" he discovered in the "heart" of life. His appeal to life here is at first puzzling, however, because it echoes the speech on the tarantulas in which he claimed that the wisest *know* the secret of life. If this is the case, what more have they now to learn from Zarathustra? As we shall see, this question can be best answered by contrasting the account of life given in "On the Tarantulas" with that given in "On Self-Overcoming."

Consider first the passage from "On the Tarantulas":

> Life wants to build [*bauen*] itself up into the *heights* with pillars and steps; it wants to look into vast distances and out toward stirring beauties: therefore it requires *height*. And because it requires *height*, it requires steps [*Stufen*] and contradiction among the steps and the climbers. Life wants to climb and to overcome itself climbing.
>
> And behold, my friends: here where the tarantula has its hole, the ruins [*Trümmer*] of an ancient temple rise; behold it with enlightened [*erleuchteten*] eyes! Verily, the man who once piled his thoughts to the sky in these stones [*wer hier einst seine Gedanken in Stein nach Oben thürmte*] —he, like the wisest [*gleich dem Weisesten*], knew the secret of all life [*das Geheimniss alles Lebens*].

That struggle and inequality are present even in beauty, and also war for power and more power [*Krieg um Macht und Übermacht*]: that is what he teaches us here in the plainest parable.[62] (emphases mine)

Consider next the corresponding remarks in "On Self-Overcoming":

Hear, then, my word, you who are wisest [*ihr Weisesten*]. Test in all seriousness whether I have crawled into the very heart of life and into the very roots of its heart.

Where I found the living, there I found will to power; and even in the will of those who serve I found the will to be master.

That the weaker should serve the stronger, to that it is persuaded by its own will, which would be master over what is weaker still: this is the one pleasure it does not want to renounce. And as the smaller yields [*hingiebt*] to the greater, that it may have pleasure and power over the smallest, thus even the greatest still yields [*also giebt auch das Grösste noch hin*], and for the sake of power risks life. That is the yielding [*Hingebung*] of the greatest: it is a hazard and danger and casting dice for death. . . .

And life itself confided this secret [*diess Geheimniss*] to me: "Behold," it said, "I am *that which must always overcome itself.* Indeed, you call it a will to pro-create or a drive to an end, to something higher, farther, more manifold: but all this is one, and one secret [*Eins und Ein Geheimniss*].

"Rather would I go-under [*noch gehe Ich unter*] than forswear this; and verily, where there is going-under [*wo es Untergang giebt*] and a falling of leaves, behold, there life sacrifices itself [*opfert sich*]—for power. That I must be a struggle and a becoming and an end and a contradiction [*Widerspruch*] of ends—alas, whoever guesses what is my will should also guess on what *crooked* [*krummen*] paths it must proceed.[63]

I have quoted these accounts of life in full, because the differences between them reflect a dramatic change in Zarathustra's self-understanding. As I previously argued in this chapter, the first account articulates a view of life that seems to be based on the experience of transcendence described in "On the Rabble" (the speech that immediately precedes "On the Tarantulas"). This view of life, which stresses life's predilection for height and hierarchy, represents it, to borrow Henry Staten's phrase, as a "self-augmenting" economy: as a flow of resources whose telos is accumulation and growth.[64] In "On the Tarantulas," in fact, life is depicted as *relentlessly* self-augmenting: building itself up with pillars and steps; revealing its secret in the process whereby the builder of an ancient temple amassed a mound of stones in order to realize his creative intention; and warring, in all its instances, to increase its store of power. Life appears here, in short, as an enterprise that persistently accumulates life and power into ever larger masses of ordered life and power.

Despite some notable similarities, the picture of life presented in "On Self-Overcoming" is significantly different from the one I have just described. To be sure, Zarathustra continues to highlight life's striving for height ("you call it a will to . . . something higher"), for hierarchy ("That the weaker should serve the stronger, to that it is persuaded by its own will, which would be master over what is weaker still"), and for the acquisition of power ("the smaller yields to the greater, that it may have pleasure and power over the smallest"). Different, however, is the emphasis he now places on life's disposition, especially as it is manifest in the greatest wills to power, *to risk and sacrifice life for the sake of power*. In "On Self-Overcoming," Zarathustra portrays life as, in effect, consuming and destroying itself. He claims that life's self-augmenting economy is connected to a "spendthrift" economy (here, again, I am borrowing Staten's terminology) that is governed by the imperative to *squander* life's energies. The spendthrift economy bolsters the self-augmenting economy because spendthrifty life spends and sacrifices itself in order to acquire and amass power.

From the perspective of "On Self-Overcoming," "On the Tarantulas" gives an incomplete portrait of life that ignores the fact that life spends itself. We should note, however, that the incompleteness of this portrait is already hinted at in "On the Tarantulas" by an irony in Zarathustra's remarks about the ruins of an ancient temple. In exhorting his friends to behold those ruins, Zarathustra invites them to look *beyond* the ruins themselves and to concentrate on the life-inspired vision of the architect who built the ancient temple. By focusing on this vision, Zarathustra lets disappear from view the ravages of time that converted the architect's creation (his "piled" up thoughts) into ruins. Looking at the temple with "enlightened" eyes, which see only what the architect imagined and then created, he *overlooks* the forces of decline that destroy creations and create ruins. In effect, he loses sight of the fact that change, destruction, and loss—what he later calls "sacrifice"—are no less essential to the economy of life than the amassing of ever larger quantities of life and power. "On the Tarantulas" is ironic, for in advancing Zarathustra's view of life it reveals a blindness in that view. Life is symbolically avenged for Zarathustra's blindness, when the tarantula, whose home is with the ancient temple's ruins, bites Zarathustra.

Life's literal revenge against Zarathustra is the suffering he expresses in "The Night Song."[65] To say that, however, is just to say that Zarathustra, in overlooking life's propensity to spend itself, perpetuates the self-estrangement that causes his suffering. Zarathustra is self-estranged, we have seen, because he disowns his power of receptivity. In "The Dancing Song," he reclaims this ability, yet cannot sustain his belief that overcoming man is possible. Zarathustra continues to acknowledge his power of receptivity in "On Self-Overcoming," but now sees that it has an indispensable contribution to make to the project of overcoming man and creating new values.

For Zarathustra, life overcomes itself when it sacrifices itself, and life sacrifices itself when it goes-under ("where there is going-under . . . there life sacrifices itself"). Going-under involves a "yielding" ("the yielding of the greatest"), Zarathustra implies, by which the will to power relinquishes power "for the sake of power."[66] More exactly, going-under requires that the will to power surrender its second-order mastery of first-order passions, and thus that it acknowledge the body's ability to receive and suffer an unmastered chaos of uncreated passions.[67] Going-under entails a "sacrifice" of life, for it involves a destruction both of particular values and of the individual self these values produce (note that Zarathustra says that the creator is an annihilator [ein Vernichter]).[68] This sacrifice is "for the sake of power," because it permits the will to power to *reassert* power and mastery through the creation of new values (that is, through the revaluation of the passions) and hence through the creation of a new self. In surrendering power, the will to power squanders an established form of life and embraces the body's capacity to be affected by passional chaos; in reasserting its power, the will to power produces a new form of life and perpetuates life's self-augmenting economy.

Because it is in the nature of the will to power to relinquish power for the sake of power, life is a "becoming" that proceeds on crooked and self-contradictory paths. When life goes-under and overcomes itself, Zarathustra suggests, it shows itself to be something other than the "smooth" and static mirror that the wisest identify as life. Indeed, life that overcomes itself has more the look of an endlessly rotating funhouse mirror, a moving looking glass of crooked surfaces that produces ever-changing and contradictory appearances of the things it reflects. Filled with lust by the will to truth, the wisest do not see that life's self-overcoming repeatedly displaces its forms and appearances only to replace them with new and contradictory forms and appearances. Rather they believe that self-overcoming is a process whereby life builds itself to a height from which it can know and appreciate its enduring forms and essential nature ("[Life] wants to look into vast distances and out toward stirring beauties: therefore it requires height. . . . Life wants to climb and to overcome itself climbing"). Although Zarathustra attributes this view of life to the wisest in "On the Tarantulas," its connection to the experience of transcendence he describes in "On the Rabble" again suggests that he is implicated in his critique of the wisest.[69] What this view implies, in any case, is that the wisest see life as an immobile reality that is impervious to transformation.

The blindness of the wisest to life's power to overcome and transform itself is in keeping with their loyalty to the will to truth. Self-overcoming entails going-under. We have seen, moreover, that where the will to power *as will to truth* prevails, the self is oblivious to the possibility of going-under. The will to power that wills the truth is a leonine will to power that has blinded itself to its intrinsic capacity to relinquish power. Put differently, the will to power per se can both relinquish power and acknowledge the body's capacity to go-under; when the will to power wills the truth, however, it loses sight of its capacity to surrender its second-order mastery of first-order passions. Yet this is simply to say that, in willing the truth, the will to power obscures the body's receptive power to be affected by unmastered, passional chaos. The blindness of the wisest to life's power to overcome itself is, in essence, the will to truth's blindness to the reality of uncreated, living passions that can affect the body independently of the will to power's assertion and transformative reassertion of mastery over those passions.[70] Where the will to truth's "smooth mirror" is the measure of the real, life's self-overcoming cannot be entertained as a real possibility.

Zarathustra proves himself to be wiser than the wisest, and to be wiser than he was when he embraced the will to truth, by showing how the will to power per se, when it surrenders and reasserts power, undermines the will to power as will to truth. By surrendering and reasserting power the will to power can create new values.

Because creating new values is the essence of overcoming man, it is reasonable to assume that the will to power is the will Zarathustra affirms at the conclusion of "The Tomb Song." Insofar as it can surrender and reassert power, and thereby bring about man's self-overcoming, the will to power can validate Zarathustra's faith that man can be overcome; it can justify that faith, in other words, precisely by effecting man's self-overcoming. Although life may involve the loss of youth's visions and hopes—and in Zarathustra's case the loss of the vision and the hope of creating new values—those visions and hopes can be renewed and sustained by exploiting the creative power of the will to power to realize and substantiate them. It is significant, moreover, that the will to power can realize Zarathustra's hope to overcome man only by admitting that, as life herself suggests in "The Dancing Song," change and loss are essential to life. By surrendering power, the will to power acknowledges the body's receptive capacity to suffer passional chaos, and in effect consigns an existing mode of individual existence *to the past*. By reasserting power, it aims to revalue the passions and thus to create *new* values. In general, Zarathustra's analysis of the will to power resolves the dilemma facing him at the end of "The Dancing Song": it shows, in fine, that even if one discards the will to truth and reclaims one's power of receptivity one can find in the creative ability of one's will to power a basis for rejecting the spirit of gravity's belief that creating new values is impossible. In the language of "The Night Song," it shows that the creation of new values involves both receiving *and* giving.[71]

"On Those Who Are Sublime," the speech that follows "On Self-Overcoming," brings to a conclusion the therapeutic self-analysis that begins with "The Night Song" and that undermines the epistemological posture Zarathustra adopts at the beginning of Part 2. The gist of this self-analysis, I have been arguing, is a critique of the will to truth. As developed in "The Dancing Song," "The Tomb Song," and "On Self-Overcoming," Zarathustra's self-analysis and critique lead him to see (1) that to create new values he has both to discard his will to truth and reclaim his power of receptivity (his "sensibility") and (2) that discarding his will to truth and reclaiming his power of receptivity need not entail the triumph of the spirit of gravity. As we have seen, Zarathustra's self-analysis explains why the lion-spirited individual cannot create new values and why the creation of new values requires the exchange of one modality of Dionysian experience for another. Zarathustra completes his self-analysis in "On Those Who Are Sublime" by making explicit the genealogy of leonine, creational impotence that it presupposes. In the same speech, he ties that genealogy to a second but closely related genealogy of modern Cartesian and post-Cartesian notions of the knowing subject.

At first glance, Zarathustra's expressed distaste for the sublime may seem little more than a corollary to Nietzsche's repudiation of Christian-Platonic metaphysics. For Kant and Schiller, whose aesthetics provide an invaluable context for appraising Nietzsche's writing on the sublime and the beautiful, the sublime announces that man, as a rational being, transcends the sensible world of nature and appearances.[72] Because Nietzsche rejects as Christian-Platonic, or "otherworldly," all philosophies that judge appearances by comparing them to a "true world" that transcends them—even if that world is equated with theoretical or practical rationality—Zarathustra's distaste for the sublime is predictable.[73]

Although this gloss of "On Those Who Are Sublime" is not without merit, it only begins to do justice to the philosophical ambition of Zarathustra's speech.[74] What it misses, I think, is Zarathustra's rejection of Kant's and Schiller's belief that the sublime is a *disclosive* mode of experience. For Kant and Schiller, the sublime heralds human transcendence by *revealing* the fact that human beings are supersensible subjects existing apart from nature and appearances. For Zarathustra, the sublime reveals no such fact, but rather prompts human beings *mistakenly* to believe that they are supersensible subjects who exist apart from nature and appearances. In Zarathustra's view, the sublime is a *generative* mode of experience leading human beings to picture themselves as supersensible subjects of the sort that Kant's and Schiller's aesthetics assume to exist.

Zarathustra's rejection of the disclosive conception of the sublime is closely connected to his completion of his self-analysis. In order to see this, we need only consider that Zarathustra himself, prior to rejecting the disclosive conception in "On Those Who Are Sublime," straightforwardly embraced it. I want to argue, in fact, that Zarathustra's description of his flight to a height above the rabble—a height of cold wells and strong winds that he later identifies with his will to truth and knowledge—involves a disclosive conception of the sublime with significant affinities to Kant's characterization of the dynamical sublime. After clarifying these affinities, I will investigate Zarathustra's interpretation of the sublime as a generative mode of experience.

In our experience of the dynamical sublime, claims Kant, our recognition that an object is *fearful*—our recognition that, were we threatened by it, physical resistance would be futile—involves the belief that, compared to the "might" (*Macht*) of the object, our "ability" (*Vermögen*) to resist it is insignificant. We call fearful objects "sublime," Kant argues, "because they raise the soul's fortitude above its usual middle range and allow us to discover [*entdecken lassen*] in ourselves an ability to resist which is of a quite different kind, and which gives us the courage [to believe] that we could be a match for nature's seeming omnipotence [*Allgewalt*]." Strictly speaking, of course, the sublime, for Kant, belongs to the human spirit and not to fearful objects. It is an experience through which the spirit surpasses its ordinary propensities and becomes conscious of a supersensible vocation (*Bestimmung*): "though the irresistibility of nature's might makes us, considered as natural beings, recognize our own physical impotence, it reveals [*entdeckt*] in us at the same time an ability to judge ourselves independent of nature, and reveals in us a superiority over nature that is the basis of a self-preservation quite different in kind from the one that can be assailed and endangered by nature outside us. . . . we regard nature's might . . . as . . . not having dominance over us, as persons, that we should have to bow to it if our highest principles were at stake and we had to choose between upholding them or abandoning them."[75]

As Kant describes it here, the experience of the sublime has a compensatory quality such that our apprehension of physical incapacity is accompanied by the revelation of our supersensible power (or ability) to resist what we cannot resist physically.[76] We delight in our sublimity, when we discover that, as rational beings capable of acting from principles, we enjoy an immunity from the might to which nature may subject us as physical creatures. As Kant understands it, the experience of the (dynamical) sublime involves a recognition of powerlessness, as well as a spiritually satisfying disclosure of a superior and countervailing power that transcends the domain (nature) within which we felt powerless.

Recall, now, Zarathustra's self-description in "On the Rabble." Zarathustra suggests there that he became nauseous when he believed that the rabble was essential to life and sensed that he was powerless to enjoy a life free of the rabble. As we have seen, Zarathustra coped with his nausea by learning to live "like a cripple who has become deaf and blind and dumb." Suddenly, however, he seemed to discover a life divorced from the life of the rabble. More exactly, he experienced a "flight" to a "height" that seemed to secure him a life separate from the life the rabble dominated. In celebrating his flight and height, Zarathustra affirmed his newfound ability to enjoy a life of which the rabble knew nothing. Like the experience of the sublime Kant describes, his experience seemed to reveal a power, or a capacity (not, now, to resist physical force through adherence to principle, but to enjoy a life free of the rabble), that transcended the domain wherein he felt powerless (not nature, but the life the rabble poisoned). No less than Kant, Zarathustra sketches a disclosive conception of the sublime, for he insists that the compensatory power he feels stems from an elevated and separately existing spiritual life that he has literally discovered or "found."[77]

In "On the Rabble," Zarathustra develops a genealogy of an experience of "height" and transcendence that he later connects to his conception of himself as a knowing subject. In "On the Sublime," he revises that genealogy in light of his critique of the will to truth in "The Night Song," "The Dancing Song," "The Tomb Song," and "On Self-Overcoming." Rather than view his leonine pursuit of a "life of knowledge" in terms that reproduce the outline of Kant's analysis of the dynamical sublime, Zarathustra will now represent his experience of sublime transcendence as an effect, caused by a heroic though self-estranging act of will, that generates an image of man as a supersensible subject. Moreover, he will imply that Kant's and Schiller's disclosive conception of the sublime, like the disclosive conception he himself sketches in "On the Rabble," is founded on the reification of such an image.

"On Those Who Are Sublime" focuses on the personification of the sublime in the figure of the hero. Zarathustra's characterization of this figure has self-critical implications, for it so clearly echoes his previous self-descriptions. Figuring the sublime hero as possessing a "swelled chest [*erhobener Brust*] . . . like one who holds in his breath" and as harboring "knowledge" (*Erkenntniss*) in the manner of "a wild beast" (*ein wildes Thier*), Zarathustra explicitly recalls his portrait of himself—his chest heaving and he proclaiming the wisdom of a wild animal—in "The Child with the Mirror": "Violently my chest will expand [*wird*

sich da meine Brust heben], violently will it blow its storm . . . and thus find relief. . . . Indeed, you too will be frightened, my friends, by my wild wisdom
[*wilden Weisheit*]. . . . Would that my lioness, wisdom [*meine Löwin Weisheit*],
might learn how to roar tenderly."[78] Similarly, when Zarathustra suggests that
the hero's retreat to the "woods of knowledge" was prompted by nausea and contempt at being close to "the earth," he reminds us of his description of his own
nausea-fleeing flight to the "cold wells" and "strong winds" of knowledge. The
sublime hero, Zarathustra says, is one "who withdraw[s]." Repenting an "earthly"
life that disgusts him (he is, we are told, a "penitent of the spirit" [*Büsser des
Geistes*]), he seems to have invented a life—a life of "hunting" for knowledge—
that compensates for the life he has renounced. Withdrawing into himself and
asserting his heroic will to knowledge and truth, the sublime hero projects the
image of a deathly and otherworldly life, appearing to be a shadowy phantom
whose essence is supersensible.[79] Standing aloof from the world of appearances,
he seems to reside beyond the reach of warm sunlight, and even beyond the
touch and warmth of *his own* sunlight, reminiscent of the leonine Zarathustra in
"The Night Song": "And only when he turns away from himself, will he jump
over his shadow [*Schatten*]—and verily into *his* sun. All too long has he been sitting in the shadow, and the cheeks of the penitent of the spirit [*Büsser des Geistes*]
have grown pale; he almost starved to death on his expectations."

Personifying a happiness that figuratively "smells" of contempt for the earth,
though *not* of the earth itself, the sublime hero disowns his power to be affected
in ways that would identify him as an "earthly" or physical being.[80] In order to
reclaim his power of receptivity, he must, like Zarathustra in "The Dancing
Song," "discard [*verlernen*] his heroic will." In other words, he must let go of his
will to knowledge and truth, admit that he is a body possessed by passions, and
accept that he is not the incorporeal and shadowy phantom he appears to be:
"When power becomes gracious [*gnädig*] and descends [*herabkommt*] into the
visible—such descent [*Herabkommen*] I call beauty." Beauty, here, entails the repudiation of sublimity: it is a movement by which a once heroic, leonine will to
power, having renounced the illusion of supersensible subjectivity, and having
ceased to hold aloof from the "visible" world of appearances, graciously conde-
scends to revalue the passions through which that world stirs and moves the human body. For Zarathustra, beauty is the cure that relieves the self-estrangement
of the sublime.[81]

"On Those Who Are Sublime" argues that the experience of sublime transcendence described in "On the Rabble" was an effect of self-estrangement, and
not of a literal discovery of a life-divorced-from-life. It suggests, moreover, that
this sort of experience *generates* the image and illusion of a supersensible life, or

subjectivity, the existence of which life, or subjectivity, Kant's and Schiller's disclosive conception of the sublime presupposes.[82] More generally, "On Those Who Are Sublime" sketches a psychoaesthetic genealogy of the modern Cartesian tendency to view human beings as knowing subjects who (1) exist apart from the world of appearances, and (2) reduce reality to what can be known. Zarathustra's genealogy is psychological, in a broad sense, because it roots this tendency in the lived experience of self-estrangement. It is aesthetic, because the psychology of self-estrangement it highlights illuminates a distinctive form of aesthetic experience.[83] For Zarathustra, the person who sees herself as a Cartesian or Kantian knowing subject has reified the fantasy that she transcends the world of sensible objects, a fantasy that has been generated by an experience of the sublime that originated in self-estrangement. Zarathustra falls prey to just such a fantasy, likewise generated by an experience of the sublime, when in "The Night Song" his identification with the "strong winds" of his "wild wisdom" moves him to see himself as a spontaneous cogito that distinguishes itself from the world of appearances whose "givenness" it denies.

In Part 1, Zarathustra is a lion who speaks a lion's speech to potential and actual lions. Only in Part 2, however, is his leonine self-estrangement plainly evident. Part 2 makes explicit the self-estrangement of the lion-spirit by depicting Zarathustra's exploration of the ramifications of his (Zarathustra's) will to truth. Part of the yield of this exploration is the genealogical insight that the self-estrangement that explains the lion-spirit's creational impotence derives from the lion spirit's will to truth. Closely related to this insight is a second genealogical claim, namely, that the lion-spirit's will to truth fosters a feeling of sublime transcendence that encourages the modern Cartesian and post-Cartesian tendency to view human beings as knowing subjects who exist apart from the world of sensible objects.

I will conclude my discussion of Zarathustra's crisis and cure by considering again, briefly, the relationship between Dionysus-Zagreus and Dionysus the coming god. "On Those Who Are Sublime" obliquely investigates this relationship, as can be seen if one compares the final sentence of that speech to the remarkably similar notebook entry that Nietzsche penned during the summer he completed Part 2. The final sentence of Zarathustra's speech reads as follows:

> For this is the soul's secret: only when the hero has abandoned her [*sie der Held verlassen hat*], she is approached in a dream by the overhero.[84]

The corresponding notebook entry alludes explicitly to the figures of Dionysus and Ariadne:

Dionysus on a tiger: the skull of a goat: a panther. Ariadne dreaming: "Abandoned by the hero [*vom Helden verlassen*], I dream the over-hero." To conceal Dionysus entirely [*Dionysos ganz zu verschweigen*]![85]

Besides glossing the concluding claim of "On Those Who Are Sublime," Nietzsche's notebook entry offers insight into the entire speech. The references to Dionysus, Ariadne, and a hero who abandons Ariadne recall the myth that Dionysus wed Ariadne after Theseus, the hero, abandoned her. To be sure, Theseus is one of Nietzsche's favorite figures for the hero. Why, however, does he invoke this figure, along with the apparently critical motif of abandonment, both in the notebook entry and in "On Those Who Are Sublime"?

By connecting Dionysus to a tiger and a panther—that is, to two beasts of prey—Nietzsche alludes to a distinct facet of the god's mythological nature: namely, to the bloodthirsty savagery that Greek myth associates with the name "Zagreus," an appellation meaning "great hunter."[86] Zarathustra recalls the imagery of Nietzsche's notebook entry when he describes the hero as a savage or "wild" beast who "stands there like a tiger."[87] And he seems implicitly to invoke the figure of Zagreus when he describes the hero as a kind of "hunter" (in the woods of knowledge).[88] It seems, then, that Zarathustra's Theseus-like hero is a Dionysian figure *in his own right*. Specifically, he is Dionysus-Zagreus. Similarly, I have argued, Zarathustra is Dionysus-Zagreus when *he* appears as a (Promethean and leonine) hero.[89]

Nietzsche's notebook entry suggests that the reference to the soul in the last sentence of Zarathustra's speech should be read as an allusion to Ariadne. What can we make of this? Without pretending to do full justice to the significance Ariadne has for Nietzsche, I will suggest here, drawing some inspiration from Nietzsche's published writings, that she signifies the human capacity to be touched and moved by passional chaos. Put succinctly, "Ariadne" names the human body's power of receptivity to the advent of the "coming" Dionysus.[90]

In *Ecce Homo*, Nietzsche remarks that "the answer" to the Dionysian night song "would be Ariadne."[91] Ariadne is the rejoinder to Zarathustra's lament, I am arguing, because she is a metaphor for the ability to go-under that Zarathustra-Zagreus or, indeed, any other sublime, Zagrean hero must reclaim in order to end his suffering. As Nietzsche suggests in *Beyond Good and Evil*, she symbolizes the connection of human beings to a Dionysus who is an agent of labyrinthine chaos.[92] Where the sublime Zagreus prevails, the Ariadnean power to be affected by chaos lies dormant (like Cupid at the well). In order to revive that power, that his soul might know something of the coming god, the Theseus-like Zagrean hero must "discard his heroic will" and hence "abandon" his soul to a life bereft of his heroic spirit. Only in the wake of this abandonment can the soul envision (dream) the advent of a chaos-bearing Dionysus, whose identity Nietzsche, in keeping with his notebook entry, *conceals* with the name "overhero."[93]

By exchanging one mode of Dionysian experience for another, the leonine Dionysian hero relinquishes his will to truth and strives to become a creator of new values. Ariadne is essential to this exchange, because she is the medium through which it transpires. The feminine middle term that mediates the relationship between two men—that is, the two Dionysuses—Ariadne is a figure for Nietzsche's attempt to think two distinct modalities of Dionysian experience as different aspects of a single configuration of human possibilities: "A labyrinthine human being never seeks the truth, but—whatever he may try to tell us—always and only his Ariadne."[94]

CHAPTER FIVE

Eternal Recurrence, Acts I and II

This . . . fantasy is of the mind unmoored, say unhinged, leaving itself
without material in which to realize and communicate itself; it is an
anxiety of progressive *inexpressiveness*, named as such in Coleridge's
"Dejection", some lines from which Mill quotes in his *Autobiography*.
. . . [Mill] characterizes "the general tone of [his] mind at this period"
as one in which he was "seriously tormented by the thought of the
exhaustibility of musical combinations", calculating . . . that the
twelve tones of the octave must have about yielded all their usable
combinations up. . . . The concept of inexpressiveness, related to a
sense of negative uniqueness, or depressed privacy, abutting the
concept of the exhaustion of the medium of art, leaving no room
for anything new or original to be said in it, is what I am calling
representative, or historical, in Mill's case.

STANLEY CAVELL, *The Claim of Reason*

All three phases of time merge . . . as the same in one single present,
a perpetual "now." Metaphysics calls the constant now "eternity."
Nietzsche too thinks the three phases of time in terms of eternity as
the constant now. Yet for him the constancy consists not in stasis but
in a recurrence of the same. . . . Such return is the inexhaustible
abundance of a life that is both joyous and agonizing.

MARTIN HEIDEGGER, "Who Is Nietzsche's Zarathustra?"

In a famous passage in *Ecce Homo*, penned literally, if not "6,000 feet beyond
man and time," then 6,000 feet above sea level, Nietzsche identifies "the thought
of eternal recurrence" (*der Ewige-Wiederkunfts-Gedanke*) as the *Grundconception*
of *Zarathustra*.[1] He implies that this thought, or idea, is the theme that "grounds"
his philosophical and literary masterpiece, the unifying raison d'être for all the
other motifs that animate *Zarathustra*.[2]

It is significant, therefore, that Zarathustra says that he is the intercessor (*Fürsprecher*) of the circle.[3] Thus, he announces that his vocation is, in part, to mediate and make intelligible the thought of recurrence, which is, figuratively, the thought of the circle. He is right, of course, for the thought of recurrence comes into view as *Zarathustra's Grundconception,* or unifying theme, through the medium of Zarathustra's speeches and actions. To make sense of the thought of recurrence as *Zarathustra's Grundconception* is to make sense of it precisely as it is revealed through those speeches and actions.

To begin to see the implications of this last claim, recall, briefly, Cleanth Brooks's once well-known argument for interpreting the concluding lines of Keats's "Ode on a Grecian Urn" as speech spoken "in character." How should one understand Keats's "'Beauty is truth, truth beauty,'—that is all / Ye know on earth, and all ye need to know"? Rather than construe this proposition as Keats's statement of a philosophical thesis on the essential natures of beauty and truth, one should interpret it, Brooks argues, as the urn's commentary "on its own nature." Keats's poem is a drama, the urn the protagonist of that drama. And the utterances of the urn, like those of *dramatis personae* generally, derive their significance from the dramatic contexts in which they are spoken. Accordingly, Brooks insists that his reading of the urn's self-referential commentary derives "from the context of the 'Ode' itself."[4]

Suppose, now, that we consider the thought of recurrence in light of Brooks's reading of Keats. What would it mean to interpret this thought as spoken and enacted "in character"? The perhaps obvious answer to this question, which I have only begun to sketch, is that to interpret the thought of recurrence this way would be to interpret it as the unifying theme of *Zarathustra.* Zarathustra's speeches and actions reveal the thought of recurrence, for through them Zarathustra *forms* the thought of recurrence. Not only does Zarathustra form the thought, he trans-forms it, not once but twice. As we shall see, Zarathustra's formation and transformations of the thought of recurrence, like the utterances of Keats's urn, draw their significance from the dramatic contexts that prompt them (e.g., the soothsayer's prophecy). Put another way, the import of Zarathustra's elaborations of this thought depends on his evolution as a character in connection to the situations and incidents that compose the drama of *Zarathustra.* Speaking and acting as an evolving character, Zarathustra speaks and acts "in character" when he forms and transforms the thought of recurrence, thereby establishing that thought as *Zarathustra's Grundconception.*[5]

Contemporary Nietzsche scholarship considers the thought of recurrence to be one of Nietzsche's philosophical doctrines. On this view, the thought of recurrence is principally *Nietzsche's* thought: either his theory of the cosmos or his response to the question "How should one live one's life?"[6] This same scholarship tends also to assume that the substance of the thought of recurrence, be it theoretical *or* practical, can be explicated without reference to *Zarathustra*. Here, I break with contemporary scholarship by holding that the thought of recurrence is (1) principally Zarathustra's thought and (2) a thought that Zarathustra defines and develops (forms and transforms) with reference, in essence, to circumstances occurring in *Zarathustra*. *As a Grundconception revealed by Zarathustra's thoughts and actions*, the thought of recurrence is best interpreted within its dramatic context. That Nietzsche's protagonist, Zarathustra, forms or transforms the thought of recurrence in "these" or "those" *particular* situations is fundamental to the identity of that thought as a theme that grounds and connects other motifs. This identity disappears from view if one conceptualizes the thought of recurrence as a thesis entailing no reference to *Zarathustra*, but that Nietzsche endorses and happens to illustrate by means of *Zarathustra*.

Let me hastily add that conceptualizing the thought of recurrence in the now usual way is not without justification—*Zarathustra* is not, after all, the only place in Nietzsche's writing in which the thought of recurrence crops up. For example, passages in the *Nachlass* imply that the thought of recurrence is a cosmological doctrine that can be stated omitting any allusion to *Zarathustra*. Similarly, number 341 of *The Gay Science* suggests that it is a practical doctrine entailing no such allusion. As I have already suggested, holding that there is a doctrine of recurrence that can be explicated absent any reference to *Zarathustra* is compatible with holding that *Zarathustra* illustrates that doctrine. Still, it is one thing to interpret the thought of recurrence as the thought of a doctrine that can be phrased (or paraphrased) without adverting to a drama that illustrates it, but quite another to construe it as intrinsically a particular character's thought as he forms and transforms it in a particular drama. As distinct from its formulation in *The Gay Science*, the *Nachlass*, and other writings, Nietzsche's representation of the thought of recurrence as a *Grundconception* easily lends itself to the latter interpretation.[7]

To be sure, I am not denying that Zarathustra invests the thought of recurrence with cosmological and practical significance. Zarathustra forms the thought in response to the soothsayer's prophecy; he transforms it, subsequently, into a thought based on a practical postulate that refers to a cosmological vision; he transforms it a second and final time when the advent of his children seems imminent. As a developing theme, Zarathustra's thought of recurrence is not a cosmological vision, although it comes to be and then ceases to be rooted in a belief concerning such a vision. Indeed, in each of its formations, Zarathustra's thought is rooted in a belief concerning a particular vision or experience that Zarathustra has in the drama that is *Zarathustra*. Qua *Grundconception*, the thought of re-currence is inextricably bound up with that drama. It is essentially a dramatic thought, a thought-in-the-mode-of-drama that I shall call the "thought-drama" of eternal recurrence.

Zarathustra forms his thought of recurrence by reasoning from the sooth-sayer's prophecy ("all is the same, all has been," etc.), as he interprets it, to the conclusion that his (Zarathustra's) existence is characterized by a recurrence of the same. When Zarathustra transforms his thought the first time, he alters his reason for endorsing this conclusion: he still holds that his existence is charac-terized by a recurrence of the same, but for the reason that, in envisioning his soul as an omnipresent "now" that encompasses and recurs in all other mo-ments, he is constituting his soul as such a "now." In transforming his thought a second time, Zarathustra again retains his belief that his existence is charac-terized by a recurrence of the same, but begins to base that belief on the con-sideration that the passions and the possibility of experiencing passional chaos have been returned to his body and to the bodies of others. Zarathustra forms his thought of recurrence by forming (for a particular reason—again, the sooth-sayer's claim) the belief that his existence is characterized by a recurrence of the same. He twice transforms his thought by twice changing his reason for main-taining that belief.

In developing the thought of recurrence, Zarathustra follows the path of the three metamorphoses of the spirit. First forming his thought in response to the soothsayer's speech, he reverts to the posture of the camel. Thus, in the first act of the thought-drama of recurrence, Zarathustra endorses the view that no new values can be created. In the defiant, second act, he transforms his thought by becoming a lion who envisions his soul as the omnipresent incarnation of an eternal "now." In the third act of his thought-drama, Zarathustra again trans-forms his thought as he becomes a child who can create new values.

As he elaborates his thought of recurrence, Zarathustra becomes a camel, a lion, and then a child. In this chapter, I focus on the first two acts of Zarathus-tra's thought-drama—"the camel's thought of recurrence" and "the lion's thought of recurrence"—in Parts 2 and 3 of *Zarathustra*. In Chapter 6, I turn to Part 4, which concludes with Zarathustra's second transformation of the thought of re-currence and his performance of the third act of his thought-drama—the for-mation of "the child's thought of recurrence."

I will conclude this preliminary discussion of *Zarathustra's Grundconception* by tying some key issues raised in preceding chapters to the "dramatic" inter-pretation of the thought of recurrence sketched here.

1. The soothsayer's prophecy prompts Zarathustra's formation of the thought of recurrence. But if that is so, does it make sense to claim that the thought of recurrence is the unifying theme of *Zarathustra*? The appearance of the soothsayer marks the beginning of the second half of *Zarathustra*, in terms of numbers of speeches.[8] Given that Zarathustra does not form the thought of recurrence in *Zarathustra*'s first half, how can his formation and transformation of the thought in the second half "ground" the motifs and incidents of the first half?

Here we need to remember that Nietzsche, at the beginning of *Zarathustra*, by parodying Paul's letter to the Philippians, expresses a skeptical appraisal of Zarathustra's will to innovate. We have seen, moreover, that, in the first half of *Zarathustra*, Zarathustra repeatedly encounters representations of repetition that revoice the skepticism evident in the parody of Paul. The soothsayer's representation of repetition is *Zarathustra*'s most forceful statement of this skepticism: it is the iteration of incredulity that Zarathustra finds most threatening and that erodes his Dionysian, Goethean faith. Responding to the soothsayer, Zarathustra's camel-spirited formation and leonine transformation of the thought of recurrence thematically "ground," or explain, the presence in the text of his earlier camel-spirited and leonine skirmishes with the skeptics of *Zarathustra*'s first half—for one point of these skirmishes, evident in retrospect, is to *prefigure* Zarathustra's responses to the soothsayer.

2. In the introduction to this book, I claimed that "the possibility of creating new values" is the unifying theme of *Zarathustra*. How can this assertion be squared with that of the present chapter: that Zarathustra's elaboration of the thought of recurrence is the unifying theme of *Zarathustra*?

By forming and transforming the thought of recurrence, Zarathustra contextualizes the issue of creating new values. More exactly, he historicizes the issue by posing it as a problem produced by the modern asceticism of the "small" or "last" man. When Zarathustra first forms the thought of recurrence, he holds that his existence is characterized by a recurrence of the same, basing his judgment on the belief that modern asceticism has destroyed the possibility of creating new values, leaving him victim to the endless perpetuation of the small man's meaningless existence (This belief expresses Zarathustra's interpretation of the soothsayer's prophecy).[9] When Zarathustra transforms his thought (when he forms the lion's thought of recurrence), he defies the specter of the small man and reasserts the possibility of creating new values. When he transforms his thought yet again (when he forms the child's thought of recurrence), he acts to realize that possibility. For Zarathustra, to elaborate the thought of recurrence is to develop the idea of creating new values, specifically in response to the historical phenomenon of the small man. Zarathustra's thought of recurrence concretizes and historically specifies *Zarathustra*'s thematic focus on the possibility of creating new values.

By fashioning his thought of recurrence, Zarathustra extends and completes *Zarathustra*'s explanation of that possibility. As philosophical explanation, *Zarathustra* shows how Zarathustra, by adopting the posture of the lion-spirit, reaffirms and maintains his commitment to becoming a new-values creator, despite the representations of repetition that accost him ("Zarathustra's Prologue"); how Zarathustra, or a disciple, could become a lion-spirit, and how a lion-spirit could remain attuned to his proper calling (which is to go-under and to become a child-creator), notwithstanding their subjection to psychological pitfalls and worldly temptations (Part 1); and how Zarathustra could become a new-values creator, despite the fact that he has become a self-estranged lion-spirit (Part 2). In the aftermath of the soothsayer's speech, we also see how Zarathustra elaborates his thought of recurrence (by forming and transforming that thought) and thereby becomes a new-values creator, notwithstanding the fact that the forces of modern asceticism have annulled the passional preconditions of self-overcoming (Parts 2, 3, and 4). By elaborating his thought Zarathustra extends and completes a narrative that shows how he could become a new-values creator despite the discouraging skepticism (of representations of repetition), the pitfalls and temptations, the self-estrangement, and finally, the modern asceticism that subvert and *appear to exclude* the possibility of new-values creation.

3. I have claimed that Zarathustra enacts the second metamorphosis of the spirit when he performs the second act of his thought-drama. But is it plausible that he should do this? After all, if the argument of Chapter 4 is correct, then Zarathustra has learned, well before he meets the soothsayer, that to enact the second metamorphosis is to estrange oneself from one's ability to go-under. Why, then, when he first decides to transform the thought of recurrence, does he decide, once again, to become a lion-spirit?

A brief answer is that Zarathustra in Part 3 becomes a lion-spirit in order to resist the soothsayer's spirit of resignation. Moreover, in becoming a lion-spirit, he attempts to reconcile lion-spiritedness with his acknowledgment of his ability to go-under. In Part 3, Zarathustra endeavors to show that, notwithstanding the self-analysis of Part 2 (beginning with "The Night Song" and ending with "On Those Who Are Sublime"), self-estrangement is a fate that the lion-spirit, qua lion-spirit, can evade. In his language, he attempts to solve the paradox of his "double will." As we shall see, Zarathustra fails in this effort.

4. At the close of Chapter 2, I left open for further analysis Nietzsche's depiction of the Promethean lion as Dionysian. Why, I asked, should the figure of Dionysus play any role *at all* in the conceptualization of the heroic, leonine posture

that animates Zarathustra's reactions to representations of repetition? In the present chapter, I provide an answer to that question, one that is suggested by the depiction of Zarathustra's struggle to effect a leonine transformation of his thought of recurrence. I argue, in essence, that the figure of the Dionysian hero is Nietzsche's mythical image of the paradoxical thesis that the possibility of going-under to passional chaos, despite its eradication by the asceticism of the last man, remains present and available as a possibility that is "waiting" to be reborn.

Let me now turn to Zarathustra's appraisal of modern, European culture, an appraisal that "sets the stage" for the first act of the thought-drama of recurrence.

Modernity's Images of Self-Transformation

I concluded the last chapter with an analysis of "On Those Who Are Sublime." The six speeches following that speech, of which "The Soothsayer" is the last, mark a decisive turning point in the plot of *Zarathustra*. The first three of these—"On the Land of Education," "On Immaculate Perception," and "On Scholars"—describe Zarathustra's past, and can be read as thinly disguised autobiography on Nietzsche's part. More important, they express Zarathustra's view of modern, European culture from the perspective of his paean, in his speech on the sublime, to the passion- and body-embracing beauty that annuls leonine self-estrangement.

Considered from this perspective, the culture of modern Europe is a "sterile" (*unfruchtbare*) affair that, while recognizing all past faiths, celebrates no faith and no passion of its own ("On the Land of Education"); that considers emasculated, passionless contemplation (*Beschaulichkeit*) essential to the perception of beauty ("On Immaculate Perception"); and that sees the dry, passionless spectator (*Zuschauer*) as the paradigm of scholarly excellence ("On Scholars").[10] Bent on banishing passion and the possibility of experiencing passional chaos from human life, this culture is the repressive, ascetic regime that Zarathustra previously represented with the limit-concept of the last man.[11] Augmenting his earlier portraits of the modern world (as sketched, e.g., in his speeches on the last man and the new idol), Zarathustra now suggests, especially in his treatments of the modern scholar and the modern conception of beauty, that modernity rationalizes repression by installing a Cartesian, or perhaps Kantian, image of dispassionate, supersensible, subjectivity—of which image he provides a genealogy in "On Those Who Are Sublime"—as a normative ideal (for scholars, for judgments of aesthetic and cultural value, etc.).[12]

Zarathustra, of course, exhorts modern Europeans to transform themselves, and so invites a comparison of his vision of a transformed human existence to rival visions of the same. He himself pursues such a comparison in the second group of three speeches following "On Those Who Are Sublime": "On Poets," "On Great Events," and "The Soothsayer"—speeches in which Zarathustra challenges himself to demonstrate the superiority of his vision. If he is now ready to meet his challenge, it is because his speeches on self-overcoming and the sublime have completed his elaboration of a post-Christian-Platonic interpretation of human being-in-time that points to the possibility of transfiguring and overcoming man. In developing this interpretation, Zarathustra's chief concern has been to cultivate lion-spirited disciples (Part 1) and to clarify for his disciples the true content of a teaching of which they have grown ashamed (Part 2, through section 8). Zarathustra's speeches of crisis and self-analysis mark a shift of concern, for they pertain less to his disciples' perceptions than to his attempt to cope with his own experience of self-estrangement. His speeches on education, immaculate perception, and scholars, in tandem with the speeches on poets, great events, and the soothsayer, mark a further shift, because they look beyond the perceptions of Zarathustra's disciples, and beyond the anguish of his crisis and self-analysis, in order to amplify and highlight his appraisal of modern European culture. The speeches on poets, great events, and the soothsayer focus in particular on what Nietzsche believes to be this culture's most compelling yet questionable images of a radically transformed human being.[13]

By analyzing these images, Zarathustra revises a central argument of *Schopenhauer as Educator*, the third of the *Untimely Meditations*. In this work, Nietzsche argues that modern, European humanity, his characterization of which prefigures his later depictions of the last man, has fallen short of the *idea* of humanity.[14] Modern Europeans might transform themselves, he suggests, and thus realize this idea, were they inspired to do so by powerful images of human possibility:

> Who is there then, amid these dangers of our era, to guard and champion *humanity*. . . . Who will set up the *image of man* when all men feel in themselves only the self-seeking snake and currish fear and have thus declined from that image to the level of animals or even of automata?
>
> There are three images of man which our modern age has set up one after the other and which will no doubt long inspire mortals to a transfiguration [*Verklärung*] of their own lives: they are the man of Rousseau, the man of Goethe and finally the man of Schopenhauer.[15]

In *Schopenhauer as Educator*, Nietzsche proclaims the superiority of Schopenhauer's image of a transformed and transfigured human being. Considered from Schopenhauer's perspective, Goethean man—"the world-traveller"—and Rousseauean man—"the world-liberator"—know only the superficial world of appearances and becoming in which "everything is hollow [*hohl*], deceptive [*betrügerisch*], shallow [*flach*] and worthy of . . . contempt."[16] For Schopenhauer, human beings can transform their animal- and machinelike lives, and so realize the idea of humanity, not by participating in the "violent revolutions" (*Revolutionen*) inspired by Rousseau, and not by nourishing themselves on "everything great and memorable" like Goethe's Faust, but by embracing a "suffering [that] serves to destroy [one's] . . . wilfulness and to prepare that complete revolution [*Umwälzung*] and conversion [*Umkehrung*] of [one's] being, which it is the real meaning of life to lead up to."[17] The only genuine revolution, Schopenhauer suggests, is a transfiguration of the self that annihilates the will, and that is prompted by knowledge that looks beyond the surface world of appearances to the inner nature of the will-in-itself.[18]

In "On Poets" and "On Great Events," Zarathustra revisits Goethe's and Rousseau's images of man, asserting again that both express a certain superficiality. As in *Schopenhauer as Educator*, the treatment of Goethe concentrates on Faust, whom Nietzsche equates with Goethe's image of man. Focusing in particular on Faust's final transfiguration, Zarathustra represents Goethe's poetic vision as paradigmatic of poetic visions generally. Zarathustra himself is a poet, of course, and so he appears to enact the paradox of the liar in insisting that "the poets lie too much."[19] Yet Zarathustra distances himself from this flirtation with paradox when he claims for himself a depth of insight that has eluded Goethe and others: "I have grown weary of the poets, the old and the new: superficial [*Oberflächliche*] they all seem to me, and shallow [*seichte*] seas. Their thoughts have not penetrated deeply enough; therefore their feelings did not touch bottom."[20] Zarathustra's poetry is not *merely* poetry, because it is more profound than that of other poets.[21] Still, Zarathustra knows that these other poets also make speeches about overmen (and not only about gods), and so implicitly grants that they too believe that human beings can transform and overcome themselves. But such speeches partake in the illusion that the transformation of man into a being beyond man entails the transcendence of our time-bound, earthly, sensual existence.[22] Goethe (whose Faust a conjured spirit in fact calls *Übermenschen*) is implicated here, for he depicts Faust's final transfiguration as the transformation of earthly "imperfection" (*Unzulängliche*) into heavenly perfection.[23] While the Goethe who converses with Eckermann symbolizes Dionysian faith, the Goethe who writes *Faust* has a shallow understanding of the sort of self-transformation and -overcoming that is available to man. Quoting the last stanza of *Faust*, Zarathustra is thus "weary . . . of all the imperfection [*Unzulänglichen*] which must at all costs become event."[24]

Because Zarathustra rejects Schopenhauer's notion of a will-in-itself, he cannot justify a claim to profundity, as could Nietzsche in *Schopenhauer as Educator*, by appealing to a knowledge that looks beyond the world of appearances. For Zarathustra, self-transformation is a matter of self-overcoming, a knowledge of which Zarathustra possesses because "life itself" has confided its secret to him (see my discussion of "On Self-Overcoming" in Chapter 4). Zarathustra is more profound than Goethe, because he knows the essential nature of all the living. If the figure of Faust personifies a certain superficiality, it is not now because he is a world traveler, too attached to the world of flux and appearances, but because he betokens Goethe's failure to see that an authentic transfiguration of human life is possible without departing our time-bound, earthly existence.[25]

Zarathustra's criticism of Rousseau's image of man attacks a view that, like his own, endorses the possibility of a "this-worldly" transfiguration of human existence. Although Zarathustra never quotes Rousseau in "On Great Events," he pictures the modern revolutionary as a "fire hound," bellowing smoke and ashes like a volcanic mountain. Thus, he echoes Nietzsche's claim, in *Schopenhauer as Educator*, that Rousseauean man "possesses the greatest fire," as well as a simile Nietzsche uses in that book to compare Rousseauean man to Typhoeus under Mount Etna.[26] According to Zarathustra, Rousseauean man has a shallow and false understanding of the "this-worldly" and earthly conditions that allow for the radical transformation of human beings' lives. More exactly, Rousseauean man mistakenly believes that the revolutionary seizure of state power can fundamentally transform human life:

> Indeed for a hound of the depth you take your nourishment too much from the surface [*Oberfläche*]! At most, I take you for the earth's ventriloquist [*Bauchredner der Erde*]; and whenever I have heard the overthrow-and-scum-devils talking, I found them like you: salty, mendacious, and superficial [*flach*].
>
> Believe me, friend hellish noise: the greatest events—they are not our loudest but our stillest hours. Not around the inventors of new noise, but around the inventors of new values does the world revolve; it revolves *inaudibly*.
>
> Admit it! Whenever your noise and smoke were gone, very little had happened. What does it matter if a town became a mummy and a statue lies in the mud. . . . This counsel, however, I give to kings and churches and everything that is weak with age and weak with virtue: let yourselves be overthrown—so that you may return to life, and virtue return to you.[27]

Rousseau's political modernism can no better effect a profound transfiguration of European humanity than can the Cartesian revolution in epistemology that locates the foundations of knowledge in supersensible, knowing subjects— or so Zarathustra implies. Putting the point a bit differently, Zarathustra believes that the modern revolutionary tradition that Rousseau initiates, because it is oblivious to the problem of creating new values, cannot hope to effect the radical changes it envisions. For Zarathustra, the only genuine modernism is a Dionysian modernism that conceptualizes human and cultural transformation as entailing a revaluation of the passions that constitute the individuals' tie to the "earth." If this sort of modernism has a potentially political significance, as I suggested it might in Chapter 3, the politics it offers is not that of bourgeois, socialist, or Marxist revolutions that aim to monopolize state power. Politics at the level of the state, Zarathustra argues, is a politics of the earth's ventriloquists: it is a shallow and superficial politics that only pretends to engage what is most fundamental to the constitution of human existence. The Rousseauean revolutionary modernist is destined to effect a *repetition*, or "return to life," of the forms of life she *intends* to overcome, because, Zarathustra suggests, she is *not radical enough*: taking her nourishment from the surface of the earth, she does not, like the overman Zarathustra imagines, speak "out of the heart of the earth . . . *the heart of the earth [that] is of gold.*"[28]

Among Nietzsche scholars, it is commonplace to see the soothsayer appearing in Part 2 as a figure for Schopenhauerian pessimism.[29] Supposing that this way of viewing the soothsayer is valid—and I believe it is—one can easily imagine a reasonable reply to Zarathustra's nemesis, a response that would emphasize the differences between Zarathustra's and Schopenhauer's concepts of the will (between the will to power and the will to live), and argue that Schopenhauer's image of man, no less than Goethe's, or Rousseau's, reflects a shallow (mis)understanding of the conditions required for self-overcoming.[30] Zarathustra shuns this reply. Rather, after hearing the soothsayer's prophecy, he succumbs to what he elsewhere calls "the great weariness": "the prophecy touched his heart and changed him. He walked about sad and weary; and he became like those of whom the soothsayer had spoken. 'Verily,' he said to his disciples, 'little is lacking [*es ist um ein Kleines*] and this long twilight will come.'"[31] Here, apparently, the renunciative spirit of Schopenhauer's pessimism so possesses Zarathustra that he is transformed. To be sure, the change he experiences is not the self-transformation he envisions in speaking of self-overcoming. Yet it is genuine and dramatic, and suggests that *something like* Schopenhauer's conception of a will-annihilating self-transfiguration remains a viable option for Zarathustra. How is this possible?

In Chapter 2, I argued that the essence of Nietzsche's rigor is his relentless practice of thinking against himself. Nowhere is this practice more on display in *Zarathustra* than in the portrait of the soothsayer. The soothsayer voices the spirit of pessimism, but without presupposing Schopenhauer's metaphysics. In fact, the soothsayer's challenge to the project of overcoming man is perfectly compatible with Zarathustra's rejection of Schopenhauerian metaphysical dualism. Moreover, it is also compatible with Zarathustra's understanding of human existence as an earthly, bodily phenomenon, and with his (putatively) post-Christian-Platonic interpretation of human being-in-time. Nietzsche thinks against himself in the figure of the soothsayer, by depicting him as a skeptic who specifically repudiates Zarathustra's Dionysian modernism. The soothsayer is the most terrifying and threatening representation of repetition in *Zarathustra*, because he personifies Schopenhauer's voice from *within* the horizon of a distinctively *Zarathustran* philosophical perspective. He cannot be dismissed as shallow, for, unlike Goethe and Rousseau, he *assents*, at least implicitly, to Zarathustra's understanding of the conditions essential to "self-overcoming." But because the soothsayer denies that these conditions can be assumed to obtain, he insinuates that Zarathustra's thinking remains flawed and that human life can be radically transfigured only through a renunciation of the will (to power).[32]

In order fully to appreciate the significance of the challenge that the soothsayer presents to Zarathustra's teaching, I want to place that challenge in the context of the critique of the God-concept that Zarathustra propounds when he speaks from his heart in "Upon the Blessed Isles." This critique not only prefigures Zarathustra's encounter with the soothsayer, but, likewise, provides an important interpretive clue as to the nature of Zarathustra's attempt to preserve his teaching in the face of the soothsayer's prophecy:

> But let me reveal my heart to you entirely my friends: *if* there were gods, how could I not endure to be a god! *Hence* there are no gods. Though I drew this conclusion, now it draws me.
>
> God is a conjecture; but who could drain all the agony of this conjecture without dying? Shall his faith be take from the creator, and from the eagle his soaring to eagle heights?
>
> God is a thought that makes crooked all that is straight [*Gott is ein Gedanke, der macht alles Gerade krumm*], and makes turn whatever stands. How? Should time be gone, and all that is impermanent a mere lie! To think this is a dizzy whirl [*Wirbel*] for human bones [*Gebeinen*], and a vomit for the stomach; verily, I call it the turning sickness to conjecture thus. Evil I call it, and misanthropic [*menschenfeindlich*]—all this teaching of the One and the Plenum and the Unmoved and the Sated and the Permanent. All the permanent—that is only a parable [*Gleichniss*]. And the poets lie too much.
>
> It is of time and becoming that the best parables should speak: let them be a praise and a justification of all impermanence.

Creation—that is the great redemption [*Erlösung*] from suffering and life's growing light. . . .

Whatever in me has feeling, suffers and is in prison; but my will always comes to me as my liberator [*Befrier*] and joy-bringer [*Freudebringer*]. Willing liberates: that is the true teaching of will and liberty—thus Zarathustra teaches it. Willing no more and esteeming no more and creating no more—oh, that this great weariness [*grosse Müdigkeit*] might always remain far from me. . . . Away from God and gods . . . [my] will has lured me; what could one create if gods existed?[33]

I argued in Chapter 4 that in some significant respects the first half of "Upon the Blessed Isles" recalls Kant's project in the first *Critique*. In considering the second half of this speech, much of which I have quoted here, Kant remains a useful touchstone, though we need now to bear in mind his second *Critique*, not his first. In particular, we need to consider Kant's general strategy in arguing for his postulates of pure practical reason.[34] Zarathustra's central concerns differ substantially from Kant's, but their strategies of argument have some affinity.

Consider, for example, Kant's practical argument for postulating the existence of God—in essence, that postulating the existence of God is essential to avoiding moral despair. According to Kant, reason requires, as an essential component of the "highest good," that happiness be distributed in proportion to virtue. Moreover, reason commands that each of us make the highest good the object of her will. Of course, none of us can succeed in realizing this object, because the "will cannot by its own strength bring nature, as it touches on . . . happiness, into complete harmony with . . . practical principles."[35] For Kant, the impotence of the will raises the pessimistic possibility that our pursuit of the highest good amounts to chasing a "fantastic . . . empty imaginary" end.[36] To avoid the hopelessness born of contemplating this possibility, we must assume the existence of a being—God—whose existence would rule it out. To postulate God's existence, then, is to suppose that there exists a cause of nature adequate to the realization of the highest good. We have reason to believe that God exists, for without that belief "the moral life to which we are called as rational beings is threatened by . . . despair in the face of nature's indifference."[37]

For Kant, then, postulating that *God exists* is necessary to avoid moral despair; absent this assumption, we should feel compelled to abandon the aims of rational morality.[38] For Zarathustra, postulating that *God does not exist* is necessary to avoid the creator's despair; absent this assumption, the would-be creator would feel driven to abandon his goal of creating an overman through the creation of new values. In both cases, the general argument-strategy is to establish that holding a particular conviction (that God exists; that God does not exist), is indispensable to preserving one's belief that one's pursuit of certain ends (the aims of rational morality; the aim of creating an overman) is not a futile quest after a fantasy that cannot be realized.

Let us consider the particulars of Zarathustra's argument. Beginning with the dictum that gods do not exist—for, if they did, Zarathustra could not bear not to be one—Zarathustra implies that, if gods existed, his merely *human* life would be intolerable. In the next paragraph, Zarathustra develops this idea, suggesting that, if God existed, specifically his (Zarathustra's) life as an aspiring new-values creator would be intolerable. But why? Zarathustra answers this question with two allusions, the first to the Book of Ecclesiastes, the second to the tragedy of the tightrope walker. The proposition "God is a thought that makes crooked all that is straight" (*Gott ist ein Gedanke, der macht alles Gerade krumm*) clearly resounds the perspective of Ecclesiastes 7:13 ("Consider the work of God for who can make that straight, which he hath made crooked" [*Siehe an die Werke Gottes, denn wer kann das schlect machen/das er krümmet*]), and indirectly invokes a vision of time that, elsewhere in Ecclesiastes (1:9–10), captures the essence of God's crooked work: "The thing that hath been, it is that which shall be; and that which is done is that which shall be done: and there is no new thing under the sun. Is there any thing whereof it may be said, See, this is new? it hath been already of old time, which was before us."[39] In the divinely ordered world of Ecclesiastes, where things past endure permanently in the present and the future, the appearance of change and impermanence (e.g., the passing of generations) belies the fundamentally *unchanging* nature of reality: time, in this world, is tantamount to *no time* in the eyes of the creator ("Should time be gone . . . ?"), because it forbids the advent of qualitatively new modes of human experience.[40] To "think" such a time is "a dizzy whirl [*Wirbel*] for human bones [*Gebeinen*]," Zarathustra says, for this is to think what (in Zarathustra's allegorical reading of the tightrope walker's tragedy) the tightrope walker thought just before *he* became a dizzy "whirlpool of arms and legs" (*ein Wirbel von Armen und Beinen*): that creating new values and transforming the character of human experience is simply impossible.[41]

Revising a line from the final stanza of *Faust*, Zarathustra extends his argument by remarking that "All the permanent—that is only a parable."[42] Goethe and Christianity come under attack here, but so too does a tradition of Platonist metaphysics that sees temporal appearances as unreal parables (or images) of timeless being and value. From the perspective of this tradition, time and impermanence constitute a mirage, a sort of "lying" or sham reality that cannot give rise to new values. As we saw in Chapter 2, Platonism holds that all values that can exist have always existed, whereas Christianity—as Zarathustra interprets it in his allusion to Ecclesiastes and, before that, in his description of the great dragon in "On the Three Metamorphoses"—claims that all values that can exist have been created. Reasoning practically, or from the heart, Zarathustra construes Platonist metaphysics and Christian God-talk as misanthropic, presumably because they entail that it would be futile to pursue the end that *he* has assigned human existence. Platonist metaphysics and Christian God-talk must be seen as *mere* parable, he intimates, so that he can preserve from the blight of their misanthropy his hope that, in the future, new values will be created.

Zarathustra begins to summarize his argument for the postulate that God does not exist, by complicating the view of value-creation he proposed in "On Enjoying and Suffering the Passions." In that speech, Zarathustra said that value-creation is a matter of transforming the passions one suffers (*Leidenshaften*) into virtues one enjoys (see my analysis in Chapter 3). In "Upon the Blessed Isles," he adds that the creative will makes sufferings into joys, and that it *redeems* those sufferings by esteeming and "liberating" them. To preserve his belief that his creative/redemptive effort to create an overman is not a futile, fantastical enterprise, Zarathustra's "practical reason" leads him to deny God's existence: "Away from God and gods . . . [my] will lured me; what could one create if gods existed?"[43] If Zarathustra held that God exists, he would fall prey to the "great weariness" that haunts individuals who have lost faith in their ability to create. Belief in God, he implies, is a sufficient, if not necessary condition for experiencing that weariness. Zarathustra succumbs to the great weariness, we have seen, upon hearing the soothsayer's prophecy. But why is this? To be sure, the answer to this query is *not* that Zarathustra has abruptly decided that God exists, thus rejecting the advice of his practical reason. Still, the belief that prompts his weariness is closely tied to the belief that God exists, for both beliefs entail that creating new values is impossible.

> And I saw a great sadness descend upon mankind. The best grew weary of their works. A doctrine appeared, accompanied by a faith: "All is empty [*leer*], all is the same, all has been!" And from all the hills it echoed: "All is empty, all is the same, all has been!" Indeed we have harvested: but why did all our fruit turn rotten and brown? What fell down from the evil moon last night? In vain [*Umsonst*] was our work; our wine has turned to poison; an evil eye has seared our fields and hearts. We have all become dry; and if fire should descend on us, we should turn to ashes; indeed, we have wearied the fire itself. All our wells have dried up; even the sea has withdrawn. All the soil would crack, but the depth refuses to devour [*die Tiefe will nich schlingen*]. "Alas, where is there still a sea in which one might drown?" thus are we wailing across shallow swamps [*über flache Sümpfe*]. Verily, we have become too weary even to die. We are still waking and living on—in tombs.[44]

The soothsayer's prophecy, in both the doctrine and the faith it foresees, anticipates a world that is strikingly similar to that of Ecclesiastes. The doctrine the soothsayer envisions—that "all is empty, all is the same, all has been!"—pithily repeats the claim of Ecclesiastes that what shall be is what has been. Moreover, the "faith" he prophesies, that human striving is pointless, succinctly echoes the beginning of Ecclesiastes: "Vanity of vanities . . . all is vanity. What profit hath a man of all his labor which he taketh under the sun?"[45]

During the time the soothsayer foretells, any and all efforts to transform the world—here depicted as so many attempts to add to the world's bounty of fruit and wine—will prove futile. By using images of a profitless harvest and a withdrawn sea to depict these futile endeavors, the soothsayer resounds the language Zarathustra uses in the prologue to promote the cause of the overman. In effect, he insinuates that Zarathustra's enterprise, no less than any other attempt to create something new, is doomed to fail.[46] The human lives the soothsayer soothsays will persist in tombs: reminiscent of human lives in the crooked world of Ecclesiastes, they will perpetuate in the future the modes of life that have shaped them in the past.

The spirit of the soothsayer's prophecy possesses Zarathustra immediately. Although the soothsayer never speaks of a god like the god of Ecclesiastes, the impact of his speech on Zarathustra is the same as it would have been had he persuaded Zarathustra to believe that he lived in the world of such a divinity. We can explain this impact if we examine (1) Zarathustra's description of his dream after hearing the soothsayer's prophecy and (2) his description in "The Convalescent" of his reaction to the soothsayer's prophecy. These descriptions show why Zarathustra cannot dismiss the soothsayer as he did Goethe and Rousseau, and shed light on the fact that, in the wake of the soothsayer's prophecy, his adherence to the practical postulate for which he argues in "On the Blessed Isles" does not by itself suffice to keep him from despairing of the possibility of creating new values.

Here, then, is Zarathustra's dream:

> I had turned my back on all life [*Allem Leben hatte ich abgesagt*], thus I dreamed. I had become a night watchman and a guardian of tombs upon the lonely mountain castle of death. Up there I guarded his coffins: the musty vaults were full of such marks of triumph. Life that had been overcome [*überwundenes Leben*] looked at me out of glass coffins. I breathed the odor of dusty eternities: sultry and dusty lay my soul. And who could have aired his soul there.[47]

In the soothsayer's premonition, the images of a depth that refuses to "devour" life and of a swamp too shallow to "drown" life suggest that life has lost its ability to go-under and overcome itself. Similarly, in Zarathustra's dream, the figure of a death that has overcome life alludes not to life's disposition to sacrifice and overcome itself (cf. "On Self-Overcoming"), but, on the contrary, to the utter demise of life's capacity for self-overcoming.[48] In Zarathustra's dream, which vividly reproduces the soothsayer's portrait of human life, the death that has overcome life has enlisted Zarathustra to guard life's remains. Having survived that death, life's remains lie awake in Zarathustra's dream, looking at him out of glass coffins and affording him a picture of what life has been and will continue to be absent the possibility of self-overcoming. Zarathustra dreams of renouncing and turning his back on life, and of becoming the guardian of life's remains, because he now believes that self-overcoming is impossible. Prompted by the soothsayer's prophecy, he sees himself enacting the only form of self-transformation that Schopenhauer acknowledges.

In "The Convalescent," in the course of describing his reaction to the soothsayer's prophecy, Zarathustra says, "man's earth [*Menschen-Erde*] turned into a cave for me, its chest sunken; all that is living became human mold and bones and musty past to me. My sighing sat on all human tombs and could no longer get up."[49] Here, by invoking the image of the earth, Zarathustra clarifies the deepest implications of the soothsayer's prophecy. In "On the Gift-Giving Virtue" and "On Those Who Are Sublime," Zarathustra affirms the earth in order to recall men to the possibility of revaluing their (first-order) passions; and in "On the Gift-Giving Virtue," he voices his Dionysian faith that "man and man's earth [*Menschen-Erde*] [remain] unexhausted." But in "The Convalescent," Zarathustra implies that the soothsayer's prophecy has led him to lose his Dionysian faith, and so to see the earth as a moldy, chest-sunken corpse whose life has been *thoroughly* exhausted.[50] Like the remains that looked at him out of glass coffins, the decaying earth he now imagines symbolizes the demise of man's ability to overcome himself and the consequent consignment of human existence to perpetuating a "musty," Christian-Platonic past that it cannot surpass. More exactly, it signifies the pandemic annihilation of the passional preconditions of self-overcoming, and hence the triumph of the ascetic ideal in the age of the last man.[51] The possibility of experiencing Dionysian chaos will be expunged from human existence, Zarathustra's dream and remarks in "The Convalescent" suggest, though Zarathustra's conscience, hinted at in his dream by the bizarre appearance of a *black* coffin that mocks him, will resist his pessimistic and renunciative response to this fact.[52]

In essence, Zarathustra's dream brings to light the connection between the soothsayer's appearance and the tragedy of the tightrope walker—a tragedy that compels Zarathustra to see that pursuing the purpose he has assigned human existence may be futile. In effect, the demise of the tightrope walker shows Zarathustra that overcoming man may be possible neither in the present nor in the future. In the final sections of the prologue, Zarathustra sees his way beyond the Schopenhauerian ending of the tightrope walker's tragedy by insisting that there still exist human beings—harvesters and fellow creators—who can go-under and create new values. Through Part 1 and much of Part 2 he persists in this insistence, as he directs his attention to disciples whom he hopes will become new-values creators. In the wake of his crisis and cure, Zarathustra's attention to his disciples wanes. Still, his critique of the normative ideal of dispassionate subjectivity (in "On the Land of Education," "On the Immaculate Perception," and "On Scholars") suggests that he retains the belief that there continue to exist individuals who can overcome themselves. Confronted with the soothsayer's prophecy, however, Zarathustra begins to doubt that belief. The soothsayer's vision of an exhausted earth persuades Zarathustra that, due to the ascetic practices of modernity, the destruction of all the (first-order) passions of all human beings is imminent ("Verily . . . little is lacking and this long twilight will come"). Like the tightrope walker beset by a victorious jester, Zarathustra sees a future before him in which what has been—Christian-Platonic man—will still be. And like the tightrope walker who quits his rope, Zarathustra responds to what he sees by embracing a spirit of resignation that renounces and turns away from life.

As we have seen, the Schopenhauerian voice Zarathustra hears in the soothsayer was invoked in *The Birth of Tragedy* to deny that historical change can facilitate a Dionysian transfiguration of human existence (see Chapter 3), and is invoked again in "Zarathustra's Prologue" (through the parody of Paul and the depiction of the tightrope walker's tragedy) and in Paul de Man's readings of Nietzsche. In all its idioms, this Schopenhauerian countervoice to the spirit of modernism speaks against the hope that Dionysus will renew modern Europe. In the mouth of the soothsayer, I have suggested, it also speaks from within the perspective of Zarathustra's post-Christian-Platonic interpretation of human existence. That Zarathustra sees this—and perhaps hears it, when the soothsayer borrows his images—is evident from his suggestion, in describing his reaction to the soothsayer's prophecy, that the soothsayer's forebodings bear on the fate of "man's earth."

For the soothsayer, human existence is a time-bound, bodily affair that has fallen victim to the ravaging effects of the ascetic ideal. This, however, is precisely what Zarathustra believes. The soothsayer, it seems, is Zarathustra's mirror image, but with one significant difference: where Zarathustra has allowed himself to hope that "man's earth" will remain unexhausted, the soothsayer knows no such hope. Zarathustra cannot dismiss the soothsayer, for confronted with the soothsayer's prophecy he has no grounds on which to justify his heart's desire. If anything, Zarathustra's failure to identify individuals who can "see" within themselves the possibility of experiencing Dionysian chaos is supporting evidence for the soothsayer's belief that such individuals, if they still exist, will soon be extinct.[53] Neither, moreover, can Zarathustra resist the soothsayer's spirit of resignation by appealing to the practical postulate that God does not exist: indeed, because the soothsayer's pessimism is perfectly compatible with that postulate (i.e., one can consistently hold that God does not exist *and* that the practice of asceticism will soon succeed in extirpating all the earth's passions), Zarathustra seems fated to see in renunciation the *only* form of radical self-transfiguration available to him. Zarathustra will not escape this view of his situation until he formulates a postulate of "practical reason" that is adequate to responding to the soothsayer's prophecy.[54]

For Zarathustra, believing that the passional basis of human life has been everywhere destroyed, like believing that God exists, would be tantamount to believing that the creation of new values is impossible. If the repression effected by the practice of asceticism has completely destroyed the earth's passions, then no one can experience passional chaos; and if no one can experience passional chaos, then no one can overcome herself by revaluing her previously repressed passions.[55] The task of formulating a *second* practical postulate, one for coping with the soothsayer's prophecy, is what Zarathustra will now devote himself to. The appearance of the soothsayer marks a decisive, halfway turning point in the plot of *Zarathustra*. Perhaps, then, we should not be surprised that soon after that appearance, in "The Stillest Hour," Zarathustra leaves his disciples in order to concentrate exclusively on developing a response to the soothsayer.[56]

Previously in this chapter I argued that Zarathustra looks beyond the perceptions of his disciples in his speeches on poets and great events; as in "The Soothsayer," Zarathustra demonstrates his distance from his disciples by shaking his head at their superficial thinking. Even Zarathustra's most beloved disciple proves lacking when he fails to penetrate the meaning of Zarathustra's dream of glass and black coffins.[57] Confronted with Goethe's, Rousseau's, and Schopenhauer's challenges to their master's teaching, Zarathustra's disciples show that they lack a subtle understanding of that teaching and that they therefore cannot defend it against modern Europe's most profound and persuasive competing voices.[58] When Zarathustra departs from his disciples, however, it is not because they are lackluster students,[59] but, rather, because the soothsayer's Schopenhauerian challenge to his teaching implies that it would now be fruitless for him to strive to make his disciples *better* students. If the extinction of the passions constituting "man's earth" is imminent, then there can be no point to exhorting even the best and most beloved disciple to overcome himself. Zarathustra's problem now, for which he will require all the resources of his "practical reason," is to find a way *not* to despair at the possibility of overcoming man, and thus *not* to remain prey to the spirit of renunciation that despair engenders, despite the historical success and triumph of the ascetic ideal.

The Camel's Thought of Recurrence

Zarathustra typically becomes a camel when, like the camel of "On the Three Metamorphoses," he accepts the proposition that the future will yield no new values and therefore no escape from the Christian-Platonic past. In his initial response to the soothsayer's representation of repetition he becomes a camel one last time, and forms the camel's thought of recurrence.

As we have seen, the advent of the soothsayer is prefigured by various other representations of repetition, characters who respond skeptically to Zarathustra's modernism, but less persuasively than the soothsayer. In the prologue, for example, Zarathustra meets the saint in the forest, the townspeople of the Motley Cow, and the jester who leaps over the tightrope walker. And in Part 2, before Zarathustra hears the soothsayer, he discovers that his enemies have distorted his teaching and transformed *his* image into a representation of repetition resembling the spirit of gravity. Still, the soothsayer remains a distinctive figure, for his prophecy is based on a specifically *Zarathustran* interpretation of human existence and prompts Zarathustra to suggest that the recurrence of man—and of the Christian-Platonic values man embodies—is the greatest and gravest obstacle facing his personal and poetic intentions.

> My torture-stake [*Marterholz*] was not the knowledge that man is evil—but I cried as no one else has yet cried: "Alas, that his greatest evil is so very small! Alas, that his best is so very small!"
>
> The great disgust with man—*this* choked me and had crawled into my throat; and what the soothsayer said: "All is the same, nothing is worthwhile, knowledge chokes." A long twilight limped before me, a sadness, weary to death, drunken with death, speaking with a yawning mouth. "Eternally recurs the man of whom you are weary, the small man"—thus yawned my sadness and dragged its feet and could not go to sleep. . . . my sighing and questioning croaked and gagged and gnawed and wailed by day and night: "Alas, man recurs eternally! The small man recurs eternally!"
>
> Naked I had once seen both, the greatest man and the smallest man: all-too-similar to each other, even the greatest all-too-human. All-too-small, the

greatest!—that was my disgust with man. And the eternal recurrence even of the smallest—that was my disgust with all existence. Alas! Nausea! Nausea! Nausea![60]

It is worth noting that Zarathustra refers in these passages not to the recurrence of all things—as will his animals—but to the recurrence of man, the small man, and the smallest man.[61] What, then, does the thought of *man's recurrence* signify?

For Zarathustra, to think this thought is, in part, to think the persistence of human life as it has been formed by Christian-Platonic values. He suggests, moreover, that the thought of man's recurrence is prompted by the soothsayer's prophecy that, in the "long twilight" to come, man's ability to create *new* values will succumb to a "yawning" and "weary . . . death."[62] To Zarathustra man's recurrence seems inevitable, and even *eternal*, for, absent the possibility of creating new values, Zarathustra sees *no end* to the subjection of human life to Christian-Platonic values, even though adhering to these values seems pointless after the demise of the ascetic ideal. Zarathustra's obsession with the small man's recurrence is significant, for *all men* have become small men in his eyes; even in the "greatest man" and his "greatest evil," Zarathustra implies, the all-too-human and all-too-small qualities that distinguish the small man are abundantly evident.[63] The small man, Zarathustra suggests, is the flealike, diminutive last man, the man who "makes everything small."[64] He is, in other words, the secular epitome of Christian asceticism, the man in whom Christian-Platonic values receive their ultimate and perfect expression (see Chapter 2). Thus, in envisioning man's recurrence as the recurrence of the small man, Zarathustra envisions the recurrence of Christian-Platonic values in their most extreme and devastating form. Man's recurrence here is the endless perpetuation of human life as it has been formed by those values, the endless perpetuation of human life as embodied in the last and ultimate legatee of the Christian-Platonic interpretation of human existence.

In Zarathustra's view, the recurrence of man entails the recurrence of nihilism. In the aftermath of the demise of the ascetic ideal, Zarathustra has assigned a new purpose to human existence. Because the soothsayer's prophecy suggests that this purpose will not be realized—viz., that man will not be overcome—it causes Zarathustra to see human existence as he saw it in the wake of the death of the tightrope walker—as worthless and without meaning ("nothing is worthwhile," he hears the soothsayer saying). As we have seen, Zarathustra cannot respond to the soothsayer's prophecy as he did to the tightrope walker's death, for he accepts the soothsayer's belief that the possibility of experiencing passional chaos will soon be banished from human existence. Suggesting, however, that he has been lashed to a torture stake or cross (*Marterholz*), Zarathustra echoes the prologue's Pauline portrait of his descent, thereby implying that he has failed to recall men to Dionysus and to assign them a feasible purpose.[65] Whereas Zarathustra once claimed that he wanted to become man *again*, he senses now that he is doomed to suffer man *again and again and again* . . . —without relief— and that the interminable, incessant recurrence of pervasively small and purposeless man is the crucifix to which modern asceticism has eternally bound him. Zarathustra thinks the camel's thought of recurrence in asserting that he has fallen victim to a recurrence of the same, and in inferring that assertion from the proposition that he has been forever yoked to the unending, uninterrupted iteration of the small man's *meaningless* existence. Nietzsche captures the nihilistic essence of this thought in one of his posthumously published notes: "existence as it is, without meaning or aim, yet recurring inevitably . . . 'the eternal recurrence.' This is the most extreme form of nihilism: the nothing (the 'meaningless'), eternally!"[66]

To summarize my argument: Zarathustra forms the camel's thought of recurrence when he judges that his existence is characterized by a recurrence of the same, basing that judgment on his belief that, due to modern asceticism, he has been eternally martyred to the endless perpetuation of the small man's existence. But what explains this belief, his *reason* for judging that his existence is qualified by a recurrence of the same? The brief answer to this question, I have suggested, is the soothsayer's prophecy. A longer answer is that Zarathustra's interpretation of that prophecy voices what Stanley Cavell, in one of the epigraphs to this chapter, calls an "anxiety of . . . inexpressiveness." In Cavell's words, Zarathustra imagines himself a "mind unmoored, say unhinged, leaving itself without material in which to realize and communicate itself." The "material" in which Zarathustra intends to realize his creation of new values is the field of bodily passions, the erosion of which the soothsayer prophecies. Envisioning the consequences of that erosion—namely, that it precludes the possibility of creating new values— Zarathustra imagines, again, to borrow Cavell's words, "the exhaustion of the medium of [his] art." Reminiscent of John Stuart Mill, Zarathustra figures his worry that he is incapable of "new or original" creation with an image of recurrence—not of musical combinations, but of the small man. In other words, he voices his anxiety of inexpressiveness by fantasizing that he has been eternally crucified to the eternal recurrence of the small man's meaningless existence.[67]

Zarathustra's formation of the thought of recurrence imaginatively dramatizes the soothsayer's suggestion that creating new values has ceased to be possible. Indeed, Zarathustra's expressed reason for believing that his existence is characterized by recurrence—that something *has happened to him*, that he has fallen prey to the plight of being eternally bound to the endless perpetuation of the small man's meaningless existence—describes the beginning of a dramatic action, comparable, I will argue, to the first scene of Aeschylus's *Prometheus Bound*. By developing this action, Zarathustra will transform the thought-drama of recurrence into a *more elaborate* thought-drama that has a leonine act of self-assertion as its "second act."[68]

Construing himself as a defiant lion-spirit, Zarathustra in this second act invents a second practical postulate and a self-deifying self-portrait that enable him to reaffirm his commitment to becoming a new-values creator.[69] In effect, he fabricates a dramatic persona that he uses to "save [the] light" of his teaching through the "long twilight" the soothsayer predicts.[70] By preserving that light, Zarathustra recuperates his belief that renunciation is not the only form of radical transfiguration genuinely available to human beings. Most important, he transforms his thought of recurrence by altering his reason for believing that his existence is characterized by a recurrence of the same.

The Lion's Thought of Recurrence I: The Meaning of Redemption

Zarathustra sketches a "script" for the second act of his thought-drama in "On Redemption." This speech, which immediately follows "The Soothsayer," distinguishes three kinds of redemption—what I shall call redemption1, redemption2, and redemption3. As we shall see, Zarathustra dramatizes the conflict between redemption3 and the camel's thought of recurrence when he enacts the script he outlines in "On Redemption" in the dream he recounts in "On the Vision and the Riddle." Subsequent to this dramatization, and for the remainder of Part 3, Zarathustra's primary aim is to reconcile redemption3 with the possibility of redemption1.

Zarathustra expounds his concept of redemption1, *the redemption of the human past*, by way of an address to friends:

> Verily, my friends, I walk among men as among the fragments and limbs of men. This is what is terrible for my eyes, that I find man in ruins and scattered as over a battlefield or a butcher field. And when my eyes flee from the now to the past, they always find the same: fragments and limbs and dreadful accidents [*grause Zufälle*]—but no human beings.
>
> The now and the past on earth—alas, my friends, that is what *I* find most unendurable; and I should not know how to live if I were not also a seer of that which must come. A seer, a willer, a creator [*Schaffender*], a future himself and a bridge to the future—and alas, also, as it were, a cripple at this bridge: all this is Zarathustra. . . .

I walk among men as among the fragments of the future—that future which I envisage. And this is all my art [*Dichten*] and striving, that I compose and carry together into One [*ich in Eins dichte und zusammentrage*] what is fragment and riddle and dreadful accident [*grauser Zufall*]. And how could I bear to be a man if man were not also a poet [*Dichter*] and guesser of riddles and redeemer of accidents [*Erlöser des Zufalls*].

To redeem those who lived in the past [*Die Vergangnen zu erlösen*] and to recreate [*umzuschaffen*] all "it was" into a "thus I willed it"—that alone should I call redemption [*Erlösung*]. Will—that is the name of the liberator and joy-bringer; thus I taught you my friends.[71]

With these remarks, Zarathustra revisits some themes he introduced in "On the Gift-Giving Virtue," where he depicted man as an experiment in whose body dwell the mistakes of millennia:

Alas, much ignorance and error have become body within us.

Not only the reason of millennia, but their madness too, breaks out in us. It is dangerous to be an heir. Still we fight step by step with the giant, accident [*Zufall*]; and over the whole of humanity there has ruled so far only nonsense—no sense.[72]

In the same speech, Zarathustra also held that a man can bring "sense" to a body that accident has bequeathed him by revaluing his repressed passions.[73] He develops this point in "On Redemption," at first by suggesting that throughout human history—"the now and the past on earth"—the play of accident has so impoverished human life that even great men have been reduced to fragments and fractions of the bodies they could have been otherwise.[74] Such fragments belong to the present and the past "on earth," presumably because they exemplify kinds of corporeal passion that have commonly claimed human existence in the past and that commonly claim it in the present notwithstanding the ravages of asceticism.[75] In the future Zarathustra envisages, individuals will re-create themselves by compelling their passions (the fragments of their bodies) to function in concert with each other. Thus, redeeming and bringing new sense to these passions will involve revaluing them and using them to create integrated selves ("And this is all my art and striving, that I compose and carry together into One what is fragment and riddle and dreadful accident"). Alluding to his talk of redemption and creation in "Upon the Blessed Isles" ("Will—that is the name of the liberator and joy-bringer; thus I taught you my friends"), Zarathustra concludes his discussion of redemption1 by reminding us that to redeem and esteem passions is to liberate them from suffering and transform them into joys.

As I have interpreted it, Zarathustra's account of redemption1 recapitulates and expands on the view of value-creation and redemption he put forth in "On Enjoying and Suffering the Passions," "On the Gift-Giving Virtue," and "Upon the Blessed Isles." His pithy summary of this view—that it envisions the transformation of "all 'it was' into a 'thus I willed it'"—highlights his idea that to create new values is to work on materials that the creator finds "already there" *prior* to creating anything. The fragments Zarathustra mentions belong to the "already there," or the "it was," not only because they claim the creator before he asserts his second-order, creative will, but, likewise, because they instance kinds of passion that have persisted in claiming human bodies despite the historical reign of the ascetic ideal. When an individual creator revalues the fragments constituting *his* body's passional life, he is responding to common, "earthly" forms of feeling that gripped human beings well before *he* existed, and thus to forms of feeling that tie him to his forebears. By investing these fragments with functional significance, he transforms the "it was" into a "thus I willed it" and so creates new values. The creator can redeem the "it was," for he recognizes in the passions that his life shares with the lives of his forebears the possibility of reviving those passions, and hence of turning forms of feeling his forebears' suffered (under the painful rule of asceticism) into joys.[76]

Zarathustra's discussion of redemption2—*the redemption of the human will in the perspective of revenge*—begins by describing a view of the past that differs markedly from that enjoyed by creators:

> But now learn this too: the will itself is still a prisoner. Willing liberates; but what is it that puts even the liberator himself in fetters? "It was" that is the name of the will's gnashing of teeth and most secret misery [*Trübsal*]. Powerless against what has been done, he is an angry spectator of all that is past. The will cannot will backwards; and that it cannot break time and time's covetousness [*der Zeit Begierde*], that is the will's loneliest misery.[77]

The will is a prisoner, Zarathustra says, because it cannot will backwards and undo the past. As he later puts it, "'that which was' is the name of the stone . . . [the will] cannot move."[78] Figuring time as covetous, Zarathustra depicts it as craving all that transpires and as ceaselessly satisfying its craving by sucking all events into a past that the will cannot alter. Revenge—"the will's ill-will against time and its 'it was'"—is, in essence, the will's aversion to time and time's covetousness.[79] It is, in other words, the will's antipathy to the fact that time never ceases to confront the will with the will's powerlessness to undo the past.[80] From the perspective of the will's antipathy to this fact, the past comes into view as exceeding the will's power, and not, as from the perspective of the creative will, as available to creative redemption.

Redemption2 can be conceptualized either practically or theoretically. Viewed as a *practical task* by a prereflective and revenge-driven will, redeeming the will is a matter of performing deeds that will free the will from the misery it suffers because it cannot will backwards:

> What means does the will devise for himself to get rid of his misery [*dass es los seiner Trübsal werde*] and to mock his dungeon? Alas, every prisoner becomes a fool; and the imprisoned will redeems himself [*erlöst sich*] foolishly. That time does not run backwards, that is his wrath. . . . And so he moves stones out of wrath and displeasure, and he wrecks revenge on whatever does not feel wrath and displeasure as he does. Thus the will, the liberator, took to hurting; and on all who can suffer he wreaks revenge for his inability to go backwards.[81]

Here, Zarathustra describes the revenge-driven will's aim of freeing itself from its misery by using inanimate objects (e.g., movable "stones") and then all living creatures ("all who can suffer") to vent its "ill-will against time and its 'it was.'" For such a will, redeeming the will is tantamount to releasing it from the misery it suffers. The prereflective, revenge-driven will attempts to release itself from the misery it suffers, and thus to redeem itself, by performing deeds that effectively discharge its wrath and ill-will.[82]

When the revenge-driven will suspends its prereflective efforts to redeem itself, it constructs a reflective, theoretical view of human existence that, in its final permutation, puts into question the revenge-driven will's prereflective understanding of redemption:

> Verily a great folly dwells in our will; and it has become a curse for everything human that this folly has acquired spirit.
>
> *The spirit of revenge*: my friends, has so far been man's best reflection [*Der Geist der Rache: meine Freunde, das war bisher der Menschen bestes Nachdenken*]; and where there was suffering one always wanted punishment too.
>
> For "punishment" is what revenge calls itself; with a hypocritical lie it creates a good conscience for itself.
>
> Because there is suffering in those who will, inasmuch as they cannot will backwards, willing itself and all life were supposed to be—a punishment. And now cloud upon cloud rolled over the spirit, until eventually madness preached, "Everything passes away; therefore everything deserves to pass away. And this too is justice, this law of time that it must devour its children." Thus preached madness.
>
> "Things are ordered morally according to justice and punishment. Alas, where is redemption [*Erlösung*] from the flux of things and from the punishment called existence?" Thus preached madness.

"Can there be redemption if there is eternal justice? Alas the stone *It was* cannot be moved: all punishments must be eternal too." Thus preached madness.

"No deed can be annihilated: how could it be undone by punishment? This, this is what is eternal in the punishment called existence, that existence must eternally become deed and guilt again. Unless the will should at last redeem itself [*sich selber erlöste*], and willing should become not willing." But, my brothers, you know this fable of madness.[83]

According to Zarathustra, reflection (*Nachdenken*) on human life in the perspective of spiritualized revenge (in the perspective of "the spirit of revenge," which is revenge that "has acquired spirit") has developed over time, issuing in what he represents as four distinct preachings of madness.[84] The belief that unites these preachings, and that seems to define the perspective of spiritualized revenge most generally, is that the misery the will suffers, due to the fact that it cannot will backwards, is a punishment to which human life is ineluctably subject ("Because there is suffering in those who will . . ."). Subjecting human life to theoretical reflection, spiritualized revenge sees everywhere the signs of time's covetousness (viz., the "law of time . . . the flux of things . . . the stone *It was* [that] cannot be moved . . . [and] existence [that] must eternally become deed and guilt again"), and thus everywhere the object of ill will. From this point of view, human life is pervasively and essentially a miserable punishment because it is pervasively and essentially a temporal phenomenon. Zarathustra suggests, moreover, that, in the theoretical perspective of spiritualized revenge, the prereflective will cannot redeem itself by performing revenge-venting deeds, for such deeds, like all deeds, simply renew the guilt and punishing misery of having done deeds that cannot be undone: "'this is what is eternal in the punishment called existence, that existence must eternally become deed and guilt again. *Unless the will should at last redeem itself, and willing should become not willing*'" (emphasis mine). In all the history of spiritualized revenge, as Zarathustra depicts it, only one view of redemption has proved to be consistent with the belief that the will's suffering from its inability to will backwards is essential to life: Schopenhauer's view that to be released from such suffering one has to resign the life—the deed-doing and the willing—that sustains such suffering.[85] As theoretically interpreted by spiritualized revenge, redemption, or release from the misery of willing, demands renunciation.

In "On Redemption," then, Zarathustra rejects the conception of revenge he advanced in "On the Tarantulas"—revenge as "repressed envy" and "aggrieved conceit"—and opts instead for the view that revenge is rooted ultimately in the human experience of time.[86] To be sure, this new view reflects Zarathustra's recognition, acquired in "The Tomb Song," "The Dancing Song," and "On Self-Overcoming,"—that change and loss are essential to life. But beyond this, it also suggests that the passing of time, and *not* the existence of social hierarchies, has been the primary cause of the revenge-driven and Christian-Platonic teachings to which Zarathustra opposes his own views in the first nine speeches of Part 2. It would seem, then, that Zarathustra cannot plausibly claim to have escaped the heritage of Christian-Platonic thought unless he can show that his teaching is *not* rooted in an ill will toward time and time's covetousness. Zarathustra expresses his sensitivity to this issue in the remarks that follow his discussion of the practical (prereflective) and theoretical (as interpreted by the *spirit* of revenge) conceptions of redemption2.

> I led you away from these fables when I taught you "The will is a creator." All "it was" is a fragment, a riddle, a dreadful accident—until the creative will says to it, "But thus I willed it." Until the creative will says to it, "But thus I will it; thus shall I will it."
>
> But has the will yet spoken thus? And when will that happen? Has the will been unharnessed yet from his own folly? Has the will yet become his own redeemer and joy bringer [*Wurde der Will sich selber schon Erlöser und Freudebringer*]? Has he unlearned the spirit of revenge and all gnashing of teeth? And who taught him reconciliation with time and something higher than any reconciliation? For that will which is the will to power must will something higher than any reconciliation; but how shall this be brought about? Who could teach [*lehrte*] him also to will backwards?[87]

It is significant that in the first paragraph cited here Zarathustra explicitly invokes his conception of redemption1 by speaking of a creative will that could appropriate the fragmentary legacy of the "it was." In this same paragraph, he suggests that he has put forth redemption1 as an alternative to the "fables" proffered by spiritualized revenge. He suggests, in other words, that he has intended to teach a conception of redemption that involves viewing the past, not as revenge views it—namely, not as exceeding and fettering the will's power—but as something that can be creatively redeemed. Yet, as Zarathustra's first two questions imply, the will has not heeded his teaching. And why is this? Why has the will not been "unharnessed yet" from the folly of revenge and of seeing the "it was" as a fetter?

Zarathustra hints at an answer to these questions when, as we have seen, he ties his conception of redemption1 to his description of the will as a liberator and a joy bringer in "Upon the Blessed Isles." An important feature of that description, it may be recalled, is Zarathustra's claim that, were the great weariness to overtake him, the kind of redemption he discusses in "Upon the Blessed Isles" *and* in "On Redemption"—again, redemption1—would no longer be possible.[88] We know, of course, that the great weariness overtakes Zarathustra when he hears the soothsayer's prophecy, and that Zarathustra sees this as a prophecy that the ravages of asceticism will soon leave all human beings bereft of the passions that redemption1 presupposes. For Zarathustra, then, the teaching that creative willing involves redemption1, though *not* rooted in revenge's ill will toward time and time's covetousness, is not, in the face of the imminent fulfillment of the soothsayer's prophecy, a viable alternative to the fables that have been "harnessed" to the human will by spiritualized revenge.

As we have seen, Schopenhauer's equation of redemption and renunciation expresses the inner logic of spiritualized revenge. The connection between Schopenhauer's thought and the spirit of revenge is significant, for it sheds light on Zarathustra's renunciative response to the soothsayer's prophecy. Granting that the soothsayer's prophecy will be fulfilled, Zarathustra also admits that his project of overcoming man and redeeming the human past is doomed. Any further pursuit of that project now strikes him as pointless. But why should believing that his project is pointless lead Zarathustra to renounce willing? The answer to this question is that Zarathustra, in the immediate aftermath of the soothsayer's prophecy, can discern no reason to reject redemption2 as theoretically interpreted. Because redeeming the past (redemption1) seems destined to disappear as an option, he cannot see a way to avoid viewing the past as a fetter, which means, however, that he himself must suffer the misery of powerlessness that gives rise to revenge and to spiritualized revenge. In short, the soothsayer's prophecy moves Zarathustra to retreat to the perspective of revenge, and ultimately to affirm that the theoretical notion of redemption2 is the only conception of redeemed human willing valid within that perspective (as we have seen, spiritualized revenge *refutes* the revenge-driven will's practical and prereflective conception of redeemed human willing).

To be sure, Zarathustra's retreat is temporary. Thus, as after the tightrope walker's tragedy, Zarathustra here struggles to see a way beyond a Schopenhauerian appraisal of his situation.[89] Zarathustra's fourth question—"Has the will yet become his own redeemer and joy bringer?"—begins to chart that way. For the will to become *its own* redeemer and joy bringer—rather than a redeemer that redeems surviving passions (fragments) by liberating *them* from suffering and transforming *them* into joys (redemption1)—it must liberate *itself* from the fetter of the "it was" and bring *itself* joy. Zarathustra's final four questions suggest that the will would succeed in doing this were it to *unlearn* spiritualized revenge ("the spirit of revenge") and *learn* to will backwards. Now, we know that for Zarathustra "willing backwards" is using one's will to undo the past. What, however, is the relation between willing backwards and unlearning spiritualized revenge? As we have seen, spiritualized revenge, like all revenge, involves the belief that the will is powerless to undo the past. Indeed, this belief is an essential component both of the will's misery and of its antipathy to time and time's covetousness. To propose, however, that the will *may be able* to will backwards, and thus that it may possess the power to undo the past after all, is to propose that this belief may be untrue. The will will become its own redeemer and joy bringer, Zarathustra implies, when it learns how to undo the past. When it learns that, however, it will (1) reject as false the belief that it is powerless to undo the past and (2) "unlearn" and relinquish the spiritualized ill will that essentially involved that belief.

Redemption3, or *the redemption of the will through the act of willing backwards*, is Zarathustra's alternative to accepting the claim that the will can redeem itself only by "not willing." From the viewpoint of spiritualized revenge, the will suffers because it cannot will backwards. But from the viewpoint of a will that believes that it can will backwards, the will suffers because it adheres to the false belief that it cannot will backwards. From the latter viewpoint, the will can free itself of its misery, *absent any acts of renunciation*, simply by learning to do what spiritualized revenge assumes the will cannot do.

The idea of redemption3 suggests an attractive "script" for the second act of Zarathustra's thought-drama. Were Zarathustra to learn to will backwards, he could undo a "past on earth" that has been dominated by Christian-Platonic man and values. To undo that past would be to undo the fact that a secularized version of these values had led to the imminent exhaustion of the earth in the person of the small and last man. In undoing the "past on earth," Zarathustra would also preclude the possibility of a future where the Christian-Platonic values that prevailed in the past persisted in governing human affairs (to will that these values *did not* prevail in the past would be implicitly to will that they *not continue* to prevail in the future; values can continue to prevail, only if they have already prevailed). Thus, he would preclude the possibility of a future wherein he, like a crucified martyr, were eternally bound to the endless perpetuation of human existence as it has been formed by those values. Undoing the earth's past and envisioning a future free of Christian-Platonic man and his values, Zarathustra would restore his hope that man will be overcome someday through the creation of *new* values. It would seem, then, that the practical postulate that he personifies redemption3 is precisely the postulate Zarathustra requires to enact the second act of his thought-drama, for it would relieve him of his despair at the possibility of overcoming man and from the spirit of renunciation that this despair has engendered in him.

At least two objections come to mind at this point. One is that it is simply absurd to suppose that an individual could "will backwards." Though understandable, this objection overlooks the fact that the issue in question is the formulation of a *practical postulate*. Considered as such, one's assertion that one personifies the act of willing backwards is not obviously more absurd than the assertions Kant entertains as practical postulates—that one's soul is immortal, for example, and that there is a God who is the author of nature. My point here is not that one absurdity justifies another; rather, it is that a practical postulate is significant, not because it asserts a convincing physical or metaphysical theory, but because it illuminates the connection between some deeply held hope or commitment and our beliefs about the self and the world.

The second objection has greater force, for it questions the efficacy of a practical postulate involving the idea of willing backwards. Put informally, this objection claims that the idea of willing backwards throws the baby out with the bath water. Stated more precisely, it notes that undoing the Christian-Platonic past entails eradicating the possibility of redemption1, which Zarathustra equates with the possibility of creating new values. Redemption1 is possible only if there exist passions exemplifying kinds of passion that have persisted in claiming human existence notwithstanding the historical reign of the ascetic ideal. If, however, the Christian-Platonic past were undone, if a backwards-willing will were to eliminate the Christian-Platonic past, then there would exist no passions exemplifying kinds of passion that have persisted in claiming human existence *despite* that past. A willing backwards that willed that Christian-Platonic man and his Christian-Platonic values be expunged from the past would, in effect, nullify the possibility of overcoming Christian-Platonic man. How, then, could the proposition that Zarathustra personifies, or embodies, the act of willing backwards work as a practical postulate to defeat his despair at the possibility of overcoming Christian-Platonic man?

This second objection is significant, for it points to the paradoxical character of redemption3. Because redemption3 purports to undo the Christian-Platonic past, it seems to provide for the possibility of a future that would not perpetuate that past eternally, and thus for the possibility of a future featuring new values. Yet this same mode of redemption, again, because it purports to undo the Christian-Platonic past, appears to foreclose the possibility of new-values creation. In freeing the future from the eternal perpetuation of Christian-Platonic values (embodied in the last man), the act of willing backwards would erase the historical reality of Christian-Platonic man. Thus, it would eliminate the possibility of a creative willing that redeemed the Christian-Platonic past (redemption₁) by revaluing kinds of passion that tie that past to the present.[90]

To explore further the paradoxical character of redemption₃, and the question as to whether it can provide the basis for a viable practical postulate, I want to consider in some detail Zarathustra's dream-vision in "On the Vision and the Riddle," Zarathustra's first attempt to add a second act to the thought-drama of recurrence. The "script" for Zarathustra's dream-performance is the idea of a backwards-willing will that undoes the Christian-Platonic past and effects the self-redemption that is redemption₃.[91]

ZARATHUSTRA'S DREAM OF A DWARF

Upward—defying the spirit that drew it downward towards the abyss, the spirit of gravity, my devil and archenemy. Upward—although he sat on me, half dwarf, half mole, lame, making lame, dripping lead into my ear, leaden thoughts into my brain.

"O Zarathustra," he whispered mockingly, syllable by syllable; "you stone of wisdom [*Stein der Weisheit*]! You threw yourself up high, but every stone that is thrown must fall [*aber jeder geworfene Stein muss—fallen*]. O, Zarathustra, you stone of wisdom, you slingshot, you star-crusher! You threw yourself up so high; but every stone that is thrown must fall [*aber jeder geworfene Stein—muss fallen*]. Sentenced [*Verurtheilt*] to yourself and to your own death by stoning [*Steinigung*]—O Zarathustra, far indeed have you thrown the stone, but it will fall back on *you*."

Then the dwarf fell silent, and that lasted a long time. His silence, however, oppressed me; and such two someness is surely more lonesome than being alone. I climbed, I climbed, I dreamed, I thought; but every thing oppressed me. I was like one sick whom his wicked torture [*Marter*] makes weary, and who as he falls asleep is a wakened by a still more wicked dream. But there is something in me that I call courage; that has so far slain my every discouragement. This courage finally bade me stand still and speak: "Dwarf! It is you or I."[92]

Because he appears here as a dwarf, Zarathustra's spirit of gravity can be identified with the *small man*. Speaking for the first time in Part 3, this diminutive representation of repetition iterates a refrain—"but every stone that is thrown must fall"—that twice proclaims what the soothsayer previously implied: namely, that Zarathustra *must* fail in his attempt to overcome man. Try as he might to hurl himself beyond man, Zarathustra cannot, in the dwarf's view, evade the pull, the burden, and the refrainlike recurrence of man, or even of the small man. Indeed, from the perspective of the dwarf/small man, Zarathustra is a comic figure whose every effort to escape the existence of the small man brutally returns him to that existence. Zarathustra will be his own "death by stoning," the dwarf insists, because his falls and failures promise to destroy the aspiration the dwarf mocks.

Envisioning himself as subject to an endless torture that yields him no sleep, Zarathustra appears to internalize the dwarf/small man's belief that freeing himself from the dwarf/small man is impossible. Prefiguring his portrait of himself as a martyr whose torture stake (*Marterholz*) is the endless perpetuation of the small man's existence, Zarathustra suggests, in effect, that his subjection to the dwarf is his subjection to the small man's eternal recurrence. Later in the dream, the dwarf reinforces Zarathustra's suggestion, insisting that "all that is straight lies. . . . All truth is crooked; time itself is a circle."[93] Echoing the perspective of Ecclesiastes ("Consider the work of God: for who can make that straight, which he hath made crooked"), as well as that of the Christian God as Zarathustra portrays him in "Upon the Blessed Isles" ("God is a thought that makes crooked all that is straight"), the dwarf, with these remarks, advances a "circular" conception of time that sees men's present and future lives as perpetuating a mode of life and experience that has formed them in the past. For the dwarf, this can only be a matter of perpetuating the mode of life that he epitomizes: namely, human life as it has been shaped by Christian-Platonic values. If Zarathustra will never escape the pull, the burden, and the refrain of the small man, it is, the dwarf suggests, because he will remain forever subject to the perpetuation of the Christian-Platonic past as embodied in the everlasting presence of the small man.[94]

Commenting on the courage he summoned to fend off the dwarf ("This courage finally bade me stand still and speak"), Zarathustra calls courage "the best slayer."[95] He likewise adds, in an aside to his sailor-companions, that courage slays "dizziness [*Schwindel*] at the edge of abysses [*Abgründen*]" and that "pity is the deepest abyss [*Abgrund*]: as deeply as man sees into life, he also sees into suffering."[96] Here, Zarathustra's talk of pity comes as no surprise, for Zarathustra ties pity to Schopenhauer's belief that life merits renunciation (as does Nietzsche) and has himself succumbed to the spirit of resignation in the aftermath of the soothsayer's prophecy.[97] If the dwarf's appraisal of Zarathustra's plight is correct; if, in other words, overcoming man and redemption1 have ceased to be possible, leaving Zarathustra to suffer endlessly the torture of the small man's existence, then a pitying renunciation of life (redemption2 as theoretically understood), demanded by an interpretation of life in the perspective of spiritualized revenge, would seem to be reasonable. Unless, of course, Zarathustra can learn to will backwards and thereby liberate himself from the "abysmal thought" that his circumstances warrant him believing that he should renounce life.

"Stop, dwarf! I said. "It is I or you! But I am the stronger of us two: you do not know my abysmal thought [*abgründlichen Gedanken*]. *That* you could not bear!"

Then something happened that made me lighter, for the dwarf jumped from my shoulder, being curious; and he crouched on a stone before me. But there was a gateway just where we had stopped.

"Behold this gateway dwarf!" I continued. "It has two faces [*Gesichter*]. Two paths meet here; no one has yet followed either to its end. This long lane stretches back for an eternity. And the long lane out there, that is another eternity. They contradict each other, these paths; they offend each other face to face [*sie stossen sich gerade vor den Kopf*]; and it is here at this gateway that they come together. The name of the gateway is inscribed above: 'Moment.' But whoever would follow one of them, on and on, farther and farther—do you believe dwarf that these paths contradict each other eternally?"

"All that is straight lies," the dwarf murmured contemptuously. "All truth is crooked; time itself is a circle."

"You spirit of gravity," I said angrily, "do not make things too easy for yourself! Or I shall let you crouch where you are crouching, lamefoot [*Lahmfuss*]; and it was I who carried you to this *height*.

"Behold," I continued, "this moment! From this gateway, Moment, a long, eternal lane runs [*läuft*] *backward*: behind us lies an eternity. Must not what-ever *can* run have run on this lane before [*Muss nicht, was laufen kann von allen Dingen, schon einmal diese Gasse gelaufen sein*]? Must not whatever *can* happen have happened, have been done, have passed by before. And if everything has been there before—what do you think, dwarf, of this moment? Must not this gateway too have been there before? And are not all things knotted together so firmly that this moment draws after it *all* that is to come? Therefore—itself too? For whatever *can* run [*laufen kann*]—in this long lane out *there* too, it *must* run once more [*muss es einmal noch laufen*].

"And this slow spider, which crawls in the moonlight, and this moonlight itself, and I and you in the gateway, whispering together, whispering of eternal things—must not all of us have been there before. And return and run in that other lane [*in jener anderen Gasse laufen*], out there, before us, in this long dreadful lane—must we not eternally return?"[98]

When Zarathustra reaches the gateway he says "I or you," thus reversing his earlier "You or I" and prompting the dwarf to jump from his shoulder. Something in the experience of the gateway relieves Zarathustra of his burden. Standing under it, Zarathustra poses a riddle to the dwarf—the riddle of time. Because the gateway is named Moment, and is in fact the *present* moment, it is plausible to suppose that the two paths are the *past*, all past moments, and the *future*, all future moments, abutting one another in the present moment. Zarathustra suggests that the two paths contradict each other eternally: he implies, in other words, that if a moment has passed away into the past then it is not a future moment (a moment yet to occur), and that no future moment has passed away into the past. Describing time as a circle, the dwarf seems to "solve" Zarathustra's riddle by denying that time is the linear phenomenon that Zarathustra's talk of contradiction suggests. As we have seen, however, the dwarf's description of time, in that it alludes to Ecclesiastes and to one of Zarathustra's earlier characterizations of the Christian God, need not be read as gainsaying the linearity that Zarathustra contemplates; rather it can be read as proposing that linear time, as Zarathustra understands it, has the "circular" property of effecting in the present and throughout the future the *perpetual* existence of Christian-Platonic man (again, as epitomized in the person of the small man): "existence *as it is*, without meaning or aim, yet recurring inevitably"(emphasis mine).

Sensing the inadequacy of the dwarf's response to his riddle, Zarathustra chides him not to make things too easy for himself. Zarathustra then calls the dwarf "lamefoot," a name that the jester, appearing in the prologue as a figure for the spirit of gravity, applied to the tightrope walker who had made danger his vocation.[99] Zarathustra's use of that name, in the context of his dream confrontation with the dwarf, suggests that the dwarf or spirit of gravity is now the one in danger. His use of "lamefoot" also suggests an analogy between Zarathustra's relation to the dwarf and the mythical sphinx's relation to the lamefoot Oedipus.[100] Here, Zarathustra appears as a sphinx posing the riddle of time to the dwarf-Oedipus—a riddle within the riddle and dream that Zarathustra conveys to his audience of sailors.[101]

Zarathustra proposes his own solution to the riddle by putting forth an apparently "cosmological" vision of eternal recurrence.[102] Appearing initially to speak of events occurring in time, but not of the moments of time, he claims that all events that can happen have happened; or in other words, that all possible events have been present at some past moment, and therefore that all possible events have "run" on the path of the past stretching behind him. Zarathustra seems subsequently to assume that the set of events that can and have happened *includes* the moments of which time consists, and then to infer, on the basis of that assumption, that the present moment, which he identifies with the gateway, has already run on the path of the past ("And if everything has been there before—what do you think, dwarf, of this moment? Must not this gateway too have been there before?"). Zarathustra implies, moreover, that the set of future moments and events contains the present moment ("And are not all things knotted together so firmly that this moment draws after it *all* that is to come? Therefore—itself too?"), and that all moments and events that *can* happen in the future ("in this long lane out *there*") belong to the set of future moments and events that *must* (and will) happen *once more*—and that, therefore, have happened already ("For whatever *can* run—in this long lane out *there* too, it must run once more"). Put succinctly, Zarathustra's thesis seems to be that the set of all past moments and events exhausts the set of all possible moments and events (all moments and events that *can* happen) and is identical to the set of moments and events that will occur again, and thus *recur*, in the future.

When an event recurs, it must recur at the time it originally occurred, for otherwise it would not be the same event.[103] Perhaps this is why Zarathustra suggests that events *and* moments recur—that events recur when the moments at which they occur later recur. But what sense is there in saying that a moment that has passed away into the past (that has, like Zarathustra's gateway, already walked on the path of the past) *later* recurs; that it recurs *as* a later time (Zarathustra's moment draws after it "itself too")? Speaking in this way boggles the mind, for it implies that one and the same moment is the occurrence of at least two distinct times (the occurrence of a past time and the occurrence subsequently of some future time), which is tantamount to implying that one and the same moment is identical to two distinct moments. To speak of recurrent moments, then, is to assert the contradiction that a self-identical moment is not self-identical.

Why is it that, though talk of recurrent moments involves self-contradiction, it seems plausible nonetheless to Zarathustra? Or, to put the question a bit differently, what is it about the way Zarathustra envisions time that permits him to see the idea of recurrent moments as somehow coherent? The answer to this question, I think, is that Zarathustra figures time in two different but related ways. On one hand, the figure of the abutting paths invites us to see the moments of past and future time as a set of *path-places* extending in two directions from the gateway. On the other hand, we are asked to think of individual moments by analogy to the gateway itself, that is, as mobile entities that can "run" on the abutting paths. Thus, when Zarathustra imagines a moment's recurrence, he imagines a mobile entity—the gateway—as having run on the path of the past and as running subsequently on the path of the future. More precisely, he envisions one and the same *single moment* as the occurrence of *two distinct times* by picturing a *single entity* in *two distinct places*. To visualize the present moment *as past* is to visualize the gateway in one place—on the path of the past. To visualize the same moment *as recurring in the future* is to visualize the gateway in a second place—on the path of the future. Since a gateway is an entity that can traverse physical space and appear in different places at different times, this way of envisioning the past occurrence and future recurrence of the present moment, or of any moment for that matter, avoids obvious contradiction and is *prima facie* coherent.

Exploring the particulars of Zarathustra's vision of time shows that it depends for its apparent coherence on the representation of time as space. Zarathustra "spatializes" time, by picturing it as two paths intersecting at a gateway that marks the place and the present moment in which he stands.[104] For Zarathustra, all places present on the paths of the past and the future are present simultaneously. Thus, each of these places is present at the same time as the place he himself occupies. By spatializing time, Zarathustra represents all times and moments as *concurrent* with the present moment.

From the perspective of the present moment, as Zarathustra depicts it, the putative past and future come into view as spatially continuous extensions of the place of the present moment (just as, in a house, the places belonging to an addition to a small hall come into view as spatially continuous extensions of the place of the original hall), but *not* as existing "before" or "after" the present moment. From this perspective, the experience of the present moment is that of a perpetual, or eternal, "now," relative to which neither earlier nor later moments exist. As envisioned from within the present moment, recurrent moments—again, mobile entities that materialize in one place and then another on the concurrent paths of the past and the future—appear not as elements of the mundane time we typically experience, but as modifications of a spatially extended, extramundane *nunc stans*.[105]

In dreaming that time is space, Zarathustra imagines that he is performing the "script" for the second act of the thought-drama of recurrence. This "script," again, is the idea of a will that wills backwards and so effectively undoes the Christian-Platonic past. In his dream, Zarathustra relates the act of willing backwards to his cosmological vision of a perpetual "now" through a reference to the Oedipus myth. As we have seen, Zarathustra's allusion to the lamefooted Oedipus likens the confrontation between the dwarf and Zarathustra to that between Oedipus and the sphinx. This reference likewise suggests an analogy to the meeting between Oedipus and Laius, because the "lamefoot" dwarf and Zarathustra, like Oedipus and Laius, clash with one another at a crossroads (the place where the paths of the past and the future meet).

After he defeats and murders Laius, Oedipus usurps his father's place in his mother's bed and in the political life of Thebes. Zarathustra's struggle with the dwarf appears to reverse this outcome, for here Zarathustra-Laius defeats the dwarf-Oedipus. Like Oedipus, the dwarf is related to murder and usurpation. As a figure for the small and last man, he signifies the small and last man's "murder" of the earth's passions. And because he sees the human future as perpetuating the Christian-Platonic past, he signifies this past's usurpation of the role of the creative will in dictating the values of the future. Zarathustra-Laius defeats the dwarf-Oedipus because, by envisioning the present moment as a perpetual "now" relative to which *no earlier moments exist*, Zarathustra-Laius seems to annul the past per se. Thus, he seems to annul the fact of a human past that has murdered the earth's passions and then usurped the role of the creative will in dictating the values of the future. Picturing himself as a resurrected Laius, returned to the crossroads to undo the criminal deeds of his son's past, Zarathustra imagines himself undoing the Christian-Platonic past, and thus as having learned to will backwards.

By casting himself in the role of a Laius who has learned to will backwards, Zarathustra denies that he has come "too late" to create new values. In other words, he denies that Christian-Platonic values as epitomized by the small man have exhausted the earth and rendered any further value-creation impossible. Like a Laius who envisioned a world in which Oedipus's crimes had never been committed, the strategy of willing backwards envisions a moment—a perpetual "now"—in connection to which there exist no prior moments, no prior value-creations, and no prior exhaustion of the earth. As if he were one of Harold Bloom's "strong poets," to whom he may be fruitfully compared, Zarathustra copes with his feeling of belatedness, and with the anxiety of inexpressiveness that that feeling engenders, by in effect denying his belatedness.[106] One can begin to see the point of this comparison by considering Zarathustra in light of one of Bloom's remarks regarding his best example of a strong poet, John Milton. According to Bloom, Milton "transumed" his precursor poets, Homer and Spenser, by creating the powerful impression that their tropes and poems were imitations of *his* achievement in *Paradise Lost*: "Milton's aim is to make his own belatedness into an earliness. . . . Troping upon his forerunners' tropes, Milton compels us . . . to accept his stance and vision as our origin, his time as true time."[107] Writing as if he were not a latecomer, Milton reinvents the time of literary history by figuratively denying the existence of earlier poetic visions. Similarly, but much more ambitiously, Zarathustra reinvents time per se by means of a spatializing representation of the present moment that denies the existence of earlier moments.[108]

For the dreaming Zarathustra, the present moment is not simply an entity that can track along the paths of the present and future; it is also and *specifically* a gateway, a distinctive kind of entity whose raison d'être typically is admission—in this case, Zarathustra's admission to a vision of time wherein the dwarf has no place. Facing in two directions, the gateway called Moment is, literally, an *Augenblick*: a glance of the eye in two directions that permits Zarathustra to see the *putative* past and future as eternally present footpaths that stretch the presence of the present moment eternally forwards and eternally backwards into an eternal *nunc stans*. Whereas the dwarf knows nothing of the present moment, Zarathustra repeatedly refers to it to highlight the image of time it affords him. It is *in* the moment that the two paths come together; it is *from* the moment that "a long . . . lane runs *backward*"; and it is the moment that "draws after it *all* that is to come." For Zarathustra, the present moment is privileged, in that it enables him to envision the *whole* of time *as* an eternally present moment.[109] The dwarf has no place in this moment, for it excludes from time the past per se, and therefore, the Christian-Platonic past, and therefore, the endless perpetuation of the Christian-Platonic past, which perpetuation the dwarf symbolizes.

Zarathustra begins to cope with his abysmal thought—again, that his circumstances justify him believing that he should renounce life—by dreaming the drama of a willing-backwards that envisions a perpetual "now" as time's ever-present moment. In Zarathustra's dream, future moments (moments succeeding the "now"), no less than past ones, disappear from view. And absent future moments, redemption1 and the creation of not yet existing values—that is, the creation of *new* values—cease to be possible. As we have seen, the act of willing backwards would have the paradoxical effect of eradicating the possibility of creating new values, even though it appeared to restore that possibility and to liberate the will from the spirit of renunciation. Zarathustra's dream-performance of this act begins to clarify its paradoxical character, by showing that an eternal "now" is *the mode of temporality that an act of willing backwards would engender.* Willing backwards would remove the possibility of creating new values, not only by nullifying the possibility of revaluing passions that have persisted historically in claiming human existence, but, more extremely, by establishing a mode of temporality that precluded the occurrence of any moments *outside* the present one—and therefore, the coming-to-be of anything new (i.e., anything not now or yet existing, such as a new person, a new object, a new event, or, as concerns Zarathustra, a new value).[110] It is as if Laius, by envisioning a world wherein his usurper son's crimes had not been committed, had foreclosed the possibility of his or anyone else having children that they had not yet had.

I can further explain the paradox that is involved in willing backwards by considering Zarathustra's spatialization of time and his allusions to the Oedipus myth as so many ways of illustrating a dreamed enactment of the second metamorphosis of the spirit.[111] Before he recounts his dream, Zarathustra describes it as "the vision of the loneliest" (*das Gesicht des Einsamsten*), thus echoing his assertion in "On the Three Metamorphoses" that the second metamorphosis occurs "in the loneliest desert" (*in der einsamsten Wüste*).[112] Burdened by the spirit of gravity, the epitome of the Christian-Platonic values that cause life to seem a desert, Zarathustra initially appears in his dream as a camel, weighed down and oppressed by the living legacy of life-denying asceticism.[113] As his dream progresses, he becomes a defiant lion who succeeds in repudiating this legacy.

As we have seen, "On the Three Metamorphoses" describes the lion-spirit's struggle against Christian-Platonic values by recalling Siegfried's clash with a dragon, Fafner, in Wagner's *Ring*. Similarly, "On the Vision and the Riddle" describes Zarathustra's struggle against the spirit of gravity by recalling Siegfried's clash with a dwarf, Mime.[114] In *Zarathustra*, these struggles are connected because the great dragon and the dwarf Zarathustra battles partake in the *same attitude* toward the values they personify. The great dragon holds to the view that Christian values are and must be the only values. Proclaiming "good for all, evil for all," the dwarf, as Zarathustra later depicts him (again in connection to the spirit of gravity), also insists on the reality and the possibility of just one system of values.[115] A figure for the endless perpetuation of Christian-Platonic man and his values, Zarathustra's spirit of gravity, like the Christian God the great dragon symbolizes, is a representation of repetition who denies the possibility of creating new values. This, again, is why he echoes the Christian God's "crooked" vision of human possibility, and why as a lion-spirit Zarathustra must oppose him.

In Chapter 1, we saw that the lion's struggle against the great dragon involves three themes: supersession, priority, and freedom. As we shall see, these themes recur in Zarathustra's dreamed confrontation with the dwarf or spirit of gravity. Taken in tandem, they frame Zarathustra's vision of himself as the dwarf's lion-spirited antagonist.

In "On the Three Metamorphoses," the lion *supersedes* the Christian God or great dragon by claiming for himself the power and the authority to create values. In "On the Vision and the Riddle," a leonine Zarathustra supersedes the dwarf by claiming for himself the same power and authority. By figuring himself as a resurrected Laius, Zarathustra purports to undo the dwarf-Oedipus's usurpation of the creative will's power and authority to dictate the values of the future. Because the dwarf sees the future as perpetuating the Christian-Platonic past he himself epitomizes, he asserts implicitly what the great dragon proclaims explicitly: "All value has long been created, and I am all created value. Verily, there shall be no more 'I will.'" By willing backwards and annulling the Christian-Platonic past, a Laius-like Zarathustra reaffirms his creative will: performing a negation of a negation, he successfully usurps a usurper, thereby insisting that his will possesses the power and the authority to create new values.

As we saw in Chapter 1, the lion denies the Christian God's *priority* by denying the existence of any will that has exhausted the possibilities of value-creation prior to the lion's assertion of his will. Like the lion, who asserts himself against the Christian God by saying "I will," Zarathustra asserts himself against the dwarf by saying "Stop dwarf! It is I or you." It is significant, of course, that Zarathustra's "I or you" reverses his earlier "You or I," and that this reversal explicitly denies the dwarf's precedence with respect to Zarathustra just after Zarathustra exhorts the dwarf to stop at the moment marked by the gateway. Pausing to stand within that moment, Zarathustra can "stop" the dwarf (the dwarf jumps down from Zarathustra's shoulder when Zarathustra reaches the gateway) because the gateway itself has "stopped" the flow of time. From the spatializing perspective of the moment, time appears not as flowing ceaselessly from the future into the past, but as two motionless footpaths, eternally extending the presence of the present moment into the eternal presence of a perpetual "now" that no moment precedes or succeeds. Because he sees time in this manner, Zarathustra holds that no moments have occurred prior to the present moment. Thus, he rejects the belief that any particular will (the Christian God's will, for instance) or any particular tradition of human willing and valuing (the Christian-Platonic tradition epitomized by the dwarf) has exhausted the possibilities of value-creation, *or even existed, before* his assertion of his will within the perpetual "now." Resembling the strong poet who transumes his precursors, Zarathustra denies that the possibilities of value-creation have been spent, for he denies that there has been *any* creative willing prior his own.

In "On the Three Metamorphoses," the lion creates *freedom* for the creation of new values by repudiating the camel's belief that the future must perpetuate the Christian-Platonic values that have ruled human existence in the past. We have seen that the dwarf also espouses that belief, and that Zarathustra, like the lion, rejects it in his dream. For Zarathustra, the camel's belief cannot be true because, again, the perpetual "now" excludes from time the past per se, and therefore the perpetuation in the future of the Christian-Platonic past. Zarathustra, like the lion, feels free and able to create new values, for he denies the view that human life in the future has to have the Christian-Platonic character it had in the past.

I have been urging that the act of willing backwards, as performed by Zarathustra in the dream he recounts in "On the Vision and the Riddle," is an enactment of the second metamorphosis of the spirit. The paradox involved in this act, I should now like to show, is an instance of the sort of paradox I ascribed to the lion-spirit in Chapter 4. I want to explain this paradox by linking it to the epistemically based self-estrangement that Zarathustra, in Part 2, discovered in the figure of the lion.

Disclaiming his capacity to be touched and moved by the chaos of the coming god, the lion-spirit is Dionysus-Zagreus, a sublime Promethean hero whose self-assertive will functions as an Apollonian mask that estranges him from his ability to go-under. In Part 2 (e.g., in "The Night Song"), Zarathustra appears as a leonine Dionysus-Zagreus and exhibits a self-masking and self-estranging will that is also his will to truth. As we have seen, self-analysis leads Zarathustra to discard his will to truth and (in "On Those Who Are Sublime") to reclaim his ability to go-under.

In the present chapter, I have argued that Zarathustra reprises the posture of the lion-spirit in "On the Vision and the Riddle." Yet I do not wish to claim that he recommits himself to the will to truth. Zarathustra "backtracks," as it were, to the self-estranging posture of the lion, but, in so doing, develops a nonepistemic *reinterpretation* of lion-spiritedness. In Part 2, Zarathustra acts as a lion-spirited proponent of the will to truth, hoping to free his teachings from distortion and to dispel the spirit of gravity. In "On the Vision and the Riddle," he again hopes to dispel the spirit of gravity, but absent any attempt to establish his version of the truth. Rather, Zarathustra now responds to his nemesis by picturing himself willing backwards. The problem presently confronting Zarathustra is practical, not epistemic: it is the problem of crafting a practical postulate predicated on a cosmological vision that is compatible with becoming a new-values creator. It is significant, therefore, that, like the will to truth Zarathustra formerly endorsed, his cosmological vision, in that it pictures his will inhabiting a perpetual "now," is a form of leonine self-estrangement.

As discussed earlier, self-estrangement is a constitutive feature of the lion-spirit, for in insisting on the absolute independence of his will, the lion-spirit disowns his power of receptivity and disclaims his ability to go-under to a chaos of uncreated passions. Because acknowledging his ability to go-under would involve admitting that his will depends on factors other than itself to create new values—for instance, that it depends on the existence of uncreated, first-order passions to create such values—the leonine individual, in order to maintain his belief in his will's absolute independence, must refuse to acknowledge that ability. As we saw in Chapter 1, the lion-spirit's supersession of the Christian God leads him to believe that, if there are created values, then, sufficient unto itself, his will and his will alone is the source of those values. The Promethean lion holds that his assertion of his will is both necessary and sufficient for the creation of new values.

In Part 2, Zarathustra expresses the lion's insistence on absolute independence by promoting a more or less idealist epistemology that denies the element of the "given" in human knowledge. Representing the will to power as the will to truth, this epistemology repudiates the view that the possibility of knowledge depends on the existence of "intuitions" (cf. Kant), or on the existence of any other elements of knowledge that the knowing subject has not created. From the perspective of this lion-spirited theory of knowledge, human knowledge involves *no* power of receptivity to uncreated passions. In "On the Vision and the Riddle," Zarathustra again expresses the lion's insistence on absolute independence, this time by envisioning dwarf-stopping courageous willing as belonging to a perpetual "now" that has no moments before it or after it. Here, not the will to truth, but the will to inhabit such a "now," masks Zarathustra's power of receptivity and causes his self-estrangement. To suppose that one's will were ensconced within an eternal, present moment would be to deny, in effect, that one's will could ever cease to will what it was willing at that moment, for whatever it was willing at that moment it would have to will eternally. Indeed, a will inhabiting a perpetual "now," or a perpetual, present moment, could never go-under, because going-under requires that the will surrender its second-order mastery of first-order passions. It requires, in other words, that the will cease to will whatever it is willing at a given moment, and hence that that moment of willing pass into the past, thereby showing that it was not perpetual. By securing itself within the temporality of a *nunc stans*, a will that willed backwards would disclaim its ability to go-under. From the viewpoint of such a will, human being-in-time would involve *no* power to suffer a chaos of uncreated passions, and thus no capacity to revalue and redeem passions of a sort that claimed generations past. In fact, acknowledging the possibility of such revaluation and redemption (redemption1) would not be possible for a will inhabiting Zarathustra's perpetual "now," for this would involve admitting that, in creating new values, the will could make use of kinds of materials (passions) that existed in the human past *before* it asserted itself. Because a will that willed backwards could not admit that such a past existed, it would deny, we have seen, the reality of such materials: it would deny the existence of passions exemplifying kinds of passion that, notwithstanding the historical reign of the ascetic ideal, have persisted in claiming human existence.

It is perhaps evident now that the paradox entailed in willing backwards is but an instance of a paradox that is essential to lion-spiritedness. On one hand, the lion-spirit who envisions his will ensconced within an eternal "now," by annulling the past per se, and therewith annulling the possibility of a future that would perpetuate past values, recommits himself to becoming a new-values creator. And yet, ineluctably, that very spirit, because he envisions his will as never surrendering its mastery and as never ceasing to will what it is willing, disowns its ability to go-under and to become a new-values creator.

ZARATHUSTRA'S DOUBLE WILL

I will conclude my discussion of "On the Vision and the Riddle" by considering the remainder of Zarathustra's dream:

> Thus I spoke, more and more softly; for I was afraid of my thoughts and
> reservations [*Gedanken und Hintergedanken*]. Then suddenly [*plötzlich*] I heard
> a dog howl nearby. Had I ever heard a dog howl like this? My thoughts ran
> back [*lief zurück*]. Yes, when I was a child, in the most distant childhood [*in
> fernster Kindheit*]: then I heard a dog howl like this. And I saw him too,
> bristling, his head up, trembling in the stillest midnight when even dogs
> believe in ghosts—and I took pity: for just then the full moon, silent as death,
> passed over the house; just then it stood still, a round glow—still on the flat
> roof, as if on another's property [*fremdem Eigenthume*]—that was why the dog
> was terrified [*entsetzte sich*], for dogs believe in thieves and ghosts. And when I
> heard such howling again I took pity again.
>
> Where was the dwarf gone now? And the gateway? And the spider? And all
> the whispering? Was I dreaming, then? Was I waking up?
>
> Among wild cliffs I stood all at once alone [*mit Einem Male, allein*], bleak,
> in the bleakest moonlight. *But there lay a man.* And there—the dog, jumping,
> bristling, whining—now he saw me coming: then he howled again, he *cried.*
> Had I ever heard a dog cry like this for help? And verily, what I saw—I had
> never seen the like. A young shepherd I saw, writhing [*sich windend*], gagging
> [*würgend*], in spasms, his face distorted, and a heavy black snake [*eine schwarze
> schwere Schlange*] hung out of his mouth. Had I ever seen so much nausea and
> pale dread [*Grauen*] on one face? He seemed to have been asleep when the
> snake crawled into his throat, and there bit itself [*da biss sie sich*] fast. My hand
> tore at the snake and tore in vain; it did not tear the snake out of his throat.
> Then it cried out of me: "Bite! Bite its head off! Bite!" Thus it cried out of
> me—my dread, my hatred, my nausea, my pity, all that is good and wicked in
> me cried out with a single cry.
>
> You bold ones who surround me! . . . You who are glad of riddles! Guess me
> the riddle [*So rathet mir doch das Räthsel*] that I saw then, interpret me the
> vision of the loneliest. . . . *What* did I see then in a parable. . . .
>
> The shepherd, however, bit as my cry counseled him [*wie mein Schrie ihm
> rieth*]; he bit with a good bite. Far away he spewed the head of the snake—and
> he jumped up [*sprang empor*]. No longer shepherd, no longer human [*nicht
> mehr Mensch*]—one changed [*ein Verwandelter*], radiant, *laughing*! Never yet
> on earth has a human being laughed as he laughed! O my brothers, I heard
> a laughter that was no human laughter [*keines menschen Lachen*]; and now
> a thirst gnaws at me, a longing that never grows still. My longing for this

laughter gnaws at me; oh, how do I bear to go on living! And how could I bear to die now![116]

After Zarathustra finishes his conversation with the dwarf, his dream further dramatizes and intensifies his struggle to cope with his abysmal thought. Speaking softly, under the moonlight, he hears a dog howl. Next, he recollects a setting from his childhood, wherein he again finds moonlight and a dog howling. Suddenly, however, he has a premonition, in which he sees his future sickness and convalescence in the person of a shepherd (speaking to the sailors, Zarathustra calls his vision a "foreseeing" [*Vorhersehn*]), and in which, once more, he finds moonlight and a dog howling.[117]

Prior to Zarathustra's aside to the sailors ("You bold ones . . ."), the second half of his dream appears to admit of at least two interpretations. On one hand, it can be viewed pessimistically as supporting the abysmal thought that Zarathustra's situation warrants the belief that he should renounce life. As if prefiguring Freud's explanation of how displacement works to construct dreams, Zarathustra's recollection and premonition seem, on this interpretation, to transfer the fear he feels in speaking to the dwarf ("I was afraid of my thoughts and reservations") first to one and then to another setting wherein that fear appears as the fear of *other* individuals.[118] When, for example, Zarathustra remembers his childhood, he sees a dog terrified by the image of a full moon that, ghost- and thieflike, suddenly stands still "on another's property." What he sees, in other words, is a dog frightened by an image of usurpation. To be sure, no dwarf appears here as a usurping, Oedipal, spirit of gravity that subjects the future to the dictates of the past. Rather the deathly full moon appears in this role, thieflike, to usurp a claim to a piece of property, and ghostlike, to subject that property to the command of a haunting past that persists in perpetuating itself.[119] When Zarathustra foresees his future, he sees his fear no longer in a howling dog, but intensified as "pale dread" in the face of a shepherd in whom he has yet to recognize himself. Pictured as (orally) penetrated by a heavy serpent (*eine . . . schwere Schlange*), the figure of the shepherd refigures Zarathustra's earlier expressed feeling of being penetrated by heavy, dripping lead that the dwarf dripped into his ear. As before, the source of Zarathustra's displaced fear—the weighty, penetrating serpent—seems to symbolize the Oedipal "spirit of gravity" (*Geist der Schwere*), that would-be usurper of Zarathustra's creative will who wishes to "gag" (*würgen*) to death the project of overcoming man.[120] Viewed pessimistically, then, the second half of Zarathustra's dream suggests that his fate in the future (e.g., the future he sees in the person of the suffering shepherd) will be what it has been in the past (e.g., his remembered childhood). It suggests, more generally, that Zarathustra will never escape his subjection to Christian-Platonic man's recurrence, and that he will be justified in the future, no less than he has been in the past, in believing that he should renounce life, pitying it as he does in his dream.[121]

Consider now an alternative interpretation of the second half of Zarathustra's dream, again as Zarathustra recounts it prior to his aside to the sailors. Concentrating on the transitions from one dream-episode to another—that is, on (1) the transition from the conversation with the dwarf to the memory of childhood, and (2) the transition from the memory of childhood to the vision of the shepherd—we notice immediately that the second half of the dream, no less than the first, concerns the nature of time. For example, the recollective act prompting the first transition—Zarathustra says that his thoughts "ran back" (presumably along the path of the past where all that "can run" has run before) until they arrived at his "distant" childhood—involves a perception of time as space that Zarathustra has already articulated. Both transitions suggest, moreover, that Zarathustra's perception of time as space continues to involve the idea of a perpetual "now." Suddenly (*plötzlich*) hearing a dog howl, Zarathustra is immediately born by his dream thoughts to a time he sees as a remote place (his "distant" childhood), in which the dwarf and the gateway are no longer present. Then, *all at once* (*mit einem Male*), he finds himself alone in a radically different setting. Just as in a movie, when a camera cuts from one scene to another, Zarathustra's dream seems to transport him instantaneously from one time (perceived as a place) to another: from the present time (the time of his colloquy with the dwarf) to a past time (his childhood), and then from that past time to a future time (his premonition). Because these cuts from time to time seem sudden and instantaneous, because, in other words, they seem to take *no time* at all, they evoke the impression that all three times are the same time.[122] Indeed, they evoke the impression that Zarathustra has never departed from the present moment, and that he experiences that time as a perpetual "now" relative to which, strictly speaking, there exist no earlier or later times.

If we read the second half of Zarathustra's dream with attention to the images, figures and symbols that constitute its content, then it seems to confirm the view that Zarathustra should renounce life. But if we read it with an eye to the cinematic form of its appearance (highlighting the transitions between episodes but slighting the images and figures), then, like the first half of his dream, it seems to allude to the idea of a perpetual "now" and to endorse the lion-spirit's antidote to the specter of man's recurrence. Which of these readings is correct? Or better, which of them reveals Zarathustra's true destiny?

Deciding between readings of his dream, Zarathustra suggests, is like guessing the answer to a riddle: "Guess [*rathet*] me this riddle," he says, "interpret me the vision of the loneliest." In the part of his dream he recounts after his aside to the sailors, we see Zarathustra presenting his own guess and solution to the interpretive riddle he has posed. Remarking that "the shepherd bit . . . as my cry counseled [*rieth*] him," Zarathustra expresses himself using the German word *rieth*. *Rieth*, however, is a form of the verb *raten* (or, in Nietzsche's spelling, *rathen*), which is also the verb Zarathustra uses to exhort the sailors to guess his riddle. By playing on the double meaning of *raten*—"to counsel" as well as "to guess"—Zarathustra intimates that his counsel to the shepherd is itself an interpretation that guesses at the meaning of the vision of the loneliest. By advising the shepherd to bite off the head of the heavy, black serpent, Zarathustra, as he appears in his vision, interprets his vision and, we shall see, reveals his own destiny. But what is the content of Zarathustra's counsel and interpretation? What does the shepherd's bite signify?

Zarathustra's vision suggests an answer to this question, with its descriptions both of the setting wherein Zarathustra encounters the young shepherd and of the events leading the shepherd to bite off the serpent's head. The gist of this answer, I shall argue, is that the shepherd's bite produces an experience of the sublime that marks the shepherd and, ultimately, Zarathustra as defiant, Promethean heroes. To construe the shepherd's bite in this way is, no doubt, to hold that Zarathustra's counsel to the shepherd interprets "the vision of the loneliest," not as portending man's recurrence, and not as hinting that Zarathustra would be justified in believing he should renounce life, but as a lion-spirited vision in which, finally, willing backwards and the temporality of the perpetual "now" triumph over the pessimistic implications of the images appearing in the second half of Zarathustra's dream (before the aside to the sailors). This construal implies, in other words, that in counseling the shepherd to bite off the serpent's head, Zarathustra interprets his vision as a parable ("*What* did I see then in a parable," he asks the sailors) of a lion-spirited victory over the spirit of gravity. Subsequently in Part 3, in "The Convalescent," we learn that Zarathustra's interpretation of his vision was *in fact* an accurate revelation and intimation of his own destiny.

"Among wild cliffs [*wilden Klippen*] I stood at once alone, bleak, in the bleakest moonlight. *But there lay a man.*" With these sentences, Zarathustra begins to describe his dream encounter with the shepherd and the serpent, sketching a contrast between nature's awesome power, as figured by the image of wild cliffs, and human beings' vulnerability to that power, as suggested by the presence of a person prostrate on the ground. The picture outlined here is reminiscent of one of the vignettes Kant uses to illustrate his concept of the dynamical sublime, and could also be used for that purpose.[123] As Zarathustra describes the setting of his encounter, it becomes clear to him that the power confronting the man he sees is not simply that of nature, but likewise the power of the serpent who has crawled into the man's mouth. It is significant, moreover, that Zarathustra's depiction of the serpent, as biting and gagging the shepherd's throat, recalls his claim in "On the Rabble" that "the bite [*Bissen*] on which [he] gagged [*würgte*] the most" was the fact that life requires "even the rabble." As we saw in Chapter 4, Zarathustra escaped the feeling of powerlessness caused him by this fact by exploiting a compensatory power (to enjoy a life free of the rabble) that engendered a sensation of sublime height and transcendence. As we shall see presently, the shepherd resorts to a similar strategy to escape his gagging subjection to the serpent who torments him. In Part 3, Zarathustra strives to emulate the shepherd and thus to realize his destiny, supposing, as he did in "On the Rabble," that the sensation of sublimity depends on the discovery of an elevated reality that is given independently of the will (see below my reading of "Before Sunrise"). Subsequently, however, he recurs to the position he proposed in "On Those Who Are Sublime": namely, that that sensation is wholly the artifact of a heroic (though self-estranging) act of the will (see, below, my reading of "The Seven Seals").

Failing to pull the serpent from the shepherd's mouth, Zarathustra is powerless to save him and, since the shepherd is a figure for Zarathustra (he prefigures Zarathustra's destiny), to save himself. But if Zarathustra cannot save himself by tearing at the serpent, he can, in the person of the shepherd, counter the serpent's bite with a bite of his own and, acting the role of a defiant lion, free himself from the onerous serpent, or spirit of gravity, who would make him into a camel. Zarathustra's failure recalls the soothsayer's suggestion that human striving is a "vain" (*umsonst*) enterprise (Zarathustra reports that he tore at the serpent "in vain") and seems to verify a judgment all camels would endorse: namely, that Zarathustra is powerless to defeat the spirit of gravity. In contrast, the action of the shepherd betokens Zarathustra's latent, unacknowledged power to do what he vainly attempts to do when, in his dream, he endeavors to save the shepherd. Eventually, Zarathustra acknowledges and exploits that power, but only in "The Convalescent."

By biting off the serpent's head the shepherd kills it, thereby demonstrating his defiant, leonine refusal to be thwarted by the spirit of gravity and by the abysmal thought (once again, that Zarathustra's circumstances justify him in believing that he should renounce life) that the spirit of gravity (in the person of the dwarf who pummels Zarathustra with the implications of the soothsayer's prophecy) prompts in Zarathustra.[124] In essence, the shepherd repudiates both the spirit of gravity's message that the small man will perpetuate himself and Zarathustra's abysmal thought.

Exercising his power of repudiation, the shepherd offsets Zarathustra's failed effort to pull the serpent from the shepherd's throat. Freeing himself from the specter of the small man, and from the abysmal thought that this specter engenders, he emulates Siegfried, the hero who slays both the small man (the dwarf, Mime) and the serpentine creature (Fafner) who oppose him.[125] Enacting Zarathustra's counsel and dream interpretation ("Bite!"), the shepherd's bite and expectoration display a compensatory power to will backwards and "kill" the spirit of gravity, deploying as a weapon the idea of a perpetual "now." The shepherd's exertion of that power renders him sublime (the effect of his biting and spewing is, literally, an act of self-elevation, of jumping up), and signals the "hermeneutical" triumph of a reading of Zarathustra's dream (or, more exactly, of the dream's second half, prior to the aside to the sailors), which, by connecting the dream's form to the idea of a perpetual "now," compensates in its own right for a pessimistic reading that cannot discern in the dream the possibility of a lion-spirited victory over the spirit of gravity.

The shepherd's laughing, bite-inspired sensation of sublimity is his exhilarating feeling that he has transcended humanity per se, and not simply that he has transcended the rabble. "No longer shepherd, no longer human" (*Nicht mehr Hirt, nicht mehr Mensch*), the shepherd personifies a sublimity that is, in essence, his *negation* of his humanity. Indeed, in the figure of the shepherd one sees a compelling portrait of what Schiller described as the *inhuman* potential of the sublime, its capacity to lift man into the sphere of the purely daemonic.[126] Should we say, then, that the figure of the shepherd is an image of the overman? Though many commentators have been tempted to do just that, my inclination here is to demur. To be sure, the shepherd has *changed*; he has, in fact, experienced a metamorphosis that recalls Zarathustra's speech on the three metamorphoses (Zarathustra uses *Verwandelter* to characterize the shepherd as "one changed," and so explicitly echoes his use of *Verwandlungen* in the title of the first speech of Part 1). But which metamorphosis has the shepherd experienced? To insist that the shepherd is an overman is to imply that he has become the creator and child who overcomes man by creating beyond himself.[127] As I have been arguing, however, the shepherd can be more plausibly interpreted as a lion-figure who, reminiscent of the lion of "On the Three Metamorphoses," speaks a "biting" *no* to the serpent–spirit of gravity who has made him into a burden-bearing camel.[128] Appearing as a *sublime* and Siegfried-like hero, the shepherd has yet to become a beautiful overhero and overman.[129] He is a laughing and sublime lion, but not yet a creator of new values.[130]

What sense can be made, then, of the claim that the laughing shepherd is no longer human? The answer to this query, I believe, is that the shepherd, by willing backwards and enjoying the sublimity of a perpetual "now," relinquishes his tie to "man." By willing backwards, the lion-spirited shepherd denies the existence of the human past (and, indeed, the existence of the past per se). Thus, he denies that there exist any passions linking that past to the present (again, in denying the existence of the human past, he denies the existence of any passions exemplifying kinds of passion that, despite the ravages of asceticism, have persisted in the past *and* in the present in claiming and shaping human existence). By willing backwards and enacting the "script" of redemption3, the shepherd obliterates the possibility of redemption1: through the very act of will with which he denies the existence of the human past and asserts that the future need not perpetuate Christian-Platonic values, he also denies that there exist passions connecting him to the human past, passions he would require to redeem that past through the creation of new values. The shepherd illustrates the paradoxical character of redemption3. He is "no longer human," because, to invoke Schiller again, his embrace of a sublime and perpetual "now" necessitates that he "omit" (*versäumen*) from his existence his ties to human history.[131]

Zarathustra alludes to this omission, and to the paradox of willing backwards, in a speech entitled "On Human Prudence":

> Not the height but the precipice is terrible. That precipice where the glance plunges *down* and the hand reaches *up*. There the heart become giddy confronted with its double will. Alas, friends, can you guess what is my heart's double will?
>
> This, this is *my* precipice and my danger, that my glance plunges into the height and that my hand would grasp and hold on to the depth. My will clings to man; with fetters [*Ketten*] I bind myself to man because I am swept up toward the overman; for that way my other will wants to go. And therefore I live blind among men as if I did not know them, that my hand not wholly lose its faith in what is firm.
>
> I do not know you men: this darkness and consolation are often spread around me. I sit at the gateway [*Thorwege*], exposed to every rogue, and I ask: who wants to deceive me? That is the first instance of my human prudence [*Menschen-Klugheit*], that I let myself be deceived in order not to be on guard against deceivers. Alas, if I were on guard against men, how could man then be an anchor for my ball?[132]

Zarathustra's precipice and danger is that his will to overcome man will cause him to let go of his connection to man (to lose his faith in what is firm). But why does Zarathustra show concern here? Shouldn't he expect that overcoming man will be a matter of breaking his ties to man? Zarathustra hints at an answer to these questions when, by depicting man as an anchor for his "ball," he revisits a metaphor he previously used to describe the goal of overcoming man: "Verily, Zarathustra had a goal: he threw his ball: now you, my friends, are the heirs of my goal; to you I throw my golden ball."[133] Zarathustra needs man to anchor his ball—that is, to anchor his effort to overcome man—for to overcome man is to trans-form man. Overcoming man is *not* a matter of creating a being bearing no tie to man, but of revaluing modes of passion that, historically, have claimed human lives. In "On Human Prudence," in the aftermath of his discussion (in "On Redemption") of willing backwards, Zarathustra worries that he will have to forsake his tie to human beings and their passions if he is to reaffirm and keep alive his commitment to becoming a new-values creator. He frets that the redemption involved in willing backwards (redemption3), and thus in preserving his belief that man can be overcome, must compromise the very connection to man that creating new values and overcoming man presupposes. The figure of a split and "double" will succinctly but aptly characterizes Zarathustra's dilemma, as well as the paradox it seems to express.

Zarathustra's effort to overcome man has become a self-defeating and therefore *imprudent* enterprise, for it threatens to subvert the attachment to man that Zarathustra's *prudence* (*Klugheit*) knows is essential to redemption1. In "On Involuntary Bliss," which immediately follows "On the Vision and the Riddle," Zarathustra still ponders his predicament. The "children of his hope," he suggests, are future companions and new-values creators *for the sake of whom* he must perfect himself.[134] Zarathustra will perfect himself when he acquires the leonine strength he discerned in the laughing shepherd—a strength he needs to defeat the spirit of gravity and to cope with the abysmal thought that that spirit has spawned in him:

> Alas, abysmal thought . . . when shall I find the strength to hear you burrowing, without trembling any more? . . . Even your silence wants to choke me, you who are so abysmally silent. . . . As yet I have not been strong enough for the final overbearing, prankish beating of the lion. Your gravity [*Schwere*] was always terrible for me; but one day I shall yet find the strength and the lion's voice to summon you. And once I have overcome myself that far, then I also want to overcome himself in what is still greater; and a victory shall seal my perfection [*und ein Sieg soll meiner Vollendung Siegel sein*].[135]

Zarathustra will emerge a victorious lion when, after summoning his abysmal thought, he achieves the even greater perfection of spitting it out and repudiating it. For the sake of his children—or, more exactly, for the sake of his hope for children—Zarathustra must achieve this perfection, for without it he will despair at the possibility of finding the progeny he seeks (without performing the second metamorphosis of the spirit, he will despair at the possibility of finding companions who can create new values). Notice, however, that Zarathustra's love for this possibility compels him to resist the call to a leonine confrontation with his abysmal thought: "The wind blew through my keyhole and said, 'Come!' Cunningly, the door flew open and said to me, 'Go!' But I lay there fettered [*angekettet*] to the love for my children."[136] Echoing his earlier suggestion that his prudence bid him fetter himself to man as his anchor, Zarathustra now suggests that he has heeded his prudence by binding himself to a love that is his passion for the possibility of finding children/creators.[137] If Zarathustra resists the call to summon and repudiate his abysmal thought, it is because it calls him *away* from a possibility his prudence endorses, even as it calls him *toward* the perfection he requires if he is not to despair at that possibility. Explicitly characterizing his situation as paradoxical and self-defeating, Zarathustra says, "I am in the middle of my work, going to my children and turning from them [*zu meinen Kindern gehend und von ihnen kehrend*]."[138]

Cleverly recalling the portrait of Wotan in the third part of Wagner's *Ring* cycle (*Siegfried*), Nietzsche begins Part 3 of *Zarathustra* by dubbing Zarathustra "The Wanderer" (*Der Wanderer*). In the third part of the *Ring*, Wotan appears as a wanderer—indeed, he too is called *Der Wanderer*—who foresees the advent of Siegfried, the fearless hero who will retrieve the ring of the Nibelung.[139] Like Wotan, Zarathustra anticipates the appearance of a hero; unlike Wotan, he is himself the hero he anticipates: "Only now are you going your way to greatness! Peak and abyss—they are now joined together. . . . You are going your way to greatness: now this must give you the greatest courage that there is no longer any path behind you."[140] The courage that will bring heroic greatness to Zarathustra will be a courage that defeats his pitying sense that his circumstances justify him in believing he should renounce life. As we have seen, Zarathustra's counsel to the shepherd is an interpretation of Zarathustra's dream that prefigures Zarathustra's acquisition of this courage. Zarathustra's counsel also intimates that Zarathustra, out of the "deepest depth" and abyss of a pitying and pessimistic reading of his dream, will leap to his highest peak and height: that is, to the sublime height figured by the Siegfried-like shepherd who bites off the serpent's head.[141] Still, the aim of Zarathustra's wandering in Part 3 is not simply to become the courageous and sublime hero of whom he dreams. More ambitiously, he aspires to become a hero who, despite his heroism and sublimity, has not cut off his connection to man. Putting the point just a little differently, the ultimate goal of Zarathustra's wandering is to "solve" the paradox of his "double will":

When Zarathustra was on land again he did not proceed straight to his mountain and his cave, but he undertook many ways and questions and found out this or that; so that he said to himself, joking: "Behold a river that flows, winding and twisting, back to its source [*der in veilen Windungen zurück zur Quelle fliesst*]." For he wanted to determine what had happened to man meanwhile: whether he had become greater or smaller.[142]

Here, Zarathustra uses the metaphor of a spiraling, serpentine river, circling back to its source, to represent his wandering journey home in Part 3. Recalling the prologue's eagle-borne serpent more than the snake who crawls into the shepherd's throat, this metaphor seems explicitly to connect the circular image of the ouroboros to the Neoplatonic idea of an epistrophic return to one's home and origin. Like the epistrophe that concludes the prologue (see Chapter 2), Zarathustra's return home will entail his recuperation of the Dionysian superfluity that marks him as a heroic, Promethean Dionysus-Zagreus. In the prologue, Zarathustra ties the figure of the ouroboros to his prudence. Thus, by invoking that figure in Part 3, he suggests that the central aim of his journey home is to cultivate his prudence. Because Zarathustra connects his return home to his interest in man (Zarathustra wants to know what has happened to man), he suggests too that the prudence he hopes to cultivate is the *human* prudence that instructs him to retain his connection to man (to fetter himself to man). In journeying home, then, Zarathustra will strive not only to become a heroic, shepherdlike Dionysus-Zagreus, but also to combine his heroism with a prudential attachment to man that his heroism would otherwise obliterate.[143]

In an important speech that he gives after he arrives home, Zarathustra proclaims that "there are many ways of overcoming. . . . But only a jester thinks: 'man can also be *over leapt* [*übersprungen werden*].'"[144] Now, it is difficult to read this passage, I think, without considering its connection to Zarathustra's description of the laughing shepherd as having *leapt up* [*sprang empor*], implicitly *over* man (the shepherd, we recall, is "no longer human"). If interpreted in light of the distinction between overcoming and overleaping man, that description seems but only a partial representation of the aims Zarathustra endeavors to fulfill in Part 3. To be sure, Zarathustra in Part 3 intends to fulfill the destiny the shepherd prefigures. As I have been arguing, however, he also intends to cultivate his prudence and to solve the paradox of his "double will." Indeed, he ultimately aims to reconcile the practical postulate that he personifies redemption3 (the postulate that he personifies the act of willing backwards) with the possibility of redemption1. In the closing speeches of Part 3, for example, Zarathustra embraces the postulate that he personifies redemption3, but not without aspiring to acknowledge his ability to go-under.

Aspiring to acknowledge that ability, even as he pictures his will as willing backwards and inhabiting an eternal "now," Zarathustra attempts to remain open to the possibility of becoming a creator of new values. As we shall see, his gesture of openness fails. Still, the gesture is significant, for it shows that Zarathustra, even as he fulfills his destiny and becomes the shepherd of his dream, *resists* the truth that his leap-up-and-over-man contradicts the instruction of his prudence; that is, he resists the truth that his leap expunges his tie to man and to the possibility of overcoming man.

The Lion's Thought of Recurrence II: The Tragedy Ends

In Chapter 2, I defended Nietzsche's view that *Zarathustra* is a tragedy by interpreting Zarathustra, as he initially appears, as a tragic hero. In the remainder of the present chapter, I will show how Zarathustra, by performing the second act of the thought-drama of recurrence, and thus by realizing the future he foresees in "On the Vision and the Riddle," fulfills his role as a tragic hero and makes *Zarathustra*, Parts 1–3, into a non-Schopenhauerian tragic drama.[145]

Recognizing in the prologue that he is implicated in the ending of the tightrope walker's tragedy—recognizing, that is, that his descent threatens to leave human beings suffering the experience of meaninglessness—Zarathustra struggles to see his way beyond the Schopenhauerian spirit of resignation that haunts the tightrope walker's demise. Thus, in the final sections of the prologue, Zarathustra renews his commitment to finding individuals who can go-under and overcome themselves. As we have seen, the soothsayer's prophecy—that such individuals will soon cease to exist—compels Zarathustra to confront the spirit of resignation once again. By formulating a second practical postulate that defeats that spirit, and by attempting to reconcile that postulate with the possibility of redemption1, Zarathustra, in Part 3, brings *his* tragedy to a non-Schopenhauerian conclusion.

References to numerous mythical and literary personae animate Nietzsche's portrait of Zarathustra as a tragic hero. Examples include allusions to Laius, Theseus, and Zagreus; Wotan and Siegfried as they appear in Wagner's *Ring*; Christ as Paul depicts him in his letter to the Philippians; and, perhaps, Byron's Manfred.[146] Still, the central figure in the depiction of Zarathustra's tragic heroism is *Prometheus*.

Appearing in the prologue as a self-spending fire bringer, whose "fire" and "gift" is his Dionysian vision of the overman, Zarathustra begins his tragedy, not by defying Zeus, but by defying the legacy of the "dead" Christian God.[147] Like Aeschylus's Prometheus, Zarathustra affirms the worth of human existence, insisting that man can serve the purpose of overcoming man.[148] As we have seen, the soothsayer challenges Zarathustra's affirmation from within the perspective of Zarathustra's post-Christian-Platonic interpretation of human existence. As we have also seen, Zarathustra responds to that challenge by imagining that, again, like Aeschylus's Prometheus, he has been "bound" for his defiant action. In Zarathustra's fantasy of inexpressiveness, the punishment for his sacrilegious (anti-Christian) attempt to dissolve the rift between Dionysus and man is the torture of being eternally chained to the endless perpetuation of the small and last man's meaningless existence. Refusing to accept that this rift marks an ir- revocable contradiction between the divine (the Dionysian) and the human, Zarathustra—in his fantasy, like Prometheus as Nietzsche depicts him in *The Birth of Tragedy*—suffers horribly for his defiance.[149]

Zarathustra again echoes *The Birth of Tragedy*'s portrait of Prometheus by ty- ing the "binding" of Zarathustra to the perpetuation of a mode of life—the small and last man's mode of life—from which Dionysus has been banished. It will be recalled, in this connection, that the title page of *The Birth of Tragedy*, to which Nietzsche refers in his "Preface to Richard Wagner," originally showed a vignette by the sculptor Rau exhibiting a defiant Prometheus just liberated by Hercules from his torture and his chains.[150] A figure for the possibility of trans- forming a culture that had bound in exile its Dionysian energies, Rau's image of Prometheus *unbound* was also supposed to symbolize the release of those ener- gies by the Herculean power of German music:

> If . . . we have rightly associated the disappearance of the Dionysian spirit with
> a . . . degeneration of the Hellenic man—what hopes must revive in us when
> the most certain auspices guarantee *the reverse process, the gradual awakening
> of the Dionysian* spirit in our modern world! It is impossible that the divine
> strength of Herakles should languish forever in ample bondage to Omphale.
> Out of the Dionysian root of the German spirit a power has arisen. . . .
> *German music* as we must understand it, particularly in its vast solar orbit
> from Bach to Beethoven, from Beethoven to Wagner.[151]

As I noted in Chapter 3, *The Birth of Tragedy* sees in Wagner's music the culmi- nation of a musical tradition expressing the Dionysian essence of the German nation. With the rise of Socratism·and the degeneration of Hellenic man, Dio- nysus was banished from the world of European humanity. Put in terms of the Prometheus myth, he was chained to a rock at the "world's limit," leaving So- cratic man—who, significantly, prefigures the figure of the small and last man (see the introduction to this volume)—to rule the world.[152] Where Socratic man persists and perpetuates a mode of life from which Dionysus has been banished,

Prometheus-Dionysus will remain *bound*. Where the Herculean power of German music announces itself, he will appear *unbound*, striding "boldly and freely before the eyes of all nations" and returning Dionysus to a world that seems otherwise to have forgotten him.[153]

The Birth of Tragedy only hints at a conception of Prometheus's effort to cope with the punishment he suffers as he awaits the appearance of Hercules. In Aeschylus's version of Prometheus's story, as Nietzsche analyzes it, the Titan delights in his "ability to create," for which he atones with eternal suffering. Yet this suffering is a "slight price" that Prometheus's creative ability more than makes good.[154] Here, Nietzsche's point seems to be that Aeschylus's Prometheus, even after Zeus has bound him and dispatched a vulture to torture him, finds joy in his capacity for artistic creation.[155] In order to evoke the spirit of that joy, Nietzsche refers his reader not to Aeschylus, but, oddly, to Goethe:

Here I sit [*Hier sitz Ich*], forming men
in my own image,
a race to be like me,
to suffer, to weep,
to delight and rejoice,
and to defy you,
as I do.[156]

For Nietzsche, the concluding stanza of Goethe's "Prometheus" finds a basis for endorsing life in the formative power of the artist. To be sure, Goethe invites this reading of his poem's final lines by penning a penultimate stanza that confronts the view that renunciation is the proper response to suffering:

Did you fancy perchance
that I should hate life
and fly to the desert
because not all
my blossom dreams ripened?[157]

Staving off the Schopenhauerian wisdom that sees misfortune and reason for renunciation everywhere, Goethe's Prometheus, as Nietzsche interprets him, vanquishes the spirit of resignation by affirming his ability to create.

In Parts 3 and 4, Zarathustra learns to cope with his punishment while awaiting the arrival of his "children"—that is, while awaiting the creators and "new philosophers" in whose company he will leave his home and go-under one final time. The advent of Zarathustra's children—"the children of his hope" in "On Involuntary Bliss"—seems imminent at the conclusion of Part 4 and promises to play a liberating role analogous to that played by the Herculean power of

German music in *The Birth of Tragedy*. Presumably, the advent of Zarathustra's children would be the appearance of individuals who could go-under and over-come themselves: that is, the appearance of individuals in whom the passions and the possibility of experiencing passional chaos had been reborn (they would be individuals of a sort that disappeared from the world during the "long twi-light" the soothsayer foresees). Zarathustra's children's arrival would signal the "liberation" of Zarathustra-Prometheus, for it would show that Zarathustra-Prometheus could now return Dionysus to a world that had forgotten him: or, again, that he could now close the rift between Dionysus and man by poetically inspiring *some* individuals to "see" within their bodies the possibility of going-under and creating new values.[158] But what of Zarathustra before his children arrive? How does he cope with the resignation-inducing punishment of being bound eternally to the small man, and cope in a way that permits him to believe that he is awaiting the arrival of human beings in whom the rift between Dio-nysus and man can finally be dissolved? When Zarathustra leaves his home with his children, he will have abandoned his Promethean (Zagrean) experience of Dionysus in order to fulfill his personal and poetic intentions. But how, in the meantime, does he live? How does he endure the exile of the coming god be-yond the bounds of possible experience in the age of the last man?

At first blush, the answer to this question is uncomplicated: like Goethe's Prometheus, Zarathustra affirms his ability to create. To be sure, a more discern-ing answer is that Zarathustra embraces the practical postulate that he personi-fies redemption3. Zarathustra embraces that postulate because, with redemption1 a dubious possibility, he realizes he has no choice if he is to avoid interpreting life in the perspective of spiritualized revenge. By supposing that he is willing back-wards, Zarathustra defiantly denies that the future must endlessly perpetuate Christian-Platonic values. Thus, in the manner of the lion-spirit, he asserts that he is free and able to create new values (*qua lion*, of course, he *cannot* create new values).[159] Zarathustra resembles Goethe's Prometheus, in other words, because by asserting his (putative) freedom and ability to create values he defeats the spirit of resignation.

By linking Zarathustra to Prometheus, I can finally address a question I posed near the end of Chapter 2: Why, I asked, does Nietzsche use the figure of Dionysus to conceptualize the heroic, lion-spirited posture that Zarathustra op-poses to representations of repetition? The answer, I think, is that Nietzsche wants the Promethean lion to symbolize new-values creation as a possibility that still can be realized despite the subversive, skeptical voices that appear to exclude it. In depicting the defiant, Promethean lion, Nietzsche pictures the Dionysian chaos essential to realizing that possibility as a superabundantly available resource that is a potential though not yet actual source of new values (a source that has still to show itself for what it is). Put a bit differently, he pictures the creation-prompting coming Dionysus as a Zagrean Dionysus: that is, as a Dionysus who can but has not yet realized his power to "come" and incite the creation of new values. When Nietzsche depicts Zarathustra in the image of Goethe's Prometheus, he again pictures the coming Dionysus in this way. Conjecturing that modern asceticism has banished (or will soon banish) from human life the possibility of experiencing the chaos of the coming god, he nonetheless thinks, or imagines, that possibility as an option that may yet be *returned* to human life and still be realized. Like Aeschylus and Sophocles, who illustrated their thinking by means of myth,[160] Nietzsche illustrates his thinking by picturing Zarathustra as a Promethean, Zagrean Dionysus.

As we have seen, it is paradoxical that Zarathustra personifies redemption3. Prior to the appearance of his "Herculean" children, Zarathustra can endure the banishment of the possibility of experiencing passional chaos from the modern world, for he supposes that, in willing backwards, he denies that the future will be tyrannized by Christian-Platonic values. Were he willing backwards, however, Zarathustra would also blot out the future, and thus reduce to nonsense the idea of children/creators who could redeem the human past (again, willing backwards directs Zarathustra both to and away from the children he desires). By striving in Part 3 to solve the paradox of his "double will"—by striving, that is, to reconcile the possibility of redemption1 and the practical postulate that he personifies redemption3—Zarathustra struggles to become a lion who does not estrange himself from his ability to go-under when he affirms his freedom to create. Consistent with Nietzsche's reading of the Prometheus myth, he aspires yet again to abolish the contradiction between the divine and the human. Zarathustra pursued this aim at the beginning of *Zarathustra*, by attempting through his descent to bring Dionysus to man. In Part 3, Zarathustra pursues the same aim, but by attempting to remain connected to man, even when he (Zarathustra) embodies the Dionysian (Zagrean), heroic, sublimity associated with redemption3. Without descending to man, Zarathustra strives to realize *in his own person* a Promethean "universality" that cancels the division between the Dionysian and the human.[161] In this way, he brings his tragedy to a non-Schopenhauerian conclusion (the closing sections of Part 3) that leaves him still awaiting the advent of his children.

In what follows, I sketch a reconstruction of the path by which Zarathustra brings his tragedy to an end. Beginning with a brief treatment of "Before Sunrise," I then proceed to consider the five speeches that directly follow "Before Sunrise." I subsequently discuss the speeches that Zarathustra delivers after he arrives home, but before he summons his abysmal thought: "On the Three Evils," "On the Spirit of Gravity," and "On Old and New Tablets." I conclude with an interpretation of the final four sections of Part 3, focusing in particular on redemption3 and on the fate of Zarathustra's effort to reconcile the practical postulate that he personifies redemption3 with the possibility of redemption1.

In "Before Sunrise," in the wake of Zarathustra's proclamation (in "On Involuntary Bliss") that he lacks the lion's voice for summoning and repudiating his abysmal thought, he reasserts that he aspires to the leonine sublimity he envisioned in "On the Vision and the Riddle":

> O heaven [*Himmel*] above me, pure and deep! You abyss of light! Seeing you, I shudder [*schaudere*] with godlike desires. To throw myself into your height, that is *my* depth. To hide in your purity, that is *my* innocence.
>
>   Gods are shrouded by their beauty; thus you conceal your stars. . . . That you came to me, beautiful, shrouded in your beauty, that you speak to me silently, revealing your wisdom—oh, how should I not guess all that is shy in your soul. . . .
>
>   And when I wandered alone, for *whom* did my soul hunger at night, on false paths? And when I climbed mountains, *whom* did I always seek on the mountains, if not you? And all my wandering and mountain climbing were sheer necessity and a help in my helplessness: what I want with all my will is to *fly*, to fly up into *you*.[162]

Recalling his earlier discussion of the sublime and the beautiful, Zarathustra sees in the luminous sky, appearing just before sunrise, a sublime height that, having become "gracious" and descended "into the visible," seduces him with a beauty that makes him "shudder [*schaudere*] with godlike desires."[163] Invoking the figure of flight, which he uses to express the lion-spirit's antipathy to the spirit of gravity as early as the speech "On Reading and Writing," Zarathustra remarks that he aspires to fly up into the sky's height to make *its* sublimity his own. It is evident, however, that Zarathustra has not yet acquired the leonine strength he needs to be the self-determining cause of his own sublimity and to defeat the spirit of gravity in the aftermath of the soothsayer's prophecy.

To be sure, Zarathustra can envision himself as sublime, but he cannot imagine that he could be *sufficient unto himself* in realizing the sublimity he envisions. Wishing to fly into a sky that *transcends* him, Zarathustra requires the fiction of a sublime height, present *apart* from his will, to imagine himself achieving the sublimity he will achieve by conquering his abysmal thought. Reverting to a version of the disclosive conception of the sublime (see Chapter 4), he holds that, to achieve this sublimity, he must put himself in touch with a reality—in this case, the sky—that he has found to exist independently of his will: "If only you are about me, pure and light, you abyss of light, then into all abysses I still carry the blessings of my saying-yes."[164] By the end of Part 3, Zarathustra has again rejected the disclosive conception of the sublime, having initially rejected it in "On Those Who Are Sublime" (see Chapter 4). Indeed, in the final speech of Part 3, he transfigures the figure of the sky, making it into a metaphor for a sublimity that is wholly the artifact of his will:

> If ever I spread tranquil skies over myself and soared on my own wings into my own skies [*Wenn ich je stille Himmel über mir auspannte und mit eignen Flügeln in eigne Himmel flog*]; if I swam playfully in the deep light-distances. . . . Are not all words made for the grave and heavy [*die Schweren*]? Are not all words lies to those who are light? Sing! Speak no more![165]

Relying no longer on the figure of a sublime sky that exists apart from his will and shrouds itself in beauty, the Zarathustra who sings at the close of Part 3 has created (over himself) and identified as "his own" the sublime and gravity-defeating skies across which he flies. Zarathustra begins to reveal *his* beauty, we shall see, only at the end of Part 4.[166]

The sequence of five speeches that immediately follows "Before Sunrise" narrates the paradox of Zarathustra's "double will": going to his children and turning from them, or going to man and turning from him, the Zarathustra who appears in these speeches, while gathering courage for the lion's sublime "I will," journeys alternately toward and away from other human beings.[167]

Consider, for example, "On Virtue That Makes Small" and "Upon the Mount of Olives." In the former, Zarathustra recounts his discovery that, during his visit to the blessed isles, man became smaller and smaller. Expressing dismay at the doctrines of virtue that have promoted man's decrease, and that have led to the exhaustion of the earth prophesied by the soothsayer ("Hourly they are becoming smaller, poor, more sterile—poor herbs! poor soil! and *soon* they shall stand there like dry grass and prairie—and verily, weary of themselves and languishing even more than for water—for *fire*"), he still invokes the figure of the great noon to reassert his hope that man will be overcome.[168] Although the smallness of the small and last man seems to pervade human life, Zarathustra is drawn to the leonine belief that man's future need not perpetuate his Christian-Platonic past. Notice, however, that he pays *no heed* to man's future in "Upon the Mount of Olives," where, in contrast to the prophet who still speaks hopefully of the great noon, the figure we hear stresses his desire for privacy and self-concealment—his desire, in other words, to distance himself from man: "Loneliness can be the escape of the sick, loneliness can also be escape *from* the sick."[169] In "Upon the Mount of Olives," Zarathustra turns from man to hide himself from man: "That no one may discern my ground and ultimate will, for that I have invented my long bright silence."[170]

In "On Passing By" and "On Apostates," Zarathustra goes again to man, only to be disappointed by what he finds. In "On Passing By," he discovers "a fool" called "Zarathustra's ape," a fellow who speaks the letter but not the spirit of Zarathustra's teaching. Perceiving in his "ape" a person driven by revenge, Zarathustra tells him that "even if Zarathustra's words *were* a thousand times right, still *you* would always *do* wrong with my words."[171] In "On Apostates," Zarathustra meets some disciples who once believed in him, but who have since "become pious again."[172] "To these believers," he warns, "whoever is of my kind among men should not tie his heart; those who know the changeful, cowardly nature of mankind should not believe in these springtimes and colorful meadows."[173]

Zarathustra's disillusioning contacts with his fellow human beings lead him again to turn from man. In "The Return Home," in fact, he chides himself for showing man too much consideration, alluding in this context to "On Human Prudence," the speech in which he first describes his "double will."[174] When he arrives home, Zarathustra seems not to have cultivated his human prudence; on the contrary, he has repudiated entirely his connection to man:

> Down there . . . all speech is in vain. There forgetting and passing by are the best wisdom: *that* I have learned now. . . . With happy nostrils I again breathe mountain freedom. At last my nose is redeemed [*erlöst*] from the smell of everything human. Tickled by the sharp air as by sparkling wines, my soul sneezes [*niest*]—sneezes and jubilates to itself: *Gesundheit!*[175]

Appearing to disavow public speech and to delight in a mode of redemption that "omits" his bond to humanity, the Zarathustra who repairs to his high mountain home embraces the pose of haughty sublimity, *turning up his nose* at all that is human.[176]

At this juncture, it is important to note that Zarathustra sees the sublimity he seeks as but a single perspective, a point of view that he could set aside in order to "go to man" again. As we shall see, Zarathustra will not literally go to man again before the ending of Part 4. After completing the trek home described in the five speeches that directly follow "Before Sunrise," he comes to a rest and ceases to journey *either* toward man or away from him. Still, the paradox of Zarathustra's "double will" continues to show itself: it is evident, for example, in the tension between (1) Zarathustra's expressed willingness in "On the Three Evils" to suspend his quest for a sublime, leonine self-sufficiency in order to attend to man, and (2) his resumption of that quest in his very next speech, "On the Spirit of Gravity."

> Measurable by him who has time, weighable by a good weigher, reachable by strong wings, guessable by divine nutcrackers: thus my dream found the world—my dream . . . how did it have the patience or the time to weigh the world? Did my wisdom secretly urge it, my laughing wide-awake day-wisdom which mocks all "infinite worlds" [*unendliche Welten*]? For it speaks: "Wherever there is force, *number* will become mistress: she has more force."
>
> How surely my dream looked upon this finite world [*endliche Welt*] . . . not riddle enough to frighten away human love, not solution enough to put to sleep human wisdom: a humanly good thing the world was to me today though one speaks so much evil of it.[177]

Here, in "On the Three Evils," Zarathustra alludes to "Before Sunrise" and calls to mind Kant's concept of the mathematical sublime.[178] In "Before Sunrise," Zarathustra described as unbounded (*unbegrenzte*) the sublime sky into which he wished to fly at dawn. In effect, he envisioned that sky as an "infinite world" from which he would have to depart once the sun arose. In "On the Three Evils," Zarathustra presses his point, suggesting that his "sunrise-" or "day-" wisdom will never appreciate the sky's unbounded infinity. Now, according to Kant's discussion of the mathematical sublime, the imagination cannot comprehend the infinite expanses that sublime reason insists it comprehend.[179] Similarly, Zarathustra's day-wisdom cannot measure and would even mock the unbounded sky, his before-sunrise wisdom notwithstanding ("you and I have in common—the uncanny, unbounded Yes and Amen," we hear in "Before Sunrise"). Like the imagination as Kant understands it, Zarathustra's day-wisdom is bound essentially to the comprehension of finite quantities. In "On the Three Evils," Zarathustra speaks from the perspective of his day-wisdom, and so defers the quest for the sublime that shaped his outlook in "The Return Home." In suspending this quest, moreover, he directs his attention to man.

Attending to man, Zarathustra aspires to "weigh humanly well" (*menschlich gut abwägen*) sex, the lust to rule, and selfishness; more exactly, he hopes to determine anew the worth of these "best cursed" phenomena ("he that taught to bless also taught to curse") from a specifically *human* point of view.[180] Having stayed his quest for the sublime, Zarathustra now focuses his comments on the pertinence of these phenomena to man's capacity for self-transformation. In evaluating sex, for example, he sees a promising parable of his "highest hope" that human beings go-under and overcome themselves.[181] Similarly, in evaluating selfishness and the lust to rule, and in thus expanding his earlier analysis of the gift-giving virtue, Zarathustra alludes to the human capacity to create new virtues by transforming the self and body:

> "Gift-giving virtue"—thus Zarathustra once named the unnameable.
>
> And at that time it also happened . . . that his word pronounced *selfishness* blessed, the wholesome healthy selfishness that wells from a powerful soul— from a powerful soul to which belongs the high body, beautiful, triumphant, refreshing, around which everything becomes a mirror—the supple, persuasive body, the dancer whose parable and epitome is the self-enjoying soul. The self-enjoyment of such bodies and souls calls itself "virtue."[182]

Zarathustra knows that embodying the selfishness and the beauty of the gift-giving virtue would require that he sacrifice his vision of himself as sublime: "that the lonely heights should not remain lonely and self-sufficient eternally; that the mountain should descend to the valley and the winds of the height to the low plains—oh, who were to find the right name for such longing?"[183] Zarathustra could embrace the possibility of redeeming man's past and overcoming man only if he lets go the pose of sublimity he adopts in "The Return Home." To embrace that possibility, he reminds us, would be to anticipate the advent of the great noon: "And whoever proclaims the ego wholesome and holy, and selfishness blessed, verily, he will also tell us what he knows, foretelling: 'Verily, it is at hand, it is near, the great noon!'"[184]

Knowing that the advent of the great noon is *not yet* imminent, Zarathustra rekindles the voice of lonely solitude in "On the Spirit of Gravity." Again echoing "On Reading and Writing," he uses the figure of flight in this speech ("He who will one day teach men to fly . . .") to resume his pursuit of a sublime, leonine self-sufficiency.[185] "One must learn to love oneself," Zarathustra insistently proclaims, "so that one can bear to be with oneself and need not roam. Such roaming baptizes itself 'love of the neighbor.'"[186] Recalling his disappointment that in going to man he met his frothing ape, Zarathustra declines now "to reside and abide where everybody spits and spews": that, he remarks, "happens to be *my* taste."[187] Zarathustra's talk here of *his* taste is fundamental to his desire to pronounce the lion-spirit's "*I* will," for it is precisely his prerogative of taste— namely, his right to estimate and to create a *new* "good and evil"—that Zarathustra wishes to oppose to the spirit of gravity's taste-leveling edict, "good for all, evil for all."[188]

In "On the Three Evils" and "On the Spirit of Gravity," the paradox of Zarathustra's "double will" no longer appears as the subject of a narrative describing Zarathustra's goings-to and turnings-from his children (which is how it appears in the five-speech sequence following "Before Sunrise"). Rather it comes to light through a juxtaposition of two voices, each of which articulates a distinct view of the situation facing Zarathustra when he returns home. Zarathustra extends his double-voiced meditation on his situation in "On Old and New Tablets," a speech whose finale and high point is the *fusion* of the voice of lonely, leonine sublimity with that of the human longing to redeem man's past. By synthesizing these two voices, Zarathustra will vividly depict himself as an ecstatic, Dionysus-Zagreus, ready to spend and sacrifice his superabundant divinity.

The first section of "On Old and New Tablets" reads as follows:

> Here I sit [*Hier sitze Ich*] and wait, surrounded by broken old tablets and new tablets half covered with writing. When will my hour come? The hour of my going down and going under; for I want to go among men once more. For that I am waiting now, for first the signs must come to me that *my* hour has come: the laughing lion and the flock of doves. Meanwhile I talk to myself as one who has time. Nobody tells me anything new, so I tell myself—myself.[189]

By explicitly repeating the first three words of the final stanza of Goethe's "Prometheus"—"Here I sit"—Zarathustra reminds us that, like Goethe's hero, he will defeat the spirit of resignation by affirming his power to create. For Zarathustra, affirming this power will ultimately involve an effort to reconcile the possibility of redemption1 with the practical postulate that he personifies redemption3—or so I have argued. As he speaks, however, Zarathustra creates nothing. Where Goethe's Prometheus defiantly creates (forms) men, even as he sits, Zarathustra has deferred his creative action (his going among men with "new tablets" of values) to an unspecified time in the future ("my hour") that he presently awaits. Zarathustra will become a creator of new values when he apprehends signs—a laughing lion and a flock of doves, which appear at the end of Part 4—that call him beyond himself (beyond the self that tells "itself—itself") to the creation of a new self.

Zarathustra thematizes both redemption3 and redemption1 in the third section of "On Old and New Tablets:"

> There it was too that I picked up the word "overman" by the way, and that man is something that must be overcome—that man is a bridge and no end: proclaiming himself blessed in view of his noon and evening, as the way to new dawns—Zarathustra's word of the great noon, and whatever else I hung up over man like the last crimson light of evening.
>
> Verily, I also let them see new stars along with new nights; and over clouds and day and night I still spread out laughter as a colorful tent.
>
> I taught them all *my* creating and striving, to create and carry into One what in man is fragment and riddle and dreadful accident; as creator, guesser

of riddles, and redeemer of accidents, I taught them to work on the future and to redeem with their creation all that *has been*. To redeem what is past in man and to re-create all "it was" until the will says, "Thus I willed it! Thus I shall will it!"—this I called redemption and this alone I taught them to call redemption [*Erlösung*].

Now I wait for my own redemption [*meiner Erlösung*]—that I may go to them for the last time [*dass Ich zum letzten Male zu ihnen gehe*]. For I want to go to men once more; under their eyes I want to go under: dying I want to give them my richest gift. From the sun I learned this: when he goes down, overrich; he pours gold into the sea out of inexhaustible riches, so that even the poorest fisherman still rows with golden oars. For this I once saw and did not tire of my tears as I watched it.

Like the sun, Zarathustra too wants to go under; now he sits here and waits, surrounded by broken old tablets and new tablets half covered with writing.[190]

In this speech, Zarathustra relates his present circumstances to a past he remembers and a future he anticipates. Recounting the past, Zarathustra refers in particular to his speeches on the overman. Moreover, with his allusions to "noon," "evening," and "the way to new dawns," he recalls his promise, near the end of Part 1, to return to his disciples to celebrate the "great noon," the "way to the evening as [man's] highest hope," and the "new morning" of man's overcoming.[191] For Zarathustra, striving to overcome man ("all *my* creating and striving") is "work[ing] on the future" to redeem the past; it is struggling to create new values and to effect what I have called redemption1. When Zarathustra leaves his home to go to men a third and final time, he will repudiate and "let die" his superabundant and Zagrean experience of Dionysus in order to recall men to the possibility of going-under and overcoming themselves ("dying I want to give them my richest gift"). Comparing himself to the sun (as in his first speech), he expects that *this time*, when he goes to men, he will find *some* individuals—his children—in whom the ability to experience passional chaos and to redeem the past has been reborn. Whereas section 3 of "On Old and New Tablets" begins with Zarathustra recalling his past commitment to the project of overcoming man, it ends with his expressed anticipation of a time when he will descend to man and see his poetic and personal intentions fulfilled.

In the meantime, Zarathustra waits—but for what? "On Old and New Tablets" answers this query by alluding to the signs that appear at the end of Part 4, tokens that the time has come for Zarathustra to go to men again. For Zarathustra, I have argued, this time is the time for the redemption of the human past (and for overcoming man). Notice, however, that the time for Zarathustra to go to men again is not the only time for redemption that Zarathustra awaits in "On Old and New Tablets." Additionally, he awaits the time for *his own* redemption: "Now I wait for my own redemption—that I may go to them for the last time." Zarathustra will be redeemed before he goes to men again, for *his* redemption is essential to his feeling motivated to go to men again.

In anticipating his redemption, Zarathustra prefigures not the ending of Part 4, but the final four speeches of Part 3. In the first of these speeches, "The Convalescent," Zarathustra refers explicitly to his redemption while recuperating from his tussle with his abysmal thought: "But now I lie here, still weary of this biting and spewing, still sick from my own redemption [*der eigenen Erlösung*]."[192] As distinct from redemption1—again, the value-creating redemption of the human past to which Zarathustra has been persistently committed—Zarathustra's redemption, his *self-redemption*, is redemption3, his redemption of his will, through the act of willing backwards, which act (in "The Convalescent") he postulates he personifies. Unless Zarathustra effects his self-redemption, and thereby summons and repudiates his abysmal thought, he cannot feel motivated to go to men, for to feel so motivated he must renew his faith that the past can be redeemed and man overcome. As we shall see, Zarathustra's second practical postulate enables him to renew this faith, because it tells him how to teach his will to will backwards.

Zarathustra's waiting in "On Old and New Tablets" is bi-telic: it has two ends, the first of which is Zarathustra's leonine metamorphosis into the laughing shepherd of his dream. As Zarathustra puts it in "On the Spirit of Gravity," he is awaiting *himself*, which is just to say that he is waiting *for* himself to effect his self-redemption.[193] The second end of Zarathustra's waiting is the redemption of the human past, an aim he is about to realize at the close of Part 4, having realized his first end in "The Convalescent." In the two speeches following "The Convalescent," Zarathustra strives to reconcile his self-redemption with his hopes for redeeming the human past. In effect, he tries to open himself to the possibility of redeeming the human past even as he embraces the postulate that he personifies the act of willing backwards. Because the possibility of redeeming the human past begins to be fulfilled only at the end of Part 4, Zarathustra still awaits its fulfillment through most of Part 4. His waiting persists in Part 4, but as a uni-telic phenomenon.

In "On Old and New Tablets," Zarathustra's double-voiced speech expresses his bi-telic waiting. Addressing past and future alike, Zarathustra articulates an antagonism toward old tablets and a desire to write new ones. Wishing to resist the perpetuation of the past, he repeatedly foregrounds the leonine posture he associates with willing backwards. Thus, he repudiates the camel's reverence for old tablets (section 10); endorses the rage and the wrath that destroy old tablets (section 8); embraces the lion's "freedom" for new creation (section 9); and praises the lion's "will" to reject the soothsayer's belief that nothing is worthwhile (section 16).[194] Wishing for a future unlike the past, Zarathustra also anticipates the creation of new values. Thus, he stresses his love for the overman (section 24); imagines the advent of the overman as the advent of a past-redeeming "new nobility" (sections 11 and 12); and depicts his "great longing" for the overman as his search for a "children's land" called "man's future" whereupon a new nobility will flourish (sections 12 and 28).[195] Vacillating between the two voices of his double will, Zarathustra both admires the self-redeeming leonine posture he aspires to emulate and looks beyond it to a redemption that will involve overcoming man.

In the final section of "On Old and New Tablets," Zarathustra fuses the two voices of his double will:

> That I may one day be ready and ripe in the great noon: as ready and ripe as glowing bronze, clouds pregnant with lightning, and swelling milk udders— ready for myself and my most hidden will: a bow lusting for its arrow, an arrow lusting for its star—a star ready and ripe in its noon, glowing, pierced, enraptured by annihilating [*vernichtenden*] sun arrows—a sun itself and an inexorable [*unerbittlicher*] solar will, ready for annihilation [*zum Vernichten bereit*] in victory!
>
> O will, cessation of all need, my *own* necessity! Save me for a great victory! Thus Spoke Zarathustra.[196]

Still waiting for himself, Zarathustra hopes one day to be "ready" for himself, and thus ready for the "hidden will" by which he will express himself; he hopes, in other words, to be ready to personify the "solar will" of the lion-spirit, a will whose "inexorable" force he first embraced in his Dionysian night song (cf. my discussion in Chapter 4) and would embrace again to defeat once and for all his abysmal thought. Speaking in the voice of the lion, Zarathustra announces the will of Dionysus-Zagreus, the inexorable bow-and-arrow will of the hunter god. Speaking in the voice of his great longing, he imparts a vision of self-annihilation, picturing his dying as an act of birth-giving that will engender the "lightning" that is the overman.[197] If Zarathustra's leonine voice seems finally indistinguishable from that of his great longing, it is because the former formulates a series of metaphors that depicts Zarathustra equivocally as a lusting arrow *and* as a pregnant ("ready and ripe") star; as a source of annihilating sun arrows *and* as a pierced sun; as an inexorable solar will *and* as a will "ready for annihilation." In short, the voice of the leonine Dionysus-Zagreus depicts the triumph of Zarathustra's (now hidden) will as collateral to an act of ecstatic self-sacrifice whereby

Zarathustra relinquishes his will and spends his superabundance (the "swelling milk udders" that accompany his pregnancy) in order to go to man and recall him to the possibility of overcoming himself.

In the final four speeches of Part 3, Zarathustra elaborates his vision of his will as at once triumphant and disposed to self-annihilation. Put more exactly, he enacts a dramatic rendition of the self-understanding he lyrically expresses when he fuses the two voices of his double will in "On Old and New Tablets." In "The Convalescent," Zarathustra performs the second act of the thought-drama of recurrence by embracing the comforting practical postulate that he personifies redemption3. In "On the Great Longing" and "The Other Dancing Song," he attempts but fails to reconcile this postulate with the possibility of redemption1. In "The Seven Seals," finally, he self-sufficiently proclaims his sublimity.

"The Convalescent" shows Zarathustra in the role of the shepherd of his dreams, summoning and repudiating his abysmal thought.[198] After seven days recuperation, Zarathustra takes an apple in hand and listens to his animals: "Step out of your cave," they say, "the world awaits you like a garden. The wind is playing with heavy fragrances that want to get to you, and all the brooks would run after you."[199] Figured here as Adam in the garden of Eden and as Orpheus stirring inanimate nature to life, the convalescing Zarathustra symbolizes the erasure of the Christian-Platonic past and the promise of a new earth.[200] Having embraced the postulate that he personifies the act of willing backwards, he appears in his animals' eyes as a prelapsarian, original man whose fall from an Orphic Eden into Christian-Platonic asceticism his act of willing backwards has undone.

Zarathustra replies to his animals with a speech about words and sounds that suggests that his connection to nature runs deeper than his animals' have let on: "for me," he proclaims, "how should there be any outside-myself? There is no outside."[201] Having a moment ago remarked that "for every soul, every other soul is an afterworld," Zarathustra now explains that his soul need not acknowledge the reality of other souls and afterworlds, for his soul is the whole of reality, beyond or "outside" which nothing else exists.[202] Zarathustra's animals' next speech expresses their interpretation of his belief that he personifies the whole of what is:

> "O Zarathustra," the animals said, "to those who think as we do, all things themselves are dancing: they come and offer their hands and laugh and flee— and come back. Everything goes, everything comes back; eternally rolls the wheel of being. Everything dies, everything blossoms again; eternally runs the year of being. Everything breaks, everything is joined anew; eternally the same

house of being is built. Everything parts, everything greets every other thing; eternally the ring of being remains faithful to itself. In every Now being begins; round every Here rolls the sphere There. The center is everywhere. Bent is the path of eternity.[203]

Alexander Nehamas is surely right to suggest that part of what Zarathustra's animals articulate here is the Dionysian view that nature's cycles infinitely repeat themselves. He is wrong, however, to claim that the animals express "nothing more" than that view.[204] Additionally, they provide an account of Zarathustra's self-understanding, the accuracy of which Zarathustra acknowledges in his playful reply to his animals' musings: "O you buffoons and barrel organs. . . . How well you know what had to be fulfilled in seven days, and how that monster crawled down my throat and suffocated me. But I bit off its head and spewed it out. And you, have you already made a hurdy-gurdy song [*Leier-Lied*] of this?"[205] Zarathustra's animals' interpretation of his belief that he personifies all of reality, or "being," invokes a metaphor that was originally used to describe the Christian God: namely, the metaphor of the infinite sphere. To be a being for whom there is no "outside," Zarathustra's animals suggest, is to resemble an infinite sphere whose center is everywhere.

The metaphor of the infinite sphere appears for the first time in the twelfth-century, pseudo-Hermetic *Liber XXIV philosophorum*. Describing God as "an infinite sphere, whose center is everywhere, whose circumference nowhere," this text identifies God as the first cause of all things whose creative vision knows no limits and thus no "outside"; the sphere of God's vision, on this account, has no circumference.[206] Furthermore, suggests the *Liber XXIV philosophorum*, God is totally present in all things: he is the omnipresent center of the entire sphere of creation. If Zarathustra's animals are correct, then Zarathustra has envisioned himself in a similar light. To embrace the practical postulate that he personifies redemption3 is, it would seem, to tie the idea of willing backwards to a picture of himself as a Godlike being whose presence pervades the "ring of being" in all its cycles and permutations.

Before exploring further the connection between the idea of willing backwards and the metaphor of the infinite sphere, it needs to be noted that Zarathustra, while endorsing his animals' interpretation of his self-understanding, still finds it wanting. As we have seen, he replies to his animals by dubbing them "buffoons" and "barrel organs" and depicting their speech as "hurdy-gurdy" singing. After his animals insist that convalescents learn to sing, Zarathustra uses the same phrases to mock them: "O you buffoons and barrel organs," he shouts, "be silent. . . . How well you know what comfort [*Trost*] I invented for myself in seven days! That I must sing again, this comfort and convalescence I invented for myself. Must you immediately turn this too into a hurdy-gurdy song [*Leier-Lied*]?"[207] It is significant that the German phrase translated here as "hurdy-gurdy song" literally means "lyre song." The lyre, of course, is one of Apollo's instruments, and while Zarathustra will indeed learn to sing, the songs *he* learns will not be Apollonian lyre songs.[208] Zarathustra's animals have *watched* him redeem himself; seeing, and singing what they see, they have made into a lyre song the Apollonian *appearance* of his redemption (redemption3).[209] Zarathustra mocks his animals' singing—even as he recognizes the insight it expresses ("How well you know . . .")—and will strive to sing differently than they sing in order to express *his* experience of *his* redemption. Although Zarathustra's animals' metaphors—that of the infinite sphere, for example—accurately represent Zarathustra's self-understanding, they leave unexpressed the lived, Dionysian experience accompanying that self-understanding.[210] The expressive deficiency of these metaphors is perhaps most obvious when, oblivious to Zarathustra's chiding about their lyre-singing, the animals proclaim near the end of "The Convalescent" that Zarathustra should fashion a *new lyre* and sing of the recurrence of all things: for all the enthusiasm of this proclamation, it is clear that nothing in what the animals say reveals the inner life of Zarathustra's soul: "When the animals had spoken these words they were silent and waited for Zarathustra to say something to them; but Zarathustra did not hear that they were silent. Rather he lay still with his eyes closed, like one sleeping, although he was not asleep; for he was conversing with his soul."[211]

In the first half of "On the Great Longing," Zarathustra begins to express his conversation with his soul and to communicate his experience of envisioning his soul as an infinite sphere. To be sure, the Dionysian experience he conveys here is that of the *lion-spirited* Dionysus-Zagreus. Thus, when Zarathustra speaks of taking "all obeying, knee-bending, and 'Lord'[*Herr*]-saying" from his soul, and of giving back to it its "freedom over the created and the uncreated," he proclaims the lion's repudiation of camel-like obedience and the lion's freedom for new creation.[212] And when he says that he "brushed dust, spiders, and twilight" from his soul, he invokes images from "The Soothsayer" and "On the Vision and the Riddle" that recall his leonine nay-saying (here figured as "brushing") to the Ecclesiastes-echoing voices of the soothsayer and the dwarf.[213] Zarathustra also clarifies his Zagrean, Dionysian experience with a set of claims that tie the figure of the infinite sphere to his vision of time as a perpetual "now":

> O my soul, I gave you new names and colorful toys; I called you "destiny" and "circumference of circumferences" [*Umfang der Umfänge*] and "umbilical cord of time" and "azure bell."

> O my soul, now there is not a soul anywhere that would be more loving and comprehending and comprehensive [*umfangender and umfänglicher*]. Where would future and past dwell closer together than in you?
>
> O my soul, I taught you to say "today" and "one day" and "formerly" and to dance away over all Here There and Yonder.[214]

In calling his soul "circumference of circumferences," Zarathustra suggests that it has no finite circumference and so no boundaries. Echoing his animals' allusion to the metaphor of the infinite sphere, he again asserts that his soul knows no "outside." What, however, are we to make of Zarathustra's claim that his soul is the "umbilical cord of time"? With this metaphor, Zarathustra complicates our understanding of his experience by maintaining that he perceives his soul as nourishing and sustaining the very being of time. His perception becomes intelligible, I think, if we suppose that, in keeping with the metaphor of the infinite sphere, he visualizes his soul as the omnipresent center of what his animals have dubbed "the ring of being." In Zarathustra's view, his soul is the living presence of a *nunc stans*, an abiding "now" that encompasses all times. In *his* experience there are no times "outside" this "now." As in his spatializing representation of time in "On the Vision and the Riddle," Zarathustra pictures the present moment as concurrent with all moments. He depicts his soul as the "umbilical cord of time," for he sees it as incarnating a moment that is the whole of time.

In the passage in which he describes his soul as comprehending and comprehensive, Zarathustra suggests that there are no past times and no future times that eclipse his soul's boundless ambit. Here again, then, he intimates that the time of his soul is the whole of time. As Zarathustra describes his soul, it stands no "nearer" to one time than to any other, for all times dwell within the "now" of his soul's eternity. Reminiscent, perhaps, of Augustine's God, Zarathustra's soul, as he envisions it, inhabits a "never-ending present" that "does not give place to any tomorrow nor . . . take the place of any yesterday."[215] Zarathustra teaches his soul to say "today" *and* "one day" *and* "formerly"—rather than "today" *or* "one day" *or* "formerly"—because he views time's different dimensions *not* as mutually exclusive, but, as Martin Heidegger writes in the second epigraph to this chapter, as "merge[d] . . . as the same in one single present, a perpetual 'now.'"[216] Picturing himself as Dionysus-Zagreus, and therefore as the leonine origin of all value, Zarathustra's intratemporal "home" is an extramundane time that subsumes and recurs in all times.

Consider, now, the following posthumously published reflections, some of which I have already quoted in this chapter:

6.

Let us think this thought in its most terrible form: existence as it is, without meaning or aim, yet recurring inevitably without any finale of nothingness: *the eternal recurrence.*

This is the most extreme form of nihilism: the nothing (the "meaningless"), eternally!

The European form of Buddhism: the energy of knowledge and strength compels this belief. It is the most *scientific* of all possible hypotheses. We deny end goals: if existence had one it would have been reached.

7.

So one understands that an antithesis to pantheism is attempted here: for "everything perfect, divine, eternal" also compels a faith in "eternal recurrence." Question: does morality make impossible this pantheistic affirmation of all things, too? At bottom it is only the moral god that has been overcome. Does it make sense to conceive a god "beyond good and evil?" Would a pantheism in this sense be possible? *Can we remove the idea of a goal from the process and then affirm the process in spite of this?—This would be the case if something were attained at every moment within the process—and always the same.* Spinoza reached such an affirmative position in so far as every moment has a logical necessity, and with his basic instinct, which was logical, he felt a sense of triumph that the world should be constituted that way.[217] (emphasis mine)

The two notes I quote here appear in a sequence of notes dated June 10, 1887, and numbered 1–16. As I have argued already in this chapter, the notion of re currence evident in note 6—the recurrence of meaninglessness—captures the nihilistic essence of the camel's thought of recurrence. But what of note 7? Here, Nietzsche identifies a notion of recurrence that differs from the notion evident in note 6. This second notion of recurrence pertains to the present discussion, for it provides a useful gloss on Zarathustra's self-portrait in "On the Great Longing." Echoing his animals' allusions to the metaphor of the infinite sphere, Zarathustra adopts a cosmology according to which "always the same" thing *is* attained "at every moment within the process."[218] As we have seen, that "always the same" thing is Zarathustra's omnipresent soul, an incarnation of an eternal "now" that is recurrently present in all times and in all things. To Zarathustra's mind, his vision of an eternal "now" expresses his lion-spirited nay-saying to the values of the moral, Christian God who, in the voice of the spirit of gravity, says "good for all, evil for all." In contrast to that god, Zarathustra sees himself as a sort of pantheistic divinity who is "beyond good and evil."[219]

In "The Convalescent" and "On the Great Longing," Zarathustra embraces the postulate that he personifies redemption3. To be exact, he embraces the proposition that, by envisioning his soul as the omnipresent incarnation of an eternal "now," he is performing a lion-spirited act of willing backwards that takes all "knee-bending" and "obeying" from his soul; or, in other words, that envisioning his soul as he envisions it in "On the Great Longing" is tantamount to personifying redemption3. One could object to Zarathustra's postulate by arguing that personifying redemption3 is impossible and that therefore the proposition that envisioning one's soul in some particular way is tantamount to personifying redemption3 is, in fact, false. Zarathustra would resist this objection, however, by noting that his postulate that he personifies redemption3 is just that: an assumption and a "comfort" that he invents for himself in order not to despair at the possibility of creating new values. As we have seen, Zarathustra suggests in "The Convalescent" that his singing will express this comfort. In "On the Great Longing," his Zagrean, Dionysian singing has just this effect, for it conveys his experience of believing that, in envisioning his soul as the omnipresent incarnation of an eternal "now," he personifies redemption3.

Zarathustra postulates that by envisioning his soul as the omnipresent incarnation of an eternal "now" he is willing backwards. Strictly formulated, in the grammar of the first-person singular, his postulate is that "I, Zarathustra, by now envisioning my soul as the omnipresent incarnation of an eternal 'now,' perform the lion-spirited act of willing backwards, thereby constituting my soul as the omnipresent incarnation of an eternal 'now.'" Or, alternatively, "I, Zarathustra, by now envisioning my soul as the omnipresent incarnation of an eternal 'now,' personify redemption3, thereby constituting my soul as the omnipresent incarnation of an eternal 'now.'" Supposing, as does Zarathustra, that this practical postulate is true, it is also true that Zarathustra has acquired the leonine strength required to will backwards (and thus to summon and repudiate his abysmal thought), presumably by teaching himself how to envision his soul as the omnipresent incarnation of an eternal "now." By teaching himself how to envision his soul in this way, and thus enabling himself to envision his soul in this way when he asserts his practical postulate, Zarathustra has acquired the force of will he needed to redeem himself, or so his practical postulate implies. Near the end of "On Redemption," Zarathustra asks, "Who could teach [the will] . . . to will backwards?" Zarathustra's second practical postulate suggests an answer to this question: namely, that Zarathustra could teach and has taught his will to will backwards by teaching himself to see his soul as a pantheistic *nunc stans*.

In "The Convalescent" and "On the Great Longing," Zarathustra transforms his thought of eternal recurrence. As we have seen, when Zarathustra first forms his thought of recurrence, as a camel's thought, he judges that his existence is characterized by a recurrence of the same, basing his judgment on his belief that due to modern asceticism he has been eternally martyred to the endless perpetuation of the small man's existence. Zarathustra transforms his thought of recurrence, forming the lion's thought of recurrence, when he judges *again* that his existence is characterized by a recurrence of the same, but now bases that judgment on the practical postulate that he personifies redemption3. Zarathustra's *lion-spirited reason* for holding that his life is subject to a recurrence of the same is his belief that, by envisioning his soul as the omnipresent incarnation of an eternal "now," he is personifying redemption3 and constituting his soul as the omnipresent incarnation of an eternal "now." Or, stated otherwise, his belief that (to borrow again the language of Nietzsche's note 7 of June 10, 1887), by envisioning his soul as a pantheistic deity that is recurrently "attained at every moment" (that is recurrently *present* in every moment), he is redeeming himself and constituting his soul as such a deity.

In first forming the thought of recurrence, Zarathustra dramatizes the soothsayer's representation of repetition. Prompted by an anxiety of inexpressiveness, he imagines that he is the protagonist of the first act of a Prometheus drama, comparable, I have suggested, to the first act of Aeschylus's *Prometheus Bound*. More exactly, he imagines that he is a Prometheus who has been eternally bound to the endless perpetuation of the small man's existence as punishment for struggling to realize his personal and poetic intentions. In the second act of his Prometheus drama, or, as I have put it, his thought-drama of recurrence, Zarathustra still sees himself as a sort of Prometheus, though now as a character like *Goethe's* Prometheus, who defeats the spirit of resignation by affirming his freedom to create. The lion-spirited Zarathustra affirms his freedom to create by postulating that, by envisioning his soul as a pantheistic god, he is willing backwards and therefore denying that the future must perpetuate past values. In effect, the lion-spirited Zarathustra "saves [the] light" of his teaching, by reasserting both his commitment to becoming a new-values creator and his belief that renunciation is not the only form of radical transfiguration available to human beings.

By transforming his thought of recurrence, Zarathustra enacts the second metamorphosis of the spirit, bringing his tragedy to a non-Schopenhauerian conclusion. As if inspired by the lion-spirited epigraph to Part 3, he terminates his tragic play and seriousness.[220] Owing to the tightrope walker's tragedy, Zarathustra lets go the optimism that initially marks him as a tragic hero, an optimism that blinds him to the possibility that his descent could leave humanity suffering the nihilistic experience of meaninglessness. Owing to the soothsayer's prophecy, he later worries that despite his efforts to find the right men (men who can go-under and overcome themselves), and thus to avert the catastrophe of nihilism, that catastrophe—intimated in the image of the small man's recurrent, meaningless existence—is imminent. Gripped by the soothsayer's spirit of resignation, Zarathustra, the crucified tragic hero, seems now to incarnate the irrevocable *Untergang* of his attempt to heal the rift between Dionysus and man— an *Untergang* that was initially forecast by the Pauline parody of his descent. Ever resilient, however, he eventually acquires the leonine strength he needs for the second act of his Prometheus thought-drama. By bringing his tragedy to a non-Schopenhauerian conclusion, Zarathustra does *not yet* end his Prometheus thought-drama, which he will end only with a *posttragic* third act, when his Herculean children appear, signaling that, finally, in the company of companions, he can forsake the tragic-heroic, defiant, posture of the Promethean lion and become a creator of new values.

In performing the second act of his thought-drama, Zarathustra (as he envisions his soul as the incarnation of an eternal "now") finds comfort in his second practical postulate, embracing which he frees himself from the spirit of resignation evoked by the soothsayer's prophecy. Like *The Birth of Tragedy*'s concept of metaphysical comfort, Zarathustra's experience of a postulate-based comfort suggests an alternative to Schopenhauer's view that tragedies properly conclude on a note of resignation. Yet the differences between the two alternatives are remarkable, for they suggest that Nietzsche, in *Zarathustra*, has revised his youthful theory of tragedy.

As we saw in Chapter 3, the older Nietzsche ultimately rejects the metaphysical dualism that the concept of metaphysical comfort presupposes. Furthermore, he spurns the concept of metaphysical comfort as a symptom of romanticism.[221] Romantics, Nietzsche says, seek "rest, stillness, calm seas, redemption from themselves through art and knowledge, or intoxication, convulsions, anesthesia, and madness."[222] They long to escape and forget their lives, and hence to be redeemed, or delivered, *from* their lives, for they fail to persuade themselves that, by expressing themselves, they have redeemed (or made good) their lives. Thus, the leonine, Promethean spirit, who finds *comfort* in his postulate that he is redeeming his life by envisioning his soul as a pantheistic god, succeeds exactly where Nietzsche's romantics have failed. Revising his early theory of tragedy, Nietzsche seeks an answer to tragedy's spirit of resignation not in the comfort of self-forgetfulness, but in a comfort stemming from his hero's belief that by seeing his soul in a certain way he is effecting his self-redemption.[223]

In the final chapter of this book, in the context of examining Zarathustra's relationship to the higher men who appear in Part 4, I return to the question of the connection between Nietzsche's revised theory of tragedy and his criticisms of romanticism. Here, however, before turning to the second half of "On the Great Longing," and to Zarathustra's final struggle in Part 3 to reconcile the practical postulate that he personifies redemption3 with the possibility of redemption1, I should like to emphasize the significant extent to which Nietzsche's revised theory of tragedy, though designed to defeat the spirit of the soothsayer, depends on Schopenhauer's philosophy. In particular, I wish to highlight the Schopenhauerian roots in Zarathustra's pantheistic, lion's thought of eternal recurrence. Consider the following passage from chapter 54 of volume 1 of *The World as Will and Representation*:

> A man who had assimilated firmly into his way of thinking the truths so far advanced, but at the same time had not come to know, through his own experience or through a deeper insight, that constant suffering is essential to all life; who found satisfaction in life and took perfect delight in it; who desired, in spite of calm deliberation, that the course of his life as he had hitherto experienced it should be of endless duration or of constant recurrence; and whose courage to face life was so great that, in return for life's pleasures, he would willingly and gladly put up with all the hardships and miseries to which it is subject; such a man would stand "with firm strong bones on the well-grounded earth," and would have nothing to fear. Armed with the knowledge we confer on him, he would look with indifference at death hastening towards him on the wings of time. He would consider it a false illusion, an impotent spectre, frightening to the weak but having no power over him who knows that he himself is that will of which the whole world is the objectification or copy, to which therefore life and also the present always remain certain and sure. The present is the only real form of the phenomenon of the will. Therefore no endless past or future in which he will not exist can frighten him, for he regards these as empty mirage and the web of Maya. Thus he would no more have to fear death than the sun would the night. . . . This point of view is . . . expressed by Goethe's "Prometheus" especially when he says:
>
> > Here I sit [*Hier sitz ich*] forming men
> > in my own image,
> > a race to be like me,
> > to suffer, to weep,
> > to delight and rejoice,
> > and to defy you,
> > as I do.
>
> The philosophy of Bruno and that of Spinoza might also bring to this standpoint the person whose conviction was not shaken or weakened by their errors or imperfections. . . . Finally, many men would occupy the standpoint

here set forth, if their knowledge kept pace with their willing, in other words if they were in a position, free from every erroneous idea, to become clearly and distinctly themselves. This is for knowledge the viewpoint of the complete *affirmation of the will-to-live.*[224]

Schopenhauer, we know, held that constant suffering is essential to life. In the passage quoted, however, he imagines someone who believes that suffering is not essential to life, who takes perfect delight in her life, and who desires her life's endless duration or constant recurrence. Such an individual, Schopenhauer implies, would not distinguish herself from the will-in-itself, and so would see the present moment as a *nunc stans* relative to which there exist neither earlier nor later moments (the appearance of these moments he would regard as "empty mirage"); in picturing her life's constant recurrence, she would envision the endless repetition of the events of her life as transpiring within a perpetual "now" that is the whole of time.

Now it is obvious, I assume, that Schopenhauer's description of a complete affirmation of the will-to-live, in that it invokes the idea of an extramundane perpetual "now," prefigures the notion of recurrence espoused in "On the Vision and the Riddle," "The Convalescent," and "On the Great Longing." It is equally clear, I hope, that Schopenhauer's allusions to Goethe's "Prometheus" and to the pantheistic metaphysics of Bruno and Spinoza also anticipate this notion. For Schopenhauer, as well as for Nietzsche when he has Zarathustra echo Goethe's Prometheus, the figure of Goethe's hero betokens a life-affirming repudiation of the spirit of resignation. Moreover, Schopenhauer's belief that Bruno's and Spinoza's pantheisms express a view of the world that sees excellence in everything—a belief that Schopenhauer develops at length in his "Epiphilosophy"—finds an echo in Nietzsche's June 1887 suggestion that Spinoza's pantheism entails the "affirmative position" that everything is "perfect, divine, eternal."[225] In short, it seems that some of the basic elements of the pantheistic, lion-spirited thought of recurrence evident in Part 3—namely, its connection to the idea of a *nunc stans*; its association with Goethe's Prometheus's nay-saying to resignation; and, obviously, its pantheistic conceptual content—appear in Schopenhauer's depiction of the person who completely affirms the will to live. To be sure, none of this is meant to deny Nietzsche's originality. Rather my point is that Nietzsche, in thinking against Schopenhauer, revises Schopenhauer. Put another way, Nietzsche, or Zarathustra, brings Zarathustra's tragedy to a non-Schopenhauerian conclusion by interpreting Schopenhauer's portrait of complete affirmation with reference to the Nietzschean and non-Schopenhauerian idea that one can defeat the spirit of resignation by embracing the practical postulate that, by envisioning one's soul as the divine incarnation of an eternal "now," one personifies redemption3.[226]

I will turn now to the second half of "On the Great Longing." In the first half of this speech, Zarathustra recites all that he has achieved on his soul's behalf. He begins the second half by inviting his soul to respond to him:

> O my soul, I gave you all, and I have emptied all my hands to you; and now—now you say to me, smiling and full of melancholy, "Which of us has to be thankful? Should not the giver be thankful that the *receiver received* [*dass der Nehmende nahm*]? Is not giving a need? Is not *receiving* [*Nehmen*] mercy?[227]
> (emphases mine)

By distinguishing his voice from that of his soul, Zarathustra dramatizes and brings into dialogue the two voices he fused in the closing section of "On Old and New Tablets." Speaking in *his* voice through the first half of "On the Great Longing," he appears as a leonine Dionysus-Zagreus who takes delight in his soul's infinite comprehensiveness. The Zagrean experience of Dionysus, we know, is one of superabundance, of being the overrich source of all possible values. Having completed his epistrophic "return home," Zarathustra rejoices in this experience and lovingly sees it mirrored in the life of his soul: "crowded and pressed by your happiness, waiting in your superabundance and still bashful about waiting."[228] In responding to this encomium, Zarathustra's soul demurs and, in a different voice, suggests that superabundance is a melancholic and merciful suffering. As Zarathustra describes it, his soul's suffering is a "longing of overfullness," or, to be exact, that "great longing" that his speech's title names and that he identifies in "On Old and New Tablets" as his longing for the "children's land" named "man's future" whereupon the overman's new nobility will flourish.[229] Contradicting Zarathustra's voice, which praises her as superabundant, Zarathustra's soul speaks in a voice that intimates her desire to spend her superabundance so that man can be overcome.

Zarathustra is adamant in endorsing and encouraging his soul's desire to spend her overfullness:

> But if you will not weep, not weep out your crimson melancholy, then you will have to *sing*, O my soul. Behold, I myself smile as I say this before you: sing with a roaring song till all seas are silenced, that they may listen to your longing—till over silent, longing seas the bark floats, the golden wonder around whose gold all good, bad wondrous things leap—also many great and small animals and whatever has light, wondrous feet for running on paths blue as violets—toward the golden wonder, the voluntary bark and its master, but that

is the vintager who is waiting with his diamond knife—your great deliverer. O my soul, the nameless one for whom only future songs will find names.[230]

We can begin to make sense of these remarks by recalling that "Ariadne" was the title of Nietzsche's fair-copy manuscript of "On the Great Longing" and thus was Nietzsche's name for Zarathustra's soul.[231] Now, according to Zarathustra, the soul is "something about the body," a claim that is consistent with my argument in Chapter 4 that Nietzsche uses the figure of Ariadne to signify the body's power of receptivity to the coming Dionysus.[232] Extending that argument here, I wish to suggest that Zarathustra's soul, whose mythical name Zarathustra never mentions, is *his* body's power of receptivity to the "coming god." In "On the Great Longing," Zarathustra's soul seems to him the mirror of his leonine, Zagrean experience of superabundance. The melancholic longing of Zarathustra's soul is her longing to cease to serve Zarathustra as his reflecting mirror and thus to be free of his will to identify her, not as a power of receptivity, but as a plentiful source, "waiting in . . . superabundance" to spend itself. It is significant, then, that Zarathustra's soul, in her response to Zarathustra, stresses her essentially *receptive* character. Hearkening to this response, Zarathustra-Zagreus acknowledges his soul's desire to be done with the identity he has foisted on her, and so to be done with his "gift" of superabundance. More than that, he fosters this desire by conjuring the figure of the coming Dionysus, the knife-wielding vintager and master of the golden bark "around whose gold all good, bad, wondrous things leap."

By invoking a familiar image of the chaos-bearing coming Dionysus, Zarathustra again pictures Ariadne between men: as the "middle term" that mediates two modalities of Dionysian experience.[233] Performing the role of the lion-spirit, he again pictures himself, in contrast to the coming Dionysus, as Dionysus-Zagreus. In Part 2, Zarathustra endorsed the lion-spirited epistemological view that his will to truth was the measure of the real, a view that entailed his estrangement from his body's power of receptivity to the chaos of the coming god. Zarathustra expressed his self-estrangement in "The Night Song," but later repudiated his Zagrean experience of Dionysus in order to reclaim his ability to experience Dionysus *as passional chaos*. In effect, he acknowledged his soul's—Ariadne's—secret that in order to go-under and overcome himself he would have to discard his heroic, leonine will, and thus abandon his soul to a life bereft of that will. In Part 3, a lion-spirited Zarathustra grapples with similar issues, although epistemological self-estrangement has now given way to a self-estrangement that derives from the cosmological vision on which Zarathustra's second practical postulate is predicated. By viewing his will as inhabiting an all-encompassing *nunc stans*, Zarathustra estranges himself from his body's power of receptivity; in effect, he estranges himself from his soul even as he envisions her as incarnating an eternal "now." Given this new experience of self-estrangement, we might expect Zarathustra again to repudiate his Zagrean experience of Dionysus in order again to reclaim his Ariadnean ability to experience Dionysus as passional chaos. But this is precisely what he does not do, at least in "On the Great Longing."

In the second half of this speech, Zarathustra *rejects* the belief that renouncing leonine heroism is a necessary condition of rehabilitating the ability to go-under. In essence he denies that he needs to repudiate his Zagrean experience of Dionysus in order to reclaim his power to experience Dionysus as passional chaos. In the first half of "On the Great Longing," Zarathustra sees his soul as the superabundant incarnation of an eternal "now." In the second half, he sees that his soul's aspiration exceeds both his Zagrean *gift* of superabundance and his Zagrean *vision* of an eternal "now." In invoking the image of the coming Dionysus (the vintager), Zarathustra looks beyond his gift and vision alike to the future to which his soul aspires—to a future, that is, in which his soul has been relieved of his gift of superabundance in order to be claimed by a god who is not "now" present.[234] In invoking this image, however, Zarathustra exhibits no sign of relinquishing his Zagrean experience of Dionysus.

Zarathustra, in other words, attempts to have his cake and eat it too. More precisely, he attempts to reconcile the possibility of redemption1 with the practical postulate that he personifies redemption3. Zarathustra postulates and believes that he is performing the act of willing backwards by envisioning his soul as an eternal "now." He asserts that redemption1 is possible when he imagines beyond this "now" a manifestation of the coming Dionysus that would satisfy his soul's "great longing." This longing, we have seen, is Zarathustra's desire for the "children's land" named "man's future" whereupon man will overcome himself. It is his still persistent yearning to find the "children of his hope," companion creators who would embody the bright ending of the soothsayer's "long twilight" because the passions and the possibility of experiencing the coming god's passional chaos had been reborn in them. Such "children" could realize the possibility of redemption1, for they could revalue in their revived bodies modes of passion that claimed human existence prior to the exhaustion of the earth in the era of the last man.[235] Zarathustra anticipates the return of previously banished passions to his life and to the lives of his future companions. Without repudiating his Zagrean experience of seeing his soul as the superabundant incarnation of an eternal "now," and without repudiating his belief that, by envisioning his soul in this way, he is effecting redemption3, he awaits the renewal of the possibility of going-under to the coming Dionysus. Thus, he seems to acknowledge his ability to go-under and therefore to open himself to the possibility of redeeming the human past, even as he postulates that he is willing backwards.

Zarathustra's effort to reconcile the possibility of redemption1 with the postulate that he personifies redemption3 is his effort to solve the paradox of his double will; it is, in essence, his attempt to retain a prudential connection to "man" and "man's future" even as he performs the second, leonine act of the thought-drama of recurrence. Reminiscent of Prometheus as Nietzsche depicts him in *The Birth of Tragedy*, Zarathustra resolves in "On the Great Longing" to eliminate in his solitary, single person the rift between the "divine" Zagreus and man, yet without descending to man as he does at the start of the prologue and at the end of Part 4.[236]

By attempting to solve the paradox of his double will, Zarathustra complicates the ending of his tragedy. Having invented a comfort (his practical postulate) sufficient to defeat the spirit of resignation, he also purports to embrace that comfort without denying the possibility of redemption1. In "The Other Dancing Song," Zarathustra tries out and tests his solitary, Promethean solution to the paradox facing him—a solution that fails, as we shall see. By the end of Part 3, Zarathustra has retreated to a lion-spirited and Zagrean posture that estranges him once again from his ability to go-under.

Recall now the dilemma Zarathustra confronted in the dancing song of Part 2: Zarathustra acknowledged his body's power of receptivity to Dionysian chaos, only to find himself falling victim to the spirit of gravity. Did Zarathustra then revert to the self-estranging posture of "The Night Song" in order to defeat his nemesis, or did he maintain his openness to Dionysian chaos? Zarathustra resolved his dilemma when he recognized that, even if he acknowledged his body's power to be affected by the coming god, he could defeat the spirit of gravity by affirming life's "secret" of self-overcoming. Very quickly, however, his affirmation of life's secret was rendered moot by the soothsayer's prophecy: going-under and creating new values would soon be impossible, and Zarathustra would soon construe himself as a martyr, crucified to the endless perpetuation of the small man. In "The Other Dancing Song," Zarathustra renews his affirmation of self-overcoming, for he believes (1) that by envisioning his soul as an eternal "now" he is willing backwards, undoing the Christian-Platonic past, and reestablishing his freedom to create new values, but (2) that his act of willing backwards, far from being paradoxical and self-defeating, leaves him free to acknowledge the possibility of going-under. As in "On the Great Longing," Zarathustra believes that he personifies redemption3 but that he has not estranged himself from his power to experience Dionysian chaos.

"The Other Dancing Song" begins with Zarathustra looking into life's eyes and seeing in them an image of a golden boat, an image that Zarathustra used in "On the Great Longing" to imagine the advent of the coming Dionysus. When life's Dionysian eyes alight on Zarathustra's foot, she rattles her rattle and he begins to dance. Leaping toward and away from life, his dance leads him, ultimately, to chase after her.[237] Vividly recalling the speech ("On Self-Overcoming") wherein he revealed life's secret of self-overcoming and described her "crooked paths" (*krummen Wegen*) as routes of "struggle" and "becoming," this chase proceeds along "crooked ways" (*krumme Bahnen*), whereupon life seems repeatedly to go-under and to transform her identity: "Here are caves and thickets; we shall get lost. Stop! Stand still! Don't you see owls and bats whirring past? You owl! You bat!"[238] In pursuing life, Zarathustra acknowledges his Ariadnean receptivity to the Dionysian flux and chaos that are essential to life's self-overcoming. At the same time, he insists on *his* identity as Dionysus-Zagreus: "I am the hunter [*Jäger*]," Zarathustra proclaims, "would you be my dog or my doe?"[239] As Zagreus, the hunter, Zarathustra sentimentally judges that life is no threat to his identity, and that he can court her with no risk to himself: "Oh, see me lying there you prankster, suing for grace. I should like to walk with you in a lovelier place. Love's paths through silent bushes, past many-hued plants. Or there along the lake. . . . Over there are sunsets and sheep: when shepherds play on their flutes—is it not lovely to sleep."[240] Life quickly challenges this judgment when, turning against Zarathustra, she proves herself to be a Circe-like witch who would make the hunter and would-be shepherd into a hunted sheep:

> Oh, this damned nimble supple snake and slippery witch! Where are you? In my face two red blotches from your hand itch.
>
> I am verily weary of always being your sheepish shepherd. You witch, if *I* have so far sung to you, now you shall cry. Keeping time [*Nach dem Takt*] with my whip, you shall dance and cry! Or have I forgotten the whip? Not I![241]

In a draft of his chapter on *Zarathustra* for *Ecce Homo*, Nietzsche writes that "there are cases where what is needed is an Ariadne's thread leading into the labyrinth."[242] In "The Other Dancing Song," a heroic, Theseus-like Zarathustra-Zagreus follows such a thread—the Ariadne's thread of his body's receptivity to the coming Dionysus he sees in life's eyes—into a labyrinthine chaos of caves and thickets and animals whirring by. Yet when, like a serpentine Circe, life attempts to transform the Zagrean hunter into sheeplike prey, he responds with his whip and violently thrashes her.[243] In effect, Zarathustra refuses here to let his Zagrean-Dionysian identity go-under to life's flux and chaos. Rather, in order to preserve that identity, he opposes himself to life's ever transformative becoming and self-overcoming. Distancing himself from his power to go-under, he now subjects life to the painful rule and rhythm of his lash.

By refusing to let his identity go-under, Zarathustra-Zagreus demonstrates the failure of his Promethean solution to the paradox of his double will. In other words, Zarathustra shows that he cannot embrace the practical postulate that he personifies redemption₃ and, at the same time, accept as part of his identity an Ariadnean soul that renders him susceptible to the coming Dionysus. In order to maintain his Zagrean identity, Zarathustra again estranges himself from his ability to go-under, this time by availing himself of a whiplike and leonine assertion of his will that abolishes life's chaos and forces her to conform to a regular rhythm and time. Notwithstanding the Promethean resolve of "On the Great Longing," Zarathustra falters in his effort to reconcile his second practical postulate and the possibility of redemption₁, because redemption₁ (again, the revaluation of historically persistent passions) requires an openness to passional chaos that cannot but undermine his sense that he possesses a stable identity, ensconced forever within an eternal "now."

In the second section of "The Other Dancing Song," Zarathustra considers the consequences of his failure. Absent a solution to the paradox of his double will, he is "stuck" with the self-defeating triumph of redemption₃ and, as in Part 2, will have to repudiate his Zagrean experience of Dionysus if he is to reclaim his receptivity to Dionysian chaos. Life seems to recognize these consequences of Zarathustra's failure when she remarks that Zarathustra is "thinking of abandoning [*verlassen*] [her] soon."²⁴⁴ To abandon life is to die, of course, and, in suggesting that Zarathustra is thinking of dying, life recalls a pronouncement he made in "On Old and New Tablets": "For I want to go to men once more; under their eyes I want to go-under; dying I want to give them my richest gift."²⁴⁵ As I have already argued in this chapter, Zarathustra's "death wish" is his desire to repudiate and "let die" his Zagrean experience of Dionysus in order to go to men and recall them to the possibility of going-under and overcoming themselves. In thinking of abandoning life, then, Zarathustra tacitly looks ahead to his final descent to men at the end of Part 4. Life worries that Zarathustra's abandonment is imminent, for she realizes that, due to his failure to make good on his intention to reconcile his practical postulate with the possibility of redemption₁, he must leave her bereft of her Zagrean hero if he is to open himself to Dionysian chaos and redeem the human past.

Life's envisioning the possibility that Zarathustra will abandon her affiliates her with Ariadne and the heroic Zarathustra-Zagreus with Theseus: "We are both two good-for-nothings and evil-for-nothings. Beyond good and evil we found our island and our green meadow—we two alone. Therefore we had better like each other."²⁴⁶ In the ancient myth of Theseus and Ariadne, Theseus carries Ariadne to an island (Naxos) after he escapes the dreaded labyrinth. Reminiscent of that myth, Zarathustra-Zagreus appears here as the hero, Theseus, who has carried Ariadne-life to an island, but only after he has disposed of the thread that led him into the labyrinth (his body's receptivity to the coming Dionysus) and used his whip to escape the labyrinth. Set in this mythical context, life's worry that Zarathustra-Zagreus will abandon her takes on an added significance relating to Zarathustra's disclosure of his soul's secret in Part 2: "For this is the soul's secret: only when the hero has abandoned her [*sie der Held verlassen hat*], she is approached in a dream by the overhero." As I glossed it in Chapter 4, Zarathustra's soul's secret is that the Zagrean hero must leave his soul —or, figuratively, his Ariadne—to a life bereft of his Zagrean, heroic experience of Dionysus, if he is to reclaim his receptivity to Dionysian chaos. And, as I suggested in the last paragraph, Ariadne-life seems to have recollected essentially *this* secret when, in the wake of Zarathustra's failure to reconcile his practical postulate and the possibility of redemptioni, she remarks that Zarathustra is thinking of abandoning her soon. Ariadne-life knows—or, again, Zarathustra's soul and life knows—that, as Zagreus, he must desert her if he is to embrace his ability to go-under. Zarathustra-Zagreus explicitly admits his desire to desert Ariadne-life, yet he seems to surprise her by knowing the soul's secret that she believed she alone knew:

> "There is an old, heavy, heavy growl bell that growls at night all the way up to your cave; when you hear this bell strike the hour at midnight, then you think, between one and twelve—you think, O Zarathustra, I know it, of how you want to abandon me soon [*mich bald verlassen willst*]."
>
> "Yes" I answered hesitantly, "but you also know—" and I said something into her ear, right through her tangled yellow foolish tresses.
>
> "You *know* that, O Zarathustra? Nobody knows that. And we looked at each other and gazed on the green meadow over which the cool evening was running just then, and we wept together. But then life was dearer to me than all my wisdom ever was.[247]

If Zarathustra appears in "On the Great Longing" not to accept his soul's secret, in "The Other Dancing Song" he seems to appease Ariadne-life by speaking her secret to her. Had Zarathustra succeeded in resolving the paradox of his double will, then, in effect, he would have acknowledged his soul's receptivity to life's chaos, but without repudiating his Zagrean experience of Dionysus. We have seen, moreover, that Zarathustra's failure to resolve this paradox meant that he would have to repudiate his Zagrean experience of Dionysus in order to acknowledge his soul's receptivity to life's chaos. In essence, then, Zarathustra's soul's secret is that, yes, the heroic, Promethean Zagreus will abandon life, "but . . ."—as Zarathustra remarks before whispering into life's ear—it is only in the wake of that abandonment that Zarathustra will be able to reclaim his ability to go-under. If Ariadne-life is dear to Zarathustra—indeed, dearer now than the wild leonine wisdom that fostered Zarathustra's estrangement in Part 2—it is because Ariadne-life and Zarathustra share Ariadne's secret that Zarathustra will be able to forswear his whip-wielding opposition to life's chaos after Zarathustra, as Zagreus, has forsaken life. Ariadne-life is astonished to discover that she and Zarathustra share this secret ("You *know* that . . ."), yet weeps joyfully with him over her discovery.[248]

Zarathustra-Zagreus will forsake life, but only when Zarathustra's children seem near at the end of Part 4. In the meantime, Zarathustra brings Part 3 to a close by singing "The Seven Seals," his "Yes and Amen Song." Here, finally, Zarathustra soars "on [his] own wings into his [own] skies," insisting that the sublime and gravity-defeating heaven he praised in "Before Sunrise" belongs to him.[249] Proclaiming that "there is no above, no below," he sees himself, like a pantheistic god, as transcending the limitations of perspective, a joyful and omnipresent deity who self-sufficiently "stand[s] over every single thing as its own heaven, as its round roof, its azure bell, and eternal security."[250] Repeatedly in "The Seven Seals," Zarathustra describes himself as lusting after "eternity and after the nuptial ring of rings [*hochzeitlichen Ring der Ringe*]," thus suggesting that the eternity he embraces is that of a *high and sublime time*—literally, in German, a *hoch Zeit*—that marries time itself to eternity.[251] In depicting this high time as a ring of rings, Zarathustra echoes his descriptions of his soul as a "circumference of circumferences" and as "comprehending and comprehensive," and so again intimates that he inhabits an eternal "now," having no "outside," that subsumes all times within itself.[252] Zarathustra's sublime time is the time of the sublime heaven he embodies, the time in which he leaps and laughs like the sublime, gravity-defeating shepherd of whom he once dreamed:

> If my virtue is a dancer's virtue and I have often leaped [*sprang*] with both feet into golden-emerald delight; if my sarcasm is a laughing sarcasm, at home under rose slopes and hedges of lilies—for in laughter all that is evil comes together, but is pronounced holy and absolved of its own bliss; and if this is my alpha and omega, that all that is heavy and grave should become light; all that is body, dancer; all that is spirit, bird—and verily, that is my alpha and omega: Oh, how should I not lust after eternity and after the nuptial ring of rings, the ring of recurrence.[253]

Conclusion

Forming and transforming his thought of recurrence, Zarathustra contributes through his actions to *Zarathustra*'s philosophical explanation of the possibility of creating new values. In the present chapter, I have concentrated on Zara-thustra's formation and first transformation of his thought of recurrence, leav-ing to Chapter 6 and my discussion of Part 4 my analysis of his second and fi-nal transformation of his thought.

In the soothsayer's speech, Nietzsche yet again expresses his skepticism toward Zarathustra's modernism, this time in the form of a prophecy that threatens Zara-thustra's personal and poetic intentions more severely than do Goethe's and Rous-seau's visions of self-transformation. Zarathustra forms his thought of recurrence when, in the spirit of the camel, he interprets the soothsayer's speech as the curse of a modern asceticism that has crucified him to the endless perpetuation of the small man's meaningless existence. He first transforms his thought, thus chang-ing his reason for believing that his existence is characterized by a recurrence of the same, when, in the spirit of the lion, and in the aftermath of his dream of a dwarf and a laughing lion, he embraces the comforting, tragedy-ending postulate that he personifies redemption3, thereby reaffirming his commitment to becom-ing a creator of new values. By showing again how, by becoming a lion-spirit, Zarathustra can sustain his commitment to becoming a new-values creator (a commitment that is a necessary precursor to this), notwithstanding the particu-larly dispiriting ramifications of the soothsayer's prophecy as Zarathustra inter-prets it, *Zarathustra* develops its unifying theme (its *Grundconception*) and ex-tends its explanation of the possibility of creating new values.

Still, the explanation remains incomplete, which is why *Zarathustra* requires a fourth part. Having struggled but failed to reconcile his practical postulate with the possibility of redemption1, Zarathustra at the end of Part 3 is a self-estranged Promethean lion, a sublime hero who must renounce his sublimity if he is to reclaim his ability to go-under and become a child-creator of new val-ues. With the advent of his Herculean children at the end of Part 4, he will re-claim that ability and transform his thought of recurrence for the second (and final) time into the child's thought of recurrence. *Zarathustra* will complete its explanation of the possibility of creating new values by showing how Zarathus-tra—notwithstanding the fact that he has *again* become a self-estranged lion-spirit, and notwithstanding the fact that modern asceticism has annulled the passional preconditions of self-overcoming—can become a child-creator in the company of other child-creators and fulfill his personal and poetic intentions.

CHAPTER SIX

Eternal Recurrence, Act III

> Vladimir: What do we do now?
>
> Estragon: Wait.
>
> Vladimir: Yes, but while waiting.
>
> SAMUEL BECKETT, *Waiting for Godot*

> Eternal return, in its esoteric truth, concerns—and can concern—only the third time of the series. Only there is it determined. That is why it is properly called a belief of the future, a belief in the future. Eternal return affects only the new.
>
> GILLES DELEUZE, *Difference and Repetition*

> I am a seer, but my conscience casts an inexorable light upon my vision, and I am myself the doubter.
>
> FRIEDRICH NIETZSCHE, *Nachlass*

"The Honey Sacrifice," the first section of *Zarathustra*, Part 4, begins with the following lines:

> And again months and years passed over Zarathustra's soul, and he did not heed them; but his hair turned white. One day when he sat on a stone before his cave and looked out—and one looks on the sea from there across winding abysses—his animals walked about him thoughtfully and at last stood still before him.
>
> "O Zarathustra," they said, "Are you perhaps looking out for your happiness?
>
> "What matters happiness," he replied; "For long I have not aspired after happiness, I aspire after my work [*ich trachte lange nicht mehr nach Glücke, Ich trachte nach meinem Werke*]."[1]

Zarathustra is happy because he has performed the second act of the thought-drama of eternal recurrence. By envisioning his soul as the omnipresent incarnation of an eternal "now," Zarathustra has, he believes, effected the self-redemption that is redemption3. As we have seen, however, he has failed to solve the paradox of his double will: that is, he has failed to reconcile his practical postulate that he personifies redemption3 with the possibility of redemption1. In "The Other Dancing Song," Zarathustra found that he could not maintain his Zagrean vision of himself as willing backwards while also acknowledging his Ariadnean receptivity to the chaos of the coming god. For the time being, then, he has disowned and distanced himself from his ability to go-under. Still, Zarathustra insists that he aspires to do his work, thus articulating his hope that he will one day reclaim that ability.

The work to which Zarathustra aspires, he reminds us in Part 4, is that of creating the overman: "I have the overman at heart," he proclaims, "*that* is my first and only concern."[2] Zarathustra's proclamation is hardly a surprise, for *Zarathustra* begins with Zarathustra descending to men to alert them to the possibility of going-under and overcoming themselves. In "The Honey Sacrifice," Zarathustra reasserts his commitment to his work, but defers his descent to men while he waits for them to ascend to his height. In effect, he announces that he will reclaim and realize his ability to go-under only if he receives a sign that the right men, the so-called "children of his hope," will soon appear atop his mountain: "Thus men may now come *up* to me; for I am still waiting for the sign that the time has come for my descent; I still do not myself go under, as I must do, under the eyes of men."[3] Zarathustra will strive to do the work to which he aspires, descending again to men and acknowledging again his receptivity to Dionysian chaos, only if he senses that the advent of his Herculean children is imminent.

Part 3 concludes with Zarathustra singing "The Yes and Amen Song," the refrain of which illuminates his deferral of his descent: "Never yet have I found the woman from whom I wanted children, unless it be this woman whom I love: for I love you, O eternity!" (*Nie noch fand ich das Weib, von dem ich Kinder mochte, es sei denn dieses Weib, das ich liebe: denn ich liebe dich, oh Ewigkeit!*).[4] Having failed to solve the paradox of his double will, Zarathustra admits that, in fact, he *wanted* to solve it: that eternity—his soul, to the extent that he envisioned it as the omnipresent incarnation of an eternal "now"—was so dear to him that he wanted to "impregnate" her with the possibility of redemption1. Zarathustra's failure to solve the paradox of his double will is, figuratively, his failure to fructify eternity with that possibility. Married to a lion-spirited vision of his soul in a sublime yet barren, self-alienating union, he delays his descent until his children, born not of eternity yet capable of redemption1, "come up" to him. Rooted in sterility and deferral, Zarathustra's story in Part 4, like that of Vladimir and

Estragon in Beckett's play, is one of hopeful, comical and, perhaps, interminable "waiting."

Reminiscent of Prometheus in the Caucasus, Zarathustra awaits his Herculean children "with both feet . . . on eternal ground, on hard primeval rock, on [the] highest, hardest, primeval mountain range."[5] Having embraced the postulate that he personifies redemption3, he has freed himself from the spirit of resignation induced in him by the soothsayer's prophecy of the endless and punishing perpetuation of man's small and meaningless existence. Like Goethe's Prometheus, Zarathustra has defied his punishment by resiliently affirming his power and freedom to create (see the closing speeches of Part 3). Embodying a honeylike and superabundant Dionysian happiness, he now depicts himself, specifically, as Dionysus-Zagreus, a hunter-god who will use his happiness to "hunt" and "fish" for the men he hopefully awaits:

> And when I desired honey, I merely desired bait . . . the best bait, needed by hunters and fisherman. For if the world is like a dark jungle and a garden of delight for all wild hunters, it strikes me even more . . . as an abysmal rich sea—a sea full of colorful fish and crabs that even gods might covet. . . . My happiness . . . I cast out far and wide . . . to see if many human fish might learn to wriggle and wiggle from my happiness until, biting at my sharp hidden hooks, they must come up to *my* height.[6]

It is significant that Zarathustra's depiction of himself here, as a fisher of men, evokes the figure of Christ no less than that of a Promethean, Zagrean hunter.[7] It is also significant that the Christ Zarathustra evokes is a martyr whose patient suffering, whose "passion," is over.[8] As we have seen, Nietzsche first portrayed Zarathustra in the image of a martyred Christ in the opening speech of the prologue. There, his parody of Paul, by figuring Zarathustra as a crucified, Dionysian savior, augured Zarathustra's unsuccessful effort to dissolve the rift between Dionysus and man. Nietzsche reprises his parody of Paul when, in "The Convalescent," he shows Zarathustra suggesting that the soothsayer's prophecy crucified him (Zarathustra) to a pervasively small and purposeless human existence. In that same section, Zarathustra also spews out his abysmal thought, thereby achieving a self-resurrecting self-redemption (redemption3) that Nietzsche's parody of Paul never hints is possible. In effect, by envisioning his soul as the incarnation of an eternal "now," Zarathustra terminates the Christlike suffering that initially beset him in the prologue, that repeatedly afflicted him in his encounters with representations of repetition echoing Nietzsche's parody of Paul, and that powerfully gripped him in the wake of the soothsayer's prophecy.

Zarathustra again evokes the figure of Christ near the conclusion of "The

Honey Sacrifice," alluding in particular to Revelations 20:4–7, when he speaks of a "great distant human kingdom, the Zarathustra kingdom of a thousand years."[9] Deferring his descent to a far-off future, he holds himself aloof from man, and thus aloof from the possibility of going-under and overcoming man that he hopes to see realized one day in his kingdom-to-come. Like the shepherd appearing in "On the Vision and the Riddle," Zarathustra (in "The Convalescent") has achieved a self-estranged, leonine sublimity that is "no longer human." Still, I have argued, he has not yet become the overman he persistently aspires to become.[10] In the final dithyramb of Part 3 ("The Seven Seals"), which Zarathustra sings to celebrate his sublimity, he mimics the Bible's image of Christ's marriage to God's holy city (Rev. 21:2) by depicting himself as the divine (pantheistic) bridegroom of the high time (*hoch Zeit*) he dubs "eternity."[11] But where the Bible figures Christ's marriage to a new Jerusalem as transpiring in the *aftermath* of his thousand-year kingdom on earth (Rev. 20:1–7), Zarathustra's marriage to an eternity that *he* blesses with *his* "alpha and omega"[12] occurs *before* the institution of the thousand-year *Reich* he anticipates. Christ weds God's holy city only after the earth on which he has reigned has passed away into the past (Rev. 21:1). Similarly, Zarathustra weds his bride in the wake of the soothsayer's prophecy of a decayed earth reduced to "human mold and bones and *musty past.*"[13] As distinct from Christ, however, Zarathustra harbors *post-nuptial* hopes: hopes that, due to the revival of the earth, he will meet other individuals—the children he awaits—in whom the earthly, bodily passions of his kingdom-to-come have been bountifully reborn; and hopes that with the appearance of these children he will finally *divorce* his beloved eternity in order to go-under and become an overman.

In general, Part 4 of *Zarathustra* tells the story of Zarathustra's adventures as he anticipates his kingdom-to-come and the advent of his Herculean children. More exactly, this "last . . . part"[14] of Nietzsche's masterpiece knits together *two* related but separable narratives, one of which tells the story of Zarathustra's transactions with the higher men and the other of which highlights his faith that, as he insists in "The Welcome," the higher men are but signs that the children he describes will soon make their way to him.

The first narrative recalls Aeschylus's *Prometheus Bound*, where Prometheus encounters a wandering, utterly miserable Io while awaiting the arrival of Hercules. Similarly, in Part 4, while awaiting the arrival of his children, Zarathustra encounters a wandering, utterly miserable group of men who fulfill the soothsayer's prophecy that the best will grow weary of their works (*ihrer Werke*).[15] Epitomizing Nietzsche's conception of romantic pessimism, these best and higher men, like the last men of the prologue, have had their passions annihilated by the asceticism of the modern world. Unlike the last men, however, the higher men *suffer* from their subjection to asceticism. Thus, with God dead, and the ascetic ideal self-destroyed, they desire a new purpose for human existence.[16] Ideally, Zarathustra would oblige their desire by exhorting the higher men to make overcoming man the new purpose of their lives. Yet the higher men lack the ability fruitfully to pursue that purpose, precisely because they possess exhausted, passionless bodies of the sort the soothsayer foresaw. As will soon become clear, they also lack Zarathustra's ability to cope with the spirit of resignation, which spirit haunts them, notwithstanding their efforts to make good their lives in the wake of the death of God. Still, the higher men know of Zarathustra and his teachings, and they want him to help them to defeat the spirit of resignation. Zarathustra brings the first of Part 4's narratives to an end when, in "The Sleepwalker Song,"[17] he grants the higher men the assistance they desire by *publicly staging* the second act of eternal recurrence as a sort of satyr play.

Intertwined with Part 4's story of Zarathustra and the higher men is a second, much briefer narrative that tells the story of Zarathustra's perseverance in anticipating the appearance of his children. Although he engages the higher men and attempts to provide them the succor they seek, Zarathustra succeeds in protecting himself and his hopes from the despairing demands of these mournful pessimists. Nietzsche's second, "anticipatory" narrative reaches its conclusion when Zarathustra, after he is done staging the second act of recurrence, announces that the arrival of his children is imminent. Looking beyond the happiness of redemption3, and beyond his involvement with the higher men's efforts to dispose of the spirit of resignation, Zarathustra now envisions the return to European modernity of the possibility of experiencing Dionysian chaos; the renewal of human beings' striving to redeem the human past (redemption1); and the reclamation in his own person of his ability to go-under. In fine, he performs the third (child's) act of the thought-drama of eternal recurrence.

How is it possible to create new values? Although Nietzsche begins and develops his answer to this question in Parts 1–3 of *Zarathustra*, he only completes it in Part 4. In Part 4, he sketches two narratives that conclude his philosophical explanation of the possibility of new-values creation. What do these narratives add to that explanation? Before I respond to this query, a brief review of the argument of Chapters 1–5 is in order.

Zarathustra strives to do his work, which is to create the overman, by struggling to fulfill his personal and poetic intentions. To create the overman, in his view, would be to become a new-values creator in his own right and to inspire others (his companions; later, his children) to become new-values creators. Were

Zarathustra to succeed in his work, he would effect a Dionysian interruption of modernity. Thus, he would realize his modernist ambition (1) to go-under to passional, Dionysian chaos, (2) to prompt others to go-under to passional, Dionysian chaos (by exhorting them to "see" and "hear" within their bodies the possibility of going-under), and (3) to join those others in revaluing human passions and thus in producing new values that stymie the perpetuation of the rationalistic culture of the last and small man.

Nietzsche shares Zarathustra's modernist aspirations but, as this chapter's third epigraph reminds us, is also prone to doubt them. As we have seen, Nietzsche's doubt, his skepticism as to the viability of Zarathustra's modernism, animates and organizes the plot of *Zarathustra*. More exactly, his skepticism is expressed in representations of repetition that, in opposing Zarathustra's personal and poetic intentions, constitute *Zarathustra* as a "stammering" text. With some affinity, perhaps, to the modern novel, as interpreted, for example, by Edward Said and Peter Brooks, *Zarathustra* frames the issue of new-values creation with reference to several personae (ranging from the forest saint to the soothsayer) who react to Zarathustra's project with insistent incredulity. Prefigured by Schopenhauer's anti-Hegelian philosophy of history (as Nietzsche articulates it in *The Birth of Tragedy*), and prefiguring Paul de Man's tropologically argued animadversions against the hubris of Dionysian modernism, these representations of repetition are resolute naysayers to the will to interrupt and radically redirect the course of human history. Still, despite such personae, *Zarathustra*, as distinct, say, from Hegel's *Phenomenology*, remains a future-oriented, modernist text (fruitfully read, I have argued, as a modernist *revision* of Hegel's great narrative) in which Nietzsche *thinks against* his skepticism by developing a putatively new and post-Christian-Platonic vocabulary for explaining the possibility of creating new values.

As philosophical explanation, the first half of *Zarathustra*—that is, *Zarathustra* prior to the soothsayer's appearance—shows how Zarathustra, notwithstanding the representations of repetition that threaten his commitment to becoming a new-values creator, could still maintain that commitment by becoming a lion-spirit ("Zarathustra's Prologue"); how Zarathustra (or a disciple), notwithstanding his exposure to the psychological pitfalls and worldly temptations that tend to derail lion-spirits (and potential lion-spirits), could still become a lion-spirit who kept attuned to the calling to become an overman (Part 1); and how Zarathustra, notwithstanding the fact that he has become a self-estranged lion-spirit, could still become an overman and overhero by learning to renounce his heroic will (Part 2). In sum, the first half of *Zarathustra* shows how Zarathustra, despite a variety of hindrances that obstruct and appear to exclude the possibility that he will become a new-values creator, could nonetheless realize that possibility.

The second half of *Zarathustra*, which is haunted everywhere by the sooth-sayer's prophecy, continues the philosophical explanation begun in the first half. By using the soothsayer's representation of repetition yet again to revoice his skepticism, Nietzsche suggests that Zarathustra, even if he were to defeat the hindrances he encounters in *Zarathustra*'s first half, could never realize his modernist intentions. In the perspective of the Schopenhauerian soothsayer, who unlike Goethe or Rousseau shares Zarathustra's post-Christian-Platonic interpretation of human being-in-time, modern asceticism's pervasive destruction of first-order bodily passions precludes the possibility that Zarathustra, or anyone else, could become a creator of new values. As we have seen, Zarathustra responds to the soothsayer's prophecy by forming the camel's and then the lion's dwarf-stopping thought of eternal recurrence. As philosophical explanation, Part 3 of *Zarathustra* shows how Zarathustra, by forming the lion's thought of recurrence, defeats the spirit of resignation that undermines his commitment to becoming a new-values creator when he forms the camel's thought of recurrence. In other words, Part 3 reasserts the explanatory claim that, despite a representation of repetition (in Part 3, the soothsayers's representation of repetition) that menaces Zarathustra's commitment to becoming a new-values creator (which commitment Zara-thustra requires to become a new-values creator), Zarathustra can reaffirm and persist in that commitment by adopting the defiant posture of the lion.

What then of Part 4? Part 3 ends with Zarathustra again having become a self-estranged lion (since he has failed to solve the paradox of his double will), and with European modernity still victim to the ascetic eradication of the passional preconditions of self-overcoming. Part 4 completes *Zarathustra*'s explanation of the possibility of creating new values by showing how Zarathustra, not-withstanding his leonine self-estrangement and the corrosive effects of the last man's modern, secular asceticism, could yet become a new-values creator who redeemed the human past. More exactly, it shows that Zarathustra, notwith-standing these apparent excluders, could yet become a new-values creator were he (1) to learn that his body had become the conduit of an epiphanic *return* to European modernity of the sort of earthly passions that tied him to the human past before secular asceticism annihilated all such passions (and, therefore, of the *return* to European modernity of the possibility of going-under to Dionysian chaos and redeeming the human past), and (2) to discard his heroic, leonine, Pro-methean will (along with the postulate that he personifies redemption3), ac-knowledge his ability to go-under, and deign to revalue his newly reborn pas-sions. As we shall see, Part 4's completion of *Zarathustra*'s answer to the question "How is it possible to create new values?" depends essentially on Zarathustra's formation of the child's thought of recurrence.

Zarathustra learns that his body has become the conduit of an epiphany and then discards his heroic will *only* in "The Sign," the very last section of Part 4. Only in this section, in other words, does Part 4 add anything to *Zarathustra's* philosophical account of the possibility of creating new values. Strictly speaking, then, the bulk of what is described in the two narratives that animate Part 4 bears little on that explanation. Still, each narrative is important. The first is significant, for it reintroduces the figure of the soothsayer, whose spirit of resignation all the other higher men echo. Prompted by the soothsayer's suggestion that Zarathustra's putative triumph over the spirit of resignation is a sham, this tale casts a retrospectively suspicious eye on the sublime and triumphant ending of Part 3. Part 4's second narrative is also significant, for, in stressing Zarathustra's perseverance in anticipating the appearance of his children, it prospectively illuminates his final metamorphosis. Moreover, the second narrative, since it includes "The Sign," describes that metamorphosis.

Zarathustra and the Higher Men

Close to the end of "The Honey Sacrifice," Zarathustra describes the children he awaits as his "in-and-for-me in all things," invoking a familiar Hegelian trope to imply that he expects these "beautiful . . . fish" to satisfy his desire to recognize himself in others.[18] In "The Cry of Distress," which directly follows "The Honey Sacrifice," the soothsayer challenges this expectation by proposing that the higher men, and thus men *other* than the children Zarathustra awaits, will satisfy this desire. Acting as a Schopenhauerian agent of the spirit of resignation, the soothsayer promotes that spirit when he proclaims that he has come to tempt and seduce (*verführen*) Zarathustra to pity men who embody it. For Schopenhauer, pity entails the apprehension of others and the misery of others as the "I once more" (*Ich noch ein mal*):[19] to pity another, he claims, is to recognize (*wiedererkennen*) oneself in her and, to the extent that pity can reveal the suffering and the vanity in *all* human endeavors, to render oneself vulnerable to the inclination to resign life.[20] The soothsayer's effort to seduce Zarathustra to pity is reminiscent of Schopenhauer, for it is his effort to persuade Zarathustra to recognize himself in the higher men—that is, to view the higher men's unhappiness as his own—and to demonstrate that Zarathustra, no less than the higher men, embodies the spirit of resignation.

When Zarathustra and the soothsayer first meet in Part 4, they shake hands as a sign that they desire "to recognize each other" (*sich wiedererkennen*).[21] More complicated than it may at first appear, the soothsayer's desire to recognize Zarathustra is, in essence, a desire for self-recognition that is implicated in his attempt to seduce Zarathustra to pity. Doubting that Zarathustra is the super-abundantly joyful person he purports to be, the soothsayer suggests that his host's putative and apparent happiness is not a genuine happiness:

> "Do you hear? Do you hear, O Zarathustra?" the soothsayer shouted. "The cry is for you. It calls you: Come, come, come! It is time! It is high time [*es is höchste Zeit*]!
>
> Then Zarathustra remained silent, confused and shaken. At last he asked, as one hesitant in his own mind, "And who is it that calls me?"
>
> "But you know that," replied the soothsayer violently; "why do you conceal yourself? It is *the higher man* that cries for you!"
>
> "The higher man?" cried Zarathustra, seized with horror. "What does he want? What does he want? The higher man! What does he want here?" And his skin was covered with perspiration.
>
> The soothsayer, however, made no reply to Zarathustra's dread, but listened and listened toward the depth. But when there was silence for a long time, he turned his glance back and saw Zarathustra standing there trembling. "O Zarathustra," he began in a sad tone of voice, "you are not standing there as one made giddy by his happiness: you had better dance lest you fall. But even if you would dance before me, leaping all your side-leaps [*alle deine Seiten-sprünge springen*], no one could say to me, "Behold, here dances the last gay man." Anybody coming to this height, looking for *that* man, would come in vain: caves he would find, and caves behind caves, hiding-places for those addicted to hiding, but no mines of happiness or treasure rooms or new gold veins of happiness. Happiness—how should one find happiness among hermits and those buried like this? Must I still seek the last happiness on blessed isles and far away between forgotten seas? But all is the same, nothing is worthwhile, no seeking avails, nor are there any blessed isles anymore.[22]

From the soothsayer's perspective, Zarathustra's putative happiness is a counter-feit delight that expresses a depth of unhappiness. Living in a kind of bad faith, Zarathustra has hidden his unhappiness from himself by allowing himself to be-lieve that he is happy—or so the soothsayer implies. With words that ironically echo Zarathustra's talk in Part 3 of leaps and heights and high times,[23] the sooth-sayer mocks Zarathustra's portrait of himself as a sublime hero who has become gay by willing backwards and defeating the spirit of resignation. Announcing that all is the same, that nothing is worthwhile, and that no seeking avails, he suggests that the spirit of resignation pervades human life and so extends to Zarathustra. For the soothsayer, recognizing Zarathustra is recognizing himself in Zarathustra, because the soothsayer believes that Zarathustra embodies the same unhappy feelings of resignation and meaninglessness that the soothsayer and the other higher men embody. By seducing Zarathustra to pity the higher men, the soothsayer would persuade Zarathustra to acknowledge that he shares in the soothsayer's and the higher men's unhappiness, and that his claim to happiness has been a lie. The soothsayer wants to compel Zarathustra to admit that the misery of the higher men mirrors Zarathustra's misery and that the soothsayer has been right to judge that, all protestations notwithstanding, Zarathustra has not freed himself from the spirit of resignation.

Because the struggle for recognition pitting Zarathustra against the soothsayer is a contest between two different views of the sort of men who will satisfy Zarathustra's desire to recognize himself in others, it is also a contest between two different interpretations of Zarathustra's identity. For Zarathustra, pitying the higher men and recognizing himself in them would amount to accepting the soothsayer's suggestion that his soul's "calm," which he (Zarathustra) attributes to his happiness, is but a symptom of a deeply felt spirit of resignation.[24] In fine, Zarathustra would be granting that his soul's calm is a disguised manifestation of the spirit of resignation and not, as it has otherwise appeared to him to be, the effect of a happiness that manifests his Promethean triumph over that spirit. Were Zarathustra to succumb to the soothsayer's seduction to pity, he would be assenting to the view that the act of willing backwards, which he postulates he performs by envisioning his soul as the incarnation of an eternal "now," expresses a will "not to will."

Zarathustra resists the soothsayer's seduction to pity by asserting, in essence, that he will vindicate his interpretation of his identity as that of a person who has triumphed over the spirit of resignation. Rather than accept the soothsayer's belief that he embodies that spirit, Zarathustra will attempt to persuade his nemesis that where Zarathustra resides the spirit of resignation can have no place. Speaking specifically of the higher men, Zarathustra insists they will not "come to grief" in *his* realm. Speaking of the soothsayer himself, he predicts that by evening this mournful prophet of gloom will dance cheerfully as Zarathustra's "dancing bear." Rejoining the soothsayer's skeptical reply to his prediction, Zarathustra is confident that he (Zarathustra) speaks the truth: "You do not believe it? You shake your head? Well then, old bear! But I too am a soothsayer [*Wahrsager*]."[25]

As a sooth-sayer, or *Wahr-sager*, in his own right, Zarathustra aspires to prove the sooth, or truth, of his self-interpretation to the soothsayer who doubts him. But how can he do this? What would, or could, *count* as proof of Zarathustra's self-interpretation in the eyes of the "old bear" who accuses him of bad faith? Zarathustra's exchange with the soothsayer hints at an answer to this question, for it suggests that Zarathustra will satisfy the soothsayer's criterion of proof if, notwithstanding the soothsayer's incredulous shaking of his head, Zarathustra's prediction that the soothsayer will dance by evening is fulfilled. More generally, it suggests that Zarathustra will vindicate his view of who he is, to the soothsayer's satisfaction, by showing that, due to his happiness, he can dispel the spirit of resignation from the soothsayer's life and the lives of the other higher men, at least temporarily. By demonstrating to the soothsayer his (Zarathustra's) power to effect the convalescence of unhappy souls—that of the soothsayer's soul included—Zarathustra will convince the soothsayer that he is not a pretender to genuine gaiety who would, were he soothful, recognize himself in the higher men.[26]

By adopting a strategy of self-vindication in response to the soothsayer, Zarathustra thematically sets the stage for what numerous commentators have rightly identified as the *comic* character of the fourth part of *Zarathustra*. Whether critics see in this finale a Shakespearean *Midsummer Night's Dream* (Alderman), a Rabelaisian carnival (Shapiro), a Menippean satire (Higgins), or a travesty of Wagner's *Parsifal* (Hollinrake), they generally accent the farcical and parodic features of Zarathustra's involvement with the higher men.[27] Still, it is Nietzsche himself who best explains the connection between the tendency to farce and parody in Part 4 and the central theme of self-vindication:

> Take care, philosophers and friends, of knowledge, and beware of martyrdom. Of suffering "for the truth's sake"! Even of vindicating yourselves [*Selbst vor der eigenen Vertheidigung*]! It spoils all the innocence and fine neutrality of your conscience; it makes you headstrong against objections and red rags; it stupefies, animalizes, and brutalizes when in the struggle with danger, slander, suspicion, expulsion, and even worse consequences of hostility, you have to pose as defenders of truth [*Vertheideger der Wahrheit*] upon earth—as though "the truth" were such an innocent and incompetent creature as to require protectors! and you of all people, you knights of the most sorrowful countenance, dear loafers and cobweb-spinners of the spirit! After all, you know well enough that it cannot be of any consequence if *you* of all people are proved right [*Recht behaltet*]; you know that no philosopher so far has been proved right. . . . The martyrdom of the philosopher, his "sacrifice for the sake of truth," forces into the light whatever of the agitator and the actor lurks in him; and if one has so far contemplated him only with artistic curiosity, with regard to many a philosopher it is easy to understand the dangerous desire to see him also in his degeneration (degenerated into a "martyr," into a stage- and platform-bawler). Only, that it is necessary with such a desire to be clear *what* spectacle one will see in any case—merely a satyr play, merely an epilogue farce, merely the continued proof that the long real tragedy *is at an end*, assuming that every philosophy was in its genesis a long tragedy.[28]

Defending himself against the soothsayer's mockery and doubts, Zarathustra in Part 4 assumes the role of the philosopher who would prove the truth of his self-interpretation. The passage I have quoted, which derives from Part 2 of *Beyond Good and Evil*, comments indirectly on Zarathustra's assumption of this role by carefully characterizing the sort of "spectacle" that a philosopher's attempt at self-vindication is bound to produce. As we shall see, the comic mood that grips the higher men as they convalesce in the milieu of Zarathustra's happiness is catching. After the higher men learn to laugh (and even to laugh satirically at Zarathustra), Zarathustra embraces that mood, recognizing that through farce and parody he can advance and bring to a culmination the higher men's convalescence. In particular, he sees that he can triumphantly demonstrate his power to dispel the spirit of resignation by publicly staging for the higher men the second, leonine act of the thought-drama of recurrence. By transmuting the second act of recurrence into a theatrical, Wagnerian "spectacle," Zarathustra, in keeping with Nietzsche's commentary, becomes a "stage- and platform bawler," a martyr who, in a sense, sacrifices himself "for the sake of the truth." More exactly, he transforms a lyric he initially sang to his soul (see "The Other Dancing Song") into a sleepwalker's song (see "The Sleepwalker Song"), his performance of which is a *degenerate rendition of the second act of recurrence*, a farcical satire of the sublime celebration of eternity that, in the closing sections of Part 3, brought his tragedy to an end. Playing the role of a *Satyrspieler*, Zarathustra "martyrs" and "sacrifices" his public image of himself as a sublime and self-redeeming tragic hero in order to enact for the higher men a comical parody of the Promethean act of will (the act of willing backwards) by which, he believes, he has transformed himself into a sublime and self-redeeming tragic hero.[29] Parodying himself, Zarathustra completes the task of vindicating himself, by establishing conclusively that he has triumphed over the spirit of resignation.[30]

I will begin to examine the depiction of the higher men in Part 4 by noting that Nietzsche portrays them as so many representations of repetition. Each of the higher men echoes Zarathustra;[31] each utters words that repeat or recall a part of a speech that Zarathustra previously delivered. For example, one of the two kings reiterates Zarathustra's question, "What do kings matter now?" Similarly, the student of the leech recites the remark that "Spirit is the life that cuts into life."[32] In each of the higher men, Zarathustra discovers a concrete instance of the soothsayer's attempt to seduce him to pity, as well as symbolic confirmation of the soothsayer's sense that, in a significant sense, the future must repeat the past. As Zarathustra traverses his mountain, in anxious pursuit of the cry of distress, he finds awaiting *him* in the future, in the persons of the men he is fated to meet, fragments, not of a new self, but of the self *he* has been in the past. The temptation to succumb to the soothsayer's seduction is, he soon realizes, equally a temptation to identify with the self he once was and to accept as true the soothsayer's assertion that self-overcoming is impossible. In "Noon," after he has conversed with each of the higher men, Zarathustra flees this temptation ("I want to run alone," he says) and takes delight, yet again, in his happiness:

> O happiness! O happiness! Would you sing, O my soul? You are lying in the grass. But this is the secret solemn hour when no shepherd plays his pipe. Refrain! Hot noon sleeps on the meadows. Do not sing! Still! The world is perfect. Do not sing, you winged one in the grass, O my soul—do not even whisper! Behold—still!—the old noon sleeps, his mouth moves: is he not just now drinking a drop of happiness, an old brown drop of golden happiness, golden wine? It slips over him, his happiness laughs. Thus laughs a god. Still! . . .
>
> What happened to me? Listen! Did time perhaps fly away? Do I not fall? Did I not fall—listen—into the well of eternity? . . . Oh, the golden round ring—where may it fly? Shall I run after it? Quick! Still! (And here Zarathustra stretched and felt that he was asleep.)
>
> "Up!" he said to himself; "you sleeper! You noon napper! Well, get up, old legs. . . . (But then he fell asleep again, and his soul spoke against him and resisted and lay down again.) "Leave me alone! Still! Did not the world become perfect just now? Oh, the golden round ball."
>
> "Get up!" said Zarathustra, "you little thief, you lazy little thief of time! What? Still stretching, yawning, sighing, falling into deep wells? Who are you? O my soul!" (At this point he was startled, for a sunbeam fell from the sky onto his face.) "O heaven over me!" he said, sighing, and sat up. "You are looking on? You are listening to my strange soul? When will you drink this drop of dew which has fallen on all earthly things? When will you drink this strange soul? When, well of eternity? Cheerful, dreadful abyss of noon! When will you drink my soul back into yourself?"
>
> Thus spoke Zarathustra, and he got up from his resting place at the tree as from a strange drunkenness, and behold, the sun still stood straight over his head. But from this one might justly conclude that Zarathustra had not slept long.[33]

Addressing his soul as he did in "On the Great Longing," and vividly recalling Nietzsche's depiction of Archilochus in *The Birth of Tragedy* (as a devotee of Dionysus, asleep at noon on a high mountain pasture),[34] Zarathustra, at noon, enjoys a seemingly drunken, Dionysian happiness while he envisions himself inhabiting a *nunc stans*. Evoking the now familiar imagery of the golden "round ring" and "round ball," he ecstatically revisits his portrait of his soul as an infinite "circumference of circumferences." In Part 3, Zarathustra formed the lion's thought of recurrence in response to an Ecclesiastes-echoing prediction that the future will perpetuate the past. Similarly, in Part 4, he renews that thought in response to his encounters with men who, like the prologue's leaping jester, symbolize that prediction.

Writing in *Ecce Homo*, Nietzsche claims that his aim in Part 4 was to invent a situation wherein pity attacks Zarathustra "like a final sin that would entice him away from *himself*."[35] Zarathustra, in fact, is at least twice drawn away from himself by pity's lure, though by the time he experiences the happiness of "Noon" he has learned not to succumb to it.[36] It is significant, then, that "Noon" begins with Nietzsche describing Zarathustra as having "*found himself*."[37] Having become firm in his disposition to say "no" to pity, Zarathustra is delighted by the self he has found. Neither a mirror image of one or more of the higher men, nor a new self of the sort he might someday create by creating new values, this euphoric "midday" self is the self-redeemed self that Zarathustra postulates he personifies by envisioning his soul as the omnipresent incarnation of a perpetual "now." Set free of the temptation that has drawn him away from that self and caused him briefly to *mistake* it for one that embodies the not at all gay spirit of resignation also evident in the higher men, Zarathustra, at noon, explicitly sets himself apart from the higher men, his solitary soul ensconced in the "well of eternity."[38]

In "Noon," which concludes the first half of Part 4, Zarathustra again celebrates the happiness he celebrated in "The Honey Sacrifice." This second celebration is, arguably, a partial vindication of Zarathustra's claim to have vanquished the spirit of resignation, for it suggests that Zarathustra's experience of a *nunc stans*, after the appearance of the higher men, suffices to keep that spirit at bay. Yet there is no reason to believe that Zarathustra's description of his happiness at noon, anymore than his allusions to his happiness in "The Honey Sacrifice," would persuade the soothsayer that Zarathustra is not self-deceived. As I have already suggested, Zarathustra's strategy of self-vindication relies on his power to effect the convalescence of souls other than his own, and therefore to prove that his triumph over the spirit of resignation has salutary consequences for persons other than himself. One might suppose, then, that the aim of that strategy would be to train the soothsayer and the other higher men to produce for themselves the happiness of noon; or, in other words, to train each of the higher men (1) to envision his soul as the omnipresent incarnation of an eternal "now" and (2) to postulate that, in envisioning his soul in this way, he is willing backwards (in fine, to train each of them to enact the second act of eternal recurrence). But this is just what Zarathustra *does not do*. Rather, he performs a parody of the second act of recurrence, which, though it dispels the spirit of resignation, falls short of inducing in the higher men the noontime happiness that he himself experiences.

Zarathustra declines to try to form the higher men in the image of his happiness. Such an effort would be fruitless, but to say why it would be fruitless, and why self-parody is the instrument Zarathustra uses against the higher men's spirit of resignation, we need to examine Nietzsche's view of the higher men. In particular, we need to specify the inherent limitations of these men, or, to put it bluntly, to explain Zarathustra's repeated suggestion that failure of a sort is their ineluctable lot.

Who, then, are the higher men? The soothsayer hints at an answer to this question when he predicts that the best will grow "weary of their works." Another higher man hints at an answer when he suggests that he and his fellows are a "remnant" of God.[39] The higher man is a remnant of God because his search for meaning presupposes the death of God. To repeat an earlier claim, the higher man wants to see a new purpose assigned to his existence in the wake of God's death and the self-destruction of the ascetic ideal. Victim to the ascetic impoverishment of life, he seeks a reason for his existence that would be the purpose of his suffering.[40] Before the higher man wearies of his works, he finds such a reason in them—or so Nietzsche suggests in *Beyond Good and Evil.*

Nietzsche clarifies his conception of the higher men with a discussion of particular higher men in section 256 of *Beyond Good and Evil.*[41] Here, Nietzsche depicts the individuals he names as supranationalist artists who embraced nationalism "only in their foregrounds or in weaker hours" (besides Napoleon, whom Nietzsche seems to have seen as a "political" artist, he identifies writers, painters, and composers: Goethe, Heine, Stendhal, Balzac, Delacroix, Beethoven, Schopenhauer, and Wagner).[42] When these men became patriots, he asserts, "they were merely taking a rest from themselves." According to Nietzsche, Europe's "higher human beings" were the "last great seekers [*Suchenden*]," geniuses who "*sought* [*suchten*] in the same way." More precisely, they were "tormented" romantics, "Tantaluses of the will," who struggled to *express* themselves through their art (they were "fanatics of expression [*des Ausdrucks*] 'at any price'"). Remarking on the romantic movement's expressivist interpretation of art,[43] Nietzsche suggests that Europe's higher men looked to their self-expressive creations—their *works*—to justify their lives; or in other words, that each of them believed that self-expression through his works was the reason he existed and the purpose of the suffering, the *Sturm und Drang*, he felt. Picturing these men as "rebels against custom . . . who soared, and tore others along, to the heights," Nietzsche seems also to hold that they each thought that self-expressive striving demanded a break with social convention by which one showed oneself to be an exceptional individual. Nietzsche argues, in fact, that it fell to the higher men, or, at least, to the ones he lists, to teach their century (the century of "the *crowd*," according to Nietzsche) the very concept of a "higher man" who distinguishes himself from the masses.

The portrait of the higher men I have sketched here agrees with the one drawn in *Zarathustra*. Each of the higher men, prior to approaching Zarathustra, has made self-distinction through self-expression the purpose of his existence. In effect, each of them has devoted himself to a mode of self-expression that sets him apart from "the rabble" or "the mob." In the case of the two kings, for example, we see individuals who have sought self-expression and self-distinction through their commitment to the values of nobility and virtue,[44] values to which (they proclaim) the rabble is oblivious. Consider, too, the student of the leech (or, strictly speaking, of the brain of the leech!) and the Wagnerian sorcerer. In the one case, science functions as the instrument of a self-expressive dedication to research wherein the specialist finds a purpose for his existence and whereby he distinguishes himself from men less conscientious than he: "The conscience of my spirit demands of me that I know one thing and nothing else: I loathe all the half in spirit, all the vaporous who hover and rave."[45] In the other case, the quintessentially expressive art of the actor is the means whereby a parodist who parodies Zarathustra's struggle with his "abysmal thought" tries to distinguish himself as a "great human being."[46]

The retired pope and the ugliest man are also self-expressive romantics. The former is "a festival of pious memories and divine services," a "black artist" who, in the aftermath of God's death, distinguishes himself from the mob by devoting himself to the remembrance of God.[47] Before he discovers that the old saint has died, leaving him bereft of a companion with whom he might have shared his pious memories, the retired pope finds the purpose of his existence in his self-expressive commitment to these memories. Responding rather differently to God's death, the ugliest man—whom Zarathustra describes as God's murderer—seeks self-distinction and self-justification in his expressed and profound respect for the great misfortune, the great ugliness, and the great failure that the "little people," the masses, pity. Contemptuous of these "little people," the ugliest man is, potentially, a criminal on the grand scale, a virtual tyrant whose murderous passion for revenge could just as well be turned against his fellow human beings as it was against God.[48]

Predicting that "the hour has come . . . for the great, bad, long, slow revolt of the mob and the slaves," the voluntary beggar, a late-nineteenth-century critic of the corruptions of modern civilization ("none of them [the rich]," he says, "is too far from the whores—mob above and mob below! What do 'poor' and 'rich' matter today?"), seeks meaningful self-expression in his relentless, antimodern effort to emulate the peaceful life of cows. "Except we turn back and become as cows," he proclaims, "we shall not enter the kingdom of heaven."[49] A similar antipathy to modernity is evident in the person of Zarathustra's shadow—the last of the higher men seeking Zarathustra—not in the longing for a simpler, animal way of life, but in a sort of Africanist, or perhaps orientalist, escapism that Nietzsche describes in *Beyond Good and Evil* as the higher man's "lusting after the foreign, the exotic."[50]

The "works" wrought by the higher men of Part 4 are the manifold modes of self-expression by which they have hoped to make sense of their lives in the aftermath of the death of God. Yet each of the higher men grows weary of his work, which is to say that each grows weary of his struggle to express himself. Put simply, a higher man grows weary of his work when he can no longer persuade himself that his chosen mode of self-expression justifies his existence; or, more precisely, that his chosen mode of self-expression is a purpose that validates and makes good his existence. A case in point is the sorcerer who wearies of his art because he fails to persuade himself that his art has redeemed his existence by making him into a great human being.[51] When the higher men mentioned in *Beyond Good and Evil* (again, see section 256) failed in their eyes to redeem their lives through self-expression, they "broke and collapsed . . . before the Christian cross."[52] In other words, when they wearied of their work, they retreated to a Christian interpretation of human existence. The weary higher men depicted in *Zarathustra* pursue a different strategy: rather than look to a Christianity they once repudiated to comfort them, they climb Zarathustra's mountain and look to Zarathustra.

In *Beyond Good and Evil*, Nietzsche argues that the romantic, self-expressive higher man is a great discoverer "in the realm of the sublime."[53] In *Zarathustra*, Nietzsche also links the higher man to the sublime, likening him to "a tiger whose leap has failed" and thus echoing Part 2's portrait of the sublime hero as "a tiger who wants to leap."[54] As we have seen, part of what makes the higher man a *higher* man is his self-expressive aspiration to achieve a self-distinguishing spiritual height that transcends and remains free of the concerns of the masses. Like Zarathustra as he appears in "On the Rabble," the higher man seeks a sublimity that would cleanse his spirit of the nausea induced by the "mob," or the "rabble."[55] As distinct from Zarathustra, however, the higher man is destined, on his "very *height*," to "stumble."[56] His failure will be evident, Zarathustra suggests, from the fact that his achievement falls short of his aspiration.

Although Zarathustra speaks specifically of the higher man's limitations in

his speech "On the Higher Man," his most illuminating gloss on these limitations, and on the higher man's proneness to falter and fail, is in "The Welcome."
Addressing the higher man in that speech, Zarathustra says, "you may indeed all
be higher men . . . but for me you are not high and strong enough. For me—
that means, for the inexorable [das Unerbittliche] in me that is silent but will not
always remain silent."[57] For Zarathustra, the higher man is in part a victim of
his own weakness. Measured against the *inexorable*, leonine will that the sublime, Zagrean Zarathustra claimed for himself in "The Night Song," and then
again in the final speech of "On Old and New Tablets," the higher man proves
neither strong nor resolute enough to foster a high and sublime vision of himself that is commensurate with his sublime aspiration. If the higher man fails to
persuade himself that in expressing and striving to distinguish himself he has
made good his existence, it is because his will is *not inexorable* and therefore *not
capable* of sustaining in him the belief that in expressing and striving to distinguish himself he has shown himself to be a truly exceptional and sublime individual. Victim to "a recurring specter of unbelief that chills and forces [him] . . .
to gobble [his] 'belief in [himself]' from the hands of intoxicated flatterers," the
higher man lacks the leonine will and determination that fosters the genuinely
sublime human being's sense of independence from the rabble.[58]

Let me summarize this discussion of the higher men's limitations and of why
Zarathustra cannot vindicate himself by forming the higher men in the image of
his happiness: Implicit in *Zarathustra*, I think, is a distinction between two modalities of the will that wills the sublime, one of which is strong, leonine, and
Promethean and the other of which is weak, irresolute, and romantic. Zarathustra himself, especially as he appears in the concluding sections of Part 3, is Nietzsche's primary and paradigmatic example of strong, Promethean willing. The
higher men are his primary examples of weak, romantic willing. For Zarathustra,
having a strong, Promethean will is a matter of being firm and successful in one's
effort to envision oneself as embodying a spiritual height that transcends the rabble, or, as in the case of the laughing shepherd who prefigures Zarathustra's appearance in "The Convalescent," as embodying a spiritual height that transcends
humanity per se. Having a weak, romantic will, on the other hand, is a matter of
being infirm and unsuccessful in this effort, notwithstanding one's aspiration.
Zarathustra cannot vindicate himself by forming the higher men in the image of
his happiness, for the higher men could never experience happiness of the sort he
experiences. Because the higher men's aspiration after the sublime is the weak, irresolute aspiration characteristic of romanticism, they cannot be trained to envision their souls as sublime incarnations of an eternal "now." Thus, they cannot be
trained to form the Promethean lion's happiness-inducing thought of recurrence

(the judgment that one's existence is characterized by a recurrence of the same, predicated on one's belief, at some particular moment, that, by then envisioning one's soul as the incarnation of an eternal "now," one is personifying redemption3), for envisioning one's soul as just such a sublime incarnation is essential to that thought.

By distinguishing Promethean willing from romantic willing, I have implied that Promethean willing is nonromantic. But one could just as well and perhaps with greater justice say that the distinction in question here is really between *two modalities of the romantic will.*[59] Like the denizens of the *"chez* Magny," as Nietzsche depicts them in an 1887 letter to Peter Gast, the higher man lacks *"la force."*[60] When the higher man acknowledges this lack, and that he is deficient in the strength of will he requires for a redemptive vision *of* his existence, commensurate in his eyes with his sublime aspiration, he begins to want to be delivered *from* his existence. Recognizing that he cannot make good his life by expressing himself, he soon becomes a romantic pessimist who hopes to escape his life. The Promethean Zarathustra avoids romantic pessimism, because, arguably, he is a strong-willed, successful, self-expressive romantic. By envisioning his soul as the incarnation of an eternal "now," he expresses a sublime view of himself that, due to his second practical postulate, seems to him commensurate with his sublime aspiration to redeem his existence by willing backwards. Thus, the Promethean Zarathustra's strong, self-expressive, romantic will appears to succeed where the higher men's weak, self-expressive, romantic wills failed.

By proposing that Zarathustra too becomes a romantic when he forms the lion's thought of recurrence, I mean to illuminate Nietzsche's complex engagement with romanticism. Despite his insistence in some of his later writings that the Dionysian excludes the romantic,[61] Nietzsche's portrait of Zarathustra as a lion-spirit suggests a different view. As I initially argued in Chapter 3, Nietzsche figures the leonine Zarathustra as a Promethean, Dionysian hero. Yet he also figures him, in the finale of Part 3 and in Part 4, as a strong romantic who has fulfilled his sublime aspirations—this, in any case, is the position I wish to defend. Nietzsche distances himself from romanticism by claiming that the Dionysian excludes the romantic, and by focusing his talk of romanticism on weak romantics who become romantic pessimists. Thus, he obscures and may even seem to overlook the strong, self-expressive romanticism of the Promethean, Dionysian hero,[62] as well as the *difference* between the Promethean Dionysian hero and the Dionysian child. As we shall see, when we examine Zarathustra's final metamorphosis in connection to the child's thought of recurrence, this difference marks Nietzsche's attempt in *Zarathustra* to break philosophically with strong romanticism.

Zarathustra's use of self-parody to vindicate his claim that he has defeated the spirit of resignation is the crowning point of the dramatic farce that follows his noontime celebration of eternity. Starting with the roasting of Zarathustra in "The Last Supper," the higher men's conversations with their host are time and again punctuated by joking, or laughter, or the praise of laughter, as in Zarathustra's speech on the higher man. Even the sadness the sorcerer's song of melancholy engenders is quite quickly dispersed by the laughter Zarathustra evokes with his rejoinder to the leech scientist's reply to the sorcerer. As the higher men "convalesce," the festive jubilation of Part 4 intensifies. Still, Zarathustra takes care to remark that his guests' laughter is not *his* laughter, and thus to suggest that their laughter is not the sort of laughter he meant to promote in his speech on the higher man: that is, not the sort of laughter that he believes betokens the Promethean sublimity the higher men desire but can never achieve.[63]

In "The Awakening" and "The Ass Festival," Zarathustra meets with a comical turn of events that catches him by surprise: namely, the sight of the higher men worshipping an ass. Zarathustra first reacts to the ass festival by rebuking his guests for awakening the old god. Confronted, however, with the higher men's articulate defense of their merry celebration, he softens his reaction and ends up praising the ass festival.[64] Entering into the spirit of his *companions'* laughter, Zarathustra increasingly appreciates *their* sense of humor. Echoing the leech scientist's claim that he (Zarathustra) could easily turn into an ass, Zarathustra even endorses the idea of an ass festival dedicated to him: that is, the idea of an ass festival in which he or, alternatively, the memory of him, displaced the ass as an object of veneration. In such a festival, Zarathustra imagines, the pious would remember him *as an ass*: "And when you celebrate it again, this ass festival, do it for your own sakes and also do it for my sake. And in remembrance of *me*."[65]

How should Zarathustra have to behave in order to be remembered as an ass? Without referring explicitly to *Zarathustra*, Nietzsche hints at an answer to this question in *Beyond Good and Evil*:

There is a point in every philosophy when the philosopher's "conviction" appears on the stage—or to use the language of an ancient Mystery:

Adventavit asinus,
Pulcher et fortissimus.[66]

An ass festival for Zarathustra's sake, a festival in which Zarathustra were remembered as an ass, would be a fete devoted to the recollection of Zarathustra's effort to vindicate his "conviction" by staging a public spectacle. It would be a commemorative tribute to Zarathustra's asinine attempt to substantiate his conviction by enacting the sort of drama that, Nietzsche maintains, philosophers inevitably enact if called upon to defend their views. Zarathustra performs such a drama in "The Sleepwalker Song," embracing the role of an ass the higher men revere and may revere again in memory someday.

We can begin to see that Zarathustra acts the ass in "The Sleepwalker Song," by noting that "Once More," the song he sings, he sang for the first time in the penultimate section of Part 3. When Zarathustra initially sang "Once More," his eyes were closed and he had begun to converse with his soul. Singing his song to his soul (figured as "life"), and meditating on the second, leonine act of recurrence, he enjoyed the still and private solitude that Gustav Mahler so exquisitely evokes when he sets "Once More" to music in the fourth movement of his Third Symphony.[67] Singing the same song to the higher men, Zarathustra transforms it, reproducing it as a sort of public, operatic theater.[68] As he sings his aria a second time, Zarathustra describes the midnight bell he hears as a "sweet lyre." Subsequently, he proposes that he is this lyre and that his song is the song of this lyre.[69] In essence, Zarathustra suggests that in performing "Once More" for the higher men he makes it into a "lyre" or "hurdy-gurdy" song that, reminiscent of the *Leier-Lied* his animals sang in "The Convalescent," cannot express his privately lived and sublime experience of self-redemption (redemption3). Insisting that he is not communicating this experience to the higher men, Zarathustra says that he speaks "before the deaf" who "do not understand" him.[70] Transmogrified into a form of public theater, "Once More" ceases to convey the pulse of Zarathustra's soul life. Rather, it stages a parody of that life, a hurdy-gurdy distortion of Zarathustra's vision of eternity that re-presents it as the drunken, asinine musing of a dim-eyed, stumbling somnambulist.

The self-parodic nature of Zarathustra's effort at self-vindication is further suggested by a consideration of his connection to the Wagnerian sorcerer. In contrast to his private, solitary rendition of "Once More," the version of the song Zarathustra sings to the higher men—punctuated as it is by his self-questioning, his exhortations to the higher men, and his abrupt, apostrophic asides to a lyre, the day, the world, and a vine—seems strained and graceless.[71] In fact, the irregular, free verse of this sleepwalking performance of "Once More" more nearly echoes the sorcerer's tortured parody of Zarathustra's struggle with his abysmal thought than it does the serene, classical style of Zarathustra's performance of "Once More" in Part 3.[72] Even Zarathustra's language in "The Sleepwalker Song"—for example his "Break, bleed, heart!" (*Brich, blute, Herz!*) and his "go, but return" (*vergeh, aber komm zürück*)—recalls the song the sorcerer sang when he first met Zarathustra.[73] Perhaps this should come as no surprise, for the sorcerer himself has prophesied that before night falls Zarathustra will have learned to laud him.[74] If imitation is the highest form of flattery, then, indeed, Zarathustra has fulfilled the sorcerer's prophecy. By echoing the song in which the sorcerer parodies Zarathustra, Zarathustra, in effect, parodies himself.

I have previously suggested that Zarathustra's self-parody entails a "self-sacrifice" whereby Zarathustra surrenders his public image of himself as a self-redeeming tragic hero. By entering into the carnivalesque mood of the higher men's religious festivity, Zarathustra relinquishes, temporarily, his elevated, Promethean depiction of himself.[75] Appearing ironically, as a Christ that has had his anti-Christian sentiments betrayed by a Judas (the ugliest man) whose Last Supper ass-worship awakened the old God, Zarathustra himself seems to betray these sentiments by abandoning his sublime self-portrait and "martyring" it to the cause of a *Satyrspiel* that deifies its leading *Spieler*. Marx's point about all world historical events—that they occur twice, first as tragedy and then again as farce—is likewise true of the second, leonine act of recurrence, the second and public enactment of which affords the higher men no occasion for tragic heroism, but the opportunity to lose themselves in revelry and carousing that the narrative voice telling the tale of "The Sleepwalker Song" would *not* have *Zarathustra's* readers confuse with the high seriousness of tragic art:

> But the old soothsayer was dancing with joy; and even if, as some of the chroniclers think, he was full of sweet wine, he was certainly still fuller of the sweetness of life and had renounced all weariness. There are even some who relate that the ass danced too, and that it had not been for nothing that the ugliest man had given him wine to drink before. Now it may have been so or otherwise; and if the ass really did not dance that night, yet greater and stranger wonders occurred than the dancing of an ass would have been. In short, as the proverb of Zarathustra says: "What does it matter?"[76]

While it would be folly to instruct irresolute romantics to envision their souls as incarnations of an eternal "now," it is not folly to use farcical self-parody to intoxicate them. Indeed, after the soothsayer fulfills the prediction that he will dance by evening, Zarathustra completes the task of self-vindication by using farcical self-parody for precisely that purpose. Like Wagner's operas, as Nietzsche describes them in *The Case of Wagner*, Zarathustra's farce excites weary nerves.[77] Appealing to the higher men's yearning for a sublimity that they cannot produce for themselves, Zarathustra enthralls his companions with his song of an unbounded eternity that encompasses all things and all oppositions. By inviting the higher men to join in his "round," Zarathustra inspires them to lose themselves in the ecstasy of a drunken singing and sleep that will relieve them, for a night, of whatever remains in them of the spirit of resignation. Zarathustra proves that he has triumphed over that spirit, not by exhorting these weak-willed romantic pessimists to do what they cannot do, but, in the manner of Wagner, by overwhelming them with intimations of the infinite. Reminiscent, perhaps, of the teachers of virtue whose promotion of sleep Zarathustra criticizes in Part 1, the higher men sing themselves to sleep, thereby escaping the unhappy feelings of meaninglessness that, with God dead, they have not been able to dissipate by expressing and striving to distinguish themselves.

Zarathustra and the Child's Thought of Recurrence

The second of the two narratives animating Part 4 tells the tale of Zarathustra's perseverance in anticipating the advent of his children. Nietzsche begins the second narrative with "The Honey Sacrifice," in which, we have seen, Zarathustra, the hunter-god, "hunts" and "fishes" for his children. He continues the story with "The Welcome," where Zarathustra compares his children to the higher men. Nietzsche concludes Part 4's second tale with "The Sign," where Zarathustra forsakes the higher men, announcing that the advent of his children is imminent.

As I have characterized it, Part 4's second narrative divides into three episodes, the first and second of which ("The Honey Sacrifice" and "The Welcome") frame Zarathustra's search for and flight from the higher men ("The Cry of Distress" through "Noon"), and the second and third of which ("The Welcome" and "The Sign") frame the evening he spends with them ("The Last Supper" through "The Sleepwalker Song"). By framing and punctuating the story of this search, flight, and evening (roughly, Part 4's *first* narrative), Nietzsche's tripartite second narrative foregrounds Zarathustra's vision of the future, attributing to him a destiny that sharply distinguishes him from the higher men.

In "The Welcome" (the second episode of Part 4's second narrative), Zarathustra renews his resolve to persevere in anticipating the advent of his children, explaining his reasons for his resolve in terms that expand on what he says in "The Honey Sacrifice." Reminiscent of Socrates' speech in the *Symposium*, Zarathustra's explanation describes an ascending order of value that terminates in beauty:

> Nor are your beautiful and wellborn enough for me. I need clean, smooth mirrors for my doctrines; on your surface even my own image is distorted. Many a burden, many a reminiscence press on your shoulders; many a wicked dwarf crouches in your nooks. There is hidden mob in you too. And even though you may be high and of a higher kind, much in you is crooked and

misshapen. There is no smith in the world who could hammer you right and straight for me.

You are mere bridges; may men higher than you stride over you. You signify steps: therefore do not be angry with him who climbs over you to *his* height. A genuine son and perfect heir may yet grow from your seed, even for me: but that is distant. You yourselves are not those to whom my heritage and name belong.

It is not for you that I wait in these mountains; it is not with you that I am to go down for the last time. Only as signs have you come to me, that those higher than you are even now on their way to me: *not* the men of great longing, of great nausea, of great disgust, and that which you call the remnant of God; no, no, three times no! It is for others that I wait here in these mountains, and I will not lift my feet from here without them; it is for those who are higher, stronger, more triumphant, and more cheerful, such as are built perpendicular in body and soul: *laughing lions* must come!

O my strange guests! Have you not yet heard anything of my children? And that they are on their way to me? Speak to me of my gardens, of my blessed isles, of my new beautiful kind [*meiner neuen schönen Art*]—why do you not speak to me of that? This present I beseech from your love, that you speak to me of my children. For this I am rich, for this I grew poor; what did I now give, what would I not give to have one thing: these children, this living plantation, these life-trees of my will and my highest hope![78]

As distinct from the ascent Socrates promotes, the movement Zarathustra depicts does not proceed from a world of bodies to a world of ideas. Rather Zarathustra envisions an ascent from one form of embodied, human being to another. To be specific, he draws on "On the Three Metamorphoses" to articulate an order of rank corresponding to the tripartite distinction between camel, lion, and child. Burdened with "reminiscences" and weighed down by the spirit of gravity—symbolized, here, by "wicked dwarfs"[79]—the higher men occupy the lowest level of the hierarchy. Recalling earlier phases of Zarathustra's development, these camel-like, weak romantics can neither rid themselves of the spirit of gravity nor see beyond their reminiscences to the possibility of a future shaped by non-Christian-Platonic values. Higher than the higher men are laughing lions, strong romantics who, presumably, like the laughing shepherd and Zarathustra in "The Convalescent," form the lion's thought of recurrence. Higher than the laughing lions, finally, are Zarathustra's children.

More needs to be said about the connection between the laughing lions and Zarathustra's children. How should this connection be understood if, as I have suggested, Zarathustra's children rank higher than laughing lions and embody the third metamorphosis of the spirit? The answer to this question, I think, is that laughing lions are not laughing lions *tout court*. Additionally, they are individuals in whom bodily passions have been reborn. Zarathustra suggests as much when he says that laughing lions are "built perpendicular in body and soul," thereby echoing his description in Part 1 of healthy bodies as "perfect and perpendicular."[80] As we saw in Chapter 3, Zarathustra associates healthy, perpendicular bodies with the Goethean, Dionysian faith that man and man's earth "remain unexhausted." In his imagination, then, laughing lions have bodies that harbor stirrings of passions that could be used to create new values. As Zarathustra pictures them, laughing lions could be prompted to "see" and "hear" within their bodies the possibility of going-under to Dionysian chaos and then becoming the children, "life-trees," and overmen who realize his "highest hope." Zarathustra calls laughing lions "his children," for they are lions who could discard their leonine wills and successfully perform the third metamorphosis of the spirit.

Zarathustra will recognize himself in his children, not because he will see their suffering as his own, but because he will see their beauty as his own. In contrast to the higher men, Zarathustra's children will be "smooth mirrors" who reflect his beautiful image without distortion. Zarathustra and the lions he awaits will *become* beautiful, precisely by enacting the third metamorphosis of the spirit. Enlivened by the energies of the blessed isles whereupon Zarathustra first envisioned "the beauty of the overman,"[81] they will realize that beauty in their own bodies by making themselves into persons of a "new beautiful kind." Zarathustra and the laughing lions will enact the third metamorphosis of the spirit when they transform the lion's thought of recurrence into the child's thought of recurrence and reclaim their abilities to go-under. Zarathustra himself seems to enact this metamorphosis in "The Sign."

This section begins with Zarathustra departing from the higher men, who remain asleep in his cave, to begin a new day. Here, again, Nietzsche's portrait of Zarathustra recalls Plato's *Symposium*, as well as Nietzsche's allusion to the *Symposium* in a discussion of the death of Socrates in *The Birth of Tragedy*: "He [Socrates] went to his death with the calm with which, according to Plato's description, he leaves the Symposium at dawn, the last of the revelers, to begin a new day, while on the benches and on the earth his drowsy table companions remain behind to dream of Socrates, the true eroticist."[82] Socrates takes leave of his companions, after arguing that a tragic poet can also write comedy. Analogously, Zarathustra takes leave of the higher men, having shown that a tragic hero, which he appears to be at the end of Part 3, can also become a comedian who parodies his own tragic heroism. In the *Symposium*, Socrates puts the spirits of tragedy and comedy behind him, confident that the final telos of his eros is the form of beauty. In "The Sign," Zarathustra puts these spirits behind him, hoping to embody an earthly beauty that, as a sublime tragic hero and a self-parodying *Satyrspieler*, remains beyond his ken.[83]

Zarathustra's movement beyond tragedy and comedy is indicated in the text, not only by the appearance of a lion that literally laughs, but by the descent of a flock of doves.[84] In the tradition of Christian iconography, an image of doves often symbolizes the holy spirit and its gifts grace (*Gnade*).[85] Zarathustra's response to the doves he sees suggests that he too associates them with a sort of grace, or graciousness, though not a grace dispensed by the Christian God. In the aftermath of the doves' appearance, Zarathustra is silent, still, and relaxed (his heart "loosens"). Thus, he resembles the portrait of the hero (see "On Those Who Are Sublime") who, in quieting his desire in beauty, stilling his passion in beauty, and releasing his body's tension in beauty, surpasses his sublimity and becomes a beautiful overhero. "When power becomes gracious [*gnädig*] and descends into the visible," says Zarathustra, "such descent I call beauty."[86] As we saw in Chapter 4, Zarathustra appears to argue here that the sublime hero becomes beautiful by reclaiming his ability to go-under and condescending graciously to revalue his passions. In "The Sign," I am suggesting, the sublimely heroic Zarathustra becomes beautiful by emulating this behavior. Zarathustra is prompted to these actions, it seems, because he reads the advent of the doves as a sign that he has been re-endowed with the capacity to personify a beauty-engendering grace or graciousness.[87] More exactly, he reads the advent of the doves as a sign that the passions of the earth (again, the kinds of passions that commonly claimed human bodies in the past, tying one generation to another) have been reborn within him—and, also, within the laughing lions he awaits—thereby enabling him and them to go-under, to redeem the human past by revaluing those passions, and to realize in their persons the third metamorphosis of the spirit.[88]

Zarathustra's belief that his enactment of the third metamorphosis would be marked by a descent of doves originated in his "stillest hour":

> Then it spoke to me again without voice: "What matters their mockery? You are one who has forgotten how to obey: now you shall command. Do you not know who is most needed by all? He that commands great things. To do great things is difficult; but to command great things is more difficult. This is what is most unforgivable in you: you have the power and you do not want to rule."
> And I answered: "I lack the lion's voice for commanding."
>   Then it spoke to me as a whisper. "It is the stillest words that bring on the storm: Thoughts that come on doves' feet guide the world. O, Zarathustra, you

shall go as a shadow of that which must come: thus you will command and commanding lead the way. And I answered: "I am ashamed."

Then it spoke to me again without voice: "You must become a child and without shame. The pride of youth is still upon you; you have become young late; but whoever would become as a child must overcome his youth too."[89]

Although Zarathustra has forgotten his camel's knowledge of "how to obey" in "The Stillest Hour," he has yet to summon the lion's "voice for commanding" that he will use to defeat his abysmal thought in "The Convalescent." After Zarathustra remarks that he lacks the voice for commanding, his conscience retorts that the stillest words bring on the storm and that thoughts that come on doves' feet guide the world. Zarathustra is ashamed that he has yet to fulfill his desire to become a lion, but his conscience foresees that stillness and dove-inspired graciousness will someday temper and displace that desire. Emphatically whispering the only words it "voices," Zarathustra's conscience anticipates his transformation in "The Sign." In the perspective of his conscience, Zarathustra, in acquiring the lion's voice for commanding, will become "a shadow of that which must come." In other words, he will become a shadow of the child he must become, the child who has relinquished the pride of the lion and enacted the third metamorphosis of the spirit.

The beautifying metamorphosis Zarathustra effects in "The Sign" distinguishes him from the laughing lions who have not yet effected the third metamorphosis of the spirit. Having become a beautiful child, Zarathustra is *oblivious* to the savage, nay-saying roar with which the laughing lion accompanying him—a figure, presumably, for the (human) laughing lions he awaits—frightens the higher men.[90] Exemplifying the "innocence" and "forgetting" of the child, Zarathustra puts out of his mind the theologically informed, leonine self-interpretation with which he envisioned his soul as an omnipresent, pantheistic deity. No longer prey to the "the final sin" of pity,[91] and now no longer a laughing lion, he will recognize his beauty only in men who, like him, have ceased to be laughing lions and effected the third metamorphosis of the spirit.

In Chapter 1, I noted that Nietzsche's child is not only "forgetting" and "innocence" but a "sacred yes." In Chapter 3, I argued that that "yes" is predicated on an experience of passional chaos. Zarathustra readies himself to say "yes" when, in the wake of the modern, ascetic annihilation of bodily passions, he takes the doves he sees to indicate that such passions, and thus the possibility of experiencing passional chaos, have been returned to European modernity. Relinquishing his view of himself as a sublime, self-redeeming tragic hero (hence, not simply relinquishing, as in "The Sleepwalker Song," the *public image* of himself as such a hero),[92] Zarathustra deigns to revalue kinds of passion that, by reoccupying his body and his future companions' bodies, have reoccupied European modernity. With these future companions near ("*My children are near*," Zarathustra proclaims), Zarathustra ceases to be a Promethean lion-spirit who, having been crucified to the endless perpetuation of Christian-Platonic values, redeems himself by (according to his practical postulate) envisioning his soul as the omnipresent incarnation of an eternal "now." Rather he becomes a child-spirit who, in going-under to the earth's reborn passions and effecting redemption1, will exhort laughing lions who are not yet children to "see" and "hear" within their bodies the possibility of doing the same. Forsaking his happiness for his work, Zarathustra will aim again to realize his personal and poetic intentions, and thus to close the rift between the coming Dionysus and man.[93]

At the conclusion of Part 4's second narrative, a sign of the return to European modernity of the possibility of experiencing passional chaos engenders the third act of the thought-drama of recurrence. In the first act of Zarathustra's thought-drama, Zarathustra judges that his existence is characterized by a recurrence of the same, predicating that judgment on his belief that he has fallen victim to the endless perpetuation of Christian-Platonic values in the person of the small man. In the second act, Zarathustra transforms his thought, judging again that his existence is characterized by a recurrence of the same, but for the reason that his soul is the incarnation of a perpetual "now" that is recurrently present in every moment, place and thing. In the third and final act, Zarathustra bases his judgment that he is tied to a recurrence of the same on his dove-inspired belief that bodily passion and the possibility of experiencing passional chaos have been returned to European modernity, thereby enabling him and the men he persevered in anticipating to play the child's game of creation. In this concluding phase of its development, the thought of recurrence motivates Zarathustra to reclaim his ability to go-under and to enact the third metamorphosis of the spirit.

As Zarathustra initially forms his thought of recurrence, it is a camel's thought that involves Zarathustra's belief that the past will repeat itself in the future; his belief, more precisely, that the values that have shaped European humanity in the past will shape it in the future. Transforming his thought the first time, Zarathustra forms the lion's thought of recurrence, which involves his belief that his soul is an omnipresent "now," or present moment, and therefore repeatedly present in all times, places, and things. Transforming his thought a second time, Zarathustra forms the child's thought of recurrence, which involves a belief neither in the repetition of the past, nor in the repetition of the present, but in the repetition of the possibility of a future that interrupts the reproduction and repetition of the past.[94] Put otherwise, the child's thought of recurrence involves Zarathustra's belief that the possibility of going-under to the chaos of the com-

ing god, and thus of making use of uncreated passions to create a future different than the past (to create a future governed by new values), has been returned
to some if not to all modern, European bodies.

The child's thought of recurrence is implicit in the metamorphosis that Zarathustra effects in "The Sign," or so I have been arguing. For an *explicit* statement
of this thought, we need only turn to the penultimate chapter of *Twilight*, where
Nietzsche envisions the eternal return as "the eternal return of life," by which I
take him to mean the eternal recurrence in life of life's inexhaustible potential to
go-under and re-create itself—even where that entails the sacrifice of life's "highest types."[95] In "The Sign," Zarathustra bases his judgment that his existence is
characterized by a recurrence of the same on his belief that the possibility of
going-under to a chaos that could be used to create new values has been returned
to his and his future companions' bodies. In *Twilight*, Nietzsche amends Zarathustra's belief, envisioning that possibility not only as an option that *has been* returned to human life, but also as one that *will be* returned to it, eternally. In the
perspective of the exuberant, final pages of *Twilight*, the soothsayer's prophecy of
an exhausted earth, if ever it were credible, shall never be credible again.

In *Zarathustra*, thinking the thought of eternal recurrence is Zarathustra's
vocation. Through his speeches and actions, Zarathustra forms and twice transforms the thought of recurrence, thus constituting it as *Zarathustra's Grundconception*, or unifying theme. As we have seen, Zarathustra's thought of recurrence, in each phase of its evolution, is intrinsically tied to critical developments
in the drama of *Zarathustra*: for example, the soothsayer's articulation of a
prophecy; Zarathustra's interpretation of that prophecy as nihilistic; Zarathustra's invention of a second practical postulate that comforts him; and the return
to European modernity of modes of passion that were previously obliterated.
Bound essentially to the drama that it thematically unifies, Zarathustra's thought
of recurrence is, I have suggested, a drama within that drama, a sort of three-act
"thought-drama" in its own right.

The end of *Zarathustra*, Part 3, is the end of Zarathustra's tragedy. It is evident, however, that the end of Zarathustra's tragedy is not the end of his three-
act thought-drama, which is a Prometheus drama whose second act marks the
conclusion of Zarathustra's tragedy. In other words, Zarathustra's tragedy ends
when Zarathustra, after imagining that he is Prometheus bound, crucified to the
perpetuation of Christian-Platonic values in the person of the small man (act 1
of the thought-drama), adopts the defiant posture of Goethe's Prometheus and
forms the lion's thought of recurrence (act 2 of the thought-drama). As Zarathustra forms the lion's thought of recurrence, he embraces the practical postu-

late that, by envisioning his soul as a pantheistic god (as the omnipresent incarnation of an eternal "now"), he is succeeding in redeeming his existence. Moreover, by embracing that postulate, he *persuades himself* that he is succeeding in redeeming his existence. Thus, Zarathustra distinguishes himself from the higher men, none of whom persuades himself that he is succeeding in that endeavor. Deriving a "tragic-heroic" comfort from a postulate that proclaims that he is redeeming his existence, Zarathustra ends his tragedy, but without losing himself in an otherworldly, metaphysical comfort that lets him forget and seem to escape his existence.[96] Exemplifying Nietzsche's critique and revision of *The Birth of Tragedy*'s theory of tragedy, Zarathustra's Promethean, heroic triumph over the spirit of resignation suggests that tragedy can end on a note of strong, not weak, romanticism.

The arrival of Zarathustra's Herculean children, which symbolically "liberates" Zarathustra-Prometheus to return Dionysus to a world that his forgotten him, initiates the third, *posttragic* act of Zarathustra's three-act Prometheus thought-drama. Because his laughing, leonine children embody the return of bodily passion to the modern world, Zarathustra can return Dionysus to that world—or, in other words, heal the rift between Dionysus and man—by inspiring his children to "see" within their bodies the possibility of going-under to the passional chaos that *is* the coming god. With his liberators near, Zarathustra forms the child's thought of recurrence, enacts the third metamorphosis of the spirit, and aspires to move his liberators to do the same. Thus, he completes the third act of his Prometheus thought-drama.

I will conclude my discussion of Part 4's second narrative by sketching some final thoughts concerning the third metamorphosis of the spirit:

1. A lion-spirited individual can effect this metamorphosis, I argued in Chapter 1, only if he abandons the leonine belief that his acts of willing are deeds done by an ego substance (a substantial subject). In Chapter 4, I complicated this picture, arguing that a lion-spirit can become a yea-saying child only if he discards his heroic will, along with his Promethean experience of Dionysus, and reclaims his ability to go-under. The two arguments are connected, for a lion-spirit can discard his heroic will and reclaim his ability to go-under only if he abandons the belief that his acts of willing are deeds done by an ego substance. What motivates this view of the lion-spirit? I sketch an answer to this question by briefly examining Nietzsche's discussion of bodily acts in section 19 of *Beyond Good and Evil*:

> A man who *wills* commands something within himself that renders obedience, or that he believes renders obedience.

But now let us notice what is strangest about the will—this manifold thing for which the people have only one word; inasmuch as in the given circumstances we are at the same time the commanding *and* the obeying parties, and as the obeying party we know the sensations of constraint, impulsion, pressure, resistance, and motion, which usually begin immediately after the act of will; inasmuch as, on the other hand, we are accustomed to disregard this duality, and to deceive ourselves about it by means of the synthetic concept "I," a whole series of erroneous conclusions, and consequently of false evaluations of the will itself, has become attached to the act of willing—to such a degree that he who wills believes sincerely that willing *suffices* for action. Since in the great majority of cases there has been exercise of will only when the effect of the command—that is, obedience; that is, the action—was to be *expected*, the *appearance* has translated itself into the feeling, as if there were *a necessity of effect*. In short, he who wills believes with a fair amount of certainty that will and action are somehow one; he ascribes the success, the carrying out of the willing, to the will itself, and thereby enjoys an increase of the sensation of power which accompanies all success.

In this way the person exercising volition adds the feeling of delight of his successful executive instruments, the useful "underwills" or under-souls—indeed, our body is but a social structure composed of many souls—to his feelings of delight as commander. *L'effet c'est moi*: what happens here is what happens in every well-constructed and happy commonwealth; namely, the governing class identifies itself with the successes of the commonwealth.[97]

On this account, a body, *B*, acts if, and only if, it has a dual nature; that is, if, and only if, it embodies (i) an act of willing, or second-order desiring, that commands an "underwill," or first-order desire, to move *B* to act, and (ii) a separate act of compliance whereby that underwill obeys the act of willing and moves *B* to act.[98] But there is more. Nietzsche claims that the use of the concept "I"—by which I believe he means the concept of an ego substance that exists apart from the acts it performs[99]—obscures the dual nature of bodies and bodily acts. More precisely, he claims that the application of that concept engenders the false belief that acts of willing and acts of moving bodies to act are "somehow one."

For Nietzsche, the concept of an I or ego substance is synthetic, because applications of that concept foster the *misrepresentation of duality as unity*. As I reconstruct it, his view is something like the following: a first judgment that an act of willing is an act of *I* willing that my body perform act *A*—where I feel that my body's performance of act *A* is "to be *expected*"—prompts me to judge that *I* willing that my body perform act *A suffices* to move my body to perform act *A*; this second judgment, in its turn, prompts a third, "synthesizing" judgment that the act of *I* willing that my body perform act *A* and the act of moving my body to perform act *A* are identical; or, alternatively, that the act of *I* willing that my body perform act *A* and the act of moving my body to perform act *A* are "somehow one." The second and third judgments obscure the dual nature of bodily acts, for they tacitly deny that the acts of compliance that actually move bodies to perform acts have a role to play in moving bodies to perform acts.

In sum, the belief that one is an ego substance engenders the illusions (i) that willing that one's body act is identical to moving it to act and (ii) that willing that one's body act suffices to move it to act. From the perspective of someone who endorses this belief, an act of willing is not directed at first-order desires (such an act is not an act of "commanding" something within oneself), and does not depend for its success on the existence and compliance of first-order desires. Indeed, from such a perspective, first-order desires disappear from view, thereby permitting bodily acts to appear as direct, unmediated manifestations of an ego substance's acts of willing: *L'effet c'est moi.*

My contention, of course, is that such a perspective belongs to the lion-spirit. The lion-spirit endorses the judgment that his acts of willing are the acts of an I or ego substance that he himself is. As we have seen, he also endorses the judgment that willing to create new values will *suffice* by itself to create them (whether promoting a quasi-idealist epistemology or embracing the practical postulate that he personifies redemption3, the lion-spirit insists on the absolute independence of his will). Why does the lion-spirit endorse both judgments? More to the point, why does Nietzsche *portray* the lion-spirit as endorsing both judgments? Section 19 of *Beyond Good and Evil* helps answer this question, for it supports the conjecture that, in Nietzsche's philosophical imagination, the lion-spirit's judgment that his acts of willing are the acts of an I substance prompts him to judge that his acts of willing to create new values will suffice by themselves to create them (the phrase "that his acts of willing to create new values will suffice by themselves to create them" abbreviates the judgment that, strictly speaking, section 19 would attribute to the lion-spirit: namely, that his acts of willing that his body create new values will suffice by themselves to move his body to create them). In the perspective of the lion-spirit, acts of willing that create new values will not be "commanding" acts of revaluation that require for their efficacy the existence and compliance of first-order desires. Indeed, in this perspective, first-order desires and passions are nowhere evident and do not exist. The lion-spirit does not acknowledge the reality of first-order desires and passions. Thus, he estranges himself from his ability to go-under to them.

Nietzsche's analysis of bodily acts helps to explain the lion-spirit's self-estrangement by connecting his self-estrangement to his view of himself as an ego substance. Nietzsche's analysis also suggests that a lion-spirit can discard his heroic will, reclaim his ability to go-under, and enact the third metamorphosis of the spirit only if he abandons his self-substantializing and self-estranging view of himself. Put otherwise, it lets us see why (in Nietzsche's view) the child-spirit, though he retains the lion-spirit's commitment to becoming a new-values creator, must eschew a substantialist self-understanding (cf. Chapter 1).

2. In *The Birth of Tragedy*, Nietzsche conceptualizes Dionysian chaos by revising Kant. In other words, he argues that experiencing Dionysian chaos entails putting oneself in touch with the Kantian thing-in-itself. In *Zarathustra*, in the aftermath of his rejection of Kant's appearances/thing-in-itself dichotomy, Nietzsche reconceptualizes Dionysian chaos, again by revising Kant. In particular, he revises Kant's doctrine of sensibility. To be precise, Nietzsche attributes a sensible "soul" (Ariadne), or power of receptivity, to the body, due to which the body can be affected by Dionysian chaos, which Nietzsche now interprets as a chaos of uncreated, bodily passions. As we have seen, the lion-spirit disowns and estranges himself from his body's power of receptivity. As we have also seen, he must reclaim and thus acknowledge this power, by reclaiming and thus acknowledging his ability to go-under, if he is to enact the third metamorphosis of the spirit.

Let me note, finally, that for Nietzsche, as well as for Kant, sensibility is epistemically significant; for Kant, because the mind's receptivity to given intuitions is essential to empirical knowledge; for Nietzsche, because the child's cognition of future possibility—that is, his "seeing" and "hearing" within his body the possibility of going-under and then becoming a creator of new values—presupposes that he has acknowledged his power to go-under and thus to receive into his experience a chaos of uncreated passions. A necessary condition of the child's distinctive knowledge is his acknowledgment of his vulnerability to the coming god.[100]

3. In Chapters 2 and 4, I argued that Zarathustra interprets his perlocutionary failure in historical terms. Oblivious to de Manian arguments, Zarathustra believes that he has failed to persuade his auditors to "see" within themselves the possibility of going-under, first, because modern asceticism has destroyed their passions, thus transforming them into men akin to the last men (see Chapter 2); and second, because his leonine self-estrangement has hindered his ability to move them (see Chapter 4). When *Zarathustra* ends, the appearance of Zarathustra's children seems imminent and Zarathustra performs the third metamorphosis of the spirit. Because Zarathustra's children embody a rebirth of bodily passions, Zarathustra expects that they will be able to "see" within themselves the possibility of going-under. And because Zarathustra enacts the third meta-

morphosis, he need not worry that leonine self-estrangement will hinder his perlocutionary efforts. Zarathustra believes that he was a perlocutionary failure (i) because his auditors had become individuals of a certain sort (men akin to the last men) and (ii) because he had become an individual of a certain sort (a self-estranged lion). As *Zarathustra* ends, Zarathustra expects to become a perlocutionary success, for he seems finally to have found auditors of the right sort and because he has become an individual of a different sort. Looking to the future, Zarathustra continues to reject the de Manian view that perlocutionary failure is ineluctable.

4. My concluding thought concerns the strong romanticism of the Promethean, Dionysian hero who fulfills his sublime aspirations. This, of course, is the romanticism that Zarathustra exemplifies in the final pages of Part 3. Nietzsche rejects even *strong* romanticism, I think (here, my remarks are largely conjectural), because it is, essentially, a form of lion-spiritedness. In other words, he holds that the strong romantic, who persuades himself that he is redeeming himself by expressing himself (who, in Zarathustra's case, embraces the practical postulate that he personifies redemption3, thereby persuading himself that he is redeeming himself by envisioning his soul as the omnipresent incarnation of an eternal "now"), is a lion-spirit committed to the fiction that the subject is an ego substance. For Nietzsche, romantic expressivism requires the view that the self-expressive poetic or otherwise artistic subject is a *substantial* subject who exists apart from his or her acts and works of self-expression. Nietzsche believes, therefore, that romantic expressivism is ultimately rooted in leonine self-estrangement.

Performing the third metamorphosis entails abandoning the substantialist self-understanding of the lion-spirit. More generally, it entails abandoning all modern philosophies of the subject that thrive on this sort of self-understanding. In Nietzsche's view, romantic expressivism is one of those philosophies, as are the Cartesianism and the Kantianism that treat dispassionate, supersensible subjectivity as a normative ideal.[101] "Forgetting" these philosophies of the subject is, he believes, essential to becoming a child-spirit who effects a Dionysian interruption of modernity.

In Lieu of a Conclusion: An Introduction to Beyond Good and Evil

In this chapter, I have presented an optimistic reading of the ending of *Zarathustra*. Taking Zarathustra at his word, I have assumed that, as he leaves his cave, his laughing, leonine, children are near. Additionally, I have assumed that the appearance of a flock of doves indicates what I interpret it to indicate to Zarathustra: namely, the return to European modernity, via Zarathustra's body and his children's bodies, of bodily passion and the possibility of experiencing passional, Dionyian chaos. In short, I have read the ending of *Zarathustra* from Zarathustra's perspective, as optimistically anticipating a Dionysian interruption of European modernity.

Needless to say, the ending of *Zarathustra* can be read differently, even if one accepts that it brings to a conclusion Nietzsche's philosophical explanation of the possibility of creating new values. In completing his philosophical explanation—that is, in completing *Zarathustra*—Nietzsche concludes an extended rejoinder to his own skepticism as to the viability of Zarathustra's modernism—a skepticism that finds expression in *Zarathustra* in the form of representations of repetition. Still, the ending of *Zarathustra* need not be interpreted as *antiskeptical*, for it can also be construed as renewing doubt and incredulity.

The key point, here, is that *Zarathustra* ends before Zarathustra's children appear. Zarathustra tells us that his children are near, but he never sees them. Thus, the ending of *Zarathustra* is marked by the *absence* of his children. That absence is significant, for it invites a skeptical appraisal of Zarathustra's outlook and a pessimistic appraisal of his situation. Because the men Zarathustra awaits remain absent, one may doubt Zarathustra's beliefs that such men exist and that bodily passion has reoccupied European modernity. Skeptical that these beliefs are true and pessimistic about Zarathustra's prospects of finding the "right men," one might also insist that, ironically, his *true children*, the children who are *truly near*, are the higher men he disavows.[102] The ending of *Zarathustra*, though it concludes an explanation of the possibility of creating new values, if read in a skeptical, pessimistic, and ironic light, suggests that Zarathustra deceives himself if he expects that he or anyone else will one day realize a Dionysian interruption of European modernity. Like the waiting of Vladimir and Estragon, Zarathustra's waiting to go-under, on this reading, will be interminable.

Like the beginning of *Zarathustra*, the ending of the book admits equally of optimistic and pessimistic readings. In Chapter 2, we saw that Zarathustra's opening speech can be read either as a parody of Neoplatonism that envisions a Dionysian renewal of human life, or, alternatively, as a parody of Paul's letter to the Philippians that questions the likelihood of such a renewal. Similarly, Zarathustra's closing talk of absent children can be read either as suggesting that the advent of Zarathustra's children and a Dionysian interruption of modernity are imminent, or, alternatively, as indicating that neither the advent of Zarathustra's children nor a Dionysian interruption of modernity is or will ever be imminent.[103] Through his construction of the ending of *Zarathustra*, Nietzsche demonstrates, once again, his tendency to think against himself. Via the figure of Zarathustra, Nietzsche expresses his vision of Dionysian interruption. Via the absenting of Zarathustra's children, he casts doubt on that vision. Yet the vision persists, and asserts itself equipollently against the doubt, which is why a de Manian reading of the ending of *Zarathustra*, one that gave the last word to skepticism and irony, would be in error. To return again to the third epigraph of this chapter, Nietzsche is a seer who doubts, but also a doubter who sees, and never one to the exclusion of the other.[104]

I will turn now to *Beyond Good and Evil*, a book whose complexities and difficulties rival those of *Zarathustra* and that I cannot begin to do justice to here. Still, I hazard an inevitably inadequate discussion of Nietzsche's "Prelude to a Philosophy of the Future" in order to make a preliminary case for my view of its relationship to *Zarathustra*. In particular, I want to defend a thesis I put forth in Chapter 1: namely, that *Beyond Good and Evil* presents itself as having been written from the perspective of Zarathustra's expectation, at the end of *Zarathustra*, that the advent of his children is imminent. The book presents itself in this way, for Nietzsche crafts it to suggest that, like Zarathustra in "The Sign," he anticipates that potential creators of new values, the men he calls "philosophers of the future" and "new philosophers," will soon ascend to him. He writes, for example, that he "see[s] such new philosophers coming up [*heraufkommen*]."[105]

Nietzsche proclaims that new philosophers are "coming up" in the second chapter of *Beyond Good and Evil*. Just a few pages earlier, in the book's preface (*Vorrede*), he readies his readers for this proclamation with an indirect allusion to the closing pages of *Zarathustra*:

> It seems that all great things first have to bestride the earth in monstrous and frightening masks in order to incribe themselves in the hearts of humanity with eternal demands: dogmatism in philosophy was such a mask; for example, the Vedanta doctrine in Asia and Platonism in Europe.
>
> Let us not be ungrateful to it, although it must certainly be conceded that the worst, most durable, and most dangerous of all errors so far was a dogmatist's error—namely, Plato's invention of the pure spirit and the good as such. But now that it is overcome, now that Europe is breathing freely again after this nightmare and at least can enjoy a healthier—sleep, we, *whose task is wakefulness itself,* are the heirs of all that strength which has been fostered by the fight against this error. To be sure, it meant standing truth on her head and denying *perspective,* the basic condition of all life, when one spoke of spirit and the good as Plato did. Indeed, as a physician one might ask: "How could the most beautiful growth of antiquity, Plato, contract such a disease? Did the wicked Socrates corrupt him after all? Could Socrates have been the corrupter of youth after all? And did he deserve his hemlock?"

But the fight against Plato, or, to speak more clearly and for the "people," the fight against the Christian-ecclesiastical pressure of millennia—for Christianity is Platonism for "the people"—has created in Europe a magnificent tension the like of which has never yet existed on earth: with so tense a bow, we can now shoot for the most distant goals.[106]

In the self-portrait Nietzsche paints here, he himself endorses wakefulness, while his fellow Europeans, in the wake of the death of God (in the wake of the triumphant struggle against Christianity and Platonism), remain prey to a sleep that is at least healthier than the slumber that produced the Christian-Platonic nightmare. In essence, Nietzsche paints himself in the image of Zarathustra as Zarathustra first appears in "The Sign": awake, and looking to the future, while his postdeath-of-god contemporaries (in *Zarathustra*, the sleeping higher men) remain drowsily oblivious to his hopes and expectations. By recalling his readers to "The Sign," Nietzsche suggests that, like Zarathustra, he aims to inspire some of his contemporaries—as we later learn, the new philosophers who are "coming up"—to become creators of new values. He likewise suggests that, in contrast to Socrates, but again like Zarathustra, he will foster the beauty of these contemporaries, not corrupt it.

If the preface to *Beyond Good and Evil* invokes Zarathustra's point of view, so too does the "Aftersong" (*Nachgesang*), a poem entitled "From High Mountains" (*Aus hohen Bergen*). In the first three stanzas of the song, with their references to a sublime "bird's-eye view" (*Vogel-Schau*) and a highest height ("For you I have prepared my table in the highest height" [*Im Höchsten ward für euch mein Tisch gedeckt*]), and with their suggestion that the poem's lyric speaker awaits friends with whom to share his honey, Nietzsche evokes images of Zarathustra as Zarathustra appears at the end of Part 3 and at the beginning of Part 4. Consider too the fifth stanza, which depicts the lyric speaker's self-estrangement as the consequence of a self-wounding victory of strength:

Am I another? Self-estranged? From me—
Did I elude?
A wrestler who too oft himself subdued?
Straining against his strength too frequently,
Wounded and stopped by his own victory?

Ein Andrer ward ich? Und mir selber fremd?
Mir selbst entsprungen?
Ein Ringer, der zu oft sich selbst bezwungen?
Zu oft sich gegen eigne Kraft gestemmt,
durch eignen Sieg verwundet und gehemmt?

In this stanza, Nietzsche revisits the theme of Zarathustra's self-estranging, leonine triumph over his abysmal thought. Friends arrive in the fourth stanza, and the seventh stanza mentions their deficiencies. In the thirteenth stanza the lyric speaker awaits *new friends*, just as Zarathustra, after noting the deficiencies of the higher men (in "The Welcome" and "On the Higher Man"), awaits the new companions he describes as his children in "The Sign." The poem ends when the lyric speaker acknowledges that his song was the song of a wizard (*Ein Zauberer*) who sang through him, a wizard he names "Friend Zarathustra" (*Freund Zarathustra*).[107]

The preface and the "Aftersong" that frame *Beyond Good and Evil*, by returning readers to *Zarathustra* and, especially, to Zarathustra's outlook in "The Sign," suggest that Nietzsche meant *Beyond Good and Evil* to promote Zarathustra's aim, at the end of *Zarathustra*, to exhort the "right men" to become creators of new values. But how was *Beyond Good and Evil* to do this? In *Ecce Homo*, Nietzsche briefly answers this question:

BEYOND GOOD AND EVIL

Prelude to a Philosophy of the Future

I

The task for the years that followed now was indicated as clearly as possible. After the Yes-saying part of my task had been solved [*Nachdem der jasagende Theil meiner Aufgabe gelöst war*], the turn had come for the No-saying, *No-doing* part: the revaluation of our values so far [*die Umwerthung der bisherigen Werthe selbst*], the great war—conjuring up a day of decision. This included the slow search for those related to me, those who, prompted by strength, would offer me their hands for *destroying*.

From this moment forward all my writings are fish hooks: perhaps I know how to fish as well as anyone?—If nothing was caught, I am not to blame. *There were no fish*.

2

This book (1886) is in all essentials a *critique of modernity* . . . along with pointers to a contrary type that is as little modern as possible—a noble, Yes-saying type. In the latter sense, the book is a school for the *gentilhomme*, taking this concept in a more spiritual and radical sense than has ever been done. . . .

When you consider that this book followed *after Zarathustra*, you may perhaps also guess the dietetic regimen to which it owes is origin. The eye that had been spoiled by the tremendous need for seeing *far*—Zarathustra is even more far sighted than the Tsar—is here forced to focus on what is nearest, the age, the around-us.[108]

I argued in Chapter 5 that Zarathustra meets his greatest challenge in the soothsayer. Of all the representations of repetition Zarathustra encounters, the soothsayer's is the most threatening, for the soothsayer shares Zarathustra's post-Christian-Platonic interpretation of human being-in-time. Zarathustra's struggle to cope with the soothsayer's prophecy reaches its culmination in "The Seven Seals." Here, as he sings "The Yes and Amen Song," in the wake of his failure to reconcile the possibility of redemption1 with the postulate that he personifies redemption3, Zarathustra envisions himself as a pantheistic god who marries time to eternity. By ending Part 3 with Zarathustra's Promethean singing, Nietzsche solves the "Yes-saying" part of the task he mentions in *Ecce Homo*. More exactly, he shows how Zarathustra, by becoming a lion-spirit, can reaffirm and sustain his commitment to become a new-values creator, despite the resignation-inspiring ramifications of the soothsayer's prophecy.

When Nietzsche solves the "Yes-saying" part of his task, his philosophical explanation of the possibility of creating new values remains incomplete. As we have seen, the ending of Part 4 concludes this explanation by showing how Zarathustra, all apparent excluders notwithstanding, can still become a child-creator. For Nietzsche, the ending of Part 4 marks a shift from the sublime, lion-spirited yea-saying that terminates Part 3 to a beautiful, child-spirited yea-saying (the child's "sacred" yea-saying).[109] It marks such a shift, because it shows Zarathustra abandoning the sublime, heroic posture of "The Yes and Amen Song" to become a child-creator who will exhort the men ascending to his height to become child-creators.

By taking up Zarathustra's hortatory ambitions, *Beyond Good and Evil* begins where *Zarathustra* ends—assuming, of course, that the new philosopher's project of *revaluing* values, featured as a no-saying and no-doing enterprise in *Ecce Homo*, is identical to the child-creator's project of *creating* new values. Nietzsche suggests as much in *Beyond Good and Evil*, when he proclaims that new philosophers, through *original* revaluations and inversions of old values, will force the will of millennia onto *"new* tracks."[110] Nietzsche's aim in *Beyond Good and Evil*, like Zarathustra's in "The Sign," is to inspire the "right men," be they called "new philosophers," "Zarathustra's children," or "better players," to become avant-garde, modernist innovators who interrupt and disrupt modernity. To promote this aim, he constructs *Beyond Good and Evil*'s "critique of modernity," the bait with which he hopes to hook his "fish," as a "school" for the modernist innovator and revaluator, depicted in *Ecce Homo* as "the *gentilhomme.*"

Zarathustra is "far sighted," for it attempts to show that a radical alternative to modernity, effected by a creation of new values, is possible. *Beyond Good and Evil* is "near sighted," for it attempts to realize what is possible by transforming what is actual. If *Beyond Good and Evil* had functioned effectively as a school for the modernist innovator, then it would have promoted and perhaps fulfilled Zarathustra's aim, at the end of *Zarathustra*, to inspire living individuals to become revaluators and creators of values. But, Nietzsche writes in retrospect, near-sightedness yielded no fish.

I will conclude this introduction to *Beyond Good and Evil* by relating it to a genre of political tracts known as "advice books," or "mirrors-for-princes," which, when they first appeared in the thirteenth century, focused on the virtues of good rulers and provided political guidance to *podestà* and city magistrates. In later years, they were written to "school" the rulers of Italian city-states.[111] In *Beyond Good and Evil*, Nietzsche lauds Machiavelli's famous advice book, *The Prince*, for "presenting the most serious matters in a boisterous *allegrissimo*."[112] Thus, he calls attention to the stylistic affinity between *The Prince* and *Beyond Good and Evil*, which is the epitome of a text that treats serious issues in a brisk and lively manner. One can also note a thematic affinity. Machiavelli wrote *The Prince* with an eye to Italian political realities. In the book's final chapter, for example, he envisions a prince-legislator who would unite Italy and save it from barbarism and chaos.[113] Similarly, in *Beyond Good and Evil*, Nietzsche envisions, on a much grander scale, a new caste of new philosophers who would unite Europe and promote a "great politics" that displaced the "petty politics" of splinter states.[114] As I argued in Chapter 3, Nietzsche's Machiavellian "great politics" is not the only politics compatible with the spirit of Dionysian, modernist innovation.[115] But it is precisely the politics in which *Beyond Good and Evil* was to school modernist innovators.[116]

Reference Matter

Notes

Abbreviations

NIETZSCHE'S WRITINGS IN GERMAN

KGW   *Kritische Gesamtausgabe: Werke*
KSA   *Sämtliche Werke: Kritische Studienausgabe*
SB   *Sämtliche Briefe: Kritische Studienausgabe*

NIETZSCHE'S WRITINGS IN ENGLISH TRANSLATION

AC   *The Antichrist*
BGE   *Beyond Good and Evil*
BT   *The Birth of Tragedy*
CW   *The Case of Wagner*
EH   *Ecce Homo*
GM   *On the Genealogy of Morals*
GS   *The Gay Science*
NCW   *Nietzsche Contra Wagner*
SE   *Schopenhauer as Educator*
TI   *Twilight of the Idols*
TSZ   *Thus Spoke Zarathustra*
UD   *On the Uses and Disadvantages of History for Life*
WP   *The Will to Power*

BIBLICAL CITATIONS

Die Bibel   All citations of passages in Martin Luther's translation of the Bible cite the edition listed in the Bibliography, which is one of two editions of Luther's translation of the Bible present in Nietzsche's library (cf. *Nietzsches Bibliothek*, ed. Max Oehler [Weimar: Die Gesellschaft der Freunde des Nietzsche-Archivs, 1942], 22–24).

Introduction: Explaining the Possibility of Modernism

1. See Cornel West, "Nietzsche's Prefiguration of Postmodern American Philosophy," *Boundary 2* 9, no. 10 (Spring–Fall 1981): 241–69.

2. See Seyla Benhabib, "Epistemologies of Postmodernism: A Rejoinder to Jean-Francois Lyotard," *New German Critique* 33 (Fall 1984): 109.

3. Allan Megill, *Prophets of Extremity: Nietzsche, Heidegger, Foucault, and Derrida* (Berkeley: University of California Press, 1985), 1.

4. See Richard Wolin, "Modernism vs. Postmodernism," *Telos* 62 (Winter 1984–85): 10; and Marshall Berman, *All That Is Solid Melts into the Air* (New York: Simon and Schuster, 1982), 23. Cf. Andreas Huyssen, "Mapping the Postmodern," *New German Critique* 33 (Fall 1984): 39.

5. See Daniel Bell, *The Cultural Contradictions of Capitalism* (New York: Basic Books, 1976), 50–51; and Jürgen Habermas, "The Entwinement of Myth and Enlightenment," trans. Thomas Levin, *New German Critique* 26 (Spring–Summer 1982): 25. See also Jürgen Habermas, *The Philosophical Discourse of Modernity*, trans. Frederick Lawrence (Cambridge: MIT Press, 1987), chap. 6.

6. See Alexander Nehamas, "Nietzsche, Modernity, Aestheticism," in *The Cambridge Companion to Nietzsche*, ed. Bernd Magnus and Kathleen M. Higgins (Cambridge: Cambridge University Press, 1996), 230–31.

7. See Robert Pippin, "Nietzsche's Alleged Farewell: The Premodern, Modern, and Postmodern Nietzsche," in *The Cambridge Companion to Nietzsche* (Cambridge: Cambridge University Press, 1996), 272.

8. For criticism of Berman's reading of Nietzsche, see my "Nietzsche's Pursuit of Modernism," *New German Critique* 41 (Spring–Summer 1987): 105–7. For critical responses to Habermas's reading of Nietzsche, see the Nehamas and Pippin pieces cited above.

9. See Paul de Man, *Blindness and Insight* (New York: Oxford University Press, 1971), 147.

10. Rosalind Krauss, "The Originality of the Avant-Garde: A Postmodernist Repetition," in *Art After Modernism*, ed. Brian Wallis (New York: New Museum of Contemporary Art, 1984), 22.

11. Ibid., 29.

12. For a related point, see Nehamas's discussion of Vattimo's analysis of postmodernism, in Nehamas, "Nietzsche, Modernity, Aestheticism," 235–36.

13. For a valuable general discussion of modernism as a philosophical problem, see Robert Pippin, *Modernism as a Philosophical Problem* (Cambridge, Mass.: Basil Blackwell, 1991). Pippin's discussion of Nietzsche, especially on pages 112–13, touches on issues similar to the ones I address in describing the way in which modernism becomes a philosophical problem for Nietzsche.

14. De Man, *Blindness and Insight*, 147.

15. Ibid., 148. Earlier commentators also emphasized Nietzsche's modernist sense of the past as a burden. For example, Thomas Mann maintained that the impulse to forget

the past and to fend off the clutches of history, evident in the second of the *Untimely Meditations*, was fundamental to Nietzsche's thinking. According to Mann, this dimension of Nietzsche's philosophy degenerated over the course of Nietzsche's career. In the late 1930s, Georges Bataille developed a different view of Nietzsche's modernism, aiming to combat Alfred Bäumler's "fascist" reading of Nietzsche. See Thomas Mann, "Nietzsche's Philosophy in the Light of Contemporary Events," in *Nietzsche: A Collection of Critical Essays*, ed. Robert Solomon (New York: Anchor Books, 1973), 358–70; and Georges Bataille, "Nietzsche and the Fascists," trans. Allan Stoekl, with Carl R. Lovitt and Donald M. Leslie, Jr., in *Visions of Excess: Selected Writings, 1927–1939*, ed. Allan Stoekl (Minneapolis: University of Minnesota Press, 1985), 190–93.

16. De Man, *Blindness and Insight*, 151.

17. David Couzens Hoy, *The Critical Circle* (Berkeley: University of California Press, 1978), 135. Joseph A. Buttigieg makes a similar complaint against de Man in his very interesting "The Struggle Against Meta(Phantasma)-Physics: Nietzsche, Joyce, and the 'excess of history,'" *Boundary 2* 9, no. 10 (Spring–Fall 1981): 188.

18. Hoy, 135.

19. BT, 97–98; KGW, III, 1: 97 (throughout these notes, in citations of KGW the Roman numerals will stand for the division, the first Arabic number for the volume number, and the second Arabic number for the page number).

20. BT, 121; KGW, III, 1: 124.

21. BT, 112; KGW, III, 1: 114.

22. I discuss the figure of the last man in greater detail in Chapter 2.

23. For a similar view, see Karl Jaspers, *Nietzsche: An Introduction to the Understanding of His Philosophical Activity*, trans. Charles F. Wallraff and Frederick J. Schmitz (Chicago: Henry Regnery, 1965), 66, 252–56.

24. The disillusion with historical dialectics is also evident in twentieth-century Marxism. For more on this point, see my "Nietzsche's Pursuit of Modernism," 105–7.

25. See Rudolph Carnap, "The Overcoming of Metaphysics Through Logical Analysis of Language," in *Heidegger and Modern Philosophy*, ed. Michael Murray (New Haven, Conn.: Yale University Press, 1978), 31–34.

26. See ibid.

27. Megill, 62–63.

28. Here, I follow a line of reasoning that Alexander Nehamas sketches in his introduction to *The Art of Living: Socratic Reflections from Plato to Foucault* (Berkeley: University of California Press, 1998). See Nehamas, *The Art of Living*, 6.

29. See Lewis White Beck, "Philosophy as Literature," in *Philosophical Style*, ed. Berel Lang (Chicago: Nelson Hall, 1979), 234–55.

30. Ibid., 242.

31. Ibid., 244.

32. See Peter Jones, *Philosophy and the Novel* (Oxford: Clarendon Press, 1975).

33. See Jean-Paul Sartre, *Literary and Philosophical Essays*, trans. Annette Michelson (New York: Collier, 1970), 84–85; and William Gass, *Fiction and the Figures of Life* (Boston: Nonpareil Books, 1971), 25.

34. Jonathan Culler, *On Deconstruction: Theory and Criticism After Structuralism* (Ithaca, N.Y.: Cornell University Press, 1982), 149–50. For the relationship between Culler's claim and the seemingly contradictory deconstructionist shibboleth that all philosophy is literature, see Richard Rorty, "Deconstruction and Circumvention," *Critical Inquiry* 11 (September 1984): 1–3.

35. See Beck, 236.

36. For an excellent discussion of the literary and fictional character of Plato's dialogues, and of Plato's use of Socratic irony to create a sense of verisimilitude, see Nehamas, *The Art of Living*, chap. 3.

37. For a related discussion of Kant's concept of the reflective judgment, of which the judgment of taste is a species, see Richard Rorty, *Consequences of Pragmatism* (Minneapolis: University of Minnesota Press, 1982), 142–43.

38. Rorty, "Deconstruction and Circumvention," 9.

39. Richard Rorty, "Philosophy Without Principles," in *Against Theory*, ed. W. J. T. Mitchell (Chicago: University of Chicago Press, 1985), 135.

40. Ibid., 136.

41. Ibid.

42. In his letter to Franz Overbeck of April 7, 1884, Nietzsche suggests that he views *Zarathustra* as having initiated new modes of philosophical thought that he will subsequently develop: "I must now proceed step by step through a series of disciplines, for I have decided to spend the next five years on an elaboration of my 'philosophy,' the portico [*Vorhalle*] of which I have built in my *Zarathustra*." See *Selected Letters of Friedrich Nietzsche*, ed. and trans. Christopher Middleton (Chicago: University of Chicago Press, 1969), 223; SB, 6: 496.

43. Here I allude to Strawson's brief remarks regarding "revisionary metaphysics" in the introduction to *Individuals: An Essay in Descriptive Metaphysics* (London: Methuen, 1987), and to Deleuze and Guattari's *What Is Philosophy?* (trans. Hugh Tomlinson and Graham Burchell [New York: Columbia University Press, 1996]), especially the introduction and chapter 1. For Deleuze's discussion of Nietzsche's use of "very precise new terms for very precise new concepts," see Gilles Deleuze, *Nietzsche and Philosophy* (New York: Columbia University Press, 1983), 52–55.

44. See Kant's introduction to *The Critique of Pure Reason*, and specifically his discussion "The General Problem of Pure Reason."

45. WP, 220; KGW, VII, 3: 206–7.

46. See Robert Nozick, *Philosophical Explanations* (Cambridge: Harvard University Press, 1981), 11.

47. Ibid., 9; emphasis mine.

48. Ibid., 9–11.

49. Essential, that is, given Zarathustra's/Nietzsche's understanding of the nature of new-values creation. I explore this understanding in Chapters 3, 4, and 5.

50. The use of a familiar style of philosophical speculation would not be intelligible as a contribution to the conversation of philosophy if the problem in question did not engage the received philosophical tradition.

To be sure, I do not mean to be arguing that the ways *Zarathustra* contributes to the conversation of philosophy are the *only* ways that a literary fiction can contribute to that conversation. Consider, in this connection, the persuasive case that Martha Nussbaum makes for the view that some novels contribute to the conversation of philosophy. According to Nussbaum, the study of certain novels is indispensable to "a fully adequate statement" of an Aristotelian ethical position. See Martha C. Nussbaum, *Love's Knowledge: Essays on Philosophy and Literature* (Oxford: Oxford University Press, 1990), 27 and *passim*.

51. Nozick represents philosophical explanations as having the form of a logical deduction. My view that they can also have the form of a story, or a narrative, is in keeping with William Dray's account of "how-possibly" explanations (of which Nozick's philosophical explanations are a species) in historical writing. See William Dray, *Laws and Explanation in History* (Oxford: Oxford University Press, 1956), 158–69.

52. See Tracy Strong, *Friedrich Nietzsche and the Politics of Transfiguration*, Expanded Edition (Berkeley: University of California Press, 1988), 356.

53. Here and elsewhere in this book, I distinguish the prologue from Part 1 of *Zarathustra*, even though, strictly speaking, the prologue belongs to Part 1. Moreover, when I speak of "Part 1," I have in mind, unless otherwise indicated, the speeches of Part 1 that follow in the aftermath of "Zarathustra's Prologue."

Chapter 1: Philosophizing with a Stammer

1. Cf. Siegfried Vitens, *Die Sprachkunst Friedrich Nietzsches in* Also sprach Zarathustra (Bremen-Horn: Dorn, 1951), 31–43; Ronald Hayman, *Nietzsche: A Critical Life* (New York: Penguin, 1982), 122, 134, 256–57; Roger Hollinrake, *Nietzsche, Wagner, and the Philosophy of Pessimism* (London: George Allen and Unwin, 1982), 16–18, 139; and Jean Pierrot, *The Decadent Imagination, 1880–1900*, trans. Derek Coltman (Chicago: University of Chicago Press, 1981), 191–206.

2. Hans-Georg Gadamer, "The Drama of Zarathustra," trans. Zygmunt Adamczewski, in *The Great Year of Zarathustra (1881–1981)*, ed. David Goicoechea (Lanham, Md.: University Press of America, 1983), 349.

3. Ibid., 355.

4. Gary Shapiro has recently argued that the structure of *Zarathustra* is rhetorical rather than dramatic. Relying on the analyses of tropes developed by Hayden White and Kenneth Burke, he maintains that the main divisions of *Zarathustra*, proceeding from "Zarathustra's Prologue" through Part 4, are, successively, symbolic, metaphorical, metonymical, synecdochic, and ironic. This reading of *Zarathustra* is not convincing, because Shapiro's rhetorical scheme does not do justice to the text. For example, one finds numerous metaphors and at least one example of catechresis in "Zarathustra's Prologue," multiple instances of irony and parody (which Shapiro interprets as a form of irony) throughout the book, and an extensive use of simile in Part 4. Shapiro never explains what makes a trope a "governing" or "tone-setting" trope in parts of the text wherein different tropes and rhetorical modes coexist. He needs some such explanation if he is to avoid the charge that his reading of *Zarathustra* oversimplifies a very complex use of

rhetorical strategies (see Gary Shapiro, "The Rhetoric of Nietzsche's *Zarathustra*," in *Philosophical Style*, ed. Berel Lang [Chicago: Nelson Hall, 1979], 347–85). For my discussion of the drama and plot of *Zarathustra*, in connection to the complex interplay of metaphor, metonymy, allegory, and irony that is already evident in the opening section of "Zarathustra's Prologue," see my analysis of Paul de Man's reading of *Zarathustra* in Chapter 2.

5. In stressing the unity of *Zarathustra*, I reject the traditional but increasingly disputed view that Nietzsche's fiction is a disorganized and disconnected set of aphorisms and sermons. For two clear statements of this view, see Arthur Danto, *Nietzsche as Philosopher* (New York: Columbia University Press, 1980), 19–20, and J. P. Stern, *A Study of Nietzsche* (Cambridge: Cambridge University Press, 1979), 157–58.

6. By speaking of the drama that "happens in the telling" of *Zarathustra*, Gadamer alludes to the critically significant distinction between the telling of a tale and the happening (fictional, in the case of *Zarathustra*) of the events of which a tale tells. In recent years, this distinction has been an indispensable premise of the most influential theories of fictional narrative. Russian formalists, French structuralists, and American critics alike take for granted an ability to discriminate "story" and "discourse." Jonathan Culler identifies the former as "a sequence of actions or events, conceived as independent of their manifestation in discourse," and the latter as "the discursive presentation or narration of events." Culler also warns against the reification of this distinction by showing in a number of cases (e.g., *Oedipus Tyrannus*, *Daniel Deronda*, and Freud's study of the Wolfman) that it is as fruitful to construe narrated actions as effects of narratives as it is to construe them as independent events. See Jonathan Culler, *The Pursuit of Signs* (Ithaca, N.Y.: Cornell University Press, 1981), 169–87.

7. TSZ, 309, 321; KGW VI, 1: 243, 258.

8. Strictly speaking, involuntary repetitions characterize one particular form of stammering.

9. It is significant that Nietzsche again uses the metaphor of "stammering" in the "Attempt at a Self-Criticism" that accompanies the 1886 edition of *The Birth of Tragedy*. In this context, he applies the metaphor to himself (see BT, 20; KGW, III, 1: 9).

10. See Stern, *A Study of Nietzsche*, 126–38. Stern is to be commended for emphasizing the need to account for the *creation* of new values. Like David Hoy, however, he does not do justice to the skepticism that Nietzsche himself brings to the project of modernism (cf. my criticism of Hoy in the Introduction).

11. Plot-centered theories may be contrasted to the "discourse-centered" approach that has recently gained prominence due to the influence of Mikhail Bakhtin's work. See Mikhail Bakhtin, "Discourse and the Novel," in *The Dialogic Imagination*, ed. Michael Holquist, trans. Caryl Emerson and Michael Holquist (Austin: The University of Texas Press, 1981), 259–422.

12. Edward W. Said, *Beginnings* (Baltimore: Johns Hopkins University Press, 1975), 137.

13. Peter Brooks, *Reading for the Plot: Design and Intention in Narrative* (New York: Vintage Books, 1985), 138–39.

14. Responding to an earlier version of a part of this chapter (see Robert Gooding-Williams, "The Drama of Nietzsche's *Zarathustra*: Intention, Repetition, Prelude," *International Studies in Philosophy* 20 [Summer 1988]: 105–16), Kathleen Higgins asks "for a further specification of the ratio—is *Zarathustra* more similar or dissimilar to the *Phenomenology*?" (see Kathleen M. Higgins, "Zarathustra's Stammer as a Way of Life," *International Studies in Philosophy* 20 [Summer 1988]: 119). I do not have an answer to Higgins's question, because I do not see how one can easily quantify the relations of similarity and difference. Still, I can say that the point of my comparison of *Zarathustra* and the *Phenomenology* is entirely pragmatic. In other words, I believe that our understanding of *Zarathustra* as a work of philosophy can be fruitfully enhanced by contrasting it to other philosophical works, including Hegel's *Phenomenology*. To be sure, any such comparison will involve an interpretation of the texts under consideration. And the specification of similarities and differences will always be relative to some such interpretation.

15. See Louis Mackey, *Kierkegaard: A Kind of a Poet* (Philadelphia: University of Pennsylvania Press, 1971), 273–75. It should be mentioned here that in Mackey's view Kierkegaard's parody of Goethe is deliberate. It should also be added that in invoking Mackey's discussion of Kierkegaard and Goethe as a model I am endorsing a philosophical analysis of literary form with affinities to the sort of analysis that Jean-Paul Sartre and William Gass propose (cf. my discussion of Sartre and Gass in the Introduction).

16. In his preface to the *Phenomenology*, Hegel writes that "*Pure* self-recognition in absolute otherness . . . is the ground and soil of Science or *knowledge in general*. The beginning of philosophy presupposes or requires that consciousness should dwell in this *element*. . . . It is this coming-to-be of *Science as such* or of *knowledge* that is described in this *Phenomenology* of Spirit." See G. W. F. Hegel, *Phenomenology of Spirit*, trans. A. V. Miller (Oxford: Oxford University Press, 1981), 14–15. For a similar point, regarding the beginning of Science, see Hegel, *Science of Logic*, trans. A. V. Miller (London: Humanities Press, 1969), 68–70. On the relation between absolute knowing and the revelation of the truth of being, see *Science of Logic*, 48–50. For Hegel, philosophy proper, or science, starts with the logic, but also includes the philosophy of nature and the philosophy of spirit. On this point, see Michael N. Forster, *Hegel's Idea of a Phenomenology of Spirit* (Chicago: University of Chicago Press, 1998), 11–12. For a useful discussion of the *Phenomenology* as a literary narrative, see M. H. Abrams, *Natural Supernaturalism: Tradition and Revolution in Romantic Literature* (New York: W. W. Norton, 1971), 225–37.

17. See Hegel, *Phenomenology of Spirit*, 486–87. For a discussion of this point, see Forster, 99–100 and 291–92.

18. Hegel, *Science of Logic*, 50.

19. Two discussions of the relationship between Hegel's phenomenology and logic from which I have benefited are Jean Hyppolite, *Genesis and Structure of Hegel's Phenomenology of Spirit*, trans. Samuel Cherniak and John Heckman (Evanston, Ill.: Northwestern University Press, 1974), 573–606, and Stanley Rosen, *G. W. F. Hegel: An Introduction to the Science of Wisdom* (New Haven, Conn.: Yale University Press, 1974), 123–50. Rosen (129) also suggests an analogy between Plato's *Symposium* and the *Phenomenology*.

20. Hegel, *Phenomenology of Spirit*, 56.

21. Cf. Abrams, *Natural Supernaturalism*, 234–37. The view I sketch in this paragraph, according to which phenomenology presupposes the perspective of science and absolute knowledge, is a version of what Michael Forster has recently called the "popular reading" of the relationship between the *Phenomenology* and Hegelian science. For Forster's detailed critique of this reading, which I cannot address here, see Forster, 270–81.

22. Consider, for example, Nietzsche's famous account in *Twilight of the Idols* of how the "true world" finally became a fable. This paragraph ends with the words "Incipit Zarathustra."

23. In his commentary on *Zarathustra*, Stanley Rosen does not systematically compare Nietzsche's fiction to Hegel's *Phenomenology*. Still, much of what he says in the way of comparing Nietzsche's philosophical thought to Hegel's bears directly on the issues I have raised in contrasting these two works. Although I disagree with Rosen on a number of issues, and am quite skeptical of his "Hegelian" interpretation of the thought of eternal recurrence (which, among other things, does not do justice to the multiple meanings that the thought acquires in the course of *Zarathustra*), I recommend his discussion of Nietzsche and Hegel for the important questions it raises. See Stanley Rosen, *The Mask of Enlightenment: Nietzsche's Zarathustra* (Cambridge: Cambridge University Press, 1995), 18, 21–22, 254–55n61. See Chapters 5 and 6 of the present book for my own interpretation of eternal recurrence.

24. See, for example, Erich Heller, *The Disinherited Mind* (New York: Harcourt Brace Jovanovich, 1975), 304–26, and Richard Perkins, "Analogistic Strategies in *Zarathustra*," in *The Great Year of Zarathustra*, ed. David Goicoechea (Lanham, Md.: University Press of America, 1983).

25. Harold Alderman has also argued that the speech on the three metamorphoses describes the structure of *Zarathustra*. As will become clear, my disagreements with Alderman concern the particulars of his interpretation of that structure. See Harold Alderman, *Nietzsche's Gift* (Athens: Ohio University Press, 1977), 19.

26. I obviously reject and hope to show to be false Erich Heller's suggestion that Zarathustra never even reaches the lion stage of the three metamorphoses. See Heller, *The Disinherited Mind*, 307.

27. GM, 162–63; KGW, VI, 2: 430.

28. TSZ, 138, 305; KGW, VI, 1: 26, 239. In general, then, I agree with Eugen Fink's claim that the camel-spirit represents "man under the burden of transcendence" (*Der Mensch unter der Last der Transcendenz*). In highlighting the camel's submission to the Christian-Platonic vision of human existence, I do not mean to overlook Zarathustra's suggestion that this figure personifies a sort of heroism ("What is most difficult, O heroes, asks the spirit that would bear much"). Like the "Schopenhauerean man" whom Nietzsche depicts in the third essay of his *Untimely Meditations*, and on whose depiction Zarathustra's portrait of the first metamorphosis seems to be modeled, the camel sacrifices himself and voluntarily embraces suffering. Still, it would be a mistake to confuse the self-denying heroism of the camel with the self-assertive, defiant, and Promethean

heroism of the lion. For Niezsche's discussion of "Schopenhauerian man," see SE, 153–55; KGW, III, 1: 367–71. For Fink's discussion of the camel-spirit, see Eugen Fink, *Nietzsches Philosophie* (Stuttgart: Kohlhammer, 1960), 70. For an interesting alternative to Fink's view, see Laurence Lampert, *Nietzsche's Teaching: An Interpretation of* Thus Spoke Zarathustra (New Haven, Conn.: Yale University Press, 1986), 316n46.

29. BT, 23; KGW, III, 1: 13. See also, in the same passage, Nietzsche's allusion to Christianity's particular antipathy to sensuality and the passions. For Nietzsche's inclination to associate the phrase "thou shalt" with "Christian, or unconditional morality," see BGE, 199; KGW, VI, 2: 121–22, and KGW, VII, 2: 101. It should be noted, finally, that while Nietzsche links Christian-Platonic values to the negation of life, he also believes that these values, in promoting the ascetic ideal, preserve life by providing it a purpose. For more on this point, see my discussion of priestly asceticism in connection to the will to truth in the opening pages of Chapter 2.

30. For a similar but more elaborate account of Nietzsche's critique of unconditional morality, see Alexander Nehamas, *Nietzsche: Life as Literature* (Cambridge: Harvard University Press, 1985), chaps. 4 and 7.

31. TSZ, 138–39; KGW, VI, 1: 26.

32. See Rev. 12:9; *Die Bibel*, "Die Bücher des neuen Testaments," 299. See Heller, *The Disinherited Mind*, 316–18.

33. My Luther interpretation is based on Hans Blumenberg's discussion of proposition 17 of Luther's *Disputatio contra scholasticam theologiam*. See Hans Blumenberg, *Work on Myth*, trans. Robert M. Wallace (Cambridge: MIT Press, 1985), 541, 545, 672.

34. The text in which Nietzsche most persuasively develops his analysis of reactive force and its relation to the negation of difference is *On the Genealogy of Morals*, especially the first essay. The best available commentary on these aspects of Nietzsche's thought remains Gilles Deleuze, *Nietzsche and Philosophy*.

35. See Alderman, 33. Alderman is right, in his discussion of Zarathustra's camel, to stress the themes of facticity and tradition. What his analysis misses is the claim of facticity and the past to *exhaust* creative possibility.

36. TSZ, 139; KGW, VI, 1: 26.

37. Ibid.

38. Karl Löwith's claim that the lion enjoys a freedom to be nothing seems to me to slight Nietzsche's claim that the lion achieves a freedom *for* new creation. See Karl Löwith, *From Hegel to Nietzsche*, trans. David Green (Garden City, N.Y.: Anchor Books, 1967), 191–92.

39. TSZ, 139; KGW, VI, 1: 26–27.

40. J. P. Clayton defends a more traditional account of the lion's freedom by assimilating it to Kant's concept of autonomy. He claims that Nietzsche is rehearsing "the classic conflict between moral laws imposed from without and moral laws generated from within, the conflict between what Kant would have called heteronomy and autonomy" (J. P. Clayton, "Zarathustra and the Stages of Life's Way: A Nietzschean Riposte to Kierkegaard," *Nietzsche-Studien* 14 [1985]: 190). Kant's *Der Wille* creates moral value in

the form of moral law. Nietzsche's lion, however, creates no value whatsoever. Clayton is mistaken, then, to attribute to the lion a self-legislated morality. For a view similar to my own, which stresses the lion's future-oriented freedom for the creation of new values, see David Goicoechea, "Love and Joy in Zarathustra," in *The Great Year of Zarathustra*, ed. David Goicoechea (Lanham, Md.: University Press of America, 1983), 41.

41. See Malcolm Pasley, "Nietzsche and Klinger," in *The Discontinuous Tradition*, ed. P. F. Ganz (Oxford: Clarendon Press, 1971), 147–48.

42. TSZ, 139; KGW, VI: 1, 27.

43. See Stern, *A Study of Nietzsche*, 181.

44. For a brief but very illuminating discussion of Nietzsche's struggles with romanticism, see Heinrich von Staden, "Nietzsche and Marx on Greek Art and Literature: Case Studies in Reception," *Daedalus* (Winter 1976): 85–93.

45. See Heller, *The Disinherited Mind*, 321–26. Heller's account of the "paradise regained" motif in romantic writers involves some oversimplification. For example, he does not distinguish a primitivist "return to nature" from the pursuit of a "second-order" or "organized" innocence that subsumes and preserves difference, multiplicity, self-consciousness, and so on. For two useful analyses of the importance of this distinction to our understanding of the writers Heller mentions, see Geoffrey Hartmann, "Romanticism and 'Anti-Self-Consciousness,'" in *Romanticism and Consciousness*, ed. Harold Bloom (New York: W. W. Norton, 1970), 46–56, and Abrams, *Natural Supernaturalism*, 141–324.

46. See Stern, *A Study of Nietzsche*, 181n1; Hollinrake, 7; Joan Stambaugh, "Thoughts on the Innocence of Becoming," *Nietzsche-Studien* 14 (1985): 164–78; and Löwith, *From Hegel to Nietzsche*, 191–92. (Löwith also discusses "On the Three Metamorphoses" in chapter 3 of his *Nietzsches Philosophie der ewigen Wiederkehr des Gleichen* [Stuttgart: Kohlhammer, 1956].) Heidegger's and Fink's interpretations of Nietzsche's playing and innocent child also deserve attention. See Martin Heidegger, *Nietzsche*, vol. 2, *The Eternal Recurrence of the Same*, trans. David Farrell Krell (San Francisco: Harper and Row, 1984), 77–78, and vol. 4, *Nihilism*, trans. Frank A. Capuzzi (San Francisco: Harper and Row, 1982), 235–37; and Fink, 187–89.

47. KGW, VII, 2: 101.

48. Stambaugh, "Thoughts on the Innocence of Becoming," 174.

49. In Chapter 3, I discuss the reflexive character of the child's will in the context of explicating Zarathustra's theory of value-creation.

50. For a useful discussion of the role of the "super-subject" in idealist philosophy *and* romantic literature, see Abrams, *Natural Supernaturalism*, 90–92 and 197–324.

51. According to Deleuze the will to ascribe established value to oneself (in the case of the lion, the established value of possessing God's power and authority) is typical of slavish or reactive dispositions. This reading is consistent with my earlier interpretation of the lion as reactive and finds textual support in BGE, 208–9; KGW, VI, 2: 222–24. See Deleuze, *Nietzsche and Philosophy*, 9–10, 81–82.

52. See BGE, 24; KGW, VI, 2: 24–25. For a further sampling of Nietzsche's criticisms both of the doer-deed dichotomy and of the assumption that the self is an ego substance, see GM, 44–46; KGW, VI, 2: 292–95, and TI, 482–83; KGW, VI, 3: 71–72.

53. TI, 501; KGW, VI, 3: 90–91.

54. See GM, 36–39, 57–58; KGW, VI, 2: 284–88, 307–8. Also, see Deleuze, *Nietzsche and Philosophy*, 113–14, and Alphonso Lingus, "The Will to Power," in *The New Nietzsche*, ed. David Allison (New York: Delta, 1977), 54, 58.

Chapter 2: A Reading of "Zarathustra's Prologue"

1. Astradur Eysteinsson, *The Concept of Modernism* (Ithaca, N.Y.: Cornell University Press, 1990), 6, 238; Eysteinsson's emphasis.

2. TI, 486; KGW, VI, 3: 75. As we shall see, "INCIPIT ZARATHUSTRA," in marking the beginning of *Zarathustra*, also marks the beginning of the going-under of Zarathustra, the book's protagonist and eponym.

3. Ibid. Here, I have altered Kaufmann's translation to accord with the Colli-Montinari critical edition. Specifically, I have substituted the phrase "'true world'" for the phrase "'true' world."

4. GM, 152; KGW, VI, 2: 418–19.

5. GM, 153; KGW, VI, 2: 419.

6. TI, 486; KGW, VI, 3: 75; emphasis in original.

7. Here, I am supposing that ethics pertains generally to the question, "How should one live?" Cf. Bernard Williams, *Ethics and the Limits of Philosophy* (Cambridge: Harvard University Press, 1985), 1–21.

8. Martin Heidegger, *Nietzsche*, vol. 1, *The Will to Power as Art*, trans. David Farrell Krell (New York: Harper and Row, 1979), 208.

9. GM, 163; KGW, VI, 2: 430. Nietzsche discusses the power of Apollonian art to "save the will" in sections 3 and 25 of *The Birth of Tragedy*. He discusses the power of Dionysian art to do the same in sections 7 and 17.

10. Mark Warren has usefully shown that in *Genealogy*, as distinct from *The Birth of Tragedy*, Nietzsche historicizes *some* suffering (i.e., that of the weak) by interpreting it as an effect of meaningless social violence rather than as intrinsic to existence as such. Still, I do not think that he is right to conclude from the argument of *Genealogy* that the later Nietzsche believes *all* suffering to have been instigated by violence. This view cannot account for Nietzsche's suggestions in *The Gay Science* (no. 370) and the "Attempt at a Self-Criticism" of the 1886 edition of *The Birth of Tragedy* that some suffering, what he calls "suffering from overfullness," obtains independently of the occurrence and institution of social violence. Neither can it explain the close affinity between the later Nietzsche's description of the Dionysian individual who suffers from overfullness and his description in the "Attempt at a Self-Criticism" of the Dionysian god depicted in the main text of *The Birth of Tragedy* (see, e.g., sections 1 and 5 of the "Attempt at a Self-Criticism"). The concurrence of these descriptions suggests that Nietzsche himself acknowledged a greater continuity between his earlier and later views of suffering than does Warren. See Mark Warren, *Nietzsche's Political Thought* (Cambridge: MIT Press, 1988),78–79.

11. In *Genealogy*, essay 3, sec. 27, Nietzsche explicitly connects his discussion of the ascetic ideal to his plans to write a history of European nihilism.

12. WP, 9; KGW, VIII, 2: 14.

13. Cf. Maurice Blanchot, "The Limits of Experience: Nihilism," in *The New Nietzsche*, ed. David Allison (New York: Dell, 1977), 122.

14. WP, 319; KGW, VIII, 2: 31.

15. GM, 162; KGW, VI, 2: 429-30.

16. For a similar view, see Stern, *A Study of Nietzsche*, 61.

17. My discussion here has some important affinities to John Caputo's account of the anti-Platonism at work in Kierkegaard's concept of repetition. I would especially emphasize Caputo's discussion of "repetition and the end of metaphysics." See Caputo, *Radical Hermeneutics* (Bloomington: Indiana University Press, 1987), 11-35. Also relevant is Gilles Deleuze's analysis of Kierkegaard's and Nietzsche's notions of repetition in the introduction to his *Difference and Repetition*, trans. Paul Patton (New York: Columbia University Press, 1994).

18. Cf., for example, the discussion of "genuine" philosophers in BGE, 136; KGW, VI, 2: 149.

19. Admittedly, Plato strictly speaking never speaks of values, grounding values, the origin of values, and so on. The account of Platonism I have sketched in the last two paragraphs is a construction of Platonism from what I take to have been Nietzsche's point of view.

20. TSZ, 121; KGW, VI, 1: 5.

21. *Die Bibel*, "Die Bücher des neuen Testaments," 72.

22. TSZ, 122; KGW, VI, 1: 5.

23. TSZ, 185; KGW, VI, 1: 91.

24. TSZ, 121; KGW, VI, 1: 5. The saint in the forest, when he first sees Zarathustra, recalls seeing him carry his ashes to the mountains. Zarathustra confirms the saint's recollection when, in "On the Afterworldly," he himself speaks of carrying his ashes to the mountains. Zarathustra's remarks seem to allude in part to Nietzsche's first book, *The Birth of Tragedy*, and can be read as indirect autobiography on Nietzsche's part.

25. My conception of "agonistic allusions" stems from Harold Bloom's writings of the early and mid-1970s. See especially *The Anxiety of Influence: A Theory of Poetry* (New York: Oxford University Press, 1973) and *A Map of Misreading* (New York: Oxford University Press, 1975). The reading of the opening section of *Zarathustra* given here revises my earlier reading of that section. Cf. my "Metaphysics and Metalepsis in *Thus Spoke Zarathustra*," *International Studies in Philosophy* 16 (Summer 1984): 27-36.

26. TSZ, 121; KGW, VI, 1: 5.

27. TSZ, 122; KGW, VI, 1: 6.

28. TSZ, 121; KGW, VI, 1: 5.

29. GS, 33; KGW, V, 2: 14. Here, I have altered slightly Kaufmann's translation.

30. I derive the notion of a "precursor text" from Harold Bloom (see above, note 25). For a discussion of Nietzsche's very early appreciation of the creative possibilities inhering in parody and, in particular, of his recognition that parody can involve the repetition and revision of received texts (and, therefore, that it need not be simply imitative), see

S. L. Gilman's interpretation of Nietzsche's juvenilia in connection to the nineteenth-century notion of the *contrafactum* (a form of musical parody) in his *Nietzschean Parody* (Bonn: Bouvier Verlag Herbert Grundmann, 1976), 13 ff.

31. My emphasis here on the *Timaeus* draws inspiration from A. O. Lovejoy's well-known classic, *The Great Chain of Being* (London: Oxford University Press, 1936), especially chapter 2. I have also benefited from M. H. Abrams's discussion of Neoplatonism in his *Natural Supernaturalism*. See especially 141 ff.

32. Quoted in Lovejoy, 47.

33. Ibid., 62–63.

34. Ibid., 63.

35. TSZ, 122; KGW, VI, 1: 6. For the importance of the chain and mirror metaphors vis-à-vis the cultural transmission of Neoplatonic cosmology, see Lovejoy, 63.

36. For the relevant passage in the fifth *Ennead*, see Lovejoy, 62. See, too, Plotinus's discussion in the third *Ennead* of the envyless productivity of cosmic reason, quoted in Lovejoy, 64–65.

37. See, for example, no. 370 of *The Gay Science* (as well as the first section of the "Attempt at a Self-Criticism," in *The Birth of Tragedy*) for Nietzsche's use of figures of fullness and overfullness to characterize Dionysus. Also relevant here is Anke Bennholdt-Thomsen's discussion of Zarathustra's relation to Dionysus in her *Nietzsche's Also sprach Zarathustra als literarisches Phänomen* (Frankfurt: Athenaum, 1974), 129–30. Bennholdt-Thomsen's reminder that "Nach Ovid . . . ist Spender des Honigs Dionysos" is no less pertinent to Zarathustra's presentation of himself in the first section of the prologue (as a bee who, since he has gathered too much honey, needs "hands outstretched to receive it") than it is to his self-depiction at the beginning of Part 4, which she emphasizes. In the former passage, Zarathustra's presentation of himself in the image of Dionysus works to reinforce the suggestion that Zarathustra is a Dionysian Demiurge.

38. Paul de Man quotes the relevant passage from Nietzsche's notebooks in his *Allegories of Reading* (New Haven, Conn.: Yale University Press, 1979), 117.

39. In *Ecce Homo*, in his discussion of Zarathustra's "Night Song," Nietzsche explicitly suggests that, in *Zarathustra*, he has used Apollonian sun imagery to symbolize Dionysus (see EH, 306–9; KGW, VI, 3: 343–47). For the details of my interpretation of Zarathustra's "Night Song," see the discussion of *Zarathustra*, Part 2, in Chapter 4.

40. I do not mean to deny here that, notwithstanding the continuity between Nietzsche's early and later conceptions of Dionysus, the later conception is predicated on a rejection of the Kantian and Schopenhauerian dualism that shapes the argument of *The Birth of Tragedy*. The fact remains, however, that the question as to whether and how there can be a Dionysian renewal of modern European culture is a central theme of *Zarathustra*, no less than of *The Birth of Tragedy*.

For the first stanza of Hölderlin's "Patmos" (in German with an English translation), see *Friedrich Hölderlin and Eduard Mörike: Selected Poems*, trans. Christopher Middleton (Chicago: University of Chicago Press, 1972), 74–75. Jürgen Habermas discusses the theme of Dionysus's absence as it appears in Hölderlin and the German Romantics in

The Philosophical Discourse of Modernity (Cambridge: MIT Press, 1987), 91–92. In fact, Habermas suggests that the god to whom Hölderlin alludes in the first stanza of "Patmos" is Dionysus (see Habermas, 92 and 92n28). Habermas also suggests that Nietzsche, notwithstanding his repudiation of Hölderlin's identification of Dionysus and Christ, retains Hölderlin's view that Dionysus's absence and seeming remoteness is a sign that his arrival among men is historically imminent. *Pace* Habermas, I have been arguing that, though the early Nietzsche may have accepted this view, the later Nietzsche did not. Indeed, the later Nietzsche, while he shares Hölderlin's belief that the god is hard to grasp (*schwer zu fassen*) grows ever more skeptical of the claim that he is near (*nah*). For further discussion of the affinities between Nietzsche's and Hölderlin's conceptions of Dionysus, see Adrian Del Caro, *Nietzsche Contra Nietzsche* (Baton Rouge: Louisiana State University Press, 1989), 44–46.

Finally, Laurence Lampert, in his discussion of "Zarathustra's Prologue," claims that the Dionysian significance of Zarathustra's descent becomes apparent only in *Zarathustra*, Part 3 (see Lampert, 16). I obviously reject Lampert's claim, for I believe that already in section 1 of the prologue Nietzsche depicts Zarathustra's descent as having a Dionysian significance. (Consistent with my argument, Del Caro discusses Nietzsche's use in the prologue of Dionysian and other imagery that Nietzsche shares with Hölderlin [see Del Caro, 45n13].) I do agree with much of Kathleen Higgins's discussion of section 1, though she seems to ignore the possibility that Zarathustra is *revising* as well as repeating Plato's use of the sun image, and thereby investing it with a new and non-Apollonian significance. I do not see, in fact, how her reading, which views the sun as a figure for an Apollonian-Socratic-Platonic and non-Dionysian sensibility, can account for Zarathustra's emphatic and anti-Platonic temporalizing of the sun (see Kathleen M. Higgins, *Nietzsche's Zarathustra* (Philadelphia: Temple University Press, 1987), 72–76). Like Higgins, Stanley Rosen offers a purely Apollonian interpretation of Zarathustra's sun. See Rosen, *The Mask of Enlightenment*, 23.

41. TSZ, 122; KGW, VI, 1: 5. Here and elsewhere in this chapter I alter Kaufmann's translation, rendering "*Also begann Zarathustras Untergang*" not as "Thus Zarathustra began to go-under," but as "Thus began Zarathustra's going-under."

42. See Zarathustra's claim that he needs hands outstretched to receive his wisdom (ibid.).

43. This translation derives from Amédée Brunot, *Saint Paul and His Message* (New York: Hawthorn, 1959), 103–4.

44. The third-person singular aorist of *kenóō* is *ekénōsen*. For a brief discussion of the theological questions raised by kenotic theories of the Incarnation, see Linwood Urban, *A Short History of Christian Thought* (New York: Oxford University Press, 1986), 95–96. See, also, the *Theological Dictionary of the New Testament III* (Grand Rapids, Mich.: Eerdmans, 1965), 661–62.

45. Charles Scott, *Christianity According to St. Paul* (Cambridge: Cambridge University Press, 1961), 272.

46. See Brunot, 104; C. Scott, 46–53.

47. See Brunot, 106–7.

48. I derive my conception of an interpretive impasse or aporia from Paul de Man. See, for example, his discussion of the aporetical character of rhetoric in his *Allegories of Reading* (see de Man, 131). For the connection between the sort of interpretive aporias that preoccupy literary critics and the notion of underdetermination familiar to philosophers of science, see Hurbert Dreyfus, "Holism and Hermeneutics," *Review of Metaphysics* 34 (September 1980): 12–13.

49. For two recent and useful discussions of irony in *Zarathustra*, see Daniel Conway, "Solving the Problem of Socrates: Nietzsche's *Zarathustra* as Political Irony," *Political Theory* 16 (May 1988): 257–80; and Robert Pippin, "Irony and Affirmation in Nietzsche's *Thus Spoke Zarathustra*" in *Nietzsche's New Seas*, ed. Michael Allen Gillespie and Tracy Strong (Chicago: University of Chicago Press, 1988), 45–71. Conway provides an insightful discussion of the irony at work in the narrative use of the word *Untergang* in section 1 of the prologue, although from a perspective somewhat different than my own (see Conway, 261–62).

50. BT, 104; KGW, III, 1: 105. I have altered slightly Kaufmann's translation by translating *Untergange* as "destruction" rather than as "end."

51. For the distinction between Nietzsche's and Aristotle's conceptions of *mythos*, see M. S. Silk and J. P. Stern, *Nietzsche on Tragedy* (Cambridge: Cambridge University Press, 1981), 229.

52. My interpretation of Aristotle follows Paul Ricoeur's discussion in his *Time and Narrative*, vol. 1, trans. Kathleen McLaughlin and David Pellauer (Chicago: University of Chicago Press, 1984), 43. See Silk and Stern, 229–30, for the somewhat questionable suggestion that Nietzsche's notion of *Vernichtung* corresponds specifically to that mode of reversal (*metabole*) that Aristotle names "peripety."

53. For Schopenhauer's analysis of tragedy, see his essay entitled "The Aesthetics of Poetry," in volume 2 of *The World as Will and Representation*, trans. E. F. J. Payne (New York: Dover, 1958). See WP, 449; KGW, VIII, 3: 203–4, for Nietzsche's discussion of the connection between pity and fear (Aristotle), on the one hand, and resignation (Schopenhauer), on the other.

54. See Northrop Frye, *Anatomy of Criticism* (Princeton, N.J.: Princeton University Press, 1957), 221–22. For a valuable discussion of K. W. F. Solger's understanding of tragic irony in connection to Nietzsche's writing about tragedy, see Ernst Behler, "Nietzsches Auffassung der Ironie," *Nietzsche-Studien* 4 (1975), 32–35.

55. Jean-Pierre Vernant, "Ambiguity and Reversal: On the Enigmatic Structure of *Oedipus Rex*," in *Greek Tragedy*, ed. Erich Segal (New York: Harper and Row, 1983), 190. For a discussion of Zarathustra's status as tragic hero that highlights the theme of failure, see Higgins, *Nietzsche's Zarathustra*, 103. For a more general discussion of Zarathustra's tragic heroism, from which my own account draws inspiration, see Heidegger, *Nietzsche*, vol. 2, *The Eternal Recurrence of the Same*, 28–62.

56. TSZ, 123; KGW, VI, 1: 6–7. Here, I have altered Kaufmann's translation of *umbringen* in such a way as accords with Hollingdale's translation. Cf. *Thus Spoke Zarathustra*, trans. R. J. Hollingdale (New York: Penguin, 1961), 40.

57. It is not difficult to see that the saint's remarks prefigure Zarathustra's later allu-

sions to his "spirit of gravity." For my interpretation of the saint as insisting on man's recalcitrant facticity, as well as for my general understanding of what is at stake in the encounter between Zarathustra and the saint, I am particularly indebted to Norman Palma's *Négation de la négativité: Structure et problematique du "Prologue de Zarathustra" reflexion sur Nietzsche* (Paris: Ediciones Hispanos Americanos, 1971), esp. 103–4 and 106.

58. Daniel Conway argues that, in asserting that he brings men a gift, Zarathustra implies that he agrees with the old saint that there is something deficient about man, that man is "too imperfect a thing." The alternative interpretation I have offered suggests that Zarathustra's assertion need not be understood as having this implication. See Daniel W. Conway, "A Moral Ideal for Everyone and No One," *International Studies in Philosophy* 22 (Summer 1990): 22.

59. By an "intellectually defensible belief," I mean a belief that admits of *prima facie* justification by appeal to prevailing standards of truth and rationality.

60. TSZ, 124; KGW, VI, 1: 7–8.

61. TSZ, 124; KGW, VI, 1: 8.

62. Ibid.

63. Ibid. Both Schacht and Nehamas convincingly argue that Nietzsche's critique of the pursuit of goals and purposes applies only to the pursuit of *some* goals and purposes. Thus, Nietzsche's advocacy of goallessness need not be seen as contradicting his belief that human beings should pursue the goal of self-overcoming. See Richard Schacht, *Nietzsche* (London: Routledge and Kegan Paul, 1983), 381, and Nehamas, *Nietzsche*, 48.

64. The secondary literature on Nietzsche's concept of the overman is by now quite extensive. For a view that, like my own, emphasizes the contrast between the overman and *Christian-Platonic* man, see Löwith, *From Hegel to Nietzsche*, 318. The interpretation of the concept of the overman that I believe is *most* misleading obfuscates Nietzsche's desire to see man become something radically other than what he is and has been: it insists that the overman is the man who fulfills the essential or true self that man is and has been all along. Advocates of this view include Palma (130); Walter Kaufmann (*Nietzsche: Philosopher, Psychologist, Antichrist* [Princeton, N.J.: Princeton University Press, 1974], 312, 316); and Arthur Danto (*Nietzsche as Philosopher*, 198). For helpful criticism of the essentialist assumptions implicit in this interpretation, see Nehamas, *Nietzsche*, 175.

65. For a reading of section 3 of the prologue that is similar to my own, see Löwith, *From Hegel to Nietzsche*, 319. What Zarathustra calls "the great contempt" is the wedding of the bad conscience to all unnatural inclinations of which Nietzsche speaks in section 24 of the second essay of *Genealogy*.

66. For two views that point like mine to the emptiness of Nietzsche's concept of the overman, see Karl Jaspers, *Nietzsche*, 128; and, more recently, Karsten Harries, "The Philosopher at Sea," in *Nietzsche's New Seas*, ed. Michael Allen Gillespie and Tracy B. Strong (Chicago: University of Chicago Press, 1988), 42.

67. TSZ; 125; KGW, VI, 1: 8. Although my understanding of the meaning of the earth echoes Palma's claim that "le sens de terre est justement la manifestation de la vi-

talité," I do not mean to be implying that to "fulfill the meaning of the earth" is to ful-fill the essence of what it is to be human. See Palma, 138, as well as note 64, above. For a detailed defence of my understanding of the role that the passions and passional chaos play in the creation of overmen, see Chapter 3.

68. TSZ, 126–27; KGW, VI, 1: 10–11. Here I have altered Kaufmann's translation by rendering *Übergang* as "going-over."

69. Alderman seems explicitly to deny the first ambiguity, though his discussion of danger seems to presuppose it. See Alderman, 29.

70. For the entirety of Zarathustra's second speech, see TSZ, 126–28; KGE, VI, 1, 10–12. Bennholdt-Thomsen's reading of this speech, which considers it to be only about forerunners, is, from my point of view, incomplete. See Bennholdt-Thomsen, 19.

71. Harries, "The Philosopher at Sea," 42–43.

72. See *Hölderlin and Mörike: Selected Poems*, 74–75. I owe to Karsten Harries the insight that Zarathustra's second speech to the townspeople can be read as echoing the language of Hölderlin's "Patmos."

73. See Vincent Vycinas, *Earth and Gods* (The Hague: Martinus Nihoff, 1961), 209–11, for the view that Hölderlin himself interprets Dionysus as the god of chaos.

74. Zarathustra's use of *Untergang* in section 4, as distinct from his use of this term in section 1, fully exploits the possibility that *Untergang* can signify ruin and destruction. Thus, his use of *Untergang* in section 4 recalls the narrative use of the term in section 1. As distinct from the narrative use, however, Zarathustra's later use of *Untergang* indicates neither the demise of Dionysus nor the irrevocable destruction of Zarathustra's effort to bring Dionysus to man. On the contrary, the later use of the term points to the self-destruction that Christian-Platonic man must undergo in order to meet with Diony-sus—that is, in order to embrace the abyss that is man's bridge to the overman.

75. TSZ, 126; KGW, VI, 1: 11.

76. TSZ, 128; KGW, VI, 1: 12. Here, I follow Hollingdale in translating *hören* as "to hear" rather than as "to listen."

77. I owe this insight to Judith Butler.

78. See J. L. Austin, *How to Do Things with Words* (Cambridge: Harvard University Press, 1962). In speaking of "perlocutionary" speech acts and of "constative" utterance, I borrow my terminology from Austin. In characterizing the former, Austin writes that "saying something will often, or even normally, produce certain consequential effects upon the feelings, thoughts, or actions of the audience, or of the speaker, or of other per-sons: and it may be done with the design, intention, or purpose of producing them; and we may say, thinking of this, that the speaker has performed an act. . . . We shall call the performance of an act of this kind the performance of a *perlocutionary act* or *perlocution*" (101). As distinct from the effects produced via illocutionary speech acts (e.g., the effect of marrying someone that is a consequence of saying "I do" in a marriage ceremony), perlocutionary speech effects are not due to social convention. Generally speaking, per-locutionary acts achieve effects *by* saying something whereas illocutionary acts achieve effects *in* saying something.

79. Cf. Higgins, *Nietzsche's Zarathustra*, 83–84, and Bennholdt-Thomsen, 20–23. Both represent Zarathustra's perlocutionary failure (in the prologue) as a failure of communication.

80. See de Man, *Allegories of Reading*, 119–31.

81. Implicitly, de Man suggests that Nietzsche's skepticism cannot be met by Cartesian and/or phenomenological arguments to the effect that human subjects can avoid error through the application of epistemological methods enabling them consciously to control their beliefs.

82. See de Man, *Allegories of Reading*, 119–23.

83. De Man seems also to suggest that the deconstructive argument appearing explicitly in the second passage is already implicit in the first. On this point, see Rodolphe Gasché, "'Setzung' and 'Ubersetzung': Notes on Paul de Man," *Diacritics* 11 (Winter 1981): 50.

84. See de Man, *Allegories of Reading*, 129–30.

85. See Austin, 14, 26, 102–3, 118. For more on the distinction between perlocutionary and illocutionary effects, see note 78.

86. See de Man, *Allegories of Reading*, 131.

87. Ibid.

88. Ibid.

89. For a clear, general discussion of the instrumental and manipulative dimensions of perlocutionary speech, see Jeff Mason, *Philosophical Rhetoric: The Function of Indirection in Philosophical Writing* (London: Routledge, 1989), 44–47.

90. See de Man, *Allegories of Reading*, 131.

91. Ibid.

92. See Richard H. Weisberg, "De Man Missing Nietzsche: *Hinzugedichtet* Revisited," in *Nietzsche as Postmodernist*, ed. Clayton Koelb (Albany: SUNY Press, 1990), 111–24.

93. See, on this point, John Searle, *Expression and Meaning* (Cambridge: Cambridge University Press, 1979), 17–18.

94. See Christopher Norris, *Paul de Man* (New York: Routledge, 1988), *passim*.

95. Cf. Frank Lentricchia, *Culture and Social Change* (Chicago: University of Chicago Press, 1983), 42–43. See also de Man's remark that

> the deconstruction of metaphor and of all rhetorical patterns such as mimesis, paronomasia, or personification that use resemblance as a way to disguise differences, takes us back to the impersonal precision of grammar and of a semiology derived from grammatical patterns. Such a reading puts into question a whole series of concepts that underlie the value judgments of our critical discourse: the metaphors of primacy, of genetic history, *and, most notably, of the autonomous power to will of the self* (emphasis mine; de Man, *Allegories of Reading*, 16).

96. See de Man, *Allegories of Reading*, 129, for de Man's reference to "Nietzsche's deconstructive procedure at its most advanced stage."

97. For de Man's suggestion that we should not read the "history" of Nietzsche's

thought as a teleological development, see de Man, *Allegories of Reading*, 116. Also, see Norris, 161 ff.

98. Arguably, a central theme of both texts is the death of Dionysus, interpreted in *The Birth of Tragedy* as due to Socratism and interpreted in *Genealogy* as due to slave morality and Christian asceticism. In any case, the Dionysian preoccupations of *The Birth of Tragedy* are obvious. For Nietzsche's suggestion that Dionysus remains a background figure in *Genealogy*, see the opening paragraph of his discussion of *Genealogy* in *Ecce Homo*.

99. See de Man, *Allegories of Reading*, 127.

100. Where Heidegger looks to the posthumous notes for the substance of Nietzsche's metaphysics, de Man looks to these notes for Nietzsche's most profound epistemological insights. It is also worth noting that de Man's deployment of the passive voice, to speak of Nietzsche's writings as having been "destined," rhetorically suggests that this writing was governed by an impersonal teleology whose fulfillment in the later book (or books) was prevented by Nietzsche's death.

101. See Lentricchia, 43 (and n29) for the tacit suggestion of a link between the arguments of these two essays.

102. I briefly discuss "Literary History and Literary Modernity" in the Introduction to this book.

103. See de Man, *Allegories of Reading*, 79–102.

104. Timothy Bahti's English translation of this essay, which I tend to follow below, is available in Paul de Man, *The Rhetoric of Romanticism* (New York: Columbia University Press, 1984), 47–65. The German original, citations from which I interpolate where appropriate, was first printed as "Wordsworth und Hölderlin," in *Schweizer Monatshefte* (March 1966): 1141–55.

105. See de Man, *The Rhetoric of Romanticism*, 57–58.

106. Ibid., 56, 58, 61.

107. Ibid., 55, 57–58.

108. See BT, 46–47, 36, 69–72, 22; KGW, III, 1: 36–38, 24, 63–67, 11. In general, I am inclined to regard de Man's politically charged repudiation of Dionysus as part of what Norris (190) describes as his "agonized reflection on his wartime experience" that "can best be read as a protracted attempt to make amends (albeit indirectly) in the form of an ideological auto-critique" (Norris points out that Geoffrey Hartmann has made a similar argument). It is from this perspective that I interpret the following remarks:

> Act and interpretation are thus connected in a complex and often contradictory manner. For the interpreter of history, it is never a simple and uniform movement like the ascent of a peak or the installation of a definitive social order. Rather it appears much more in that twilight in which for Wordsworth the crossing of the Alps was bathed, in which the coming-to-consciousness is in arrears vis-à-vis the actual act, and consequently is to be understood not as a conquest but rather as a rectification or even a reproach. The future is present in history only as the remembering of a failed project that has become a menace. (*The Rhetoric of Romanticism*, 58–59)

Here, I leave open the question as to whether, as some critics suggests, de Man's episte-mological skepticism leads necessarily to a sort of political quietism (see, on this point, Lentricchia, *Culture and Social Change*, 38–52, and Norris, 1–17).

109. See de Man, *Allegories of Reading*, 115–16.

110. Ibid., 146, 16, 15.

111. For clear definitions of the terms "vehicle" and "tenor," which were originally in-troduced into modern literary criticism by I. A. Richards, see M. H. Abrams, *A Glossary of Literary Terms* (New York: Holt, Rinehart, and Winston, 1971), 61.

112. For a general discussion of the relationship between metonymy and *kenosis* (*kenosis* is a noun that corresponds to the verb *kenóō* and signifies the *act* of emptying out), see Harold Bloom, *A Map of Misreading*, 98–99. For Bloom's earlier treatment of the concept of *kenosis*, see *The Anxiety of Influence*, 14–15, 77–92.

113. Paul de Man, "The Rhetoric of Temporality," in *Interpretation: Theory and Prac-tice*, ed. C. S. Singleton (Baltimore: Johns Hopkins University Press, 1969), 207.

114. Ibid.

115. Ibid., 206, 190.

116. Cf. Edward Said's remark that "a 'beginning' is designated in order to indicate, clarify, or define a *later* time, place, or action. . . . We might not actually say as much every time, but when we point to the beginning of a novel, for example, we mean that from *that* beginning in principle follows *this* novel. Or, we see that the beginning is the first point (in time, space, or action) of an accomplishment or process that has duration and meaning. *The beginning, then, is the first step in the intentional production of mean-ing.*" See Said, *Beginnings*, 5; emphasis in original.

117. See de Man, *Allegories of Reading*, 115–16. On the notion of an "allegory of irony," see de Man, "The Rhetoric of Temporality," 207–9.

118. See Carol Jacobs "Allegories of Reading Paul de Man," in *Reading de Man Read-ing*, ed. Lindsay Waters and Wlad Godzich (Minneapolis: University of Minnesota Press, 1989), 105–20, for a related but complicated discussion of the ironization of alle-gory in connection to the allegorization of irony.

119. By "decided authority" I mean authority that is decided in the sense of being be-yond question.

120. In both the passages I cite in this sentence the emphasis is mine.

121. De Man, *Allegories of Reading*, 131.

122. De Man's "Rhetoric of Tropes" (103–18 of *Allegories of Reading*) originally ap-peared under the title "Nietzsche's Theory of Rhetoric" in an issue of *Symposium* (*Sym-posium* 28, no. 1 [Spring 1974]: 33–51) that includes a discussion of de Man's essay in which de Man, Walter Kaufmann, Peter Heller, and others participate. In the course of this discussion, de Man explicitly confirms his commitment to an ironic and anti-Dionysian reading of *Zarathustra*, arguing that his deconstruction of a "truth-centered Dionysian reading of *The Birth of Tragedy*" (published as "Genesis and Genealogy," in *Allegories of Reading*) can be considered preparatory to a similar reading of *Zarathustra* (48–49). Writing in a more general vein, Ernst Behler echoes de Man in also suggesting

that Nietzsche uses irony to distance himself from the Dionysian motifs that animate his writing. See Behler, "Nietzsches Auffassung der Ironie," 35. See, also, Ernst Behler, *Irony and the Discourse of Modernity* (Seattle: University of Washington Press, 1990), 92–100.

Rudolph Kuenzli's reading of *Zarathustra* ("Nietzsche's Zerography: *Thus Spoke Zarathustra*," *Boundary 2* 9, no. 3, and 10, no. 1 [Spring–Fall 1981]: 99–117) owes a great deal to recent poststructuralist readings of Nietzsche (though Kuenzli criticizes Derrida and Blanchot for concentrating on Nietzsche's notes and fragments at the expense of his more coherent works) and can be read as an attempt, following de Man's suggestion, to deconstruct those "truth-centered" readings of *Zarathustra* that ascribe a doctrinal unity to it, especially to its first three parts (Kuenzli presents Eugen Fink's discussion of *Zarathustra* in Fink's *Nietzsches Philosophie* as a typical example of such readings). The essence of Kuenzli's de Man–inspired reading of *Zarathustra* is his claim that *Zarathustra*, Part 4, at each and every turn, ironically mocks and undermines the teachings of Parts 1–3, thus destroying whatever doctrinal coherence could otherwise be ascribed to the text. I differ with Kuenzli on two counts: first, and as I hope to have shown by way of my reading of the opening section of *Zarathustra*, one need not wait to read the fourth part of this book to see that and how it puts into question its own fundamental teachings; second, I think that Part 4, if viewed in the perspective of the antithesis of intention and repetition and, most important, in light of the evolution of the thought of eternal recurrence, can be shown to be "doctrinally" of a piece with the parts of *Zarathustra* that precede it. For my interpretation of Part 4, see Chapter 6.

123. I agree, therefore, with Karl Jaspers (see Jaspers, 10) who claims that "self-contradiction is the fundamental ingredient of Nietzsche's thought." I also agree with Jaspers's claim that contradiction in Nietzsche's thinking is "a sign of truthfulness rather than of incompetent thinking" (see ibid.). Nietzsche is often if not always reprising and retesting perspectives that he himself has criticized ann questioned (his Dionysianism, for example). Thus, I reject Walter Kaufmann's suggestion that Nietzsche's thought progresses by way of the correction of errors to a state of organic coherence (see Kaufmann, 90–91).

As regards more recent commentators, Maurice Blanchot has usefully distinguished two forms of writing in Nietzsche: one coherent and philosophical, the other discontinuous and fragmented. In Blanchot's view, Nietzsche's more coherent discourse has been "always already surpassed" by that of the fragment. The latter discourse eludes definitive interpretation, says Blanchot, because it is a discourse of "unlimited difference" (see Maurice Blanchot, *L'entretien infini* [Paris: Gallimard, 1969], 228–31). Though I agree with Blanchot, as far as he goes, I think that he presents a view of Nietzsche's writing that, like de Man's, overlook's Nietzsche's relentless effort to question his own questioning of philosophical speculation: yes, the discourse of the fragment has always already surpassed that of philosophy, but the opposite is true too.

Another perspective worth mentioning here is that of Richard Rorty, who insists on a view of Nietzsche that ends up standing de Man and Blanchot on their heads. Rorty argues, in essence, that Nietzsche's thought ultimately falls prey to a "relapse from irony into metaphysics, his final surrender to a desire for power" (see Richard Rorty, *Contingency, Irony, Solidarity* [Cambridge: Cambridge University Press, 1989], 117). Although Rorty rightly perceives that Nehamas's "Proustian" reading of Nietzsche ignores some important features of Nietzsche's speculative, Dionysian philosophizing (my notion of Nietzsche's speculative, Dionysian philosophizing roughly corresponds to what Rorty describes as Nietzsche's "metaphysics" and "ironic theorizing" [97–108]), Rorty's belief that Nietzsche's thought surrenders to and comes finally to rest in such philosophizing is no less false than de Man's belief that, ultimately, Nietzschean irony supersedes Nietzschean speculation. In my view, de Man's and Rorty's views of Nietzsche are equally one-sided.

For a critique of deconstructionist appropriations of Nietzsche that parallels in some important respects my critique of de Man, see Peter Heller, *Studies on Nietzsche* (Bonn: Bouvier Verlag Herbert Grundmann, 1980), 218–26. And finally, for the view that the contradictions in Nietzsche's thought stem from his philosophy of contradictions, see Wolfgang Müller-Lauter, *Nietzsche: His Philosophy of Contradictions and the Contradiction of His Philosophy*, trans. David J. Parent (Urbana: University of Illinois Press, 1999).

124. See, for example, the penultimate section of *Twilight* in which Nietzsche calls himself "the last disciple of the philosopher Dionysus" (TI, 563; KGW, VI, 3: 154).

125. TSZ; 130; KGW, VI, 1: 15.

126. Cf. UD, 104–5. See Lampert, 25, for a view that also stresses the last man's conception of history as progress.

127. Hollingdale, for example, translates *erfunden* as "discovered."

128. See, for example, TSZ, 399–400; KGW, VI, 1: 344. The smallness motif in this passage echoes Zarathustra's claim that the last man makes everything small, as well as his comparison of the last man to a flea. For further development of the idea that the last man is a utilitarian, see Gary Shapiro, "Festival, Carnival, and Parody in Zarathustra IV," in *The Great Year of Zarathustra (1881–1981)*, ed. David Goicoechea (Lanham, Md.: University Press of America, 1983), 52.

129. Gilles Deleuze (*Nietzsche and Philosophy*, 150–51, 165) ignores completely the optimism of the last man. For a view that accords more closely with my own, see Palma, 205, 207.

130. Cf. GM, first essay, sec. 13.

131. Cf. Nehamas, *Nietzsche*, 33, 112–13.

132. This is Hollingdale's translation.

133. My thinking about the details of Zarathustra's speech on the last man has benefited primarily from Palma's discussion. See especially 210 and 215–16. For my references to the speech on the last man, see TSZ, 129–31; KGW, VI, 1: 12–15.

134. Cf. Deleuze, *Nietzsche and Philosophy*, 138–39, on the theme of domestication. Deleuze notes that, as distinct (implicitly) from Hegel, Nietzsche views universal history as the triumph of reactive forces, the primary effect of which is the domestication of man, not the fulfillment of self-consciousness. See, also, Michel Foucault, *The Order of Things* (New York: Vintage, 1973), 262–63, for the claim that Nietzsche turns Hegel's conception of the "end of history" on its head.

135. For Zarathustra's explicit suggestion that the last man has annihilated the possibility of experiencing chaos, see TSZ, 129; KGW, VI, 1: 13. For the classical interpretation of European modernity as a form of secularized asceticism, see Max Weber's *The Protestant Ethic and the Spirit of Capitalism*, trans. Talcott Parsons (New York: Scribner, 1930) For a complicated treatment of affinities between Nietzsche and Weber that also highlights Weber's *suppression* of central Nietzschean motifs, see Georg Stauth and Bryan S. Turner, *Nietzsche's Dance: Resentment, Reciprocity, and Resistance in Social Life* (Oxford: Basil Blackwell, 1988), especially chaps. 2 and 3.

136. TSZ, 129; KGW, VI, 1: 13.

137. Cf. Nietzsche's discussion in *The Birth of Tragedy* of the banishment of Dionysus from the Greek theater. Cf., too, Palma's discussion of the exclusion of negativity, which, in essence, corresponds to what I have interpreted as the banishment of the possibility of experiencing Dionysian chaos (Palma, 201, 222.)

138. GM, 96; KGW, VI, 2: 352.

139. Lukács even goes so far as to claim that Nietzsche's "whole life's work was a constant polemic against Marxism and socialism," even though "he never read a single line of Marx and Engels" (see Georg Lukács, *The Destruction of Reason*, trans. Peter Palmer [Atlantic Highlands, N.J.: Humanities Press, 1981], 313). Leo Strauss, speaking specifically with reference to Nietzsche's conception of the last man, offers a similar view: "Regardless of whether or not Nietzsche knew of Marx's writings, he questioned the communist vision of society more radically than anyone else. He identified the man of the communist world society as the last man" (Leo Strauss, *Studies in Platonic Political Philosophy* [Chicago: University of Chicago Press, 1983], 32). Like Strauss, Palma (212–13) and Lampert (25) also interpret the last man as the symbol of a communist social ideal.

To be sure, these accounts of the last man and of Nietzsche's (implied) evaluation of Marxism and communism have some basis in Nietzsche's writings. Still, they tend to obfuscate some important affinities between Nietzsche's and Marx's appraisals and criticisms of modern egalitarianism. We should note, for example, that Nietzsche's conception of the last man resembles more the conception of "crude communism" that Marx develops in his *1844 Manuscripts* than it resembles the conception of "utopian communism" that Marx develops in that same text. It is also significant that Nietzsche's interpretation of resentment as the driving engine of modern egalitarianism echoes Marx's discussion of the role of envy in bringing about the leveling of differences that marks the transition from capitalism to crude communism. Finally, we should consider the close kinship between Nietzsche's vision of creative human flourishing and Marx's vision of human existence subsequent to the advent of utopian communism (see Karl Marx, *Early Writings*, trans. Rodney Livingstone and Gregor Benton [New York: Vintage Books, 1975], 345–58).

140. See Jaspers, 261–62. He (in his discussion of Nietzsche's reaction to the "democratic age") captures better than most commentators the scope of Nietzsche's critique of European modernity.

141. By a "limit-concept" I mean a concept that defines the utmost limit of certain

tendencies (here, ascetic tendencies). Such concepts constitute valuable contributions to social thought by functioning heuristically as ideal types. Thus, simplifications like Nietzsche's concept of the last man, notwithstanding the fact that they *are* simplifications, help us to understand the way things are in the world (cf., on this point, Stern, *A Study of Nietzsche*, 132), and need not be treated as fallacious applications of a melodramatic aesthetic to the analysis and explanation of social phenomena (cf. Wylie Sypher, "Aesthetic of Revolution: The Marxist Melodrama," in *Tragedy: Vision and Form*, 2nd ed., ed. Robert Corrigan (New York: Harper and Row, 1981). For another view of Nietzsche that also stresses his belief that there is a continuity between Christian-moral and liberal-democratic cultures, albeit without treating asceticism as the connecting link between these cultures, see Warren, 214.

142. See GM, 76; KGW, VI, 2: 328–29, for an exceptionally clear statement of this complaint. It is worth adding here that one can reconcile the modernist ideal of self-transformation with the defence of capitalism if one dissociates this ideal from the sexual, bodily, and Dionysian energies that capitalist rationalization deprecates. Among recent writers, Richard Rorty provides the most thoroughgoing attempt to finesse this reconciliation, and thus to succeed theoretically at being both a modernist aesthete and a committed advocate of the socioeconomic status quo (see Rorty, *Contingency, Irony, and Solidarity, passim*). Richard Poirier has likewise attempted to dissociate the valuable activity of private self-creation from the project of radical social change; thus, like Rorty, he repudiates those apocalyptic strains in Nietzsche's thought that I have characterized as Nietzsche's "Dionysian modernism" (Richard Poirier, *The Renewal of Literature* [New Haven, Conn.: Yale University Press, 1987], 170, 185, 191–92, 202). What links Rorty and Poirier, and what allows them to escape the Nietzschean/Weberian conclusion that secularized asceticism and self-re-creation mutually exclude each other, is their shared commitment to a purely *linguistic* model of self-transformation. (This is by no means to deny the subtle differences that *separate* Rorty and Poirier and that become most apparent when one attends to their differing responses to Harold Bloom's "humanist" literary criticism.) For an incisive and contemporary contrast to Rorty's and Poirier's view of self-transformation, see Daniel Bell's neo-Weberian *The Cultural Contradictions of Capitalism*. Because Bell presupposes a *psychological* as distinct from a linguistic model of self-transformation, and thus takes quite seriously the sexual and Dionysian affirmations of would-be self-creators, he sees a genuine contradiction between the ascetic ethos that sustains the capitalist economy and the (in his view) subversive psychological impulses at work in the modernist and postmodernist celebration of the self's pursuit of new modes of self-existence.

143. GM, final section; KGW, VI, 2: 429–30.

144. Here, my account of the last man owes something to Dan Conway's acute criticism of an earlier account.

145. For Nietzsche's clearest discussion of the creative potency of Dionysian sufferers, see GS, no. 370; KGW, 301–4.

146. TSZ, 131; KGW, VI, 1: 15.

147. Earlier in this chapter I explained and made use of Paul de Man's concept of allegory. Here, however, I rely on a simpler and more traditional concept of allegory, according to which an "allegory is a narrative in which the agents and the action, and sometimes the setting as well, are contrived not only to make sense in themselves, but also to signify a second, correlated order of persons, things, concepts, or events" (see Abrams, *A Glossary of Literary Terms*, 4).

148. TSZ, 133; KGW, VI, 1: 17.

149. Cf. Lampert, 26. I agree with Lampert that the phrase "the good and the just" is, for Zarathustra, a more comprehensive designation than the phrase "the last man."

150. See TSZ, 324-25; KGW, VI, 1: 261-63, and EH, 330; KGW, VI, 3: 367.

151. TSZ, 163-64; KGW, VI, 1: 61-62.

152. See CW, no. 6; KGW, VI, 3: 17-20, also BGE, no. 256, no. 269; KGW, VI, 2: 209-12, 232-35. Cf. also the descriptions of the jester and the magician who appear in Part 4.

153. BT, 104; KGW, III, 1: 105.

154. TSZ, 131; KGW, VI, 1: 15.

155. The interpretation of the tightrope walker as a "mask" of Dionysus is justified, I believe, by the more fundamental claim that we should regard him as a figurative personification of the Dionysian possibility of overcoming man. The details of my reading of section 6 seem to be consistent with Higgins's general suggestion that the jester is the voice of the tradition that Zarathustra wants to overcome. Yet Higgins and I disagree on the question as to whether the tightrope walker's activity is "goal-oriented." Her suggestion is that it is not (see Higgins, *Nietzsche's Zarathustra*, 86). Yet, without supposing that the tightrope walker deliberately aims to reach the end of the course before the jester, I do not see how one can explain the fact that the tightrope walker falls precisely as a consequence of "seeing his *rival* [*Nebenbuhler*] win."

156. BT, 86; KGW, III, 1: 83.

157. For the later Nietzsche, the theater of Wagnerian romanticism, rather than that of Euripedean aesthetic Socratism, marks the cultural triumph of anti-Dionysian asceticism.

158. TSZ, 132; KGW, VI, 1: 17.

159. All the quoted material in this and the preceding paragraph derives from TSZ, 132; KGW, VI, 1: 16-7.

160. Ibid.

161. TSZ, 133-35; KGW, VI, 1: 17-19.

162. It is not insignificant to note that the hermit offers Zarathustra and his companion *bread and wine*, the vehicles and symbols of the Christian communion (the Eucharist sacrament). Nietzsche's parody of the communion ceremony reinforces the suggested identification of Zarathustra and the dead tightrope walker: Christians, by participating in this ceremony, commemorate and partake in the death of Christ; Zarathustra, by participating in the communion offered by the hermit, symbolically commemorates and partakes in the dead possibility represented by the dead tightrope walker.

By using imagery pertaining to the death of Christ, Nietzsche recalls his readers to his parody of the first half of Paul's letter to the Philippians in section 1 of the prologue. Perhaps, too, he means to recall them to Hölderlin's great poem "Brot und Wein," which, significantly, ties the imagery of the communion to the figure of Dionysus.

163. TSZ, 135; KGW, VI, 1: 19.

164. Ibid. Morning, for Zarathustra, is the time of the child's self-overcoming. Noon (see Zarathustra's claim near the end of Part 1, for example, that man stands in the middle of his way between beast and overman at the "great noon"; Zarathustra's experience of noon in Part 4; and Nietzsche's reference to noon in "How the 'true world' finally became a fable") is the time of leonine readiness that precedes going-under (evening) and going-over (the advent of a new morning). Midnight, finally, is the dark obverse of noon: the time of the leonine solitude that is the counterpart of leonine readiness and that marks Zarathustra's solitary singing of "Once More" in "The Other Dancing Song." Midnight is also the time of the "The Sleepwalker Song," with which Zarathustra parodies his solitary singing of "Once More" in "The Other Dancing Song" (see my discussion of the "Sleepwalker Song" in Chapter 6).

165. TSZ, 135; KGW, VI, 1: 19.

166. TSZ, 136; KGW, VI, 1: 20-21.

167. TSZ, 136; KGW, VI, 1: 20. Zarathustra's use of the figure of the harvester in section 9 recalls his use of the figure of the planter in his speech on the last man.

168. TSZ, 190; KGW, VI, 1: 98.

169. Daniel Conway also suggests that Zarathustra, unlike Nietzsche, "misreads" the time of his descent. For his analysis of this misreading, which differs from my own, see "A Moral Ideal for Everyone and No One," 21-22. On the significance of noon in *Zarathustra*, see note 164, above.

170. Harold Alderman has also noticed that the three metamorphoses play an important role in structuring the action that occurs in the last few sections of the prologue. See Alderman, 30 ff. The particulars of his account differ from my own.

171. For a discussion of some of the *possible* meanings that can be ascribed to the figures of the eagle and the serpent, see David S. Thatcher, "Eagle and Serpent in *Zarathustra*," *Nietzsche-Studien* 6 (1977): 240-60.

172. TSZ, 137; KGW, VI, 1: 21.

173. See Abrams, *Natural Supernaturalism*, 160. Also worth noting here is Abrams's general discussion of the transmission of Hermetic thought in the West after the Renaissance (160 ff). See, finally, Perkins, "Analogistic Strategies in *Zarathustra*," for a discussion of Nietzsche's use of Hermetic imagery, including the image of the ouroboros.

174. See Abrams, *Natural Supernaturalism*, 148.

175. TSZ, 137; KGW, VI, 1: 21.

176. Lampert is certainly right to note that Luther's Bible describes the serpent using the word *listig* (see Lampert, 315n29). However, he misses the fact that Luther uses *klug* to depict Eve's belief that she will become wise as a result of eating from the tree of knowledge. See Gen. 3:1, 3:6; *Die Bibel*, "Die Bücher des alten Testaments," 3.

177. Gen. 3:5; *Die Bibel*, "Die Bücher des alten Testaments," 3.

Chapter 3: Dionysus, the German Nation, and the Body

1. It is worth noting that, in his 1886 preface to *The Birth of Tragedy* (his "Attempt at a Self-Criticism") Nietzsche explicitly describes his first book as a "stammering" attempt to speak as a disciple of Dionysus. See BT, 20; KGW, III, 1: 8–9.

2. BT, 95–96; KGW III, 1: 95; emphasis in original.

3. BT, sec. 19; KGW III, 1: 116–25. See especially Nietzsche's claims that "out of the Dionysian root [*Grunde*] of the German spirit a power has arisen which, having nothing in common with the primitive conditions of Socratic culture, can neither be explained nor excused by it"; that "the birth of a tragic age means simply a return to itself of the German spirit, a blessed self-rediscovery after powerful intrusive influences had for a long time compelled it . . . to servitude under their form [*Form*]"; and that this birth points to a "new form of existence [*Daseinsform*]." In these passages, Nietzsche seems to presuppose the modern, "expressivist" thesis, often linked to Herder, that forms of individual and collective spirit acquire determinateness only through self-expression. For an insightful discussion of this thesis, see Charles Taylor, *Hegel* (Cambridge: Cambridge University Press, 1975), 11–29.

4. BT, 136–37; KGW III, 1: 143. I have altered the translation slightly. For Nietzsche's references to Bach and Beethoven, see BT, 119; KGW III, 1: 123. In tying Dionysus to Martin Luther's Reformation, Nietzsche seems to belie his assertion in the "Attempt at a Self-Criticism" that Christianity is treated with a hostile silence throughout *The Birth of Tragedy* (cf. Silk and Stern, 121). For Wagner's celebration of Luther's chorale, which Nietzsche echoes, see Richard Wagner, *Beethoven*, trans. Edward Dannreuther (London: W. W. Reeves, 1903), 95. For a related and instructive discussion of Luther's influence on the development of German music from Bach onward, see Henry A. Lea, "Mahler's Extraterritoriality," *Massachusetts Review* (Autumn 1990): 344.

5. Nietzsche writes: "Let no one try to blight our faith in a yet-impending rebirth of Hellenic antiquity; for this alone gives us hope for a renovation and purification of the German spirit through the fire magic of music [*den Feuerzauber der Musik*]" (BT, 123; KGW III, 1: 127). The reference here to the "fire magic of music" alludes to the "magic fire music" that marks the conclusion of Wagner's *Die Walküre*.

6. For Nietzsche's extended statement of the argument I have summarized in this paragraph, see BT, sec. 23; KGW, III, 1: 141–45.

7. BT, 139; KGW III, 1: 145.

8. BT, 121; KGW III, 1: 124–25.

9. For a useful discussion of Herder's use of such language, see Isaiah Berlin, *Vico and Herder* (New York: Vintage Books, 1976), 182.

10. For a discussion of the concept of nationalism that illuminates the social history and intellectual traditions shaping Nietzsche's nationalism in *The Birth of Tragedy*, see Isaiah Berlin's essay entitled "Nationalism," in his *Against the Current*, (New York: Penguin, 1982), 333–55.

11. See Etienne Balibar and Immanuel Wallerstein, *Race, Nation, and Class*, trans. Chris Turner (London: Verso, 1991), chap. 3, for Balibar's discussion of supranationalism.

12. For Nietzsche's notion that Dionysus signifies the dissolution of all national and, more generally, social boundaries and differences, see BT, 37, 59; KGW, III, 1: 25–26, 51–52. See, also, Silk and Stern, 64, especially their claim that in the Dionysian state there is "in fact, no place for *any* distinctions" (emphasis mine).

13. Here, I should note that I follow Robert E. McGinn in reading Nietzsche (in *The Birth of Tragedy*) as using the term "culture" (*Kultur*) primarily to refer "to a complex of forms of human intellectual and artistic activity (e.g., music, philosophy, drama, etc.; or, more generally, Kunst, Wissenschaft, etc.) . . . as an interlocking web of such forms viewed as the incarnations of the Geist of the social unit in question." For the early Nietzsche, a culture is an interrelated group of practices that expresses the unifying spirit of a *Volk* or other social group. See Robert E. McGinn, "Culture as Prophylactic: Nietzsche's *Birth of Tragedy* as Culture Criticism," *Nietzsche-Studien* 4 (1975): 77–80.

14. See BT, 119–21, 138; KGW, III, 1: 122–25, 145. Here and in what follows, my discussion of the rhetoric of exclusion and collection draws on James A. Snead's discussion of the same in his very fine analysis of what he calls "the European notion of 'universality.'" See James A. Snead, "European Pedigrees/African Contagions: Nationality, Narrative, and Communality in Tutuola, Achebe, and Reed," in *Nation and Narration*, ed. Homi Bhaba (New York: Routledge, 1990), esp. 244–46.

15. For Nietzsche's view that Dionysus is the one and only truly existent being, see BT, 45, 50, 71, 73; KGW, III, 1: 34, 41, 66, 68. For his description of the world of appearances as "unreal" or "truly nonexistent," see BT, 45; KGW, III, 1: 35. I will add that I maintain a more or less traditional interpretation of Nietzsche's notion of the Dionysian ground of appearances, notwithstanding Werner Hamacher's argument that Nietzsche in *The Birth of Tragedy* holds that "the Apollonian principle of division and differentiation is already at work in the original unity of Dionysian" (see Werner Hamacher, "'Disgregation of the Will': Nietzsche on the Individual and Individuality," trans. Jeffrey S. Librett, in *Reconstructing Individualism*, ed. Thomas Heller, Morton Sosna, and David Wellbery [Stanford, Calif.: Stanford University Press, 1986], 114). Hamacher defends this view by citing two passages from *The Birth of Tragedy*:

> Individuation, "dismemberment [*Zerstückelung*], the properly Dionysian affliction" (I, 61), torments the "originally unified, the eternally afflicted and self-contradictory" (I, 32), not as violence from without, but as the accomplishment of its immanent process. And if Dionysus finds deliverance from the affliction of individuation, it is only in the fleeting forms of interpretation, appearance, and therefore, yet again, individuation. What inflicted the wound is supposed to heal it, but the wound, individuation, is also the life of the original unity of the whole. (Hamacher, 114)

Hamacher's citations of Nietzsche's text refer to *Werke in drei Bänden*, ed. K. Schlecta (Munich, 1966); for the same passages in BT and KGW, see BT, 73, 45; KGW, III, 1: 68, 34. As far as I can see, neither of Hamacher's citations supports the view he wishes to encourage. The first occurs in a passage in which Nietzsche is discussing the Greek myth of the Dionysus of the Mysteries "of whom wonderful myths tell that as a boy he was torn to pieces by the Titans." Read as metaphysical allegory, this myth would appear to pertain not to the presence of distinct individuals *within* the Dionysian ground of appearances (Hamacher's reading), but to the painful emergence *from* that ground of the individual forms that Hamacher describes as "fleeting forms of interpretation, appearance." The full statement from which Hamacher draws his first citation is consistent with this alternative interpretation and reads as follows: "Thus it is intimated that this dismemberment, the properly Dionysian affliction, is like a *transformation [Umwandlung]* into air, water, earth, and fire, that we are to regard the state of individuation as the origin and primal cause of all suffering, as something objectionable in itself" (emphasis mine). The second citation supports Hamacher's reading only if one assumes that, in Nietzsche's view, the occurrence of affliction and self-contradiction in the Dionysian ground of appearances necessitates that this ground consist of distinct individual parts. Yet I see nothing in Nietzsche's text to justify the assumption that he held such a view.

16. See BT, 62–64; KGW, III, 1: 55–58.

17. BT, 137; KGW, III, 1: 143; emphasis in original.

18. BT, 64; KGW, III, 1: 57.

19. In section 21 of *The Birth of Tragedy*, Nietzsche explicitly links the Roman *imperium*'s preoccupation with political/civic affairs to "the most extreme secularization" (BT, 125; KGW, III, 1: 129).

20. These include the state and society, as well as other spheres of activity separated by the "hostile barriers that necessity, caprice, or 'impudent convention' have fixed between man and man" (BT, 59, 37; KGW, III, 1: 52, 25).

21. BT, 63; KGW, III, 1: 55.

22. BT, 59; KGW, III, 1: 52.

23. BT, 39; KGW, III, 1: 28.

24. For Sloterdijk's analysis of this compromise, which I have found extremely helpful, see his *Thinker on Stage*, trans. Jamie Owen Daniel (Minneapolis: University of Minnesota Press, 1989), 24–32.

25. BT, 39; KGW, III, 1: 28. Here, I have altered slightly Kaufmann's translation.

26. BT, 37; KGW, III, 1: 25.

27. For the Dionysian barbarian's desire for fusion with his neighbor, see ibid. For Nietzsche's explicit association of Dionysus with excess (*Uebermaass*), see my discussion of Nietzsche and de Man in Chapter 2, as well as BT, 46–47; KGW, III, 1: 36–38. For a useful, general analysis of Nietzsche's notion of Dionysian excess, see John Sallis, *Crossings* (Chicago: University of Chicago Press, 1991), 50–59.

28. BT, 40; KGW, III, 1: 29–30. My emphasis.

29. BT, 40; KGW, III, 1: 28–29.

30. Ibid.

31. BT, 39; KGW, III, 1: 28. For a discussion of the political implications of Nietzsche's Apollonian compromise, see Sloterdijk, 27–28. Also relevant, in this context, is the link McGinn draws (McGinn, 86) between the Apollonian compromise and Herbert Marcuse's notion of repressive or institutionalized desublimation.

32. For Nietzsche's representation of the Hellenic chorus as deriving from the Dionysian Greek festivals, see BT, 62; KGW, III, 1: 55.

33. BT, 109−10; KGW, III, 1: 111−12.

34. For Nietzsche's reference to the will's "true, undissembled voice," see BT, 104; KGW, III, 1: 104. On the connection between the opening passage of section 18 and Nietzsche's discussion of the symbolic revelry of the Dionysian Greeks, see Henry Staten, *Nietzsche's Voice* (Ithaca, N.Y.: Cornell University Press, 1990), 207.

35. BT, 104; KGW, III, 1: 105.

36. In section 21, Nietzsche claims that, in tragedy, Apollonian illusion (viz., the dramatic aspect of Greek tragedy) is broken and annihilated. According to McGinn (88−89), this claim shows that section 18's proposition, that tragic culture is a form of illusion, expresses Nietzsche's belief that tragedy is a form of temporary, *Apollonian* illusion that gives way, ultimately, to a "Dionysian effect" that Nietzsche associates with metaphysical comfort. McGinn's reading of section 18 should be rejected, however, because it overlooks the fact that Nietzsche, in characterizing tragic culture as a form of illusion, refers explicitly to the "*metaphysical comfort* [emphasis mine] that beneath the whirl of phenomena eternal life flows on indestructibly," *not* to a temporary Apollonian illusion that gives way to a Dionysian and metaphysical comfort. To put the point a bit differently, McGinn's reading of section 18 will seem plausible only if one mistakenly identifies the *Apollonian* illusion Nietzsche discusses in section 21 with the *metaphysically comforting* illusion ("that beneath the whirl of phenomena . . .") he discusses in section 18, notwithstanding the fact that throughout *The Birth of Tragedy* Nietzsche distinguishes the "dramatic" and Apollonian aspect of tragedy from the metaphysical comfort with which, he proclaims in section 7, "every true tragedy leaves us." (Nietzsche alludes to the musical source of this comfort when, in section 21, he says that "in the total effect of tragedy, the Dionysian predominates once again. Tragedy closes with a sound which could never come from the realm of Apollonian art.")

For an alternative and compelling interpretation of section 18 that differs from the one offered in this chapter, see Maudmarie Clark, "Language and Deconstruction: Nietzsche, de Man, and Postmodernism," in *Nietzsche as Postmodernist*, ed. Clayton Koelb (Albany: SUNY Press, 1990), 75−85.

37. Quoted in Paul de Man, *Allegories of Reading*, 96.

38. See Staten, 187−216.

39. Ibid., 199.

40. Ibid., 209.

41. BT, 59; KGW, III, 1: 52. I have slightly altered Kaufmann's translation.

42. Quoted in Taylor, *Hegel*, 389.

43. See ibid., 390.

44. Schopenhauer, *The World as Will and Representation*, 1: 273−74, 2: 442−43.

45. Ibid., 2: 443.

46. Ibid., 1: 182−83 (for the German original, on which I have based my interpolations, see Arthur Schopenhauer, *Zürcher Ausgabe: Werke in zehn Bänden* (Zurich: Diogenes Verlag, 1977), 1: 236−37, 2: 443.

47. BT, 24–25; KGW, III, 1: 13–14.

48. EH, 270–71; KGW, VI, 3: 308.

49. For Nietzsche's interpretation of the modern state as a "cold monster," see *Zarathustra*, Part 1, "On the New Idol."

50. WP, 281; KGW, VII, 2: 202. See also TSZ, 146–49; KGW, VI, 1: 35–40, and BGE, 19–21, 25–27; KGW, VI, 2: 20–21, 25–28. Also, cf. Schacht, 272; and Nehamas, *Nietzsche*, 187–88.

51. TSZ, 171; KGW, VI, 1: 71.

52. Ibid., 72.

53. I explore below, in some detail, Nietzsche's view that virtues are valued characteristics.

54. TSZ, 187; KGW, VI, 1: 94–95. For a different though illuminating reading of some of the passages I have quoted here, see Gary Shapiro, *Nietzschean Narratives* (Bloomington: Indiana University Press, 1989), 54–60. As far as I can tell, Shapiro's treatment of Zarathustra's use of "proportional metaphor" is perfectly compatible with my interpretation of the relationship between embodiment and virtue.

55. Nietzsche also links self-creation to the creation of new values in *The Gay Science*. See GS, 255–56; KGW, V, 2: 243–44. Cf. Schacht, 413.

56. This is the position I take Nietzsche to be sketching in the second section of the preface to the second edition of *The Gay Science* (GS, 33–35; KGW, V, 2: 15–17). The values in question here, and throughout my discussion of Nietzsche's view of value-creation, are what Richard Schacht (403–4) describes as "second-order" or "explicit" values.

57. TSZ, 171; KGW, VI, 1: 71.

58. TSZ, 148; KGW, VI, 1: 39. Here, I have slightly altered Kaufmann's translation.

59. See Lester Hunt, *Nietzsche and the Origin of Virtue* (New York: Routledge, 1991), 73–74.

60. Cf. Daniel Breazeale, "The Meaning of the Earth," *The Great Year of Zarathustra*, ed. David Goicoechea (Lanham, Md.: University Press of America, 1991), 117. Here, I should note that I reject Breazeale's view (122–33) that there is in *Zarathustra* an opposition between a "naturalist" theory of value-creation that finds the roots of our values in our facticity (for Nietzsche, the passions and drives that claim human existence) and an "existentialist" theory that sees our values as stemming from our interpretive activity. Against this view, I will be arguing that the theory of value-creation Nietzsche adumbrates in *Zarathustra* involves both a factical dimension—Zarathustra holds that human values have a basis in uncreated passions—*and* an interpretive one—passions become values when, through an act of interpretation, they are assigned a purpose. In the theory of value-creation appearing in *Zarathustra*, that is, facticity and interpretation complement one another.

61. TSZ, 171, 227–28; KGW, VI, 1: 71, 145.

62. TSZ, 226; KGW, VI, 1: 143–44.   63. Ibid.

64. GM, 77; KGW, VI, 2: 329–30.   65. GM, 117–18; KGW, VI, 2: 381.

66. Cf. Breazeale, "The Meaning of the Earth," 119.

67. WP, 207; KGW, VIII, 3: 159.

68. TI, 490; AC, 572; KGW, VI, 3: 79, 170.

69. For essentially the same view, see Nehamas, *Nietzsche*, 187–89.

70. GS (no. 290), 232; KGW, V, 2: 210.

71. I agree, therefore, with Bernd Magnus's claim that "*Übermenschlichkeit* is a second-order diagnostic principle." See Bernd Magnus, "Perfectibility and Attitude in Nietzsche's *Übermensch*," *Review of Metaphysics* 36 (March 1983): 635.

72. TSZ, 187; KGW, VI, 1: 94.   73. TSZ, 189; KGW, VI, 1: 96.

74. TSZ, 188; KGW, VI, 1: 95–96.   75. TSZ, 144–45; KGW, VI, 1: 33.

76. See GM, 122, 141; KGW, VI, 2: 386, 408.

77. TSZ, 186; KGW, VI, 1: 95.

78. TSZ, 186; KGW, VI, 1: 93.

79. TSZ, 171; KGW, VI, 1: 71.

80. Lampert identifies the gift-giving virtue with the will to power and believes it significant that Nietzsche does not use the term "will to power" to name the gift-giving virtue in Part 3 of *Zarathustra*. In my view, the gift-giving virtue is not identical to the will to power per se, but with the will to power in its specific capacity as a means of self-resurrection. See Lampert, 194–95.

81. TSZ, 188–89; KGW, VI, 1: 95–96. Here, I have altered Kaufmann's translation, rendering *herrschender Gedanke* as "ruling thought," not as "dominant thought."

82. TSZ, 301–3; KGW, VI, 1: 234–36.

83. My use of the distinction between first- and second-order desires derives from Harry Frankfurt's essay "Freedom of the Will and the Concept of a Person," in Frankfurt's *The Importance of What We Care About* (Cambridge: Cambridge University Press, 1988), 11–25.

84. The characterization of the will to power as a second-order passion that revalues first-order passions more or less summarizes my reconstruction of Nietzsche-Zarathustra's understanding of the process by which human beings overcome themselves, create new values, and so on. Commentators who rely on the same or a similar distinction in their analysis of the will to power and/or value-creation include Alderman (see *Nietzsche's Gift*, 72–81); Nehamas (see Nehamas, *Nietzsche*, 188, as well as 252n17); and Maudmarie Clark (*Nietzsche on Truth and Philosophy* [Cambridge: Cambridge University Press, 1991], 210–12, 228–29). See also, in this connection, Deleuze's analysis of the relation between will to power and force (*Nietzsche and Philosophy*, 49–52), and Blondel's suggestion that, for Nietzsche, the creation of values stems from "evaluations of life by itself as *will to power*" (Eric Blondel, *Nietzsche: The Body and Culture*, trans. Seán Hand [Stanford, Calif.: Stanford University Press, 1991], 69). Wolfgang Müller-Lauter insists that, for Nietzsche, all passions and drives are will to power (and, contra Heidegger, that there exists a plurality of wills to power). To be sure, many of Nietzsche's writings support this view. It nonetheless seems to me that Zarathustra presents the will to power as, exclusively, a kind of second-order passion (Müller-Lauter, "Nietzsche's Teaching of Will to Power," trans. Drew E. Griffin, *Journal of Nietzsche Studies* 4–5 (Autumn 1992–Spring 1993), 57–59.

Finally, I will note that the interpretation of the will to power as second-order desire answers Meredith Williams's objection that the concept of the will to power cannot explain value-creation. Williams's view seems plausible, only because she identifies the will to power with the desire to dominate violently. But this narrow construal of "the empirical content of the notion of the will to power" (Williams) should be rejected, for it captures neither (1) the connection Zarathustra draws between willing and esteeming, nor (2) his identification of esteeming and valuing. Once these features of Zarathustra-Nietzsche's understanding of value-creation are taken into consideration, the interpretation of will to power as second-order desire seems a natural one, and one can begin to see just how Zarathustra-Nietzsche accounts for the content of created values. See Meredith Williams, "Transcendence and Return: The Overcoming of Philosophy in Nietzsche and Wittgenstein," *International Philosophical Quarterly* 28, no. 4 (December 1988): 403-19.

85. TSZ, 189; KGW, VI, 1: 96-97.

86. TSZ, 142; KGW, VI, 1: 30.

87. My reading of "On the Teachers of Virtue" agrees in essence with Lampert's reading (see Lampert, 36-37). For another useful discussion of this speech, see Werner Dannhauser, *Nietzsche's View of Socrates* (Ithaca, N.Y.: Cornell University Press, 1974), 253. Finally, I will add that I also follow Lampert in interpreting "On the Afterworldly" and "On the Despisers of the Body" as elaborations of the attack on the "old" or Christian-Platonic teachers of virtue begun in "On the Teachers of Virtue."

88. All the references in this paragraph are from TSZ, 142-47; KGW, VI, 1: 31-37. I have altered Kaufmann's translation slightly, rendering *Absterbende* not as "[the] decaying" but as "[the] dying."

89. Ibid.

90. For Nietzsche's description of the ascetic priest as a sick purveyor of sickness, see GM, 125-26; KGW, VI, 2: 390-91. The overall development of Part 1 suggests that "the afterworldly" and the "despisers of the body" have contributed to the spread of asceticism and sickness, for their "nonsensical" teachings of virtue have come to dwell in the body, led human spirit and virtue away from the earth, and made human beings into sick physicians who need to help themselves (see "On the Gift-Giving Virtue").

91. TSZ, 142, 189; KGW, VI, 1: 30, 96.

92. TSZ, 145; KGW, VI, 1: 34.

93. Nietzsche's general preoccupation with the themes of exhaustion and fatigue is clearly evident in numerous passages collected in *The Will to Power*. For a superb discussion of these themes that highlights the affinities between Nietzsche and his contemporaries, see Anson Rabinbach, *The Human Motor: Energy, Fatigue, and the Origins of Modernity* (New York: Basic Books, 1990), 19-44. For a related treatment of similar motifs, see George Steiner, "The Great Ennui," in *Bluebeard's Castle* (New Haven, Conn.: Yale University Press, 1970), 3-25. Rabinbach focuses on the writings of medical writers and scientists, as well as on the works of philosophers, poets, and novelists. Steiner limits his attention to the philosophical and literary culture of the nineteenth century.

94. Quoted in Kaufmann, 155.

95. See Johann Wolfgang von Goethe, *Conversations with Eckermann*, trans. John Oxenford (San Francisco: North Point Press, 1984), 101. For the corresponding passages in an edited version of Eckermann's German text, see Johann Peter Eckermann, *Gespräche mit Goethe*, ed. Conrad Hofer (Leipzig: Heffe und Beder Verlag, 1913), 156. For a critical

discussion of Goethe's treatment of the problem of "poetic exhaustion," see Walter Jackson Bate, *The Burden of the Past and the English Poet* (Cambridge: Harvard University Press, 1970), e.g., 5–6, 111–12.

96. TI, 554; KGW, VI, 3: 145.

97. TI, 554; KGW, VI, 3: 146.

98. Blondel, 112.

99. Cf. ibid., 69, for a view similar to my own regarding Nietzsche's rejection of the nature/culture distinction.

100. Here and in the remainder of this paragraph I sketch an answer to the question Blondel poses when, having shown that Nietzsche eschews the nature/culture distinction and makes "culture . . . the object of a *Naturgeschichte*," he writes: "[A] difficulty now presents itself: within the 'determinist' framework of genealogy, what can possibly act as the source of a *new* culture . . . ? If culture is just a name for a nature that is trying to fill its own lack, what will be the source of the overcoming that Nietzsche constantly demands, what will be the source of the *Übermensch's transcendence*, even one that falls back on the imminent horizons of the Earth and the body?" Moreover, I provide an account of the relationship between self-overcoming and cultural change that argues for an alternative to Meredith Williams's view that, for Nietzsche, a person can "generate afresh a new set of values" only if he stands "fully outside the form of life of which he is a part." See Blondel, 69–70; Meredith Williams, 415.

101. Here, I want to flag the connection between some of the issues I raise in this paragraph and, indeed, throughout this section, and Stanley Cavell's recent, engaging effort to engage Nietzsche and Spengler by way of Wittgenstein in "Declining Decline," the first of two essays contained in his *This New Yet Unapproachable America*. Cavell's essay emphasizes the Nietzschean and Spenglerian themes of cultural exhaustion and spiritual nausea. Moreover, his discussion of cultural transfiguration (in his words, "the power of the ordinary to move the ordinary") has real affinities to the conception of "listening to the body and the earth" that I attribute to Zarathustra:

> I have suggested that the biological interpretation of form of life is not merely another available interpretation to that of the ethnological, but contests its sense of political and social conservatism. My idea is that this mutual absorption of the natural and the social is a consequence of Wittgenstein's envisioning of what we may as well call the human form of life. In being asked to accept this, or suffer it, as given for ourselves, we are not asked to accept, let us say, private property, but separateness; not a particular fact of power but the fact that I am a man, therefore of *this* (range or scale of) capacity for work, for pleasure, for endurance, for appeal, for command, for understanding, for wish, for will, for teaching, for suffering. The precise range or scale is not knowable a priori, any more than the precise range or scale of a word is to be known a priori. Of course you can *fix* the range; so you can confine a man or a woman, and not all the ways or senses of confinement are knowable a priori. The rhetoric of humanity as a form of life, or a level of life, standing in need of something like transfiguration—some radical change, but as

it were from inside, not *by* anything; some say in another birth, symbolizing a different order of natural reactions—is typical of a line of apparently contradictory sensibilities, ones that may appear as radically innovative (in action or in feeling) or radically conservative: Luther was such a sensibility; so were Rousseau and Thoreau. Thoreau calls himself disobedient, but what he means is not that he refuses to listen but that he insists on listening differently while still comprehensibly.

See Stanley Cavell, *This New Yet Unapproachable America* (Albuquerque: Living Batch Press, 1989), 44.

102. Both Laurence Lampert and, more recently, Greg Whitlock have seen the importance of the camel-lion-child scheme for interpreting the speeches of Part 1. On particular points of interpretation, I sometimes agree and sometimes disagree with them. Where these points of agreement and disagreement strike me as significant, I mention them, not in the main body of my discussion, but in a footnote. See Lampert, 50–51; also Greg Whitlock, *Returning to Sils-Maria* (New York: Peter Lang, 1990), 72–73.

103. See Whitlock, 73.

104. See TSZ, 150–51; KGW, VI, 1: 42–43. I interpret the pale criminal's soul's desire for "blood" as a desire that the pale criminal's bodily desire (his "greed and lust") be fulfilled, for it seems to me that the pale criminal's soul's desire for blood is predicated on its interpretation of his body's desire as a desire for blood. His soul's desire for blood is a desire, simply, to see his body's desire for blood sated.

105. Here again I rely on Harry Frankfurt (11–16), who defines a second-order volition as a second-order desire to render some first-order desire effective as a motive. See Frankfurt.

106. TSZ, 150–51; KGW, VI, 1: 42–43. Emphasis mine.

107. WP, 133; KGW, VIII, 3: 156.

108. In the third essay of *Genealogy*, as in WP, 133, Nietzsche uses the figure of the hen stopped by a chalk line to investigate the concept of sin. In the same essay, he explicitly links the concept of sin to the interpretive perspective of Christian (priestly) morality. See GM, 140–41; KGW, VI, 2: 406–7.

109. Thus, the pale criminal rejects Nietzsche's claim in *Genealogy* that "man's 'sinfulness' is not a fact but merely the interpretation of a fact" (GM, 129; KGW, VI, 2: 394).

110. TSZ, 152–53; KGW, VI, 1: 44–46.   111. TSZ, 305; KGW, VI, 1: 239.

112. TSZ, 131; KGW, VI, 1: 15.   113. TSZ, 153; KGW, VI, 1: 45.

114. TSZ, 153; KGW, VI, 1: 46.

115. All the quotations in this and the preceding paragraph, with occasional alterations to Kaufmann's translations, come from TSZ, 152–56; KGW, VI, 1: 44–50. With regard to the youth on the mountainside, I reject Whitlock's claim (78) that the youth has "successfully metamorphosed through the camel and lion stages." My view that the youth has not yet completed the second metamorphosis seems to me to be more in accord with Lampert's reading (47–50).

116. Lampert (50–51) claims that this speech can be construed as a description of the lion-spirit, but offers no justification for this assertion.

117. To his "brothers in war" Zarathustra says, "I know of the hatred and envy in your hearts." Before he says this, the youth on the mountainside speaks of his *envy* of Zarathustra and of his *hatred* of the flier. For these assertions, as well as for Zarathustra's remark about waging war for one's own thoughts, see TSZ, 155, 159; KGW, VI, 1: 48, 54. As other commentators have noted, the remark about waging war for one's thoughts suggests that the warfare Zarathustra has in mind is an inner, spiritual warfare (see Whitlock, 80; Lampert, 53). Dannhauser, however, suggests that Zarathustra aims to address "real warriors" (Dannhauser, 38-39). For an insightful interpretation of "On War and Warriors" that approaches this speech from a perspective different from my own, see Thomas L. Pangle, "The 'Warrior Spirit' as an Inlet to the Political Philosophy of Nietzsche's Zarathustra," *Nietzsche-Studien* 15 (1986): 140-79.

118. TSZ, 160; KGW, VI, 1: 55.

119. TSZ, 160; KGW, VI, 1: 56. According to Whitlock (80), the warrior is "not yet the lion, he is the camel (= 'thou shalt' is more agreeable than 'I will')." Lampert (51-53), however, seems to ignore the apparent contradiction between his claim that the speech "On War and Warriors" describes the lion-spirit and Zarathustra's assertion that his warriors prefer "thou shalt" to "I will."

120. In suggesting that, with the transition from "On War and Warriors" to "On the New Idol," Zarathustra redirects his attention from merely potential lions to individuals who have completed the second metamorphosis of the spirit, I differ with Dannhauser (38-39), Pangle (142-43), and Lampert (50-51, 321). Each of these commentators reads "On the Preachers of Death," "On War and Warriors," "On the New Idol," and "On the Flies of the Marketplace" as expressing Zarathustra's attitudes toward current institutions and culture. As regards the third and fourth of these speeches ("On the New Idol" and "On the Flies of the Marketplace") I agree with this reading. But I see little, if any, evidence that Zarathustra is addressing the contemporary military establishment (not be confused with what Pangle calls "the warrior spirit") in "On War and Warriors." Neither do I see evidence that "On the Preachers of Death" is directed against the religious establishment per se. Indeed, in this speech, in addition to attacking religious teachers like the Buddha (cf. Lampert, 51), Zarathustra seems to criticize philosophers (e.g., "'Life is only suffering,' others say . . ." has the ring of an allusion to Schopenhauer); seemingly secular and utilitarian opponents of childbirth ("'Giving birth is troublesome,' says another group; 'why go on giving birth? One bears only unfortunates!'"); and contemporary proponents of the work ethic ("And you too, for whom life is furious work and unrest . . . your industry is escape and the will to forget yourselves"). As I have argued, "On the Preachers of Death" and "On War and Warriors" are best interpreted in light of Zarathustra's encounter with the youth he meets in "On the Tree on the Mountainside."

121. TSZ, 161; KGW, VI, 1: 58.

122. TSZ, 162-63; KGW, VI, 1: 59.

123. See *Symposium*, in *The Collected Dialogues of Plato*, ed. Edith Hamilton and Huntington Cairns (Princeton, N.J.: Princeton University Press, 1961), 564, 216a.

124. TSZ, 163; KGW, VI, 1: 59.

125. TSZ, 189; KGW, VI, 1: 97.

126. TSZ, 164; KGW, VI, 1: 62.

127. TSZ, 163; KGW, VI, 1: 61. For Zarathustra's reference to "good tidings" (*gute Botschaft*), see TSZ, 189; KGW, VI, 1: 96. For a helpful, detailed discussion of "On the Flies of the Marketplace," see Pangle, 146–48.

128. TSZ, 166; KGW, VI, 1: 65. Here, I have altered Kaufmann's translation, translating *Wald* as "woods" rather than as "forest."

129. TSZ, 166; KGW, VI, 1: 65.

130. TSZ, 167–68; KGW, VI, 1: 65–66.

131. Zarathustra also uses the figure of mud to describe the "new idol." See TSZ, 162; KGW, VI, 1: 59.

132. See TSZ, 169, 173–74; KGW, VI, 1: 67–68, 74. My interpretation of "On the Friend" agrees substantially with Lampert's interpretation (Lampert, 57–58).

133. See TSZ, 167–68; KGW, VI, 1: 67.   134. TSZ, 161; KGW, VI, 1: 57.

135. Ibid.   136. TSZ, 172; KGW, VI, 1: 72.

137. TSZ, 161; KGW, VI, 1: 57.

138. TSZ, 171–72; KGW, VI, 1: 71–72. I agree with Lampert that Zarathustra envisions the founding of a new *people*. Whitlock speaks of new *peoples*, but I see no textual basis for this, at least in "On the Thousand and One Goals." I also agree with Lampert in interpreting this speech as an expression of Zarathustra-Nietzsche's political philosophy. I thus reject Whitlock's view that Nietzsche's thought in *Zarathustra* is apolitical. See Lampert, 63–64; Whitlock, 83, 91.

139. TSZ, 132; KGW, VI, 1: 17.

140. See my discussion in Chapter 2 of Zarathustra's thoughts in the immediate aftermath of the death of the tightrope walker.

141. In "On the Thousand and One Goals," Zarathustra's use of *fehlt* (translated as "lacking") to characterize the nihilistic experience of not having a goal prefigures Nietzsche's discussion of this sort of experience in the last section of *Genealogy*.

142. BGE, 131; KGW, VI, 2: 144. Here, I have altered Kaufmann's translation to render *grossen Politik* as "great politics." Kaufmann's translation has "large-scale politics." Lampert also notes the connection between "On the Thousand and One Goals" and Nietzsche's "great politics" (see Lampert, 63–64 and 323n107).

143. For what seems to be a similar view, see Bonnie Honig, *Political Theory and the Politics of Displacement* (Ithaca, N.Y.: Cornell University Press, 1993), 74.

144. For Nietzsche's explicit espousal of a patriotic sensibility, see the "Preface to Richard Wagner," which opens *The Birth of Tragedy*.

145. In *Beyond Good and Evil*, Nietzsche overtly conceptualizes "peoples" or "nations" as fabrications (BGE, 188; KGW, VI, 2: 202).

146. TSZ, 174; KGW, VI, 1: 74–75.

147. TSZ, 173; KGW, VI, 1: 74.

148. TSZ, 174–75; KGW, VI, 1: 76. Obviously, I reject Lampert's view that this speech describes the spirit of the child. (Lampert claims, in fact, that speeches 16–21 of

Part 1 describe the child-spirit. As will become clear, I reject this view too. The only one of these speeches that can be plausibly construed as describing the child-spirit is "On the Gift-Giving Virtue.") On this point, my view accords more closely with Whitlock's account (see Lampert, 51, 64; Whitlock, 93).

149. TSZ, 174; KGW, VI, 1: 76.

150. TSZ, 177; KGW, VI, 1: 79.

151. On my reading, Zarathustra's tears are tears prompted by the painful experience of separation. In this respect, they seem to me to resemble the tears Zarathustra sheds at the end of "The Stillest Hour." Lampert's claim (66) that Zarathustra's tears certify his addressee's fitness for solitude remains a puzzle to me; I do not see, I confess, how tears can be taken to certify such fitness, or to certify anything at all for that matter.

152. Cf. Charles Rosen, *Sonata Forms* (New York: W. W. Norton, 1988), 304, 324.

153. Lampert's phrase "provisional maxims" could appropriately be applied here. As far as I can tell, Lampert does not say which of Zarathustra's speeches, other than "On Free Death," should be taken as identifying such maxims. My intuition is that he would include under this rubric more of Zarathustra's speeches than I have. This is in part because he does not read "On the Way of the Creator" as having the special significance I attribute to it (see Lampert, 73).

154. Both Lampert (66–73) and Whitlock (94–99) offer useful discussions of these speeches.

155. TSZ, 190; KGW, VI, 1: 97.

156. TSZ, 190; KGW, VI, 1: 97–98.

Chapter 4: Cartesian Subjects, Promethean Heroes, and the Sublime

1. See TSZ, 195; KGW, VI, 1: 101. Following Hollingdale, I have made a small change in Kaufmann's translation, rendering *erschrak* not as "startled," but as "frightened."

2. In this respect, the spirit of gravity resembles the great dragon of "On the Three Metamorphoses" (see my discussion in Chapter 2). When, in Part 3, Zarathustra relates the spirit of gravity to the view that one "good and evil" is binding on *all*, he suggests, again, that the spirit of gravity acknowledges none but Christian-Platonic values and morality (see TSZ, 306; KGW, VI, 1: 239). I follow Lampert, 87, in interpreting the image of the devil appearing in "On the Child with the Mirror" as an image of Zarathustra's spirit of gravity. Zarathustra explicitly identifies the devil with the spirit of gravity in "The Dancing Song."

3. Lampert's suggestion that Zarathustra's disciples remain innocently loyal to him, and that their denial seems to them an affirmation, leaves unexplained Zarathustra's suggestion that they have become ashamed of him. What evidence is there for believing that Zarathustra is wrong? And if he is wrong, what are we to make of his error? See Lampert, 85–88.

4. TSZ, 195; KGW, VI, 1: 102. Translation slightly altered.

5. TSZ, 197; KGW, VI, 1: 103.

6. My sense of the significance of Zarathustra's blessed isles largely agrees with Lampert's (83). Daniel Conway suggests that Zarathustra sees the blessed isles as a "utopian community," but for this claim I see no basis. Moreover, Conway's suspicion that the allusion to the blessed isles "further suggests that Zarathustra has engineered an afterworldly redemption of his pedagogical struggles," seems to overlook the fact that the blessed isles of early Greek myth, unlike the Christian afterworld of which Zarathustra is the enemy, may be found *at the ends of the earth*. (For an excellent overview of the figure of the blessed isles in early Greek myth, see Timothy Gantz, *Early Greek Myth* [Baltimore: Johns Hopkins University Press, 1993], 132–35.) For Conway's discussion of the figure of the blessed isles, see his "Nietzsche Contra Nietzsche: The Deconstruction of *Zarathustra*," in *Nietzsche as Postmodernist*, ed. Clayton Koelb (Albany: SUNY Press, 1990), 96–97.

7. For Zarathustra's reference to a new speech, see TSZ, 196; KGW, VI, 1: 102.

8. TSZ, 198; KGW, VI, 1: 105–6. I have slightly altered Kaufmann's translation, rendering *erst* as "at first" rather than as "only."

9. For a clear and succinct account of Descartes's reduction of reality and experience, see Harries, "The Philosopher at Sea," 36–40; also Charles Taylor, *The Sources of the Self: The Making of Modern Identity* (Cambridge: Harvard University Press, 1989), 145–46. In *The Birth of Tragedy*, Nietzsche ties a similar reduction of experience to the figure of Socrates.

10. For a reading of "Upon the Blessed Isles" that stresses like mine the epistemological and especially Kantian motifs in the first half of the speech, see Whitlock, 126–30.

11. I mark the shift in Zarathustra's speech as beginning with his "But let me reveal my heart to you entirely, my friends . . ." (TSZ, 198; KGW, VI, 1: 106).

12. TSZ, 200; KGW, VI, 1: 109.

13. TSZ, 200–201; KGW, VI, 1: 109–10. On the themes of pity and shame, See also the last five aphorisms of Book 3 of *The Gay Science*.

14. TSZ, 202; KGW, VI, 1: 112.

15. TSZ, 202; KGW, VI, 1: 111. For Nietzsche's explicitly stated conception of the connection between pity and Schopenhauer's doctrine that life ought to be renounced, see AC, 572–73; KGW, VI, 3: 170–72.

16. Cf. Pangle, 152–53.

17. All the material in this paragraph quoted from "On Priests" derives from TSZ, 202–5; KGW, VI, 1: 113–15.

18. TSZ, 152; KGW, VI, 1: 44.   19. TSZ, 203; KGW, VI, 1: 113.

20. TSZ, 206; KGW, VI, 1: 117.   21. Ibid.

22. Here, one may wonder whether the anger of Zarathustra's disciples, when they hear from Zarathustra that he does not advocate a "reward" theory of virtue, is psychologically compatible with their being ashamed of him for (in their view) adhering to a (Christian-Platonic) conception of virtue they thought he repudiated. The answer, I think, is yes. Even though his disciples have become ashamed of him, they continue to have expectations based on an interpretation of his teaching that is the source of their

shame—for example, the expectation that they will be rewarded for their efforts to enact what they perceive to be Zarathustra's teaching of virtue. In fact, one can even imagine a disciple's desire for a reward being intensified by his feeling that Zarathustra had let him down: he would want a reward, not only as payment for his virtuous behavior, but as recompense for his disappointment in Zarathustra.

23. For a similar, recent critique of utilitarianism that emphasizes the moral value of maintaining one's integrity, see Bernard Williams's remarks in J. J. C. Smart and Bernard Williams, *Utilitarianism: For and Against* (Cambridge: Cambridge University Press, 1973), 108–18.

24. I borrow this formulation from Lampert, 94.

25. TSZ, 208–11; KGW, VI, 1: 120–23. "Conversation with the Kings," the third section of Part 4, emphasizes the egalitarian character of the rabble's public culture.

26. Here, my reading is indebted to Whitlock, 137–38.

27. TSZ, 209–10; KGW, VI, 1: 121–22.

28. TSZ, 210; KGW, VI, 1: 122.

29. TSZ, 152; KGW, VI, 1: 44. In "On Reading and Writing," Nietzsche speaks of the "rabble" or the "mob" using the term *Pöbel*. In "On the Rabble," he uses the term *Gesindel*. In Part 4, in "Conversation with the Kings," he uses both these terms.

30. TSZ, 210–11; KGW, VI, 1: 122–23.

31. All the quoted material in this paragraph is from TSZ, 211–13; KGW, VI, 1: 124–26.

32. For a similar formulation, see Harries, 37.

33. All the quoted material in this paragraph derives from TSZ, 214–17; KGW, VI, 1: 128–31.

34. TSZ, 217–18; KGW, VI, 1: 132.

35. In "The Night Song," Kaufmann translates *Brunnen*, and also the more poetic *Born*, as "fountain." In "On the Rabble" and "On the Famous Wise Men," he translates *Brunnen* as "well," and uses "fountain" to translate both *Born* and *Quell*.

36. EH, 306; KGW, VI, 3: 343; emphasis mine.

37. TSZ, 218–19; KGW, VI, 1: 133–34.

38. In his essay "Experience," Ralph Waldo Emerson bemoans his inability to be touched and moved by objects and emotions, grief included. Prefiguring the central theme of Zarathustra's night song, he writes of "the Indian who was laid under a curse that the wind should not blow on him, nor water flow to him nor fire burn him, is a type of us all." Emerson, "Experience," in *Selections from Ralph Waldo Emerson*, ed. Stephen E. Whicher (Boston: Houghton Mifflin, 1960), 256–57.

39. All the quoted material in this paragraph derives from Kant, *Critique of Pure Reason*, 92–93.

40. Heidegger, perhaps more than any other commentator, has stressed the centrality of the concept of sensibility in Kant's thought. See, especially, Martin Heidegger, *Kant and the Problem of Metaphysics*, trans. James S. Churchill (Bloomington: Indiana University Press, 1962).

41. My reference to Fichte is meant as a useful analogy. I do not wish to suggest,

however, that Zarathustra has become a *strict* Fichtean, or that he has a Fichtean notion of the absolute self. (On Fichte's notion of the absolute self, see John Lachs, "Is There an Absolute Self?" *Philosophical Forum* 19 [Winter–Spring 1988]: 169–81). For a useful, general discussion of Fichte's unwillingness to preserve the Kantian distinction between spontaneity and receptivity, see Robert Pippin, *Hegel's Idealism* (Cambridge: Cambridge University Press, 1989), 51–59.

42. EH, 308; KGW, VI, 3: 346.

43. In his literary use of Plotinus's images of the emanation of the One, Nietzsche is heir to a tendency well established in European romanticism. For the Romantics' use of Plotinus's images, see Abrams, *Natural Supernaturalism*, 147, and *The Mirror and the Lamp* (London: Oxford University Press, 1953), 58–59. In *The Mirror and the Lamp*, Abrams connects the Romantics' use of Plotinian metaphors of the mind to Kant's Copernican revolution in epistemology. My reading of "The Night Song," especially my suggestion that Zarathustra personifies in this section a pure spontaneity, points to a similar connection in Nietzsche.

44. BT, 73–74; KGW, III, 1: 66–68.

45. Here, I follow Kathleen Higgins's excellent discussion of "The Night Song" in "The Night Song's Answer," *International Studies in Philosophy* 18 (Summer 1985): 40–42. As will be evident to anyone who consults Higgins's essay, my use of *The Birth of Tragedy* to interpret "The Night Song" builds on her seminal insights. I should also like to mention, in this context, Daniel Conway's insightful reading of "The Night Song" in his "Nietzsche Contra Nietzsche," 97–100. My chief difference with Conway is, perhaps, insignificant: where he sees a tension between an Apollonian text and a Dionysian subtext, I see a tension between two Dionysian texts, each of which represents a distinct modality of Dionysian experience. I should add, finally, that I am in complete sympathy with Conway's critique of Pangle's reading of "The Night Song" (see Conway's note 23).

46. "De-individuation," here, refers to the destruction or "going-under" of a distinct individual self, that is, of a distinct functional ordering of first-order passions that has been effected by the will to power. It need not involve the destruction of the body within which these passions exist. The existence of numerically distinct bodies is a necessary though not sufficient condition for the creation of numerically distinct selves. On this point, I follow Nehamas's account of the self-body relationship in Nietzsche's thought. See Nehamas, *Nietzsche*, 180–81.

47. Nietzsche's reference to the "coming Dionysus" reflects the tendency in Greek antiquity to see Dionysus as "the god who comes, the god of epiphany, whose appearance is far more urgent, far more compelling than that of any other god." See Walter F. Otto, *Dionysus: Myth and Cult*, trans. Robert B. Palmer (Bloomington: Indiana University Press, 1965), 79 ff. For a discussion of Dionysus as Zagreus, see ibid., 191–92.

48. It may seem odd that Nietzsche associates Zagreus, and therefore dismemberment, with the figure of the hero, while dissociating Zagreus from chaos. Wouldn't one expect Dionysus-Zagreus, to the extent that he was born through dismemberment, to be intimately attuned to "chaos"? Perhaps. My alternative suggestion, however, is that Nietz-

sche interprets dismemberment, or, in German, *Zerstückelung*, as connoting partition and division. Zarathustra-Zagreus is a figure of division, or self-division, precisely to the extent that he is self-estranged. More exactly, he is estranged from his ability to experience Dionysian chaos.

49. TSZ, 218; KGW, VI, 1: 133.

50. Daniel Conway also argues that "The Night Song" points to Zarathustra's responsibility for his own pedagogical difficulties. See Conway, "Nietzsche Contra Nietzsche," 99–100. See TSZ, 218; KGW, VI, 1: 133, for Zarathustra's plotting of revenge.

51. TSZ, 220; KGW, VI, 1: 135–36.   52. Ibid.

53. Ibid.   54. TSZ, 153; KGW, VI, 1: 45.

55. For the quoted material in this paragraph, see TSZ, 219–22; KGW, VI, 1: 135–37.

56. Lampert's reading of "The Dancing Song" (*Nietzsche's Teaching*, 104–9) I find questionable, for it rests on the assumption that Zarathustra, when he describes life as "unfathomable," speaks from the perspective of his leonine wild wisdom, and not from the perspective of someone who has begun to look beyond his wisdom's vision of life (though Higgins makes a similar assumption [see Higgins, *Nietzsche's Zarathustra*, 142–44], I am generally sympathetic to her discussion of "The Dancing Song," which emphasizes Zarathustra's confusion over the relationship between life and wisdom). Zarathustra's wild wisdom, with which he clearly identifies at the end of "On the Famous Wise Men," generates the sunlit perspective of the ironically titled section that follows "On the Famous Wise Men," "The Night Song." In "The Dancing Song," Zarathustra speaks from a different perspective, namely, that of his "darkness" and "night." His description of life as "unfathomable" reflects the fact that, from this perspective, which is bereft of wisdom, he can find no basis for resisting the spirit of gravity.

Finally, I believe that Alan White (*Within Nietzsche's Labyrinth* [New York: Routledge, 1990], 83) is right to suggest that Zarathustra's questions at the end of "The Dancing Song" express his doubt regarding the viability of the project of overcoming man. White moves too quickly (and with too little argument), however, when he judges that Zarathustra's questions involve a definitive "casting aside" of this project. As far as I can see, there is no textual basis for this judgment. Moreover, I do not see how White's judgment can be easily reconciled with Zarathustra's later claim—in "On the Higher Man"—that he still has the overman "at heart" and that the overman is his "first and only concern" (TSZ, 399; KGW, VI, 1: 353). If we take Zarathustra at his word here, then the project of overcoming man has remained a central concern for him through all of Part 3 and most of Part 4.

57. TSZ, 222–23; KGW, VI, 1: 138–39. For a helpful discussion of Nietzsche's autobiographical allusions in this section, see Whitlock, 148–50.

58. TSZ, 225; KGW, VI, 1: 141.   59. TSZ, 225; KGW, VI, 1: 142.

60. TSZ, 198; KGW, VI, 1: 105–6.   61. TSZ, 226; KGW, VI, 1: 143.

62. TSZ, 213–14; KGW, VI, 1: 126–27.

63. TSZ, 226–27; KGW, VI, 1: 143–44; emphases in original. I have altered Kaufmann's translation slightly, by substituting "go-under" and "going-under" for "perish"

and "perishing." I have also translated *Widerspruch* as "contradiction" rather than as "opposition."

64. See Staten, 8–15.

65. In "On the Tarantulas," life's figurative revenge (the tarantula's bite) gives rise to the spirit of revenge in Zarathustra (see TSZ, 214; KGW, VI, 1: 127). As we have seen, and as we might expect, Zarathustra's suffering in "The Night Song" likewise inspires Zarathustra with the spirit of revenge.

66. Here, it should be noted that *Hingebung*, which Kaufmann translates as "yielding," also connotes sacrifice.

67. For my interpretation of the will to power as a second-order passion, see Chapter 3.

68. TSZ, 228; KGW, VI, 1: 145.

69. The proposition that Zarathustra explicitly attributes to the wisest—"that struggle and equality are present even in beauty; and also war for power and more power"—I read as a pithy summary of the account of life he has proposed just prior to his speech about the ruins of the ancient temple.

70. To the extent that the will to truth is blind to the reality of uncreated passions, it consigns those passions to "nothingness." Thus, the will to truth remains a "will to nothingness" (cf. my discussion of the will to truth in Chapter 2). To the extent that the will to truth is blind, moreover, it is also a will to error (cf. BGE, 35; KGW, VI, 2: 37–38). My argument that, in Part 2, the error concerns the *body* (the body's capacity to go-under to a chaos of uncreated passions) appears to find some support in Nietzsche's 1881 sketch of the four parts of *Zarathustra*. Of Part 2, Nietzsche writes: "Flüchtig-skeptisch-mephistophelisch. '*Von der Einverleibung der Erfahrungen.*' Erkenntnis = Irrthum, der organisch wird und organisirt" (Fleeting-skeptical-mephistophelian. 'About the corporealizing of experience.' Knowledge = error, which becomes organic and organized) (see KGW, V, 2: 418). It should be noted, of course, that the meaning of these remarks is not altogether clear, and that they can be taken to support interpretations of Part 2 other than my own. See, for example, Stanley Rosen's treatment of the 1881 sketch in Rosen, *The Mask of Enlightenment*, 18.

71. Zarathustra states this point explicitly in Part 3: "He shall be known and tested whether he is of my kind and kin, whether he is the master of a long will, taciturn even when he speaks, *and yielding so that in giving he receives*—so that he may one day become *my companion and a fellow creator* and fellow celebrant of Zarathustra" (TSZ, 273; KGW, VI, 1: 200; emphases mine).

72. See Immanuel Kant, *Critique of Judgment*, trans. Werner S. Pluhar (Indianapolis: Hackett, 1987), 120–23; Friedrich von Schiller, "On the Sublime," in *Naive and Sentimental Poetry, and On the Sublime*, trans. Julius A. Elias (New York: Frederick Ungar, 1966), 198–204. Schopenhauer is less useful than Kant and Schiller in approaching Nietzsche-Zarathustra's remarks regarding the sublime and the beautiful, for unlike Kant and Schiller he does not draw a sharp distinction between these two modes of aesthetic experience. Nietzsche, however, notwithstanding his revised conception of the sublime

and his apparent repudiation of Kant's conception of the beautiful (e.g., in Zarathustra's speech, "On Immaculate Perception"), develops the distinction in a way that still echoes Kant's and Schiller's thinking. For a brief but clear discussion of Schopenhauer's departure from Kant on this issue, see Kathleen M. Higgins, "Arthur Schopenhauer," in *Routledge History of Philosophy*, vol. 6, *The Age of German Idealism*, ed. Robert Solomon and Kathleen M. Higgins (New York: Routledge, 1993), 350.

73. Cf. Nietzsche's reference to Kant's practical philosophy in "On How the 'True World' Finally Became a Fable" (TI, 485; KGW, VI, 3: 74).

74. This, roughly, is the gloss Pangle (168–70) gives.

75. See Kant, *Critique of Judgment*, 120–21, for the passages quoted in this paragraph. For the German original, see *Kants Werke* (Berlin: de Gruyter, 1968), 5: 261–62.

76. For a valuable critical discussion of Kant's compensatory conception of the dynamical sublime, see Thomas Weiskel, *The Romantic Sublime: Studies in the Structure and Psychology of Transcendence* (Baltimore: Johns Hopkins University Press, 1976), 84–85. For a persuasive argument that Kant distinguishes two varieties of the dynamical sublime, only one of which I sketch, see Paul Crowther, *The Kantian Sublime* (Oxford: Clarendon Press, 1989), 116–17.

77. TSZ, 210; KGW, VI, 1: 121. For Zarathustra, the experiences of power and powerlessness are successive. In Kant's discussion of the dynamical sublime, they seem to be simultaneous. Kant's discussion of the mathematical sublime is ambiguous on this point. For a further discussion of the temporality of the Kantian sublime, see Crowther, 123–25.

78. For the quotations from "On the Child with the Mirror," see TSZ, 196–97; KGW, VI, 1: 103. For the quotations in this paragraph from "On Those Who Are Sublime," see TSZ, 228–31; KGW, VI, 1: 146–48. I have altered Kaufmann's translation of *wildes*, rendering it as "wild" rather than as "savage."

79. Zarathustra rejects Cartesian dualism. He seems to be claiming, however, that self-estrangement in the domain of bodies and appearances can produce appearances that give the (false) impression of being appearances *of* supersensible subjects.

80. For the quoted material in this paragraph, see TSZ, 228–31; KGW, VI, 1: 146–48.

81. Nietzsche's portrait of the sublime hero as someone who stands aloof from the world of appearances may owe something to Wagner's depiction of Beethoven's sublime genius in Wagner's *Beethoven* (a book to which Nietzsche alludes in *The Birth of Tragedy*'s "Preface to Richard Wagner"); see Wagner, 20, 54, 56, 102–3. I thank John Sallis for pointing out the relevance of Wagner's book to my interpretation of "On Those Who Are Sublime."

82. For a more detailed treatment of Nietzsche's critique and subversion of Kant's concept of the sublime, see Bianca Theisen, "Rhythms of Oblivion," in *Nietzsche and the Feminine*, ed. Peter J. Bugard (Charlottesville: University of Virginia Press, 1994), 98–101.

83. For an insightful interpretation of the sublime as involving a psychology of self-estrangement, see Weiskel, 34–48. The critique of the modern, Cartesian concept of the knowing subject that is evident in "On Those Who Are Sublime" (and, more generally, in the first thirteen sections of Part 2), in highlighting the theme of self-estrangement,

suggests that, in *Zarathustra* at least, Nietzsche's attempt to "overcome epistemology" involves what Charles Taylor describes as an attempt to "show us more of what we really are like." In *Zarathustra*, in other words, Nietzsche's treatment of epistemology has greater affinity with the line of thinking that Taylor admires in Heidegger and Merleau-Ponty than with the "neo-Nietzscheanism" he criticizes in Foucault and Derrida. See Charles Taylor, "Overcoming Epistemology," in *After Philosophy: End or Transformation?* ed. Kenneth Baynes, James Bohman, and Thomas McCarthy (Cambridge: MIT Press, 1987), 464–88.

84. TSZ, 231; KGW, VI, 1: 148.

85. KGW, VII, 1: 453. Here, I have slightly altered the translation David Farrell Krell gives in his *Postponements: Women, Sensuality, and Death in Nietzsche* (Bloomington: Indiana University Press, 1986), 113.

86. See Otto, 111–14, 191–92.

87. TSZ, 229; KGW, VI, 1: 146.

88. Ibid.

89. Nietzsche may well have drawn on the literature of European romanticism for his conception of the hero. In pursuing this idea, it would be useful to note the affinities between Nietzsche's portrait of the sublime hero and the figure of Manfred in Byron's *Manfred* (cf. the first epigraph to this chapter). Manfred, like Nietzsche's hero, is a withdrawn figure who, as Michael Cooke puts it, "rises above the things he rejects." Yet, eventually, Byron's protagonist is befallen by a serenity that prefigures Nietzsche's description of the beautiful overhero the sublime hero becomes when he discards his heroic will. Nietzsche's great admiration for Byron's *Manfred* is evident from his remarks on the poem in *Ecce Homo* (EH, 245–46; KGW, VI, 3: 284). For Cooke's discussion of *Manfred*, which provides the basis for my brief remarks, see *The Blind Man Traces the Circle* (Princeton, N.J.: Princeton University Press, 1969), 64–74. For a valuable discussion of the adolescent Nietzsche's passion for Byron, and especially for *Manfred*, see Graham Parkes, *Composing the Soul* (Chicago: University of Chicago Press, 1994), 28–33.

90. For a view that, like my own, relates the figure of Ariadne to the human body, and to the human body's ability to experience chaos, see Harries, "The Philosopher at Sea," 36–40. See also Bernard Pautrat, *Versions du Soleil: Figures et système de Nietzsche* (Paris: Seuil, 1971), 325–26.

91. EH, 308; KGW, VI, 3: 346.

92. In *Beyond Good and Evil*, Nietzsche says the following words of Dionysus: "Thus he once said: 'Under certain circumstances I love what is human'—and with this he alluded to Ariadne who was present—'man is to my mind an agreeable, courageous, inventive animal that has no equal on earth; it finds its way in any labyrinth. I am well disposed towards him.'" (BGE, 236; KGW, VI, 2: 249). My reading of this passage involves the assumption that, for Nietzsche, the labyrinth is a figure for Dionysian chaos. For a similar interpretation of the figure of the labyrinth, together with textual evidence to support it, see Philip Grundlehner, *The Poetry of Friedrich Nietzsche* (New York: Oxford University Press, 1986), 229, 239. See also, on this point, Harries, "The Philosopher at

Sea," 39–40. I should add, finally, that the claim that Ariadne symbolizes the connection of human beings to Dionysus echoes Grundlehner's remark (229) that "Ariadne as the personification of womanhood becomes Nietzsche's human representative of Dionysus."

93. For a similar view, see Adrian Del Caro, "Symbolizing Philosophy: Ariadne and the Labyrinth," *Nietzsche-Studien* 17 (1988), 139–40. I should like to add here that the distinction between Dionysus-Zagreus and Dionysus the coming god offers a useful perspective on Nietzsche's poem "Ariadne's Lament." Described in the poem as a "hunter," the Dionysus who abandons Ariadne (lines 90–95) seems to be Dionysus-Zagreus. On the other hand, the Dionysus whose epiphany introduces the poem's epilogue ("A bolt of lightning. Dionysus becomes visible in emerald beauty"), and who tells Ariadne, "I am your labyrinth," can plausibly be identified as the chaos-bearing coming god (cf. Grundlehner, 214–20, 227). Consistent with my readings of "On Those Who Are Sublime" and Nietzsche's corresponding notebook entry, the coming god appears in Nietzsche's poem only *after* Ariadne has been abandoned by the hunter-god, Zagreus.

94. KGW, VII, 1: 127. The translation is from Krell, 15.

Chapter 5: Eternal Recurrence, Acts I and II

1. EH, 295; KGW, VI, 3: 333.

2. The idea that literary themes can function as "grounds" or sufficient reasons is at least as old as Alexander Baumgarten's *Reflections on Poetry* (1735). According to Baumgarten, "By *theme* (*Thema*) we mean that whose representation contains the sufficient reason of other representations supplied in the discourse, but which does not have its own sufficient reason in them." Quoted in Werner Sollors, ed. *The Return of Thematic Criticism* (Cambridge: Harvard University Press, 1993), 5.

3. Kaufmann translates *Fürsprecher* as "advocate." See TSZ, 328, KGW, VI, 1. 267.

4. Cleanth Brooks, *The Well Wrought Urn* (New York: Harcourt Brace Jovanovich, 1975), 151–66.

5. Harold Alderman (84) has also suggested that Zarathustra and the idea of recurrence "develop together" in *Zarathustra*. For an earlier sketch of the argument I develop here, see my "Comments on Bernd Magnus's 'A Bridge to Far: Asceticism and Eternal Recurrence,'" in *Southern Journal of Philosophy* 37, supplement (1999), 117.

6. For an excellent overview of the key issues raised by the "cosmological doctrine or practical doctrine?" approach to Nietzsche's writings on recurrence, see Clark, *Nietzsche on Truth and Philosophy*, 245–70. Clark also summarizes and discusses with insight some of the most engaging recent secondary literature on the topic of eternal recurrence.

7. For a very useful and perhaps exhaustive overview of the variety of Nietzsche's formulations of the idea of eternal recurrence, see Schacht, 253–66. For an approach to eternal recurrence with affinities to my own, and which emphasizes that Nietzsche's different characters, in different contexts, develop different formulations of eternal recurrence, see James Winchester, "Of Scholarly Readings of Nietzsche: Clark and Magnus on Nietzsche's Eternal Return," *New Nietzsche Studies* 3, nos. 3–4 (Summer–Fall 1999): 77–97.

8. *Zarathustra*, including Part 4, contains eighty speeches (twenty-two in Part 1; twenty-two in Part 2; sixteen in Part 3; and twenty in Part 4). "The Soothsayer" is the nineteenth speech of Part 2 and, therefore, the forty-first speech of the entire book. Robert Pippin counts differently, identifying "The Stillest Hour," the last speech of the second of the four parts, as the midpoint of *Zarathustra*. See Pippin, "Irony and Affirmation," 51.

9. A persistent theme in twentieth-century Nietzsche scholarship is the suggestion that there is a tension, or a contradiction, between the doctrine of the eternal recurrence and the future-oriented ideas of an overman and a creative will to power. I believe that this suggestion is correct, at least to the extent that it captures the conflict between (1) Zarathustra's modernist (personal and poetic) intentions to overcome man through the creation of new values and (2) his *initial* formation of the thought of recurrence, which denies that these intentions can be realized. However, I also believe that Zarathustra transforms his thought of recurrence, and that his second transformation of his thought (resulting in the child's thought of recurrence, which involves the belief that the passions and the possibility of going-under to passional chaos have been returned to human existence) *reconciles it* with his modernist aspirations. For several scholarly discussions of the issues in question here, extending from the 1930s to the 1990s, see Alfred Bäumler, *Nietzsche: Der Philosoph und der Politiker* (Leipzig: P. Reclam, 1931), 79 ff; Löwith, *Nietzsches Philosophie der ewigen Wiederkehr des Gleichen*, esp. chap. 4; Barker Fairley, "Nietzsche and the Poetic Impulse," *Bulletin of the John Rylands Library* 19 (July 1935): 356–57; Lukács, 376, 394; Megill, 114–15; Erich Heller, "Nietzsche's Terror," *Salmagundi* 68–69 (Fall 1985–Winter 1986): 88; Strauss, 185; and S. Rosen, *The Mask of Enlightenment*, 201.

10. TSZ, 231–38; KGW, VI, 1: 149–58. Near the end of "On Immaculate Perception," Zarathustra speaks of a solar love of the earth that "would suck at the sea [*Am Meere will sie saugen*] and drink its depth into her heights." In effect, he adduces the image of a sun fraught with sexual fever ("Do you not feel the thirst and the hot breath of her love?"), a sun that passionately desires the earth's seas, to displace "The Night Song's" image of a cold sun that cannot love: "She would suck at the sea and drink its depths into her heights; and the sea's desire rises towards her with a thousand breasts. It wants to be kissed and sucked by the thirst of the sun." By reimagining the night song's sun, Zarathustra figures the creator as having discarded his will to truth and reclaimed his body's capacity to be moved by "earthly" passion (figured here as the sea's desire). Thus, he affirms that the creative longing of the creative self involves a power of receptivity to the passions, a power that, I have argued, Nietzsche associates with Ariadne. My interpretation of the sun imagery of "On Immaculate Perception" finds support in a remark Zarathustra utters in "On the Great Longing," the fair copy of which Nietzsche gave the title "Ariadne" (see KSA, 14, 324). That remark, which addresses Zarathustra's Ariadnean soul, explicitly echoes "On Immaculate Perception:" "O my soul, I taught you to persuade so well that you persuade the very ground—like the sun who persuades even the sea to its own height" (TSZ, 334; KGW, VI, 1: 274–75). For a general discussion of the sexual imagery in "On Immaculate Perception," see Higgins, *Nietzsche's Zarathustra*,

128–29. For a further discussion of Zarathustra's Ariadnean soul, see my interpretations of "On the Great Longing" and "The Other Dancing Song" in this chapter.

11. Lampert (123) also connects these speeches to Zarathustra's earlier portrait of the last men. In general, Nietzsche's portrait of the detached and passionless character of modern European culture may be usefully compared to Kierkegaard's often similar portrait in *The Present Age*.

12. As Whitlock notes (161), Zarathustra portrays the scholar ("I must go out into the open and away from all dusty rooms. But they sit cool in the cool shade [*Schatten*]: in everything they want to be mere spectators, and they beware of sitting where the sun burns the steps") in terms that recall the shadowy image of the sublime hero who withdraws from the sun and seems to exist apart from the world of bodies and appearances. In "On Immaculate Perception" (cf. Higgins, *Nietzsche's Zarathustra*, 128), Zarathustra describes the Kantian/Schopenhauerian subject of aesthetic judgment as imagining that she is a "pure" subject-perceiver whose perceptions need not be affected by bodily will and desire ("'To be happy in looking, with a will that has died and without the grasping and greed of selfishness, the whole body [*am ganzen Leibe*] cold and ashen, but with drunken moon eyes . . . ,' thus the seduced seduces himself").

13. Here, I refer to the discussion of the Goethean, Rousseauean, and Schopenhauerian images of man in *Schopenhauer as Educator*. I discuss these in greater detail below.

14. See, for example, the discussion of the cultured man's simulation of happiness, in SE, 149; KGW, III, 1: 362.

15. SE, 150; KGW, III, 1: 364–65.

16. SE, 152, 155; KGW, III, 1: 366, 370.

17. SE, 151–52; KGW, III, 1: 365–67. I have slightly altered Hollingdale's translation here, rendering *Umwälzung* as "revolution" rather than as "overturning."

18. See, for example, Schopenhauer, *The World as Will and Representation*, 1: 404, and *Zürcher Ausgabe*, 2: 499–500. Note in particular Schopenhauer's claim that with the self-suppression of the will "man's whole inner nature is fundamentally changed [*geändert*] and converted [*umgekehrt*]." I have slightly altered Payne's translation here, rendering *umgekehrt* as "converted" rather than as "reversed." Nietzsche's use of *Umkehrung* to describe Schopenhauer's position (see note 17 and the corresponding passage cited in the main text) obviously echoes Schopenhauer himself.

19. Note, especially, the following remarks: "But what was it that Zarathustra once said to you? That the poets lie too much? But Zarathustra too is a poet. Do you believe that he spoke the truth here? Why do you believe that?" (see TSZ, 239; KGW, VI, 1: 159). Strictly speaking, Zarathustra would create a paradox only if he remarked that all poets always lie. For an insightful reading of "On Poets" that treats it as a critical and self-critical demystification of metaphor, see Shapiro, *Nietzschean Narratives*, 66–67. For a further discussion of Zarathustra in connection to the liar's paradox (which discussion first prompted my own thinking about this topic), see David Luban's unpublished manuscript, "The Liar and the Circle: A Semiotic of Eternal Recurrence."

20. TSZ, 240; KGW, VI, 1: 161.

21. Lampert (127–30) makes a similar point. See also Higgins, *Nietzsche's Zarathustra*, 148.

22. TSZ, 240; KGW, VI, 1: 160. Whitlock (163–64) also reads Zarathustra's critique of other poets' "overmen" as a critique of otherworldly visions of *human* possibility.

23. See the last stanza of Goethe's *Faust*, part 2. For Goethe's use of *Übermenschen*, see *Faust*, part 1, line 490.

24. TSZ, 240; KGW, VI, 1: 161. Avital Ronell has reminded us recently that Nietzsche preferred the *Conversations with Eckermann* to *Faust*. See Avital Ronell, "Namely, Eckermann," in *Looking After Nietzsche*, ed. Laurence A. Rickels (New York: SUNY Press, 1990), 251.

25. Here, my discussion echoes Whitlock's claim (164) that Zarathustra, as distinct from the poets he criticizes, "knows that *the future is a possible ground for the perfection of man, whereas the Beyond is not*" (emphasis in original).

26. See TSZ, 241–45; KGW, VI, 1: 163–67; and SE, 151; KGW, III, 1: 365. See also Lampert, 134, 332n79. For a discussion of Typhoeus in early Greek myth, see Gantz, 48–51. Higgins links the figure of the fire hound to the Greek myth of Hades and the Christian doctrine of hell, yet admits that these allusions do not provide "the crucial key to the meaning of [On Great Events]." This meaning, she suggests, "has something to do with political developments" (Higgins, *Nietzsche's Zarathustra*, 129–31).

27. TSZ, 243; KGW, VI, 1: 164–65.

28. TSZ, 244; KGW, VI, 1: 166. The suggestion that the heart of the earth consists of gold may be taken, I believe, as an allusion to the gift-giving virtue and to its role in resurrecting the body and the earth.

29. See, for example, Lampert, 136; Whitlock, 166; Harries, "The Philosopher at Sea," 27; Hollinrake, 80; and Richard Drake, "Shepherd and Serpent: Zarathustra's Phantasmagoria," in *Friedrich Nietzsche*, ed. Harold Bloom (New York: Chelsea, 1987), 225.

30. Zarathustra has already alluded to the differences between his and Schopenhauer's conceptions of the will in "On Self-Overcoming," where he describes Schopenhauer's will to live as "the will to existence." See TSZ, 227; KGW, VI, 1: 144–45.

31. TSZ, 245–46; KGW, VI, 1: 168–69. In "The Cry of Distress," Zarathustra calls the soothsayer "you soothsayer of the great weariness" (TSZ, 353; KGW, VI, 1: 297).

32. Zarathustra explicitly links the soothsayer's talk of weariness and his claim that "all is the same" to the Schopenhauerian doctrine of renunciation in "On Old and New Tablets": "And this is always the manner of the weak: they get lost on the way. And in the end their weariness still asks, 'Why did we ever pursue any way at all? It is all the same.' *Their* eyes appreciate the preaching, 'Nothing is worthwhile! You shall not will'" (TSZ, 318; KGW, VI, 1: 254).

33. TSZ, 198–99; KGW, VI, 1: 106–7.

34. See Immanuel Kant, *Critique of Practical Reason*, trans. Lewis White Beck (Indianapolis: Bobbs-Merrill, 1956), 114–39.

35. Ibid., 129.

36. Ibid., 118.

37. See Thomas McCarthy, "Critical Theory and Political Theology: The Postulates of Communicative Reason," in his *On Reconstruction and Deconstruction in Contemporary Critical Theory* (Cambridge: MIT Press, 1991), 204–5. I follow McCarthy's interpretation of Kant in treating Kant's argument for postulating God's existence as an attempt to show that the avoidance of moral despair requires the assumption that God exists.

38. Cf. ibid., 213.

39. For Luther's translations of the biblical passages that I cite from Ecclesiastes (one of which translations I also cite), see *Die Bibel*, "Die Bücher des alten Testaments," 654, 658. Luther, it may be noted, uses *schlect* (straight, plain, or simple), rather than *gerade*, where the King James Bible has "straight."

40. Cf. R. Y. B. Scott's account of the "philosophical nihilism" of Ecclesiastes: "The generations come and go, mankind moves across the stage from darkness to darkness in endless procession—while the stage itself goes round and round. Everywhere there is constant weary movement, but no real change. Nothing is new, nothing new happens, nothing becomes memorable (I 3–11). The reason for this is that God has decreed that the world should be what it is—from man's standpoint a warped and defective world which no effort of man can alter (I 15, vii 13)." See *The Anchor Bible*, vol. 18, *Proverbs, Ecclesiastes*, ed., with intro. and notes, R. B. Y. Scott (New York: Doubleday, 1965), 202.

41. I discuss Zarathustra's allegorical interpretation of the tightrope walker's tragedy in Chapter 2.

42. In the last stanza of *Faust*, part 2, Goethe describes the impermanent as but a parable.

43. Zarathustra explicitly relates his creative effort to the goal of creating an overman in the remarks that conclude "Upon the Blessed Isles" (TSZ, 199–200; KGW, VI, 1: 107–8).

44. TSZ, 245; KGW, VI, 1: 168.

45. Eccles. 1.2 3; *Die Bibel*, "Die Bücher des altens Testaments," 654.

46. See TSZ, 125, 136; KGW, VI, 1: 9, 20. Cf. Whitlock, 166–67.

47. TSZ, 246; KGW, VI, 1: 169.

48. Whitlock (167) may be intending to make a similar point in his discussion of the ambiguous meaning of *ueberwinden*.

49. TSZ, 331; KGW, VI, 1: 270. Richard Drake (225) has also noted the connection between these remarks and Zarathustra's dream in the wake of the soothsayer's prophecy.

50. Here, I am inspired by Drake's (ibid.) reading. I will also add that Zarathustra's *loss* of Dionysian faith, which is prompted by the soothsayer's prophecy, should not be confused with his *betrayal* of that faith. The latter, which I discuss in Chapter 4, is a function of Zarathustra's leonine self-estrangement.

51. Gilles Deleuze also links the soothsayer and the last man, though his line of analysis is somewhat different from my own (see Deleuze, *Nietzsche and Philosophy*, 50–51, 165). In a section of *Twilight of the Idols* entitled "Critique of Modernity," Nietzsche notes explicitly that modernity's annihilation of the passional preconditions of self-overcoming thwarts modernist aspirations of the sort Zarathustra exemplifies: "The whole of the West no longer possesses the instincts out of which institutions grow, out

of which a *future* grows: perhaps nothing antagonizes its 'modern spirit' so much" (TI, 543; KGW, VI, 3: 135).

52. As I interpret it, the black coffin symbolizes the passions and the possibility of experiencing passional Dionysian chaos, both of which have been repressed from human existence through the triumph of the ascetic ideal. Higgins (*Nietzsche's Zarathustra,* 149–51) makes a similar point, though she blames Zarathustra's self-estrangement, and not the historical efficacy of the ascetic ideal, for burying Dionysus. On my view, Zarathustra's estrangement from his ability to experience Dionysian chaos, though evident, say, in "The Night Song," is something he has overcome (at least temporarily) by the time he hears the soothsayer's speech (see my discussion of Zarathustra's "crisis and cure" in Chapter 4). Thus, I reject Higgins's suggestion that the black coffin symbolizes a chaos that would be available to Zarathustra to experience were he not self-estranged. On the contrary, it signifies a chaos that would be available to no one to experience, not even to persons who were not self-estranged, were the soothsayer's prophecy fulfilled.

The black coffin mocks Zarathustra, and then throws him to the ground, for figuratively it embodies a return of the repressed in the mode of a guilt-creating Dionysian conscience—a conscience that has come to punish Zarathustra for permitting himself to be possessed by the Schopenhauerian soothsayer's spirit of renunciation. This conscience returns to haunt Zarathustra in "The Stillest Hour," where it encourages him in his struggle to free himself from this spirit of renunciation.

For a very different interpretation of the significance of the black coffin, see Lampert, 138–39, where the black coffin is "only more of the same, another coffin, but one filled with mocking laughter for the one who dreams of a redemptive future." Although this reading is plausible, it can be faulted for not doing justice to the difference in significance (for Zarathustra) of the transparent glass coffins and the opaque black coffin. In my view, the former represent what is left of life after the dark, Dionysian energies figured by the latter have been expunged from life.

53. Zarathustra's recognition that he is both connected *and* opposed to the soothsayer is evident in one of his remarks near the end of "The Soothsayer": "The soothsayer . . . shall eat and drink by my side; and verily, I shall show him a sea in which he can drown" (TSZ, 248; KGW, VI, 1: 172). Dan Conway and Stanley Rosen have also noticed the connection between Zarathustra and the soothsayer (see Conway, "Nietzsche Contra Nietzsche: The Deconstruction of *Zarathustra*," 101–2; S. Rosen, "Nietzsche's Image of Chaos," 16–17). For a reading that highlights Zarathustra's *opposition* to the soothsayer, arguing along lines somewhat similar to my own, see Pippin, "Irony and Affirmation," 51–55.

54. Lampert (136) argues that though "Zarathustra acknowledges immediately the truth of the [soothsayer's] prophecy . . . [he] does not assent to the despairing teaching itself." My own view is that Zarathustra does assent to the teaching, which is precisely *why* he comes to resemble those of whom the soothsayer speaks. In other words, Zarathustra renounces, for the time being, the hope that creating an overman and new values will be possible in the future. Zarathustra eventually recovers this hope, and over-

comes his despair (which is his central preoccupation and project in Part 3), but only by formulating a *second* practical postulate. Lampert's claim (136), alluding to "On Great Events," that "Zarathustra knows that the Schopenhauerian pessimism of the Soothsayer is false, for 'the heart of the earth is made of gold,'" lets Zarathustra beg the question against the soothsayer, and so misses the severity of the challenge that the soothsayer's prophecy poses for Zarathustra.

55. Nehamas seems to believe that Nietzsche would deny that an individual's passions could be completely rooted out. Whether or not Nehamas is correct, I think that Nietzsche, in *Zarathustra*, entertains the hypothesis that this could happen and, indeed, that it has happened (or is about to happen) to everyone. More exactly, he uses the figures of the soothsayer and the last man (see my discussion in Chapter 2) to envision the worst sort of nihilism as stemming from the triumph of a secularized version of the will to nothingness. See Nehamas, *Nietzsche*, 122–23.

56. See TSZ, 259; KGW, VI, 1: 186.

57. TSZ, 247–49; KGW, VI, 1: 170–72.

58. In "On Poets," the disciple at whom Zarathustra shakes his head fails to appreciate the implication of Zarathustra's play with the "liar's paradox." Moreover, he is angered when Zarathustra suggests that his teaching, like that of other poets, might be critically challenged. This is a disciple who dogmatically adheres to Zarathustra's teaching, not so much because he has understood it, but out of loyalty to Zarathustra.

The disciples at whom Zarathustra shakes his head in "On Great Events" are impressed more by the *myth* of Zarathustra—that is, the story of Zarathustra's flight and descent into hell—than by what Zarathustra has to say. In the context of a chapter intended to criticize the view that sensationalized "great events" make a difference to the way of the world, these disciples' behavior is obviously ironic and suggests that they have not genuinely grasped the point of Zarathustra's story of his encounter with a "fire hound" (cf. Lampert 132–33).

59. Here, then, I reject Lampert's claim (126) that Zarathustra ultimately severs himself from his disciples because he is disenchanted with them.

60. TSZ, 331; KGW, VI, 1: 270. Here, I have followed Hollingdale in translating *Marterholz* as "torture-stake" rather than as "torture."

61. Nehamas and Clark make the same point. See Nehamas, *Nietzsche*, 147–48, and Clark, *Nietzsche on Truth and Philosophy*, 261.

62. Zarathustra originally links the figure of the "long twilight" to the soothsayer's prophecy shortly after he hears that prophecy (see TSZ, 246; KGW, VI, 1: 169).

63. For a similar reading, see Bernd Magnus, Stanley Stewart, and Jean-Pierre Mileur, *Nietzsche's Case: Philosophy as/and Literature* (New York: Routledge, 1993), 152.

64. Clark (*Nietzsche on Truth and Philosophy*, 275–76) rejects the "usual assumption," which she attributes to Nehamas (*Nietzsche*, 148), that the small man is related to the last man. It seems to me, however, that there is substantial textual evidence supporting the "usual assumption." First, the passages I cite in the main text (TSZ, 129; KGW, VI, 1: 13) strongly suggest that Nietzsche means for us to think of the last man as di-

minutive. Second, much of what Zarathustra says of the small man—that he is prudent, disposed to maximize happiness, and inclined to make life agreeable—clearly echoes Zarathustra's description of the last man as proceeding carefully, as purporting to have invented happiness, and as seeking agreeable dreams (cf., for instance, the speech on the last man to the discussion of "small people" and their "small virtues" in "On the Higher Man," no. 3). Third, Zarathustra seems to blame both the small man and the last man for the domestication of human existence (cf. TSZ, 282; KGW, VI, 1: 210; to TSZ, 129; KGW, VI, 1: 13), thereby suggesting that he means *not* to distinguish them. Fourth, the most straightforward reading of Zarathustra's claim that "small people . . . are the over-man's greatest danger" (see TSZ, 399; KGW, VI, 1: 345) is that it is meant to develop fur-ther his earlier suggestion that the last man "represents the greatest danger for all of man's future" (TSZ, 325; KGW, VI, 1: 263). Finally, I believe that Clark is correct to identify the small man as one of those cruel "accusers of life" who, Zarathustra tells us, take delight in "tragedies, bullfights and crucifixions." But this identification does not suffice to distinguish the small man from the last man, the latter of whom Zarathustra sees as a species of the "good and the just." According to Zarathustra, the good and the just "*crucify* him who invents his own virtue" (emphasis mine). For the textual basis for this last point, see TSZ, 324–25, 330; KGW, VI, 1: 262–63, 269.

65. According to Richard Drake (225), "since the word for 'torture-stake' in German (*Marterholz*) suggests the crucifixion, Zarathustra's paranoia transforms him into a Christ who dies from man's powerlessness."

66. See WP, no. 55, 35–36; KGW, VIII, 1: 217. Clark (*Nietzsche on Truth and Philos-ophy*, 270–71) conflates the notion of recurrence expressed here with the distinct notion evident elsewhere in Nietzsche's writing that cosmic cycles of world history eternally re-cur. If we keep these notions separate, then we can begin to see that Zarathustra's worry about the recurrence of the small man admits of at least two interpretations. The first, which I give, argues that the recurrence causing Zarathustra anxiety is a recurrence he equates with the eternal perpetuation of a meaningless existence (viz., the meaningless existence of the small man): this interpretation sees a connection between the recurrence of the small man and WP, no. 55. The second interpretation, which Clark gives, claims that Zarathustra's anxiety about the recurrence of the small man should be understood with reference to some version—for her, an "unrealistic" version—of the cyclical notion of recurrence (see Clark, *Nietzsche on Truth and Philosophy*, 268–72). For a brief reading of WP, no. 55, that is careful *not* to confuse the notions of recurrence in question here, see Nehamas, *Nietzsche*, 144–45.

67. See Stanley Cavell, *The Claim of Reason: Wittgenstein, Skepticism, Tragedy, and Morality* (Oxford: Oxford University Press, 1979), 472.

68. Here it strikes me that my conception of the thought of recurrence—as an evolv-ing drama that is, in part, a drama of liberation through self-assertion—has some affinity to Magnus, Stewart, and Mileur's (155) conception of recurrence "as concept and as en-abling rhetoric, as self-descriptive and therapeutic."

69. In "The Convalescent," Zarathustra speaks of the "comfort . . . I invented for

myself" (*den Trost erfand Ich mir*) (TSZ, 332; KGW, VI, 1: 271). Lampert (260) entertains very briefly the idea that Kant's notion of a practical postulate may be of use in interpreting the thought of eternal recurrence. My own attempt to conceptualize recurrence as a practical postulate was prompted by Hans Blumenberg's remarks regarding Kant's postulate of the soul's immortality. See Blumenberg, *Work on Myth*, 262-95; see, too, Robert M. Wallace's introduction to this book, esp. xxxii-xxxvii.

70. TSZ, 246; KGW, VI, 1: 169.

71. TSZ, 250-51; KGW, VI, 1: 174-75. Here, following Hollingdale, I have altered Kaufmann's translations of *Dichten, dichte,* and *Dichter.*

72. TSZ, 189; KGW, VI, 1: 96.

73. For my account of Zarathustra's account of value-creation in "On the Gift-Giving Virtue," see Chapter 3.

74. Here, I refer to Zarathustra's discussion of "inverse cripples." The notion this discussion advances, that men have been reduced to a part of what they are or might otherwise be, echoes the sixth letter of Schiller's *Letters on the Aesthetic Education of Man*; Marx's claim, in the *1844 Manuscripts,* that where private property prevails, the sense of having supersedes all the physical and intellectual senses; and Friedrich Hölderlin's *Hyperion.* See Friedrich von Schiller, *Letters on the Aesthetic Education of Man,* trans. Reginald Snell (New York: Friedrich Ungar, 1965), 37-45, and Karl Marx, *Early Writings,* 351-52. For the relevant passage from *Hyperion,* see Adrian Del Caro, *Nietzsche Contra Nietzsche,* 45.

75. See my discussion of the figure of the earth in Chapter 2.

76. In interpreting the passages in question, Higgins writes the following: "Our wills are able to reformulate the spectrum of materials that our past bequeaths us by focusing them into patterns of aspiration. . . . Redemption . . . involves converting the materials of the past into constructions that the presently active individual views as valuable. The materials of the past are redeemed . . . by actually being reconstructed along lines suggested by our aspirations" (see Higgins, *Nietzsche's Zarathustra,* 187). My view differs from Higgins's in that I see (first-order) aspirations themselves—what I have called "passions"—as the materials the creative will acts upon.

77. TSZ, 251; KGW, VI, 1: 175-76. I have slightly altered Kaufmann's translation here, rendering *Trübsal* as "misery."

78. Ibid.

79. Ibid.

80. As I see it, my own view is in essential agreement with Heidegger's claims that "Revenge is the will's ill-will toward time and that means toward passing away, transiency. Transiency is that against which the will can take no further steps, that against which its willing constantly collides. . . . Time, as passing away, is repulsive; the will suffers on account of it" (Martin Heidegger, "Who Is Nietzsche's Zarathustra," in *Nietzsche,* vol. 2, *The Eternal Recurrence of the Same,* trans. David Farrell Krell [San Francisco: Harper and Row, 1984], 224). Thomas Pangle (171-72) has criticized Heidegger's interpretation of Nietzsche's conception of revenge by arguing (1) that Nietzschean revenge is not a reaction to transience and (2) that it is a reaction to the fact that "every action is

inescapably shaped . . . by the 'crippled' past against which the 'ascendent' present and future defines itself." It seems to me, however, that there are elements in Zarathustra's speech not mentioned by Pangle—for example, the reference to "time's covetousness," as well as the clear suggestion that the will is enraged *not* by the fact that all willing is de-pendently shaped by the past but by the fact that the transience caused by time's cov-etousness leaves the will powerless to undo and alter the past—that support Heidegger's view. (Lampert [145, 333n88], though he seems to recognize that Zarathustra's reference to time's covetousness supports Heidegger's reading of the relevant text, still endorses Pangle's view.) It also seems to me that Zarathustra's remarks regarding the redemption of the human past (redemption1 in my interpretation), precisely because they concern *the past*, explicitly endorse a dependence on the past that, according to Pangle, stimulates the will's aversion to "time and its 'it was.'" Thus, *pace* Pangle, I am not persuaded to the view that the *new* issue Zarathustra introduces, when he says "But now learn this too: the will itself is still a prisoner," is the issue of dependence on the past.

Wolfgang Müller-Lauter has also criticized Heidegger's interpretation of revenge as a reaction to transience. In "On Redemption," argues Müller-Lauter, Zarathustra addresses "the theme of transitoriness as such" only when he begins to discuss spiritualized revenge (the spirit of revenge). This seems wrong to me, however, for, on my reading, Zarathus-tra has already figuratively invoked the theme of transitoriness in speaking of "time's cov-etousness." See Wolfgang Müller-Lauter, "The Spirit of Revenge and the Eternal Recur-rence: On Heidegger's Later Interpretation of Nietzsche," trans. R. J. Hollingdale, *Journal of Nietzsche Studies* 4–5 (Autumn 1992–Spring 1993): 137–38.

81. TSZ, 251–52; KGW, VI, 1: 176.

82. I wish to claim, in other words, that Nietzsche here is prefiguring the view he de-velops subsequently in the third essay of *Genealogy*, namely, that venting affects such as resentment and revenge can be a way of deadening pain and displeasure (GM, 127; KGW, VI, 2: 391–92).

83. TSZ, 252–53; KGW, VI, 1: 176–77. Here, I have slightly altered Kaufmann's translation, translating *der Menschen bestes Nachdenken* as "man's best reflection" rather than as "the subject of man's best reflection."

84. Both Strong and Lampert relate these preachings to particular moments in the history of European culture (Strong, *Friedrich Nietzsche*, 225–31, and Lampert, 146).

85. For the connection between Schopenhauer's thought and the Christian notion that all doing and willing is sinful and steeped in guilt, see Schopenhauer's defense of Augustine and Luther in chapter 70 of *The World as Will and Representation*, vol. 1.

86. In "On the Tarantulas," Nietzsche prefigures this change in Zarathustra's con-ception of revenge by locating the vengeful tarantula's home amidst the ancient ruins that symbolize the forces of decline to which, I argued in Chapter 4, Zarathustra is oblivious. This suggests, I take it, that the spirit of revenge is rooted in the human expe-rience of change and loss, which is the human experience of time.

87. TSZ, 253; KGW, VI, 1: 177.

88. In *Ecce Homo*, Nietzsche explicitly invites the view that Zarathustra's teaching in

"On Redemption" of what I call "redemption1" is, in substance, the same teaching Zarathustra sets forth when discussing creation, esteeming, and redemption in "On the Blessed Isles" (EH, 308–9; KGW, VI, 3: 346–47).

89. Heidegger has also suggested that the discussion of revenge in "On Redemption" can be read as involving an engagement with Schopenhauer. See Martin Heidegger, *What Is Called Thinking*, trans. Fred D. Wieck and J. Glenn Gray (New York: Harper and Row, 1968), 93–94.

90. Here, I should note a point of agreement between my thinking and Leo Strauss's remark that, for Nietzsche, "the history of man hitherto, i.e., the rule of non-sense and chance . . . is the necessary condition for the subjugation of non-sense and chance." Strauss's further remarks make it clear that, when speaking of the subjugation of non-sense and chance, he has in mind, among other texts, the discussion in "On Redemption" of what I call "redemption1." The point of agreement between us is the thought that redeeming fragments and dreadful accidents, to paraphrase Zarathustra, is a future oriented task that presupposes as a necessary condition "the history of man hitherto." See Strauss, 189–90.

91. In "The Convalescent," in Part 3, Zarathustra realizes in his own person the performance of which he dreams in "On the Vision and the Riddle."

92. TSZ, 268–69; KGW, VI, 1: 194–95. I have made some slight alterations in Kaufmann's translation.

93. TSZ, 270; KGW, VI, 1: 196.

94. Yirmiyahu Yovel has also drawn a connection between Nietzsche's thoughts about recurrence and the Book of Ecclesiastes, though he seems to assume that this part of the Bible played no role in the development of these thoughts (see Yirmiyahu Yovel, "Nietzsche and Spinoza: *Amor Fati* and *Amor Dei*," in *Nietzsche as Affirmative Thinker*, ed. Yirmiyahu Yovel [Dordrecht: Martinus Nijhoff, 1986], 198). My belief that Nietzsche echoes and invokes the perspective of Ecclesiastes in *Zarathustra* (in "Upon the Blessed Isles" and "On the Vision and the Riddle," as well as in "The Soothsayer") suggests *prima facie* that the roots of Nietzsche's thinking about recurrence are *not only* Greek (cf. Karl Löwith, "Nietzsche's Revival of the Doctrine of Eternal Recurrence," in Löwith, *Meaning in History* [Chicago: University of Chicago Press, 1949], 219–20). The issue is complicated, however, by scholarly speculation that the vision of time set forth in Ecclesiastes is itself of Greek origin. For more on this issue, see Isidore Levy, "Rien de nouveau sous le soleil," *La Nouvelle Clio* (1953): 326–28, and Scott, 196–201.

95. TSZ, 269; KGW, VI, 1: 195.

96. Ibid. Gary Shapiro (*Nietzschean Narratives*, 76) helpfully points out that Zarathustra's address on courage is directed to the sailors, not to the dwarf.

97. See my discussion of "On the Pitying" in Chapter 4; also AC, 572–73; KGW, VI, 3: 170–72.

98. TSZ, 269–70; KGW, VI, 1: 195–96. Here I have altered slightly Kaufmann's translation by rendering *laufen* and its cognate forms using the verb "to run" rather than the verb "to walk." In this respect, I follow Hollingdale's translation.

99. I proposed that the jester can be read as a figure for the spirit of gravity in my discussion in Chapter 3 of "On Reading and Writing."

100. I first developed this line of analysis in my "Recurrence, Parody, and Politics in the Philosophy of Friedrich Nietzsche" (Ph.D. diss., Yale University, 1982), 48–49. For a more recent discussion, along similar lines, see Higgins, *Nietzsche's Zarathustra*, 257–58n7. Magnus, Stewart, and Mileur (151) also note Zarathustra's allusion to the figure of Oedipus in "On the Vision and the Riddle." Richard Drake (225) observes that a related allusion occurs in "The Convalescent," when Zarathustra describes a "long twilight" (which he associates with both the soothsayer's prophecy and the recurrence of the small man) as limping before him.

101. It will be remembered that the sphinx's riddle—"What walks on four legs in the morning, two in the afternoon, and three in the evening?"—is also about time: namely, the time of human existence.

102. As will become clear in the course of this chapter, Zarathustra's cosmological vision, as I interpret it, is a vision of a perpetual "now" and not the putatively scientific doctrine that recent literature on the subject tends to designate as "cosmological." For an excellent summary of some of this literature, see Robert John Ackermann, *Nietzsche: A Frenzied Look* (Amherst: University of Massachusetts Press, 1990), 153–57. Nehamas (see Nehamas, *Nietzsche*, 142–53) and Clark (see Clark, *Nietzsche on Truth and Philosophy*, 247–54) provide the two most compelling recent efforts to develop alternatives to the cosmological interpretation as typically understood. Of continuing importance in this connection is Bernd Magnus's older *Nietzsche's Existential Imperative* (Bloomington: Indiana University Press, 1978).

103. Magnus (ibid., 107–8) provides a clear discussion of this point.

104. My thinking about the spatialization of time draws its primary inspiration from Joseph Frank's influential "Spatial Form in Modern Literature," the first chapter of his book, *The Widening Gyre* (New Brunswick, N.J.: Rutgers University Press, 1963). Gary Sha piro (see *Nietzschean Narratives*, 95–96) has also suggested that Zarathustra's thinking about eternal recurrence involves a spatialization of time. Joan Stambaugh (*Nietzsche's Thought of Eternal Return* [Baltimore: Johns Hopkins University Press], 39–40), in her reading of "On the Vision and the Riddle," attempts to distinguish what is "spatial" from what is "temporal" in Zarathustra's remarks; thus, she overlooks the way in which Zarathustra uses spatial relations to represent temporal relations.

105. I borrow the distinction between mundane and extramundane time from Bernd Magnus, though I conceptualize it somewhat differently than he does. See Magnus, *Nietzsche's Existential Imperative*, 109–10.

106. By linking Cavell's notion of inexpressiveness to Bloom's conception of belatedness, I mean to highlight a significant point of convergence between Cavell's reading of Wittgenstein's "private language argument" and Bloom's theory of modern poetry. Not surprisingly, Bloom and Cavell both invoke Walter Jackson Bate's book *The Burden of the Past and the English Poet* as a point of reference central to their thinking about the modern artist's mission of originality (see Cavell, *The Claim of Reason*, 472–73, and

Harold Bloom, *The Anxiety of Influence* [New York: Oxford University Press, 1973], 8). Significantly, Bloom also cites Nietzsche as a "prime" influence on his thinking, though the book he mentions is *Genealogy*, not *Zarathustra*. Nietzsche's thought about the issue of artistic belatedness was doubtlessly informed by Goethe's reflections on the issue in the *Conversations with Eckermann* (see, e.g., the conversations of January 2, 1824 and January 29, 1826).

107. Harold Bloom, *A Map of Misreading*, 131-32.

108. For an earlier and in many ways different version of my effort to tie Bloom's theory of poetry to the drama of "On the Vision and the Riddle," see my "Metaphysics and Metalepsis," esp. 33-34. For a more recent effort along similar lines, which also relates eternal recurrence to Zarathustra's attempt to cope with the experience of belatedness, see Magnus, Stewart, and Mileur, 139-54.

109. For my earlier interpretation of the idea that Zarathustra privileges the moment, which I here revise, see my "Recurrence, Parody, and Politics," 51 (see also my "Metaphysics and Metalepsis," 30-31). Higgins quotes at length from this earlier interpretation in order to buttress her own views regarding Zarathustra's emphasis on the moment (see Higgins, *Nietzsche's Zarathustra*, 176). The interpretation of Zarathustra's conception of the moment that I have found most instructive is the one Heidegger puts forth in *Nietzsche*, vol. 2, *The Eternal Recurrence of the Same*, 37-62. Also instructive is Alan White's discussion in *Within Nietzsche's Labyrinth*, 87-88.

110. Here I assume that the coming-to-be at a given time of something new has as a necessary condition that at all preceding times that particular "something" did not exist.

111. Lampert (35) asserts that the transformation Zarathustra undergoes in "On the Vision and the Riddle" "cannot be subsumed under the imagery" of the "On the Three Metamorphoses." According to Lampert, "the images employed in describing that later transformation are completely different." My own interpretation of Zarathustra's transformation in "On the Vision and the Riddle," in that it argues that this transformation *can* be "subsumed" under Zarathustra's conception of the second metamorphosis, clearly and explicitly contradicts Lampert's view. To be sure, Lampert is correct to note that "On the Vision and the Riddle" uses different images than "On the Three Metamorphoses," but from this claim it hardly follows that these different images have been used to describe a different sort of transformation. The particulars of my interpretation of Zarathustra's "leonine" transformation I give in the main text.

112. See TSZ, 268, 138; KGW, VI, 1: 193, 26.

113. For Zarathustra's belief that the dwarf or spirit of gravity's Christian-Platonic and ascetic values cause life to seem a desert, see TSZ, 305; KGW, VI, 1: 239. For a reading that likewise relates Zarathustra's subjection to the spirit of gravity to the figure of the camel, see Magnus, *Nietzsche's Existential Imperative*, 165-67.

114. J. P. Stern (*A Study of Nietzsche*, 165) relates the dwarf to Alberich, Mime's brother. I mention Mime rather than Alberich, because Mime is the dwarf Siegfried *slays* after having slain Fafner (see *Siegfried*, act 2).

115. TSZ, 306; KGW, VI, 1: 239.

116. TSZ, 270–72; KGW, VI, 1: 196–98. I have made some slight alterations in Kaufmann's translation.

117. For Zarathustra's reference to his vision of the shepherd as a foreseeing, see ibid.

118. For Freud's conception of the dream-work as involving the displacement of "psychical intensities," see Sigmund Freud, *The Interpretation of Dreams*, trans. James Strachey (New York: Avon, 1965), 340–44. For a useful discussion of some examples, see David Stafford-Clark, *What Freud Really Said* (New York: Schocken, 1971), 77 ff. For a brief, philosophically informed discussion, see Paul Ricoeur, *Freud and Philosophy* (New Haven, Conn.: Yale University Press, 1970), 93–94.

119. The reference in Zarathustra's dream to thieves and ghosts and a moon silent as death may be a veiled allusion to a dream that Nietzsche had as a child, in the immediate aftermath of his baby brother's death:

> I heard the church organ playing as at a funeral. When I looked to see what was going on, a grave opened suddenly, and my father arose out of it in a shroud. He hurries into the church and soon comes back with a small child in his arms. The mound on the grave reopens, he climbs back in, and the gravestone sinks back over the opening. The swelling noise of the organ stops at once, and I wake up. In the morning I tell the dream to my dear mother. Soon after that little Joseph is suddenly taken ill. He goes into convulsions and dies within a few hours.

Quoted from Hayman, 18.

120. In "On Involuntary Bliss," Zarathustra himself links the figure of the "half dwarf, half mole" (*Maulwurf*) spirit of gravity to that of the serpent: "Alas, abysmal thought that is *my* thought . . . my heart pounds to my very throat whenever I hear your burrowing [*graben*]. . . . Even your silence wants to choke [*würgen*] me. . . . Your gravity [*Schwere*] was always terrible enough for me." Zarathustra's depiction of his thought as "burrowing" I read as an allusion to the molelike character of the spirit of gravity. His portrait of his thought as "choking" I read as an allusion to the serpent appearing in "On the Vision and the Riddle" (see TSZ, 274; KGW, VI, 1: 201). Note, finally, that in "The Convalescent," Zarathustra connects his choking to his disgust with man and to the soothsayer's prophecy (see TSZ, 331; KGW, VI, 1: 270). That Zarathustra makes this connection is no surprise, for the soothsayer's prophecy implies that man cannot be overcome and thus prefigures the spirit of gravity's suggestion that Zarathustra cannot evade the refrainlike recurrence of man, the object of Zarathustra's disgust.

121. In speaking of pity in the second half of his dream, Zarathustra uses *erbarmen*, not *mitleiden*.

122. Nietzsche's "cinematic" literary technique can also be found in Flaubert's *Madame Bovary*. For a discussion of Flaubert's use of the literary "cut" and its relation to the spatialization of time, see Frank, 14–16. Nietzsche, we know, was familiar with *Madame Bovary*, though neither his published nor unpublished remarks on the novel comment on Flaubert's literary technique (see CW, 176; KGW, VI, 3: 28, and VIII, 3: 306).

123. Kant himself, it may be recalled, used the example of "bold, overhanging and,

as it were, threatening rocks" to illustrate his conception of the dynamical sublime (see Kant, *Critique of Judgment*, 120).

124. To claim that the dwarf/small man is the source of Zarathustra's abysmal thought is not to deny Zarathustra's claim that the dwarf could not bear his (Zarathustra's) thought. What Zarathustra claims, on my reading, is that the dwarf could not bear to think that his (the dwarf's) circumstances justify the belief that he (the dwarf) ought to renounce life. Zarathustra bears to think this about his own circumstances (i.e., he bears to think that his [Zarathustra's] circumstances justify the belief that he [Zarathustra] ought to renounce life), for he is not crushed by his thought. Zarathustra frees himself from his thought when, like the leonine shepherd of his dream, he defiantly spits it out and repudiates it (cf. "The Convalescent"). The circumstance that threatens Zarathustra with the spirit of renunciation (resignation)—namely, the meaningless recurrence of the small man—does not, in the dwarf/small man's eyes, warrant the belief that he (the dwarf/small man) ought to renounce life. As we saw in Chapter 2, the small man for whom the dwarf is a figure (i.e., the last man) is oblivious to the nihilism he represents.

125. The characterization of Fafner, the dragon, as serpentine occurs in scene 1 of act 2 of *Siegfried* when Mime attributes to the dragon a serpent's tail (*ein Schlangenschweif*). It is also worth noting that in the final scene of *Siegfried*, Siegfried, prefiguring the shepherd of Zarathustra's dream, appears as a hero who *laughs*. Brünnhilde depicts him as a hero who laughs when she sings: "O Siegfried! Herrlicher! Hort der Welt! Leben der Erde! Lachender Held!"

126. See Schiller, "On the Sublime," 210.

127. Zarathustra explicitly links the creator who creates new values to the figure of the overman in section 9 of the prologue. There, he suggests that it is precisely the creator of new values who follows the rainbow path to becoming an overman (see TSZ, 135–36; KGW, VI, 1: 19–21).

128. Whitlock (200) argues that the shepherd's bite is not an act of force by which the shepherd rids himself of the notion that nauseates him, but an act of facing and accepting that notion. Whitlock's reasoning, however, is not clear to me. The act of biting *is*, after all, an act of force performed by the mouth. Moreover, the shepherd *spits out* the serpent's head after biting it off, thus ridding himself of the serpent's head and, symbolically, of whatever notion or thought the serpent's head is interpreted to represent.

129. Zarathustra ascribes beauty to the overman in "Upon the Blessed Isles." In "On Those Who Are Sublime" he appears to argue that one can attain the beauty of the overman by becoming an overhero who has overcome the sublimity of the hero.

130. In "On Old and New Tablets," Zarathustra remarks that he is awaiting the arrival of a laughing lion. And in "The Welcome," in Part 4, he suggests that the children he awaits are laughing lions. Finally, in "The Sign," when the arrival of his children seems imminent, Zarathustra is surprised by the appearance of an actual lion who does in fact laugh.

131. See Schiller, "On the Sublime," 211; *Schillers Sämtliche Werke: Säkular-Ausgabe* (Stuttgart and Berlin: Cotta, 1904–5), 12: 281. In translating *versäumen* as "to omit," I have altered slightly Elias's translation.

132. TSZ, 254; KGW, VI, 1: 179–80.

133. TSZ, 186; KGW, VI, 1: 91. Here and in what follows I assume that, through a detailed reading of "On Human Prudence," it could be shown that Zarathustra sees all four instances of the human prudence he mentions in "On Human Prudence" as functioning to maintain his connection to his anchor, man.

134. TSZ, 273; KGW, VI, 1: 199.

135. TSZ, 274–75; KGW, VI, 1: 201–2. Zarathustra has previously suggested that he lacks the leonine strength he needs to cope with his abysmal thought in "The Stillest Hour."

136. Ibid. I have slightly altered Kaufmann's translation.

137. I follow Lampert (173) in reading Zarathustra's talk of lying fettered to his children as alluding to his opening remarks in "On Human Prudence."

138. TSZ, 273; KGW, VI, 1: 200. Here, I follow Hollingdale in translating *kehrend* as "turning" rather than "returning."

139. In scene 1 of act 2 of *Siegfried*, Wotan speaks to Alberich of Siegfried: "Whom I love I leave to fend for himself; he stands or falls, but is his own master: I avail myself only of heroes."

140. TSZ, 264–65; KGW, VI, 1: 190.

141. In "The Wanderer," Zarathustra says that "It is out of the deepest depth that the highest must come to its height" (see TSZ, 266; KGW, VI, 1: 191).

142. TSZ, 279; KGW, VI, 1: 207.

143. I noted in Chapter 2 that in section 10 of the prologue Zarathustra's heroic, leonine pride (his eagle) interprets his prudence (his serpent) to be *allied* to his lion-spirited effort to envision himself as the Dionysian origin of all values. I suggested too that this prideful, pride-driven interpretation of his prudence finds an echo in section 10's image of an eagle-borne ouroboros, which image, whether viewed from a Hermetic or a Christian perspective, seems to mark Zarathustra as *the* being in whom all values originate. In Part 3, Zarathustra evinces a more mature, *human* interpretation of his prudence (hence his emphasis on his *human* prudence) that discerns a conflict between his prudence and his leonine pride. Having recognized that the heroic posture of the lion is self-alienating, and that willing backwards may involve a reiteration of leonine self-alienation that, by severing his connection to man, defeats his effort to overcome man, Zarathustra now sees that his prudence, which bids him to fetter himself to man, cannot be so easily reconciled with the aspirations of the lion-spirit. Still, in the closing sections of Part 3, Zarathustra will strive (but fail) to effect some such reconciliation, and thus to solve the problem of his double will.

144. TSZ, 311; KGW, VI, 1: 245. I have slightly altered Kaufmann's translations.

145. The view that *Zarathustra*, Parts 1–3, is a tragedy contradicts Hayman's assertion (6) that Nietzsche never wrote a tragedy; Megill's claim (74) that, in his later writings, Nietzsche "no longer attributes to tragedy the important role he did in *The Birth of Tragedy*"; and McFadden's remark (George McFadden, "Nietzschean Values in Comic Writing," in *Why Nietzsche Now?* ed. Daniel O'Hara [Bloomington: Indiana University Press 1985], 343) that *Zarathustra* is "anything but tragic."

146. For my discussion of a possible allusion to Byron's *Manfred*, see Chapter 4, note 89.

147. See Chapter 2 for my discussion of Nietzsche's explicit suggestion, in no. 342 of *The Gay Science*, that the beginning of *Zarathustra* is the beginning of a tragedy.

148. In *Prometheus Bound*, Prometheus affirms the worth of human existence by rescuing humankind from Zeus's plans to destroy it. See Aeschylus, *Prometheus Bound*, trans. David Grene in *Aeschylus II*, ed. David Grene and Richmond Lattimore (Chicago: University of Chicago Press, 1956), 147–48.

149. See BT, 71; KGW, III, 1: 65–66.

150. On this point, see Blumenberg, *Work on Myth*, 606.

151. BT, 119; KGW, III, 1: 122–23.

152. For the figure of the "world's limit," see Grene's translation of *Prometheus Bound*, 139.

153. BT, 121; KGW, III, 1: 124–25.

154. BT, 70; KGW, III, 1: 64.

155. Blumenberg (*Work on Myth*, 619) notes that Nietzsche's representations of the Prometheus story characterize the bird that tortures Prometheus as a vulture, not as an eagle.

156. BT, 69; KGW, III, 1: 63. I am indebted to Blumenberg for my thinking about Nietzsche's use of Goethe's poem to interpret Aeschylus's tragedy. See Blumenberg, *Work on Myth*, 613.

157. For a full translation of Goethe's "Prometheus Ode," see *Twenty German Poets*, ed. Walter Kaufmann (New York: Random House, 1962), 9–11.

158. Nietzsche's view that "man" (e.g., Zarathustra's children) must play the "Herculean" role of liberating Prometheus-Dionysus in a (modern) world that has forgotten him is evident not only in the apotheosis of German music in *The Birth of Tragedy*, but, subsequently, in the first two sentences of the Prometheus sketch of 1874: "Prometheus und sein Geier sind vergessen worden, als man die Welt der Olympier und ihre Machte vernichtete. Prometheus ewartet seine Erlösung einmal vom Menschen" (KGW, III, 4: 461). For commentary on this sketch, see Blumenberg, *Work on Myth*, 618 ff.

159. On this point, see my discussion of the lion's freedom for new creation in Chapter 1.

160. See BT, 67–72; KGW, III, 1: 60–67.

161. On Prometheus's "heroic effort . . . to attain universality," see BT, 71; KGW, III, 1: 66.

162. TSZ, 276; KGW, VI, 1: 203–4. I have made some minor changes in Kaufmann's translation.

163. Lampert (174) also notes the allusion in this speech to "On Those Who Are Sublime," but interprets it differently than I do.

164. TSZ, 277; KGW, VI, 1: 205 (I have altered slightly Kaufmann's translation). Nietzsche later quotes this passage (as well as a related passage in "On Old and New Tablets") in *Ecce Homo*, where he unequivocally links it to Zarathustra's effort to contend with his abysmal thought:

... he [Zarathustra] that has the hardest most terrible insight into reality, that has thought the "most abysmal idea," nevertheless does not consider it an objection to existence [*Dasein*], not even to its eternal recurrence—but rather one reason more for being himself the eternal Yes to all things, "the tremendous, unbounded saying Yes and Amen."—"Into all abysses I still carry the blessings of my saying yes."— *But this is the concept of Dionysus once again.* (EH, 306; KGW, VI, 3: 343)

In my view, Zarathustra's abysmal thought ("idea") is the thought that his circumstances justify him in believing he should renounce life. To say that Zarathustra does not consider this thought to be an objection to his existence, *even* when his existence is characterized by "eternal recurrence," is to say that *even* when his circumstances are characterized by "eternal recurrence" (again, by the endless perpetuation of Christian-Platonic values in the person of the small and last man), Zarathustra does *not* believe that his thought that his circumstances justify him in believing he should renounce life is a good reason for him to object to and renounce life (it should be noted here that I am assuming that the reference to eternal recurrence in the passage I quote from *Ecce Homo* alludes to the "first act" of the thought-drama of recurrence; it should also be noted that, in writing of the eternal recurrence of "existence" (*Dasein*) in this passage, Nietzsche echoes his description of an eternally recurring and meaningless existence in *Will to Power*, no. 55, which description, in my view, captures the substance of Zarathustra's "first act" vision of the small man's recurrence [cf. note 66, above]). Rather, Zarathustra regards his abysmal thought to be a good reason for becoming a sublime and leonine being *who rejects his abysmal thought*, a Dionysian creature (in the mode of Dionysus-Zagreus) whose yea-saying obliterates all abysses, including the "abyss" of his abysmal thought (Zarathustra becomes precisely this sort of being when, in "The Convalescent," he initiates the "second act" of the thought-drama of eternal recurrence by embracing the practical postulate that he personifies the act of willing backwards). For Zarathustra, the thought that his circumstances constitute a reason (or a justification) for believing he should renounce life is not a reason to object to and renounce life but a reason to become the sort of being who renounces his thought. Yea-saying for Zarathustra, somewhat like the faith of Kierkegaard's knight of faith, involves a paradoxical "reasoning" that rejects the voice of rational belief.

For two different but important alternative readings of the passage quoted from *Ecce Homo*, see Nehamas, *Nietzsche*, 148, and Clark, *Nietzsche on Truth and Philosophy*, 261–62.

165. TSZ, 343; KGW, VI, 1: 287.

166. I have not done justice here to the beauty and richness of "Before Sunrise." Of particular significance in this speech is Zarathustra's vision of a world set free of God-given purposes and Christian "good and evil," both of which he later associates with the spirit of gravity (in "On Old and New Tablets" and "On the Spirit of Gravity"). Only when Zarathustra acquires the leonine strength he requires to cope with his abysmal thought will he be able fully to embrace this vision.

167. Here I differ with Gary Shapiro, who sees Zarathustra, in Part 3, simply moving away from the public world he shares with others, not moving toward that world. See Shapiro, *Nietzschean Narratives*, 72.

168. TSZ, 284; KGW, VI, 1: 213.

169. TSZ, 287; KGW, VI, 1: 217.

170. TSZ, 286; KGW, VI, 1: 216.

171. TSZ, 290; KGW, VI, 1: 221.

172. TSZ, 290; KGW, VI, 1: 222.

173. TSZ, 291; KGW, VI, 1: 223.

174. Zarathustra alludes to "On Human Prudence" when he says, "Disguised I sat among them . . ." (TSZ, 297; KGW, VI, 1: 229).

175. TSZ, 296, 298; KGW, VI, 1: 228, 230.

176. Cf. Shapiro, *Nietzschean Narratives,* 72 ff. Here, it should be noted that in German *niesen* can mean "to turn one's nose up at something" as well as "to sneeze." Zarathustra wishes to invoke both meanings, I think, at the end of "The Return Home."

177. TSZ, 299; KGW, VI, 1: 231–32. Translation slightly altered.

178. Lampert (191–92) also notes the connection between "Before Sunrise" and "On the Three Evils."

179. See Kant, *Critique of Judgment,* 103 ff.

180. TSZ, 299; KGW, VI, 1: 232.

181. TSZ, 300.; KGW, VI, 1: 233. Zarathustra speaks explicitly of his highest hope in connection to the figure of the overman in "On the Gift-Giving Virtue." See TSZ, 190; KGW, VI, 1: 98.

182. TSZ, 302; KGW, VI, 1: 234.

183. TSZ, 301–2; KGW, VI, 1: 234.

184. TSZ, 303; KGW, VI, 1: 236.

185. TSZ, 304; KGW, VI, 1: 238. Zarathustra also echoes "On Reading and Writing" in speaking of his taste and love for blood. See TSZ, 306; KGW, VI, 1: 240.

186. TSZ, 305; KGW, VI, 1: 238.

187. TSZ, 306; KGW, VI, 1: 240.

188. TSZ, 306; KGW, VI, 1: 239.

189. TSZ, 308; KGW, VI, 1: 242.

190. TSZ, 310; KGW, VI, 1: 244–45.

191. TSZ, 190; KGW, VI, 1: 98.

192. TSZ, 330; KGW, VI, 1: 269.

193. In "On the Spirit of Gravity," Zarathustra says, "Verily, I too have learned to wait—thoroughly—but only to wait for *myself*" (TSZ, 307; KGW, VI, 1: 240).

194. The figure of the raging bull, especially because section 8 contrasts this figure to that of the "plowing bull," recalls the portrait of the hero who has yet to become "a white bull walking before the plowshare" in "On Those Who Are Sublime"; in section 9, Zarathustra seems to be identifying a version of the second metamorphosis of the spirit, namely, the transition from camel to lion; finally, the development of Zarathustra's speech in sections 13 through 16 (cf., especially, section 16 to sections 13 and 14) suggests that the soothsayer's belief that nothing is worthwhile is a new version of an old view familiar from the "old tablets" (see Whitlock, 219, for a similar point and for a discussion of the apparent allusion to Ecclesiastes in section 13).

195. In connecting the figure of a "new nobility" to Zarathustra's concept of the overman I echo Whitlock's reading of this figure (218–19). For a very different and, I think, less plausible view, see Lampert, 207.

196. TSZ, 326–27; KGW, VI, 1: 264–65. I have followed Hollingdale in translating *zum Vernichten bereit* as "ready for annihilation."

197. Zarathustra first uses the figure of lightning to describe the overman in the prologue.

198. Zarathustra's remarks in the second section of "The Convalescent"—"and how that monster crawled down my throat and suffocated me. But I bit off its head and spewed it out"—clearly suggest that in the first section of that speech, in summoning and confronting his abysmal thought, he has enacted the role of the shepherd. See TSZ, 330; KGW, VI, 1: 269.

199. TSZ, 328; KGW, VI, 1: 267–68.

200. In interpreting the animals as alluding to Orpheus and to Adam in Eden, I follow Richard Drake's (219–20) interpretation.

201. TSZ, 329; KGW, VI, 1: 268.

202. Ibid.

203. TSZ, 329–30; KGW, VI, 1: 268–69.

204. Nehamas, *Nietzsche*, 146–47.

205. TSZ, 330; KGW, VI, 1: 269.

206. I follow here Karsten Harries's translation of the passage I quote from the *Liber XXIV philosophorum*. See Karsten Harries, "The Infinite Sphere: Comments on the History of a Metaphor," *Journal of the History of Philosophy* 13 (January 1975): 7–8. My interpretation of the *Liber XXIV philosophorum* derives directly from Harries's article. For Harries's provocative suggestion that there is a connection between Nietzsche's doctrine of the eternal recurrence and Nicolaus Cusanus's metaphors for God's infinity—the metaphor of the infinite sphere, for example—see Harries, "The Philosopher at Sea," 42. Robin Small also attempts to make sense of Zarathustra's animals' allusion to the metaphor of the infinite sphere, but along lines quite different from my own (see Robin Small, "Nietzsche and a Platonist Cosmos: Center Everywhere, Circumference Nowhere," *Journal of the History of Ideas* 44 [January–March 1983]: 89–104). Finally, Nietzsche revives the metaphor of the infinite sphere to describe the kingdom of God in *The Anti-Christ*: "The 'kingdom of God' is nothing that one expects; it has no yesterday and no day after tommorow, it will not come in 'a thousand years'—it is an experience of the heart; it is everywhere, it is nowhere" (AC, 608; KGW, VI, 3: 205).

207. TSZ, 332; KGW, VI, 1: 271.

208. Richard Drake (227–28) also notes the tacit allusion to the art of Apollo in Zarathustra's talk of a *Leier-Lied*.

209. For Zarathustra's reference to his animals' observation of his redemption, see TSZ, 330; KGW, VI, 1: 269.

210. Both Gary Shapiro and Laurence Lampert make a similar point. See Shapiro, *Nietzschean Narratives*, 81–82, and Lampert, 220.

211. TSZ, 333; KGW, VI, 1: 273.   212. TSZ, 334; KGW, VI, 1: 274–75.

213. Ibid.; see also White, 94.   214. TSZ, 333–35; KGW, VI, 1: 274–75.

215. St. Augustine, *The Confessions*, trans. R. S. Pine-Coffin (New York: Penguin, 1982), 262–63.

216. See Martin Heidegger, "Who Is Nietzsche's Zarathustra," 218. Heidegger's in-

terpretation of the temporality of eternal recurrence in this essay—which interpretation is based on his reading of "The Great Longing"—corresponds roughly to what I understand to be the "second act" of the thought-drama of recurrence. Alan White offers a different interpretation of Zarathustra's claim that he has taught his soul to say "'today' and 'one day' and 'formerly,'" but without relating that claim to Zarathustra's allusion to the metaphor of the infinite sphere (see White, 93–94).

217. See WP, no. 55; KGW, VIII, 1: 217–18.

218. During the Renaissance, Giordano Bruno also used the metaphor of the infinite sphere to adumbrate a pantheistic cosmology, but I do not know whether Nietzsche was aware of this when he wrote *Zarathustra*. For Bruno's use of this metaphor, see Hans Blumenberg, *The Legitimacy of the Modern Age*, trans. Robert M. Wallace (Cambridge: MIT Press, 1983), 572–78.

219. In his notebooks, Nietzsche explicitly connects the ending of *Zarathustra*, Part 3, to the lion-spirit's "I will" and to the achievement of a perspective that is "beyond" the good and evil of traditional morality. See KGW, VII, 1: 547–48.

220. See TSZ, 260; KGW, VI, 1: 188. For the connection of Zarathustra's speech, "On Reading and Writing," to the spirit of the lion, see Chapter 3.

221. See BT, 26; KGW, III, 1: 16.

222. See GS, 328; KGW, V, 2: 302.

223. Against Zarathustra, one might argue that the affirmation of eternal recurrence at the end of Part 3 (my second act of the thought-drama of recurrence), Zarathustra's assertions to the contrary notwithstanding, *expresses* rather than triumphs over the spirit of resignation. Bearing in mind that, from the perspective of spiritualized revenge, resignation (renunciation) is the only form of radical transfiguration available to human beings, one might additionally argue that Zarathustra's affirming of eternal recurrence means he has not freed himself from spiritualized revenge, but only confirmed its Schopenhauerian proclamations (Heidegger argues that the affirmation of eternal recurrence is linked to the spirit of revenge (see Heidegger, "Who Is Nietzsche's Zarathustra," 228–29), as does Peter Berkowitz, who explicitly aligns his view with Heidegger's (Berkowitz, *Nietzsche: The Ethics of an Immoralist* [Cambridge: Harvard University Press, 1995], 177–78, 207). In Part 4, Zarathustra addresses these arguments, for he is forced to confront them in the person of the soothsayer. Indeed, Part 4 is primarily about Zarathustra's efforts to vindicate his claim to a happiness that, *pace* the soothsayer's charges, he believes liberates him from the spirit of resignation (see my discussion of Part 4 in Chapter 6).

224. Schopenhauer, *The World as Will and Representation*, 1: 283–84. I have slightly altered Payne's translation of the final stanza of Goethe's "Prometheus" in order to bring it into accord with Walter Kaufmann's translation mentioned in note 157 of this chapter.

225. Schopenhauer, *The World as Will and Representation*, 2: 642–46. For a fascinating discussion of the tendency to see a connection between Goethe's "Prometheus" and Spinoza's pantheism in the German intellectual tradition that Schopenhauer and Nietzsche both inherited, see Blumenberg, *Work on Myth*, 397–429. See also George di Gio-

vanni's "The Unfinished Philosophy of Friedrich Heinrich Jacobi," introduction to Friedrich Heinrich Jacobi, *The Main Philosophical Writings and the Novel Allwill*, trans. and ed. George di Giovanni (Montreal: McGill-Queens University Press, 1994), 67–116.

226. My view that Zarathustra envisions himself as a pantheistic god in the concluding sections of Part 3 has some affinity to Peter Berkowitz's view that Zarathustra, in these same sections, adopts a self-deifying image of himself. Notwithstanding this affinity, Berkowitz and I differ on numerous issues of interpretation regarding (1) the precise significance of Zarathustra's "self-deification" and (2) the role of Zarathustra's self-deification vis-à-vis the development of his self-understanding and the development of *Zarathustra* as a whole (see Berkowitz, 176–210). For a critique of Berkowitz's discussion of self-deification that raises insightful questions regarding its treatment of Nietzsche's Dionysianism and the theme of self-overcoming—questions that, I believe, my interpretation can accommodate—see Michael Allen Gillespie, "Nietzsche and the Premodernist Critique of Postmodernity," *Critical Review* 11, no. 4 (Fall 1997): 543–53.

227. TSZ, 335; KGW, VI, 1: 275.   228. TSZ, 334; KGW, VI, 1: 275.

229. TSZ, 335; KGW, VI, 1: 275.   230. TSZ, 335–36; KGW, VI, 1: 276.

231. See KSA, 14, 324. For Alan White's commentary on this point, see White, 99. See also Lampert, 233–34, and Whitlock, 225–26. For a reading similar to my own, see Harries, "The Philosopher at Sea," 40.

232. TSZ, 146; KGW, VI, 1: 35.

233. For a discussion of the ancient sources of this image, see Whitlock, 226. Also see Otto, chap. 5, and Bennholdt-Thomsen, 125. Lampert (233–34) notes the play of Dionysian imagery in "On the Great Longing," as well as in "The Other Dancing Song," but attributes no philosophical or other significance to the distinction I have stressed between Dionysus as Zagreus and Dionysus as the coming god.

234. That Zarathustra is looking beyond the "now" and toward the future is strongly suggested by his rhetorical emphasis on the "now" in the passages immediately *preceding* his discussion of his soul's "longing of overfullness": "O my soul . . . you now stand there . . ."; "O my soul, now there is not a soul anywhere . . ."; "O my soul . . . now—now you say to me . . ."; "O, my soul . . . now your own overrichness. . . ." See TSZ, 334–35; KGW, VI, 1: 275.

235. Zarathustra's rhetoric of family connectedness—for instance, "In your children you shall make up for being the children of your fathers: thus you shall redeem all that is past"—suggests a continuity of life and experience between the children-creators who redeem the past and their predecessors (see TSZ, 316; KGW, VI, 1: 251). In this chapter, and in connection to my discussion of redemption1, I have interpreted this suggestion of continuity to imply that the children in whom the passional basis of human existence is reborn (the children who appear at the end of Part 4) suffer the same *kinds* of passions as their Christian-Platonic predecessors.

236. This is what I previously described (note 161, above) as Zarathustra's attempt to achieve Promethean "universality."

237. Lampert (235) reads Nietzsche as portraying life at the beginning of Zarathus-

tra's dance as a Dionysian maenad; Drake (230) reads him a portraying her here as a sort of Medusa.

238. TSZ, 337; KGW, VI, 1: 279.

239. Ibid.; cf. Lampert, 235.

240. TSZ, 337; KGW, VI, 1: 279.

241. TSZ, 338; KGW, VI, 1: 279-80. For the insight that Nietzsche depicts life as a Circe-like figure, I am indebted to Drake, 230-31.

242. Quoted in Harries, "The Philosopher at Sea," 37. See also, in connection to my interpretation of "The Other Dancing Song," Harries's discussion of Nietzsche's remark.

243. See Drake, 231, for a similar point.

244. TSZ, 338; KGW, VI, 1: 281. Here, I have altered slightly Kaufmann's translation.

245. TSZ, 310; KGW, VI, 1: 245. It seems to me that this passage must play a key role in any attempt to answer the questions that Alan White usefully raises in attempting to make sense of Zarathustra's admission that he is thinking of abandoning life (see White, 97-98). It also seems to me that White is right to claim that Zarathustra is not intending *literally* to commit suicide.

246. TSZ, 338; KGW, VI, 1: 280; cf. Lampert, 236.

247. TSZ, 338-39; KGW, VI, 1: 281. I have altered slightly Kaufmann's translation.

248. For a statement of the traditional view—which I reject here—that the secret Zarathustra communicates to life is some conception of eternal recurrence, see Lampert, 238. For a different interpretation, see Higgins, *Nietzsche's Zarathustra*, 155-56. For a more detailed discussion, see M. Platt, "What Does Zarathustra Whisper in Life's Ear?" *Nietzsche-Studien* 17 (1988): 179-94.

249. TSZ, 343; KGW, VI, 1: 287.

250. Ibid. See also TSZ, 277; KGW, VI, 1: 205.

251. TSZ, 340-43; KGW, VI, 1: 283-87. Alan White (98) has also noted Nietzsche's play on the expression *hoch zeit*.

252. The fourth seal, the fair copy of which was entitled "Of the Ring of Rings," supports this interpretation, for it portrays Zarathustra as celebrating a ring, and thus a sort of "circumference," that is *all-comprehensive*. See, on this point, White's discussion of the fourth seal (98-99).

253. TSZ, 342-43; KGW, VI, 1: 286-87. I have altered slightly Kaufmann's translation.

Chapter 6: Eternal Recurrence, Act III

1. TSZ, 349; KGW, VI, 1: 291. Here, I have altered slightly Kaufmann's translation.

2. TSZ, 399; KGW, VI, 1: 353.

3. TSZ, 351; KGW, VI, 1: 293. Zarathustra announces that he will reclaim (acknowledge again) and realize his ability to go-under, which he deliberately disclaims in "The Other Dancing Song," only if he receives a sign that the time has come for him to do so. Notice, however, that in thus announcing his intentions, Zarathustra *alludes* to his ability to go-under and hence acknowledges it. In other words, with the very speech

act by which he purports to *defer* his acknowledgment and realization of his ability to go-under, he acknowledges that ability. Zarathustra's performative self-contradiction, like the bad faith it seems to express, may be inevitable, for his decision to disown and distance himself from his ability to go-under, in the aftermath of (1) his acknowledgment of that ability in Part 2 (see my discussion of Zarathustra's "crisis and cure" in Chapter 4), and (2) his failure to reconcile his second practical postulate with the possibility of redemption1 (see my discussion of "The Other Dancing Song" in Chapter 5), is a decision to disown a dimension of his existence (his ability to go-under) that he has *already* acknowledged.

4. TSZ, 340–43; KGW, VI, 1: 283–87.

5. TSZ, 352; KGW, VI, 1: 294.

6. TSZ, 350–51; KGW, VI, 1: 292–93.

7. See Matt. 4:19 and Mark 1:17, where Christ appears as a fisher of men who will make his disciples fishers of men. For the tendency in Christian and European romantic interpretations of the Prometheus story to relate Prometheus to the figure of Christ, see Harold Bloom, *The Ringers in the Tower: Studies in Romantic Tradition* (Chicago: University of Chicago Press, 1971), 120–21. For the suggestion that Nietzsche's depiction of Zarathustra as a fisher echoes Lucian's portrait of the philosophical fisher in his *Piscator,* see Bennholdt-Thomsen, 127–28.

8. Zarathustra has "forgotten patience . . . because his 'passion' is over [*die Geduld verlernt hat,—weil er nicht mehr 'duldet'*]." See TSZ, 351; KGW, VI, 1: 293.

9. TSZ, 352; KGW, VI, 1: 294.

10. Several commentators have recently argued that Zarathustra ultimately abandons the idea of overcoming man (of creating an overman), some of them insisting that Zarathustra embraces the teaching of eternal recurrence at the expense of his teaching that man can and should be overcome. See, for example, Lampert, 258; Daniel W. Conway, "Overcoming the *Übermensch*: Nietzsche's Revaluation of Values," *Journal of the British Society for Phenomenology* 20, no. 3 (October 1989): 215 ff.; and Clark, *Nietzsche on Truth and Philosophy,* 253, 270–77, 284. In contrast to this view, I hold that Zarathustra retains his commitment to overcoming man through the end of Part 4, which commitment is compatible with the child's thought of recurrence (cf. Chapter 5, note 9). For a valuable critique of Conway's and Lampert's positions on this issue, see Ansell-Pearson, 185–94.

11. In thinking about Nietzsche's use of the figure of the divine bridegroom, I have benefited from M. H. Abrams's discussion of the Book of Revelations in his *Natural Supernaturalism,* 37–46.

12. TSZ, 342; KGW, VI, 1: 286. Cf. Rev. 21:6.

13. TSZ, 331; KGW, VI, 1: 270; emphasis mine.

14. William Schaberg has established that when Part 4 was initially printed, in April 1885, its title page bore the legend "Fourth and Last Part" (cf. KGW, VI, 289). Schaberg also argues persuasively that, by March 1885, Nietzsche had conclusively decided that *Zarathustra* would end with Part 4. See William H. Schaberg, *The Nietzsche Canon: A Publication History and Bibliography* (Chicago: University of Chicago Press, 1995),

87–88, 101–9. For the argument that, subsequent to the initial printing of Part 4, Nietzsche still toyed with the idea of adding to Zarathustra's story, see David. E. Cartwright, "The Last Temptation of Zarathustra," *Journal of the History of Philosophy* 31, no. 1 (January 1993), 69.

15. TSZ, 245; KGW, VI, 1: 168. For the encounter between Prometheus and Io, see Aeschylus, *Prometheus Bound*, 160–71.

16. Cf. my discussion of the last man and the higher man in Chapter 2.

17. Cf. KGW, VI, 1: 391, where the title given to the penultimate section of Part 4 is "Das Nachtwandler-Lied."

18. TSZ, 352; KGW, VI, 1: 294.

19. See Arthur Schopenhauer, *On the Basis of Morality*, trans. E. F. J. Payne (Indianapolis: Bobbs-Merrill, 1965), 211; *Zürcher Ausgabe*, 6: 312. See, also, Cartwright, 55.

20. See Schopenhauer, *On the Basis of Morality*, 209; *Zürcher Ausgabe*, 6: 310–11. For Schopenhauer on the connection between pity and resignation, see *The World as Will and Representation*, 1: 374–98; *Zürcher Ausgabe*, 2: 464–92. See also Cartwright, 55.

21. TSZ, 353; KGW, VI, 1: 297.

22. TSZ, 354–55; KGW, VI, 1: 297–98.

23. The soothsayer suggests that Zarathustra is not the happy man he seems to be, and that he is evading and not acknowledging the fact that he is unhappy, in part by punning on the expression *Seitensprünge*, which literally means "side leaps," but which can also mean "evasions."

24. For Zarathustra's reference to his soul's calm, see TSZ, 349; KGW, VI, 1: 292.

25. TSZ, 356; KGW, VI, 1: 299. Francesca Cauchi, in her otherwise insightful discussion of Zarathustra's encounter with the soothsayer, slights the theme of self-vindication and mistakenly suggests that Zarathustra resigns himself to the soothsayer's view of him (see Francesca Cauchi, *Zarathustra Contra Zarathustra* (Aldershot, Eng.: Ashgate, 1998), 76–86, esp. 85–86. For a reading that more closely corresponds to my own, see Rosen, *The Mask of Enlightenment*, 212–13.

26. If Zarathustra succeeds in vindicating himself in the eyes of the soothsayer, it is less clear that he has succeeded in vindicating himself in the eyes of his critics and detractors (including, e.g., Martin Heidegger and, more recently, Peter Berkowitz), some of whose criticisms of Zarathustra can be read as echoing the soothsayer's criticism. Cf. Chapter 5, note 223.

27. See Alderman, 115; Shapiro, *Nietzschean Narratives*, 107 ff.; Higgins, *Nietzsche's Zarathustra*, 203–32; and Hollinrake, 152–71. See also Kuenzli, 109–14, and, most recently, Cauchi, 5–8, 147–68.

28. BGE, 35–37; KGW, VI, 2: 38–39. I have made some small changes in Kaufmann's translation.

29. As we have seen, it is the public image of Zarathustra as a figure who enjoys the heights and high times of the sublime that draws the soothsayer to him. Presumably, it is also this image that draws the other higher men to him. For a brief discussion of the historical origins of the satyr play in fifth-century B.C.E. Athens, with useful biblio-

graphical references, see Daniel W. Conway, *Nietzsche's Dangerous Game* (Cambridge: Cambridge University Press, 1997), 122–23.

Laurence Lampert (309–10) suggests that the sleepwalker song accurately conveys the grounds of the doctrine of recurrence that Zarathustra affirms in the final sections of Part 3. Consistent with that suggestion, Kathleen Higgins holds that, with this song, Zarathustra gives his insights "the most apt expression they could have" (see Higgins, *Nietzsche's Zarathustra*, 236). For a view closer to my own, which argues that the sleepwalker song *imitates* Zarathustra's earlier affirmations of recurrence, but without genuinely communicating the experiential content of those affirmations, see Rosen, 242–44. Consider too, in this connection, Hans-Georg Gadamer's argument (361–62, 366–67) that Zarathustra knows that there is something false and illusory about the higher men's celebration of eternal recurrence in "The Sleepwalker Song."

30. Both Bennholdt-Thomsen (210–11) and Conway (*Nietzsche's Dangerous Game*, 127) also use the notion of the satyr play to discuss Part 4. See, also, Fink, 114–18. For a discussion of the limitations of the satyr-play analogy in the interpretation of Part 4, see Shapiro, *Nietzschean Narratives*, 99–100.

31. For a similar point, see Magnus, Stewart, and Mileur, 163.

32. Zarathustra explicitly notes that the kings have repeated his words. The student of the leech repeats a statement Zarathustra made in "On the Famous Wise Men." See TSZ, 357–58, 216, 363; KGW, VI, 1: 301–2, 130, 308.

33. TSZ, 389–90; KGW, VI, 1: 339–41.

34. BT, 49–50; KGW, III, 1: 40.

35. EH, 228; KGW, VI, 3: 268–69.

36. See TSZ, 361, 376; KGW, VI, 1: 306, 324.

37. TSZ, 387; KGW, VI, 1: 338; emphasis mine.

38. The point here is that Zarathustra—to the extent that he briefly experiences pity—does, at least twice, for a moment in each case, recognize himself in the higher men (come to see in their misery the mirror image of his own soul). However, Niezsche's remark in *Ecce Homo* and his characterization of Zarathustra at noon suggest that these momentary lapses occur precisely when Zarathustra *erroneously* takes the self he is at noon (and, earlier, when he performs the honey sacrifice) for one that embodies the unhappy spirit of resignation. When he *finds* himself he signals that he is no longer given to making this mistake.

39. Presumably, the higher men are a remnant of God, if not the last remnant. See TSZ, 393–94; KGW, VI, 1: 345–46. For possible biblical sources of the figure of the remnant, see, for example, Lev. 5:13, 2 Kings 19:4, Isa. 37:4, Ezra 9:8, Isa. 1:9. See, also, Isa. 11:11 and 16:14, as well as Jer. 44:28, Ezek. 6:8, Joel 2:32, Rom. 11:5, and Rev. 11:13. Thanks to Andrew Frisardi for alerting me to these sources.

40. The higher men suffer from themselves, says Zarathustra. See TSZ, 401; KGW, VI, 1: 355.

41. According to Peter Berkowitz, the higher men portrayed in Part 4 of *Zarathustra* ("pathetic buffoons") exemplify a type of individual very different from the type portrayed

in *Beyond Good and Evil* ("worthy precursors to the new philosopher"). I differ with Berkowitz on this point, for it seems to me that Nietzsche's discussion of the higher men in *Beyond Good and Evil* is often of a piece with and a further meditation on the colorful characters he depicts in Part 4 (see, e.g., BGE, no. 256, which I discuss in detail in the present chapter, and BGE, no. 269). Thus, much of what Nietzsche writes about higher men in *Beyond Good and Evil* pertains directly to these characters. Still, I do not deny that at least some of Nietzsche's talk about higher men in *Beyond Good and Evil* seems to refer to figures quite unlike the higher men appearing in Part 4. See Berkowitz, 230, 300n2.

42. All the source material in this paragraph derives from BGE, no. 256 (BGE, 196–98; KGW, VI, 2: 209–12).

43. For European romanticism's expressivist interpretation of art, see M. H. Abrams's influential study, *The Mirror and the Lamp, passim*. See, also, Michael Cooke, *The Romantic Will* (New Haven, Conn.: Yale University Press, 1976), 145–50. For a more recent discussion, see Taylor, *The Sources of the Self*, 374–81. For a perceptive and important critique of Abrams's view, see Charles Larmore, *The Romantic Legacy* (New York: Columbia University Press, 1996), 7–16.

44. TSZ, 356–60; KGW, VI, 1: 300–304.

45. TSZ, 363; KGW, VI, 1: 308.

46. TSZ, 369; KGW, VI, 1: 315. For Nietzsche's suggestion that Wagner is a sort of sorcerer, or magician, see his claim, in *The Case of Wagner*, that Wagner is "the Cagliostro of modernity" (CW, 166; KGW, VI, 3: 17). For Nietzsche's emphasis on the *expressivist* character of Wagner's music and drama, see his discussion "Wagner as a Danger," in *Nietzsche Contra Wagner* (NCW, 666–67; KGW, VI, 3: 419–21). Other commentators who argue that the sorcerer parodies Zarathustra include Alderman (119); as well as Magnus, Stewart, and Mileur (164).

47. TSZ, 370–71; KGW, VI, 1: 317–18.

48. TSZ, 375–79; KGW, VI, 1: 323–28.

49. TSZ, 381–83; KGW, VI, 1: 330–32.

50. BGE, 197; KGW, VI, 2: 211. For the escapist, orientalist/Africanist exoticism of the wanderer who is Zarathustra's shadow, see the song the wanderer sings in "Among Daughters of the Wilderness." For an insightful discussion of this song, which stresses its orientalist exoticism, see Shapiro, *Nietzschean Narratives*, 116 ff. For a close reading of the song as a whole, see C. A. Miller, "Nietzsche's 'Daughters of the Desert': A Reconsideration," *Nietzsche-Studien* 2 (1973): 157–95.

51. See TSZ, 363–70; KGW, VI, 1: 309–16.

52. BGE, 197; KGW, VI, 2, 211. Cf. BT, 26; KGW, III, 1: 16; and GS, 329; KGW, V, 2: 303, where Nietzsche also ties romanticism to Christianity.

53. BGE, 197; KGW, VI, 2: 210.

54. TSZ, 229, 404; KGW, VI, 1: 146, 359.

55. For my discussion of "On the Rabble," see Chapter 4.

56. TSZ, 402; KGW, VI, 1: 357.

57. TSZ, 394; KGW, VI, 1: 346.

58. BGE, 219; KGW, VI, 2: 234.

59. For the related though not identical argument that the romantic mind, in engaging the phenomenon of the will, moves between the poles of Prometheanism and stoicism, see Cooke, *The Romantic Will*, 216–22. For a more general discussion of the Prometheanism of the romantic spirit, see Harold Bloom's influential essay "The Internalization of Quest Romance," in Bloom, *The Ringers in the Tower*, 13–35 (see, also, in this connection, Bloom, *The Anxiety of Influence*, 79–80). For an insightful discussion of *Zarathustra* that draws inspiration from Bloom's essay, see Magnus, Stewart, and Mileur, 138–46.

60. See SB, 8, 191–92. Peter Heller also refers to Nietzsche's letter to Gast in his helpful discussion of Nietzsche's critique of romantic pessimism. See Peter Heller, "Nietzsche's Struggle with Romantic Pessimism," in Heller, *Studies on Nietzsche*, 204.

61. See GS, 327–31; KGW, V, 2: 301–4.

62. Cf., in this connection, Adrian Del Caro's remarks regarding Nietzsche's appraisal of romanticism: "Just as Nietzsche envisaged two kinds of nihilism, depending on whether strength or weakness is the motivating factor, so too are there two kinds of romanticism, a fact he frequently overlooked; the romanticism that he usually described as weak, passive, and pathological; and the image of romanticism that represents the *transition* from passive to active, namely, a cheerful, strong, destructive, creative romanticism." Del Caro, *Nietzsche Contra Nietzsche*, 24.

63. See TSZ, 422; KGW, VI, 1: 382.

64. For a discussion along related lines, see Higgins, *Nietzsche's Zarathustra*, 226–30.

65. TSZ, 429; KGW, VI, 1: 390.

66. BGE, 15; KGW, VI, 2: 15.

67. For a musically informed discussion of Mahler's setting to music of Zarathustra's song, see Peter Franklin, *Mahler: Symphony No. 3* (Cambridge: Cambridge University Press, 1991), 66–68.

68. For a similar point, see Cauchi, 159.

69. TSZ, 433–44; KGW, VI, 1: 395–97.

70. TSZ, 434; KGW, VI, 1: 397.

71. When Zarathustra sings "Once More" to the higher men, he skips the third and fourth lines of the song. He sings lines 1–2 and 5–11 of the song at the ends of sections 3–11 of "The Sleepwalker Song." The higher men join Zarathustra in singing "Once More" in section 12 of "The Sleepwalker Song."

72. Cf. Hollinrake, 99–106, 153.

73. TSZ, 364–67; KGW, VI, 1: 309–13.

74. TSZ, 415; KGW, VI, 1: 374.

75. Both Shapiro (*Nietzschean Narratives*, 108) and Hollinrake (167 ff.) note the religious parody at work in Part 4. Hollinrake makes a detailed and convincing case that the parody primarily concerns Wagner's *Parsifal.*

76. TSZ, 430; KGW, VI, 1: 392.

77. CW, 166; KGW, VI, 3: 17.

78. TSZ, 394–95; KGW, VI, 1: 346–47; I have altered slightly Kaufmann's translation. In suggesting that, in this passage and elsewhere in Part 4, Nietzsche means to recall his readers to Plato's *Symposium*, I am mindful that Plato's dialogue on love made a profound impression on Nietzsche, even as a young man, leading him to describe it, when he graduated from Pforta, as his *Lieblingsdichtung*. See, on this point, Kaufmann, *Nietzsche*, 23, 160.

79. Zarathustra explicitly figures the spirit of gravity as a dwarf in "On the Vision and the Riddle."

80. TSZ, 145; KGW, VI, 1: 34.

81. See TSZ, 199–200; KGW, VI, 1: 107–8.

82. BT, 89; KGW, III, 1: 87. Other commentators who have noted the apparent allusion to Plato's *Symposium* in "The Sign" include Higgins (*Nietzsche's Zarathustra*, 236–37), Hollinrake (113–14), and Shapiro (*Nietzschean Narratives*, 122–23).

83. For a similar view, which relates the creation of the new to Zarathustra's movement beyond the perspectives of tragedy and comedy, see Deleuze, *Difference and Repetition*, 92, 298–99. Note, also, in this connection, aphorism 150 of *Beyond Good and Evil*, which Heidegger used as the epigraph to the published edition of his 1937 University of Freiburg lecture course on the eternal recurrence of the same (see Heidegger, *Nietzsche*, vol. 2, *The Eternal Recurrence of the Same*, 3): "Around the hero, everything turns into a tragedy; around the demi-god, into a satyr play; and around God—what? perhaps into 'world'?" (BGE, 90; KGW, VI, 2: 99). At the conclusion of Part 3, Zarathustra triumphs as a tragic *hero*. In Part 4, he appears temporarily as a *Satyrspieler*, whom the higher men revere as a *demi-god*. At the conclusion of Part 4, Zarathustra experiences the return to European modernity of the possibility of going-under to the coming *god*, Dionysus. By going-under to the coming god and creating new values, Zarathustra and his children will attempt to remake the *world* of European modernity.

84. Zarathustra initially predicts the appearance of the lion and the doves in the speech, "On Old and New Tablets," in Part 3. See, TSZ, 308; KGW, VI, 1: 242.

85. For a useful discussion of the figure of the dove in Christian iconography, see George Ferguson, *Signs and Symbols in Christian Art* (New York: Oxford University Press, 1954), 10–12.

86. TSZ, 230; KGW, VI, 1: 148.

87. This, then, is an occasion in Nietzsche's writing on which, as J. P. Stern acknowledges, the heroic "morality of strenuousness" gives way to the spirit of grace and equanimity. See Stern, *A Study of Nietzsche*, 156, 161, 169–70.

88. In "The Sign," Zarathustra makes reference to the laughing lions he awaits when he says, "'*My children are near, my children*'" (TSZ, 438; KGW, VI, 1: 402). According to Peter Berkowitz, Zarathustra in "The Sign" (1) abandons the project of self-deification and (2) abandons the perspective of the child for that of the lion. On my view, (1) is true but (2) is false. Berkowitz errs, I believe, in assuming that Zarathustra becomes a child with his triumphal self-deification at the conclusion of Part 3. As I attempted to show in Chapter 5, a careful reading of Part 3 supports a different view: namely, that Zarathustra

becomes a lion with his triumphal (pantheistic) self-deification at the conclusion of Part 3. The appearance of laughing lions at the conclusion of Part 4 is the appearance of individuals like Zarathustra, men who can forsake the project of self-deification and enact the third metamorphosis of the spirit because their bodies embody the return to European modernity of the possibility of going-under to Dionysian chaos. See Berkowitz, 226–27, 301n11.

89. TSZ, 258–59; KGW, VI, 1: 185.

90. Cauchi (167) suggests that the lion's actions—his turning away from Zarathustra, his jumping toward the cave, and his roaring at the higher men—signify Zarathustra's hostility toward the higher men. This interpretation strikes me as implausible, because these actions are not initiated by Zarathustra (Zarathustra does not instruct the lion to act as he acts) and because Zarathustra seems to be unaware of the lion's actions.

91. For Zarathustra's suggestion that pity is his final sin, see TSZ, 439; KGW, VI, 1: 404. For the interesting argument that Zarathustra uses the word "sin" (*Sünde*) ironically, see Higgins, *Nietzsche's Zarathustra*, 235–38.

92. In "The Sleepwalker Song," Zarathustra lets go his public *image* of himself as a sublime, Promethean hero, but does not cease to understand himself as such. In "The Sign," he does cease to understand himself as a sublime, Promethean hero and finally performs the beautifying third metamorphosis of the spirit.

93. In "The Sign," as in "The Honey Sacrifice," Zarathustra proclaims that he is concerned with his happiness, not his work (see TSZ, 439; KGW, VI, 1: 404). Magnus, Stewart, and Mileur (273–74n2) stress the fact that Zarathustra, in this context, uses the term *Werk* and not *Arbeit*, arguing that his reference to his work is a reference to his "literary production." For analysis and criticism of this argument, see Cauchi, 166n315.

94. The three repetitions I discuss here correspond, roughly, to the three repetitions Deleuze identifies in his discussion of *Zarathustra* in the final chapter of *Difference and Repetition* (298–99). See, also, ibid., 90, from which I derive this chapter's second epigraph.

95. TI, 561–62; KGW, VI, 3: 153–54.

96. In the final section of his "Attempt at a Self-Criticism," which he added to the 1886 edition of *The Birth of Tragedy*, Nietzsche explicitly distinguishes *The Birth of Tragedy*'s notion of metaphysical comfort from the notion of a "this-worldly" comfort that he associates with "that Dionysian monster who bears the name Zarathustra." On my view, the "this-worldly" comfort Zarathustra enjoys is the tragic-heroic comfort he invents for himself by adopting the practical postulate that he personifies redemption3 (cf. my discussion in Chapter 5). See BT, 25–27; KGW, III, 1: 15–16.

97. BGE, 26–27; KGW, VI, 2: 26–27.

98. The terminology of second- and first-order desire is, of course, mine, not Nietzsche's. I introduce and explain this terminology (which I borrow from Harry Frankfurt) when I develop my interpretation of the will to power in Chapter 3.

99. Sections 16 and 17 of *Beyond Good and Evil* provide the basis for my interpretation of Nietzsche's conception of the "concept 'I'" in section 19. See BGE, 23–24; KGW, VI, 2: 23–25.

100. For a related discussion of Kant's doctrine of sensibility in connection to his notion of the "passive self" and to Nietzsche's and Hölderlin's notions of time and recurrence, see Deleuze, *Difference and Repetition*, 85–93.

101. Cf. my discussion in Chapter 5 of Zarathustra's belief that modernity treats dispassionate, supersensible subjectivity as a normative ideal. For a view of Nietzsche's view of romanticism that is similar to my own, and that holds that Nietzsche's critique of the idea of a unitary, substantial subject cuts equally against the ideals of disengaged reason (corresponding to what I describe as the ideal of dispassionate, supersensible subjectivity) and those of romantic, expressivist fulfillment, see Taylor, *The Sources of the Self,* 462–63. For more general and comprehensive treatments of Nietzsche's engagement with romanticism, see Heller, *Studies on Nietzsche,* 192–231; Del Caro, *Nietzsche Contra Nietzsche, passim*; and Ernst Behler, "Nietzsche's Challenge to Romantic Humanism," in *Nietzsche: Critical Assessments,* ed. Daniel W. Conway with Peter S. Goff (London: Routledge, 1998), 1: 24–46.

102. Daniel Conway (*Nietzsche's Dangerous Game,* 166) gestures in the direction of a reading along these lines.

103. With an eye to a somewhat different set of concerns, Magnus, Stewart, and Mileur (178–85) also argue that the ending of *Zarathustra* admits of both optimistic and pessimistic readings.

104. I want to stress here that Nietzsche presents no *argument* for undecidability; rather he constructs the ending of *Zarathustra* with an eye to displaying the possibility of opposed but equally potent interpretations. In this context, then, his philosophical-literary "method" may have an affinity to Sextus Empiricus's practice of *isosthenia,* which, on at least one account, "works not be arguing that there are conflicts that can never be rationally resolved, but by *displaying* antitheses in which the conflicting opinions and arguments are felt to be equally plausible" (see Michael Williams, "Skepticism Without Theory," *Review of Metaphysics,* 41, no. 3 [March 1988]: 572). I am particularly grateful to Adrian Slobin for prompting me to think seriously about the Pyrrhonian motifs in Nietzsche's writing. For a more extensive examination of affinities between Nietzsche and Sextus, see Daniel W. Conway and Julie K. Ward, "Physicians of the Soul: Περιτσοπή in Sextus Empiricus and Nietzsche," in *Nietzsche und die antike Philosophie,* ed. Daniel W. Conway and Rudolph Rehn (Trier: WVT Wissenschaftlicher Verlag, 1992), 193–223. For an account of the rhetorical stance that Nietzsche adopts at the end of *Zarathustra,* similar to the account that I outline, see Pippin, "Irony and Affirmation," 63 ff., esp. 65.

105. BGE, 11; KGW, VI, 2: 11. I wish to thank Joshua Andresen for calling my attention to this passage. Peter Berkowitz also argues that the perspective from which *Beyond Good and Evil* is written corresponds to Zarathustra's outlook in "The Sign." Berkowitz and I differ, however, in our interpretations of the content of this outlook. According to Berkowitz (212, 222–27), Zarathustra ceases to be a child and becomes a lion in "The Sign." My own view, for which I have argued at length in this chapter, is that just the opposite is true. In "The Sign," Zarathustra ceases to be the lion he becomes at the end of Part 3 (see Chapter 5) and becomes a beautiful child.

106. BGE, 1–2; KGW, VI, 2: 4–5.

107. For the "Aftersong" of *Beyond Good and Evil*, from which the quoted material in this paragraph largely derives, see BGE, 240–45; KGW, VI, 2: 253–55. See, too, R. J. Hollingdale's translation of *Beyond Good and Evil* (222–23), on which I have also relied for translations of parts of the "Aftersong."

108. EH, 310–11; KGW, VI, 3: 348–49.

109. It is worth recalling here that the leonine yes-and-amen with which Part 3 ends is rooted in Zarathustra's defiant, leonine "nay-saying" to the prophecy of the soothsayer, the spite of spirit of gravity, and so on. Thus, unlike the "yea-saying" of the child, it is rooted in reaction (cf. my discussion of the lion-spirit in Chapter 1).

110. BGE, 117–18; KGW, VI, 2: 128–30; see also BGE, 135–36; KGW, VI, 2: 148–49. In *Ecce Homo*, Nietzsche describes the creative project of revaluation as a no-doing, no-saying project of destruction. Thus, he highlights the fact that it is in the nature of new-values creation to disrupt and subvert prevailing cultural practices. For Nietzsche's explicit suggestion that no-doing destruction is *essential* to the creative activity of the yea-saying, Dionysian creator (in *Zarathustra*, the yea-saying, Dionysian child), see GS, 329; KGW, V, 2: 303.

111. For a useful discussion of the history of the "advice book" genre, see Quentin Skinner, *The Foundations of Modern Political Thought*, vol. 1, *The Renaissance* (Cambridge: Cambridge University Press, 1978), 28–48.

112. BGE, 41; KGW, VI, 2: 43.

113. See Niccolò Machiavelli, *The Prince*, trans. and ed. Mark Musa (New York: St. Martin's Press, 1964), 216–25.

114. BGE, 131; KGW, VI, 2: 144.

115. For a fine discussion of the Machiavellian character of Nietzsche's great politics, with which I largely agree, see Ansell-Pearson, 192–94, 201–24.

116. Here, obviously, I am in sympathy with what Maudemarie Clark has recently described as the "standard view" of *Beyond Good and Evil*. According to this view, *Beyond Good and Evil* expresses the hope "that a group of philosopher-aristocrats will eventually bring about a revaluation of the values of the modern democratic-liberal order by imposing their own new values on the larger society in which they will live—through force and violence, if necessary." For Clark's analysis and criticism of the standard view, see Maudmarie Clark, "Nietzsche's Antidemocratic Rhetoric," *Southern Journal of Philosophy* 37, supplement (1999): 119–41. For a careful critique of Clark's criticism and a defense of the standard view, see, in the same issue, A. Todd Franklin, "The Political Implications of Nietzsche's Aristocratic Radicalism," 143–49.

Bibliography

Nietzsche's Writings in German

Kritische Gesamtausgabe: Werke. Ed. Giorgio Colli and Mazzino Montinari. Berlin: de
Gruyter, 1967–.
Sämtliche Briefe: Kritische Studienausgabe in 8 Bänden. Ed. Giorgio Colli and Mazzino
Montinari. Berlin and Munich: de Gruyter and Deutscher Taschenbuch
Verlag, 1986.
Sämtliche Werke: Kritische Studienausgabe in 15 Bänden. Ed. Giorgio Colli and Mazzino
Montinari. Berlin and Munich: de Gruyter and Deutscher Taschenbuch
Verlag, 1980.

Nietzsche's Writings in English Translation

The Antichrist. In *The Portable Nietzsche*, ed. and trans. Walter Kaufmann. New York:
Viking, 1954.
Beyond Good and Evil. Trans. Walter Kaufmann. New York: Vintage Books, 1989.
The Birth of Tragedy. In *"The Birth of Tragedy" and "The Case of Wagner,"* ed. and
trans. Walter Kaufmann. New York: Vintage Books, 1967.
The Case of Wagner. In *"The Birth of Tragedy" and "The Case of Wagner,"* ed. and
trans. Walter Kaufmann. New York: Vintage Books, 1967.
Ecce Homo. Trans. Walter Kaufmann. In *"On the Genealogy of Morals" and "Ecce
Homo,"* ed. Walter Kaufmann, trans. R. J. Hollingdale and Walter
Kaufmann. New York: Vintage Books, 1969.
The Gay Science. Trans. Walter Kaufmann. New York: Vintage Books, 1974.
Nietzsche Contra Wagner. In *The Portable Nietzsche*, ed. and trans. Walter Kaufmann.
New York: Viking, 1954.
On the Genealogy of Morals. Trans. R. J. Hollingdale and Walter Kaufmann. In *"On the
Genealogy of Morals" and "Ecce Homo,"* ed. Walter Kaufmann. New York:
Vintage Books, 1969.
On the Uses and Disadvantages of History for Life. Trans. R. J. Hollingdale. In *Untimely
Meditations*, trans. R. J. Hollingdale. Cambridge: Cambridge University
Press, 1983.

Schopenhauer as Educator. Trans. R. J. Hollingdale. In *Untimely Meditations,* trans.
    R. J. Hollingdale. Cambridge: Cambridge University Press, 1983.
Selected Letters of Friedrich Nietzsche. Ed. and trans. Christopher Middleton. Chicago:
    University of Chicago Press, 1969.
Thus Spoke Zarathustra. In *The Portable Nietzsche,* ed. and trans. Walter Kaufmann.
    New York: Viking, 1954.
Thus Spoke Zarathustra. Trans. R. J. Hollingdale. New York: Penguin, 1961.
Twilight of the Idols. In *The Portable Nietzsche,* ed. and trans. Walter Kaufmann. New
    York: Viking, 1954.
The Will to Power. Ed. and trans. Walter Kaufmann. Trans. R. J. Hollingdale. New
    York: Vintage Books, 1968.

Other Works

Abrams, M. H. *A Glossary of Literary Terms.* New York: Holt, Rinehart, and Winston,
    1971.
———. *The Mirror and the Lamp.* London: Oxford University Press, 1953.
———. *Natural Supernaturalism: Tradition and Revolution in Romantic Literature.*
    New York: W. W. Norton, 1971.
Ackermann, Robert John. "Current American Thought on Nietzsche." In *Nietzsche
    Heute: Die Rezeption seines Werks nach 1968,* ed. Sigrid Bauschinger, Susan L.
    Cocalis, and Sara Lennox, 129–36. Bern and Stuttgart: Francke Verlag, 1988.
———. *Nietzsche: A Frenzied Look.* Amherst: University of Massachusetts Press, 1990.
Adorno, Theodor. *In Search of Wagner.* Trans. Rodney Livingston. Great Britain: NLB,
    1981.
Adorno, Theodor, and Max Horkheimer. *Dialectic of Enlightenment.* Trans. John
    Cumming. New York: Seabury Press, 1972.
Aeschylus. *Prometheus Bound.* Trans. David Grene. In *Aeschylus II,* ed. David Grene
    and Richmond Lattimore, 138–79. Chicago: University of Chicago Press,
    1956.
Aiken, Henry David. "Introduction to *Zarathustra.*" In *Nietzsche: A Collection of
    Critical Essays,* ed. Robert Solomon. Garden City, N.Y.: Anchor Books, 1973.
Alderman, Harold. *Nietzsche's Gift.* Athens: Ohio University Press, 1977.
Allison, David. "Nietzsche Knows No Noumenon." *Boundary 2* 9, no. 10 (Spring–Fall
    1981): 295–310.
Ansell-Pearson, Keith. *Nietzsche Contra Rousseau: A Study of Nietzsche's Moral and
    Political Thought.* Cambridge: Cambridge University Press, 1991.
Augustine, St. *The Confessions.* Trans. R. S. Pine-Coffin. New York: Penguin, 1982.
Austin, J. L. *How to Do Things with Words.* Cambridge: Harvard University Press, 1962.
Bakhtin, Mikhail. "Discourse and the Novel." In *The Dialogic Imagination,* ed.
    Michael Holquist, trans. Caryl Emerson and Michael Holquist, 259–422.
    Austin: University of Texas Press, 1981.

Balibar, Etienne, and Immanuel Wallerstein. *Race, Nation, and Class.* Trans. Chris
    Turner. London: Verso, 1991.
Bataille, Georges. "Nietzsche and the Fascists." Trans. Allan Stoekl, with Carl R. Lovitt
    and Donald M. Leslie, Jr. In *Visions of Excess: Selected Writings, 1927–1939,*
    ed. Allan Stoekl, 182–96. Minneapolis: University of Minnesota Press, 1985.
Bate, Walter Jackson. *The Burden of the Past and the English Poet.* Cambridge: Harvard
    University Press, 1970.
Bäumler, Alfred. *Nietzsche: Der Philosoph und der Politiker.* Leipzig: P. Reclam, 1931.
Beck, Lewis White. "Philosophy as Literature." In *Philosophical Style,* ed. Berel Lang,
    234–55. Chicago: Nelson Hall, 1979.
Behler, Ernst. *Irony and the Discourse of Modernity.* Seattle: University of Washington
    Press, 1990.
———. "Nietzsches Auffassung der Ironie." *Nietzsche-Studien* 4 (1975): 1–35.
———. "Nietzsche's Challenge to Romantic Humanism." In *Nietzsche: Critical
    Assessments,* ed. Daniel W. Conway with Peter S. Goff, 1: 24–46. London:
    Routledge, 1998.
Bell, Daniel. *The Cultural Contradictions of Capitalism.* New York: Basic Books, 1976.
Benhabib, Seyla. "Epistemologies of Postmodernism: A Rejoinder to Jean-Francois
    Lyotard." *New German Critique* 33 (Fall 1984): 103–26.
Bennholdt-Thomsen, Anke. *Nietzsche's* Also sprach Zarathustra *als literarisches
    Phänomen.* Frankfurt: Athenaum, 1974.
Berkowitz, Peter. *Nietzsche: The Ethics of an Immoralist.* Cambridge: Harvard
    University Press, 1995.
Berlin, Isaiah. *Against the Current.* New York: Penguin, 1982.
———. *Vico and Herder.* New York: Vintage Books, 1976.
Berman, Marshall. *All That Is Solid Melts into the Air.* New York: Simon and Schuster,
    1982.
Blanchot, Maurice. *L'entretien infini.* Paris: Gallimard, 1969.
———. "The Limits of Experience: Nihilism." In *The New Nietzsche,* ed. David
    Allison, 121–27. New York: Dell, 1977.
Blondel, Eric. *Nietzsche: The Body and Culture.* Trans. Seán Hand. Stanford, Calif.:
    Stanford University Press, 1991.
Bloom, Harold. *The Anxiety of Influence: A Theory of Poetry.* New York: Oxford
    University Press, 1973.
———. *A Map of Misreading.* New York: Oxford University Press, 1975.
———. *The Ringers in the Tower: Studies in Romantic Tradition.* Chicago: University
    of Chicago Press, 1971.
Blumenberg, Hans. *The Legitimacy of the Modern Age.* Trans. Robert M. Wallace.
    Cambridge: MIT Press, 1983.
———. *Work on Myth.* Trans. Robert M. Wallace. Cambridge: MIT Press, 1985.
Breazeale, Daniel. "The Meaning of the Earth." In *The Great Year of Zarathustra,* ed.
    David Goicoechea, 113–41. Lanham, Md.: University Press of America, 1991.

————. "Nietzsche: Life as Literature." In *Journal of the History of Philosophy* 26, no. 1 (January 1988): 167–69.

Brecht, Bertolt. "The Modern Theater Is the Epic Theater." In *Brecht on Theater*, trans. John Willett, 33–42. New York: Hill and Wang, 1964.

Brooks, Cleanth. *The Well Wrought Urn*. New York: Harcourt Brace Jovanovich, 1975.

Brooks, Peter. *Reading for the Plot: Design and Intention in Narrative*. New York: Vintage Books, 1985.

Brunot, Amédée. *Saint Paul and His Message*. New York: Hawthorn, 1959.

Buttigieg, Joseph A. "The Struggle Against Meta(Phantasma)-Physics: Nietzsche, Joyce, and the 'excess of history.'" *Boundary 2* 9, no. 10 (Spring–Fall 1981): 187–207.

Byron, George Gordon, Lord. "Manfred." In *The Complete Poetical Works of Byron*, ed. Paul E. More, 478–97. Boston: Houghton Mifflin, 1905.

Caputo, John. *Radical Hermeneutics*. Bloomington: Indiana University Press, 1987.

Carnap, Rudolph. "The Overcoming of Metaphysics Through Logical Analysis of Language." In *Heidegger and Modern Philosophy*, ed. Michael Murray, 23–34. New Haven, Conn.: Yale University Press, 1978.

Cartwright, David E. "The Last Temptation of Zarathustra." *Journal of the History of Philosophy* 31, no. 1 (January 1993): 49–69.

Cauchi, Francesca. *Zarathustra Contra Zarathustra*. Aldershot, Eng.: Ashgate, 1998.

Cavell, Stanley. *The Claim of Reason: Wittgenstein, Skepticism, Tragedy, and Morality*. Oxford: Oxford University Press, 1979.

————. *Disowning Knowledge: In Six Plays of Shakespeare*. New York: Cambridge University Press, 1987

————. *This New Yet Unapproachable America*. Albuquerque: Living Batch Press, 1989.

Clark, Maudmarie. "Language and Deconstruction: Nietzsche, de Man, and Postmodernism." In *Nietzsche as Postmodernist*, ed. Clayton Koelb, 75–90. Albany: SUNY Press, 1990.

————. "Nietzsche's Antidemocratic Rhetoric." *Southern Journal of Philosophy* 37, supplement (1999): 119–41.

————. *Nietzsche on Truth and Philosophy*. Cambridge: Cambridge University Press, 1991.

Clayton, J. P. "Zarathustra and the Stages of Life's Way: A Nietzschean Riposte to Kierkegaard." *Nietzsche-Studien* 14 (1985): 179–200.

Connolly, William E. *Identity/Difference*. Ithaca, N.Y.: Cornell University Press, 1991.

Conway, Daniel W. "A Moral Ideal for Everyone and No One." *International Studies in Philosophy* 22 (Summer 1990): 17–29.

————. "Nietzsche Contra Nietzsche: The Deconstruction of *Zarathustra*." In *Nietzsche as Postmodernist*, ed. Clayton Koelb, 91–110. Albany: SUNY Press, 1990.

————. *Nietzsche's Dangerous Game*. Cambridge: Cambridge University Press, 1997.

———. "Overcoming the *Übermensch*: Nietzsche's Revaluation of Values." *Journal of the British Society for Phenomenology* 20, no. 3 (October 1989): 211–24.

———. "Solving the Problem of Socrates: Nietzsche's *Zarathustra* as Political Irony." *Political Theory* 16 (May 1988): 257–80.

Conway, Daniel W., and Julie K. Ward. "Physicians of the Soul: Περιτσοπή in Sextus Empiricus and Nietzsche." In *Nietzsche und die antike Philosophie*, ed. Daniel W. Conway and Rudolph Rehn, 193–223. Trier: WVT Wissenschaftlicher Verlag, 1992.

Cooke, Michael G. *The Blind Man Traces the Circle.* Princeton, N.J.: Princeton University Press, 1969.

———. *The Romantic Will.* New Haven, Conn.: Yale University Press, 1976.

Crowther, Paul. *The Kantian Sublime.* Oxford: Clarendon Press, 1989.

Culler, Jonathan. *On Deconstruction: Theory and Criticism After Structuralism.* Ithaca, N.Y.: Cornell University Press, 1982.

———. *The Pursuit of Signs.* Ithaca, N.Y.: Cornell University Press, 1981.

Dannhauser, Werner. *Nietzsche's View of Socrates.* Ithaca, N.Y.: Cornell University Press, 1974.

Danto, Arthur. *Narration and Knowledge.* New York: Columbia University Press, 1985.

———. *Nietzsche as Philosopher.* New York: Columbia University Press, 1980.

———. "Philosophy as/and/of Literature." *Proceedings and Addresses of the American Philosophical Association* 58 (1984): 5–20.

Del Caro, Adrian. *Nietzsche Contra Nietzsche: Creativity and the Anti-Romantic.* Baton Rouge: Louisiana State University Press, 1989.

———. "Symbolizing Philosophy: Ariadne and the Labyrinth." *Nietzsche-Studien* 17 (1988): 125–57.

Deleuze, Gilles. *Difference and Repetition.* Trans. Paul Patton. New York: Columbia University Press, 1994.

———. *Nietzsche and Philosophy.* Trans. Hugh Tomlinson. New York: Columbia University Press, 1983.

Deleuze, Gilles, and Félix Guattari. *What Is Philosophy?* Trans. Hugh Tomlinson and Graham Burchell. New York: Columbia University Press, 1996.

de Man, Paul. *Allegories of Reading.* New Haven, Conn.: Yale University Press, 1979.

———. *Blindness and Insight.* New York: Oxford University Press, 1971.

———. "Nietzsche's Theory of Rhetoric." *Symposium* 28, no. 1 (Spring 1974): 33–51. Issue contains a discussion by de Man and respondents to his paper, including Walter Kaufmann and Peter Heller.

———. *The Rhetoric of Romanticism.* Trans. Timothy Bahti. New York: Columbia University Press, 1984.

———. "The Rhetoric of Temporality." In *Interpretation: Theory and Practice*, ed. C. S. Singleton, 173–209. Baltimore: Johns Hopkins University Press, 1969.

————. "Wordsworth und Hölderlin." *Schweizer Monatschefte* (March 1966): 1141–55.

Derrida, Jacques. *Spurs: Nietzsche's Styles.* Trans. Barbara Harlow. Chicago: University of Chicago Press, 1979.

di Giovanni, George. "The Unfinished Philosophy of Friedrich Heinrich Jacobi." Introduction to Friedrich Heinrich Jacobi, *The Main Philosophical Writings and the Novel Allwill,* trans. and ed. George di Giovanni. Montreal: McGill-Queens University Press, 1994.

Donnellan, Brendan. *Nietzsche and the French Moralists.* Bonn: Bouvier, 1982.

Drake, Richard. "Shepherd and Serpent: Zarathustra's Phantasmagoria." In *Friedrich Nietzsche,* ed. Harold Bloom, 213–44. New York: Chelsea, 1987.

Dray, William. *Laws and Explanation in History.* Oxford: Oxford University Press, 1956.

Dreyfus, Hurbert. "Holism and Hermeneutics." *Review of Metaphysics* 34 (September 1980): 3–23.

Eckermann, Johann Peter. *Gespräche mit Goethe.* Ed. Conrad Hofer. Leipzig: Heffe und Beder Verlag, 1913.

Emerson, Ralph Waldo. "Experience." In *Selections from Ralph Waldo Emerson,* ed. Stephen E. Whicher, 254–74. Boston: Houghton Mifflin, 1960.

————. "Self-Reliance." In *Selections from Ralph Waldo Emerson,* ed. Stephen E. Whicher, 147–68. Boston: Houghton Mifflin, 1960.

Eysteinsson, Astradur. *The Concept of Modernism.* Ithaca, N.Y.: Cornell University Press, 1990.

Fairley, Barker. "Nietzsche and the Poetic Impulse." *Bulletin of the John Rylands Library* 19 (July 1935): 344–61.

Ferguson, George. *Sign and Symbols in Christian Art.* New York: Oxford University Press, 1954.

Fink, Eugen. *Nietzsches Philosophie.* Stuttgart: Kohlhammer, 1960.

Forster, Michael N. *Hegel's Idea of a Phenomenology of Spirit.* Chicago: University of Chicago Press, 1998.

Foucault, Michel. *Language, Counter-Memory, Practice.* Trans. Donald F. Bouchard and Sherry Simon. Ithaca, N.Y.: Cornell University Press, 1977.

————. *The Order of Things.* Trans. Alan Sheridan. New York: Vintage Books, 1973.

Frank, Joseph. *The Widening Gyre.* New Brunswick, N.J.: Rutgers University Press, 1963.

Frankfurt, Harry. *The Importance of What We Care About.* Cambridge: Cambridge University Press, 1988.

Franklin, A. Todd. "The Political Implications of Nietzsche's Aristocratic Radicalism." *Southern Journal of Philosophy* 37, supplement (1999): 143–49.

Franklin, Peter. *Mahler: Symphony No. 3.* Cambridge: Cambridge University Press, 1991.

Freud, Sigmund. *The Interpretation of Dreams.* Trans. James Strachey. New York: Avon, 1965.

Frye, Northrop. *Anatomy of Criticism*. Princeton, N.J.: Princeton University Press, 1957.

Gadamer, Hans-Georg. "The Drama of Zarathustra." Trans. Zygmunt Adamczewski. In *The Great Year of Zarathustra*, ed. David Goicoechea, 339–69. Lanham, Md.: University Press of America, 1983.

Gantz, Timothy. *Early Greek Myth*. Baltimore: Johns Hopkins University Press, 1993.

Gasché, Rodolphe. "'Setzung' and 'Übersetzung': Notes on Paul de Man." *Diacritics* 11 (Winter 1981): 36–57.

Gass, William. *Fiction and the Figures of Life*. Boston: Nonpareil Books, 1971.

Gillespie, Michael Allen. "Nietzsche and the Premodernist Critique of Postmodernism." *Critical Review* 11, no. 4 (Fall 1997): 537–54.

Gilman, S. L. *Nietzschean Parody*. Bonn: Bouvier Verlag Herbert Grundmann, 1976.

Goethe, Johann Wolfgang von. *Conversations with Eckermann*. Trans. John Oxenford. San Francisco: North Point Press, 1984.

———. *Faust*. Trans. Charles E. Passage. Indianapolis: Bobbs-Merrill, The Library of Liberal Arts, 1965.

———. *Faust: Eine Tragödie*. Munich: Deutscher Taschenbuch, 1977.

———. "Prometheus." Trans. Walter Kaufmann. In *Twenty German Poets*, ed. Walter Kaufmann, 9–11. New York: Random House, 1962.

Goicoechea, David. "Love and Joy in Zarathustra." In *The Great Year of Zarathustra, (1881–1981)* ed. David Goicoechea, 33–44. Lanham, Md.: University Press of America, 1983.

Gooding-Williams, Robert (see also Williams, Robert). "Comments on Bernd Magnus's 'A Bridge Too Far: Asceticism and Eternal Recurrence.'" *Southern Journal of Philosophy* 37, supplement (1999): 113–18.

———. "The Drama of Nietzsche's *Zarathustra*: Intention, Repetition, Prelude." *International Studies in Philosophy* 20 (Summer 1988): 105–16.

———. "Literary Fiction as Philosophy: The Case of Nietzsche's *Zarathustra*." *Journal of Philosophy* 83 (November 1986): 667–75.

———. "Nietzsche's Pursuit of Modernism." *New German Critique* 41 (Spring–Summer 1987): 95–108.

———. "Zarathustra's Descent: Incipit Tragoedia, Incipit Parodia." *Journal of Nietzsche Studies.* 9–10 (Spring–Autumn 1995): 50–76.

Grundlehner, Philip. *The Poetry of Friedrich Nietzsche*. New York: Oxford University Press, 1986.

Habermas, Jürgen. "The Entwinement of Myth and Enlightenment." Trans. Thomas Levin. *New German Critique* 26 (Spring–Summer 1982): 13–30.

———. *The Philosophical Discourse of Modernity*. Trans. Frederick Lawrence. Cambridge: MIT Press, 1987.

Hamacher, Werner. "'Disgregation of the Will': Nietzsche on the Individual and Individuality." Trans. Jeffrey S. Librett. In *Reconstructing Individualism*, ed. Thomas Heller, Morton Sosna, and David Wellbery, 106–39. Stanford, Calif.: Stanford University Press, 1986.

Harries, Karsten. "Boundary Disputes." *Journal of Philosophy* 83 (November 1986):
    676–77.
———. "Hegel and the Future of Art." *Review of Metaphysics* 27 (1975): 677–96.
———. "The Infinite Sphere: Comments on the History of a Metaphor." *Journal of
    the History of Philosophy* 13 (January 1975): 5–15.
———. "The Philosopher at Sea." In *Nietzsche's New Seas*, ed. Michael Allen Gillespie
    and Tracy B. Strong, 21–44. Chicago: University of Chicago Press, 1988.
Hartmann, Geoffrey. "Romanticism and 'Anti-Self-Consciousness.'" In *Romanticism
    and Consciousness*, ed. Harold Bloom, 46–56. New York: W. W. Norton,
    1970.
Hayman, Ronald. *Nietzsche: A Critical Life.* New York: Penguin, 1982.
Hegel, G. W. F. *Phenomenology of Spirit.* Trans. A. V. Miller. Oxford: Oxford
    University Press, 1981.
———. *Science of Logic.* Trans. A. V. Miller. London: Humanities Press, 1969.
Heidegger, Martin. *Kant and the Problem of Metaphysics.* Trans. James S. Churchill.
    Bloomington: Indiana University Press, 1962.
———. *Nietzsche.* Pfullingen: Neske, 1961.
———. *Nietzsche.* Vol. 1, *The Will to Power as Art.* Trans. David Farrell Krell. San
    Francisco: Harper and Row, 1979.
———. *Nietzsche.* Vol. 2, *The Eternal Recurrence of the Same.* Trans. David Farrell
    Krell. San Francisco: Harper and Row, 1984.
———. *Nietzsche.* Vol. 3, *The Will to Power as Knowledge and as Metaphysics.* Trans.
    Joan Stambaugh, Frank A. Capuzzi, and David Farrell Krell. New York:
    Harper and Row, 1987.
———. *Nietzsche.* Vol. 4, *Nihilism.* Trans. Frank A. Capuzzi. New York: Harper and
    Row, 1982.
———. *What Is Called Thinking.* Trans. Fred D. Wieck and J. Glenn Gray. New York:
    Harper and Row, 1968.
Heller, Erich. *The Disinherited Mind.* New York: Harcourt Brace Jovanovich, 1975.
———. "Nietzsche's Terror." *Salmagundi* 68–69 (Fall 1985–Winter 1986): 78–90.
Heller, Peter. *Studies on Nietzsche.* Bonn: Bouvier Verlag Herbert Grundmann, 1980.
Higgins, Kathleen M. "Arthur Schopenhauer." In *Routledge History of Philosophy*,
    vol. 6, *The Age of German Idealism*, ed. Robert Solomon and Kathleen M.
    Higgins, 330–62. New York: Routledge, 1993.
———. *Nietzsche's Zarathustra.* Philadelphia: Temple University Press, 1987.
———. "The Night Song's Answer." *International Studies in Philosophy* 18 (Summer
    1985): 33–50.
———. "Zarathustra's Stammer as a Way of Life." *International Studies in Philosophy*
    20 (Summer 1988): 117–22.
Hölderlin, Friedrich. *Friedrich Hölderlin and Eduard Mörike: Selected Poems.* Trans.
    Christopher Middleton, with facing German originals. Chicago: University
    of Chicago Press, 1972.

Hollingdale, R. J. *Nietzsche*. London: Routledge and Kegan Paul, 1973.

Hollinrake, Roger. *Nietzsche, Wagner, and the Philosophy of Pessimism*. London: George Allen and Unwin, 1982.

Honig, Bonnie. *Political Theory and the Politics of Displacement*. Ithaca, N.Y.: Cornell University Press, 1993.

Hoy, David Couzens. *The Critical Circle*. Berkeley: University of California Press, 1978.

Hunt, Lester. *Nietzsche and the Origin of Virtue*. New York: Routledge, 1991.

Huyssen, Andreas. "Mapping the Postmodern." *New German Critique* 33 (Fall 1984): 3–52.

Hyppolite, Jean. *Genesis and Structure of Hegel's Phenomenology of Spirit*. Trans. Samuel Cherniak and John Heckman. Evanston, Ill.: Northwestern University Press, 1974.

Irigaray, Luce. *Marine Lover of Friedrich Nietzsche*. Trans. Gillian C. Gill. New York: Columbia University Press, 1991.

Jacobs, Carol. "Allegories of Reading Paul de Man." In *Reading de Man Reading*, ed. Lindsay Waters and Wlad Godzich, 105–20. Minneapolis: University of Minnesota Press, 1989.

Jaspers, Karl. *Nietzsche: An Introduction to the Understanding of His Philosophical Activity*. Trans. Charles F. Wallraff and Frederick Schmitz. Chicago: Henry Regnery, 1965.

Jones, Peter. *Philosophy and the Novel*. Oxford: Clarendon Press, 1975.

Kant, Immanuel. *Critique of Judgment*. Trans. Werner S. Pluhar. Indianapolis: Hacket, 1987.

———. *Critique of Practical Reason*. Trans. Lewis White Beck. Indianapolis: Bobbs-Merrill, 1956.

———. *Critique of Pure Reason*. Trans. Norman Kemp Smith. New York: St. Martin's Press, 1965.

———. *Kants Werke*. Vol. 5. Berlin: de Gruyter, 1968.

Kaufmann, Walter. *Nietzsche: Philosopher, Psychologist, Antichrist*. Princeton, N.J.: Princeton University Press, 1974.

Kierkegaard, Søren. *The Present Age*. Trans. Alexander Dru. London: Collings, 1962.

Krauss, Rosalind. "The Originality of the Avant-Garde: A Postmodernist Repetition." In *Art After Modernism*, ed. Brian Wallis, 13–29. New York: New Museum of Contemporary Art, 1984.

Krell, David Farrell. *Postponements: Women, Sensuality, and Death in Nietzsche*. Bloomington: Indiana University Press, 1986.

Kuenzli, Rudolph. "Nietzsche's Zerography: *Thus Spoke Zarathustra*." *Boundary 2* 9, no. 3, and 10, no. 1 (Spring–Fall 1981): 99–117.

Lachs, John. "Is There an Absolute Self?" *Philosophical Forum* 19 (Winter–Spring 1988): 169–81.

Lampert, Laurence. *Nietzsche's Teaching: An Interpretation of* Thus Spoke Zarathustra. New Haven, Conn.: Yale University Press, 1986.

Larmore, Charles. *The Romantic Legacy*. New York: Columbia University Press, 1996.

Lea, Henry A. "Mahler's Extraterritoriality." *Massachusetts Review* (Autumn 1990): 341–54.

Lentricchia, Frank. *Culture and Social Change*. Chicago: University of Chicago Press, 1983.

———. *After New Criticism*. Chicago: University of Chicago Press, 1980.

Levy, Isidore. "Rien de nouveau sous le soleil." *La Nouvelle Clio* (1953): 326–28.

Lingus, Alphonso. "The Will to Power." In *The New Nietzsche*, ed. David Allison, 37–63. New York: Delta, 1977.

Lovejoy, A. O. *The Great Chain of Being*. London: Oxford University Press, 1936.

Löwith, Karl. *From Hegel to Nietzsche*. Trans. David Green. Garden City, N.Y.: Anchor Books, 1967.

———. *Nietzsches Philosophie der ewigen Wiederkehr des Gleichen*. Stuttgart: Kohlhammer, 1956.

———. "Nietzsche's Revival of the Doctrine of Eternal Recurrence." In Löwith, *Meaning in History*, 214–22. Chicago: University of Chicago Press, 1949.

Luban, David. "The Liar and the Circle: A Semiotic of Eternal Recurrence." Unpublished ms.

Lukács, Georg. *The Destruction of Reason*. Trans. Peter Palmer. Atlantic Highlands, N.J.: Humanities Press, 1981.

Luther, D. Martin. *Die Bibel, oder die ganze Heilige Schrift des alten und neuen Testaments nach der deutschen Übersetzung Luthers*. 127th ed. Halle, 1818.

———. *Die gantze Heilige Schrifft Deudsch*. Ed. Hans Volz and Heinz Blanke. Munich: Rogner and Bernhard, 1972.

Machiavelli, Niccolò. *The Prince*. Trans. and ed. Mark Musa. New York: St. Martin's Press, 1964.

MacIntyre, Aladair. *After Virtue*. Notre Dame, Ind.: University of Notre Dame Press, 1981.

Mackey, Louis. *Kierkegaard: A Kind of a Poet*. Philadelphia: University of Pennsylvania Press, 1971.

Magnus, Bernd. "The Deification of the Commonplace." In *Reading Nietzsche*, ed. Robert C. Solomon and Kathleen M. Higgins, 152–81. New York: Oxford University Press, 1988.

———. *Nietzsche's Existential Imperative*. Bloomington: Indiana University Press, 1978.

———. "Perfectibility and Attitude in Nietzsche's *Übermensch*." *Review of Metaphysics* 36 (March 1983): 633–59.

Magnus, Bernd, Stanley Stewart, and Jean-Pierre Mileur. *Nietzsche's Case: Philosophy as/and Literature*. New York: Routledge, 1993.

Mann, Thomas. "Nietzsche's Philosophy in the Light of Contemporary Events." In *Nietzsche: A Collection of Critical Essays*, ed. Robert Solomon, 358–70. New York: Anchor Books, 1973.

Marx, Karl. *Early Writings.* Trans. Rodney Livingstone and Gregor Benton. New York: Vintage Books, 1975.

Mason, Jeff. *Philosophical Rhetoric: The Function of Indirection in Philosophical Writing.* London: Routledge, 1989.

McCarthy, Thomas. "Critical Theory and Political Theology: The Postulates of Communicative Reason." In McCarthy, *On Reconstruction and Deconstruction in Contemporary Critical Theory,* 200–215. Cambridge: MIT Press, 1991.

McFadden, George. "Nietzschean Values in Comic Writing." In *Why Nietzsche Now?* ed. Daniel O'Hara, 337–58. Bloomington: Indiana University Press, 1985.

McGinn, Robert E. "Culture as Prophylactic: Nietzsche's *Birth of Tragedy* as Culture Criticism." *Nietzsche-Studien* 4 (1975): 75–138.

Megill, Allan. *Prophets of Extremity: Nietzsche, Heidegger, Foucault, and Derrida.* Berkeley: University of California Press, 1985.

Miller, C. A. "Nietzsche's 'Daughters of the Desert': A Reconsideration." *Nietzsche-Studien* 2 (1973): 157–95.

Mink, Louis. "History and Fiction as Modes of Comprehension." *New Literary History* 1 (1970): 541–58.

———. "Narrative Form as a Cognitive Instrument." In *The Writing of History: Literary Form and Historical Understanding,* ed. Robert Canary and Henry Kozicki. Madison: University of Wisconsin Press, 1978.

Montinari, Mazzino. "The New Critical Edition of Nietzsche's Complete Works." Trans. David. S. Thatcher. *Malahat Review* 24 (October 1972): 121–33.

Müller-Lauter, Wolfgang. *Nietzsche: His Philosophy of Contradictions and the Contradiction of His Philosophy.* Trans. David J. Parent. Urbana: University of Illinois Press, 1999.

———. "Nietzsche's Teaching of Will to Power." Trans. Drew E. Griffin. *Journal of Nietzsche Studies* 4–5 (Autumn 1992–Spring 1993): 37–101.

———. "The Spirit of Revenge and the Eternal Recurrence: Heidegger's Later Interpretation of Nietzsche." Trans. R. J. Hollingdale. *Journal of Nietzsche Studies* 4–5 (Autumn 1992–Spring 1993): 127–53.

Nehamas, Alexander. *The Art of Living: Socratic Reflections from Plato to Foucault.* Berkeley: University of California Press, 1998.

———. *Nietzsche: Life as Literature.* Cambridge: Harvard University Press, 1985.

———. "Nietzsche, Modernity, Aestheticism." In *The Cambridge Companion to Nietzsche,* ed. Bernd Magnus and Kathleen M. Higgins, 223–51. Cambridge: Cambridge University Press, 1996.

———. "The Postulated Author: Critical Monism as a Regulative Ideal." *Critical Inquiry* 8 (Autumn 1981): 131–49.

Nietzsches Bibliothek. Ed. Max Oehler. Weimar: Die Gesellschaft der Freunde des Nietzsche-Archivs, 1942.

Norris, Christopher. *Paul de Man.* New York: Routledge, 1988.

Nozick, Robert. *Philosophical Explanations.* Cambridge: Harvard University Press, 1981.

Nussbaum, Martha C. *The Fragility of Goodness*. Cambridge: Cambridge University Press, 1986.

———. *Love's Knowledge: Essays on Philosophy and Literature*. Oxford: Oxford University Press, 1990.

———. "The Transfiguration of Intoxication: Nietzsche, Schopenhauer, and Dionysus." In *Nietzsche: Critical Assessments*, ed. Daniel W. Conway with Peter S. Goff, 1: 331–59. London: Routledge, 1998.

Otto, Walter F. *Dionysus: Myth and Cult*. Trans. Robert B. Palmer. Bloomington: Indiana University Press, 1965.

Palma, Norman. *Négation de la négativité: Structure et problematique du "Prologue de Zarathustra" reflexion sur Nietzsche*. Paris: Ediciones Hispanos Americanos, 1971.

Pangle, Thomas L. "The 'Warrior Spirit' as an Inlet to the Political Philosophy of Nietzsche's Zarathustra." *Nietzsche-Studien* 15 (1986): 140–79.

Parkes, Graham. *Composing the Soul*. Chicago: University of Chicago Press, 1994.

Pasley, Malcolm. "Nietzsche and Klinger." In *The Discontinuous Tradition*, ed. P. F. Ganz, 146–57. Oxford: Clarendon Press, 1971.

Pautrat, Bernard. *Versions du soleil: Figures et système de Nietzsche*. Paris: Seuil, 1971.

Perkins, Richard. "Analogistic Strategies in *Zarathustra*." In *The Great Year of Zarathustra*, ed. David Goicoechea, 316–38. Lanham, Md.: University Press of America, 1983.

Pierrot, Jean. *The Decadent Imagination, 1880–1900*. Trans. Derek Coltman. Chicago: University of Chicago Press, 1981.

Pippin, Robert. *Hegel's Idealism*. Cambridge: Cambridge University Press, 1989.

———. "Irony and Affirmation in Nietzsche's *Thus Spoke Zarathustra*." In *Nietzsche's New Seas*, ed. Michael Allen Gillespie and Tracy Strong, 45–71. Chicago: University of Chicago Press, 1988.

———. *Modernism as a Philosophical Problem*. Cambridge, Mass.: Basil Blackwell, 1991.

———. "Nietzsche and the Origin of the Idea of Modernism." *Inquiry* 26 (1983): 151–80.

———. "Nietzsche's Alleged Farewell: The Premodern, Modern, and Postmodern Nietzsche." In *The Cambridge Companion to Nietzsche*, ed. Bernd Magnus and Kathleen M. Higgins, 252–78. Cambridge: Cambridge University Press, 1996.

Plato. *The Collected Dialogues of Plato*. Ed. Edith Hamilton and Huntington Cairns. Princeton, N.J.: Princeton University Press, 1961.

Platt, M. "What Does Zarathustra Whisper in Life's Ear?" *Nietzsche-Studien* 17 (1988): 179–94.

Poirier, Richard. *The Renewal of Literature*. New Haven, Conn.: Yale University Press, 1987.

Rabinbach, Anson. *The Human Motor: Energy, Fatigue, and the Origins of Modernity*. New York: Basic Books, 1990.

Ricoeur, Paul. *Freud and Philosophy*. New Haven, Conn.: Yale University Press, 1970.

———. *Time and Narrative*. Vol. 1. Trans. Kathleen McLaughlin and David Pellauer. Chicago: University of Chicago Press, 1984.

Ronell, Avital. "Namely, Eckermann." In *Looking After Nietzsche*, ed. Laurence A. Rickels, 233–57. New York: SUNY Press, 1990.

Rorty, Amelie Oskenberg. "Experiments in Philosophic Genre: Descartes *Meditations*." *Critical Inquiry* 9 (March 1983): 545–64.

Rorty, Richard. *Consequences of Pragmatism*. Minneapolis: University of Minnesota Press, 1982.

———. *Contingency, Irony, Solidarity*. Cambridge: Cambridge University Press, 1989.

———. "Deconstruction and Circumvention." *Critical Inquiry* 11 (September 1984): 1–23.

———. "Philosophy Without Principles." In *Against Theory*, ed. W. J. T. Mitchell, 132–38. Chicago: University of Chicago Press, 1985.

———. "Two Meanings of 'Logocentrism': A Reply to Norris." In *Redrawing the Lines: Analytic Philosophy, Literary Theory, and Deconstruction*, ed. Reed Dasenbrock, 204–16. Minneapolis: University of Minnesota Press, 1989.

Rosen, Charles. *Sonata Forms*. New York: W. W. Norton, 1988.

Rosen, Stanley. *G. W. F. Hegel: An Introduction to the Science of Wisdom*. New Haven, Conn.: Yale University Press, 1974.

———. *The Mask of Enlightenment: Nietzsche's Zarathustra*. Cambridge: Cambridge University Press, 1995.

———. "Nietzsche's Image of Chaos." *International Philosophical Quarterly* 20 (March 1980): 3–23.

Said, Edward W. *Beginnings*. Baltimore: Johns Hopkins University Press, 1975.

———. "On Originality." In *The World, the Text, and the Critic*, 126–39. Cambridge: Harvard University Press, 1983.

———. "On Repetition." In *The World, the Text, and the Critic*, 111–25. Cambridge: Harvard University Press, 1983.

Sallis, John. *Crossings*. Chicago: University of Chicago Press, 1991.

Sartre, Jean-Paul. *Literary and Philosophical Essays*. Trans. Annette Michelson. New York: Collier, 1970.

Schaberg, William H. *The Nietzsche Canon: A Publication History and Bibliography*. Chicago: University of Chicago Press, 1995.

Schacht, Richard. *Nietzsche*. London: Routledge and Kegan Paul, 1983.

Schiller, Friedrich von. *Letters on the Aesthetic Education of Man*. Trans. Reginald Snell. New York: Friedrich Ungar, 1965.

———. "On the Sublime." In *Naive and Sentimental Poetry, and On the Sublime*, trans. Julias A. Elias, 198–204. New York: Frederick Ungar, 1966.

———. *Schillers Sämtliche Werke: Säkular-Ausgabe*. Stuttgart and Berlin: Cotta, 1904–5.

Schopenhauer, Arthur. *On the Basis of Morality*. Trans. E. F. J. Payne. Indianapolis: Bobbs-Merrill, 1965.

————. *The World as Will and Representation*. Vols. 1 and 2. Trans. E. F. J. Payne. New York: Dover, 1958.

————. *Zürcher Ausgabe: Werke in zehn Bänden*. Zurich: Diogenes Verlag, 1977.

Schutte, Ofelia. *Beyond Nihilism: Nietzsche Without Masks*. Chicago: University of Chicago Press, 1984.

Scott, Charles. *Christianity According to St. Paul*. Cambridge: Cambridge University Press, 1961.

Scott, R. Y. B., ed. *The Anchor Bible*. Vol. 18, *Proverbs, Ecclesiastes*. New York: Doubleday, 1965.

Searle, John. *Expression and Meaning*. Cambridge: Cambridge University Press, 1979.

Shapiro, Gary. "Festival, Carnival, and Parody in Zarathustra IV." In *The Great Year of Zarathustra (1881–1981)*, ed. David Goicoechea, 44–62. Lanham, Md.: University Press of America, 1983.

————. *Nietzschean Narratives*. Bloomington: Indiana University Press, 1989.

————. "The Rhetoric of Nietzsche's *Zarathustra*." In *Philosophical Style*, ed. Berel Lang, 347–85. Chicago: Nelson Hall, 1979.

Silk, M. S., and J. P. Stern. *Nietzsche on Tragedy*. Cambridge: Cambridge University Press, 1981.

Sloterdijk, Peter. *Thinker on Stage*. Trans. Jamie Owen Daniel. Minneapolis: University of Minnesota Press, 1989.

Skinner, Quentin. *The Foundations of Modern Political Thought*. Vol. 1, *The Renaissance*. Cambridge: Cambridge University Press, 1978.

Small, Robin. "Nietzsche and a Platonist Cosmos: Center Everywhere, Circumference Nowhere." *Journal of the History of Ideas* 44 (January–March 1983): 89–104.

Smart, J. J. C., and Bernard Williams. *Utilitarianism: For and Against*. Cambridge: Cambridge University Press, 1973.

Snead, James A. "European Pedigrees/African Contagions: Nationality, Narrative, and Communality in Tutuola, Achebe, and Reed." In *Nation and Narration*, ed. Homi Bhaba, 231–49. New York: Routledge, 1990.

Soll, Ivan. "Reflections on Recurrence: A Re-Examination of Nietzsche's Doctrine, *Die ewige Wiederkehr des Gleichen*." In *Nietzsche: A Collection of Critical Essays*, ed. Robert Solomon, 322–42. Garden City, N.Y.: Anchor Books, 1973.

Sollors, Werner, ed. *The Return of Thematic Criticism*. Cambridge: Harvard University Press, 1993.

Staden, Heinrich von. "Nietzsche and Marx on Greek Art and Literature: Case Studies in Reception." *Daedalus* (Winter 1976): 79–96.

Stafford-Clark, David. *What Freud Really Said*. New York: Schocken, 1971.

Stambaugh, Joan. *Nietzsche's Thought of Eternal Return*. Baltimore: Johns Hopkins University Press, 1972.

————. "Thoughts on the Innocence of Becoming." *Nietzsche-Studien* 14 (1985): 164–78.

Staten, Henry. *Nietzsche's Voice*. Ithaca, N.Y.: Cornell University Press, 1990.

Stauth, Georg, and Bryan S. Turner. *Nietzsche's Dance: Resentment, Reciprocity, and Resistance in Social Life*. Oxford: Basil Blackwell, 1988.

Steiner, George. *Bluebeard's Castle*. New Haven, Conn.: Yale University Press, 1970.

Stern, J. P. "Nietzsche and the Idea of Metaphor." In *Nietzsche: Imagery and Thought*, ed. Malcolm Pasley, 64–82. Berkeley: University of California Press, 1979.

———. "Nietzsche's Aesthetics." *Journal of European Studies* 5 (1975): 213–22.

———. *A Study of Nietzsche*. Cambridge: Cambridge University Press, 1979.

Strauss, Leo. *Studies in Platonic Political Philosophy*. Chicago: University of Chicago Press, 1983.

Strawson, P. F. *Individuals: An Essay in Descriptive Metaphysics*. London: Metheuen, 1987.

Strong, Tracy. *Friedrich Nietzsche and the Politics of Transfiguration*. Expanded ed. Berkeley: University of California Press, 1988.

———. "Oedipus as Hero: Family and Family Metaphors in Nietzsche." *Boundary 2* 9, no. 10 (Spring–Fall 1981): 311–35.

Sypher, Wylie. "Aesthetic of Revolution: The Marxist Melodrama." In *Tragedy: Vision and Form*, 2nd ed., ed. Robert Corrigan, 216–24. New York: Harper and Row, 1981.

Taylor, Charles. *Hegel*. Cambridge: Cambridge University Press, 1975.

———. "Overcoming Epistemology." In *After Philosophy: End or Transformation?* ed. Kenneth Baynes, James Bohman, and Thomas McCarthy, 464–88. Cambridge: MIT Press, 1987.

———. *The Sources of the Self: The Making of Modern Identity*. Cambridge: Harvard University Press, 1989.

Thatcher, David S. "Eagle and Serpent in *Zarathustra*." *Nietzsche-Studien* 6 (1977): 240–60.

Theisen, Bianca. "Rhythms of Oblivion." In *Nietzsche and the Feminine*, ed. Peter J. Bugard, 83–103. Charlottesville: University of Virginia Press, 1994.

Theological Dictionary of the New Testament III (Grand Rapids, Mich.: Eerdmans, 1965.

Urban, Linwood. *A Short History of Christian Thought*. New York: Oxford University Press, 1986.

Vernant, Jean-Pierre. "Ambiguity and Reversal: On the Enigmatic Structure of *Oedipus Rex*." In *Greek Tragedy*, ed. Erich Segal, 189–209. New York: Harper and Row, 1983.

Vitens, Siegfried. *Die Sprachkunst Friedrich Nietzsches in* Also sprach Zarathustra. Bremen-Horn: Dorn, 1951.

Vycinas, Vincent. *Earth and Gods*. The Hague: Martinus Nihoff, 1961.

Wagner, Richard. *Beethoven*. Trans. Edward Dannreuther. London: W. W. Reeves, 1903.

Warren, Mark. *Nietzsche's Political Thought*. Cambridge: MIT Press, 1988.

Weber, Max. *The Protestant Ethic and the Spirit of Capitalism*. Trans. Talcott Parsons. New York: Scribner, 1930.

Weisberg, Richard. "De Man Missing Nietzsche: *Hinzugedichtet* Revisited." In

    Nietzsche as Postmodernist, ed. Clayton Koelb, 111–24. Albany: SUNY Press, 1990.

Weiskel, Thomas. *The Romantic Sublime: Studies in the Structure and Psychology of Transcendence.* Baltimore: Johns Hopkins University Press, 1976.

West, Cornel. "Nietzsche's Prefiguration of Postmodern American Philosophy." *Boundary 2* 9, no. 10 (Spring–Fall 1981): 241–69.

White, Alan. *Within Nietzsche's Labyrinth.* New York: Routledge, 1990.

Whitlock, Greg. *Returning to Sils-Maria.* New York: Peter Lang, 1990.

Wilcox, John. *Truth and Value in Nietzsche.* Ann Arbor: University of Michigan Press, 1974.

Williams, Bernard. *Ethics and the Limits of Philosophy.* Cambridge: Harvard University Press, 1985.

Williams, Meredith. "Transcendence and Return: The Overcoming of Philosophy in Nietzsche and Wittgenstein." *International Philosophical Quarterly* 28, no. 4 (December 1988): 403–19.

Williams, Michael. "Skepticism Without Theory." *Review of Metaphysics* 41, no. 3 (March 1988): 547–88.

Williams, Robert (see Gooding-Williams, Robert). "Metaphysics and Metalepsis in *Thus Spoke Zarathustra.*" *International Studies in Philosophy* 16 (Summer 1984): 27–36.

———. "Recurrence, Parody, and Politics in the Philosophy of Friedrich Nietzsche." Ph.D. diss., Yale University, 1982.

Winchester, James. "Of Scholarly Readings of Nietzsche: Clark and Magnus on Nietzsche's Eternal Return." *New Nietzsche Studies* 3, nos. 3–4 (Summer–Fall 1999): 77–97.

Wolin, Richard. "Modernism vs. Postmodernism." *Telos* 62 (Winter 1984–85): 9–20.

Yovel, Yirmiyahu. "Nietzsche and Spinoza: *Amor Fati* and *Amor Dei.*" In *Nietzsche as Affirmative Thinker,* ed. Yirmiyahu Yovel, 193–203. Dordrecht: Martinus Nijhoff, 1986.

Index

Abrams, M. H., 323n31, 351n43, 379n11

Adorno, Theodor, 1

Aeschylus, 205, 236–37, 256, 272, 372nn148,156

Alderman, Harold, 279, 318n25, 319n35, 327n69, 336n170, 342n84, 356n5, 382n46

allegory, 79–82, 90–94, 335n147

allusions, 322n25, 359n26, 381n39; to Book of Revelation, 272, 379n11; to Christian God, 35, 36, 37–38, 39, 42–43, 217, 222, 225, 254, 320n51, 373n166; to Christian iconography, 294, 302–3; to Ecclesiastes, 196–97, 198, 215, 217, 252, 282, 366n94; to the Fall, 97–98; to Goethe, 40, 191, 196; to Gospel of Luke, 50–51; to Jesus, 50–51, 55–56, 124, 236, 271–72, 290, 335n162, 362n65, 363n65, 379n7; to Neoplatonism, 52–53, 55, 57–60, 79, 80, 96–97, 303; to Oedipus, 217, 219–20, 222, 227; to Paul's letter to the Philippians, 55–60, 61, 62, 75, 78, 79–80, 81, 89, 93, 96, 114, 187, 200, 204, 236, 257, 271, 303, 336n162; to Plato, 51, 52, 53, 291–92, 293, 324n40, 384nn78,82; to Wagner, 21–22, 35, 90, 92, 222, 231, 234, 236, 279, 283, 289, 337n5, 368n114, 370n125, 371n139, 382n46, 383n75. See also parody

"Among Daughters of the Wilderness," 382

Andresen, Joshua, 386n105

Antichrist, The, 375n206

Antigone, 60

Apollo and the Apollonian, 47, 69, 252, 339n31, 351n45, 375n208; vs. the Dionysian, 54, 77, 104, 106–8, 110, 111–12, 165, 321n9, 323n39, 324n40, 338n15, 340n36. See also Birth of Tragedy, The; Dionysus and the Dionysian

apparent excluders, 14–16, 307; representations of repetition as, 15–16, 17–18, 19, 23–24, 25–26, 29, 32–33, 38, 84, 89, 99, 132, 149, 150, 165, 187, 188, 194, 275, 303

appearance and reality, 176–80, 229–30, 241–42, 257, 354n79; appearance vs. thing-in-itself, 105, 107–17, 131, 165, 191–92, 224–25, 301, 338n15; Christian-Platonic views on, 47, 48–49, 51, 176; Dionysus as metaphysical ground of appearances, 105, 106–12, 114, 116, 338n15

Archilochus, 281

Ariadne: and Dionysus, 180–82, 261–62, 270, 355n92, 356n93; as life, 265–67; and receptivity to passional chaos, 181–82, 261–62, 264–65, 266, 270, 357n10; as Zarathustra's soul, 261–62, 264–65, 266, 301, 357n10

"Ariadne's Lament," 356n93

Aristotle, 13, 59–60, 325n52

asceticism, 321n11, 335n157; ascetic priests, 47, 86, 88, 128–29, 155, 319n29, 343n90; and Christian-Platonic values, 34–36, 46, 50–51, 52, 65, 86–87, 88, 121–23, 124, 133, 155, 165, 203, 213–14, 222, 250, 319n29, 329n98, 368n113; and death of God, 90, 93, 283; demise of ascetic ideal, 88, 90, 93, 203, 283; of the last man, 86–87, 88–89, 187, 189, 199; in modern culture, 16, 19, 23, 33–34, 71, 86–89, 129, 131, 160, 187, 188, 189–90, 200–202, 203–4, 211, 240, 256, 268, 273, 275, 295, 301, 333n135, 334n142, 358n11, 360n51, 361n52, 362n55, 386n101; and will to truth, 46–48, 51

"Ass Festival, The," 288

Aufhebung, 28–31

Austin, J. L., 74, 327n78

PHILOSOPHY

By combining a close study of the text with imaginative, original, and rigorous interpretive concepts, Gooding-Williams breaks new ground. He opens new avenues of insight into Nietzsche which cry out for further exploration. This book casts fresh light on Nietzsche; it will decisively alter the debate around this great philosopher of modernity.

—Charles Taylor, *McGill University*

This study of Nietzsche's *Zarathustra,* at once elegant and meticulous, bold and comprehensive, allows us to grasp this ever enigmatic work in a way never before realized—as an altogether unique engagement with modernism in which the creation of new values is affirmed in the very face of nihilism. The nuance of the analysis, in its encounter with deconstructive and other contemporary readings of Nietzsche, is extraordinary.

—Edward S. Casey, *State University of New York at Stony Brook*

Drawing from diverse traditions of scholarship across numerous academic disciplines, Robert Gooding-Williams delivers a compelling, original interpretation of Nietzsche's most influential work, *Thus Spoke Zarathustra.* Bringing his estimable gifts to bear on this enigmatic book, Gooding-Williams presents *Zarathustra* as a momentous engagement with the problem of modernity. Scholars and enthusiasts alike will appreciate the author's balanced scholarship, exhaustive research, keen intellect, and lucid prose. *Zarathustra's Dionysian Modernism* is an interpretive tour de force.

—Daniel W. Conway, *The Pennsylvania State University*

ATOPIA: PHILOSOPHY, POLITICAL THEORY, AESTHETICS

Robert Gooding-Williams is Professor of Philosophy and Jean Gimbel Lane Professor of the Humanities at Northwestern University. He is the editor of *Reading Rodney King, Reading Urban Uprising.*

Stanford University Press

WWW.SUP.ORG

ISBN 0-8047-3295-7

90000

9 780804 732956